45603

Economics of Wages and Labour

Economics of
Wages and Labour

L. C. HUNTER
D. J. ROBERTSON

AUGUSTUS M. KELLEY · PUBLISHERS
NEW YORK 1969

First published in the UK in 1969 by
MACMILLAN AND CO LTD

Published in the United States by
AUGUSTUS M. KELLEY · PUBLISHERS
New York, New York 10010

SBN 678 07002 4

Library of Congress Catalog Card Number
70-83359

Printed in Great Britain by
R. & R. CLARK LTD
Edinburgh

Contents

6 Contents

Preface

This book is intended to be a textbook on labour economics designed to meet the needs of students of economics pursuing a course on this topic within their degree curriculum. Unlike authors of American textbooks on labour, we have not produced a full account of trade unionism – for two reasons. First, there is already a considerable literature on British trade unionism, reflecting the fact that this aspect of work on industrial relations in Britain has had a long history and a substantial amount of academic attention. Secondly, to have included an adequate account of trade unionism would have meant a considerable extension to the size of the book. We have instead offered only a single chapter on this matter. With this exception, however, we hope that the book will be found sufficient for the needs of undergraduates throughout their course.

We have given considerable emphasis to the practical aspects of the labour market, both because we think that these are of great importance to a full understanding of how the labour market in Britain works, and because we wish our book to be of interest to managers and others whose interests in labour are not merely academic. The book should be within the capacity of people who are not studying formal courses in economics, and we would hope it would command their interest.

Our work originated in three different circumstances. First, when Macmillans suggested that a book on the economics of wages, by one of the present authors (D. J. R.), should be prepared for a second edition, it became apparent that this would require a substantial revision. Secondly, the other of the present authors (L. C. H.) had been doing some preliminary work towards a possible book on the labour market with special emphasis on labour supply. Thirdly, both authors have been very conscious of the need for a volume which would cover all the main topics of labour economics in the British context. Discussions between us about our separate and joint interests resulted in the decision to produce the present book. While it is intended that this book should serve instead of a second edition of *The Economics of Wages*, it is a new work and by no means just a second edition. It covers many more subjects and is more than twice as long. Even those sections which are based upon *The Economics of Wages* have been very considerably rewritten. It is not surprising that this should be so; apart from the obvious impact of joint-authorship and a wider frame of reference upon earlier work, discussion of wages, especially in its practical aspects, has moved forward very rapidly in Britain over the eight years since the original book was completed. The result is a joint new effort in which we have both played a full and equal part.

In writing this book we have accumulated debts to our colleagues which we would wish to acknowledge. The very high degree of informal co-operation and discussion in the University of Glasgow is one of the great pleasures of working in it; but this makes individual acknowledgements rather difficult. We have benefited over the years from association with all of our colleagues, and our true debt is to the community of Glasgow economists and other social scientists as a whole. On this particular occasion, however, we are particularly indebted to Mr D. I. Mackay and Mr G. L. Reid for most helpful advice, and to Mr G. L. Reid for kindly making available to us a chronology of prices and incomes policy under the Labour Government which he prepared for teaching purposes and appears here as an Appendix to Chapter 21. We are also happy to recognise our constant and continuing debt to Miss A. M. Strang and her colleagues, and to the secretaries of the Department of Social and Economic Research, and on this occasion in particular to Mrs S. Hazelton, Miss C. Macdonald, Mrs D. Ryder and Miss M. D. Simpson.

L. C. H.
D. J. R.

Department of Social and Economic Research
University of Glasgow
July 1968

Part I

Introduction

1 Labour in the Economy

This book is concerned with the part played by labour in the operation of the economy, and the issues which arise in trying to ensure that labour's contribution is effective, appropriate and suitably rewarded. Such a subject is so important that it needs no apology. It is also remarkably complicated. Labour is after all only a collective term for a very substantial part of the population with domestic responsibilities and duties, ambitions and aspirations, likes and dislikes. The supply of labour is not simply a matter of the allocation of an inanimate resource without opinions. Moreover, labour supply is highly differentiated by education and training, ability, location and other factors. The demand for labour has to take account of human strengths and weaknesses, and reflect society's view of the appropriateness of the tasks that may be given to workers. The Government and social institutions such as the trade unions affect both the demand for and the supply of labour in all manner of different ways. The payments made to labour have all the characteristics of a price like any other price, but in addition they have to reflect the way in which people respond to monetary inducements and to vary with the amount and type of work undertaken; and, for most of us, they represent all, or the larger part, of the income on which we and our families live. Only the purest of theoretical economists can hope to live out the assumption that labour is a resource for productive purposes like any other resource. The interest of the subject for most of its students is the intermingling of market and of human factors. For the economist who becomes involved in labour problems there is a special fascination in reconciling the problems of pricing and of resource allocation, with which economics as a whole is greatly concerned, with the particular issues that arise in applying the economist's concepts in a context of institutional complexity and for a resource with a mind of its own.

II. Labour's Contribution

Though it is fashionable to comment on the need for more investment and advanced technology as the means of achieving rising output and improved productivity, the essential and important place of labour in our economic life remains undisputed. It is, of course, true that modern technology has taken over a lot of tasks that previously fell to manual workers, and it is also true that our hopes of a rising standard of living are quite largely dependent on improved machinery. The initiating force for all these changes is, however, the human brain. Even the computer is like a brilliant idiot which can perform calculations at tremendous speed, but still requires to be told what calculations it should do. There are many problems to be sorted out in integrating the new technologies into the production process and adapting the labour force to them – these are discussed in Chapter 16 – but the primacy of human labour as the motivating agent is unquestioned.

The presumed antithesis between machinery and labour is really based on a misunderstanding of the real nature of labour's contribution to production. It is easy enough to prove that machines can work harder than men, and develop more power as well. Men can move mountains, but it is a great help to take some bulldozers and mechanical shovels along as well! The essential point, however, is not to show what machines can do, but to remember that machinery lacks full adaptibility. Ever since man began to invent implements, it has been clear that the main task of workers has been to know how and when to use their equipment. The more complex the equipment has become, the more complex the range of issues for workers to assess and control. Machinery makes most work easier in terms of physical effort, but the essential task of labour has still to be done – to show judgment, to be adaptable, to have forethought, and generally to do the kind of work which machines cannot readily do, including the development of new technologies. The real issue for our modern society – provided that we do not develop a volume of production power beyond our abilities to consume, and there is little immediate sign of this as yet – is then not that of the replacement of labour by the machine, nor any suggestion that labour is not needed. After all, in the ultimate, nothing at all would happen and no improvements would take place unless labour organised them. The issue is rather one of obtaining labour's full potential contribution to production in a changing economy with changing tasks and increasing complexity and specialisation.

The type of labour force which our modern economies now need is both specialised and flexible. It does not necessarily follow that there is no room for simple jobs and unskilled workers, since this depends on the actual way in which labour supplements technology, and many simple tasks are yet very difficult to mechanise, or the unit of production or service is on too small a scale, or too diversified, to warrant the extensive use of capital equipment. There will, however, be an increasing need for specialist training, and for managerial and administrative competence. The utilisation of labour in the production process now requires both a trained labour force in many different categories and levels of skill, and a capacity to change the pattern of specialism with changes in demand and in technology. Managers and administrators, technologists, technicians, skilled trades and semi-skilled workers are all required in an infinity of different types, and the types required may be expected to change frequently.

Each of such broad subdivisions of the labour force – managers, professional workers and technologists, technicians, skilled tradesmen and the more routine grades of salaried staff, semi-skilled and unskilled workers – have their own characteristic patterns of supply and demand. In each case also there are likely to be particular issues of the appropriate type, and the circumstances, of payment. As the economy develops, the demands upon it alter, while changes in production methods are both a reflection of rising incomes and changed demands, and a response to them. The desirable utilisation of labour resources must reflect these changes as well as alterations in the relative costs of labour and other resources. The problem of allocation is not merely a matter of moving labour in general into the right work, but requires adjustments for all these different types of labour. The position is further complicated by the existence of further subdivisions of the labour force – by sex, by age, by location (since both supply and demand characteristics for labour as a whole, and for different types of labour, are variable, for example, between regions and between urban and rural locations), and by quality (since, for example, in a broad category such as managers, and even within narrower specifications of particular managerial types, there are many quantitative factors that arise in selection, suitability and allocation).

Since the labour market is so subdivided and yet so subject to changes, it is evident that the efficiency of its operation will be dependent on the powers and processes of adjustment of the price (or wage) structure of the labour market, on the adequacy and balance of initial training, on the availability of retraining and other means of adjusting the occupational structure by operating on existing members of occupational groups, on the ease or difficulty of moving workers from one location to another, and on the adequacy, accuracy and use of information. All these subjects – wage structure, training, retraining, flexibility and mobility, information flow and information service – therefore require study as part of labour economics. Such study is needed to understand how the labour market works and how it might be improved. The whole subject, however, also has a much wider importance. Labour is a key and a scarce resource, and our prospects of economic growth, therefore, depend on our ability to move labour to where it is needed and, in general, to keep the adjustment of our labour force in pace with the needs of the developing economy.

III. Labour's Reward

The importance of labour's role in the production processes of our economy is matched by the importance of income from work in determining expenditure. Income from employment amounts to 70 per cent of the British national income. The way in which income from employment is distributed is, therefore, the largest single factor in determining the distribution of purchasing power in the economy. How this money is spent will broadly determine the composition of demand. This point is obviously relevant to market research organisations who try to discover the extent and prospects of markets for particular goods or services. It is equally important for economic policymakers, since it is very difficult to envisage adjustments to the level of expenditure in the economy – and especially to the level of consumption expenditure – which do not have to operate to a large degree upon income from employment. While a large part of investment in the economy is carried through by companies and by governments, much of the flow of savings depends upon income from employment.

Indeed, income from employment is one of the great macro-economic variables which determine the whole pattern of operation of the economy. Thus study of the labour market which helps us to understand how income from employment is obtained and distributed is an essential part of the framework of our understanding of the economy as a whole, and a prerequisite of successful policy-making. This point has, of course, been specially emphasised in recent years when so much attention has been directed to the tendency of wages and salaries to grow more rapidly than is compatible with stable prices, and incomes policy has become a very active economic and political issue. While this is the topical demonstration of the link between the labour market and general economic policy, it is not the only reason for the assertion that those who wish to understand how the economy works, and still more those who wish to regulate its working by policy measures, need to know how the labour market operates. For example, discussion of the movement of personal savings, and of the effects of changes in policy on personal savings, cannot readily be divorced from a consideration of how income from employment is earned and distributed. While incomes policy is the crucial issue in the short-term, any discussion of the longer-term prospects of economic growth for the British economy must give particular attention to the utilisation of labour and to problems of labour supply, and to demand for labour and income from work. The examination of work on the labour market and wages is not a diversion from the broad study of macro-economics and of national economic policies; it is a necessary part of that study.

IV. Standard of Living

For the majority of people, income from employment determines their standard of living, since a discussion of the distribution of income, such as that in Chapters 13 and 14 of this book, shows that investment income or income from property is generally relatively unimportant, except for the top few per cent of income receivers. While money is by no means the only key to a full and satisfying life, it is a prerequisite of many types of fuller living, especially in leisure and recreational activities. It is hardly surprising that the movement of the level of wages in our economy should be a matter of great interest to us all. But to understand the way in which incomes from employment are changing it is necessary to do more than simply look at the barometer of the level of wages as compared with prices. The individual's well-being is more closely related to the fortunes of his own particular category of employment, so that the wage or income structure is quite as relevant as the average movement of wages. Moreover, an individual's purchasing power is constrained not only by his total income but by the way in which it is obtained. A secure income, protected against the hazards of redundancy or sickness and free from large fluctuations with changing bonuses or overtime, is much more useful for some types of committed expenditure – like buying a house – than an income which is highly variable. Discussions of wage structure and of security of employment and methods of wage payment also, therefore, bear closely on the standard of living of those in employment.

V. Households

Most discussions about labour are based on the individual worker as the relevant unit of reckoning, whether for purposes of payment or for determining the supply of labour. It is, of course, true that in our modern economy the worker is employed and paid as an individual, but it is much less true that his decisions on income and work are made solely as an individual. While men and women come into the labour market as individuals, they belong to households. Unfortunately most of the data available to analysts of the labour market are in terms of individuals rather than households, and the importance of thinking of households as well as individuals may not therefore emerge as clearly as we might wish in succeeding chapters. It is, therefore, specially important to stress the point here. It impinges upon analysis of the labour market by affecting the supply of labour and the distribution of spending power.

Most men of working age have to work to live, the alternative being an existence at a somewhat low level on unemployment pay or Social Security benefits. It cannot really be said, therefore, that the fact of having dependants greatly affects the usual decision to offer oneself for employment. In any event the desire to do something is sufficiently strong in most of us that we would be unlikely to do absolutely nothing, even if the unlikely were to happen and we could expect to be adequately paid without working. On the other hand the actual or potential existence of dependants is an important factor in determining the kind of job we aim at, or are prepared to accept. Most adult males of working age in Britain have a wife and pass through a spell of twenty years or so with dependent children, and they may also have all the problems associated with aged relatives. The existence of dependants is an undoubted spur to attempts to maximise income opportunities, and hence to ambition. On the other hand, many of the difficulties that arise in securing adequate labour mobility stem from the existence of family responsibilities, and the limitations these impose on full freedom of movement. For example, housing is an important factor in geographical mobility which presents problems for the man with domestic responsibilities. The immediate drop in income and the longer-term uncertainty which are likely to go with a decision to seek a new type of employment, perhaps requiring retraining, are particularly difficult when family responsibilities have to be considered – and so on the other hand is the decision to hang on to an occupation for which there are declining opportunities.

The position of women is, of course, somewhat different. Young single women, though subject to somewhat greater social constraints, are like young men in being relatively free of household responsibilities, but as they become older they are apt to acquire them. The position of married women is different again. The decisions of married women on whether or not to take a job are in current circumstances a chief determinant of changes in the size of the British labour force, and in recent years more married women have been seeking employment. But their decisions to work are taken against a much more complex set of constraints created by their household responsibilities, and their periods in, and away from, employment naturally reflect their family responsibilities. They are less mobile than male workers and may want special conditions such as part-time work. The circumstances of their employment may also limit their husband's choice of job and create a situation in which the well-being of the household requires a husband – or a wife – to accept a more limited employment opportunity than might otherwise be available if their partner's employment had not also to be considered. In the actual choice of a job a wife may sometimes be as impressed by the desire to have something useful to do which is compatible with her husband's employment or their joint social responsibilities as by any view of maximising her own income.

For most of us the income we earn becomes household income, and both the manner in which we want to receive it and the way it is spent are household rather than individual issues. Though it is conventional to discuss living standards and wages in relation to individual incomes, the effective unit ought to be the household rather than the individual. A wage which may be mildly inadequate for a single man can mean poverty to a man with a large family – a point which is well illustrated by the problems which can arise when rates of payment for State-controlled welfare schemes, which take account of family size, are found to be in excess of wage-earnings for low-paid men with large families. The range of normal earnings for manual workers in Britain tends to be sufficiently small that whether or not the wife is working becomes a more important indication of the family's standard of life than the husband's status as a skilled or unskilled man. Discussions of the effect of rising wages on spending and savings habits should again reflect the household's rather than the individual's income. The emphasis which is nowadays placed on security as an influence on the decisions taken by workers is again directly traceable to the household. Security of employment is specially necessary for those with dependants. A family's income – unlike that of single men – is likely to be committed to a number of regular expenditures – on a house mortgage or rent, on hire purchase, and so on, with the result that the head of a household has a special interest in keeping his pay coming in regularly and in predictable amounts, and this increases his interest both in security of employment and in the security of his income when in employment.

VI. The Employer–Employee Relationship

We are apt nowadays to take it as axiomatic in our kind of society that most workers are employees. There are, of course, employers, but the typical employing unit is one in which the employers are a somewhat shadowy group of shareholders or taxpayers who are very likely to be employees also in their other capacity. The self-employed have tended to be congregated in distinct special categories such as fee-earning professionals, farmers, or small shopkeepers.

This familiar situation, however, is far from universal in the world today and is of comparatively recent origin. If, for example, one were to look over the sweep of history to find what status has been typical for workers, slavery would appear more characteristic than the present situation, while for many parts of the world the usual situation is that of the self-supporting peasant. The slave society, being, in contemporary terminology, able to direct labour, had fewer problems of mobility than contemporary society, while employee rights, which restrict the uses of labour and create occupational barriers, were naturally much weaker. The slave also worked in a context in which his livelihood and his family's domestic circumstances and activities were both part of the same system. The peasant society in underdeveloped countries today creates many difficulties for the development of a wage-earning industrial structure, but so long as workers remain peasants no special markets for labour need develop as distinct from the market for goods sold off the peasants' holding. In peasant communities, as in pre-industrial Britain, the craftsman is likely to be self-employed, negotiating directly with the final consumer, or perhaps with a wholesaler, for his services without the intermediate stage of selling his labour to an employer. Since the employer–employee relationship developed, the change has gone beyond a simple context in which both are easily identifiable individuals. The scale of the employing unit has grown enormously over the last hundred years, and this has meant both that employers have become corporate personalities rather than individuals, and that workers have become members of groups or categories rather than individuals.

The development of the employer–employee relationship and the growth in scale of the typical employing unit have combined to create a number of distinctive features of current industrial relations. First, the trade unions, as distinct from the earlier craft guilds, are associations of employees based on the assumption of a clear separation of the interests of workpeople and of employers in the work to be done. Secondly, a statement of the relationship between the worker and his employer, in terms of the price offered and payable for the workers' services, and separate from the price of the goods, must develop where workers sell their labour. This statement need not be formalised, but the increased scale of enterprises and the advent of trade unions as the bargaining unit have produced increasing formality in the contracts negotiated, and an increasing distance between those who settle terms and conditions of employment and those who work to them. It is worth commenting, however, that there are contrasts between different countries on this point; contracts are, for example, much more formal in the U.S.A. than in the U.K. In the U.S.A. they tend to bargain for each plant or establishment separately, whereas here bargains are generally first struck at the level of a whole industry and nationally, though the terms set are often supplemented locally. Thirdly, the establishment of wage or salary earning as the typical method of payment for work has created a series of customs and laws governing the way in which men provide their service, protect their 'capital' as trained men and negotiate to secure improvements in their conditions. Fourthly, the social context of the employee is in many ways very different from that of his predecessors. His work and his home are quite distinct. He is a specialist very little of whose work is for his own consumption. Finally, the emergence of employee status as a usual condition brings with it unemployment, redundancy and all the other issues that arise when a man and his work can be separated. On the other hand, in the previous context under-employment or starvation could follow from a subsistence economy or from self-employment, and it is more readily possible nowadays to separate a man from his work on retirement and to make provision in the scheme of things for ill health and other misfortunes.

In brief, the employer–employee relationship is the basic assumption of current thinking and experience on labour matters, and as such it sets aside many of the labour problems of the last two centuries from those of preceding generations, while the increased scale of the employing unit may now be setting aside contemporary problems once more from those that preceded them.

VII. Productivity and Leisure

The return which the society in which he lives receives from a man's work is one of the most important matters about which labour economists should enquire. It is also, however, one of the most difficult to elucidate. There are problems both of concepts and of measurement, and the problems raised are coterminous with our whole subject-matter rather than a single confined topic.

The easiest way to look at labour's output is simply to argue that the harder a man works the more he will produce. This is, of course, true, but achieving efficiency in the utilisation of labour and improvements in productivity involve more than simply inviting everybody to work a bit harder. We have to ask other questions as well. Have they the right equipment? The seeds of growth come from much broader changes than simply the rate of working. If we wish to improve productivity, we need to look first to the level and content of investment and then to whether the labour is fully effective in its use of the available equipment. This latter question is partly a matter of an effective rate of work – a way of putting the matter that correctly infers that steady work is at issue rather more than erratic peak performances – and partly one of seeing to it that labour is deployed in the best possible way. Within a place of work this raises questions about the efficiency of management, the method of payment, supervision, and the existence of impediments to effective working in the form of restrictive practices or out-dated conventions. More generally, the deployment of labour to achieve effective work takes us on to all the topics of labour economics – the adequacy of education and training in quality and volume, the structure of the labour force, mobility and immobility, and the extent to which the wage structure is an efficient allocating agent.

The amount of work actually produced is also a function of the division between work and leisure. Again this is a topic which will recur in various guises throughout this book. There is first the theoretical issue of what determines the preferences of individuals for work or for leisure. We shall be discussing this, but unfortunately no simple answer will emerge. Family commitments, changing social conventions, including the availability of facilities for leisure activities, the level and the pattern of income, including the extent to which payment is available when not at work, and interventions by the legislature, are all factors that will affect the choice between leisure and work. Efficiency of operation and the organisation of work are also very much influenced by the way in which leisure is taken. Many issues arise here. The normal age of retirement and the extent to which people choose to postpone retirement influence the size and age distribution of the working population. The length of annual holidays and the incidence of annual and public holidays determine the pattern of working throughout the year. The length of the standard working week and its division between the days of the week, the extent and pattern of overtime working, the use of shift working, and the availability and use of part-time workers determine the rhythm of work during the day and set problems of organising that work effectively. In sum, both the total volume of time spent at work and the way in which that time is allocated are important parts of discussion of the operation of labour markets, and hence of productivity.

The measurement of productivity of labour is subject to at least two major difficulties. First, output has to be related to time at work. Both in terms of comparisons over periods of time and at any given point of time it is, therefore, more accurate to look at productivity as output per man-hour. On the other hand, if we wish to discuss the amount of work achieved, comparisons per man-hour do not sufficiently reflect possible losses of work through increased leisure. It is not by any means necessarily true, however, that the loss of output due to more leisure is directly proportional to the increase in leisure. When hours of work averaged more than sixty in a week, a number of studies suggested that the marginal increase in output from the last few hours worked was probably very small or negative, but this is less likely to be true now, when the average week's work comprises about forty-five hours.

The second problem in measuring the productivity of labour is by far the greater. It is simply that we have the very greatest difficulty in practice in knowing whether an increase in output is to be attributed to labour or to better organisation of work, more capital or better technology, and, further, whether the contribution of labour is due to harder work or to an increase in education and training. It is apparent, for example, that a measure of productivity which is derived simply by dividing increases in output by changes in the size of the labour force or the total number of hours worked contains all sources of productivity improvement and not only those contributed directly by harder work. Indeed, the very concept of continuing improvement of productivity from harder work is itself illusory. We cannot in reason expect people to do their work first at a brisk walk, later at a canter and eventually at a record-breaking run. We come back again to labour's contribution in terms of effective work based on adequate educational foundations, using appropriate equipment, and with good organisation. But to disentangle the contributions to productivity of capital, technology and organisation from those of labour is by no means simple, so that by and large productivity measures require to be treated with caution, while increasing sophistication in the measures makes them less easy to comprehend or operate.

VIII. Differing Viewpoints on Industrial Relations

While this book is mainly concerned with labour economics, it also has a bearing on problems of industrial relations. A brief discussion of the scope of industrial relations as a subject of academic interest and endeavour is therefore needed at this point, to place this book in perspective and to indicate the aspects of industrial relations which are stressed here and those that have appropriately been played down in this treatment.

A number of disciplines have contributed to the contemporary academic study of the employer–employee relationship. Most of the writing on the subject until recently has been in the form of social or institutional history, or detailed description of the working of particular institutions. The lawyers have naturally been concerned with some aspects of industrial relations as a part of their study of industrial law. More recently economists and sociologists have become active in developing their disciplines in this area. It is unfair and difficult to characterise the contribution of these various methods of thinking in a few brief sentences, but it will be helpful to try, looking first to the approaches other than that of the economist and then relating these to the task set before the labour economist.

(1) THE HISTORICAL/INSTITUTIONAL APPROACH

The historical/institutional descriptive tradition had one great strength but several weaknesses. Its strength lay in its insistence on accurate and detailed knowledge of the precise circumstances and the personalities which formed the fabric of the development of the employer–employee relationship over the last two centuries. This tradition of scholarship has given us a close knowledge of institutional development and an appreciation of the ever-important truth that in industrial relations facile generalisations or theorising can be no substitute for a knowledge of the facts – a knowledge which particularly reminds us that decisions in this area can be subjectively as well as objectively taken. The main weakness of the approach is the obverse of its strength – too much institutionalised discussion may conceal the underlying forces in our economy and society which influence our work as much as any other part of our life. In addition, those writing on these lines were for the most part interested in working-class movements and in trade unions rather than in the development of employers' organisations or in the evolution of the administration and ethos of the enterprises themselves. As a consequence, we have inherited a somewhat one-sided view of the history of industrial relations, knowing far more about the trade unions than about any other aspect. In circumstances in which current description and historical development form a larger part of our knowledge than that achieved by analysis of the contemporary situation and forecasts of changes in it, there is always a risk that opinions will be formed too much on analogy with past circumstances and there will be too little emphasis on change. This risk has materialised in the study of industrial relations. The history of trade unionism is one of a struggle for recognition and power while the people they represented have often worked in conditions of irregular employment and poverty. This is not at all the contemporary context of strong trade unions and full employment, and many of the historical attitudes of trade unions are quite irrelevant to the contemporary scene. This kind of statement does not of course invalidate the historical or institutional approach or necessarily devalue the work that has been produced on these lines. It does, however, suggest that an analytical framework is necessary. It is unfortunate that economists and sociologists were slow to turn their minds to industrial relations but helpful that they have done so. On the other hand, it is impossible and wrong to proceed to analyse events in the labour sector without drawing on institutional knowledge, since the institutions provide the framework within which the action takes place.

(2) THE LEGAL APPROACH

The other approach to industrial relations which has a long history is that of the lawyers. It is natural that this should be so. A relationship so important as that between employers and workers has inevitably been the subject of legislation and of legal debate. On the other hand, the British system of industrial relations, unlike that of some other countries, notably the U.S.A., has up to the present been largely organised by the parties to agreements, without much intervention from the law. There are no legal procedures by which unions are recognised as representing particular categories of workers in the employment of particular employers. Collective agreements are not designed as legal documents. Shop stewards operate without benefit of any kind of clear statement of their legal position. The law is, indeed, a bystander in much of British industrial relations. Strikes are unregulated by law provided that the strikers do not behave in a way which would be illegal in the ordinary course of events. The law has acted to remove obstacles to the shaping of our industrial relations, for example, in the long series of Acts relating to trade unions, but has been a prior condition to the process of trade-union development rather than an initiating force. The law in matters of contract is concerned with the relationship between the individual employee and the individual employer, and thus most of the issues settled by collective bargaining are brought into force by agreement rather than by legal obligation, the position in law being one of some complexity.

Two qualifications to this general thesis about the relative unimportance of the law in industrial relations in Britain should be mentioned. First, there are parts of our industrial relations where the law is important. For example, we operate a selective system of minimum wage fixing, and the law prescribes the areas in which, and the way in which, minimum wages are to be fixed, and how they should be enforced. The Factories Acts, and other legislation such as that relating to road transport, limit the ways in which workers can be employed, while legislation related to trade unions defines the freedom of operation which they enjoy. Secondly, British governments have in recent years shown a tendency to want to intervene in industrial relations and in the operation of the labour market much more than they used to do. For example, since 1963 the law has required an employer to give a contract of employment to a worker specifying a period of notice of termination of employment of at least a week, with longer notice for those with longer service, and this procedure has been supplemented since 1965 by an obligation on the employer in cases of redundancy to make redundancy payments according to a prescribed pattern based on length of service. The State has recently also begun to play a major part in the training of workers through the Industrial Training Act of 1964. In discussing recent developments, therefore, it is necessary to take considerable account of changes in the law. On the other hand, the issues that require discussion are not those of interpretation and judgment of a long series of statutes and cases – in which the lawyer is much more at home than economists and sociologists, for example – so much as the implications for policy of such recent statutes, and this is a suitable subject area for discussion by social scientists.

The Royal Commission on Trade Unions and Employers' Associations reported just before this book went to press. It was expressly invited to consider whether changes in the law were required, and received and recommended a number of suggestions for such changes. Again, after a long number of years of voluntary incomes policies, we have begun to take steps which seem bound to limit severely the autonomy of collective bargaining. The 'wage freeze' and 'period of severe restraint' in 1966 and 1967 have not been the first attempts to control the movement of wages, but on this occasion the Government has supplemented its efforts by introducing Prices and Incomes Acts in 1966 and succeeding years. It seems likely, therefore, that in the future the law will become much more important in British industrial relations.

(3) THE SOCIOLOGICAL APPROACH

There are two strands to the investigation of labour and industrial relations by sociologists. The older of these is associated with social reformers as well as social analysts and consists of studies concerned in one way or another with the conditions of life of the working poor. More recently, however, industrial sociologists have developed studies of the motivations of workpeople, of supervision, and of the informal and formal organisation of the work group, the factory or the enterprise. Description of social conditions has an honourable place in the history of social welfare in Britain, since it has been the familiar precursor of social action to alleviate the conditions which it has illuminated. While this type of work continues, however, it is inevitable and appropriate that it should now be increasingly replaced by social analysis, which is a more useful policy-making instrument in that it helps us to appreciate the process of social adjustment to change as well as to see the need for it. Though some of the work of the sociologist in industrial relations barely impinges on that of other scholars – for example, studies of small group organisation and the interaction of personalities within the group are an important contribution to the art of management but do not need to be greatly studied by those concerned with the general operation of the labour market – most situations in industrial relations demand some social understanding. In any study of the reaction of the labour market to change, social as well as economic and institutional factors are clearly highly relevant. The currently important example of this is in research on the possibilities and effects of automation. The reactions of workers to such changes affect the return in improved efficiency which it is hoped to gain. Changes in the demand for labour raise questions of occupational and other forms of mobility, training and retraining. New technology sets up new patterns of working and supervisory relationships. New methods affect the security of work and of payment. All of these have social implications and produce social reactions.

Industrial relations is concerned with people. The most important organisations involved are social organisations building up and adapting their own rules and defining their own purposes; and work and payment, while they are essentially economic, have also considerable social implications. In consequence, while it is possible to set aside much of the specialised sociological literature in approaching an industrial relations topic from some other viewpoint, it is not possible to forget the social background or the social problems.

(4) THE RELATIONSHIP BETWEEN THE ECONOMIC AND
     OTHER APPROACHES

This book is concerned with labour economics. We must therefore ask what is the special economic approach to industrial relations. But first, we should sum up the foregoing, try to give an impression of the perspective on these other viewpoints of industrial relations which is appropriate to the labour economist, and hence indicate the minimum level of knowledge of such matters which will suffice for the student of labour economics. This minimum is, of course, much less than the desirable level of knowledge, and certainly much less than is required by the student of industrial relations as a whole.

Perhaps the least important approach for the labour economist is that of the lawyers. The minutiae of legal discussion need not greatly concern us. The operation of the labour market is influenced by what the law permits and this has to be discussed, but detailed legal analysis is not part of our remit. Again, the minutiae of institutional observation and of procedure need not generally receive much attention from the economist, nor is it essential for the student to know the details of the history of trade unionism, though the broad sweep of that history can illuminate many contemporary problems. And the detail of social survey material relating to social welfare, and the detail of analysis of the work group and social relations in the work place, and of supervisory roles, can generally be set aside, though an awareness of such matters is important to the labour economist. Those aspects of sociological investigation, however, which relate to matters such as the supply of labour, reactions to change, attitudes to security and incentive, and to the mobility of labour are most important to the labour economist, though in practice they hardly appear as social issues to be considered apart from economic analysis, since this type of social awareness is a necessary part of much of the study of labour economics.

In brief, the student of labour economics must know something about the institutional background, and also of the social factors which condition utilisation of labour in the economy. Since institutional factors will differ between one economy and another, and the social background and attitudes can also be somewhat different in different countries, it is almost inevitable that each country has to develop its own labour economics in which the social and institutional environment can be taken into account. This necessary degree of localisation is, of course, unfortunate, but in this context we must accept it and concentrate mainly on the particular character of the British labour market.

(5) THE ECONOMIC APPROACH

What are the distinctive characteristics of the economic approach to the study of industrial relations – and hence of labour economics? Economics itself is concerned with the process of balancing all the many demands upon the resources of the economy with the supply of resources that can be deployed to meet these demands. It studies such relationships at the level of the individual's means and expenditure, from the point of view of the firm, and for the economy as a whole. Economists analyse, but also in practice prescribe and criticise policy measures designed to improve the operation of the economy in some way. Labour economics does all the same things, but with particular reference to labour. Thus labour economics looks at the individual's decision to supply his work and the factors that determine his income. It considers the way in which a firm adjusts its demand for labour relative to technology and capital supply, how it obtains workers, the methods by which it pays for work, and how these wages are settled. At the national level the labour economist is concerned with the structure of the labour force, the wage level and the balance between the demand for labour and its supply. Since these are matters of public importance and, have therefore been the subject of many policy pronouncements and policy measures, the labour economist as well as analysing will inevitably find himself engaged in commenting on and criticising labour market policies.

While the subject-matter of labour economics has a close affinity with the usual subject-matter of economics, it is also true that there are distinctions, and it is these distinctions that mark labour economics out from other parts of the subject. Three distinctions are of special importance. Briefly, labour economics is a separate branch of economics mainly because (a) labour is not a single undifferentiated resource but a complex assortment of people with different training, characteristics and capabilities, (b) a wage is a price, but a special sort of price with characteristics of its own, and (c) the labour market, and especially the supply of labour, is greatly influenced by institutional and social factors which are relevant to it, and not to the same degree to other markets. Many economists have written of wages in an aggregative way, regarding them simply as the price of labour. The labour economist begins to develop with the realisation that labour is not homogeneous, that wages are a system of prices, and that the labour market is in reality a whole interrelated system of markets. While economists in some other branches of economics can keep going without much social or institutional understanding – though perhaps to their detriment – the labour economist cannot do so.

IX. The Contents of this Book

This book has four main Parts which attempt to cover the principal parts of labour economics. The next Part (Part II) describes the British labour market. It first gives an introduction to the institutions that influence the labour market. This is followed by a discussion of wages in Britain – the structure of wages, how they are paid, and how they are fixed. Discussion of the structure of the labour force and of full employment and unemployment end the section. Part III is for the most part analytical rather than descriptive. It discusses the demand for and supply of labour, including the mobility of labour, and the determination of wages. Part IV discusses rather wider issues, being concerned with the way in which incomes of all kinds have grown and been distributed in Britain, both before and after taking account of taxation, and with the long-standing question of what determines the share of wages in total income. Part V discusses some of the current issues which are affecting the operation of the labour market.

Some of the issues chosen were self-selecting – inflation and incomes policy, and technical change and automation, for example. It is not possible, however, to discuss all possible issues, and we have chosen the others as those which seem to us to be of special importance: training, manpower planning, security and migration. It is our hope that the book as a whole will be found to have sufficient depth to be a satisfactory basis for the teaching of labour economics to students throughout their undergraduate course, as well as meeting the needs of managers and others who require a survey of labour market topics.

SUGGESTED READING

While we have not set out to eliminate footnotes, we have not thought it necessary in a book of this type to give extensive references for each point made. On the other hand, the student will wish to have some guidance on further reading. We have therefore appended a few appropriate references to each chapter. Since this chapter is introductory, it offers a convenient point at which to list some general textbooks on labour. All of these are American; except for the second which is by a distinguished British economist, but was written for an American series.

G. F. Bloom and H. R. Northrup, *Economics of Labor Relations*, 5th ed., Homewood, Ill., 1965.

E. H. Phelps Brown, *The Economics of Labor*, Yale, 1962.

A. M. Cartter and F. R. Marshall, *Labor Economics: Wages, Employment and Trade Unionism*, Homewood, Ill., 1967.

N. W. Chamberlain, *The Labor Sector*, New York, 1965.

M. W. Reder, *Labor in a Growing Economy*, New York, 1957.

L. G. Reynolds, *Labor Economics and Labor Relations*, 4th ed., Englewood Cliffs, N.J., 1964.

Part II

The British Labour Market

2 Institutions in the Labour Market

I.

It is not unusual for economists to be concerned with problems which cannot be divorced from their institutional setting: for example, monetary discussion in Britain must assume the existence of the Bank of England, and require some knowledge of the characteristic features of that august institution. But labour economics is specially influenced by institutional factors. There is therefore a strong temptation to write a book on labour economics mainly from the institutional point of view, and to devote perhaps the first half of the book to a discussion of trade unions and employers' associations and the like. This approach is deliberately forsworn here, partly, as Chapter 1 has already suggested, because trade unions in particular are quite adequately discussed in a number of British books, and a lengthy account is not needed here. (An indication of such fuller sources of information is given as Suggested Reading at the end of this chapter.) Moreover, to give great emphasis to institutional description in a book on labour economics might tend to give institutional factors unreasonable priority in the reader's mind, and so obscure many other important aspects of the subject. It is essential to remember that institutions lie in the background of the discussion; it is wrong, and probably harmful to understanding, to give undue emphasis to the institutional aspects at the expense of the more theoretical, and in the longer run perhaps more important, factors. Nevertheless some knowledge of the institutional background is a necessary first step, and so we must at this stage give preliminary treatment of some important features.

This chapter will discuss trade unions, employers' associations and the Government as the relevant institutional forces. It is, however, important to stress at the outset that the interests of institutions and of their members are not always the same thing. Workers and employers may have different interests from all of the trade unions, the employers' associations and the Government. The employer is interested in his own special labour requirements, which may not be coincident with the views of his employers' association and may not necessarily fall into line with

B

Government policy. The individual worker has to consider his own life and his own interests. The trade union may get its members as much money as possible; but a worker may be a member of a minority group in a particular trade union and have particular aspirations different from those of most of the membership. His work is, to the individual employee, not just a means of obtaining money, but a way of life, and any extra money a trade union may get for him is not just an addition to a pay packet once a week but the means to a particular standard of life. Both the individual worker and the individual employer have unique interests in the labour market, and the presence of these interests must always be borne in mind. It is sometimes possible in aggregative discussion about wages and labour supply to think only of the views of representative institutions and forget the people we are talking about!

II. Trade Unions

Trade unions are not purely economic institutions. We ought not to expect them to act as a kind of collective economic man. We ought not, indeed, even to expect that their actions will always be consistent, either with each other or with some kind of preconceived economic theory, economic policy, or social policy. They are social institutions, and like all social institutions they are from time to time somewhat confused in their ideas about what they are trying to do. Like all institutions in a democratic society they are subject to doubts, and to conflicting policies put forward by different parts of the organisation. It would be wishful thinking to build trade unions into an economic theory as rational economic decision-takers. They have, of course, an important part in discussion of the way in which labour is supplied, and the terms on which it is supplied, but the part they play cannot be adequately summed up in a word or two of economic rationalisation. And if we look at the way in which trade union activity expresses itself, we may find a number of confused voices and results. Despite this lack of safe generalisations about trade unions, the economist may be tempted to go on to see whether any objective economic processes may be discovered working behind the front of social and institutional processes associated with trade unions. While analysis of the outcome of trade-union actions may yield useful economic results, it is wise to be wary of attributing oversimplified motives to trade unions.

Certainly collective institutional statements of the motives and objectives of workers must be treated with some caution.

The complex organisational pattern of British trade unions is one reason for the general suggestion that a trade union may be expected to speak with many voices. They are organised at different levels: the branch, the district, the national level, possibly the workshop as distinct from the branch, probably the shop steward as distinct from the local official. The problems facing these different levels of the trade union are different and the answers they give can be different. Thus, for example, a national agreement negotiated by trade union national officers may be much more clear-cut and much more simple than the complex pattern of problems that face a shop steward or a local official in dealing with the wage structure and payment methods of one particular place of work. One symptom of this has been the conflict which has from time to time arisen in recent years between shop stewards and the full-time officials of trade unions. This has come out in unofficial strikes, and in shop stewards from time to time taking control of the detailed problems out of the hands of the central organisation. If, then, we ask who decides trade-union tactics and policy, we may get a different answer depending upon what organisational level we are thinking about.

Another organisational problem which produces some confusion of counsel, and is a source of frequent criticism by managements, is that there is no great coincidence between the pattern of unions of different types and the pattern of industry in Britain, or indeed of the pattern of firms. It is customary to say that there are three or four major types of union in Britain, though this statement is somewhat more simple than the facts. The craft union is organised on the principle of a single craft, or a group of crafts, no matter in what industry these craftsmen may occur, such as the Patternmakers' Union, or the Boilermakers. The general union purports to recruit workers whatever their industry or grade of work. In theory anyone can join a general union provided he is an employee and is not already in a union. In practice the general unions are the strongholds of the unskilled and semi-skilled factory operatives. They are particularly important in the newer industries where skilled trades of the older types are less numerous, and they have big memberships in transport and public authority employment. Then, thirdly, there is what appears to be the clear and tidy principle of organisation, the industrial union; but there are no clear-cut examples of industrial unions in Britain. Perhaps the best example would be the National Union of Mineworkers; but it does not organise all the people in the mining industry or all the people with whom the National Coal Board negotiates. For the most part attempts by industrial unions to become the sole union for one industry have not succeeded. Finally there is the growing group of non-manual workers' unions, which, generally speaking, overlap from one industry to another, though some are by their nature confined to one industry or one group of employers (as in the case of the National and Local Government Officers' Association or the Civil Service Clerical Association). Some professional organisations, though they have had considerable success in promoting the interests of their workers in negotiating salary changes and controlling the terms of entry into their professions, combine these trade-union activities with more general professional concerns such as promoting research and publishing learned journals. Such associations would probably not accept a trade-union label but are nevertheless part of the increasing organisation of non-manual workers for labour market purposes.

The result of this pattern of different types of union is that when an industry comes to negotiate with its employees' representatives, it finds that it is in fact negotiating with many unions. There are over thirty unions party to the agreement in the engineering industry; and it is difficult to think of any industry where only one union is involved. It cannot be assumed that the different unions have an agreed point of view on labour matters; indeed, the opposite is very often the case. For example, the past history of disputed wage claims between the British Railways Board and the railway unions is largely a history of attempts by the Board to conciliate first one union and then another.

At the particular level of the firm the same kind of pattern emerges again. A giant firm like Imperial Chemical Industries has a large group of almost twenty signatory unions, but smaller firms also have a number of unions. An engineering firm, for example, is likely to have to negotiate with one or both of the big general workers' unions, the Transport and General Workers' Union and the National Union of General and Municipal Workers: it will certainly have to deal with the Amalgamated Union of Engineering and Foundry Workers; it probably has the Pattern-makers and the Draughtsmen, and frequently some others.

Naturally, the answers given by the union side in these circumstances are complex. Moreover, some disputes in the post-war period allegedly between the employers and unions have in fact been disputes among two or more unions, with the employers standing by. Disputes between unions on which union should represent a particular group of workers (jurisdictional disputes) are likely to be matters which affect the organisation and the output of a factory, but the employer can usually intervene in them only at his peril. The same is true of demarcation disputes, where union members quarrel over who should carry out particular work and have the employment that goes with the work. While it is possible to form the general impression that trade unionists are all alike, or at least all differ from the rest of humanity rather more than they differ from each other, in practice this is just not true. There is all the difference in the world between the problems of the old-established craft and its trade union, and the problems of the unskilled labourer. In the printing industry, for example, the craft unions have always taken a line which has tended to preserve the differential position of the craft and the status of the craft. The general workers' unions were not blessed by the ready co-operation of the craft unions in their early development. At present the differentials accorded to skill in different industries depend to quite an extent on relative power either within a single union, or within a group of negotiating unions where craft as well as less skilled elements are represented. It would be absurd in the extreme to suggest that there is only one viewpoint in a union such as the Transport and General Workers' Union, which includes in its membership female semi-skilled operatives in mass-production factories, ship pilots on Merseyside, dockers in most parts of the country, road passenger transport workers, heavy lorry drivers – and so on through a very long list.

This general problem of the conflict between the organisational pattern of the trade unions and the pattern of their relations with employees has led to a growth of federations of trade unions, so that for particular negotiations a large federation of unions meets as one and presents a united front, though the united front must be compounded of a great many diversities in individual attitudes. Some of these federations, such as the National Federation of Building Trades Operatives, have a tight constitution; others, such as the Confederation of Shipbuilding and Engineering Unions, where many different elements are included, have a very loose constitution.

The structure of the leadership of the trade unions and its relationship to the membership is another matter which requires consideration if we are to understand how the trade unions function. Union constitutions differ widely, and the authority delegated to officials, the position of officials in the formal union structure, the period and the terms of office of officials, and the method by which officials are selected, can all differ radically from one union to another. Nevertheless, the formal differences created by the constitution-makers appear to have relatively little effect from union to union in the way in which the leadership is related to the members. Each union has one or two highly important officials at the centre of affairs. Normally these officials are the general secretaries of their unions, though sometimes the president is the most important personality. In most cases the general secretaries are elected in one way or another, though this is not always true and their periods of office between elections differ; but it is very rare for a general secretary to lose his office before he retires or gives it up. This point is of central importance because it indicates the true nature of the power of the general secretary, or whatever the equivalent official may be in a particular union. He is an elected official, normally, and he appears to be under the control of the members. More immediately he is likely to be under the control of an Executive Committee. Sometimes, to ensure that control, he is not a member of the Executive Committee but accepts instructions. But despite the formal checks to his authority, the general secretary, by virtue of his superior knowledge and experience, can usually dominate the counsels of his union. This is not to say that he can get away with anything at all, but within the broad remit of the union's policy he can be very influential. Union business is nowadays highly complex and expert, and above all very time-consuming. The lay working members of the union cannot compete with the full-time officials in knowledge and understanding, and are therefore bound to some extent to accept advice from their full-time officials. Much of the important union business does not excite the interest and enthusiasm of the members and is left to the officials who shape policy by a series of decisions which are sometimes apparently unexciting and on points of detail. A number of consequences flow from this position of the trade-union leaders.

(a) Since union authority is, for most purposes, concentrated on one man or a few men at the centre of the union, we get rather greater continuity of decision than might otherwise appear likely. On the whole also we have enjoyed, in Britain at least, greater moderation than some sections of the union movement might approve. What degree of success was achieved in the period of the income standstill policy in 1966–7, for example, was largely a reflection of the political wisdom and maturity of the union leaders. On the other hand the policy of a union may alter quite substantially as a result of a change in their full-time officials.

(b) This system throws tremendous responsibility on the shoulders of a few men. It is not clear whether the trade-union movement has yet learned the art of training such men in the context of mature trade unionism. The unions are no longer fighting for a position and do not as obviously require a militant personality for their leader. They are now expected by the public and the Government to conduct themselves with statesmanship and have a sense of responsibility. And they must always be very well aware that they are extremely powerful, and are more vulnerable to accusations of using too much power than of being considered too weak for the situations with which they may be confronted. To be elected by the members from their own number, and then to gain experience after election, may not always be enough to train a satisfactory modern trade-union leader. Moreover, it is not clear that trade-union leaders in modern Britain are given the status and income from their unions that they need if they are to act with a sense of well-being and security. If we assume that most of the local work of a trade union is simple and is done on a voluntary basis, then a few officials to carry out central negotiations may do; but where so much is left to the official as at present, and when it seems clear that the trade unions ought to be playing a greater part in formulating policies all the way down to the factory, there appear to be too few officials to do the job adequately. Those officials that the unions do have are therefore not only underpaid but overworked. One of the greatest barriers to improved collective bargaining in Britain is the lack of sufficient competent trade-union officials to handle the matter from their end.

(c) Since a few overworked officials carry great responsibilities, there is a strong tendency for the principal officials of unions to find themselves at cross-purposes with their members. A difference of outlook between the central leadership and the members is likely to produce an alternative source of authority. The members cannot easily express their dissatisfaction individually, and probably lack the initiative to do so, but they can be led into open protest by local leaders such as shop stewards. Such a situation can result in unofficial strikes designed to remedy specific local grievances, or strike action may possibly be only nominally against the employer and actually aimed at the union's own authority. Alternatively, the local leaders may take decisions and even negotiate agreements without the sanction of the central body of the union, and so lead local policy, and possibly local conditions of work, away from those set by the union. Thus quite a lot of detailed policy has been created at the factory level, not by the union officials, but by the members themselves acting through shop stewards, and it is not always possible to reconcile actions at the local level with declared policies from the centre.

There is always a tendency among the general public to suggest that the Trades Union Congress ought to do something about the current labour problem, whatever that may be. In other words, the general public assume that the T.U.C. has strong executive authority over its member unions.

This is very far from the truth. Certainly the T.U.C. is a kind of parliament of trade unions in Britain, but its decisions are not binding on the constituent unions. It is true that the T.U.C. has a disciplinary committee, but the extreme of that committee's powers is to expel a union from the T.U.C. Such expulsion does not affect the union's collective agreements and really boils down to saying that a union which cannot agree with what is being said at the T.U.C. will not take part in the debate. If a union has already quarrelled with the T.U.C. it may feel that it is as well out of it. The sanction of expulsion is not therefore of final and devastating importance to the union. On the other hand it is comforting to have the moral and sometimes active support of the T.U.C. and to have the comradeship and sense of approbation that comes from being members of a common body of trade unionists. Trade unions do not like to be thrown out of the T.U.C.

If we then realise that the powers of the T.U.C. are formally extremely limited, we have, of course, to go on to ask wherein lies the T.U.C.'s power, if any. Its main source of authority is in its ability to decide on policies or topics where unions are generally in agreement but no clear line has been formulated, rather than in its ability to turn unions back from policies to which they are strongly attached. This shepherding role of the T.U.C. arises from the facts that it is the central body of trade unionism, that it has, over the years, built up prestige and, probably most importantly, because the body which promulgates the T.U.C.'s views, the General Council, is itself composed of the most important trade unionists in Britain. Most of the important general secretaries of the big trade unions are on the T.U.C. General Council, and when it speaks it has authority in its voice and unions listen to it with respect. But they need not obey it!

The actual strength of the trade unions differs very considerably from one industry to another. In some, such as coal mining, all or almost all the employees from the top downwards are in trade unions, while in others, such as retail trades, both membership and degree of organisation are very uneven. The extent of organisation and the attitudes to trade unionism vary between regions, and trade unions are markedly more important for men than for women. On the other hand, the effectiveness of trade unionism is only partially to be reckoned by counting heads. Trade unions are a part of the recognised fabric of our economic life, and this is nowhere more apparent than in the general acceptance of voluntary collective bargaining – negotiation and agreement between employers and recognised representatives of workers – as the way in which terms and conditions of work are settled.

This institution of collective bargaining is a characteristic feature of the operation of the British labour market. The way in which it works, and the extent to which the labour market in practice departs from its formal frameworks, are discussed in later chapters. At this point the methods by which trade unions influence the operation of the labour market may be listed. It will be readily seen that most of them are in practice related to collective bargaining; but even without the presence of some *special* technique or power over events in the market, the trade unions have an important part to play, simply because they now enjoy the *general* right to be heard and to make formal or informal representation to individual employers or employers' organisations on matters that interest them. This right to be heard extends to governmental as well as industrial matters, since governments of both main political parties now follow a well-established practice of consulting the trade unions, and sometimes deferring to their views, on subjects which appear to affect their interests. Indeed governments tend to use trade-union officials – and particularly the influential members of the General Council of the T.U.C. and its General Secretary – as multi-purpose advisers on public affairs.

To an extent which varies with circumstances, trade unions affect the supply of labour to particular occupations or industries, and this control, where it exists, can naturally influence the differential price payable for certain types of work. The extent to which control over the supply of a category of workers is possible is related not only to trade-union strength, but also in a very clear way to the actual degree to which any given occupation is distinct from other occupations. The term 'demarcation' has developed the unsavoury air of an attempt by workers in one occupation to prevent others from doing particular types of work which the occupation claims for itself. But in its neutral sense 'demarcation' simply indicates a process of distinguishing between one thing and another. The labour force is highly demarcated in this sense – and nowhere more so than among the professions. When we say that a particular job requires qualifications we are demarcating it from other jobs. It does not, of course, follow that there is anything wrong in doing this. We all feel much more comfortable in the knowledge that doctors, lawyers, dentists and the rest have been trained for their jobs and have satisfied prescribed tests of their competence. On the other hand, the effect is that we create a separate group in the labour force subject to separate supply by justifiable attention to qualifications and not only by unwarranted attempts to create a monopoly. We must not therefore assume that where a group of workers gains control over the conditions of entry into its occupation, this is an unreasonable interference

B 2

with the free operation of the labour market, since this power rests with, for example, the General Medical Council rather more fully than with a dockers' union. Equally, however, control over qualifications always involves in greater or lesser degree elements of both monopoly and the preservation of quality, whether in motive or in results, and this must be borne in mind whether we are discussing, for example, the way in which lawyers demarcate their professional groups or how the shipbuilding trade unionists specify distinctions in the work and qualifications of riveters and welders.

If we set aside proper concern for qualifications and standards (realising that in practice there can be much debate about what 'proper' means in this context), then we may list the other ways in which trade unions may control entry into an occupation. In British industry the most usual form of such control is by limiting the number of apprentices. A trade union may specify a particular ratio of apprentices to craftsmen, and hold to this ratio without reference to whether the ratio chosen is a reasonable reflection of the number of apprentices that can be trained by a given number of jour- neymen, or to the industry's need to secure an adequate supply of trained workers. As a corollary to this policy such craftsmen, or for that matter professional groups, will also oppose the use of workers who have not qualified by apprenticeship (referred to as dilutees) and will seek agreements limiting or eliminating their entry to the market. The intention of such restrictions is to keep the supply of craftsmen at the lowest feasible level, thus ensuring full employment and better wages and conditions for the craftsmen concerned, while guarding against the possibility that too great a shortage might become a special cause of attempts to find alternative means of production, avoiding the use of the scarce occupation.

Craftsmen, and sometimes also professional groups, have an obvious means of limiting entry into their occupation through defining the skill required and controlling the wages of acquiring it. Trade unionists without this means of operating can still, however, influence the entry of workers who will compete for their supply of jobs by various versions of the 'closed shop'. Sometimes this term means that a man must join a union, and usually a specified union, if he takes a particular job in a particular place of work. In these circumstances, which are usually described as a 'union shop', especially in the American literature, the influence of trade unionists will depend on the extent to which they can persuade employers not to employ particular types of worker. Obviously, workers who are unaccept- able to the union could be eliminated, but they will be employed before the union's view is determined, and this is a weaker position than if a man must be a member of the union before he can be employed. In this latter situation – a closed shop in the full meaning of the term – the union can control the supply of labour for the types of work which it represents. The degree of control is, of course, a function of the way in which admission rules to the union are operated.

Seniority rules provide another method by which workers can control the labour force in their section of the labour market and in so doing improve their own security of employment and promotion prospects. Perhaps the most familiar version of such rules relates to the 'last in, first out' principle which results in increasing the security of the established worker at the expense of increasing the risk of unemployment for the newcomer when demands for labour vary. This in itself strengthens the promotion prospects of the established men who acquire experience and status from service, but seniority rules may also be devised to cover promotion by length of service. Other versions of seniority arrangements may perhaps be operated by a union as a guide to the hiring of new workers, requiring that the first in line be given the job, in determining internal promotion, and in regulating re-employment after a temporary reduction in the labour force.

All these rules help to improve the control of the unions over the way in which workers are supplied. Another means to control can come from influencing the amount of work done and the way in which it is done. Conditions of work range from the facilities provided for workers, and the supplementary benefits which they enjoy over and above their wage and which increase labour cost, to the hours of work for normal pay, the availability of holidays with pay, the tea breaks and so on. These are the most usual parts of collective bargaining and influence either the cost of the work done or the volume of work done in terms of hours or days worked.

Other controls on the amount of work done may, however, depend less on collective bargaining and more on initiatives or understandings, which may be developed by a group of trade-union members in a factory, or possibly simply by a small informal group of workers acting collectively, but not in a formally organised way or as members of a union. Workers may decide on a 'reasonable' work load among themselves, and bring into existence an informal but effective code of behaviour on the volume of work to be done, using social pressures in the work group to keep all members of it in line. In some cases this 'norm' may become institutionalised as the task which a worker is expected to do each day, and a rule or custom may develop which permits the worker to go home early when his task is done. Sometimes the group sets sensible standards of work, sometimes not. The latter circumstance, if backed by a strongly entrenched work group, may be very difficult for the management to alter unless the whole situation in which it exists can be changed.

Workers may also organise some controls over the way in which work is carried out, and again these may be informal understandings or simply habits, or they may go further and become established rules, imposed by union authority or incorporated in collectively bargained agreements. Some habits of work will grow up among any group of people faced with common tasks. We all do this and it is only natural that we should. Sometimes the habits are good and reasonable. Sometimes the circumstances in which habits are established alter with changing technology or changing products and the habits live on beyond their usefulness. It is part of management's job to keep habits of work in line with the needs of production. Techniques such as work study and methods study are devised to do this, and to some extent the technique of productivity bargaining is simply a means of changing habits. Good new habits may simply be a matter for effective supervision. Productivity bargaining is discussed again in later chapters.

Habits may develop into deliberate efforts to share out or spin out work, and union members may purposely devote themselves to devising rules to regulate their own conduct, or to put pressure upon managements. This result may be achieved in one of two ways. First, rules may be devised on how the job is to be done. A union may enforce particular standards for the manning of a machine – maintaining a labour force for it which is larger than is technically necessary – and which offset the cost advantages of its introduction and use. This might be a matter of working practice confirmed by union solidarity or it may form part of an agreement. In some cases, even where there is no specific plant or machine involved, the union may insist on craftsmen being accompanied and helped in their work by a craftsman's mate, frequently on a one for one basis. Restrictions of this type may dissuade managers from embarking on changes in production methods which appear to be technologically justified, as well as keeping costs high in new production processes. Secondly, unions may bring about the splitting up of jobs to a greater degree than managements would like by demarcating jobs to correspond with, and as an essential complement to, the demarcation of occupations which was discussed above. Again there is the necessary reservation that a job, to be properly done, may need a special skill, but overdue insistence on the right of a group or type of workers to be the only people allowed to perform a particular task may split up a natural sequence of operations among several different workers with consequent loss of productivity, as well as preserving of work for each of those who have to be allowed to do their part.

A trade union may attempt to secure its objectives by advocating changes in the law. The regulation of conditions and methods of work by legal changes is a part both of our history and of our current practice. Historically, the law was probably a much more important method of regulating conditions of work and working practices in the nineteenth century than it has been up to now in the twentieth. Certainly, trade unions attempted to use this way of meeting their ends in the labour market, as well as their more general political aims, more exclusively then than now, when the emphasis has shifted to collective bargaining. On the other hand, the trade unions were by no means the sole or, in many instances, the most important agents of improvements in work and working conditions in the nineteenth century. The main agent of change was undoubtedly the rising income of the community, but social reformers of all kinds played their part in specific legislative changes as well. From our present viewpoint these changes in the law have a necessary and desirable look. The limitation of children's work, the regulation of women's work, the improvement of conditions of work in the mines, in merchant shipping, and in the factories, are all part of this story, as are regulations for safety, the careful control of dangerous processes, delimitation of the rights of apprentices and so on. Such changes, however, must be recognised as limiting the operation of the market mechanism and output potentialities, and influencing the cost of labour, even though they may be accepted as desirable and necessary, and current attempts by unions to push new changes in the law have to be considered from this point of view as well as others. For example, restrictive legislation relating to shop hours affects the efficiency of retailing and hence the numbers of workers required in this activity. Regulations affecting road transport and the hours or spells of duty that may be worked in that industry again affect costs and payments. Proposals to ensure control over 'proper' training and qualifications of hairdressers are quite likely to put up the price of hairdressing. These remarks are not intended to suggest that changes in the law are undesirable or unnecessary, but to underline the points that their cost is a relevant factor, and that pressure upon Parliament and political action may be important weapons in a union's attempt to improve the well-being and income of its members.

The last method of achieving trade-union objectives which must be mentioned here is that of strike action. In the nineteenth century strikes were generally long and bitter struggles, often to secure recognition of the right to bargain and be recognised more than to influence one particular bargain. They could, indeed, be regarded as trials of strength from which the outcome was that one side gave in completely rather than that an agreement was finally reached. In practice, the workers usually lost the argument and always suffered during the strike. Now that collective bargaining and all its adjuncts are so well established, the well-organised official strike or a threat of official strike action is more likely to be introduced as a lever to the bargaining situation than as a way of achieving results on its own. The contemporary official strike aims to achieve at minimum cost and duration the maximum impact upon the employers in the industry concerned, and also upon the Government and the public so that the Government will be persuaded to help in pushing the employers towards a more attractive outcome at the bargaining table. The possibility of strike action may be regarded as an underpinning of the realities of collective bargaining. The usefulness of strikes to unions need not be judged solely by the frequency with which they actually happen, and the threat of strike action has been an important part of trade-union policy in advancing their interests in collective bargaining. It is inevitable that the function of a strike as a demonstration or hint in the process of collective bargaining should have resulted in more short strikes rather than the full-scale long-duration strike which is now somewhat rare. Selective strike action, falling on different places or different firms at different times, working to rule (which in practice is the same thing as a 'go-slow'), one-day or token stoppages, and so on, will serve the purpose of indicating the unions' latent strength. There are also, of course, unofficial strikes, which may again occur in many different forms, but these are either related to local bargaining situations, or are best regarded as an indication of protest or unrest in small-scale situations, and it would take us too far from the present context to discuss them here.

It would be possible to go on discussing trade unions and trade-union policies at much greater length, but with the objective of this chapter in mind – to provide only as much institutional material as is necessary for background – it is now time to stop. We have attempted to sketch in some of the characteristic features of union organisation and leadership, and some of the most important means of achieving the general purpose of regulating and bettering the workers' position in the labour market. In so doing we have incurred the risk of leaving the impression that unions spend all their time in conspiring to 'rig the market'. This impression, it may be said in conclusion, is an exaggeration. The compressed nature of this account, while it gives necessary prominence to trade-union actions and their effects, does not sufficiently illustrate the limitations of their powers in many circumstances, obscures the routine character of much trade-union participation in the labour market, and finally plays down the effect of the operation of the market itself, a subject with which much of the rest of the book will be concerned.

III. Employers' Associations

Employers' associations are associations of employers formed to conduct negotiations on wages and conditions of work and to look after, collectively, the labour problems of their members. Less need be said about them here than about trade unions, and less can be said, since there is a surprising lack of research knowledge about them, relative to the large volume of information about trade unions.[1] We do know that most industries now have one or more employers' associations, which are increasingly members of a larger federation, but comparatively little can be said about the constitutions or the practices of such associations in general. The main reason for this lack of knowledge is that employers' associations are often fairly secretive about their doings. Their leaders seem less inclined to make speeches than trade-union officials. Their membership is, of course, smaller in number and so their proceedings can be kept more secret, and in general they do not appear to be specially anxious to make their dealings widely known. While a few industries have associations for labour purposes only – associations of businessmen in their capacity as employers – the situation is somewhat confused by the fact that most industries combine in one association the function of an employers' association for labour matters and a general trade association which deals with commercial and industrial problems. In these associations labour issues such as collective bargaining, advice on manpower problems, and procedures for dispute settlement are dealt with as they arise, along with a continued interest in such matters as production methods, competition, quality, new raw materials, and all the various things that form the business of a general-purpose trade association.

Perhaps the most important thing to remember about employers' associations is that they originated mainly as a form of collective defence

---

[1] To some extent this has recently been remedied by the work of the Royal Commission on Trade Unions and Employers' Associations, notably in the evidence of various individual associations and in the Royal Commission Research Paper No. 7, *Employers' Associations*, H.M.S.O., 1967.

against trade-union pressures. As such, one of their main functions is in the negotiation of basic rates for the industry or section of industry they represent, and in trying to keep member firms in line with these rates. Pressure from the association is often felt to be necessary, either to prevent firms from paying less than the negotiated rates (which would give some cost advantage to the wage-cutter but which is very exceptional in a situation of full employment and labour shortage) or to prevent members from paying above the rate. This latter case is much more prevalent in the labour shortage context of the post-war period, in which member firms with a need for more labour may be tempted to raise basic rates to attract labour from competing firms. To some extent associations may be able to persuade firms not to raise basic rates in this way, but even so there are many alternatives open to the firm which wishes to poach labour: for example by guaranteeing a high level of overtime or, where piece-work systems of payment exist, by loosening the norms. The average employers' association has little or no control over this kind of practice, though there do appear to be a few exceptions where the common interest of constituent firms is strong enough to persuade them that the association should be given effective power over non-conforming firms.

The difficulty here is that there is not always an effective sanction available to the association. Where the functions of employers' and trade associations are combined in one body, the threat of expulsion may mean that a firm would lose certain advantages, such as the exchange of technical information, discounts on purchases, and the like. Elsewhere the benefits may be less tangible, as for example where the advantage of membership is confined to the existence of a collective mouthpiece to Government or other important bodies by means of the association, or to the presence of advisory services, or a forum for general discussion, which an individual firm may not use much in any case. In such cases the threat of expulsion or of a fine may mean little to the recalcitrant firm and the authority of the association is weak. In general it seems to be very much the case that the scope and authority of associations is determined by the nature of members' interests and by the kind of functions the member firms wish the association to perform.

The staff of the association act as professional negotiators whose job is to negotiate as tight an agreement as possible with the trade unions. Since they act as negotiators rather than as employers, they can on the one hand concede an increase without necessarily being tied to the economic position of individual members, and on the other hand may not negotiate wage increases large enough to satisfy the recruitment needs of some of their members.[1] The extent to which the association tries to set a realistic and effective maximum rate, as opposed to one which is essentially a minimum basis for additional payments, varies from case to case; but on the whole the latter is much the more common, especially in view of the rather limited sanctions available to most associations. We must expect to find, from time to time, a gap between the policies recommended by associations and the needs of particular employers, with the corollary that individual employers fill in the somewhat negative and defensive prescriptions of their association with more positive wage policies of their own construction, designed to meet their own special needs and circumstances.

Employers' associations generally carry out many other functions in addition to negotiation, though the precise range of activities varies a great deal. The range of activities is determined only to a small extent by the members' subscriptions and the extent of the employer coverage in the trade, which on average appears to be around 75 per cent of potential. Much more important seems to be the desire of members for either a forum of *discussion* of broad policy issues or a really effective means of implementing group decisions. In most cases, however, important non-wage activities include the development of machinery for dispute settlement and the provision of special staff to negotiate over disputes and strike action on behalf of member firms, the provision of information and advisory services for management, the representation of employers' interests to Government, assistance with special manpower problems such as recruitment, training and safety, and the collection of trade statistics, particularly on employment and wages.

Associations of employers for labour matters, those with mixed trade and employer functions, and general trade associations are in most cases members of the Confederation of British Industries. The Confederation has a role in relation to Government which is broadly similar to that of the T.U.C. By virtue of its size and representative character it too is a multi-purpose adviser on all industrial and employment matters, sometimes pushing its advice unasked on a reluctant Government and often being called in for consultations. In this way it has come to be influential in many broad labour issues, such as incomes policy. It was, for example, one of the three signatories to the Joint Declaration of Intent on Incomes Policy in 1964.

[1] However, many associations have local or regional branches, whose staffs may be called in to assist in negotiation of wages above the minimum in the individual firm. In this way the association is able to keep some degree of control over the inter-firm variation of wage rates.

IV. Government

The Government is both a very large employer and, as the actual political and administrative authority of the country, has a natural interest in, and influence upon, the labour market. It has the usual point of view of an employer in securing good value for its wage and salary bill, and additionally its expenditure is under continual scrutiny by the taxpayers and their elected representatives. But there is also a tendency for people to feel that the Government should set a good example. Government is usually expected to be enlightened – a term which in this context is probably a synonym for generous – in its investment policy, its wage and salary arrangements and the other conditions of service which it offers. But at other times, especially when the Government is appealing for restraint in increasing incomes, or other unpopular measures, the idea that the Government should set a good example is likely to mean that Civil Servants, and others whose pay and conditions are to some measure under Governmental guidance, should be treated in a specially strict way. These conflicting forces make the study of the Government as an employer especially intriguing. This is unfortunately not a topic that can be pursued at length in this book. Two points may, however, be made. First, the normal way in which Government tries to avoid these dilemmas is to try, whenever possible, to pass the burden of difficult decisions on the pay and conditions of its employees on to independent bodies, the most permanent and important being the Civil Service Arbitration Tribunal, and to base its own decisions on 'objective' evidence, mainly in the form of comparisons with outside employment provided by the Pay Research Unit, with, in the recent past, additional guidance from the National Board for Prices and Incomes. Secondly, this process, and the general situation, are likely to weaken the Government's control over its own labour policy, which may then lack decisiveness and flexibility. The fact that its labour policy tends to be publicly stated and precisely delineated is not always compatible with the degree of flexibility and adaptability necessary to promote the optimal deployment of the labour force in terms of productivity.

The broadest aspects of the policy by which a Government influences the labour market lie in its ability to adjust the overall level of demand for labour, its concern for full employment and unemployment, and also its influence, through deflation and inflation, and, more directly, by incomes policy, on the level of wages. These matters will be discussed in Chapters 7, 20 and 21. The Government also influences the labour market's operation in many more detailed ways, which need only be mentioned here since they come up for more detailed discussion in later chapters.

The main direct efforts of the Government in the labour market are administered by the Department of Employment and Productivity (formerly the Ministry of Labour).[1]

(a) The Department is responsible for promoting and co-ordinating the work of the Industrial Training Boards and providing Government Training Centres.

(b) It provides a number of different types of machinery for settling industrial relations disputes which, while they can be concerned even with issues affecting individuals, are often the means by which big issues on conditions of labour supply and payment are settled. Some parts of collective bargaining – notably the Joint Industrial Councils – are run by the Department, and the Wages Councils procedures set minimum wages which are enforced by the Wages Inspectorate of the Department.

(c) There exists a large volume of legislation on working conditions, safety, and the like, resulting from a long series of Factory Acts and related legislation. This legislation is administered by the Department through the Factory Inspectorate.

(d) One of the most important needs of the labour market is for information – the essential prerequisite of any market. The employment services of the Department – the network of local employment exchanges, Youth Employment Officers and so on – are an important source of market information provided through official Government agencies. At a more general level, an understanding of the labour market both for policy and

---

[1] Parts of the Department of Economic Affairs concerned with prices and incomes policy were added to the Ministry of Labour in April 1968, and the Ministry was then rechristened the Department of Employment and Productivity, under Mrs Barbara Castle as First Secretary of State. This change seems to be broadly in line with the view of the functions and objectives of the Ministry of Labour which informs much of the discussion of Part III of this book. Moreover, incomes policy was the most important part of Governmental activity in the labour market not fully under the guidance of the Ministry of Labour prior to April 1968. It will, however, be too early to give a full assessment of the practical influences of this administrative change before this book goes to press. Since it has an established meaning and history, the title Ministry of Labour will be used throughout the book wherever the reference is to the past, but the new title will be used in references to the contemporary situation and to the future. The Ministry of Labour *Gazette*, to which frequent reference is made in this book, changed its name to the *Employment and Productivity Gazette* in June 1968. The older title is used here since all the references are to issues bearing that title.

other purposes depends upon a reliable flow of statistical information, the main source of which is the Department of Employment and Productivity.

Five further major areas in which the Government influences the operation of the labour market, mainly through other Ministries, are worth listing here. First, the provision of education, as well as being an obligation on society and a source of non-monetary profit to the individual, is also a major factor in labour supply (Chapter 17). Secondly, the labour market in Britain is underpinned by social security arrangements, notably relating to unemployment, sickness and redundancy (Chapter 18). Thirdly, the Government may by its policies on technical change influence the occupational pattern of the labour market's operations (Chapter 16); and fourthly by its regional policies influence its locational pattern (Chapter 19). Finally, taxation changes the take-home pay of workers and affects their incentive to work (Chapter 14).

The foregoing is something of a catalogue rather than a discussion. This is partly because so many of the ways in which Government is involved are discussed in later chapters. It is also true, however, that in a country in which the Government embarks on active social and economic policies it is difficult to find any aspect of the labour market in which such policies are not an influential factor. British Governments have been active in social policy related to the labour market at most times in our history, but have in recent years become increasingly interventionist both in general economic policy and in regarding the labour market as an important sector in which to exercise influence.

SUGGESTED READING

E. H. Phelps Brown, *The Growth of British Industrial Relations*, 1959.
G. D. H. Cole, *An Introduction to Trade Unionism*, 1953.
A. Flanders and H. A. Clegg (eds.), *The System of Industrial Relations in Great Britain*, 1954.
A. Flanders, *Trade Unions*, 1952.
A. Flanders, *Industrial Relations: What is Wrong with the System*, 1965.
A. Flanders, *Collective Bargaining: Prescription for Change*, 1967.
K. G. J. C. Knowles, *Strikes*, 1952.
Ministry of Labour, *Industrial Relations Handbook*, revised ed., 1961.
B. C. Roberts, *Trade Unions in a Free Society*, 2nd ed., 1962.
B. C. Roberts (ed.), *Industrial Relations, Contemporary Problems and Perspectives*, 2nd ed., 1968.
Royal Commission on Trade Unions and Employers' Associations, *Report*, 1968.
Royal Commission, Research Paper No. 7, *Employers' Associations*, 1967.
E. L. Wigham, *Trade Unions*, 1956.
J. Woodward, *Industrial Organisation: Theory and Practice*, 1965.

3 Wages and Methods of Wage Payment

I. The Meaning of 'Wage'

The word 'wage' is used so frequently in the English language that it might seem reasonable to take it for granted that everybody knows what it means. This, however, is a most dangerous assumption; a word in such frequent use acquires many shades of meaning according to context. Indeed, in the case of 'wage', or 'wages', these various shadings have so proliferated that preliminary separation of the different varieties is essential, especially since much of the discussion that follows is concerned with distinctions between different types of wage.

'Wages' can have either a very broad meaning or a rather narrow one. At the widest, wages are the reward to the factor of production labour, and so include any payment for work, whether it is work done for an employer or that of a self-employed man. For example, the element in a trader's takings which is reckoned to be due to his own personal services, assessed at the value they would command in the labour market, can be regarded as an imputed wage and so part of the remuneration of the factor of production labour. Similarly, fees earned by professional people can be regarded as part of wages in this context in economic theory. 'Wages', when the term is used with reference to employed persons only, sometimes means all forms of direct labour cost, including fringe benefits, while more frequently it refers only to the elements of payment that figure in the pay packet. When economic statisticians discuss the wage bill, they are frequently including salaries as well. At other times wages are carefully distinguished from salaries as being the reward of operatives rather than supervisors, of hourly or weekly paid workers rather than of monthly paid, or of manual workers rather than clerical or white-collar workers. The division between wages and salaries is, however, always somewhat arbitrary. Shop assistants, for example, used to be thought of as salaried but now seem to have become wage-earning, presumably because their job, while 'white collar', is weekly paid, and at a low level. More narrowly still, a man's wage is sometimes identified with his *wage rate*, the stated amount at which he is hired, expressed on a time basis in relation to an hour or a day or a week's attendance at work net of any additions in the form of bonus, overtime payments, etc. Because of the possibility of many other kinds of payment, a man's wage rate may differ from his 'wages' – which in the colloquial sense usually means the amount he takes home at the end of the week. Further, the amount which goes home with the worker (his 'take-home pay' in the American terminology) will differ from the gross amount he has earned because of such things as social security and income tax deductions. It is perfectly possible to find 'wages' being used to mean the gross amount of a man's earnings, or the net amount which he customarily takes home with him, while an amount smaller than the first of these and probably smaller than the second – his negotiated wage rate – may also sometimes be described as his wage.

The distinctions between his wage rate, his earnings and other elements of payment are most important for the worker concerned, and also for our understanding of how the labour market works. They involve a recognition of several different types of wage payment which fill out the worker's pay packet. Each of these methods of payment has its own purposes, characteristics and peculiarities, and this chapter is devoted to their examination. To begin with we look at each payment method separately, but in practice it is very usual for a worker to be paid several different types of payment at once; an obvious and simplified example would be that of a worker receiving a basic time payment plus bonus earnings and overtime payment.

II. Time Payments

The salary is perhaps the most simple payment based on time. It is a pure time payment, since it is drawn up as a statement of so much money payable to an individual, or to each member of a group of people with given and known characteristics, for a certain period of time.

In the case of salaried workers the period of time involved is a month or possibly a year, whereas for wage earners the period involved is generally a week or less. In itself this point is no more than a difference in description of the payment contract; but it is accompanied by a real distinction in the period of notice voluntarily given by employers, as distinct from the minimum requirements of the Contracts of Employment Act of 1963. Even so, the difference between a month's and a week's notice is not very substantial, and the actual differences between salary earners and wage earners owe rather little to this formal distinction in the timing of payment and much more to differences in the type of work commonly remunerated by each type of payment and to associated differences in conditions of service.

Non-manual workers are usually salaried, while most operative grades are wage-earning. Supervisory, administrative, managerial and professional employees tend to be, and indeed are almost invariably, salaried. The result is that senior employees of a firm are paid salaries while, generally speaking, the lower grades are paid wages. The status difference, which gives to the salary earner a social position within and outside the firm which is not accorded to the wage earner, is perhaps partly a reflection of this. Marginal groups such as clerical workers (and until recently shop assistants), by being given salaries have shared in this social esteem which has, in consequence, led to dissatisfaction among the more highly-skilled and responsible wage earners. A highly-skilled tradesman, with a daughter who has completed her secondary education and has a clerical job in the same firm, could find himself in respect of his conditions of service in an inferior position to his daughter.

Salaried workers tend to have other advantages in conditions of service besides greater social status. The formal monthly contract with its obligation to give a month's notice has its importance; but perhaps more important is the usual inference that the salaried worker must be given more notice and should, in general, be less readily made redundant than the wage earner. Of course this is in part due to the fact that the senior staff in a firm will be salaried workers, and to the general nature of the jobs which lead to salaries. Salaried workers in industry may have an office of some sort rather than be on the work-floor, the volume of their activities does not fluctuate widely with the volume of output, and within an organisation of a given size fluctuations in the numbers of salaried workers will tend to be slight. Their cost as workers is commonly assessed on an overhead rather than a variable or direct cost basis. There is less short-run variation in numbers employed in service industries and public administration, which have high proportions of salaried workers, and the same is true of the professions. Perhaps because their jobs are more secure, salaried workers tend to have given to them many formal security provisions which add to their well-being and improve their conditions of service. For example, retired salaried workers are much more usually found enjoying a pension provided wholly or partly by the firm than retired wage earners. Salaried workers tend to be treated more generously when they are ill, and special provisions for sickness are more common for salaried than for wage-earning employees. Further, hours of work in Britain for office staffs and for administrative people generally tend to be formally shorter than those of wage-earning employees; since such people are salaried, this means that salaries are usually associated with somewhat shorter weekly hours of work. On the other hand, informal overtime is perhaps more usual for salaried workers than for wage earners, and extra payment for overtime is less usual. One very important distinction is that salaried workers often have a salary scale which ensures regular annual increments as experience increases, and this is very rare for wage earners. In sum, a salary is a straight time payment calculated on a monthly basis; but the main distinctions between it and a wage are derived largely from the kinds of job that are remunerated by wages and salaries respectively, and the supplementary conditions of service that have been developed for salaried workers.

Among wage earners time payment can take a number of different forms, but its formal expression will be the same in each case – a certain sum of money for a certain grade of worker or a certain individual worker for a certain period of time. Normally in the case of wage earners the period of time will be expressed either as an hour, or as a shift, or as a week of so many hours' duration. The most obvious type of time payment for wage earners, and the closest parallel to the salary, is the standard time rate, which is intended to be paid without additions or supplementation. Many collective agreements provide for such standard time rates for workers of particular grades in the industry concerned. The agreement assumes that workers in individual firms will actually be paid the standard time rates; but the needs of particular employers, and possibly the different characteristics of particular workers, may mean that standard time rates are, in practice, supplemented. In consequence we can have two standard time rates applicable to the same workers – the standard time rates in the national agreement, and the further standard time rates which are actually valid in particular factories (the latter being greater than the former).

Collective bargaining agreements may also express time rates in the form of minima. For example, an agreement may specify a minimum rate for a certain category of workers for a certain number of hours. All Wages Council wage determinations are in the form of minima of this general type. The category of workers for whom the minimum is prescribed may be large or small; a very elementary agreement would merely recommend one minimum payment for all workers in an industry, or for men and women separately. The minimum time payment may take different forms. It may, for example, be expressed in terms which suggest that the workers in the industry are paid on a time basis and that this is the minimum time rate which would be appropriate. On the other hand the minimum may take the form of a guaranteed minimum which simply indicates that no matter how workers are paid they should be guaranteed not less than a fixed amount for a fixed period of time. Sometimes the minimum payment appears as a 'fallback' rate, which expressly indicates that the worker is paid on other than a time basis but also says that he or she is to be able to fall back on to the minimum time payment if earnings from other sources do not exceed it.

The major characteristic of the time payment is that it is a payment which is conditional only on the worker turning up for his job for the recognised period of hours. It has no direct relationship to performance or to the quality of work which the man does, though of course a scale of time payments associated with promotion has the aspect of satisfactory and above average performance built into it. Secondly, the time payment is relatively predictable and secure. For example, one way in which the salaried worker is on the whole more secure than the wage earner is simply that the salary is predictable, whereas many wage earners are not completely paid in such predictable ways, for example because they may have variable bonus or premium payments. Thirdly, because a time payment can be clearly expressed, and is frequently clearly recorded in some form of agreement, there is the greater security that formal procedures are required to alter its level; it is not really very easy for a time payment to be eroded or altered by informal action.

III. Payment by Results

The essential characteristic of systems of payment by results, of whatever type they may be, is that payment is related directly to work done. Their main purpose is to ensure extra output from workers by providing the incentive of a direct and immediate relation between work and payment. Formal systems of payment by results tend in practice to divide into two main groups, which may be called piecework and time allowances; though the general intention is the same in both cases and distinctions between them are more technical than analytical.

(1) PIECEWORK

The idea behind piecework is that the worker is remunerated according to the number of units of output he produces, and the unit of output is therefore priced. Many piecework systems, especially the older varieties, have behind them a formal price list, some of which have a long history; the cotton textile industry in Lancashire, for example, has negotiated most elaborate price lists for a long number of years. The boot and shoe industry has printed price lists covering each particular type of shoe produced by the industry (with a separate list for army boots!). These lists indicate the prices to be paid, for example, for each inch of stitching the uppers of various types of shoe, and show the variations in price that may occur with every conceivable variation in the design of the shoe. Whether or not the price list is published, the essence of payment based on piecework is that a price should be agreed for a unit of output and that the worker should be remunerated according to the number of units he produces. Piecework may be based on the individual or on the group. In individual piecework the individual worker is remunerated according to an estimate of his own output, while in group piecework the group's output is reckoned up and there must be some agreed principle of division of the rewards payable to the group. Piecework is frequently accompanied by some form of time rate. Thus a further variety of time rate, which may occur in agreements, and which may occur in the same or in a somewhat different form in factories, is the pieceworker's basic time rate. Such a basic time rate would be payable to the pieceworker before the calculation of his piecework earnings and in addition to those earnings. It would provide to the pieceworker some guarantee of stability and some certain payment in addition to that which depends upon his own output.

(2) TIME ALLOWANCES

In systems of payment based on time allowances, output is timed rather than priced. There are a number of such systems, but all rely on some kind of standard time which is allowed to the worker for the performance of a given quantity of output. Payment is based on the time allowed rather than the time actually taken, or on some relationship between the time allowed and the time taken. Some form of time rate is used as the basis of payment – either the time rate which would apply to the worker if he were a time worker, or a specially designed time rate. It is usual to safeguard the situation where the worker takes a longer time than he is allowed by providing that payment under an incentive scheme shall not be less than time rates alone would give him. (Of course, if the time taken exceeded the time allowed, the bonus earnings of the worker could otherwise be negative.) Because, in practice, the time allowed is almost always in excess of the time taken, the difference between the time allowed and the time taken is referred to as the time saved.

The simplest version of such a time-allowance system is that where the worker is paid at a time rate for the hours he has been allowed for the various jobs he has done rather than the hours he has actually taken. This is known as '100 per cent bonus', because one way of expressing this payment is to say that the worker is paid his time rate for the hours he has actually been at work, plus 100 per cent of the time he has actually saved on the jobs he has done against the time allowed for them. (The time taken plus the time saved equals the time allowed.)

More complicated versions of payment by results based on time allowances involve quite opposite ideas of the relationship between output and payment which ought to be followed under an incentive scheme. It is possible either to pay an increasing return as the output of the worker greatly exceeds the calculated time, i.e. as he saves more and more time, or alternatively to pay a smaller return as output greatly exceeds the time allowed. In the latter case the assumption would appear to be that a worker who is succeeding in saving a specially high proportion of the time allowed must be in some way taking advantage of a flaw in the system. In other words it is assumed that, generally speaking, workers may be expected to exceed the output laid down for them, i.e. to save time against the allowed time, by a moderate and reasonably predictable amount, but that a very large saving does not result from extra effort so frequently as from a flaw in the calculation of the time allowed. The alternative system, on the other hand, does not concede possible errors in calculation of the time allowed and follows the view that if a worker works greatly in excess of the rate laid down for him he should receive an increasing return for his effort. If one accepts the view that the times calculated or allowed are correct, then the justification for an increasing return is fairly clear. From the point of view of the management it rests on the statement that an increasing output without extra equipment or extra overhead costs is at lesser total cost to themselves and so justifies proportionately greater reward to the worker. It is based from the worker's point of view on the proposition that additional effort is marginally more difficult, that he is more reluctant to provide that additional effort, and that he ought to be rewarded more than proportionately for it. It is perhaps a reflection of management doubts about either the accuracy of times calculated for incentive schemes, or about the possibility of exceptionally high output from particular workers, that where schemes diverge from 100 per cent bonus they tend to favour the decreasing rate of return type of differential system rather than the increasing rate of return.[1]

Systems of payment based on time allowances can of course be operated on a group as well as on an individual basis. The group's output is measured against the times allowed for the performance of different jobs, and the workers in the group are paid bonus on an agreed basis of division according to the extent to which the time allowed has been exceeded by the group.

Payment based on an incentive scheme should be used only if output can be satisfactorily measured. In the older piecework systems measurement was probably more a matter of bargaining than anything else. In present-day practice, especially with time allowances, managements prefer to time output by use of a stop-watch and to claim that the timing, once carried through, offers an objective indicator of how quickly a job can be done. One difficulty in accepting the idea that timing by stop-watch is objective is that it assumes that the worker who is being timed for measurement purposes is carrying through the work at the kind of pace which he would normally use if he were not being observed: this is a somewhat doubtful proposition. Moreover, factories are subject to difficulties and delays in the flow of production, and timing one operation may give a very different result from the kind of experience of a worker who day by day performs a large number of the same operation. All the delays build up and can amount to a considerable departure from the smooth flow of production which is assumed when one operation only has been timed, and while allowance may be made for this, in calculating times for whole jobs it is difficult to do this adequately or accurately. A further development of time study is to add into the calculation of the time allowed for a job allowances for the various difficulties that may arise, and also allowances for what can be regarded as reasonable periods for pauses and rests in the worker's flow of output. We can thus get a complex and synthetic estimate of the time allowed which, by being more complex, can take into account more factors, but which still rests on the initial need to get an objective measurement of the flow of work. Where time study is not readily possible, the tendency has been to use rate fixing. This system involves the use of a highly experienced man who assesses time, usually by looking at all the steps that are necessary to carry through a job and providing a standard estimate for each step, which is then adopted as the basis for payment on this job.

[1] Such arrangements are known as premium bonus systems, and the best-known example of the decreasing return type is probably the Halsey or Weir system. In this system the worker is paid a fixed proportion (normally 50 per cent) of the time he saves.

Both in time study and in rate fixing, unfortunately, there are plenty of opportunities for argument. If the output to be measured is standardised and large, times and prices have an opportunity to settle down, the rate of work can be assessed with some accuracy, and there is less possibility of argument. If there is only a small flow of work of a non-standardised variety, payment by results can be used only if managements and men are prepared to accept inaccurate measurements. If the unit is produced only slowly, then the period for which output must be reckoned may well be longer than the period of payment. To take an extreme example, even if we supposed that the shipbuilding industry were engaged in the production of nothing but standard ships, it would be farcical to measure the units of production in terms of the number of ships, when only one is built every few months or longer. Parts of the job have to be measured rather than the job in total. Systems of payment by results of the type we have been describing are not really very suitable for 'one-off' jobs or for jobs in which there is no standardisation of flow of work.

The second point of importance about systems of payment by results is that they tend almost invariably to stress output as the objective of work and effort. This is not wholly true, since some incentive schemes are, for example, based on avoidance of waste. One typical scheme of this type, where the workers are dealing with a valuable commodity and where the rate of work is, on the whole, controlled by a factory flow and is not in the worker's control, provides that the worker will be paid bonus in inverse proportion to the weight of the waste produced. But although this kind of example could be duplicated, in general it is true to say that payment by results is designed to elicit output rather than anything else. This means that it can be appropriately used only where output is indeed the main objective of the activity of the workers. This is possibly generally true, but physical output, or measurable output, is not the usual end of managerial or professional skill, at least in the normal sense of output. Nor is output alone to be taken into account where considerations of high quality come in, or where responsibility, for example, is largely involved. This suggests that payment by results should be used as a major item of payment only where the work is relatively routine. For example, the large group of maintenance workers cannot readily be brought on to payment by results since they are not engaged in work which is to be measured only in output terms. (Cases are, however, known in which maintenance workers are paid in effect a bonus according to how little work they have to do – a bonus related to the amount of time lost through breakdowns of machinery they maintain.)

Thirdly, payment by results can produce uncertainties and insecurities in payment. If the scheme is working perfectly it may be possible to say that the uncertainty is entirely under the workers' own control, that it is only the kind of uncertainty that arises from an inability to work hard in one week which results in a smaller pay packet. But there is also a wider sense in which incentive schemes result in uncertainty and insecurity for workers. Workers, like everyone else, have regular outlays on rent, on household expenditures, on food, and other regular commitments such as hire purchase. These claims have to be met week by week, and can, of course, be more readily provided for out of a regular income. Income security is obtainable from a time rate, but is hardly obtainable from fluctuating payment by result earnings, and even though actual fluctuations may be small, the risk of their occurring is strongly present in the system of payment and in the worker's mind. Thus there are advantages for workers in time rates, though the extra earnings of payment by results are, undoubtedly, welcome to them.

In summary, incentive payment schemes of the piecework and time-allowance types are based on the measurement of output and are therefore suitable where output is the objective and where output can be readily measured. They are much less suitable in conditions where output is not routine. Standardised objects, such as can be produced in a steady flow, provide the best conditions for incentive payment systems. In other cases they can become both costly and inefficient. The advantage of high earnings which payment by results can give to workers should be offset a little by the disadvantage of irregular earnings.

V. Other Incentive Payments

All of the foregoing discussion of time payments and of payment by results is somewhat oversimplified. The possible permutations of payment systems are legion, and it is a criticism of British payment practices that we tend at times to be somewhat too inventive in this matter. Though this classification into time work and piecework or payment by results is the most useful single division that may be attempted, it omits some other important types of payment and some newer developments to be discussed in this section.

Historically, one of the most interesting types of payment by results is the contract system. Under it the workers can in many respects be regarded as independent contractors rather than as employees. A well-known example, of which elements still survive, is that where a squad of men engaged in erecting ships contracted with the shipyard for large sections of the work on the ship. The squad elected its own leader, and changes in the composition of the squad were by agreement among the skilled men. The contract was really with the skilled men in the squad, and the skilled men employed the unskilled on some kind of agreed basis of division of the contract price. The management paid progress payments, and when the work was finished the squad received the final payment on the contract. How quickly the work was done depended on the squad. It is relatively rare to find pure examples of a contract system of this type nowadays. In the shipyards, for example, this kind of thing would perhaps now be better described as rather unsatisfactory group piecework pricing for large sections of work. One version of the contract system which is expanding at present is giving the building industry considerable cause for concern. It is known as 'labour only sub-contracting'. In it the main contractor supplies materials and equipment but does not employ the workers directly. They are either employed by a sub-contractor who is likely to pay them on piecework, or they are self-employed. This system naturally has major implications for the organisation and co-ordination of the industry's labour force, and gives those responsible for its product very little control over the quality of the work done. It also raises problems of insecurity for workers and considerable possibilities of avoiding taxation.[1]

Another type of incentive payment related to work loads, which still survives in some places, is the task system. It may, for example, be used as a rough means of controlling the volume of work done by workers, who are sent out to do jobs on their own and are given a quota of a certain number of calls or tasks to carry out in a day. Under piecework or systems based on time allowances it is assumed that the worker will stay in the factory for the whole period of the normal working day. The levels of output and of payment vary, not the normal hours of work. Under the task system the worker is set a task, and once it is completed he can go home. The word 'stint' is sometimes used in preference to task, to describe the quantity of work set for the worker to carry out. (Words like 'stint' or 'doggie' are also used to describe informal limits set by the workers themselves when they try collectively to limit the level of output achieved under an incentive scheme.

[1] Cf. A. I. Marsh and W. E. J. McCarthy, *Dispute Procedures in Britain*, Royal Commission on Trade Unions and Employers' Associations, Research Paper No. 2 (Part 2), 1968. Labour only sub-contracting was recently the subject of an official Committee of Enquiry under Professor E. H. Phelps Brown. (Cmnd. 3714, 1968.)

Fear of reductions by management in the prices or times allowed for jobs is the usual reason for such actions.)

It is impossible to specify or detail all the other kinds of bonus that may occur. But it is important to realise that a bonus payment can be regarded as a clear incentive to output only if, in some way, it is related to output, and if the output can in some way be measured. It would be proper to regard such things as a Christmas bonus, which has no specific relationship to work done, as an extra payment rather than as an incentive payment. It does not follow, however, that this type of extra payment gives no return for the outlay since a feeling of belonging or of being well treated is clearly a factor in retaining the services of workers and in keeping them loyal. The bonus rate, and commission, are among the many possible types of direct bonus payments other than those mentioned above. The bonus rate is a system whereby particular levels of output, as well as receiving the appropriate return on an incentive scheme based on piecework or time allowances, also result in the rate on which bonus is calculated being increased. Thus, for example, a scale may be constructed showing various levels of bonus performance (i.e. the extent to which actual outputs have exceeded the level which the times allowed would suggest) and against them bonus rates or supplementations to the rate which will occur as the level of bonus performance rises. Commission is really a form of piecework applied to those whose work consists of selling or providing a service. The typical example is that of the commercial traveller who receives commission on the volume of his sales. The same kind of thing would apply to a hairdresser who might be offered commission on the number of heads of hair he cuts above a certain minimum number. A manager of a shop might well be receiving a bonus related to sales.

There are also a large number of possible indirect bonus arrangements, in which the level of bonus payable to the worker is not calculated directly on his performance but on the performance of other people. Thus, for example, a maintenance worker may receive a bonus geared to the level of output of the factory as a whole. He may feel that he can influence the factory output, and if so the bonus is indirectly calculated but direct in its effect. If he does not feel this then the bonus is merely a device to bring his earnings up to the level of those who can be placed on direct bonus and is not an incentive to him. It is, indeed, sometimes argued that putting some workers on direct and some on indirect bonus causes those who are on indirect bonus to feel that they are merely being compensated and not encouraged. If a bonus is assessed over the whole of a factory and is applicable to everyone, then all may feel that they ought to encourage each other; but if some are paid according to the level of output of a factory whereas others have arrangements based on the individual or small groups, those who are remunerated on the basis of output in the factory at large may simply feel that they are being carried along. A rather formal version of the indirect bonus is known as a 'lieu' rate: bonus is paid as a rate in lieu of direct bonus earnings. This type of remuneration may be payable either to workers who work along with others earning direct bonus, or to workers who are expected to work at a speed appropriate to bonus earnings but cannot have any direct measurement made of their output. The more payment by *direct* bonus develops, the more arrangements to pay *indirect* bonus are likely to develop. Payment by direct bonus results in increased earnings, and those whose earnings are increased move out of their previous relation in earnings and in status to other workers in the factory who are not on bonus. In other words the internal factory wage structure is altered by the introduction of a direct bonus, and the more it is affected the more it becomes necessary to do something about those who are not on bonus. And so the development of direct bonus also results in attempts to apply bonus of one kind or another to everyone, even if everyone cannot be provided with a *suitable* bonus.

It is necessary to secure a satisfactory level of output, and studies of schemes of incentive payment worked in suitable circumstances suggest, though they rarely prove, that the incentive has resulted in an increase in output. On the other hand, the payment by results schemes produce their own costs, and difficulties, so that in order to obtain an increase in output managements may find themselves making difficulties in other directions. Moreover, output is a matter of having the right kinds of worker with the right qualifications and experience, in the right quantity and doing their work correctly – and not only one of obtaining a particular rate of working. Concern for volume of production produces an increasing interest in payment by results, but while payment by results continues to be important, and is unlikely to be abandoned in many types of production for a long time, in recent years there has been increasing interest in trying to find methods of payment which reflect the broader aspects of a full contribution from the workers.

Three of the stock problems of payment by results schemes are that they can produce instability in earnings which accords badly with the desire of managements to maximise the long-term attraction of the payment they offer and the stability of their labour force; that they emphasise a rather narrow view of factors that contribute to high output, concentrating upon the workers' immediate tasks rather than on the total organisation, method

C

and flow of production; and that they set problems in finding means to remunerate those whose work cannot readily be put on to a direct incentive scheme in ways which preserve some appropriate structure of payment between different types of labour. This last problem is related to the situation which arises when payments schemes, which are planned badly or become out of date, begin to produce differences in payment between workers which appear to be at variance with effort and distort the wage structure. On the other hand, there is a growing recognition of the importance of studying and attempting to measure output by individuals, groups and the factory as a whole, using up-to-date techniques of work study, work measurement and production control. Reflection on these problems has produced a developing interest in schemes of payment which as far as possible are applicable to employees as a whole, which are accompanied by general acceptance of methods of controlling and measuring work flows, and which if possible lead to co-operation by the workers in management plans to improve productivity by changes in work practices and technical innovations.

As a result of a shift in emphasis towards group or factory-wide incentives which emphasise co-operation among employees and present fewer problems of wage structure, 'measured day work' appears to have been gaining popularity, though it is still very much less common than the forms of payment by results discussed in the last section. The idea of measured day work is to devise a structure of time rates applicable to all the different grades of workers in the factory, to pay workers these time rates but to associate the time rates with strong production control and very careful and frequent measures of the output of the factory or group, and to adjust the level of the rates regularly to reflect changes in output performance. This system has the advantages of stability in payment and preservation of the structure of relative payment levels, while encouraging high output. Since all workers benefit from increased output, there is some inducement to accept changes in production methods, though this will be less true if redundancy is in question. The incentive offered is to the group rather than the individual, and this, while it diminishes the personal incentive for individuals, encourages co-operation, and has the advantage of pulling together the efforts of the maintenance workers and those on the production line. On the other hand, the incentive effect of the payment system must be kept in being between reviews, and this sets up a need for effective communications and good supervision.

While it is not clear how much they are being used in practice, there has certainly also been a growth in discussion of schemes relating payment to much more broadly-based measures of performance. Several such plans are current in the literature, those associated with the names of Rucker, Scanlon and Kaiser probably being the most discussed. The Scanlon Plan is the best known, and may be used as an illustration. It is intended to be applied to all employees in an enterprise, including salaried workers, and stresses the view that productivity and good industrial relations both stem from widespread employee co-operation and participation. The Plan associates a machinery for processing employees' suggestions, and for ensuring their consultative participation in improvements in productivity, with an arrangement which relates all payments to improvements in the performance of the enterprise. This requires a structure of committees and a developed communications system, together with a formula for gearing wages to performance. Generally the formula relates changes in labour costs and in payment in some way to the sales value of goods produced. The method of assessing improvements in performance varies with the circumstances of the company, but will always require that the employees develop some appreciation of the financial and cost implications of such improvements. The advantages of the Plan, if it succeeds, will come as much from a general improvement in co-operation within the firm as from productivity. Conversely, it can hardly succeed without considerable willingness on the part of workers and their trade unions to co-operate and to understand the managers' problems and their views on the criteria of successful performance. Stripped of its overtones of co-operation and participation in the development of the enterprise, the Scanlon Plan is really a group incentive scheme for the enterprise as a whole based on a complex assessment of output. It does, however, illustrate the trend in thinking about incentives towards group schemes, steady payments with frequent reviews, and more comprehensive concepts of productivity accompanied by sophisticated management techniques of measurement, control and improvement of work flows, and these are features that now play a greater part in thinking about incentives in general, as well as in the specific context of such payment plans.

V. Hours of Work, Shift Work and Overtime

In this section we shall discuss first the emergence of 'standard' working weeks in Britain, then the arrangement of the actual pattern of hours in the working week (including the special and important case of shift working), and overtime.

The working week in British industry has been consistently reduced over a fairly long number of years. At first this was achieved by legislation directed at governing the hours of work of women and children and only indirectly affecting the hours of work of men. In this century, however, standard working weeks have been established mainly by collective bargaining agreements. Over the years, the standard has been reduced in the bargaining process, and the existence of standard weeks together with reductions in their length have created a situation in which overtime has made its appearance. Before the First World War there were wide differences in the hours of work of wage earners, but the average level was over 50 and probably around 52. After the First World War a large number of agreements brought the standard number of hours of work down to roughtly 47 hours. After the Second World War a further series of negotiations around 1945–7 brought standard hours down again to 44 or 45 in most cases. In the latter part of the fifties further negotiations began, which have now made the 40-hour week customary, though the move downwards from 44 has in many cases been with a temporary pause at 42 hours, and some industries are still around that level. The hours of work of salaried workers and offices are usually shorter, but reductions in their hours have occurred at broadly the same time as those of factory workers.

When wage earners work hours beyond those of the standard week they are paid overtime. Short-time occurs if they do not work the full standard hours. If short-time is due simply to a man's own failure to turn out, then he will be paid at his hourly rate for the hours he works. If, however, the short-time is created by his employer failing to give him work for the full week, then there is usually some kind of guaranteed-week provision which ensures that a worker gets some, if not all, of his standard week's wages when he has been available for work which his employer has not been able to provide. The actual arrangements for guaranteed weeks, however, vary a good deal from case to case and special arrangements are likely to apply when short-time working occurs on a large scale. At their extreme, large-scale short-time arrangements in a firm can take the form of sharing unemployment by taking turns of being 'temporarily stopped' and of drawing unemployment benefit.

The reduction in the length of the working week has been associated with marked changes in the distribution of hours in the working week – first to reduce the length of the day's work on Saturday and then to eliminate regular Saturday working altogether in almost all manufacturing industries and in many forms of office employment. As a result overtime premium rates are now payable for both Saturday and Sunday working, and the five-day week – roughly from 8 a.m. to 5 p.m. on Mondays to Fridays with one hour for lunch – is now usual. In those industries such as public transport in which week-end working is necessary, special arrangements tend to be made for time-off and for payment for week-end working.

Shift working is by no means a new idea in British industry. It has always been customary in mining and in any industry, such as iron and steel, where for technical reasons the process is continuous, or in cases such as public transport, where a service has to be provided for longer hours than those of the normal working day. There are innumerable methods of organising the pattern of shifts, though these are usually varying combinations of a day (or early) shift – say from 6 a.m. to 2 p.m. – a back (or late) shift – say from 2 p.m. to 10 p.m. – and, if required, a night shift. The shift arrangements are often so made as to allow a regular change for the worker from working one shift to another. The number of hours in a shift worker's week is normally less than that of the day worker and a premium rate for shift working (for example, time-and-a-fifth) is often paid, with special extra payments for night work.

While shift working is not new, the general reduction in the length of the working week and the current trends in technology are likely to make it increasingly important in the future. Shift working can develop from three broad causes, first because the process in question is technically continuous and cannot be shut down each day; secondly, because the work provides a service which is required for more than the length of the working day; and thirdly because the capital equipment required for the work needs for economic reasons to be used more intensively than just for forty or so hours in the week. The first of these is the traditional reason for a shift-working industry – an ironworks or an oil refinery are good examples. Some industries have always had to reckon with the second point – provision of services for periods longer than the working day – but the shorter the working day the more shift working of services will be needed, and the more shift working in general develops, the more will be the demand for services outside conventional hours. For example, the possibility of shift working is now becoming a real issue in the retail trades, and to an increasing extent in catering.

If a unit of production is capital intensive it is naturally important to make the best use of the capital installation. This need will always be there, but if the capital is likely to become obsolescent, making the most effective use of it involves getting the most out of it in the period of time before it is superseded by newer equipment. It may be possible, with this consideration in mind, to increase output during the day by increasing the labour force which works with the machinery, or by putting in ancillary machinery, but this will increase unit costs as well as output. Shift working is likely also to increase unit costs because of the extra payments to shift workers and the costs of keeping the factory open. The exact point at which shift working becomes the right economic answer depends on the circumstances of the case, but the shorter the normal working day becomes as standard hours are reduced, the more the need to utilise the capital equipment fully before its effective life is past, and the higher the ratio of capital to labour cost in production costs, the more the bias towards a decision in favour of shift working.

Do reductions in the standard week such as those which have recently taken place increase wages or increase leisure? In a sense, reductions in the length of the standard week accompanied, as they have been, by no reductions in the size of the previously agreed weekly wage, are wage increases, since they mean extra payment per hour; but it is also possible to regard them as an improvement in the general conditions of work. If a worker is able to attain the same standard of payment and the same standard of life with more leisure, then he has gained as against his previous condition. At first sight the advantage of a reduction in the standard working week appears to be just such an increase in leisure. The test is, however, a purely factual one. Have the hours actually worked been reduced in proportion to the reduction in the standard working week? If they have not, then there has been a shift from standard hours to overtime hours and here the provisions for overtime payment become highly relevant.

The facts of the matter are these: over the long period, actual hours of work have gone down, with variations, roughly according to the reductions in the standard week. Indeed overtime has not, in general, been of crucial significance till recently. The reductions to 44 and then to 40 hours since the Second World War have produced a substantially different picture. As standard hours have been reduced there has tended to be a similar increase in average overtime working for men, though less so for women, so that hours actually worked by men have on average remained roughly similar to pre-war. The only periods when this has not happened have been those of recession, when the demand for labour has fallen and the average of actual hours worked has fallen. This effect was particularly marked in the deflationary period which accompanied the wage freeze of 1966–7: it is too early to say whether we may expect to see hours go up again much with expansion after devaluation. The effect of a change in standard hours in the post-war period has, therefore, generally been an increase in payment, especially for men, since the same amount of money has been earned for a shorter number of hours and the difference between the new standard week and the old has been made to yield additional payments, both at the normal rate and the extra rate applicable to overtime working.

Overtime working may be described as work beyond the standard hours laid down for any particular industry, or, more accurately, as work outside the particular pattern of hours which has been laid down as standard. This qualifying remark is added because it is not necessarily true that a worker must work the full quantity of standard hours before he moves on to overtime. If, for example, he is missing from one of the regular standard working periods, he may nevertheless still earn overtime by turning up at an overtime period outside the normal times of work. There is indeed a close affinity between overtime payments and all extra payments for work at unusual times. Hours worked on overtime are subject to a premium rate payment for wage earners, though not generally for salaried workers. Whether or not the man is a time worker or is paid by results, these premium payments are usually expressed by reference to the time rate or to some special time rate used for overtime premium calculations. Thus when a man is working overtime he will be earning payment for the work he is doing, or the time he is putting in, in the normal way depending on whether he is paid by results or is a time worker, and in addition will be receiving an overtime premium rate. The level of these premium rates differs from industry to industry and for different periods of the week. They are usually expressed as a fraction of the time rate, and it is usual for week-day evening overtime to attract from one-third to two-thirds of the time rate as an overtime premium payment, for Saturday to attract something of the same kind if a five-day week is in operation, and for Sunday to carry an overtime premium rate of the same size as the time rate (i.e. double time). Night work generally carries special premiums.

Possible generalisations about overtime payment differ according to whether overtime is being worked rarely or regularly. Historically the former is the more important case. There seems little doubt that overtime premium payments were first introduced into agreements as a means of discouraging employers from being so inconsiderate as to call workers consistently out for work beyond the normal hours, and also as a means of recompensing workers in some measure for the inconvenience of having their leisure disrupted. The general inference of this attitude is that over-time premium payments are means of discouraging employers from resort-ing to overtime and that overtime will be rather rarely worked, and will be unlikely to bulk largely either in the remuneration of the worker or in the costs of the management. To the employers it would then be the source of an occasional extra cost, either as a penalty for their own failure to time their operations successfully, or as a special item attributable, and perhaps chargeable, to an impatient customer. In these circumstances it is only in industries with an erratic demand pattern that we would expect overtime working to be frequent and extensive, and in these industries, such as the docks, overtime will be a regrettable but accepted part of life which keeps turning up from time to time.

The other kind of situation which has been common in the post-war period in Britain is where overtime becomes a general and frequent, indeed a customary and regular, part of the life of the factory and of the lives of both employers and workers. In these circumstances the effect of the overtime premium is that it tends to become not so much a discouragement to employers as an incentive to workers. If pressure of demand keeps employers in the position of trying to meet delivery dates by constant overtime working, and if shortage of workers makes it necessary for them, even if they do not need the extra output, to offer the extra payment which overtime gives so as to recruit and keep workers, then overtime working becomes a widely accepted phenomenon, and workers begin to seek it as an additional source of income upon which they count.

From the employer's point of view overtime of this type cannot any longer be regarded as an occasional and not very large extra cost; it becomes a regular part of his pattern of costs on which output for meeting his regular deliveries becomes dependent. In these circumstances he is forced to wonder whether it is really wise to have a standard working week which is clearly too short for his needs and then to supplement this by further production at an inconvenient time and with the less adequate control which can be exercised over overtime working. Is it wise to substitute Sunday and a couple of evenings a week for an extra hour each day? The employer would almost certainly prefer a system which would get the work done within the standard week, and if necessary he could probably pay the same amount as he is presently paying for the standard week and overtime combined. The worker is unlikely to want to lose the leisure of the week-ends and evenings, but overtime earnings, though occasionally unpredictable and therefore subject to some disadvantages, are large and cannot be forgone. There is thus a considerable dilemma in regular overtime working: neither side can do without it, and yet if some form of compromise could be reached it might be possible to achieve the same results without the inconveniences. One thing seems fairly certain – that as long as a situation of this type continues, reductions in the standard working week are only likely to make the immediate prospect worse. Faced with the alternative of a reduced week or extra payments, the employers might very frequently be wise to offer the extra pay. Even though it is easy to make out a good case for a long-term reduction in the length of the standard working week, there is a problem of the timing of proposed reductions: the existence of regular overtime working in an industry is likely to suggest that it is not ready for a reduction in the standard working week. Incidentally a factory which did not conform to the standard working week and the national agreements might be in a much better position to avoid constant overtime, though it would meet with other difficulties. Regular overtime working also leads on to discussions about shift working.

VI. Other Kinds of Payment

The list of other kinds of payment is potentially enormous. The group known as fringe benefits is of considerable importance and is discussed in the next section. Sliding-scale arrangements which relate increments in all or part of the wage to some variable, most typically the cost of living, and alter the level of payment as that variable alters, are discussed as a method of wage settlement in the next chapter. This section discusses only two types of payment. First, it completes the general picture of the wage earner's pay packet by giving some samples of additional rates which may be payable to him. Secondly, for the sake of convenience, the opportunity is taken here to discuss briefly a quite different type of payment – fee earning.

Extra rates of one sort or another for wage earners are very common. It is always possible to supplement the wage earner's pay for special reasons. For example, a docker's piece rate for unloading may be amended because of some special circumstances attached to unloading one particular ship. It follows from what was said earlier about minimum rates in national agreements that some extra rate payments may merely be necessary additions made by the factory for recruitment purposes and may not be specially attached to any one particular reason for an extra payment. This is perhaps the biggest category of extra rates, if they can be so described, that occurs. Extra rates for special reasons are, however, many and various. The possible use of a bonus rate has already been mentioned. In addition extra rates are paid to people of special merit or to people who, though not

c 2

employed in a completely supervisory capacity, have some extra responsibilities. The former is known as merit money, the selection of particular individuals for special extra payment on grounds of special merit. It is not promotion, which, of course, always exists and takes a person from one grade into another, but rather the designation of people within particular grades as being specially deserving. Because there is this element of selection or differentiation between workers who are otherwise classed as the same, merit money is not particularly welcomed by trade unions and indeed is frequently opposed. The payment of a little extra for special responsibilities is usual and not subject to disagreement of this type. The charge hand or the leading hand may get a few pence an hour extra. Extra rates are also payable where the work has to be conducted in specially adverse or awkward circumstances. For example, danger money may be paid for work where there is a special risk, or dirty money where the work is specially dirty. There are particular variations of this; for example in ship-repairing an oil-ship repair allowance is payable to whose who have to work in the holds of tankers which have contained oil.

Fee earning is a quite distinct payment situation. The man who earns fees is self-employed. In other types of business which are operated by self-employed men in producing goods or marketing them, the earnings of the proprietor are generally concealed within his gross profits and he ought to put in an estimate of the value of his own services in the labour market before deciding that his capital and his labour are wisely employed in this way. (It is probable that many people in their own business – for example, as shopkeepers – do not make anything like an adequate allowance for their own work, and especially the hours they put in, when they decide that their businesses are profitable.) In the case of the self-employed man who is fee-earning, the service traded in is his own professional expertise, for in this case capital employed is usually very much secondary to the personal services of the self-employed proprietor or proprietors.

The fee earner is basically a pieceworker paid by the unit of service he provides. Like any pieceworker his earnings are, therefore, variable according to his own efforts and the vagaries of the pricing system which makes some jobs easier in relation to their payment than others. Typically he will, since he is self-employed, have no fall-back payment if his fee earnings are poor or likely to decline. For example, the dentist, whose earnings are closely related to his output, has a pronounced tendency to reduced earnings as he gets older. The fee earner will also be responsible for making provision for his own holidays, pension and sickness. This insecurity of earnings and the need to provide for his own other benefits and risks means that the fee earner has to earn more in gross terms to have the same real income as the wage earner. The fee which the fee earner charges may be settled by some form of collective action or by convention. The fee-earning professions other than those attached to the National Health Service generally have established scales of fees set up by their professional institutes, either after consultation with clients or with an eye on the possible reactions of clients. Sometimes the fees to be charged are simply a matter of conventional practice. The element of convention is, however, present in all cases and conventions are slow to respond to changes in the value of money – a point which is well established in relation to the not totally dissimilar cases of conventional giving to charity – and, in consequence, the fee earner's income can be slow to rise with inflation.

Two factors modify this picture of the fee earner's position. First, in many types of fee earning it is customary to work in groups rather than as individuals. It then becomes possible for the group or partnership to iron out some of the variability of payment and to share some of the risks that would otherwise trouble the individual. A legal partnership, for example, may agree on a stated proportionate share of income to each partner and devise schemes for sickness, holidays and pensions very like those of the employee. Secondly, some of the largest fee-earning groups such as general practitioners or dentists are attached to the National Health Service and are in a mixed fee-earning/employee position. Most of them are designated as self-employed, but their fees are fixed by a process akin to that of collective bargaining and they have a varied collection of conditions of service relating to pensions, minimum earnings and the like provided by the Health Service.

VII. Fringe Benefits

The term 'fringe benefits' is used to describe a number of advantages resulting from a wage earner's employment which do not come directly within the normal definition of his weekly wage and do not appear directly in his pay packet. It is possible to divide such fringe benefits into those which in one way or another take the form of money payments and those which are non-monetary. But the division is somewhat artificial since non-monetary fringe benefits are, nevertheless, benefits to the worker which it would probably cost him something to obtain in other circumstances and which are usually a cost to his employer. What is perhaps more relevant is that some fringe benefits, such as a pension scheme, are directly and individually applicable to workers, whereas others, such as the provision of sports facilities, are much more general and are of less specific benefit to any particular worker.

The full range of fringe benefits has been enjoyed much more frequently by salaried workers than by wage earners and indeed, as was pointed out earlier, this constitutes one of the major distinctions between salaried and wage-earning employees. Historically speaking, the main fringe benefits available to wage earners have taken the form of 'payment in kind'. Payments in kind were important to farm labourers, the main class of employed labour in pre-industrial Britain. In some cases farm workers occupied a tied house on a rent-free basis, while most farm workers received some part of their food from the farm produce, a quantity of free milk, vegetables and potatoes. Given the low standard of income which was customary, these things must have added up to a considerable proportion of the total amount which the farm labourer could expect to obtain of worldly things. Many such payments to farm workers continue but have not now the same value either in total or relative to the changed real standard of living of these workers. The miner's coal is another celebrated example of a payment in kind. The police force offers a very good example of the continued importance of payments in kind in some occupations: a policeman normally has the occupancy of a police house, a uniform allowance, and so on. Nevertheless, in general, payments in kind are less important than they used to be. One of the most important examples nowadays occurs among middle-class salaried workers who receive what are colloquially known as 'perks'. Perquisites of office have always been well known, but the effect of marginally high rates of taxation has been to increase the importance of having such perquisites instead of a direct money payment. It would be impossible to find out the precise extent of this kind of thing, and the Inland Revenue would be as interested as anyone in the result; but there can be no doubt that the provision of a company car, for example, is highly valuable to someone who would otherwise have to pay for it out of post-tax income.

Holidays with pay are now a well-established form of fringe benefit. It has for a long time been the custom to grant a certain number of paid public holidays; but since the Second World War annual holidays with pay have become universal in organised employment. Some growth of payment for annual holidays had already taken place when a committee on the subject in 1938 recommended that every effort should be made to encourage the practice and that statutory bodies such as Trade Boards, as they then were, should be empowered to introduce it. Most agreements started with a one-week annual holiday, but two weeks is now usual, and there have been recent negotiations to increase this by a few days. Claims for three weeks have already occurred and, since Britain lags behind the Continent in length of holidays, it seems likely that longer holidays will in time arrive. The present position is roughly that a worker who has been with a firm for a whole year is entitled to at least a fortnight's holiday with pay, plus five or six public holidays. The question of the rate of payment for holidays has been in some dispute. Many agreements and statutory orders simply specify that the minimum or the time rate of payment shall be payable on holidays. For workers earning high bonuses this means a substantial drop in payment for the holiday period, and attempts are made to make the holiday pay equivalent to the average earnings of the worker. The question of which public holidays should be chosen is usually settled by agreement and discussion between both sides in the industry in each area. In some areas there is also agreement on which fortnight is to be the annual holiday, but in others the firms make their own decisions, or annual holidays are staggered. It is usual to find an agreement which specifies what proportion of the entitlement to holidays and holiday payment is applicable to those with less than a year's service.

The main contemporary fringe benefits are those which provide security against loss of income through sickness or redundancy and give pensions on retirement. The employer offering this type of benefit does so to improve his conditions of employment so as to keep or recruit workers. When a particular fringe benefit has become customary, he will find difficulty in avoiding a commitment to it, if he wishes to offer good conditions of employment. (For example, it is now very difficult for an employer to avoid the cost of a subsidised factory canteen or equivalent provision.) When he wants to increase the relative attractiveness of his employment and encourage his workers to feel secure and attached to his firm, he will seek to improve their conditions of employment, and improved fringe benefits are a principal way of doing this. For the worker fringe benefits offer some increase in income mainly by taking over some expenditures which he would have to incur himself – or *should* incur himself, since men are not always as careful to provide for future contingencies as they ought to be, and in consequence do not always value fringe benefits as highly as their cost merits. On the other hand the general increase in security which fringe benefits provide is valued – though not necessarily at its full cost. The cost to employers of fringe benefits is naturally somewhat variable depending on the extent of the benefits offered. Pensions and sick pay are the most expensive items. At present only a limited number of wage earners have such benefits, but they are available to most salaried workers. The cost of fringe benefits to employers in Britain probably amounts on average to something approaching 15 per cent of the wage bill. This, while it is low by European standards, is hardly negligible, and certainly suggests that the cost of fringe benefits, and not only the wage, should always be included in estimating the cost of employing workers.

Security of employment and income are matters of wide social policy. The State has, for example, a great interest in unemployment payment and in pensions and has influenced security in a number of other ways. It is not really possible to discuss security of income and employment without considering the policy of the State. This matter will therefore come up again later in this book – in Chapter 18. Again, additions to labour cost over and above wage payments include the cost of social security charges and taxation, which is a direct levy on numbers employed, and these aspects will be discussed in Chapter 14. For the present the subject can be set aside in seven summary points. 1. Fringe benefits are advantages from employment additional to the pay packet. 2. They usually cost money and are an addition to the cost of employing labour. 3. Salaried workers are more likely to have a full range of fringe benefits than wage earners. 4. Holidays with pay are now universal. 5. Payments in kind are not specially important. 6. The important developing fringe benefits are those concerned with security in one form or another. 7. Since security is also a matter in which the State is interested, public and private policies on this subject are very much intermingled.

VIII. Some Comments on Methods of Wage Payment

Up till now this chapter has been descriptive, and, while it has attempted to discuss some issues in passing, its main purpose has been to explain the whole series of complicated and interrelated items that come within the term 'wages', and which are not generally as carefully distinguished in discussion as they ought to be. This section raises a few important issues.

1. The large number of different types of payment that are in use can produce an extremely complicated pattern of remuneration for an individual worker, since one worker does not necessarily receive only one type of payment. He may be paid a time rate, but will be subject to possible supplementary rates and to complex arrangements for overtime and other

supplementary payments. If he is paid by results he will nevertheless be likely to have a time rate as a basis of payment and be subject to a more or less complex arrangement for further earnings, as well as for overtime payments, and may again have other supplementary payments.

2. Since bonus has become more usual and overtime more frequent in the post-war period, both these payments have become more important in the total pay packet. In consequence, the average worker relies to a greater extent than formerly upon obtaining these forms of income. They are somewhat less regular and certain than a time payment and the worker's pay packet is therefore less regular and certain than it used to be. On the other hand, full employment has made his job more secure, and increased job security may counteract his lack of income security.

3. Different methods of wage payment have different effects on wage structure. The idea that a wage has the function of getting workers into the right jobs and keeping them in the right payment relationship to each other leads on to the concept of a wage structure. A wage structure implies some kind of fairly permanent relationship, though one which may, nevertheless, be changed from time to time by economic circumstances, between workers of different types and between individual workers in a factory. Such a structure may be somewhat distorted when overtime and payment by results earnings are important and variable. We may, for example, find ourselves tending, in practice, though perhaps not in intention, to emphasise the output of the semi-skilled operative on payment by results as against the skill and responsibility of the highly-skilled maintenance man. Those who use complex payment methods have to look at their structural effects. It seems doubtful if these effects have been considered sufficiently in post-war Britain.

4. No one method of wage payment is a universally suitable answer to all workers. This is particularly true of the incentive scheme where conditions of measurability, standardised output, and so on, have to be met before the scheme can work adequately. But in all cases it is wise to think of a payment both in relation to the particular job that has to be done and to the needs and wishes of the particular worker or group of workers that has to do it.

5. The methods of payment discussed here can be roughly divided into two groups : those payments normally designated as rates and payable on a time basis, which are fixed by some formal process at the national level, and the remainder, especially payment by results and overtime, which are added into the worker's pay packet at his place of employment and make up with rates the total of his earnings. It is important to remember this

distinction in the discussion of formal wage bargaining in Chapter 4, where it is mainly the fixing of rates that is at issue. The distinction also comes into the discussion of wage policy under inflationary conditions in Chapter 21, where the problem is that of controlling both the formal and the informal sources of wage determination. The formal methods of wage settlement tend to alter individual payments by pushing up the rates on which the total payments are built; but control of the formal processes cannot be said to result in control of the pattern of factory payments, since on top of the formal determination of wage rates there is a large number of other methods of payment subject to other influences. In wage structure discussions this distinction leads to conflicts of purpose between alternative structures based on rates and on earnings and to difficulties of under-payment, and of a different basis of comparison, in the case of those, such as most salaried workers and very large numbers of wage earners working outside manufacturing industry, who have limited access to additional earnings opportunities. At the same time we have to be conscious of difficulties in expressing this distinction between rates and earnings, mainly because rates are so variable in character. In the foregoing, examples of formally negotiated rates can be found in very different forms – as standard rates, minimum rates, basic rates for pieceworkers and so on. We have to make the distinction between rates and earnings especially to stress the contrasts between national and local and between formal and informal methods of settling wages, but the distinction is based on rather uncertain and shifting foundations.

6. Over the last few years there has been growing interest in devising ways to improve on our present methods of payment and methods of wage settlement. This interest has been stimulated partly by a direct reaction against over-complicated and somewhat inaccurate payment schemes, and overtime, which appears to exist more as a habit and as a somewhat cumbersome method of increasing weekly pay than as a necessary source of extra output. In part the cause has been a desire to stimulate broader aspects of productivity, introduce improved occupational structures and work organisation, and remove restrictive work practices which hamper productivity. In part the objective of this interest in reform, and its most urgent concern, has been to try to damp down the repetitive wage increases which have been a standard feature of post-war inflation and to associate increases with improvements in productivity and the utilisation of labour generally.

7. The questioning attitude towards payment by results schemes which is referred to in earlier sections of this chapter, and the current interest in

measured day work and schemes such as the Scanlon Plan, are evidence of a desire to develop more satisfactory systems of payment, and to try to achieve both more flexible group-working, with consequential improvements in productivity and more stability in earnings and in wage structures. Improved payment systems are regarded as one way of relating increases in payment more closely to a general improvement in productivity and performance.

8. Another way of moving towards the same objective, which will come up for discussion again in later parts of this book, is that of 'productivity bargaining', a term which has recently obtained wide currency as a means of describing wage negotiations which seek to ally improved payment with more effective working. This may be a matter of changing working practices to allow more flexibility in the use of labour, or doing away with unnecessary ancillary workers by reorganising working methods. At times flexibility of working will require the abandonment of out-of-date or 'degenerate' payment systems. It may mean accepting additional responsibilities or duties, or a restructuring of the grading of occupations and their duties. It may be associated with a reorganisation of working routine to concentrate work in the normal working day and minimise overtime, and one of the sources of current interests in productivity bargaining is the widespread feeling that the volume of regular overtime now worked in Britain is not strictly needed to obtain the current levels of output. It will be evident that changes of this type require detailed attention to particular situations, and the exact form of the changes to be sought is dependent on close study and will differ from case to case. Indeed, the chief features of productivity bargaining are its attention to detail and the attempt to link changes in payment to improvements in productivity and working methods. It involves a necessary emphasis on measurement and recording of the value of improvements; but, on the other hand, neither the use of measurements nor the emphasis on productivity are, or should be, intended simply to equate productivity with output in any narrow sense, the more appropriate concept being something like 'effective working'.

9. In offering criticisms of payment by results schemes it is important to distinguish between the method of payment and the methods of study which preface the introduction of such a payments scheme. Time study and studies of methods of doing a job can become too closely associated with payments methods and not be sufficiently regarded as tools of general management. Time study is a process of attempting to assess the time that under normal circumstances a worker should take for a job. It is subject to

imperfections especially because it involves timing men at work who may, because they are being studied, be adjusting their speed of work. But the process of timing is not merely a matter of finding a basis of payment, it is also a study of how the job is being done and how it might be done – especially by examining the constituent steps in a job and alternative ways of doing it. Work study, which includes time study, methods study and motion study, can be used to assess the best sequence of steps to do a job and the appropriate layout of equipment. As well as indicating an appropriate speed of work it can give the possibility of changes in technique which can yield productivity improvements, and is, therefore, to be used as much as an instrument of change as simply an instrument of measurement.

10. Devices designed to improve the utilisation of labour by careful study have been becoming more important in the analysis of occupational structure – a topic which strictly belongs more to wage structure analysis than to discussion of methods of wage payment. In assessing the relative importance of jobs as a basis for payments policy, managers have to work partly with an occupational structure – of skilled trades and professions – imposed from outside the firm, and react to a wage structure partly determined by the wage at which such occupations may be hired in the market. But there are many categories of job inside a firm which are not precisely within the scope of a defined external occupation, and there are gradations in the importance of different tasks to be given to members of any one occupational grouping. Analysis of the work content of a particular job – job specification – is an important means of defining the type of individual required for it, and may also indicate desirable reorganisation between jobs to provide a better allocation of workers within a section or department. Additionally, the technique of job evaluation can assess what is expected from a worker in a particular job – for example, degree of responsibility, degree of skill, concentration, etc. – and can give an indication of the appropriate weight to give to that job in a scale of payments. Job evaluation can also be used to analyse how a job fits into the overall pattern of labour utilisation in the establishment. Such an analysis may also indicate the appropriate method of payment required to emphasise what is essentially required from the worker. In the last resort, however, both the level and structure of payment have to reflect the firm's need for an adequate supply of labour.

11. One of the most distinctive features of the conditions of employment of the salaried worker, particularly in well-organised public employments, is the salary scale which gives a worker a series of increments in payment

so that over the years in which he gains experience he proceeds from the minimum payment for his grade to the maximum. This has been regarded as a reasonable reflection of the increased value over time of a salaried worker, the effectiveness of whose work is often dependent on his own experience and judgment. Such arrangements have not, however, usually applied to wage earners, although in some industries – such as steel – seniority is the main route to promotion, and small 'seniority payments' are made in other cases. While it is arguable that experience specially enhances the contribution of the salaried worker in the types of work, such as teaching, administration or management, in which many salaried workers are employed, it is hard to see this clearly unless the increase in competence is subject to verification. In industry especially – though not generally in other salaried employments – the salary scale has been giving way to salary ranges and annual reviews. The purpose of the reviews is to examine the salaried employee's progress in his work and to relate his progress through the range of payment to this. These reviews at their best involve a detailed consideration of the main aspects of the man's work using objective indicators, where available, and detailed assessments by supervisors. This procedure is, of course, a separate matter from promotion, which naturally always involves an assessment of suitability and performance.

12. The fact that wage earners often make up a largish proportion of their pay by overtime and payment by results is a major distinction between them and salaried workers. On the other hand the salaried worker, in taking on his job for a salary, is expected to accept the obligation to be to some extent flexible in his hours of work, so as to cope with emergencies and finish the day's task before he goes home – though large amounts of working beyond the usual hours are not normally acceptable. If the wage earners can have their work reorganised into the normal day without overtime, and can be put on a basis of incentive which does not involve variable weekly earnings, their payment may be consolidated into a salary, and it may become possible also to expect a little flexibility in working hours from them if they can be given a salary and staff status. Staff status (or salaried status), with its implications for security and regularity of payment but also the inference of flexible working, is another of the current ideas for improving work and payment.

SUGGESTED READING

J. Backman, *Wage Determination*, 1959.
S. Cunnison, *Wages and Work Allocation*, 1966.
International Labour Office, *Payment by Results*, Geneva, 1951.
R. Marriott, *Incentive Payment Systems*, 2nd ed., 1961.
Ministry of Labour, *Industrial Relations Handbook*, revised ed., 1961.
National Board for Prices and Incomes, Report No. 65, *Payment by Results Systems*, 1968.
National Board for Prices and Incomes, Report No. 83, *Job Evaluation*, 1968.
G. L. Reid and D. J. Robertson (eds.), *Fringe Benefits, Labour Costs and Social Security*, 1965.
D. J. Robertson, *Factory Wage Structures and National Agreements*, 1960.
G. P. Shultz and R. B. McKersie, 'Stimulating Productivity: Choices, Problems and Shares', *British Journal of Industrial Relations*, vol. v, no. 1, March 1967.
G. Strauss and L. R. Sayles, *Personnel*, Englewood Cliffs, N.J., 1960.
W. B. Wolf, *Wage Incentives as a Managerial Tool*, 1957.

4 Processes of Wage Settlement

I.

The twentieth century has seen a rapid growth in institutionalised wage determination. The central process is that of collective bargaining, and other forms of organised wage determination may be regarded as supplementary or complementary to it. Formal methods of settling payment and other terms and conditions of employment now cover the big salaried groups as well as almost all wage earners. On the other hand, as will have become evident from the last chapter, actual payments to workers are complicated and include items which are determined more by factory policy than by formal agreement. 'Unorganised' or 'non-institutionalised' wage settlement, therefore, still has a part to play.

This chapter discusses various forms of wage settlement before concluding with some comments. Since the forms of organised wage settlement presuppose the existence of trade unions and employers' associations covering large sectors of the labour market, and include some of the activities of the Government in the labour market, this chapter links back with the discussions of the motives and activities of these institutions in Chapter 2. As well as also being obviously connected with Chapter 3, this chapter has affinities with the theoretical discussion of wage determination in Part III, and especially Chapter 12, and with the current issues of policy discussed in Chapters 20 and 21.

II. Collective Bargaining

Most wage earners in Britain are covered by some form of collective agreement. Collective bargaining may be sharply contrasted with individual negotiation by asserting that the one is concerned with organised groups of workpeople, while the other deals only with the individual case of a single employee, without any formalised connection between the decision made for one employee and that which may determine the wages and conditions of any other employee. In fact a distinction based only on numbers would be misleading. It is quite possible for collective bargaining negotiation to be concerned with the rights of one individual. And it is quite possible for an employer to introduce similar terms for a group of employees without bargaining with them collectively. Indeed, any economic analysis of labour-market operation suggests that similar workers in similar circumstances will receive a broadly similar level of payment. Three features pinpoint the special characteristics of collective bargaining. First, the workpeople are concerned *collectively* in wage settlement. This implies, and indeed explicitly requires, that they should be *organised*. Hence collective bargaining means that the workpeople will be represented by organisations devoted to improving their wages and conditions of work. The classic definition of a trade union, provided by the Webbs, fits this situation neatly. A trade union, according to the Webbs, is 'a continuous association of wage-earners for the purpose of improving the conditions of their working lives'.[1] Secondly, collective bargaining implies that there is some established arrangement by which negotiation on employees' conditions of work can take place. Thirdly, and most obviously, collective bargaining implies that workpeople's associations have the right to bargain or to negotiate on their members' behalf: there can be no question of unilateral decisions by employers. It is difficult to compress the concept of collective bargaining into a single definitional statement, but the Ministry of Labour has made a noble effort which should be reproduced. 'The term "collective bargaining" is applied to those arrangements under which the wages and conditions of employment are settled by a bargain, in the form of an agreement made between employers or associations of employers and workpeople's organisations.'[2]

Within this general framework of arrangements for the collective settlement of wages and conditions by bargaining, conducted on the workers' side through trade unions, there is room for very considerable variation in actual collective bargaining situations. We now list a number of points about the character and scope of collective bargaining.

1. First, while collective bargaining requires that the employees should be organised, the same need not be true of the employers, and there are many variations in the level at which negotiations with employers are conducted. Sometimes collective bargains are concluded with individual employers, while in other cases the employers in an industry are organised into an employers' association which bargains on behalf of all the em-

[1] S. and B. Webb, *History of Trade Unionism*, 1920, p. 1.
[2] Ministry of Labour, *Industrial Relations Handbook*, revised ed., 1961.

ployers in the industry. During this century employers' associations have become much more numerous, and for the most part fully independent collective bargains, not attached to those for an industry, occur only with very large organisations such as I.C.I. Some smaller firms, however, also prefer to stay out of the employers' associations because they feel that it restricts their freedom in settling wages suited to their conditions. Many American firms operating in Britain bargain independently. In America plant bargaining is much more common than industry-wide bargaining and this may predispose American firms here to favour the same kind of arrangement. On the other hand many collective bargains, often of a somewhat informal type, are concluded between firms and trade unions to supplement industry-wide bargains covering the same group of employees. While such agreements may be for a firm as a whole, they often take the form of shop-floor bargains in which the appropriate shop stewards may figure much more prominently than the full-time trade-union officials. The dividing line between informal local collective bargaining and managerial decision-taking associated with informal consultation with employees can be difficult to draw in practice.

2. Secondly, the scope of agreements may differ greatly. Agreements can relate to any aspect of the relationship between employers and workers, the terms and conditions of employment, and can therefore cover conditions of work generally as well as those which have a monetary expression. The agreements relating to wage payments may be presented in great detail and exactness, or may at the other extreme cover only a very general statement of minimum payments. Most agreements give details on such things as standard hours of work, paid holidays, the nature of overtime and overtime premium payments, and the characteristics of shift work and shift payments, and thus provide regulations which extend the relevance of agreements to payments beyond the immediate area of wage rates. But this can still leave many issues to be settled. For example, the volume of overtime available, or the basis of incentive schemes and the payments they offer, may greatly affect the level of payment of particular workers. Some agreements go further than others into the details of working conditions; but for the most part British collective agreements settled on an industry-wide basis leave the detail of the operation of payment and of labour utilisation to be filled in, sometimes by less formal local collective bargaining, and sometimes with no procedural formality at all.

3. Thirdly, the scale of collective bargains has tended to grow, and so has their coverage of the labour force. While collective bargaining developed during the nineteenth century, it was by no means as usual before

1914 as it is today, and the trade unions were neither as powerful nor as well recognised. The period of the First World War saw a very rapid development of collective bargaining procedures, and the Second World War, after an intervening period of fluctuating success but some progress, established collective bargaining for most wage earners. In each war, Government encouragement and Government procedures helped the development of collective bargaining ; and in each case the Government was particulary anxious to secure as much agreement as possible on wage changes on a national scale. Thus the First World War largely initiated a change towards national bargaining which, despite difficulties in the inter-war years, and the early twenties especially, was completed during the Second World War. The development of employers' associations was a necessary condition of national bargaining on behalf of whole industries. Employers were slower to combine than workers: most organisations of employers belong to the twentieth century. The development of national bargaining and of employers' organisations was thus interdependent. On the other hand, the growth of national collective bargaining has been accompanied by a growth of local bargaining which has in recent years assumed more prominence and received wider recognition in the literature. As to the coverage of collective bargaining, the next two sections of this chapter discuss the extent of statutory wage regulation and of decision-taking by arbitrators and by Government intervention; but the form of statutory regulation has many affinities to collective bargaining, and arbitration and Government intervention arise out of collective bargaining. While there are many circumstances in which wages and conditions of work are determined in an unorganised way – these are discussed in Section V of this chapter – almost all wage earners, other than those subject to statutory regulation, are covered by collective bargaining in some degree. While collective bargaining is less usual for salaried workers, many are covered by collective agreements, and collective bargaining for salaried groups has extended rapidly in post-war years.

4. Fourthly, the organisational forms of collective bargaining differ. In some, the organisation is largely informal; for example, the very large engineering industry depends upon an interchange of letters between the two sides and meetings convened by arrangement. In other cases, there is a standing body composed of members from trade unions and employers' associations with a neutral chairman, or with the chair being alternatively taken by representatives of each side. These more formal organisations are called Joint Industrial Councils, which as well as discussing bargaining matters are usually by their constitutions also involved in discussion of

matters of wider import to the industry. They originated in one of the many important recommendations of the Whitley Committee of 1916. While many of them date from a first wave of enthusiasm for this type of organisation immediately after the First World War, the majority were in fact created during and after the Second World War.

5. Fifthly, it has been customary in Britain to distinguish rather carefully between joint consultation and collective bargaining, the former being regarded as a process of discussion and communication on matters other than wages and conditions of work. The Joint Industrial Councils have, therefore, been to a degree unusual in being intended to have wider functions of discussing the industry's needs and problems. Perhaps because they were unusual in this respect they have tended to play down these wider aspects of their remit. The result of making such a marked distinction between discussions of wages and conditions of work and discussions of other matters of interest to the firm has been the development of separate machinery for joint consultation in many firms on matters other than those reserved to collective bargaining, though often such machinery has been somewhat ineffective because managements have been reluctant to put their wider plans before such a joint body, even for consultation, and have therefore been rather poor communicators; while wage earners have not always been keen to put much effort into discussions which are expressly not directly concerned with matters affecting the return to them from their work. A result of crucial importance to the operation of the labour market, however, also follows from the separation of these two subject areas: determination of wage levels has tended to become divorced, at the level both of the industry and of the firm, from discussion of the economic prospects of the industry or the firm and of its efficiency and productivity. The movement towards productivity bargaining, which will be frequently mentioned in this book, owes much of its importance to its being associated with bringing these matters fully back into discussions of the return to labour from work. It may be argued that collective bargaining has been suffering from a serious weakness because of its tendency to concentrate so much on labour's reward and not enough on the firm's prospects and productivity.

6. Sixthly, we should make some reference to sliding scales as a particular form of collective agreement, since some part at least of the pay of about two million wage earners has been affected by the most important type of sliding scale, that related to cost of living, though relating wage movements to cost of living movements is frowned upon in the context of incomes policy (see Chapter 21), and this method of determining wage movements

looks as though it may decline, and possibly rapidly. While they are governed by collective agreements, sliding-scale arrangements provide an alternative to separate negotiations of each wage change, by specifying a scale of wage changes related to different levels of an indication of the cost of living. If wage levels do not keep up with price changes, the real standard of life of the wage earner will fall. There is therefore always a strong social argument to suggest that the cost of living should be used as a measure of necessary wage change. There are obvious difficulties in applying this argument if economic reasons suggest that money-wage costs should not rise, and this is why this type of 'automatic' wage increase sets difficulties for incomes policy. It is also obvious that such sliding scales will decline in popularity if the retail price index (commonly known and used as the cost of living index) starts to fall and wages slide down the scale with it. Moreover, changes in the circumstances of occupations and industries may require differential changes in wages within an industry or between industries and these are unlikely to correspond with cost-of-living alterations. Nevertheless, several industries, of which the most notable in post-war years have been building, boot and shoe manufacture, and iron and steel, have made use of cost-of-living sliding scales.[1]

7. Finally, there are three broad categories of agreement within collective bargaining. The most basic agreement is simply the agreement to bargain. This is of course the fundamental condition of any form of collective bargaining; but as it is prior to the present framework of agreements, we are inclined to forget it. Nevertheless, claims by trade unions to be recognised by employers, and to have the right to negotiate and make agreements with them, were at the root of industrial strife in the nineteenth century, and the most significant change in this century in relations between masters and men, and in methods of wage settlement, is simply the fact that negotiations are accepted as the normal way of proceeding. Strikes, when they occur as deliberate acts of policy, are now designed to influence negotiations rather than to establish the right to negotiate, though there may still be disputes about which unions should be involved in particular

---

[1] Cost-of-living sliding scales are not the only possible form which such arrangements may take. For example, before the war the iron and steel industry used a scale based on the selling prices of a standard unit of product in each section of the industry. The selling prices were periodically determined and wages appropriately changed. A somewhat similar arrangement was operated in the coalmining industry before the war whereby uniform percentage additions in wage districts were added to the very different 'basic rates' of each pit, or lesser unit. These percentage additions were calculated from data relating to the net proceeds of the district assessed in a somewhat complicated way.

negotiations. Secondly, there is the whole portfolio of current agreements relating to conditions of work. Thirdly, there are agreements relating to the procedure to be followed in disputes about conditions of employment. These latter agreements have three distinct forms. Every collective bargaining set-up must include agreement, even though it is very informal, on how to set about negotiating a new arrangement. Many have procedures which are to be followed in a dispute on interpretation of an existing agreement. Some also have their own built-in procedures on how to invoke conciliation or arbitration if a new negotiation should result in failure to agree. Thus if a new claim is contemplated there is an agreement, whether formal or informal, on how to proceed. If people quarrel about the implications of an existing agreement, then the dispute will normally be handled, or should be handled, by an agreed procedure. Even if discussion on a new claim makes it quite clear that there is no basis on which agreement is likely, there can still be an agreement on the next steps, towards conciliation or arbitration, which follow a failure to agree.

A bald statement of procedure such as the above leaves a strong impression of orderliness in collective bargaining – the parties knowing how to begin negotiating and how to conduct themselves if they do not find a ready basis for harmony in new decisions. The observer who reads about disputes in the press and watches the harassed, despondent, angry, or anxious statements of leaders of both sides on television, is bound to feel that it is not quite like this in reality. To some extent the anxious and angry comings and goings of negotiators are not wholly reality either, since as anyone knows very well who has tried to buy or sell a second-hand motor-car or buy at a street market, the term bargaining requires acting the part of taking up a position with a great show of determination and also a hidden willingness to depart some way from it in arriving at a settlement. It would be quite wrong, however, to go on to suggest that the whole thing was at best play-acting and at worst a farce. The anger may be genuine. Discontent with an existing agreement may spring up among the men and come to the surface in unofficial action which ignores all the established procedures. While an official strike may simply be a part of the process of establishing the strength of a bargaining position, it depends for its success on the support of the members of the trade union who have to go on strike. When the employers react angrily against a claim they may to some extent be following the accepted drill for collective bargaining, but they are also reflecting the strength and weakness of their own competitive position in relation to their workers and the trade unions, and hence in the market for labour, but also more widely in their ability to meet the market situation for their products and services.

Collective bargaining is, then, essentially a matter of sorting out and reconciling conflicting interests and contrasting strengths: the statements of case put in by the sides to the bargaining discussions are, or certainly should be, directed at exploring these. Some of the relevant factors may be drawn from the sort of institutional forces discussed in Chapter 2. Some of them may reflect the wider context of contemporary social opinions, the state of the economy, the movement of prices, and economic growth; some ought to relate more specifically to the economic circumstances of the employers concerned, their costs, their production policies, capital investment and the strength of technical change, pricing policy, and the state of the market for their products. All these various influences come to bear on the central issue of the position in the labour market of the workers concerned. This raises questions of the employers' manpower policy and labour-force development and utilisation, while for the workers the terms and conditions of employment being discussed are the means of achieving a decent standard of living compatible with the value of their services.

On the whole collective bargaining is fully capable of sorting out all these factors. Criticism of the system should not be based on its tendency to erupt into crises. It can do so, but the crises are sometimes exaggerated and are less frequent than, for example, in the U.S.A. The real grounds for criticism should be on the extent to which our present collective bargaining machinery is effectively carrying through its remit. Has it become too much a routine – and thoughtless – performance with all concerned carrying out rituals which bear some resemblance to the figures of country dancing – meet your partners, link hands, go back, come forward, reverse and go the other way, etc.? In particular, is the present national scale of bargaining a sensible way of arriving at a wise allocation of labour and determination of its rewards? Should there be more formal local bargaining? Should productivity bargaining be further developed to introduce a wider range of issues relating to efficiency more directly into the bargaining situation? Should collective agreements be more detailed and more formally binding on the parties? Should agreements run for a fixed length of time, as is the usual practice in the U.S.A., or should they be open-ended, as usually happens in Britain? How can collective bargaining discussions and decisions be reconciled with full employment without inflation? Some of these questions have already been briefly raised, others will come up later in this chapter, and some will be referred to later in the book; though it would, of course, be unwise to pretend that they will be fully answered.

III. Statutory Wage Regulations: Wages Councils

The State in modern times has been reluctant to take over the job of regulating wages on any kind of permanent basis, though it has, through industrial legislation such as the Factories Acts, done much to regulate conditions of work. In earlier periods there was not the same reluctance and the State was prepared to lay down fairly detailed arrangements for assessing the payment of workers, as in the Elizabethan Statute of Artificers.

The first re-entry of the State into the field of wage determination in the modern period came with the Fair Wages resolutions of the House of Commons, which broadly limit the ability of employers who are not party to collective agreements to pay wages below those 'customarily paid in the trade'. The first resolution was passed in 1891, when the House resolved that all Government contracts should contain a clause which required the employers concerned to pay 'such wages as are generally accepted as current in each trade for competent workmen'. Similar resolutions have been passed from time to time since then. As it now stands, following on the latest revision in 1946, the resolution compels a Government contractor, and his sub-contractors, to accept the collectively-determined or observed rates in the trade as the minimum which he can pay. These are resolutions of only one of the Houses of Parliament, and their direct effect has been on Government purchasing policy. Their indirect effect has been to encourage the process of collective bargaining, since they put those employers who are out of line at a disadvantage for Government contracts, even as sub-contractors. A resolution of this type does not, however, determine the general level of payments. It merely provides protection of a rather indirect and incomplete type for the minimum wage level of some workers. The Terms and Conditions of Employment Act of 1959, however, prescribes a more general statutory procedure which can compel an employer who is not a party to a collective agreement to observe terms and conditions of employment as favourable as those which have been collectively determined for his trade. This provision is in effect the last relic of a much more general series of provisions for compulsory arbitration which were introduced during the war and continued for a few years after it. The Act continues only one of the provisions of the abolished

Industrial Disputes Order, itself a modified version of the wartime Order. Any trade union which has regularly taken part in the settlement of wages and conditions in an industry can report to the Department of Employment and Productivity an 'issue' on whether a particular employer is observing the recognised terms and conditions of employment in the industry. Such an issue, which would under the Order have been referred to the Industrial Disputes Tribunal which disappeared with the abolition of the Order, can under the Act of 1959 be referred to the Industrial Court. If the Court considers that these are recognisable terms and conditions in the industry, it can make an award requiring the employer to observe them, or conditions at least as favourable. This, then, is a direct legislative provision to underpin the collective bargaining system, and to secure observance of recognised conditions, but only in specific circumstances and on request.

By the first decade of this century the public conscience in Britain was ready to be aroused by accounts of the exceptionally poor conditions of work and payment which prevailed in some British industries. Agitation about these 'sweated industries' resulted in the Trade Boards Act of 1909, and the State found itself launched on a process of compulsorily fixing minimum wage levels in selected industries. Subsequent legislation, up to and including the Wages Councils Act of 1959, considerably expanded this role so that over three million workers are now covered by the Wages Council system. There is no general British minimum wage legislation; selective excursions into individual industries which have Wages Council have up to the present substituted for a general legal minimum.

The first Trade Boards related only to industries which seemed to be specially bad examples of sweated trades: at first only four industries were affected – ready-made tailoring, chain-making, paper-box-making, and machine-made lace finishing – but another four were added later. These industries paid specially low wages to their workers, many of whom were women and outworkers, and the principal function of the Trade Boards was to fix minimum rates of wages for specified periods of work. By 1918 the idea had been sufficiently well tested to justify extension, and a new Trade Boards Act allowed the Minister of Labour to set up a Trade Board for any trade if he thought that 'no adequate machinery exists for the regulation of wages'. At the end of the War the Wages Councils Act of 1945 superseded the Trade Board legislation. The legislation in effect is designed to create and retain a Wages Council in a trade where representative organisations of employers and workers have not developed adequate machinery of negotiation, which looks as though it is likely to remain in effective existence, and which seems capable of prescribing a reasonable standard of remuneration in the trade.

There are now around sixty Wages Councils, the post-war creations being mainly in the retail trades. Separate Wages Boards were set up in the catering industry by an Act of 1943, but the four Boards which were constituted under that Act became Wages Councils by the Act of 1959. (There are also Wages Boards under separate legislation for agricultural workers.) The powers of the Wages Councils, like the Trade Boards, centre on fixing minimum remuneration which can be enforced by law, but in addition to determining such remuneration and standard hours of work the Councils also consider other aspects of employment, such as overtime arrangements and holidays with pay. The Councils are composed of equal numbers of employers and workers and three independent members (including at least one woman if there are women in the trade). The employers and workers are chosen to represent as far as possible the various parts of the trade. They are selected as individuals rather than as officials or members of organisations, but in practice organisations are consulted, their important officials are included, and the strength of each organisation in the trade can be roughly gauged by the number of its representatives on the Council. On both sides of the table there will be people who are actually working at the trade as well as officials. The independent members, one of whom is Chairman of the Council, are drawn mainly from lawyers and university teachers. The voting in the Council, though it can be one man one vote, is usually taken by 'side', in which case each of the employers' and workers' sides have one vote and the independent members can exercise a casting vote. Once a Council has come to a decision this is sent, after a period for representation, to the Secretary of State for Employment and Productivity who is asked to make an Order to bring the proposals into effect. He has at times sent proposals back for further consideration, particularly during periods of incomes policy. Apart from temporary provisions of the Prices and Incomes Act since 1966, the Secretary of State has either to make an Order or send proposals back for reconsideration. He cannot simply reject them. Once an Order is made it is sent round to all known establishments in the trade. It has the force of law, and the Wages Inspectorate of the Department have power to inspect the books of employers. There are fines for non-compliance.

There are a number of notable characteristics of this system. In one light it can be regarded as Government interference in wage settlement; but, if we look closely, this point of view begins to take on a rather elusive character. It is true that Government interfered to set up the machinery of Trade Boards, and later Wages Councils, but having done so, it left the process of deciding on the wages and conditions to be fixed to a mixture of people in the trade and 'independent persons'. The Government contribution can be put in five points. (*a*) It created the Councils. (*b*) It provides the secretariat and pays the expenses of the process. (*c*) It ensures, through the machinery of the Office of Wages Councils and the Wages Inspectorate, that all establishments in each trade both know about the conditions fixed by the Councils and observe them. (*d*) Since the representatives of employers and workers who sit on the Councils naturally tend to be the active members of the trade, who are perhaps least likely to have been left behind in changing conditions, or are trade-union officials, it is probably true that the Government can be said to have ensured that the better employers lead the rest, and that the organised workpeople are ensured a say in conditions in their industry. (*e*) By establishing uniform machinery in a number of trades, a common secretariat, and, especially in the persons of independents, some elements of common membership, the Government has ensured that important sections of industry and retail trade will settle their conditions with considerable reference to each other and possibly to the community. It would be an exaggeration to suggest that this results, even in the limited sector to which it applies, in a uniform minimum wage corresponding to what might result from national minimum wage legislation. It does, however, result in a minimum wage pattern in the sectors it covers which, while taking account of differences in the trades, has some general consistency.

In some ways Wages Councils can be regarded as examples of collective bargaining procedures, while in other ways they resemble conciliation and sometimes they look more like arbitration. It is an indication of the development of the collective relations in the trade if the workers and employers address their remarks to each other and with only a friendly word from the Chairman arrive at an amicable settlement. In these circumstances the meeting becomes something like a well-conducted collective bargain. But if there is some real disagreement between the parties, then the independents hold the casting vote and cases and argument will tend to be directed at the independents. The independents can then try, having heard the arguments, to talk the two sides into agreement in joint meetings and in private meetings with each side: this is a process of conciliation where outsiders try to get the parties concerned to agree. The independents can also give a decision by their casting vote, if they find that their conciliatory efforts are not successful. This process of outsiders giving a decision in a dispute between two sides in an industry can be described as arbitration. In this case, however, the arbitration process is restricted, since the independents cannot initiate a decision, but must cast their vote for a motion put up by one of the sides. If neither side can be persuaded to put up a motion acceptable to the independents, then the business could end in a deadlock for the time being.

Wages Councils can be regarded as supplementing collective bargaining or as replacing it. Despite the element of compulsion in the enforcement of their decisions, which contrasts strongly with the more usual voluntary agreements, the Councils do provide *collective* settlement of wages and conditions where this did not previously exist. But once a Wages Council is in operation it can be suggested that there is no longer any compelling reason to devise private collective bargaining arrangements and so the Wages Council can be said to be replacing the growth of collective bargaining. Some industries have developed collective bargaining and their Wages Councils have fallen into disuse, or have been abolished. In many other cases the presence of the Wages Council has resulted in a considerable increase in personal contact between employers and workers. In some cases employers and workers have favoured the continued presence of a Wages Council when most decisions have in fact been taken by them in prior collective bargaining. This is more than just a rubber-stamping situation, and even in such cases the Wages Council can be regarded as having a function supplementary to that of collective bargaining (though the Department of Employment and Productivity probably regards Wages Councils of this type as going outside the purpose for which they were established and might well like to do away with them). Two functions for such Councils can be mentioned. First, they offer a means by which decisions taken by good, or at any rate organised, employers can be passed on to the unorganised sections of a trade. For the unions at least there is point in seeing that agreements reached with most employers can be forced on the less willing. Secondly, even though most matters may be agreed by collective bargaining, the Council and the independent members can be used as a private arbitration body on matters in dispute. This latter kind of point is worthy of special notice since it hints at a rather important feature of Wages Council decisions which is common to all the Councils. The machinery of the Councils is very well adapted to enable employers' or workers' representatives to make the best bargain possible and to compromise, while telling their members that they took up a position and refused to give in. Suppose, for example, that the workers ask for an increase of 5 per cent and the employers refuse to concede anything. In the course of discussion it may become apparent that the just and sensible

D

and inevitable compromise is 3 per cent. One side or the other may refuse to vote for the compromise, leaving it to be carried by the vote of the other side and of the independent members.

In some ways Wages Councils can be regarded as favouring the growth of trade unions and in other ways as retarding this growth. The need to present an agreed view at Wages Councils has almost certainly stimulated the development of employers' associations, but in the case of trade unions this is less certain. It seems clear that in Wages Council industries the power of the trade unions to obtain at any rate minimum conditions has been improved, since no matter how poorly organised they may be, they have ready-made machinery for obtaining enforceable minima, and they are, unless their membership is completely negligible, likely to be represented on the workers' side of the Council. But it is not necessary for all or anything like all the workers in the industry to join a union in order to get the security of Wages Council provisions. It can therefore be suggested that the presence of the Councils has retarded the growth of union membership. It is certainly true that trades in which there are Wages Councils tend to be relatively under-organised. This does not, however, prove the point. These trades became subject to Wages Councils in part because they were unorganised and tend in any case to be in sectors where, because of unskilled workers, small establishments, or a high proportion of female workers, we would expect union organisation to be low.

There has recently been some discussion of the case for reform of the Wages Council system stimulated by a controversial Report (Number 27) of the National Board for Prices and Incomes. That Report, while it was based on a rather narrow study of a specific event in the history of one Wages Council, offered some general criticism of Wages Councils. The question of reform had already been mooted in evidence to the Royal Commission on Trade Unions and Employers' Associations, and further discussion on reform may perhaps follow from the Report of the Royal Commission. One of the current problems of Wages Council legislation is that a Council is difficult to abolish even though it may seem to have lost its usefulness. It is an insufficient condition for the abolition of a Council, for example, to show that wages in the trade are not specially low. It is also necessary to meet the other criterion for the existence of a Wages Council, that of under-organisation, and before a Council may be abolished collective organisations of workers and employers must have established effective machinery for regulating wages and conditions, and this machinery must be likely to remain in effective existence. It is difficult in such circumstances to push a trade into independent collective bargaining if one side or the other is reluctant to assume responsibility for independent bargaining.

The question of a more general national minimum wage raises much wider issues. The case for it is that of ensuring that no worker falls below a socially acceptable minimum level of payment. Despite the Wages Councils there are undoubtedly pockets of underpayment throughout the economy – though in the nature of the case it is difficult to specify them. There are, however, plenty of problems which would require to be thought over before such a step might be taken. What should be the level of such a minimum wage? On social grounds it may be argued that it should be pushed as high as possible. But the higher the minimum wage the more it will impinge on the normal functioning of the labour market. Many people are low-paid not by malice, inadvertence or under-organisation, but simply because in our present state of economic development, and with the existing market for labour, it is all the price that their services command. There would be a strong argument on social grounds for making the same minimum apply to men and women, but if the level were fixed at any level likely to be thought reasonable for men, given the usual rates of payment of men, this would in practice disrupt a large part of the market for women's services. If there is a case for choosing different minimum levels for different circumstances, we come back to something like the Wages Councils. It is also true that a national minimum wage would not fulfil one of the main facilities of the Wages Councils, that of providing a semblance of collective bargaining in under-organised trades. Moreover, the problems of enforcement would be much greater than for the Wages Council system. On the other hand, a society like ours ought to keep thinking of the ways and means of ensuring the well-being of its poorest-paid members, and full discussion of a national minimum wage is a good way of sorting out the problems.

IV. Conciliation, Arbitration and Courts of Enquiry

Though the idea of collective bargaining is to seek an agreement, this is not always easy to achieve. Disputes may arise either over an unsettled collective bargaining claim, or about the interpretation of an existing agreement, or about some matter which is not covered by an agreement at all. While all disputes are in one sense or another about terms and conditions of employment, wage issues are most likely to come up in the first two types of situation, and a large wage issue is most likely to occur in the first – when the process of obtaining a new agreement is making little progress. A failure to agree may result in direct action by the parties – a strike or, very rarely, a lockout – but the alternative of conciliation or arbitration is generally used, and even when there is direct action it usually leads on to conciliation or arbitration. Many wage claims are therefore settled by this means. Conciliation is a process by which the two sides are brought together and a third party attempts to secure an acceptable compromise by persuasion. In arbitration both sides present their case to a third party who makes an award on what he considers to be the merits of the case. There are also procedures which are rather difficult to classify under either heading: in these the dispute is ventilated by enquiry and the opinions of both sides are canvassed. The enquiry offers its own opinion, which cannot be regarded as an attempt at conciliation in that the sides are not persuaded to adopt the opinion, but it is a strong hint about a possible solution. It is not an *award* in the arbitration sense, in that the sides have not agreed, or are not compelled, to accept it, but it is an independent *judgment* on the dispute, in the sense of a third-party verdict.

While the possible procedures under the heading of conciliation and arbitration are numerous, they all have the same general objective: to secure settlement of a dispute. They all have several features in common. First, each involves calling in a third party who has not been involved in the dispute and asking his advice or opinion. Secondly, the kinds of people who appear as arbitrators or conciliators tend to be the same. Department of Employment and Productivity officials can act as conciliators; but if a dispute is referred to outside independents, then, as with Wages Councils, the independents tend to be drawn from members of the legal profession, or academics. Some methods, however, also include as conciliators or arbitrators representatives of employers and workers from other industries who either act as assessors to an independent chairman or serve as members under an independent chairman. Thirdly, all these procedures involve the introduction of outside comment on the internal affairs of particular industries. There is always a duty upon arbitrators or conciliators to give primacy to the issue they are asked to resolve; but public and journalistic comments, and sometimes Government hints about 'public interest', that ought to be, or might be, forwarded are often evident on the more important occasions. Finally, all forms of conciliation and arbitration are voluntary. Even if the sides agree in advance to accept an arbitration award they cannot be compelled to do so, and in some types of procedure need not even co-operate. From 1940 until early in 1959, when the Industrial

Disputes Tribunal went out of existence, there was a form of compulsory arbitration which included until 1951 a prohibition on strike action, but at present arbitration requires to be preceded by the agreement of those concerned, though agreement need not be secured for informal attempts at conciliation or for formal enquiry of the Court of Enquiry type. There is therefore no final source of solution of wage disputes in Britain, which could theoretically drag on for as long as the parties concerned are prepared to keep them going, and strike action may take place between the beginning of an unresolved dispute and its settlement by conciliation or arbitration.

The list of conciliation and arbitration procedures begins with those that are privately organised by some industries. The nationalised industries each have arrangements for conciliation or arbitration built into their negotiating machinery in order to deal with cases of failure to agree. The boot and shoe industry has a well-established procedure. Many other industries have agreements stating the procedure to be followed in passing on undecided wage claims to conciliation and arbitration bodies.

If a wage claim goes through all the procedures provided by an industry without being settled, the central figures in the next act are the Secretary of State for Employment and Productivity and his officials. If conciliation or arbitration are agreed to by the sides to the dispute, the Secretary of State has then to decide in consultation with the parties concerned how best to handle it. He can keep discussions informal: in the early stages he will probably, either himself or through his Industrial Relations Department, have had contact with employers and workers in trying to get some agreement on next steps and he can continue his conciliation work in this informal way. Alternatively, he can use some more formal method: he can, for example, appoint a single arbitrator or conciliator. He may appoint a Board of Conciliation or of Arbitration, or make use of the Industrial Court or of a Court (or Committee) of Enquiry. Normally each of these bodies consists of three persons, the chairman always being an independent.

The Industrial Court is a permanent arbitration body which was first set up in 1919. Though it is called a court it has no legal standing: its awards are not legally binding, but if they are accepted and operated they become part of the contract of employment. The Court normally sits under a full-time President and two members representing employers and workpeople, though there are panels of chairmen, employers and workers who may be drawn on as required. The Court deals in all manner of disputes as well as wages. It is brought into use by the Secretary of State for Employment and Productivity once all other methods of settlement at the disposal of the industry have been exhausted and the parties have agreed to its use.

In important disputes the Secretary of State may set up a Court of Enquiry. This is a particularly useful device in cases where other methods of settlement have failed, and it has been a feature of a number of major disputes in post-war years. Since it is an enquiry it does not need to have the consent of the parties, nor need the dispute have been formally reported to the Secretary of State, and it offers an opinion rather than directly attempting to settle the dispute. In its report, which is directed to Parliament, and of course also to the public, the Court of Enquiry sets out the whole story of a dispute and draws its conclusions. To help it in getting at the story it can be given powers by the Secretary of State to take information under oath. In other words the Court of Enquiry is mainly a device to clarify the facts and to build and use public opinion to settle a dispute. On the other hand, since the Court looks into all the issues and makes its views known, it is in effect an instrument of settling disputes as well as simply of enquiry. On occasion the slightly less formal device of a Committee of Enquiry is used instead of a Court, and in complex and broad issues a Committee is set up which is composed, and functions, in much the same way as any other Committee appointed by the Government to report on an issue.

While conciliation and arbitration are to a very considerable extent organised and run by the Government acting through the Department of Employment and Productivity, it is important to realise that they are devices for helping the parties to settle disputes and not instruments for promoting Governmental policy. The conciliators and arbitrators are, for example, given rather precise terms of reference and the Department studiously avoids exerting influence on them. They represent the final stage of a process of settling wages and other labour issues between the parties and are complementary to collective bargaining rather than an alternative system. Courts of Enquiry, or Committees, by comparison, are usually given broader terms of reference. They are much more investigational in character and can pursue issues to a greater depth, and they can report broadly and can more readily present general argument and conclusions. It is perhaps for this reason that Courts of Enquiry have been more frequently used in recent years. They have in the past, though less specifically, tended to be part of the same process of complementing collective bargaining rather than substituting for it. It would, however, be possible to change the character of Courts and Committees of Enquiry in this respect, and there have been some signs of a tendency to do this.

V. The Place of Unorganised Wage Settlement

This chapter has up to now been concerned with various organised methods of wage settlement. Some people, however, still have their payment determined by wholly informal methods – and this was the typical situation before the development of collective bargaining. Moreover, as the last chapter indicated, wage earners today may draw together their pay from a number of different types of payment, and some of these are settled outwith the formal context of collective bargaining.

The direct approach to wage settlement takes the simple form of an employer deciding on a change in the wages he proposes to offer and notifying his workers, or of the worker asking for an increase. In the form in which unorganised, or individual, wage settlement commonly took place before the advent of strong trade unions, it produced a wide miscellany of rates of payment. The price of a worker's services can be quoted in different ways which convey radically different impressions to different people: a wage may mean either the actual amount which a worker takes home or a minimum basic payment below which he will never fall, or any variation in between. Moreover, labour is a highly diversified 'product' or 'resource'. It is, of course, quite meaningless to go into the labour market seeking one unit of labour without indicating the kind of labour and the kind of job. Labour is subdivided into innumerable occupations, and with an unorganised labour market there can be many different versions, and even titles, of each occupation. These points create one of the major handicaps to the working of any market, the handicap of lack of knowledge. This lack of knowledge is further emphasised by the process in which in an unorganised labour market such information as is available is actually transmitted. Studies of the operation of the labour market's mechanism for transmitting information about wages and prospects place great emphasis on casual sources of information, which continue to prevail even though an employment exchange service is available.

In the historical context the unorganised labour market tended to be one in which the balance of competitive strength was weighted in favour of the employer. The employers of any given type of labour are almost invariably very much less numerous than the workers concerned. Besides, the effective area of recruitment and supply of labour of any given type tends to be less than the whole economy, and to be limited to the representatives of one industry in a local area. The area can be very small if travel is not easy and knowledge of other places is poor, as was the case in Britain at the time when unorganised bargaining was most usual. In situations of this kind a small number of employers could group together to determine the wage level which they were prepared to pay, and so, unless in conditions of special labour shortage, keep labour's price down. Indeed, in an isolated community a single employer might find himself in a strong bargaining position of this type. On the other hand, the forces of competition in the product market may require some employers to expand output and employment. To pursue a policy which keeps the supply of labour in excess of demand may mean that employers are deliberately rejecting opportunities for expansion. Unless an employer is a monopolist in the sale of his product and can keep a high price and a low output, he will find it difficult to restrict his demand for labour. Practical questions of bargaining strengths, however, also influence the relative positions of employer and worker in unorganised wage settlement. The individual employer inevitably presents a more impressive aspect than a single worker, while workers as a group require to make a conscious effort to become united in an organisation and have still a further, and probably difficult, step to take before their organisation can play any part in a bargaining process. Moreover, the employer, as the buyer, has the initiative in making a contract with new labour: he makes the offer which the prospective employee can accept or reject. Existing employees are under the discipline of the management, who again have the right of initiating new contracts or new methods of payment. We may put the position simply by saying that in conditions of unorganised wage settlement the workers' powers of bargaining tend to become a right of protest or request rather than of negotiation. Of course, the protest can be strong or weak depending on the actual labour situation of the particular employer at a particular time. It is difficult, however, not to feel some sympathy with the imaginary picture of the cartoonists who seem to make frequent portrayals of the employee asking his boss for a rise: in their minds it is clear the boss is always domineering and the employee is always a little frightened man mentioning a very touchy subject. This may be an exaggeration, but it has some truth.

In the contemporary scene almost all wage earners, except very unorganised small groups, who probably need the protection of minimum-wage regulation, have the basic elements of their pay determined by organised processes. While collective bargaining of salaries has been developing rapidly, informal negotiation (which can be simplified to the point at which it consists of the employer laying down the rates and scales of payment he proposes to offer) still forms the sole procedure for some salary earners. Many lower-paid salaried workers are subject to collective wage negotiation, especially if they work in a public service or for a large employer, and quite a number of professional people in one way or another also have their payment arrangements determined by collective means. But substantial numbers of salaried workers, especially in industry and commerce, are paid salaries which are very much a matter for individual bargain, so that many firms are able to arrange salary scales according to their own ideas, without being bound to consider the wishes of outside parties or to keep within the terms of some binding agreement. Direct negotiation, or unilateral action by employers, is still, moreover, the most usual arrangement for promotion. The result of this type of bargaining situation for the salaried worker depends very much on whether he is one of a broad group of people with similar and not very unusual qualifications, or alternatively is a scarce type of worker for whom a number of employers are looking. The managerial and professional types of salaried workers are often in the latter position and can, therefore, make use of their monopoly position to keep up their payments; and, indeed, it would be difficult to arrange collective bargaining for some higher-salaried people who are very much recruited and paid as individuals. The lower-paid salaried groups, however, are likely to have only the disadvantage of an unorganised situation, especially in a period when rapid wage movements are occurring elsewhere.

The importance of unorganised wage settlement for wage earners is in the determination of the level of their earnings, supplementary payments, bonuses and fringe benefits, rather than their basic rates and conditions. While collective agreements may settle some of the basis upon which these supplementary payments are built, there can still be a considerable degree of freedom from collective bargaining in the determination of substantial parts of a worker's wages and conditions. To some extent it is an exaggeration to suggest that all these items are left to unorganised wage settlement. There exist in Britain all manner of local bargaining arrangements between local representatives of unions (often shop stewards) and individual employers. On the other hand, while not precisely unorganised, this type of arrangement is likely to share some of the features of the unorganised process.

This distinction between formal collectively-bargained wage settlement for the basis of a worker's pay packet and conditions and much less well-organised settlement of earnings and supplementary conditions is of the greatest importance in understanding the actual operation of the British labour market. In effect it means that while formal bargaining influences

D 2

earnings by establishing their basis component, and while there may also be local bargaining, the actual levels of earnings and conditions are determined in an unorganised process to which some of the above comments about such a process apply. In particular, the unorganised settlement of earnings and supplementary conditions creates problems of information and of undisclosed, or unknown, differences between similar groups of workers. The determination of actual bonus arrangements, pension plans and the rest is in such circumstances in the hands of the employer, and the worker's powers, as we have already noted, are those of protest or request rather than negotiation. In a tight labour market such as has been characteristic of Britain in the post-war period, it is unlikely that this will generally lead to employees suffering from a weak competitive position. On the other hand, the onus of providing effective knowledge and communications in the labour market, and of developing effective manpower policy in relation to all manner of arrangements for payment, promotion, and development both of their labour force and of their conditions of service, rests upon the employers, to an extent that is not always appreciated even by the employers themselves. Yet it is in the development of such policies that much-needed improvements in the operation of the labour market and the utilisation of labour depend.

VI. Some Comments

In this final section of the present chapter we bring together some more general comments on the processes of wage settlement in Britain, amplifying and to some extent repeating by way of conclusion some points that have already been made, and voicing a few others.

1. Argument and compromise play a very large part in current wage settlement. At almost every stage in our catalogue we are visualising a committee, a board, a council, or a group of some kind debating the arguments for and against a change, and quite frequently the group will include independents of one kind or another who will expect to be swayed by argument rather than prior preferences or commitments. Thus ability to present an argument ranks high in the qualifications of a wage negotiator (plus the ability to sit out a long succession of committee meetings). Moreover, because arguments are never altogether clear-cut and can for the sake of bargaining be much exaggerated, and because the whole aim of the procedures is to arrive at a solution of some sort, the result is frequently

a compromise of one kind or another. Argument, bargain and compromise are essential features of the present situation. Since underneath all this discussion we are dealing with a market situation, and with the need to secure the wise deployment and use of a very scarce resource, it is most important that our society makes a conscious effort to sort out the essential elements of the argument and put it on a sound basis.

2. The position of the trade unions is nowadays securely recognised in wage settlement procedures. This raises several issues for trade unions. For example, the need to bargain and to argue in committees suggests that the type of trade-union leader who makes his way by the vigour of his leadership and his success in rousing his members may not be well suited to the present context, where a patient, skilled (and trained?) negotiator might be more appropriate. There is also a bigger issue, of the future of trade unions: they were designed as agencies for establishing the rights of workers and their history has for the most part been one of struggle against society for acceptance. Now that their rights and position have been accepted, their history may perhaps be thought to be a little irrelevant to their current problems, and indeed there may be a stronger case for going against precedent than for following it. The difficulties that beset a conservative and tradition-minded organisation faced with this kind of change in its outlook and fortunes can be very great, and much of recent trade-union history could be couched in terms of the reaction to these difficulties.

3. The most distinct break in the catalogue of methods of wage settlement occurs between the methods that presuppose and require the presence of trade unions, imply the existence of employers' associations, and stress *organised* settlement, and those which do not. This point has already been put in terms of types of wage payment in the previous chapter. The main line of effort in organised wage settlement is to fix an agreed and broadly based rate of payment. Collective bargaining, arbitration, and the rest go on to set broad presumptions for extra payments, and sometimes supplementary and more detailed agreements are negotiated, but for the most part payments beyond the nationally-settled rate are the subject of less formal and more direct settlement. So long as this situation continues, the development of good payment practices in Britain – and hence the development of more effective labour-market policy – is quite largely within the initiative of employers. Changes require negotiation and give rise to difficulties but they begin when the appropriate people – in this case the employers and managers – make a start on them.

4. Another way of putting the same point would be to suggest that more and better organised local bargaining is needed. There has been a lot of

debate about the relative merits of national and local bargaining. As it has proceeded, the differences of view have narrowed. Most people now accept that national bargaining is needed as a framework of pay and conditions, but also that this framework has to be filled out in a purposive way for each employer, or at any rate for all sizeable employers. To do this will require far more detailed thinking and discussion, and there would be little point in beginning unless changes were contemplated. One of the difficulties in this type of development is the shortage of union officials with the time and training to take a full part.

5. In the last chapter we discussed the arguments which are now going on about productivity bargaining, suggesting that the real issue behind such bargaining was not simply to relate pay to output, but to relate it much more widely to the organisation and utilisation of labour. This implies detail in argument, in negotiation, and in agreements.

6. Yet another way of pointing to the same issue is to suggest that British collective bargains are on the whole rather thin and skeletal by comparison, for example, with U.S. agreements. It is, for example, true that most fringe benefits are developed by employers with comment from their workers rather than in full negotiation. There are advantages of flexibility in this, and, if properly used, of co-ordinated policy development by employers less affected by negotiated compromises. On the other hand, some greater degree of detail in agreements would help to improve the sense of relevance of the negotiations and the state of knowledge of the labour market. More detail would be an inevitable corollary of any move to make agreements more fully contractual than they are at present.

7. One other contrast between U.S. agreements and our own is that the American agreements generally run for a fixed period of time whereas ours continue until altered. Ours is a more flexible system and less given to last-minute crises before an agreement lapses. On the other hand the American system does mean that the whole range of agreement has to be fully surveyed at stated intervals. This helps to produce a sense of detail and consistency and a thorough revision. These are features which we need, though they should be attainable without necessarily putting all our agreements on to a fixed time period.

8. We have in the Wages Councils a system of developing arrangements for under-organised trades and of fixing minimum remuneration for them which has served us well. On the other hand, it is not without faults, and it may leave aside other unprotected low-wage sectors. A debate on the case for a national minimum wage is likely to develop, though the wise outcome is difficult to discern.

9. Wage negotiation and settlement is no longer as private a matter as it used to be. Collective bargaining on a large scale attracts the attention of commentators. Courts of Enquiry inform Parliament and the public and bring them into the debate. Independent members of Wages Councils, arbitrators and conciliators represent an outside view. This increase in public attention is bound to continue and even develop. Current interest in incomes policy, and the increased flow of fuller documents on wages, not least those from the National Board for Prices and Incomes, will ensure this, and, it is to be hoped, will help along the process of reform of attitudes to wage bargaining, and to the utilisation of labour.

10. While there is a long-established tradition in Britain of governmental intervention in the determination of conditions of employment, as distinct from wages, through a whole series of Acts governing conditions of work, British governments have for most of this century adopted a long-term attitude of encouraging collective bargaining and not interfering in the determination of wage levels by collective bargaining processes. There were temporary powers to avoid strikes and to require compulsory arbitration in both wars, and parts of this system remained in being until 1959, when the only trace of it that was left became the 'issues' procedure of the Terms and Conditions of Employment Act of 1959, which is referred to in Section III above. These powers, however, as well as being temporary, were concerned with the way in which collective bargaining proceeded, and more particularly with avoidance of strikes and the use of arbitration, and not with the freedom of collective bargaining to determine wage levels, or with their implementation. (While employment was strictly controlled in the Second World War, wages were not.) Collective bargaining as described in Section II above is a voluntary system encouraged by the Government and complemented where necessary by statutory wage regulations and by procedures for conciliation and arbitration. Apart from the provisions relating to statutory wage regulations which are operated through independent Wages Councils, the prospect of using Courts of Enquiries as a broader instrument for influencing decisions, and, of course, the Government's direct concern with the machinery for determining the payment of its own employees and related groups, there is nothing in the situation outlined in this chapter about State intervention to guide wage levels. This long-term attitude of support for free determination of wage levels is in contrast to the growing interest of successive governments after the Second World War in means of securing an incomes policy. Even so, prior to 1966 governments proceeded in incomes policy largely by means of advice and voluntary understanding, so that the structure described in

this chapter was prior to 1966 influenced to some degree by governmental views on incomes policy, but was not as a general rule directly inhibited from taking its decisions with all its previous authority. The situation since 1966 has been somewhat different, since the Prices and Incomes Acts from 1966 onwards introduced governmental powers to influence the amount of wage increases and to determine their date of application. In other words, the discussion of methods of wage settlement in this chapter has to be supplemented by consideration both of the influences of incomes policy and, for the most recent period, of governmental powers. Some part of the current practice of wage settlement in Britain is excluded from this chapter and deferred for discussion in Chapter 21, which is concerned with incomes policy.

SUGGESTED READING

F. J. Bayliss, *British Wages Councils*, 1962.
N. W. Chamberlain, *Collective Bargaining*, 1951.
A. Flanders and H. A. Clegg (eds.), *The System of Industrial Relations in Great Britain*, 1954.
P. Ford, *The Economics of Collective Bargaining*, 1958.
C. W. Guillebaud, *The Wages Council System in Great Britain*, 1958.
A. I. Marsh, *Disputes Procedures in British Industry*, Royal Commission on Trade Unions and Employers' Associations, Research Paper 2 (Part 1), 1966.
A. I. Marsh and W. E. J. McCarthy, *Disputes Procedures in Britain*, Royal Commission on Trade Unions and Employers' Associations, Research Paper No. 2 (Part 2), 1968.
Ministry of Labour, *Industrial Relations Handbook*, revised ed., 1961.
National Board for Prices and Incomes, Report No. 36, *Productivity Agreements*, 1967.
D. J. Robertson, *Factory Wage Structures and National Agreements*, 1960.

5 The Structure of Relative Wages in Britain

I.

When we talk of the price of a commodity we frequently mean a range of prices of a related group of articles: for example, the price of bread really refers to a very closely set range of prices covering different varieties of loaf and centring on the standard type of loaf. While for some purposes in economic theory it is perfectly proper to refer to wages as the price of labour, in actual fact we are talking about a large range of prices of diverse types of workers. The working population of Britain totals about twenty-five million persons, and this would be one way of adding up the number of units into which the labour market can be divided; to present the pattern of relative wages in Britain in its fullest detail, it would be necessary to look at each person's position separately and to build up the total pattern from this level. It would, of course, be clearly impossible for any expositor to give details of this kind. It is customary, therefore, to split up this highly diversified resource, labour, by broad characteristics, which can be used to identify some of the main divisions of the labour force; though in doing so it must be remembered that dealing in aggregates means losing something of the total picture. The pattern of relative wages disclosed when the labour market is looked at in divisions based on such broad characteristics is usually known as a wage structure.

These remarks, of course, assume that it is possible to find convenient ways of dividing up the labour force which bring out different levels of relative wages. The main ground on which such a division may be attempted is that particular categories of the labour force have clearly distinguishable characteristics which allow the supply of labour from such groups to be separately identified, both by employers and for statistical purposes, and that such groups display sufficiently different characteristics from the point of view of their utilisation in the production process as to cause differences in demand. Analysis of these matters is to be found in Part III. The factual position can be put in a few simple statements. First, there are a number of obvious distinguishing characteristics which can separate workers out from each other, for example differences in sex, age, occupation, geographical location, etc. Secondly, employers are not always prepared or able to accept one worker as completely interchangeable with another. Thirdly, workers are not always willing, or able, to change their distinguishing characteristics (obviously enough in the case of sex or age). Finally, significant differences can, in fact, be observed in relative wage levels when wage payments are split up by these major characteristics. This chapter will be concerned with looking, in turn, at each of the main elements of the British wage structure; the first step is to set out the differences between rates and the composite total of payments accruing to workers for a period's work, which may be termed 'earnings'. But within each of these categories, rates and earnings, further distinctions can be made. There is the subject of fringe benefits to which reference was made in Chapter 3 and which will come up again. Moreover, there is yet another slightly different but relevant term – income – which refers to the total of all sources of payment accruing to individuals. The prefix 'earned' or the suffix 'from work' are needed to indicate income from labour, and further definition still is needed to make the term refer to employees and not self-employed as well, while there is also the most important distinction between 'pre-tax' and 'post-tax'. We leave income aside for the present, though we return to it in Chapters 13, 14 and 15. We should also stress the limited objective of this chapter at its outset. It is not, nor can it be, a full analysis of wage structure in all its interrelations. It is simply an attempt to provide a background of the broad structure of wages in the British economy. Some of the more important of the issues raised will be discussed in later chapters, especially Chapter 11.

II. Rates and Earnings

The relative movements of wage rates and earnings in Britain can be most readily looked at by using the Department of Employment and Productivity, monthly indices of wage-rate movements and earnings and also their more detailed six-monthly enquiries into earnings and hours, all of which appear in the *Employment and Productivity Gazette*. The wage-rate index is based on weighted averages of changes in wage rates in about eight broad industry groups and gives details for men, women and juveniles separately as well as a composite figure. This index is a useful guide but, while the same wage changes are consistently selected for each industry, different types of wage rates are used in different industries. It is difficult to say whether the index measures standard rates or minimum rates, or perhaps percentage increases on piecework prices, since it is, in fact, an amalgam of all these things. It can, however, be said that the rates used are industry-wide rates and do not reflect local complications. The present official index only dates back to 1947, but there are earlier indices from official and unofficial sources. The London and Cambridge Economic Service *Bulletin* has linked the current index to an earlier official index back to 1938. This index, back to 1938, is shown in Table 5.1, and linked to later figures from the *Gazette*.

The Department's monthly index of earnings only dates from 1963. The Department has, however, collected data on earnings and hours worked from a large sample of firms in a wide range of industries twice a year, in

Table 5.1

Indices of Wage Rates and Earnings since 1938

Date	Wage rate index	Earnings index
1938	*100*	*100*
1946	163	190
1948	178	220
1950	186	240
1951	202	265
1952	219	285
1953	229	301
1954	239	322
1955	255 (*100*)	351 (*100*)
1956	108	108
1957	113	113
1958	117	117
1959	121	122
1960	124	130
1961	129	138
1962	134	143
1963	138	149
1964	145	162
1965	151	175
1966	158	185
1967	164	192

Sources: Wage-rate index: London and Cambridge Economic Service *Bulletin* and *Gazette*. Earnings index: To 1955 constructed from the average weekly earnings figures published in the Ministry of Labour *Gazette*. The figures taken were those for 'all workers included in the enquiry' in October in each year. From 1955–*Gazette*. Average of April and October figures (now the *Employment and Productivity Gazette*).

April and October, for a much longer period and publishes its results in its *Gazette*. It is the average level of earnings given by these enquiries which forms the basis for the index in Table 5.1. This earnings enquiry is undoubtedly useful but again we must remember its deficiencies. First, it is based on a large range of industries but not on all industries. (Other sources provide data on some, but not all, of the industries not given in the Department's earnings enquiry. Agriculture and the railways, for example, are covered by separate enquiries but distribution is not.) Secondly, information on the composition or dispersion of earnings in other respects than by industry and men, women, boys and girls is not as fully or regularly available.

Table 5.1 suggests that the rate of growth of earnings was much more rapid than that of wage rates between 1938 and 1950. It continued to be faster except in the recession of 1951–2 and in the 1956–8 and 1961–2 periods. While this is not evident from the annual figures in Table 5.1, more detailed information on a monthly basis suggests that during the wage-freeze period in 1966–7 wage rates almost stopped increasing and weekly earnings fell. These results will be subject to further discussion in later chapters, but a number of points can be made now.

First, this is a big change from earlier periods. Before the First World War difficulties in the availability of data, and in the less clear-cut definitions of standard negotiated rates and the standard week, make the distinction between earnings and rates more difficult to draw. In the inter-war years the levels of earnings and of rates were sometimes little different, and earnings in a number of instances moved below rates due to short-time working. But earnings and rates did not show any marked tendency for the one to diverge from the other.

Secondly, it is clear that we cannot examine any relative wage pattern solely in terms of wage rates but must also look at earnings, since there will be a substantial difference between the well-being of those who have obtained increased earnings in line with the average and those who have only received wage-rate increases.

Thirdly, the wage-rate figures relate to the determination of wages at the national level in some form of institutional process, while earnings include all other types of direct monetary payment. Thus the explanation of the gap between rates and earnings must in some way reflect the different forces, institutional, economic and social, which influence wage-rate determination for the industry on the one hand and the actual pattern of payments to individuals on the other.

Fourthly, to some extent this gap between rates and earnings reflects alterations in the occupational composition of the labour force and the upgrading of workers, so that higher proportions of workers are now at higher occupational levels and levels of payment. The main part of the gap must, however, derive from those sections of the weekly pay packet of a wage earner which are additional to rates paid on the scale determined nationally for each industry as a whole. The extra elements are payment by results and bonuses of every kind, extra rate payments of whatever variety, and overtime earnings. The area between rates and earnings is undoubtedly subject to some influence from national agreements, and some of the conditions on which extra earnings are made are set by national agreements; but this is much less than saying that the actual *level* of extra earnings is determined by national bargains. Some parts of extra earnings,

Table 5.2

Dispersion of Weekly Earnings of Adult Male Manual Workers
in 1906, 1938 and 1960

	1906			1938A[1]			1938B[1]			1960		
	Amount		% of median	Amount		% of median	Amount		% of median	Amount		% of median
	s	d		s	d		s	d		s	d	
Lower quartile	20	9	78	55	6	83	58	0	83	234	2	83
Median	26	7	100	66	6	100	70	0	100	283	4	100
Upper quartile	34	3	129	77	9	117	82	0	117	344	9	122

[1] 1938A is based on those working 44–48 hours for comparison with the full-time basis of the figures for 1906, while 1938B is for those who worked 44 hours or more and may be compared with the 1960 figures for those who worked full-time or more.
Source: G. Routh, op. cit.

such as extra rates, are clearly outside the province of national agreements. Some details on the composition of earnings are given in Table 5.5.

Average earnings naturally conceal variations in the earnings levels of different workers. Some workers receive less than the average and some more. Unfortunately, it is possible to see how these variations from the average look like only in the years when data were collected – 1906, 1938 and 1960. Table 5.2, taken from the work of Dr G. Routh,[2] is based on the data for these years. It shows the weekly earnings expected to be

[2] Guy Routh, *Occupation and Pay in Great Britain, 1906–60*, 1965.

obtained by the man in the middle position of the manual workers, ranked in terms of earnings, and then one-quarter from the top and from the bottom, in income terms, of the total group of manual workers. Thus, for example, one-quarter of manual workers may be expected to have received less than the lower quartile figure, and one-half more than the median.

The figures in Table 5.2 speak for themselves. One-quarter of male manual workers were receiving less than 83 per cent of average earnings, and one-quarter more than 22 per cent above average earnings in 1960.

There is less spread in earnings now than in 1906, but more of an upward spread in 1960 than in 1938. On a finer comparison, 10 per cent of male manual workers had earnings over 40 per cent above the average in 1960, and more than 10 per cent had earnings which were less than three-quarters of the average. Figures such as these indicate that there is a stronger tendency for some workers to earn well above the average than to fall below it, since the extent to which the top 10 per cent of workers exceed the average is greater than the extent to which the bottom 10 per cent fall below the average.

III. Regional Differences

Differences in formally negotiated wage agreements between one district and another are now relatively small. Agreements which are negotiated nationally for an industry as a whole have generally developed from a set of regional agreements which have, in turn, emerged from agreements for smaller districts. Each step towards centralising wage bargains has been accompanied by a tendency to rationalise and reduce differentials between the areas being brought within one settlement. There can be no doubt that before there were formalised wage agreements many quite irrational differences between wage levels in neighbouring areas were allowed to coexist, and the trade unions set themselves the elimination of these differences as an important part of their work. The same is true of statutory wage boards: being empowered to set up statutory minimum rates of payment, they naturally tended to work towards raising wage payments in specially low-wage districts. They began with a large number of areas divided into several grades and have gradually eliminated some of the lowest grades. Among skilled building workers, for example, the lowest rate was 39 per cent below the highest in 1913, 6 per cent in 1946 and 2 per cent in 1951. This change is quite typical of the reduction in regional differentials in negotiated rates in many industries.

It is much less easy to be certain about the regional pattern of earnings. Comparisons over time are difficult because there are few official sources of information and private enquiries have concentrated on particular aspects of the story rather than the whole. On the other hand, enough is known of parts of the story to suggest that regional differences in earnings have a strong tendency to persist over long periods of time.

For example, the differential in earnings between Scotland and the rest of Great Britain has existed for generations. It seems indeed to have widened as between 1906 and the late 1950s, though it has narrowed quite a bit in the very recent past, mainly as a result of the earnings levels enjoyed by manual workers in some of the newer firms introduced into Scotland since the war, especially in the metal industries. (The difference in the wider category of earned incomes – as distinct from manual workers'

Table 5.3

Earnings in Regions in October 1967

Region	Average weekly earnings	Average hourly earnings
South-East	104	103
East Anglia	92	91
South-Western	93	94
West Midlands	104	108
East Midlands	97	97
Yorkshire and Humberside	94	94
North-Western	98	98
Northern	97	98
Scotland	97	97
Wales	99	101
Northern Ireland	86	87
United Kingdom	*100*	*100*

Source: Ministry of Labour *Gazette*. Figures are for men in all industries included in the earnings enquiry.

earnings – has yet to show clear evidence of narrowing.) While there is this degree of constancy in the regional earnings pattern, however, it would not be true to suggest that it is completely unchanging. The Midlands area, for example, has in this century moved with the growth of the motor industry from being a low-paid farming area to a highly-paid industrial centre. Short-period changes can also occur, such as the very marked improvement in the position of engineering workers in Northern Ireland during the war. Again, there can be, with the ebb and flow of particular firms, quite marked changes in the relative position of particular districts within a region.

While it is difficult to give any historical depth in overall comparisons of earnings, the Department of Employment and Productivity has recently begun to publish details of regional earnings from their bi-annual earnings enquiries. The latest available figures, which are for adult males only, are given in Table 5.3.

In summary, regional differentiation in the payment of manual workers has been greatly reduced, if not altogether eliminated, in their negotiated wage rates but not in their earnings. Changes in the pattern of regional earnings have occurred, but regional differences arising within particular industries, as well as from differences in the industrial pattern of particular regions, have persisted. In general, the present position is that earnings are highest in the South-East and Midlands of England and lower in the more northerly parts of the British economy.

IV. Age Differentials

Differences in wages directly related to age are not very prevalent among wage earners. It is not the usual custom to have graduated payments which alter solely with age except at the stage where juveniles are progressing towards the adult rate. Comparisons of payments based on age distinctions must, therefore, largely be comparisons of juveniles and adults.

This does not mean, however, that no age patterns are discernible in the actual payment of adult wage earners. Promotion can, of course, come with age and can create a ladder of payment increases which appears to be related to age but should rather be related to ability. But relatively few wage earners are promoted beyond their skilled or appropriate occupational grade, and they reach that grade relatively early. If they are engaged on a job where their work is assessed mainly on output, they may then find themselves with a pattern of age differentials in earnings which shows a decline as they get older and less quick and dexterous. This is a fact of considerable social importance in thinking about wage earners' attitudes to their work. Unlike the salaried worker, who has a reasonable prospect of being on an incremental scale based on age, and who generally has reasonable promotion prospects also, the wage earner matures in his earning power relatively early. He may then have little to look forward to but many years at the same job and the possibility of a steady, though slow, decline in his relative payment. In some specially heavy jobs it may not even be possible for a worker to continue at the same occupation till he retires. Thus a face worker in the mines, by the time he is forty or so, may have to move to lighter work which he and those who work with him regard as less important and which is less well paid. There can be no doubt that this type of situation affects the social and economic status of many older workers and the social outlook of many wage earners. It may also in part explain why the annual (or almost so) round of wage increases in post-war years has appeared to be rather more important to wage earners than to salaried workers who have some prospects of progression up a salary scale.

Most salary workers are exempt from the prospect of earnings declining with age because they are paid on a time basis, and because of better promotion opportunities and incremental salary scales, but it does affect some professional groups who are paid on something like an output basis. The biggest group involved are the doctors and dentists who are in general practice, and some interesting documentation of their position, which illustrates the problem of all those who are paid by results, became available through the work of the Royal Commission on Doctors' and Dentists' Remuneration (Cmnd. 939, 1959). Dentists' earnings depend on the amount of work they get through, and older dentists do not seem to be able to keep up the same effort. A survey of the earnings of dentists in 1955–6 carried out by the Royal Commission showed that dentists' earnings fall off after they reach the age of 45, and the average level of general dental practitioners' earnings between the ages of 55 and 65 was only 63 per cent of that of dentists aged 40 to 45. General medical practitioners' earnings in single practice under the National Health Service depend on the size of their list of patients and on some extra payments they may earn, for example by doing maternity work. While their earnings in 1955–6 did not vary as much with age as did those of the dentists, again there was a marked falling off with age. G.P.s between the ages of 55 and 65 averaged 89 per cent of the earnings of those between the ages of 45 and 55. The same kind of experience, though to a lesser extent, was also true of professions such as accountants, barristers and surveyors where earnings are again related to output, but was not true of doctors in salaried posts or of salaried occupations such as those of university teachers or actuaries.

The contrast between the levels of payment of juveniles and adult wage earners may be most clearly seen by looking at the results of the Department of Employment and Productivity's earnings enquiries as shown in Table 5.4. At present the young man under 21 may, on average, expect to be receiving between 40 and 50 per cent of the payment of the adult male wage earner, while a girl under 18 may expect about two-thirds of the earnings of women. In both cases this represents an improvement in the relative position of young people as against 1938 (more so in the case of girls than in the case of boys).

Within the juvenile age groups there is almost invariably a gradation of wage rates, and usually of earnings, between leaving school and attaining

Table 5.4

Weekly Earnings of Juveniles in British Industry, 1938–67

Year	Boys		Girls		Boys as % of men	Girls as % of women
	s	d	s	d		
1938	26	1	18	6	37·8	56·9
1946	46	6	38	8	38·5	59·2
1950	63	9	53	5	42·4	64·7
1954	85	7	69	5	41·8	64·1
1958	112	0	86	9	43·6	64·7
1962	141	9	104	1	44·7	64·7
1966	191	9	135	9	47·2	67·4
1967	201	8	140	0	47·2	66·3

Source: Ministry of Labour Gazette. The figures are for 'all industries' in October of each year.

adult status, but the way in which this growth of payment takes place depends on the kind of job in question. Where there is a process of apprenticeship or learnership the growth of payment is generally slower and payments are lower than they would be in other circumstances. But, on the other hand, the payment position of apprentices was very poor indeed in pre-war days and they have had especially substantial increases since then. Those who are set on to a semi-skilled or unskilled job after they leave school usually grow rapidly towards adult status and adult payment, especially if they are on incentive payment, so that this kind of job, especially in a factory with an individual incentive bonus scheme, yields the most immediate short-term fruits to the young wage earner as against the long-term benefits of apprenticeship. Apprentices, however, may similarly benefit from participation in incentive earnings if their employer gives them this opportunity. Young girls tend to go into production work directly rather than take long training courses and, in any case, women tend to be in the labour market for a relatively short period before marriage. Both these factors are doubtless of importance in making 18 rather than 21 the conventionally-accepted age at which women in the industrial labour market are usually regarded as adult, and girls progress towards adult payment more quickly than boys. There are, however, exceptions to the statement that girls are paid as women at an earlier age than boys are paid as men: notable exceptions exist in retail trading and salaried work.

V. Occupational Differentials

The labour force in Britain, as in any industrial economy, is split up into an enormously large number of occupations. (Every ten years when the full Census of Population appears it is accompanied by a classification of occupations which takes up the whole of one of the larger census volumes!) Of course, some of these occupations are very similar to each other and can readily be lumped together. Others do not require any very great expert knowledge and can be classed as not very different from unskilled labour. But we are still left with a large number of occupational groupings sufficiently distinct to deserve a separate place in an exposition of wage structure. The number of professions, for example, is large and their characteristics are highly individual, while the same is broadly true of skilled tradesmen.

Faced with this complexity the best we can do is to make some heroic simplifications. First, we may split off the salary earners as a separate group to be considered presently. Then we can follow the usual simplification of dividing wage earners into three main categories of skilled, semi-skilled and unskilled. But we have also to remember the dangers of this procedure. The significance of the term 'skilled' as applied to wage earners has been changing in recent years: it is no longer possible to assume that it invariably means the man who has served an apprenticeship. Apprenticeships are now less hedged in with legal obligations, and premium payments made to the master for training are unusual. Government Training Centres are offering training courses designed to produce skilled men by a supplementary route to that of the apprenticeship. The newer industries have tended to substitute their own training programmes and courses for formal apprenticeship arrangements. In general, skill no longer means simply manual dexterity and experience but also involves in many cases a course or a period of study. Yet because the newer forms of skilled men are, by their nature, specially trained and separate, and are not always formally classified as skilled, they cannot easily be identified in a broad analysis of wages. In practice, therefore, we are obliged to quote the wage structure position of skilled men largely in terms of the old and readily recognisable apprenticeship grades of skill. We should beware, however, of assuming that all skilled men are in anything like the same position. (We know, for example, from research studies that different types of skilled men in the engineering and shipbuilding industries can command quite substantially different earnings.)

The same kind of criticism of aggregation into big groups applies also to the use of semi-skilled and unskilled as descriptive categories. Our usual habit of thinking of the typical semi-skilled man or woman as a machine operator carrying out a limited range of repetitive tasks is probably justified by the facts for manufacturing industry at least, but in addition a large number of other types of workers with differing experience and differing capabilities can be classed as semi-skilled. For example, people like lorry-drivers, storemen, crane drivers or postmen (whose work is relatively simple but who carry a measure of responsibility) are all usually regarded as semi-skilled, and some men are formally called semi-skilled because their training has not conformed to an accepted pattern, even though their work appears to the outsider to be highly skilled. One might think that the category of unskilled workers is simple enough in that it is a catch-all for those who cannot by some special experience or attribute be given a higher title. But this leaves us with all sorts of marginal decisions to make. We may say that a general labourer is unskilled, but can we say the same of an agricultural labourer or of a mate to a skilled tradesman? In fact, the semi-skilled category has been getting confused in recent years by a tendency to up-grade the unskilled into semi-skilled by giving them some special attribute. We are left with the residue as the unskilled and with a considerable problem of definition.

Though we have discussed these important detailed criticisms of the habit of showing occupational differentials for the wide categories of skilled, semi-skilled and unskilled, we have to go on and confess regretfully that even for such wide categories full documentation is difficult. The whole subject is of considerable complexity and the best source of data at present[1] is itself a complex study. No official statistics have been regularly available until the last few years, when some occupational earnings data have begun

[1] Routh, op. cit.

to appear regularly for some trades in the *Gazette*. Statistics are, however, generally agreed on the following propositions, though the whole field is not by any means covered and there are a good number of special cases.

1. At present wage rates normally result in the unskilled rate being around 80 to 85 per cent of the skilled rate, though there are examples outside these limits.

2. There is frequently a range of semi-skilled rates in each industry which are fitted into the gap between skilled and unskilled rates in a way which has meant that the pre-eminent position of the skilled is much less apparent in comparison with semi-skilled than with unskilled wage rates.

3. The present differentials in rates are much narrower than they were before the First World War or in any earlier periods for which data have been forthcoming. They have been subject to two main periods of narrowing, the period from the beginning of the First World War to about 1920 and the period from 1939 onwards, though recent years have seen a tendency in most industries for the gap expressed in percentage terms to acquire some stability.

4. The proximate cause for this narrowing in each period has been the practice, in times of war and rising prices, of granting cost-of-living wage advances on a flat-rate basis. On this basis all grades of wage earners receive the same amount of increase in money terms, which means a smaller percentage increase for the skilled men and hence a narrowing of the percentage differential.

5. This narrowing has not occurred in all cases. For example, Professor H. A. Turner[1] points out several cases, such as cotton and coalmining, where the narrowing cannot be observed, but the generalisation that narrowing has taken place is valid for most industries.

6. It is less possible to be certain about narrowing in differentials expressed in terms of the average *earnings* as against the *rates* of skilled and other workers. However, such data as we have, mainly for shipbuilding, engineering and the railways, suggests that a similar narrowing has taken place here also, though it appears to be generally true that if we compare *averages,* the gap between payments made to skilled and unskilled is wider when looked at in terms of earnings rather than in terms of rates. There seems little doubt, however, that for most industries the pay packet of unskilled men is closer to that of the skilled men than it used to be. On the other hand, in recent years differentials in earnings have shown a tendency to widen again.

[1] 'Trade Unions Differentials and the Levelling of Wages', *Manchester School,* 1952.

Some occupational earnings figures for manual workers have been produced by the Ministry of Labour since January 1963 and are published in its *Gazette*. These enquiries now cover an increasing range of industries, especially in the engineering and metal industries. Since the data include contrasts between timeworkers and payment by results workers, and overtime premium payments, they also permit some exposition of the composition of earnings. For reasons of simplicity of exposition Table 5.5 looks at the situation for the biggest industrial group covered by the Ministry's enquiries, the engineering industry, but its conclusions broadly apply to the other industries – shipbuilding, chemicals, iron and steel, and construction – for which data are now available.

Table 5.5 demonstrates a number of points which have already been made verbally in this chapter. First, on average, skilled workers receive

Table 5.5

Earnings of Manual Workers in the Engineering Industries
in January 1967

	Average weekly earnings including overtime premium	Average weekly earnings excluding overtime premium	Hours worked Average hours actually worked	Hours worked Average hours of overtime worked
	s d	s d		
Timeworkers				
Skilled	446 7	422 2	44·7	6·0
Semi-skilled	373 10	353 6	44·2	5·9
Labourers	314 3	293 8	45·1	7·1
Payment-by-results workers				
Skilled	463 7	447 11	42·6	4·3
Semi-skilled	405 2	392 7	42·1	4·2
Labourers	332 10	313 4	44·9	6·7

Source: Ministry of Labour *Gazette*.

more than semi-skilled workers, and unskilled less than either. The ratios in this table show that the unskilled worker was on average taking home around 70 per cent of the pay of the skilled, and the semi-skilled about 85 per cent of the skilled – these proportions being much wider than a comparison of wage rates would yield. Secondly, payment by results workers earn more than timeworkers on average, and for fewer hours of work. Thirdly, the less skilled tend to work longer hours on average than the skilled to increase their weekly earnings. Fourthly, overtime is an important factor in payment. The figures for overtime working in January 1967 are low because of the 'squeeze' which was then operating on the economy, but even so overtime premium payments were adding something over a pound a week to earnings. Total payments for overtime were of course much greater than this, since, for example, the skilled timeworker was receiving an average of six hours' pay for overtime working plus his premium payment. Since the standard week was forty hours and the average hours worked by skilled timeworkers were 44·7, these figures reveal the presence of some short-time working as well as overtime. The table makes amply clear the importance of both payment by results and overtime in the average worker's pay packet.

Some historical perspective on this position can be gleaned by comparing these results with data on earnings in engineering in an earlier article.[1] A comparison of the data in that article with Table 5.5 shows that the gap in earnings between unskilled and skilled, having narrowed between 1926 and 1948, has widened again, though not quite back to where it was in 1926. The difference between the earnings of timeworkers and payment by results workers – excluding overtime effects as far as possible – has on the whole narrowed since 1948, which no doubt is a reflection of increasing concern on the part of managements to attend to the position of timeworkers. Compared with 1948, the overtime element in pay has become much more important, even in January 1967 when overtime was lower than it had been for some years, a result which is the joint outcome of a reduction in the standard hours in a labour shortage situation and the general acceptance of some degree of 'right' to overtime opportunities as a part of current approaches to the payment of manual workers.

When we turn to differentials between wage earners and salary earners, and differentials within the salary structure, we again come up against the difficulty of lack of information. It is not possible to give a complete account of the movements of salaries as against wages or of the distribution of salaries.

An illuminating approach to a discussion of the position of salaried workers in the payment structure is to look at the way in which the total salaries and wages bills in manufacturing industry have moved since 1948. The figures in Table 5.6 are based on those in the Blue Book on *National Income and Expenditure*. These estimates are derived from very broad

[1] K. G. J. C. Knowles and D. J. Robertson, 'Earnings in Engineering 1926–1948', Oxford Institute of Statistics *Bulletin*, 1951.

general figures and should not be expected to give precise accuracy, but they do indicate the general trend. They suggest two firm conclusions – that the number of salary earners has been rising more rapidly than the number of wage earners, so that since 1948 the salary bill in total has grown more than the wage bill in total, but that the average salary has not grown as

Table 5.6

Wages and Salaries in Manufacturing Industry since 1948
(1948 = 100)

Year	Total wage bill	Total salary bill	Estimated average annual wage	Estimated average annual salary
1948	100	100	100	100
1952	135	147	130	123
1956	187	209	172	149
1960	225	284	212	184
1964	269	372	257	223
1965	306	448	293	249

Source: National Income and Expenditure.

much as the average wage, at least in part because of a relatively rapid increase in the number of salaried workers at the lower end of the salary range.[1]

Professor D. Seers[2] has provided estimates of changes in the average level of salaries and wages between 1938 and 1949. His calculations suggest that wages rose by 136 per cent in that period and salaries by only 72 per cent. The growth since 1948 in the number of salary earners relative to wage earners is a trend which, in the present state of the British economy, we ought to expect. It has been going on for many years, though it was possibly interrupted to some extent during the war years and the immediate post-war period. Any developed economy is likely to carry a larger number of administrative and technical staff in industry, and this means more salary earners per operative. In addition a developed economy with a growing standard of living has more of its income to spare for service

[1] These matters will be further discussed in Chapters 13 and 15.
[2] *Levelling of Incomes since 1938*, 1951.

trades and for professional services, and this, too, is reflected in a growth in the relative number of salaried workers.

There seems little doubt, then, that the average salary earner fared less well than the average wage earner during and after the war. Indeed some salary earners, even before we consider taxation, are likely to have lost ground in real terms, since prices may have moved more rapidly than the growth in their incomes. On the other hand the picture since 1956 is somewhat different. This has been a period in which salaries in manufacturing industry appear to have moved as rapidly as manual earnings. The same general point emerges from the rather broader figures for the 1955–6 to 1960 period in Table 5.9 below, and from the comparison in Table 5.7 of an index based on average weekly earnings of all manual workers,

Table 5.7

Indices of Average Weekly Earnings and Average Salary Earnings since 1955

Year	Weekly rate of wages	Average weekly earnings	Average salary earnings
1955	100	100	100
1957	113·4	113·0	114·8
1959	120·6	122·2	126·3
1961	128·8	138·0	139·9
1963	138·4	148·9	155·8
1965	151·2	174·8	178·4
1966	158·2	185·0	186·1
1967	164·2	192·3	194·7

Source: Statistics on Incomes, Prices, Employment and Production.

derived from the Ministry of Labour's earnings enquiry, with an index of average salary earnings collected by the Ministry of Labour once a year in October. For convenience of reference and to complement Table 5.1, the index of weekly rates of wages is also shown in Table 5.7.

However, the group of salaried workers is a very large one and the idea of 'the average salary earner' is not specially helpful. How has the distribution of salaries – the salary structure – been developing? It is again difficult to set this out simply and the remainder of this paragraph is frankly impressionistic. In broad terms we can divide the salary earners into five major groups, though there is a good element of arbitrariness in such a division and the comments made about each group are necessarily general-isations. The first two groups cover the lower salaried workers: the kind of people for whom being called salaried is a question of status, reflects the fact that they wear a white collar, and typically indicates that they are clerks of some kind, junior administrators, shop assistants (though these have recently been classed as wage earners), and the routine staff of firms and institutions. If such people are organised and have agreements they have probably managed rather better than if they have been unorganised. Both groups have probably lagged behind wage earners, but the organised group by less than the unorganised. The third and fourth categories we might suggest are the professional groups, organised and unorganised, counting the term profession in a very wide sense to include not only the traditional professions but also specialist managers, specialist administra-tors, the civil service and so on. Here, too, it is probable that the organised category has done better than the unorganised over the whole period since before the war, though both have probably fared less well than the organised lower grades of salaried workers, and the unorganised have probably been doing rather better in recent years. The fifth category, roughly, is the straight managerial element, those whose salaries are dependent on private industry, who are unorganised and who are not covered by specific agree-ments, being each dealt with personally. Such people may have gone a little ahead of the professional groups in recent years in their rate of salary earning.

Most salaried workers have one important advantage over wage earners – their payment is based on scales which ensure that the worker enjoys regular increments. In general, these scales now have fewer steps than they had before the war and the percentage gap between the top and the bottom step is smaller than it was. This has happened, for example, in the civil service and teachers' scales. A narrowing process is therefore evident in the salary scale. In discussing age differentials we cited cases of pro-fessions where earnings declined with age, but it should be said again that this is not usual.

Can the present position of the salary structure be set out with any accuracy? Professor M. P. Fogarty in an article a few years ago[1] drew up a salary tree for males in Great Britain in the 1950s. The sources of this information will be found in Professor Fogarty's article along with some of the qualifications to be attached to its use. Two qualifications ought specially to be mentioned here. First, it should be remembered that the descriptions given to people at various levels on the tree are rather broad

[1] 'The White-Collar Pay Structure in Britain', *Economic Journal*, 1959.

and cover very diverse kinds of work, and that while the ranges given will include the majority of cases, there will be plenty of exceptions. Secondly, the numbers of people at different levels of the tree (which incidentally is shown upside down in the table) are very different: we ought not to expect very many people on the very high levels. Professor Fogarty's work

Table 5.8

The Salary Tree (Males) in Great Britain in the 1950s

Unskilled (85–90)	Unskilled clerk (70)
Average male industrial worker = 100	
Skilled (110)	Skilled clerk (100)
Supervision (130–150) to 200	Foreman, supervisor, sergeant (Army)
Lower management to 400	Superintendent, station-master, lieutenant, teacher, ship's officer, ward sister, welfare worker. Farmer (100 +acres) marginal to this and next category.
Middle management (ceiling, trade-union jobs, 400–500) to 1000	Department manager, colliery manager, principal (Civil Service), major or lieut.-col., headmaster and other senior teachers, university lecturers, most industrial or public service medical officers and hospital registrars. General practitioners marginal to this and next category.
Senior management (ceiling, public service c. 1000–2000) to 2000 + ceiling, private industry	Managing director, senior dept. or division manager: medical consultants and about half of general practitioners: under-secretary (Civil Service) (asst. secretary marginal) : area and higher managers – Coal Board and nationalised industries : professors, colonel and general.

Source : M. P. Fogarty, art. cit.

E

is reproduced here as Table 5.8. The various items in the table are expressed as percentages of the average earnings of male industrial workers.

These data in Table 5.8 can give no more than broad impressions, the chief of which is that of very wide differentials indeed between those few who are at the top of the salary tree and the many who are at the lower levels. It is perhaps particularly noteworthy that the unskilled clerk on Professor Fogarty's estimates is below the position of the average male industrial worker. A salary may confer status but it is by no means always true nowadays that it also confers a preferential position in terms of income. Professor Fogarty is firmly of the opinion that white-collar salaries were squeezed considerably between 1938 and 1950, though by 1950 he thinks that the squeeze was coming to an end. In particular he suggests that 'since 1948–49, clerks' rates have increased as fast as rates for operatives, and not much slower than operatives' earnings', though the position with regard to higher salaries is much less certain.

Table 5.9

Average Annual Earnings of Men in Seven Occupational Classes
in 1960 compared with 1913/14 and 1955/6

Occupational class	Average annual earnings in 1960 (£)	Percentage increase on average for 1913/14	Percentage increase on average for 1955/6
Higher professional[1]	2034	620	132
Lower professional[2]	847	546	139
Managers, etc.	1850	925	125
Clerks	682	689	130
Foremen	1015	898	129
Skilled manual	796	804	128
Semi-skilled manual	581	842	124
Unskilled	535	849	123

[1] e.g. Doctors, dentists, solicitors.
[2] e.g. Qualified school-teachers, librarians.

Source: G. Routh, Occupation and Pay in Great Britain, 1906–60.

Dr Routh's work on occupational pay was based on an adaptation of the structure of occupations given in the Census. He classified these occupations into the eight categories shown in Table 5.9, and then carefully assembled all the bits and pieces of information he was able to obtain for occupations falling within these categories. Some of his information was broadly based – such as the admirable census of earnings in 1906 – while other parts of his data were much less comprehensive. He then put all these data together to construct broad averages, some of which are shown in the table.

There are two cautions to be offered in interpreting Table 5.9. The occupational class headings are extremely general, and the figures themselves, while the product of extremely careful research, are assembled from many diverse sources. The figures nevertheless confirm and give depth to the impressions attempted in the preceding paragraphs. Over the period since before the First World War, but with some evidence of a reversal of trend after 1955, those earning lower incomes have tended to increase their earnings more than the better-paid, the exceptions being managers and foremen, and these are both categories which have changed in relative importance in our society, while the jobs themselves have become more difficult with advancing technology and increasing scale of operations.

VI. Inter-Industry and Inter-Firm Differentials

Definitions of industries are peculiarly difficult, because manufacturing activities in Britain, as in any developed country, are complex and are not easily fitted into neat categories. The difficulty of presenting the facts of inter-industry differentials is increased, if not rendered nearly impossible, in comparing the period before 1948 with later years by a major change in the classification of industries which took place in that year, when the Ministry of Labour went on to the Standard Industrial Classification, and there were further revisions to that classification in 1958. If, however, we remember that an 'industry' will often include very diverse types of enterprise and conditions, and if we make reservations on that account, there is some interest in looking at patterns of payment by industry. There can be no doubt that these do alter over the years: for example, between 1924 and 1938 the relative positions of the staple industries, the new industries and 'other industries', to use very broad classifications indeed, altered markedly, particularly in 1931 when the earnings position of workers in the staple industries fell quite sharply whereas that of the new industries hardly fell at all, and the 'other industries' category actually increased very slightly.[1]

[1] G. Rottier, 'The Evolution of Wage Differentials: A Study of British Data', in J. T. Dunlop (ed.), *Theory of Wage Determination*, 1957.

Reynolds and Taft[1] reckon that between 1938 and 1948 inter-industry wage differences decreased in Britain. They also note that there was in

Table 5.10

Average Weekly Earnings of Men Manual Workers in Industry Groups in October 1966 compared with April 1960

Industry group	Average weekly earnings in October 1966		October 1966 as on index April 1960 = 100
	s	d	
Agriculture	301	4	154·9
Mining and quarrying (except coal)	400	7	147·7
Food, drink and tobacco	394	8	151·3
Chemicals and allied industries[1]	424	7	148·1
Metal manufacture[1]	429	5	135·8
Engineering and electrical goods	411	8	139·9
Shipbuilding and marine engineering[1]	425	9	152·1
Vehicles[1]	439	5	125·5
Other metal goods[1]	406	5	138·2
Textiles	370	8	143·4
Leather, leather goods and fur[1]	352	9	139·7
Clothing and footwear	355	9	141·5
Bricks, pottery, glass, cement, etc.	417	2	146·0
Timber, furniture, etc.	390	0	145·0
Paper, printing and publishing[1]	477	0	145·7
Other manufacturing industries[1]	406	7	139·7
Construction	411	2	153·5
Gas, electricity and water	382	4	150·6
Transport and communication (except railways and sea transport)	417	8	152·4
Certain miscellaneous services	347	11	146·8
Public administration	312	9	145·1

[1] October 1966 was very much within the deflationary period following the restrictive measures of July 1966, and in these cases earnings were lower than in April 1966. Average weekly earnings for men fell by just under 4s between April and October 1966. By far the most marked fall was in vehicle manufacture where earnings declined from 474s 11d to 439s 5d.

Source: Statistics on Incomes, Prices, Employment and Production.

[1] L. G. Reynolds and C. H. Taft, *The Evolution of Wage Structure*, 1956.

that period considerable flexibility in the pattern of differentials. 'Over half the industries which ranked among the twenty lowest in 1938 were no longer in that group by 1948, and of the twenty industries which ranked highest in 1938, nine were no longer in the highest bracket in 1948.' They comment on the three most obvious changes in the inter-industry pattern. Agriculture has come up markedly from its very low position in the inter-war years and, in 1948 at least, cotton and coalmining had improved their relative position substantially, though more recently neither of these two has fared just as well. On the other hand, comparisons of broad classifications of industries can be misleading, since some sections may be much more prosperous than others, while changing categorisation of the labour force, and changing demands for labour relative to the supply of various types, lie behind any simple comparisons of industrial averages. It remains true, however, that rapidly expanding industries, such as the motor-car industry, will tend to pay more, occupation by occupation, than others which are less prosperous. Some indication of the position is given in Table 5.10, which compares the movement of weekly earnings for men manual workers in the industry groups of the 1958 Standard Industrial Classification between April 1960 and October 1966 and gives the average weekly earnings in October 1966 in these industry groups.

The data available on differentials between firms in the same industry suggest that the size of the firm in which a worker is employed may be just as important a factor in his earnings as the industry itself. The Ministry of Labour analysed its earnings enquiry for October 1958 by the size of establishment in which adult male workers were employed, and came to the conclusion that 'the figures show that there was a tendency for both average weekly earnings and average hourly earnings to rise according to the size of the establishment as covered by the return. . . . In 107 industries where an average has been calculated for establishments with less than 25 wage earners, 83 had the lowest average weekly earnings and 78 had the lowest average hourly earnings. Conversely for establishments with 500 or more wage earners for which an average has been calculated, 71 out of 92 industries had the highest average weekly earnings and 72 the highest hourly earnings.' Though again the story has exceptions: in 15 industries the two smallest size ranges included the highest average weekly earnings. An examination of the list of industries where small firms tended to pay the highest earnings suggests that this occurs in industries where the *typical* firm is very small, with the inference that efficiency in these industries is not much increased with growth in the size of the establishment.

VII. Men and Women

Any account of changes in differentials between the payment of men and that of women must look first at the very large changes in the employment position of women. Table 5.11, which is drawn from Dr Routh's work, and uses the same occupational class structure as Table 5.9, therefore first shows, in columns 2 and 3, the changes in the occupational structure of the female labour force between 1911 and 1951, before giving the differential position in other columns.

During the period between 1911 and 1951 women became a much more important constituent part of the labour force, both proportionally and in absolute numbers, and at the same time there was a very striking change in the occupational pattern of their employment. The most important change was the emergence of a very large group of female clerical workers. There was a growth in the proportion of women in professions. There was an absolute reduction in the number of women in skilled occupations, which reflects the declining importance of skilled textile workers and dress-makers. The decline in the proportion of semi-skilled workers[1] is associated with the decreasing relative importance of women agricultural workers and domestic servants and the increasing importance of female shop assistants, catering workers, and women in semi-skilled occupations in industry.

In view of such major changes in occupational structure, generalisations about the differential between men's and women's work must be carefully phrased and taken with caution, since one will be comparing very different occupational structures, both when looking at women at different rates and when comparing women's payment with that of men. In the broadest terms Dr Routh's work suggests that men's and women's earnings increased by roughly the same amount between 1913/14 and 1960, and that, therefore, the overall differential between their payment levels has been largely unaltered. On the other hand, as columns 4–7 of Table 5.11 show, this result is the product of differences in the experience of different groups. In fact, the only occupational class which has deteriorated in its relative position, according to Dr Routh's work, is that of female semi-skilled manual workers. The data for this class showed above-average increases in earnings between 1913/14 and 1960 for most women in semi-skilled work in industry, and below-average increases for the expanding category of shop assistants

[1] In fact in this case there was a small increase in the numbers in this group during the period.

and the declining group of women in private domestic service. In other words, women have enjoyed greater increases in payment than men, and the differential between men's and women's earnings has narrowed, except in the two substantial categories of shop assistants and domestic service. The general position is that women in employment on average receive somewhere between 50 and 60 per cent of men's average annual earnings.

Table 5.11

Occupational Distribution of Women in Seven Occupational Classes in 1911 and 1951, and Average Annual Earnings in 1960 compared with 1913/14 and 1955/6

(1)	(2)	(3)	(4)	(5)	(6)	(7)	(8)
	Percentage of gainfully occupied women		Average annual earnings in 1960	Percentage increase on average for		Percentage of men's average 1913/14 1960	
Occupational class	in 1911	in 1951	(£)	1913/14	1955/56		
Higher professional	0·2	0·5	(1425)	—	(138)	—	(75)
Lower professional	6·5	8·2	606	680	138	57	72
Managers, etc.	6·6	6·0	1000	(1250)	125	(40)	54
Clerks	3·3	20·4	427	949	135	42	61
Foremen	0·2	1·1	602	1056	126	50	59
Skilled manual	24·8	12·8	395	898	125	44	50
Semi-skilled manual	53·4	43·1	339	678	126	72	58
Unskilled	5·0	7·9	283	1000	125	44	53

Source: G. Routh, *Occupation and Pay in Great Britain, 1906–60.*

In the professions, where equal pay is an important factor and supplementary, and probably less equal, earnings are less important, the ratio is nearer to three-quarters. These figures are, of course, still broad averages which tell us little about detailed experience. For example, in the case of the professions, it is probable that men, with generally longer and less-interrupted service, occupy a higher proportion of the more responsible positions.

The more recent situation may be gleaned from a comparison of column 6 of Table 5.11 with the equivalent column of Table 5.9. Such a comparison shows a tendency for women to improve their differential position very slightly as against men between 1955/6 and 1960. On the other hand, column 6 itself gives the same impression for women as was found in other tables, that in the more recent past the salaried occupations have been doing slightly better in their increases than the lower-paid. Table 5.12 takes a more detailed look at the situation in respect of men and women in manufacturing industry since 1938.

This table brings out four points of importance to the preceding discussion. First, average weekly earnings of women have gained relative to those for men since 1938. Secondly, however, there has been a deterioration in this position over the last decade. Thirdly, women's earnings have improved rather more decisively in hourly than in weekly terms, reflecting the greater volume of overtime working by men. Fourthly, on average women's earnings in manufacturing industry are about 50 per cent of those of men in weekly terms and 60 per cent when earnings for one hour's work are compared.

VIII. Symmetry and Diversity in the Structure

Though this chapter so far will no doubt have seemed sufficiently complicated to the reader, it has had all too great an appearance of simplicity as against the actual facts. The impression that workers divide neatly into categories is misleading; the appearance of symmetry is therefore also misleading. Any one individual will fall into several categories at the same time: he will work in a particular region and be of a particular age and of a particular occupation in a particular industry – and so on. The classification of differentials shown here can be defended on the ground that it shows up some of the broad patterns; but there are other underlying patterns, and for many of these we do not have much information. Smaller areas within regions, for example, may possibly, though it seems a little unlikely, have just as diverse a pattern of earnings as that which we have conveyed for large regions; we do not know with any accuracy to what extent small districts within an area like Scotland or Yorkshire differ radically in earnings levels from other parts of the same general area.

Discussion of the diversity of earnings at the personal level requires participation in a guessing game. Table 5.2 gave an indication of the average range of diversity in earnings, but not of the variability of the individual's personal position. All the differentials discussed in this chapter bear on the individual's earnings opportunities, and the composition of his earnings by method of payment is also highly relevant. One of the main criteria of a worker's well-being in the post-war years is whether or not he is being paid his negotiated rate or has access to extra payment. We know very little in detail about extra rates. We do know that about

Table 5.12

Earnings of Men and Women in British Manufacturing Industry, 1938–67

Year	Average weekly earnings			Average hourly earnings		
	Men	Women	Women as % of men	Men	Women	Women as % of men
	s d	s d		d	d	
1938	69 0	32 6	47·1	17·4	9·0	51·7
1946	120 9	65 3	54·0	30·4	18·4	60·5
1950	150 5	82 7	54·9	37·9	23·6	62·3
1954	204 5	108 2	52·9	50·6	31·0	61·2
1958	256 8	134 1	52·2	64·6	39·2	60·6
1962	317 3	160 10	50·5	81·0	49·0	60·5
1966	406 1	201 4	49·6	105·9	63·4	59·9
1967	427 6	211 2	49·5	111·0	66·3	59·7

Source: Ministry of Labour *Gazette*. The figures are for 'all industries' in October of each year, and for women working 'full-time' (i.e. for more than 30 hours in the week).

two-fifths of workers in manufacturing industry are on payment by results, and that on average about a third of the manufacturing labour force do some overtime in any one week. In some cases extra rates, payment by results and overtime together can make up 50 per cent of a worker's pay packet. This is perhaps a little high for most workers, but one-third must be quite a usual figure in manufacturing industry. In general, service trades and salaried workers are paid an amount nearer to their rates than those who are on direct and measurable production work, and thus a large group outside manufacturing industry is subject to a quite different pattern, and generally a much smaller quantity, of extra payments.

The personal differential will now be seen to be the result of many possible complicating features. Even if we classify a man according to his occupation, region, and so on, and determine the types of payment he has, we may still be short of knowing his full position. The intensity with which he works at payment by results, for example, or the ease with which his

E 2

payment by results may be earned, will determine how much he takes home. Also he may work much or little overtime, or he may experience short-time; and these short-time or overtime hours may be at his own wish or at the dictate of his type of work. At the level of individual incomes the broad differentials we have been discussing will not be anything like as clear-cut.

This chapter has dealt exclusively with the British wage structure, which has a number of unique features that are unlikely to be duplicated elsewhere. The influence of particular institutional circumstances, for example, cannot be overlooked. Nevertheless, there is a broad similarity between the wage structures of developed economies of the Western type. It is important to notice this point here since later chapters discuss the causes of our present wage structure and we want to know how general such causes may be. Fortunately there are excellent books which deal with this subject[1] and which the reader should consult for further details. Since this work is available it is possible to be brief in presenting the broad general picture here.

The points of agreement between various national wage structures of industrial economies are really rather remarkable against a background of quite different experiences and timing of industrialisation, and different institutions. There are, of course, some differences in the patterns disclosed but on the whole these are less obvious than the similarities. Each industrial economy has broadly the same collection of important differentials. In each case these differentials, or most of them, have been narrowing over the last forty-odd years. The degree of narrowness which has now been reached differs according to circumstances: for example, occupational differentials in the United States, with more flexibility of labour supply and less trade-union control, are wider than they are in Britain, but the long-run tendency to narrow is there just the same. Other economies have the same, though not as pronounced, tendency for earnings, especially in inflationary circumstances, to diverge from rates, and the same lack of certainty about whether the narrowing in differentials has been carried as far, or has not perhaps been sometimes reversed, in earnings as against rates. Regional differentiation for large areas still remains in other economies, depending upon the industrial and economic circumstances of the different regions, and despite attempts at elimination. In other words, we can speak of the British wage structure as a fairly good example of general

[1] Reynolds and Taft, op. cit.; Organisation for Economic Co-operation and Development, *Wages and Labour Mobility*, Paris, 1965; United Nations, *Incomes in Post-War Europe*, 1967.

propositions. Making allowances for different institutional backgrounds and so on, we could reasonably expect other economies to show similar developments.

SUGGESTED READING

J. R. Crossley, 'Collective Bargaining, Wage Structure and the Labour Market in the United Kingdom', in E. M. Hugh-Jones (ed.), *Wage Structure in Theory and Practice*, 1966.

J. T. Dunlop (ed.), *Theory of Wage Determination*, 1957.

M. P. Fogarty, 'The White-Collar Pay Structure in Britain', *Economic Journal*, 1959.

Organisation for Economic Co-operation and Development, *Wages and Labour Mobility*, Paris, 1965.

E. H. Phelps Brown, 'Wage Drift', *Economica*, 1962.

L. G. Reynolds and C. H. Taft, *The Evolution of Wage Structure*, 1956.

D. J. Robertson, *Factory Wage Structures and National Agreements*, 1960.

Guy Routh, *Occupation and Pay in Great Britain, 1906–60*, 1965.

United Nations, *Incomes in Post-War Europe*, Economic Commission for Europe, Geneva, 1967.

6   Employment Trends and Structure

I. Population and Employment

An understanding of the labour market of any country requires not only a grasp of the institutional and wage-fixing arrangements but also an appreciation of the size of the labour force, the trends in its growth and changes in its composition, and the efficiency with which manpower resources are brought into employment. This chapter and the next are concerned with these issues as they arise in the British context.

The first question to be taken up is the growth of the labour force. This at once necessitates some discussion of the relation between population and employment, for if the population as a whole is growing it is probable also that the labour force will be growing or will at least possess some built-in potential for growth. However, there is no simple relationship between population and employment, since many demographic, institutional and economic factors affect the extent to which the population engages in labour market activity. More is said about these influences in Chapter 9 below.

The population growth of any country is determined by three factors: the birth rate, the death rate, and the net inflow or outflow of people by migration.[1] So long as the birth rate exceeds the death rate, and the migratory flows balance, the total population will grow. In the first half of the nineteenth century the population of Great Britain doubled, and by 1871 population totalled about twenty-six million, compared with only ten and a half million in 1801. Although there is some probable imprecision in the statistics for this period, it seems likely that this rapid growth was due to a high and increasing birth rate coupled with a (lower) death rate that was certainly not rising as rapidly as the birth rate and may even have been steady or declining. After 1871 the picture is a little clearer, and as Fig. 6.1 shows, the population of the United Kingdom grew from about twenty-seven million in 1871 to fifty-three million in 1961. By 1871

---

[1] The birth and death rates referred to here are the 'crude' rates. Demographic analysis uses more refined measures but the crude figures are enough to show the broad pattern of change.

the birth rate was beginning a long downward trend which lasted until 1931 and only recovered in the post-war period. Meanwhile the death rate was also falling, but after 1881 its rate of decline was not sufficient to keep up the previous rate of population growth (aside from the effects of migration balance, of course). Since the 1930s the death rate has been fairly stable.

Fig. 6·1

Population growth, births and deaths per 1000 population in the United Kingdom, 1871–1961

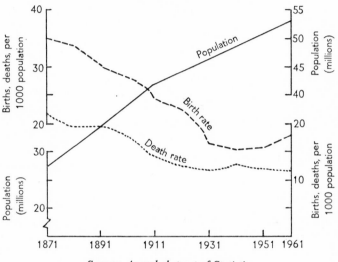

Source: Annual abstract of Statistics

Throughout the period, birth rates were in excess of death rates, but the full effects of this natural increase in population have been moderated by the fact that the country has historically been a net exporter of population, with the only real exception being the decade of the 1930s when there was a small net gain through immigration.

The future prospect is somewhat obscure, due to the sensitivity of population growth to small changes in birth rates and in migration flows. At the time of writing, there is some indication that the recent rise in birth rates has stopped and even been reversed, so that recent estimates of a United Kingdom population of seventy-five million by the year 2000 may be too high. This of course has implications for the size of the labour force in the future and for the number of jobs that have to be provided if full employment is to be maintained, though of course a great deal also depends on the age structure of the population. If the recent growth in the birth rate was to continue, and if life expectancy continues to increase as it has been doing, there is every likelihood that the population over the next two or three decades will be relatively heavily weighted in the younger and older age groups which do not normally contribute to production of economic goods and services. The result of this would be that a proportionately smaller working population would have to support a proportionately greater population that is economically inactive.

The upper limits of a country's potential labour force will be determined by the size and demographic composition of the population. The total population at any time will include three components: those who are in paid employment; those who are not in employment but who are actively seeking work and who can therefore be added to the first group to provide a measure of the country's labour force or total supply of workers; and those who are generally described in Census of Population returns as being 'economically inactive'. This last group includes young people who have not yet entered the labour force, older people who have probably been in the labour force in the past, and others of whom some may have independent means which free them from the necessity of earning money by work, while the remainder will include people who are chronically sick and unable to work, and women (especially those who are married) who are committed to full-time work in the household and in the bringing up of children. Domestic and household work does of course have an economic as well as a social value. If this work was not done by housewives and mothers, domestic servants, children's nurses, etc., would have to be employed for the purpose at the going rate for such labour. But just as it is a convention of national income accounting that household activity is not included as part of the national product, so it is conventional in labour force measurement to exclude full-time housewives unless they have a paid employment. Inevitably, the composition and size of this 'inactive' group is subject to change as alterations take place in the demographic structure of the population and as shorter-run changes occur in the social and economic factors influencing decisions to participate in labour market activity. Thus, as we shall see subsequently, one of the most striking changes in the pattern of labour market activity in recent years has been the growth in the proportion of women, and married women in particular, in the labour force.

Obviously enough, the labour force will be considerably smaller than total population, but just how much smaller will depend on a variety of circumstances. In most countries there is, for example, a statutory minimum age at which children can give up full-time education. In Great Britain at present this age is 15, though the limit is shortly to be raised to 16. Again, there is some conventional retirement age for workers in most developed countries, and comparatively small proportions of the labour force reaching that age continue in employment. Current practice in Britain is for men to retire at age 65 and for women to retire at age 60, though there are important exceptions on both sides of that limit. When a population includes a relatively high proportion of young and old persons, it is to be expected that the ratio of labour force to population will be lower, and the size of the 'inactive' group larger, than in a country where the proportion of young and old together is smaller.

The influence of demographic factors does not end there. Labour force activity has to be seen in relation to the life cycle of the individuals who comprise the population, and for many people the degree of availability for employment changes markedly over the cycle. For instance, in the years between leaving full-time education and marriage, most women are members of the labour force. Marriage and the raising of families bring about a sharp drop in the numbers of these at work but then, as families grow up and require less than full-time care, housewives again become available for paid employment. Thus any trend towards a reduction in the average age of marriage for women will reduce the proportions in the relevant age group who remain in the labour force. And if this trend or some other influence causes a lengthening of the child-bearing and rearing phase, the average labour force activity of women will fall.

Between 1911 and 1951, the total population of Great Britain increased from 40·83 million to 48·85 million, the average annual rate of increase being around 0·5 per cent. Over the same period the numbers recognised by the Censuses of Population as at work or seeking work rose from 17·80 million to 22·61 million, an average annual rate of increase of almost 0·7 per cent. Thus, despite the raising of the minimum school-leaving age over the period, the labour force actually grew more rapidly than population as a whole, probably due in large measure to the improvements in health and working-life expectation in the population, but helped also by the growth in labour demand. The net result of these changes was that whereas in 1911, 43·6 per cent of the whole population was in the labour force, by 1931 the proportion had risen to 47 per cent, though it fell back again slightly to 46·3 per cent in 1951, owing mainly to the swelling of the population under working age resulting from the post-war rise in the birth rate.

For the more recent period from 1951 to the mid-1960s, it is more convenient to use a different measure of labour force. It is worth while mentioning here that British statistics offer a variety of possible labour force measures, most of which will be met as we proceed. The choice of series to some extent depends on the purpose in hand, and to some extent on the availability of data. We are frequently obliged to use a statistical series which is not quite as appropriate for the purpose as we would like it to be, but it has to be remembered that the cost of collection of statistics must be weighed against the value to be derived from them. For the above consideration of long-term trends it was possible to use data derived from the decennial Census of Population, but for shorter-run comparisons it is usually preferable to refer to Department of Employment and Productivity statistics. In Table 6.1, which illustrates the growth of labour force and population in the period 1951–1966, the labour force

Table 6.1

Population and Working Population in Great Britain, 1951 and 1966

	1951	1966	% change 1951–66
Total working population (000s)	23,239	25,644	+10·3
Males	15,798	16,651	+5·4
Females	7441	8993	+20·9
Total population (000s)	48,854	53,266	+9·0
Males	23,450	25,882	+10·4
Females	25,404	27,384	+7·8
Working population as a percentage of total population	47·6	48·1	+1·1
Males	67·4	64·3	−4·6
Females	29·3	32·8	+11·9

Source: *Annual Abstract of Statistics*

Note: The 1951 figure for population is obtained from the 1951 Census of Population; the 1966 figure is a mid-year estimate. Working population data are for June in each year and are unadjusted for seasonal variations.

measure used is that of *total working population*, which is the most inclusive statistic available, incorporating employers, self-employed, employees in employment, those registered as unemployed under the National Insurance scheme, and members of the Armed Forces.

The table shows that in both 1951 and 1966 rather less than half the total population of Great Britain were in the labour force, and that men comprised roughly two-thirds of the working population. While the total population has been growing over this period at an annual average rate of 0·6 per cent, working population has been growing slightly faster (at 0·7 per cent). But the striking feature is that the male working population has grown by less than 6 per cent over the whole period, compared with a rise of over 20 per cent in the female labour force. This is reflected in the fact that the male working population as a percentage of the total male population has actually declined by over 4 per cent during the period, in contrast to the rise of almost 12 per cent in the equivalent ratio for women.

Since population and labour force have been growing at different rates over the period 1951–66, there must have been some change either in the age structure of the population or in the economic and other circumstances which determine the relationship between the economically active population and population as a whole. To discover what influences have been at work we must consider the problem in more detail.

II. Labour Force Participation

Differences in the age structure of the population can give rise to apparent differences in the level of labour force activity. Part of this difficulty comes from the fact that there may be a high proportion of young persons under school-leaving age in the population. If a now conventional practice is adopted, namely to exclude those under school-leaving age from the population, we can to some extent neutralise the demographic influences, and focus attention more directly upon participation in labour market activity by those who are 'eligible' for employment. This allows us to calculate the *activity rate* (or labour force participation rate), which shows, for every 100 members of the population who are 'eligible' for employment, how many are actually in the labour force. The overall activity rate in a country where the school-leaving age is fifteen would be estimated as follows:

$$\text{Activity rate} = \frac{\text{No. of persons in the labour force}}{\text{No. of persons aged 15 and over in the population}} \times 100.$$

In Britain in 1965 the overall activity rate was 62·6 per cent; for men alone the figure was 85·7 per cent, and for women it was 41·5 per cent.

Even this device, however, does not eliminate the problems of comparing activity rates between countries or within one country at different times.

Since only a small proportion of persons are likely to remain in the labour force after normal retirement age, it follows that a population heavily weighted by the post-retirement age groups will have a lower activity rate than otherwise. Again, even within the working age groups, differences in the population structure may give rise to some further variations in activity rates, though here the differences due to purely demographic factors are likely to be very small. Their effect may, however, be exaggerated by educational factors, at least for men. In this country, as in many others, there is at present a large and growing proportion of young people remaining in full-time education beyond the minimum school-leaving age, and for the most part these must be counted among the economically inactive. Wherever continuation in full-time education is important in this way there will be some diminution of the activity rate, and of course, the larger the proportion of the population in the 15- to 20-year age group, the more considerable will this dampening effect be. The age distribution of women of working age may also have some influence on the activity rate for women. If in a particular period the 'middle' age group, say 25 to 40 years, is a relatively high proportion of the total, the activity rate is likely to be lower than if it was small in relation to the high activity rate groups below the age of 25 and above the age of 40.

Activity rates can be used for a variety of purposes, including forecasts of the labour force. Just as an overall activity rate can be estimated, so it is possible to arrive at activity rates specific to individual age and sex groups which, as we have seen, will vary because of demographic and educational factors. The size and age structure of the population of working age at future dates, at least over the next ten years or so, can be forecast with a good deal of accuracy. If existing activity rates for each age and sex group are known, it is possible to make adjustments to allow for changing educational, social and other influences. The resulting 'expected' activity rate can then be applied to the forecasts for each age–sex group, and from this a picture is built up of the future size and composition of the working population.

Alternatively, activity rates may be used as a basis for estimating potential reserves of labour among the inactive population. Unfortunately there are no available British statistics at regional level which would allow us to estimate activity rates on the previous basis. Official procedure, which we follow in Table 6.2, is to make use of what data are available to arrive at an *employee activity rate*: the percentage of employees (including the unemployed) in the population aged 15 and over. Since this excludes the self-employed and employers working on their own account, as well as the

Armed Forces, and since there is no certainty that these are equipro-
portionally distributed among regions, the resulting rate is lower than that
derived earlier, and may not be a true reflection of overall activity levels in
the regions. Nevertheless the broad indication of the figures is probably
adequate for the present purpose.[1]

This table at once reveals substantial differences in 'total' activity rates
among the regions, ranging from a high of 61·4 per cent in the Midlands to
48·1 in the South-Western region and Wales. Some of the possible sources

Table 6.2

Employee Activity Rates, for Males and Females, by Region and
for Great Britain, 1964

Region	Males	Females	Total
South-East	78·3	41·4	58·8
South-Western	65·6	32·0	48·1
Midland	80·9	42·8	61·4
North Midland	75·6	37·2	56·0
East and West Ridings	80·1	39·5	58·9
North-Western	79·3	41·9	59·4
Northern	72·3	33·5	52·5
Scotland	76·5	38·8	56·5
Wales	68·2	29·1	48·1
Great Britain	76·7	39·2	57·1

Source: Ministry of Labour *Gazette*.

of variation have already been introduced. We have mentioned differences
in the age structure of the adult population and in other demographic
characteristics, differences in educational experience after the age of
fifteen, and the possibility that there are regional differences in the proportions of employers and self-employed persons. Regional differences in the
age at which women marry and in the average size of family may also give
rise to variation in activity levels. Finally, there may be differences in the
proportions of people not in the labour force due to chronic sickness. The
preponderance in some areas of heavy industries like coalmining, steel and
shipbuilding, which are most liable to produce high rates of partial or total
disablement, will have some effect in pulling down the activity rate.

It is probable that in some measure all those influences are reflected in

[1] For further discussion of the problems involved here, see Ministry of Labour
Gazette, March 1965, pp. 107–9.

the figures above, but there is little doubt that other purely economic and social factors also have a part to play. Of the five regions with a long-term average unemployment rate equal to or above the national average, only one (North-Western) has an activity rate above the all-regions average, whereas in the regions with lower than average unemployment rates, the activity rate is (again with one exception, North Midland region) above the average. Though the relationship between unemployment and activity rates is not precise, and though this series of observations does not prove the proposition, it is reasonable to suppose that activity rates vary inversely with employment opportunity as reflected in unemployment rates: that is to say, where job opportunities are plentiful a higher proportion of the population will be encouraged to seek employment than where job openings are scarce. This kind of difference will be brought about mainly by differences in the proportions of married women entering the labour market, and in the proportions of people of retirement age remaining in the market. Thus, for example, in North-Western region, where the female activity rate is exceptionally high, the long tradition of job opportunity for women in the cotton industry affords part of the explanation, whereas in areas such as the South-West and Wales there has been little employment opportunity available, and female activity rates are well below average.

It is sometimes argued that social attitudes are important, particularly with respect to women in employment. In some areas, such as Wales, it is conceivable that the low degree of participation in labour market activity on the part of women could be explained by a traditional social outlook which disapproved of women taking jobs, particularly in factories, and which regarded women's place as being at home. There is undoubtedly some truth in the contention that different regions exhibit different social attitudes, but in the particular case of Wales it seems far more probable that the traditional heavy industries have afforded little opportunity for employing women. It is also the case that activity rates for women tend to be lower in rural than in urban areas. This, again, is partially due to lack of job opportunity in the rural areas compared with the towns, but another part of the explanation is probably to be found in the fact that many women in rural areas, particularly those attached to farming communities, have relatively less freedom to take paid employment because of demands made on their time by unpaid work on and around the farm.

This discussion also gives some clue to the changes that have been taking place in the British labour force. The marked growth in the number of women in the labour force has coincided with a prolonged period of very full employment, and there is little doubt that the high demand for labour and the almost chronic problem of labour shortage have led to an expansion in the supply by drawing in those who might otherwise have remained inactive. In many cases work previously done by men has been taken over by women, and employers have frequently adapted the job to suit the supply, by modifying the hours of work and conditions of employment. But it would be wrong to suggest that the changes which have occurred are due solely to alterations in the demand situation. Undoubtedly the Second World War did a great deal in a short space of time to change attitudes to female employment, especially in factories where assembly work and precision tasks were involved. At that time employers were obliged to replace men serving in the Armed Forces by women, and many were agreeably surprised at the results. What was evidently economically acceptable in terms of national emergency became much more socially acceptable in the succeeding peace-time years.

However, even the opportunity provided by the availability of jobs for women and the removal of lingering doubts about the social position of women at work would not have been enough in themselves. Paid employment normally involves regular attendance at work, and even where part-time employment is concerned there is usually a requirement for an unbroken 'block' of hours during the day when the job can be done. As subsequent figures show, a great deal of the growth in female employment has been due to the increasing number of married women in the labour market, and these are women who have household responsibilities which are traditionally time-consuming. Over the last 15 to 20 years especially there have been many innovations in the 'capital equipment' of the household (one only needs to mention the widespread use of refrigerators, automatic cookers and washing machines) which have saved time in the household and made a significant contribution to the possibility of married women taking paid employment outside the home.[1]

Some idea of the growth of the importance of married women in the labour force can be derived from the official estimates of the number of employees in Great Britain. In 1951, 3 million (42·3 per cent) of the 7·09 million women in the employee population were married. By 1965 the number of female employees had grown to 8·49 million, of whom 4·63 million (54·6 per cent) were married. Thus, although the number of women in the employee part of the labour force had been growing fairly rapidly,

[1] An additional factor which is hard to quantify is the possibility that some of the married women at work have taken jobs out of economic necessity, i.e. where their husbands do not earn enough to keep the family, and where without the extra earnings the family would fall below what is regarded as the poverty line.

the proportion of married women had been growing still more quickly. The whole question of the supply of different types of labour and further discussion of the factors influencing the growing importance of women in the work force is encountered again in Chapter 9, where the economic significance of labour force participation and factors influencing job choice are more closely examined.[1]

III. Part-Time and Seasonal Employment

A distinction has to be made between part-time work and irregular employment. Many more people actually work in any given year than are counted as being in the labour force on a particular day or in a particular week. This means of course that there is a continual inflow and outflow of workers, not only on account of retirement and new entries from schools and from higher education but also because people are obliged to leave work on grounds of ill health or because they find that their personal circumstances now prevent them from continuing in employment, or allow them to come into employment where previously that was not possible. From another point of view many people whose circumstances permit them to do so will not want to work regularly throughout the year but will be prepared to enter the labour force for limited periods,[2] particularly where there is suitable opportunity for employment resulting from a seasonal peak of demand in certain sectors, such as the distributive trades and the Post Office at Christmas-time, and hotel and tourist employment during the summer. Part-time employment is rather different. There is at any time some number of hours of work per week which is regarded as full-time. At present in Britain this is around forty hours per week for the manual worker, and about thirty to thirty-five hours for the office worker. There are, however, many people who are employed for considerably less than this full-time equivalent, and it is these people whom we have to regard as being in part-time employment. They will normally work right throughout the year, but are employed for only part of a day or for two or three complete days per week.[3]

[1] For further discussion of women at work, see Amelia Hart, *A Survey of Women's Employment* (Government Social Survey), 1968.

[2] Many of these will not be recorded as unemployed when not actually at work.

[3] The official Department of Employment and Productivity definition of part-time employment is work which does not exceed 30 hours per week.

Part-time employment, especially for women, is a growing phenomenon. In 1950 the Ministry of Labour estimated that 324,000 women were in part-time employment in manufacturing industry – about 11·8 per cent of total female employment in manufacturing. In 1966 there were 500,000 women in part-time manufacturing employment, over 17 per cent of the total female employment in manufacturing. The causes of this trend exist both on the demand and on the supply side. On the demand side, mention has already been made of the persistent labour shortage in Britain which has obliged many employers to provide conditions which will attract into employment those who would otherwise be economically inactive but who are nevertheless capable of providing useful skills and services. As a result, employers have become much more ready to offer part-time employment to those who feel that they cannot commit themselves to full-time, regular work. On the supply side we have already mentioned some of the important factors, such as the greater opportunities for women to seek employment outside the home. But among the labour reserves who are willing to consider part-time employment there has to be included the higher proportion of people who now reach retirement age in good health and want to stay on in some kind of paid employment, possibly with a reduced load of responsibility and at a lower level of pay. Again, young people in full-time education very often have some spare time during which they can take part-time work, quite apart from vacation periods during which they may take seasonal employments.

We have so far been talking only about those people whose main activity in the labour market is part-time or irregular employment. There is, however, another trend which has been growing in importance in this country and particularly in the United States in the post-war period – the taking of a second job on a part-time and often 'unofficial' or private basis. On the supply side the motives are easy enough to discern. First, there is the possibility of avoiding disclosure of income on work done by private arrangement so that the value of every pound earned in this way is greater than that earned and taxed in more regular circumstances. This of course also has the effect of making it difficult to obtain any reliable estimates of the number of people engaging in double job-holding. Secondly, there is likely to be a strong motive among those who have low basic incomes for a forty-hour week and who have little opportunity for overtime work in their regular job. Additionally, as standard weekly hours of work are reduced, the possibility of more leisure time becomes a reality – but leisure is an activity which frequently requires money to be spent upon it. For some people the balance between leisure time and expenditure possibilities may be unsatisfactory so that they have to consider giving up some of their available leisure time in order to derive additional income. Their ability to do so will depend on the labour demand situation, and in this respect the persistent labour shortage in post-war Britain has been a factor favouring the increase of second-job activities. Much still depends, however, on the type of skill the person has to offer. It may be rather easier to follow a second employment where there is a private demand from individuals rather than from firms. In this way workers in household trades, such as painters, and professional and some white-collar workers, such as accountants, typists, etc., may be able to find a market for their services fairly readily, in contrast to the skilled fitter in the engineering trades or the locomotive driver. There is of course still another aspect of this, in that many professional workers who are in relatively short supply are employed on a part-time basis for the purposes of consultancy, both in private industry and in the public sector.

IV.   Employment Status and Occupational Structure

There are various ways in which we can view the working sector of the population. Here we look particularly at the broad employment status of the population – its division into economically active and inactive, and the division between self-employment and other categories – and at the occupational structure of employment. In the final section of this chapter we shall briefly review the changing industrial structure of employment. Differences in the social and economic environment of countries and even of regions within a single country are likely to give rise to variations in the relative importance of the various groups. In the case of employment status, for example, it seems probable that a private enterprise economy is likely to have a higher proportion of its working population in the 'employer' and 'self-employed' categories than an economy based on socialist principles where businesses are mainly State-owned and workers are State employees. From a different point of view it is again probable that an economy with a large agricultural sector under private enterprise will have relatively more employers and self-employed than one with a small agricultural population. The British economy is a 'mixed' economy in the sense that while the private enterprise sector is still dominant there is an important and growing public sector, including a number of nationalised industries. Since much of the development of the public sector has taken place since the 1930s, it might be expected that there would have been some significant changes in the distribution of the labour force by employment status over the period, owing to a reduction in the importance of the self-employed and employer category and a complementary rise in the proportion of employees.

An impression of the changes in employment status between 1931 and 1961 is given in Table 6.3. The division of the population of working age into economically active and inactive has remained unaltered, though in fact this masks a number of changes. For example, the raising of the school-leaving age in the interim, from fourteen to fifteen, would have the effect of reducing the size of the potentially active group, while the trend towards longer education should also have reduced the active proportion. At least one of the factors acting as a counterweight to this is the rise in activity rates of married women, as already discussed. Within the economically active population there has been, as we might expect, a reduction in the proportion (and numbers) working on their own account. The managerial class has increased quite significantly, but if we add those out of work to the employees in employment, we again find no change between 1931 and 1961, though of course the proportion in employment has increased with the passing of the depression of the inter-war period.

This very general classification inevitably obscures great changes within the broad groupings. A rather better impression of the trend of change can be derived from classifications according to occupational groups, though, as we shall see subsequently, even these conceal a great deal of the changes which have been taking place.

There are, however, difficulties in determining the actual extent of such changes. The reason for this is largely the alterations in definition between Census dates which make the problem of long-term comparison extremely difficult. We are, however, helped by some recent research by Dr Guy Routh, who has ironed out some of the inconsistencies in Census data and reclassified Census tabulations in a way that is useful for our present purpose.[1] Routh identifies seven main occupational classes and shows the trend in these from the Census of 1911 down to 1959. The classes are as follows:

Class 1a. Higher professional (e.g. judges, lawyers, professional accountants, authors, etc.)

Class 1b. Lower professional (e.g. actors, draughtsmen, teachers, musicians, etc.)

[1] Routh, *Occupation and Pay in Great Britain, 1906–60*, chap. 1.

Table 6.3

Employment Status of the Working-Age Population of Great Britain, 1931 and 1961[1]

Employment status	1931		1961	
	Numbers (000s)	As percentage of total population of working age	Numbers (000s)	As percentage of total population of working age
Total occupied	21,074	60·8	24,014	60·7
Economically inactive (unoccupied and retired)	13,587	39·2	15,554	39·3
Self-employed without employees (working on own account)	1273	3·7	1002	2·5
Employers, directors, managers, etc.	1181	3·4	2012	5·1
Employees in employment	16,096	46·4	20,324	51·4
Out of employment	2524	7·3	676	1·7

[1] Working-age population included persons aged 14 and over in 1931, as opposed to persons aged 15 and over in 1961.

Source: Annual Abstract of Statistics.

Class 2a. Employers and proprietors (all employers, except professional)

Class 2b. Managers and administrators (e.g. civil servants, administrative and executive officers, bankers, police inspectors, etc.)

Class 3. Clerical (e.g. clerks, book-keepers, typists)

Class 4. Foremen, inspectors, supervisors

MANUAL WORKERS

Class 5. Skilled (e.g. craftsmen, hairdressers, police other ranks, railway signalmen, etc.)

Class 6. Semi-skilled (e.g. drivers of passenger and goods vehicles, salesmen, agricultural workers)

Class 7. Unskilled (e.g. labourers, porters, charwomen, watchmen, etc.).

As we can see from Table 6.4, the manual worker is today rather less dominant than in 1911, although this category still accounts for two-thirds of the labour force. In 1911 about 80 per cent of the labour force worked in manual grades, while in 1959 this proportion had been reduced to 67 per cent. Within the manual worker category between 1911 and 1951, there was a considerable reduction both in the proportions of skilled and

Table 6.4

Changes in the Occupational Class Distribution of the Occupied Population of Great Britain, 1911, 1951 and 1959

Occupational class	Percentage of total occupied population in		
	1911	*1951*	*1959*[1]
1a. Higher professional	1·0	1·9	2·3
1b. Lower professional	3·1	4·7	5·5
2a. Employers and proprietors	6·7	5·0 ⎱	10·1
2b. Managers and administrators	3·4	5·5 ⎰	
3. Clerical workers	4·8	10·7	12·0
4. Foremen, inspectors, supervisors	1·3	2·6	2·7
5. Skilled manual	30·6	25·0	24·6
6. Semi-skilled manual	39·5	32·6	31·2
7. Unskilled	9·6	12·0	11·6
Total (per cent)	100·0	100·0	100·0

[1] 1959 figures are estimates; those for 1911 and 1951 are derived from Census data.

Source: Adapted from Routh, op. cit., table 1, pp. 4–5.

semi-skilled workers, but some increase in the unskilled category. However, since 1951, although the downward trend in skilled and semi-skilled workers seems to have continued, the growth in the unskilled worker category does appear to have been reversed. This is perhaps what we might expect from current trends in technology which tend to do away with the less skilled type of operation. If we look at the employers and proprietors and managers and administrators together, we find that between 1911 and 1959 there has been very little change in the relative proportion. However, within this group there does seem to have been a relative decline in the importance of employers and proprietors and a corresponding growth in the importance of managers and administrators – a finding which bears out the earlier conclusion about the decline of the self-employed. The professional groups, on the other hand, have quite definitely increased in importance, and now account for something like 8 per cent of the total working population, compared with only about 4 per cent in 1911. The most significant increase of all has taken place among clerical workers, who have increased from less than 5 per cent of the total to around 12 per cent at the present time. Finally, there has been roughly a doubling in the relative importance of foremen, inspectors and the supervisory grades. These changes are instructive, but when we turn to a still more detailed occupational classification we find that even larger changes have taken place within the groups themselves.[1] Only a few of the more prominent changes can be commented upon here.

Among the professional occupations there have been very considerable changes. In 1911 about 70 per cent of those in the higher professions were in the 'traditional' occupations of the Church, medicine, law and the armed forces, compared with little over 40 per cent in 1961. Professional engineers, who were relatively few in 1911, were in 1961 by far the most important single group, accounting for almost one-third of the whole class. In the lower professions, some occupations which had hardly existed in 1911 or even in 1921, such as laboratory technicians, librarians and social welfare workers, had grown considerably in size, though still remaining a small proportion of the total. Teachers and nurses, however, still accounted for over half of this class in 1961 as they had done in the earlier period (though they had of course grown a great deal in absolute numbers).

Skilled manual workers include not only those who have served a formal apprenticeship but also many others who acquire skill by considerable

---

[1] The Census of Population in 1961 identified over 200 occupational categories, though in so doing it had to standardise many more job-titles attaching to roughly similar work.

periods of training, often on the job. It is not therefore a completely unambiguous description, but there is some agreement that a training period of two years or more can reasonably be regarded as leading to the acquisition of a skill. Since a great deal of skilled work is involved in manufacturing industry, it is to be expected that the composition of the skilled manual class will have changed a great deal over the last few decades, with some of the traditional trades such as blacksmiths and riveters all but disappearing, and new trades appearing and rapidly increasing. There is little doubt that such changes have occurred, but it is difficult to give numerical substance to them because many occupational titles still prevail although the content of the work performed has changed out of all recognition. However, Routh has shown that skilled textile, leather and coal-face workers have declined as a proportion of the whole skilled group from 42 per cent in 1911 to less than 20 per cent in 1951, and this trend has undoubtedly continued in the same direction since then.[1] The metal-working trades have increased greatly in importance, now accounting for well over one-third of the class, while building craftsmen have made some moderate gains.

Among semi-skilled workers, similar problems of comparison arise. For instance, the relative importance of vehicle drivers has increased, but the composition of their group has changed almost completely, owing to the replacement of horse-drawn by motor-driven vehicles. In general, however, the composition of the semi-skilled group (and indeed the un-skilled, which is virtually impossible to classify on a detailed occupational basis anyway) has altered very much in line with the changing importance of industries in the national employment situation. Agriculture, mining and textiles were all significant employers of semi-skilled and unskilled workers, and with their decline there has been a run-down in semi-skilled jobs available in these industries. This tendency has, however, been counterbalanced by the growth of other industries employing semi-skilled labour, such as metal manufacture and engineering in general.

This leads to an important point. The changes in the overall occupational structure of employment in the economy are due to two sets of forces. To some extent, these changes are due to fairly direct technological and organisational changes *within* industries, leading to alterations in the occupational mix required to produce a particular range of products. But since many occupations are to be found in more than one industry, it follows that changes in the relative employment size of these industries, even without a shift in the relative importance of different occupations

[1] Routh, op. cit., pp. 31–2.

within them, can have an influence on the total occupational structure. It is conceivable that these two different influences, which may be called the 'occupational' and 'industrial' effect respectively, could operate in opposite directions, but in practice it seems that they have tended to work in the same direction, with only a few exceptions. There is some evidence, however,[1] that the change in the relative importance of some occupational groups, such as clerical workers, scientists, engineers and technologists, proprietors and managers, has been determined more by the occupational effect, while the industry effect has been more important in other cases, for example manual workers in industries such as textiles and clothing. Obviously, then, the changing industrial structure of employment is also important, and it is to this that we now turn.

V. Industrial Distribution of the Working Population

The industrial classification of the labour force depends on the allocation of people on the basis of the product or service with which they are mainly concerned, as opposed to the occupational classification which tells us more precisely what jobs workers perform, irrespective of industry. Some jobs are of course fairly narrowly limited to one industry, such as the melter in the steel industry or the printing craftsman, but others, such as secretaries, drivers, crane operators and electricians, perform a specific set of tasks which can be carried out in a variety of industries. This is of importance when we come, in Chapters 11, 16 and 19, to consider the mobility of the labour force between jobs, for those workers whose skills can be employed in a variety of industries are likely to have greater opportunities for changing industry than those whose job is specific to one industry.

For the moment, however, the important question is the way in which the labour force divides itself up among industries and how this pattern of industrial distribution has changed over time. There are perhaps four main reasons why the industrial distribution of the labour force should alter over time. (*a*) In the first place the production pattern of a country will to some extent reflect the availability of natural resources in the country, but as some kinds of resource are run down (coal is an obvious example) or as substitutes are discovered and new uses found for hitherto

---

[1] Cf. Routh, op. cit., chap. 1; and *Occupational Changes 1951–1961* (Manpower Studies No. 6), Ministry of Labour, H.M.S.O., 1967, p. 15.

unused resources, the pattern of production and hence of employment is likely to change. (b) Labour is usually demanded not for its own sake but for the services it provides; and the demand for labour is thus derived from the demand for the goods it can produce, or more directly from the demand for labour services themselves. This demand for goods and services will be affected not only by relative prices but also by changes in the tastes of consumers and in the real income available to consumers (or in the distribution of income among consumers). But the actual amount of labour required will depend also on two other factors: (c) the technology of production, and (d) the organisation of work. The influence of technology can be readily enough appreciated. Many goods can be produced by a variety of methods, ranging from capital-intensive to labour-intensive, and the stage of industrial development reached will have a considerable effect on the way in which labour is industrially distributed. The influence of the organisation of production is perhaps less obvious, but there are two important points here. First, an industry which is comprised of a large number of small companies or production units is likely to use different amounts of labour from the same industry organised on a large-scale basis, though this may in the end be largely a reflection of the degree of technological development. But secondly, it may well be that institutional arrangements in the industry lead to differences in the manning of equipment, management structure and so on, so that when we compare employment in an industry in different countries at the same stage of economic development, or when we study an industry's employment within a country over time, the way in which labour is utilised may be found to be different. This might be due, for example, to differences in the attitude of trade unions to income or employment security or to differences in the power of unions to enforce control over manning, but it may be due to quite different circumstances such as the extent to which sub-contracting from one industry to another is possible or profitable. This may seem to be an artificial source of difference, but in trying to explain inter-country or inter-temporal differences, such factors – and of course differences in the method of classifying industry and differences in the method of measuring employment – may be important too.

Having identified, if only in outline, the main influences which may alter the industrial distribution of the labour force, we can go on to consider the changes in the British situation. The last fifty years or so have seen very great changes in resource availability and utilisation, in the income of the population and its distribution among consumers in taxation levels and patterns, and in the organisation and technology of industry. We might also expect that the major educational and social changes superimposed on these would have been responsible for great changes in taste. It would not be surprising therefore if the present labour force distribution among industries now bore little resemblance to that of the early years of this century. As can be seen from Table 6.5, however, the changes are not perhaps as striking as we might expect, at least at the level of broad industrial groupings. Whereas employment in agriculture and in the mining industry has declined considerably between 1911 and 1959, manufacturing industry, taken as a whole, accounted for little more of the total labour force in 1959 than it did in 1911. The construction industry, the public utilities, and transport, taken together, account for very little more of the total labour force now than they did in 1911, and the distribution among these industries has changed comparatively little. More important changes have obviously taken place in public administration and defence and in the professional services, which doubled their share of the working population between 1911 and 1959. On the other hand there has been a significant decline in the miscellaneous services group, almost certainly due to the decline in the importance of people employed in domestic service. The distributive trades have remained fairly static over the whole period, although it may be that technical and organisational changes are now taking place which may eventually reduce the importance of this group in total employment.

The two final columns in Table 6.5 (which unfortunately have to be on a different basis from the earlier figures[1]) suggest the trend of development since 1959. Agricultural and mining employment are still declining in importance, and there is some indication that the growth of manufacturing employment has levelled off, though it is too early yet to be dogmatic on that point. It may, however, be significant that in the United States the share of the manufacturing sector in total civilian employment began to decline or at least to stabilise around 1958–9. It is quite possible that this country may be moving in the same direction, though recent innovations on the part of Government, such as the Selective Employment Tax, could have some effect in countering this trend in the longer run. The trend in the distributive and service industries sector still seems to be continuing upwards, but since 1959 the relative size of the public administration and defence sector has declined. This last change is mainly to be accounted for by the cessation of compulsory National Service since 1962, leading to a rundown in the size of the armed forces between 1959 and 1964. This has,

[1] See note 2 to Table 6.5.

Table 6.5

Changes in the Industrial Distribution of the Occupied Population of Great Britain, for Census Years 1911, 1931 and 1951, and for 1959 and 1964

Percentages

Industry group	1911[1]	1931[1]	1951[1]	1959 a^1	1959 b^2	1964[2]
Agriculture, etc.	8·4	6·1	5·0	4·2	4·2	3·5
Mining and quarrying	6·3	5·7	3·8	3·5	3·4	2·6
Manufacturing	34·6	34·4	37·7	38·4	35·6	35·4
Construction	5·3	5·5	6·4	6·4	6·5	7·1
Gas, electricity, water	0·6	1·2	1·6	1·6	1·6	1·6
Transport	7·9	8·2	7·7	7·1	7·3	6·9
Distribution	11·9	13·2	12·1	12·6	13·4	13·7
Professional services	4·4	5·2	6·9	8·4 ⎫		
Miscellaneous services	15·5	14·0	9·3	7·6 ⎬	20·4	22·1
Banking and finance	1·8	1·8	2·0	2·3 ⎭		
Public administration and defence	3·9	4·9	7·7	7·9	7·6	6·8
Total (per cent)	100	100	100	100	100	100

[1] *Source*: Routh, op. cit., table 18, p. 40. Data for 1911, 1931 and 1951 are from Census sources: the 1959 (*a*) figures are based on the 1948 Standard Industrial Classification.
[2] *Source*: Ministry of Labour. The 1959 (*b*) figures are based on the revised Standard Industrial Classification of 1958; and therefore differ from those in the previous column. It is necessary to include this as a link between the pre-1959 figures and 1964. Unfortunately there is another break in the series which makes it impossible to continue the table after 1964.

F

however, disguised the continuing growth of public administration employment both at local and national level.

It would be somewhat misleading to leave this brief discussion of the changing industrial structure without going on to indicate that within the broad sectors just considered there have been a great many further changes in the relative employment size of different industries. Many of these sectors are capable of much finer classification, and a full analysis of the changes in the more narrowly-defined industries would reveal a much greater degree of change than has been evident here. In fact even at the more detailed level of classification it is difficult to find industries that existed at the beginning of the century that are not in some way still represented, but their relative importance in terms of employment may have greatly diminished. At the same time new industries like electronics, plastics, and aircraft production have come into existence and grown to become major sources of employment. The closer we look at the detailed figures, the more evident does it become that the kind of changes in employment structure that we might expect to follow from technological and other forms of progress are in fact taking place in a fairly continual process.

In conclusion, this chapter has considered the growth of the population and the consequent changes in the economically active sector within the total. We have looked at the structure of employment from a number of different points of view, and brought to light some of the major influences which determine and alter the structure over time. Changes such as these clearly make considerable demands on the flexibility of the labour force and on the adjustment mechanisms on which labour market operations depend. The success of the labour market in effecting adaptation to change will be reflected in the efficiency with which the labour force is brought into use: in other words, in the effective rate of employment of the labour force. The aim of the next chapter is to investigate just this problem.

SUGGESTED READING

Ministry of Labour, *Occupational Change 1951–61* (Manpower Studies No. 6), 1967.
B. C. Roberts and J. H. Smith (eds.), *Manpower Policy and Employment Trends*, 1966.
Guy Routh, *Occupation and Pay in Great Britain, 1906–60* (National Institute of Economic and Social Research), 1965.

7 Full Employment and Unemployment

I. A Historical View

The consistent achievement of the policy goal of national full employment is a fairly recent phenomenon in this country. In the 1920s and 1930s the problem of widespread unemployment was one of the main economic issues of the day, which at times dominated thinking on economic matters. Today, the unemployment problem has not disappeared in Britain but its character has changed radically; what was once a national issue is currently much more a regional issue on a quite different scale. Policies designed to reduce unemployment are still very much in evidence, but they now exist in a fairly selective form, as we shall see subsequently. On the evidence of over twenty years of peace-time experience, the major problem of achieving an acceptable degree of employment stabilisation at a high level of economic activity is now much less pressing. It is worth while considering how this has come about, and how unemployment in the present situation differs from that of earlier periods.

The phenomenon of the business (or trade) cycle is now well documented. Since the time of the earliest available records of industrial activity, there have been persistent swings of economic activity from high demand, production and employment to low demand, low output and heavy unemployment. The length of this cycle seems to have varied in this country from about five to eleven years; furthermore, the cycle is not a purely British phenomenon, but one which is international and roughly coincidental in timing among countries – due, no doubt, to the transmission of effects through international trade. Prior to the First World War, the effect of these cycles was to cause considerable instability in the labour market, with estimates of national unemployment running from a low of 2 per cent of the labour force to about 8 per cent, or rather more in extreme cases. Though there were years in which acceptably high levels of employment, even in relation to today's standards, were achieved, on average over the 50 years or so before 1914 unemployment seems to have been of the order of 5 per cent.[1]

[1] Inevitably, these measures of unemployment are rather rough, since it is only comparatively recently that comprehensive and systematic unemployment

During the First World War itself, the level of demand was kept at a high level and unemployment was low; but with the return to peace unemployment rose sharply and remained consistently high until preparations for a new war began to improve the demand for labour in 1938–9. In the eighteen years 1921–38, unemployment in Great Britain as a whole only once fell below 10 per cent, and rose to over 21 per cent in 1931 and 1932. The average for the period was about 14 per cent, and even this does nothing to indicate the still more severe problems of particular regions and localities. These figures are indicative of the size of the problem, but much more lies behind them. Not only was there an average of one worker in seven unemployed at any moment of time, but many members of the labour force went without jobs for years at a time and it was this feature, as much as the number of unemployed, that gave rise to the social and psychological problems of the period, in addition to the purely economic losses incurred through the failure to achieve the levels of production and income possible in a better-managed economy.

The inter-war period was in fact a prolonged depression in which many of those who were normally regarded as the main bread-winners of the family unit were reduced for much of the time to an often hopeless trek in search of work. Undoubtedly this had serious implications for the family.[1] Among other consequences, it often meant that women, if they could get work, became the main family earners. It is probable, too, that many young persons who might otherwise have stayed longer at school, or entered some kind of training scheme, were obliged at the earliest opportunity to take what work was going to boost family income, even though the jobs they took were likely to lead nowhere. Further, there were the effects on the principal earners themselves. Long periods spent in idleness (except for the search for work) are undoubtedly demoralising, and the ability to exercise normal skills and judgment declines with lack of use, so

---

figures have become available. In the 1920s and 1930s the usual index of unemployment in Britain was derived from Unemployment Insurance records, which did not, however, cover all workers. The unemployment rate quoted was therefore for insured workers only and on the whole it is probable that the real overall level of unemployment was rather overstated, since the workers not covered by the scheme were less likely to experience unemployment to the same degree as the mass of lower-paid workers in manufacturing, who *were* covered. This has to be borne in mind in the following discussion.

[1] For a discussion of the sort of family and personal problems raised by unemployment in this period, see *Men Without Work* (a Report made to the Pilgrim Trust), 1938; also J. Jewkes and A. Winterbottom, *Juvenile Unemployment*, 1933.

that for those remaining unemployed for long periods of time there was a gradual deterioration in morale and skill which was only with difficulty recovered as employment conditions improved. While there are no figures to indicate its extent, it is certain that many workers with considerable skills and abilities, though in employment, were unable to find work which brought these into use. Thus not only was there an economic loss from direct employment itself, but there was also the economic, social and personal loss brought about by such misemployment of manpower.

The return to a war economy in 1939 and the mobilisation of large armed forces rapidly brought about a situation of labour shortage rather than the surplus which had prevailed for the previous twenty years. By 1943, when peace again seemed a possibility in the near future, attention began to be turned back to the difficulties of keeping the economy at a high level of activity both during and after the transition period. Although it may now seem surprising, in view of the continuous full employment of the post-war period, there was at this time a great anxiety, coloured by the experiences after 1918, that the economy on its return to peace would experience the same depressed conditions that had persisted in the inter-war period. But there were now two main differences which, though they involve us in something of a digression, are essential elements in the background to an understanding of the change in circumstances between 1935 and 1945.

First, in 1936, J. M. Keynes (later Lord Keynes) in his *General Theory*[1] had developed both a new theory of employment and a new framework for employment policy. The conventional economic wisdom and most public policy approaches to the employment problem had previously rested on the theory that unemployment was caused by a rise in money-wages to levels which employers could not afford, given the prices their products could fetch in the market. To re-establish a full-employment equilibrium, it was believed to be necessary that money wages should fall sufficiently to allow the existing supply of labour to be employed, thus clearing the market. For Keynes, on the other hand, unemployment was the result of lack of effective demand, which comprised expenditure on consumption and investment by individuals and businesses in the private sector, and spending by Government. A level of effective demand lower than that required for the generation of full employment could occur because, in general, those who saved and those who spent money on investment projects were different groups of people whose decisions were not wholly

[1] J. M. Keynes, *The General Theory of Employment, Interest and Money*, 1936.

co-ordinated. If savings increased, while no attempt was made to spend an equivalent amount on investment (owing for example to a lack of investment opportunities expected to bring in an acceptable rate of profit), the national income – and effective demand – would fall. This would continue until income fell to a level where the amount of savings and the amount of investment were equalised. An equilibrium situation would be reached but it would not be one of full employment. Cuts in money-wages would not help, for if carried out over the whole economy this could only lead to a decline in consumption, and hence in prices, providing little incentive for businessmen to invest. Wage cuts would be self-defeating. In any case, Keynes believed that the 'money illusion' was an important factor in preventing money-wages from falling very far: in other words, workers would resist cuts in money-wages even if prices were falling at an equivalent rate and real wages remained stable. Money-wages were, therefore, 'sticky' in response to downward pressures, and the flexibility of money-wage rates postulated by the pre-Keynesian theory, and required for a restoration of full employment equilibrium, did not exist.

There were many – politicians and academics alike – who found it hard to accept and to adjust to the Keynesian analysis.[1] Still more was it difficult to find immediate acceptance for the policy implications of the analysis, which were that government expenditure would have to be increased, if necessary by running a budget deficit, whenever the level of effective demand from the private sector and existing public expenditure was insufficient to produce full employment. However, the outbreak of war and the problems of financing war-time expenditure gave rise to a change in official attitudes. This was the second change in circumstances that helped to shape the post-war experience differently from that of the inter-war years. Keynes went to the Treasury, and in 1941 the first Keynesian budget (dealing in fact with the inflationary, rather than the unemployment problem, but from the same Keynesian standpoint) was introduced by Kingsley Wood. The exigencies of the war economy required strict and wide-ranging control of incomes and expenditure, and this could only be achieved by a great increase in government control of the economy. The solution of increased government intervention, regarded by many as intolerable in peace-time conditions, now became essential. Experience in flexible budgetary control under these circumstances, recognition that at least for some time after the war the economy would require to be managed more actively by the Government than before, and

[1] There had of course been precursors, but it was Keynes who gave the first widely accepted analytical account of the theory and its policy implications.

the carrying over into peace of the nation's tolerance of emergency measures, were all in some way responsible for the development in the use of the Budget as a device to balance the economy, in contrast to the pre-war situation where, by and large, the Budget had been balanced irrespective of its economic consequences.

While changes in analysis of the problem and in policy towards it are crucial elements in our post-war confidence that we may have escaped from massive under-utilisation of labour resources, in fact, despite a slight rise in the level of unemployment in 1946–7 from the war-time low, it soon became increasingly obvious that the main post-war problem was not to be one of unemployment, as had been feared, but rather of labour shortage. In this country at least, active management of the economy by Government has become an established feature, and very low levels of unemployment have been achieved, certainly well within the 3 per cent unemployment mark which was regarded by Lord Beveridge in his 1944 Report[1] as fulfilling the full employment target. Between 1948 and 1966 the highest average annual rate for Great Britain in any year was 2·5 per cent (1963) and the lowest 1·1 per cent (1955), the average for the whole period being 1·6 per cent.[2] In fact for much of the time the condition of the labour market can be described as being in a state of 'overfull employment', a condition which is characterised by an excess of vacant jobs over workers available to fill them, persistent labour shortages in some occupations and considerable upward pressure on wage and salary earnings.

Fluctuations in economic activity and in employment have continued during the post-war period, but on a scale much more moderate than between the wars, so that it is possible to speak of recessions in the economy rather than depression. In 1951–2, 1958–9 and 1962–3, unemployment rose above the long-term average and output stagnated or even declined somewhat. Even so, the rate for the nation as a whole has remained under the 3 per cent mark regarded by Beveridge as the fulcrum of full employment. As we shall see subsequently, however, all parts of the country and every section of the work force have not fared equally well. And it is questionable whether in modern conditions the 3 per cent unemployment

[1] *Full Employment in a Free Society*, 1944. It is interesting to note that Beveridge, in the prologue to his second edition of 1960, observed that Keynes himself thought 3 per cent unemployment a good target to aim at, but believed it unlikely to be achieved (loc. cit., p. 1).

[2] Since 1948, the unemployment rate has been determined by expressing the number of people registered as unemployed with the Ministry of Labour (since 5 April 1968 the Department of Employment and Productivity) as a percentage of the total number of employees in the labour force.

rate is a realistic full employment equivalent – indeed whether full employment can properly be measured in this way at all.

But just before passing on to that question, it is perhaps as well to observe that not all countries have been as successful in achieving the goal of high employment. In the United States, for example, although during the Korean War period of 1951–2 unemployment fell below 3 per cent, it has for most of the period 1949–66 ranged between 4 and 8 per cent.[1] There has been much debate how far this is due to inadequate effective demand as opposed to an increase in structural dislocation. Official policy-makers have taken the view that the main problem was lack of effective demand, and tried to tackle this directly by a massive tax cut beginning in 1964. Comparatively little was done to remedy any structural unemployment that might exist. In the event, unemployment has fallen to around 4 per cent (by U.S. measures), but it is difficult to tell how far this was due to the tax cut and how far to the expenditure of Government on the Vietnam War. While we cannot go into this in detail here it is perhaps valuable to have pointed out that full employment is not yet a universal and guaranteed characteristic of the advanced economy.

II. The Concept of Full Employment

Full employment does not mean the complete absence of unemployment. In an economy subject to no changes in demand or technology, without international contacts and possessing a perfectly accurate system of communications involving instantaneous dissemination of knowledge, it is conceivable that unemployment might be entirely eliminated, but this is clearly unrealistic. In fact, the technological structure of the economy is continually altering, and with it the demand for goods and services, the demand for labour, and hence the whole pattern of output and employment. It is inevitable in such circumstances, notwithstanding the presence of potentially powerful government policies to sustain demand at full employment levels, that workers should change jobs from time to time either from their own choice, because new and better opportunities become available, or because existing employers cannot any longer use their

---

[1] Owing to differences in statistical treatment, and in methods of collecting data, the British and United States figures are not strictly comparable. According to adjustment ratios which have been calculated, however, we can equate the 4 to 8 per cent U.S. rate to $2\frac{1}{2}$ to $5\frac{1}{2}$ per cent in British terms.

services. Although much can, and has, been done to improve the flow of information about labour availability and job opportunities in the labour market, it is also inevitable that in some instances there will be a delay before a new job or a new recruit to a firm can be found, with the result that workers seeking employment, and hence constituting part of the labour force, are (temporarily at least) unemployed. This unemployment is simply a result of the dynamism of the economy, and although the degree of this dynamism is variable, it is never really absent.

These introductory remarks underline the curiosity of the concept of full employment, that it is much easier to define in terms of what it is not, than to say more positively what it comprises. Much seems to depend on the starting point for the discussion. Because it exists as part of the economic policy of virtually every government, the full employment goal is in some senses as much a political as an economic conception, and as such it has often tended to acquire a concreteness which may not be entirely consistent with the meaning accorded to it by economic analysis. Thus, in the British case, the ideal of full employment as no more than 3 per cent unemployment was for many people the right goal for policy. But since events have now proved that a lower level of unemployment can be consistently achieved over a considerable period of time, the politically acceptable level of unemployment has fallen, so that a rise above the long-run average of $1\frac{1}{2}$ per cent to 2 or $2\frac{1}{2}$ per cent is frequently regarded as verging on departure from full employment and the signal for remedial action to be taken. From this point of view full employment is simply a numerical target, stated in terms of the country's own measures of un-employment,[1] which policies must try to achieve. But from the standpoint of economic analysis something more sophisticated is necessary.

In tackling this problem we are forced to go back to the efficiency of the economic system under consideration. Full employment must in some way be defined in terms of the effective use of the existing labour supply in a period of time. Thus we might start with a definition which stated that full employment is a situation where the best possible use is made of labour resources, consistently with the need of a dynamic economy for flexibility in production and employment. This definition evidently excludes the existence of unemployment due to a lack of effective demand, but would permit some degree of unemployment arising from necessary changes in the structure of the economy and in the distribution of labour among firms. But this unemployment stemming from economic change

[1] Thus, for example, in the United States the full employment goal has usually been stated as 4 per cent unemployment.

would, on the efficiency definition, have to be kept to an absolute minimum in terms of amount and duration, which in turn implies that the time-interval between leaving one employer and joining another should be as short as possible. In what circumstances will this condition be satisfied?

If a worker, on quitting a job or on becoming redundant, is rapidly to find another job, another job must exist which requires work of which he is capable and which he is prepared to accept. Taken over the labour market as a whole, this implies that the number of job vacancies at any time should at any rate be *not less than* (and possibly rather greater than) the number of unemployed workers. This in fact is close to the definition of full employment, as opposed to its numerical expression in terms of unemployment, used by Lord Beveridge in his 1944 Report:

> 'Full employment . . . means having *always more* vacant jobs than unemployed men, not slightly fewer jobs. It means that the jobs are at fair wages, of such a kind, and so located that the unemployed men can reasonably be expected to take them; it means, by consequence, that normal lag between one job and finding another will be very short.'[1]

On this definition, which considers that full employment exists only when vacancies *always exceed* unemployment, Britain has not had the continuous full employment often claimed for the post-war period. But more important from the present point of view, such a definition says something quite specific about the composition and character of the job vacancies, the pay associated with them, their location in relation to the unemployed who might fill them, and their composition in relation to the attributes of the unemployed.

Whether one completely accepts this definition or not, with its implications of a sellers' market for labour and the dangers inherent in that situation (which Beveridge himself recognised), one has to accept that full employment cannot simply be regarded in quantitative terms. The qualitative composition of vacancies and unemployment must also be taken into account, and it is this which raises real difficulties for full employment policies, in two ways. First, the amount of unemployment resulting from the need for flexibility in the industrial and regional distribution of output and employment must be minimised. In fact the 'magic number' of 3 per cent unemployment is probably best regarded as a 1944 estimate of the amount of 'short-term' unemployment likely to result from the institutional arrangements of the labour market in this country, which will clearly have a major influence on the ease with which people find jobs actually in existence. The more efficient the information networks operat-

[1] Op cit. (2nd ed., p. 18). Italics not in original.

ing in the various sectors of the national labour market, the more possible it will be to reduce the amount of such 'frictional' unemployment. And, indeed, the developments that have taken place in the British system of labour market communications since the 1939–45 period are substantial, which could be part of the explanation for the continued low unemployment rates achieved in the post-war period. But, secondly, it is almost inevitable that the required changes in employment structure will not be attainable simply by the retirement of the labour becoming redundant and by the diversion of new labour force entrants to the expanding industries and occupations. Many of those who still have much of their working life to live out will be obliged to change jobs. The question then is to what extent these workers can readily step into jobs in the developing sectors of the economy, since their existing skills – in so far as they possess a degree of skill at all – may not be required elsewhere in the economy and may be difficult to modify for immediate use in other industries. We are therefore brought sharply up against the problem of adapting the skills and abilities of much of the labour that becomes redundant through structural change, and this again has to be considered in the context of full employment policy, as indeed does the willingness of workers in this situation to accept the need for change.

In a sense, what we have just described is the evolution of a set of policies which started out with the goal of achieving full employment and, that immediate aim largely being attained, progressed to the more complex level of what is now recognised as 'active manpower policy'. In the simplest terms, this policy accepts the existence of a satisfactory level of employment in the economy as a whole and seeks to go further in widening the choice of jobs for labour in general, by improving labour force skills, by encouraging the mobility of labour between occupations, industries and localities where the economy requires it, and by developing the system of communications in the labour market as a whole. It is this wider choice, which requires more complete and more accurate information, that is believed to be the key not only to ensuring that everyone who wants work can obtain it, but to the fulfilment of the objective of having people at work in jobs which make the fullest use of their potential and give them real job-satisfaction. All this is not, of course, absent from the earlier discussions of Beveridge, but at that time, before an acceptable level of unemployment had really been achieved, the priority was rather different.

Full employment is by no means a clear-cut conception, and one that cannot readily be stated in a sentence. It is, at best, misleading to think of full employment simply in terms of an unemployment rate, which can conceal the underlying pattern of unemployment and job-opportunity. Essentially it comprises a qualitative balance between the amount of unemployment an economy generates by its industrial development, and the new job opportunities being opened up by the same disturbing factor. It is, in addition, a situation in which the institutional framework of the labour market is efficiently arranged so as to prevent both the non-utilisation and the mis-utilisation of labour resources. And finally, full employment is a condition of the economy in which the labour force is sufficiently educated and sufficiently adaptable both to understand the need for changes of employment and to be capable of undertaking the transfers that economic development requires.

Some of the problems raised here, such as mobility and training, will be encountered again in more detail in later chapters. But now we must return to a consideration of the pattern and characteristics of unemployment in Britain.

III. The Incidence of Unemployment

Are some workers more inclined to experience unemployment than others, and if so, who are they? Does unemployment generated in the course of a downswing in the trade cycle affect all industries equally, or do some fare better than others? Is unemployment more severe in some areas than in others? These are questions concerning the incidence of unemployment on the labour force, and it is this aspect that we now go on to investigate. The discussion introduces various types of unemployment which economists find useful in the analysis of causes and cures for specific problems, but it should be added that too much stress should not be put on the classification, which must to some extent be arbitrary. Many economists would argue that the fluctuations of the trade cycle are caused by variations in the level of investment; and that these, in turn, are determined by changes in the profitability of production due to advances in technology. If, then, technological change is a major cause of the trade cycle fluctuations, can we say dogmatically whether the unemployment created in the downswing is due to lack of effective demand or to technological factors? And if, over and above this, there is a secular decline in the importance of some industries, how far can we separate out the unemployment produced in them by the cycle from that which would probably have occurred anyway as a result of the long-term change in the production pattern? Despite such difficulties, the ability to identify some of the principal types of unemployment can be useful in the analysis of particular situations.

(1) UNEMPLOYMENT BY REGION

In commenting upon the high employment levels achieved in post-war Britain, we observed that not all parts of the country had fared equally well. For administrative purposes, statistics have long been collected for a number of 'standard regions', and use can be made of these to illustrate the pattern of unemployment over the country as a whole. Once again it has to be pointed out that the definition of areas has changed over time, and in some cases regional boundaries have been radically altered. However, despite the difficulties, a picture can be built up.

Looking back in history to the time just before the First World War, we find distinct regional differences in unemployment. At that time the higher unemployment rates were in the south of England, especially in London and its environs, while Scotland, Wales and the north of England were much better off, with rates below 3 per cent in each case in 1912–13. Since then, however, this pattern has been almost completely reversed. The great change came with the post-1918 slump in the heavy industries such as steel, coal and shipbuilding, which were largely concentrated in Wales, the north of England and Scotland, and by the mid-1930s the pattern which has persisted until the present time was in evidence. In 1937, unemployment in the south of England and in the Midlands averaged about 7 per cent, compared with about 15 per cent in the remainder of the country. This distribution has continued since the end of the Second World War, as is shown in Fig. 7.1, although of course the severity of unemployment has declined markedly. Four regions – Wales, Northern, North-Western and Scotland – have consistently remained at levels of unemployment a good deal higher than the long-run British average; and Northern Ireland has been still worse off, with a long-term average of over 7 per cent. Even if the position is a vast improvement on that of the pre-war period, it is disturbing that there should be such a continuing discrepancy in the economic performance of the regions, and much debate and analysis has taken place in an effort both to understand why this should be so and to remedy the imbalance.

There is, of course, an immediate difference between the pre-war and post-war circumstances. Prior to 1939, the cause of the trouble in general was a deficiency in the demand for labour in the country as a whole, whereas in the post-1945 era, overall demand has been adequate. But this

deficiency of demand, simply because of its implications of mass unemployment and the priority action which that demanded, tended to obscure the
underlying regional imbalance even though unemployment was much

Fig. 7·1

Regional unemployment, averages 1953-63

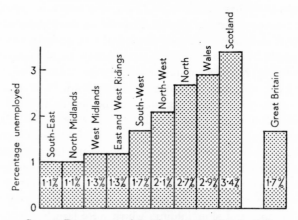

Source : Department of Employment and Productivity.

heavier in some regions than in others in the 1930s. Only once the general
problem had been solved, as it seemed to be by 1950, did it become possible
to divert attention to the regional issue. The roots of the problem were not
hard to discover. At the end of the war the economies of the regions of
higher unemployment were still largely based on heavy industry, which had
not only tended to suffer more severely from cyclical depressions, as in the
1930-2 period, but also ran into difficult conditions after the immediate
post-war boom and the drive towards recovery. Conversely, many of the
more rapidly growing industries were poorly represented in the high unemployment regions. In effect these parts of the country were suffering
largely (though not exclusively) from *structural* unemployment: in other
words from unemployment due not to a lack of effective demand but to
major changes in the structure of demand for certain key products in the
national economy.

The problem then was apparent. A rise in the total volume of expenditure on goods and services would not provide a real solution, for given
the new pattern of demand, such an increase would simply exaggerate the

pressure on the already fully-employed regions, without doing very much to improve the situation in the rest of the country. It would mean a greater stress on the labour and production facilities of industries and regions which, with low unemployment, were already running into bottleneck problems, and would thus amplify the inflationary tendencies which are never far away when full employment is present. And so experience in the 1950s and 1960s has proved, for whenever the level of demand in the economy as a whole has brought down the rate of unemployment in the less prosperous regions, the resulting inflationary pressure, mainly in the Midlands and South, has necessitated governmental policies to ease the situation by reducing demand – even though unemployed resources existed in other parts of the country.

This is, inevitably, only the briefest glimpse of the regional problem, and it would be wrong to view that problem simply as one of unemployment, which is only one symptom of the malaise. If this were a textbook on British regional economics, much more would have to be said on the details of industrial structure, the problems of generating growth of employment, output and income in the less favoured areas, the policies that have been devised to improve the situation, and on the duration of unemployment. For the moment, however, we must return to the problem of unemployment *per se*, though some further discussion of regional matters occurs in Chapter 19.

(2) UNEMPLOYMENT BY INDUSTRY

The extent to which workers in different industries are prone to unemployment will depend on a variety of factors, including the role of the industry in the economy, the organisation of the sector of the labour market in which it operates, the influence of seasonal factors and the composition of the labour force. What, firstly, is meant by the role of the industry in the economy? Some goods are more durable than others, while some are more necessary to the preservation of life than others. At the onset of a business recession, usually involving a fall in the demand for investment goods, the initial unemployment and loss of income cause those families affected to reappraise their expenditure plans: expenditure will be concentrated largely on the necessities of life and expenditure on consumer durables such as washing-machines, refrigerators, and cars is postponed. These industries in turn are affected by falling sales and labour is laid off, so that the effects are rapidly but not instantaneously spread through the economy. Thus not all industries are immediately hit by recession, and this is reflected in the gradual transmission of unemployment through the economy. But again, not every industry is equally affected by recession: in general, the greatest fluctuations in activity – and unemployment – are in the investment goods sector of manufacturing industry and in construction, while some industries suffer only minor setbacks. In an economy like that of Britain, which is so dependent on international trade and its ability to sell an important part of its output abroad, a slump in the world demand for exports can have the effect of inducing recession conditions concentrated particularly in a limited sector of industry. In the British case, textiles have been especially subject to this kind of influence. Indeed, the recession of 1952–3 was very largely due to the slump in textiles, and since the textile industry mainly employs women, this aggravated female unemployment more than male.

Another aspect of the role of the industry in the economy is the possibility that its importance as an employer may be altering. The point has already been made that the structure of demand for goods and services alters over time, and that employment will change in consequence. For an industry in the process of decline for structural reasons, there will be a continuous reduction in the number of jobs available, and where that reduction is proceeding rapidly, perhaps accentuated by a cyclical downturn, the possibility of absorbing the redundant labour immediately is slight. As a result, the unemployment rate for such an industry will tend to be higher than the all-industry average. The same kind of argument will of course apply where there is a rapid application of new labour-saving techniques of production which are not, in the first instance at any rate, matched by an increase in demand for the product concerned. In that case there is *technological unemployment*, due to the displacement of workers by improved productive plant, in contrast to the *structural unemployment* mentioned earlier.

Secondly, the industrial incidence of unemployment may be affected by the organisation of the labour market for the industry. In some industries, notably the docks, construction and parts of the printing industry, casual labour is still an important factor. The problem of casual labour is essentially that of excess supply for a given number of jobs with no regular occupants. The jobs are filled, often on a daily basis, according to some kind of rota system or similar hiring custom, so that some of the labour force is always out of work though its composition varies on a fairly regular pattern. Although casual employment has not disappeared, it is, however, true to say that it is now a much smaller problem than it was even thirty years ago.

Thirdly, many industries are affected by seasonal variations in demand, and employment may vary in consequence. The construction industry, for example, is one which is hampered by bad weather and, in the winter months of January and February especially, unemployment in construction rises. Other industries severely affected by seasonal factors are hotels and tourism, agriculture and the distributive trades, the latter of course being subject more to fluctuations due to seasonal peaks of expenditure, as at Christmas. But such seasonal variations in demand need not result in unemployment. Industries experiencing seasonal upsurges in demand are frequently able to call on regular reserve supplies of labour, such as house-wives, and students during vacation periods, who do not want or are unable to participate in all-the-year-round employment. When the seasonal rise in demand diminishes, the extra workers will largely return to their other activities. Again, as in the case of the tourist industry, employees know that they cannot expect all-the-year-round work, and normally have some other activity to which they can turn during the winter months. Finally, in some industries the seasonal nature of demand for production is not reflected to any great extent in employment or unemployment figures, since much can be done by stockpiling, diversification and even exporting to stabilise employment. Despite this, a certain seasonal pattern of unemployment does persist over industry as a whole and, according to the regional composition of employment and climatic variations, such a pattern also appears regionally.

Fourthly, there is the influence on industrial unemployment of the com-position of the labour force. As we shall see subsequently, the incidence of unemployment on white-collar and manual workers varies, as does its incidence on skilled, semi-skilled and unskilled workers in the manual category. Thus an industry which includes a high proportion of unskilled workers, who are more subject to unemployment than others, will tend to be characterised by higher than average unemployment rates. It is, however, a moot point whether the characteristics of the labour force or those of the industry are the prime cause of higher unemployment. On the one hand, it is probable that turnover – both voluntary and involuntary – is higher among unskilled workers and the consequence of this, plus perhaps a poorer system of job information (since there is less at stake),[1] will be higher unemployment. But on the other hand, an industry subject to cyclical or seasonal fluctuations in demand may find it most economical to lay off a higher proportion of its unskilled labour force (who in labour shortage situations will be more readily replaceable in the upswing than

[1] See below, Chapter 9.

skilled operatives). In the first case it would seem to be the type of labour that matters; in the second, the nature of the industry and its employment structure seems more important. It is probable in fact that the situation will alter from industry to industry.

What, then, is the recent experience of industrial unemployment in this country? Table 7.1 provides a statement of the rates of unemployment by major industry heading in June 1963 and June 1966; since the month is the same in each case it can be assumed that seasonal influences are absent, but 1963 was a year of recession while the first half of 1966 was the peak of the next cycle.

The important points from the table can be quickly appreciated. First, it is significant that four industries were above the national average in both 1963 and 1966: agriculture, forestry and fishing; shipbuilding and marine engineering; construction; and miscellaneous services. Of these, the ship-building and construction industries on both occasions were more than twice the all-industry rate, but almost certainly for different reasons. In construction there tends to be a high level of labour turnover among firms as jobs come to an end, and new jobs are not always immediately available so that there is a time-lag, involving unemployment, between jobs. This is fairly typical of the kind of unemployment known as *frictional unemployment*, which is normally of short duration and arises out of the impediments, such as lack of information or lack of mobility, to adjustments in the supply of labour. In construction, therefore, the frictional element is probably rather greater than normal, and in 1963 there was an added cyclical factor. In shipbuilding, too, there is some element of frictional unemployment stemming from the problems of achieving a smooth flow of production and regular employment for many workers who, in consequence, habitually move from yard to yard. But there is also, in addition to the frictional and of course the cyclical element, an important structural component in the 1963 shipbuilding unemployment rate. At that time the industry was suffering severely from the secular decline in the world demand for new ships and from the problem of world excess capacity for ships. Furthermore, it is probable that there was, at least in the 1963 figure, some technological unemployment, since some of the older shipbuilding trades, such as that of riveter, had been disappearing, leading to redundancy. This example, incidentally, shows how difficult it is to separate out the different factors giving rise to unemployment, and it is virtually impossible to quantify the importance of each type with any accuracy.

Only a few points need be made on the remaining industries. Textiles, as has already been mentioned, is particularly sensitive to downturns in world trade, and this is reflected in the 1963 figure, though by 1966 it was well below the national average. On the other hand, industries like the paper, printing and publishing group, the public utilities, and financial, professional and scientific services, though clearly affected by the cycle, still have very low levels of unemployment even in recession.

Table 7.1

Unemployment Rates by Industry Group, 1963 and 1966 (Great Britain)[1]

Industry	Unemployment rate (%) 1963	1966
Agriculture, forestry and fishing	2·5	1·9
Mining and quarrying	1·4	1·0
Food, drink and tobacco	2·1	1·1
Chemicals and allied industries	1·5	0·9
Metal manufacturing	2·6	1·2
Engineering and electrical industries	1·4	0·6
Shipbuilding and marine engineering	8·1	2·3
Vehicles	1·2	0·7
Metal goods n.e.s.	2·1	0·9
Textiles	2·4	0·8
Leather, leather goods and fur	2·5	1·0
Clothing and footwear	2·0	0·6
Bricks, pottery, etc.	2·1	1·1
Timber, furniture, etc.	2·2	1·1
Paper, printing and publishing	1·0	0·5
Other manufacturing	2·0	0·9
Construction	4·4	2·2
Gas, electricity and water	0·9	0·6
Transport	1·7	1·3
Distributive trades	1·9	1·0
Insurance, banking and finance ⎫ Professional and scientific services ⎭	0·6	0·5
Miscellaneous services	2·3	1·3
Public administration	1·8	1·1
All industries	2·1	1·1

[1] Unemployed as percentage of employees, mid-June in each year.
Source: Department of Employment and Productivity.

(3) UNEMPLOYMENT BY OCCUPATION

Only a few general comments can be made on the occupational incidence of unemployment. Official figures on the numbers unemployed in different occupations have been available for some time now; but we are still without a comprehensive occupational analysis of employment itself, except in Census years, which allows us only a snapshot, rather than a moving picture of events. Another consequence is of course that occupational unemployment *rates* can be derived only for Census years. These gaps in knowledge are important, not just for analytical purposes but also for policy. It is of course a help to know how unemployment affects different *industries*, but it frequently happens that technological change has the effect of changing the employment opportunities open to certain occupations represented in a range of industries. Unless there is some indication of the relative intensity of unemployment on occupations as a result of such changes, it is difficult to estimate the current and future scale of the problem and to devise appropriate measures to deal with it. On the other hand, we do have an adequate knowledge of the occupational composition of the reserves among the unemployed and this is of considerable help for some policy purposes.

However, the available evidence indicates that in the high-employment conditions of post-war Britain, unemployment has been mainly concentrated among the unskilled and low-skilled workers, except where an industry, such as shipbuilding, has suffered a major structural decline and unemployment in the transition phase has spread more generally through all occupations in that industry. The study of occupational unemployment data consistently reveals that more than half of the unemployed men at any time are classed as 'general and other labourers' or as 'normal occupation not stated' – the latter being mainly those with no fixed occupational attachment and hence basically unskilled. Furthermore, there is evidence to suggest that a large proportion of these labouring categories are subject to long-term unemployment, so that it is not simply a matter of labourers being more mobile between jobs and thus more prone to frictional unemployment. In August 1961 a Ministry of Labour Survey revealed that one-half of this labouring category had been out of work for 26 weeks or more.[1] Among women, too, there was a strong association between lack of skill and unemployment.

Some indication of the differential in unemployment experience among occupations can be derived from the 1961 Census of Population. For the

[1] Ministry of Labour *Gazette*, April 1962, p. 136.

purposes of illustration, we have calculated unemployment rates for a number of occupations in each of the main occupational classes defined by Routh and introduced in Chapter 6 above, so that a cross-sectional impression of unemployment experience can be obtained. The results are shown in Table 7.2.

Table 7.2

Unemployment Rates for Selected Occupations,
April 1961 (Great Britain) by Occupational Class[1]

Occupational class		Unemployment rate %
1a. *Higher professions*		
Professional accountants	(296)	0·5
Medical practitioners	(280)	1·2
Authors, journalists, etc.	(293)	1·2
Clergy, ministers, etc.	(298)	0·5
1b. *Lower professions*		
Draughtsmen	(312)	0·5
Teachers n.e.c.	(287)	0·5
Pharmacists, dispensers	(283)	1·4
2. *Employers, proprietors, administrators and managers*		
Farmers, farm managers	(001)	0·8
Managers in engineering	(272)	0·6
Managers in building and contracting	(273)	0·7
Proprietors and managers, food sales	(230)	1·5
3. *Clerical workers*		
Clerks, cashiers, office machine operators	(221)	1·5
4. *Foremen, supervisors, inspectors*		
Transport inspectors and supervisors	(198)	0·8
Inspectors, metal and electrical	(077)	1·7
5. *Skilled manual*		
Carpenters and joiners	(080)	1·7
Electricians	(053)	1·3
Machine-tool setters/operators	(064)	1·3
Furnacemen (metal)	(040)	2·9
Compositors	(132)	0·7
Bricklayers	(150)	2·4

[1] Unemployment rates are found by expressing the numbers out of employment as a percentage of the number enumerated in the occupation. The Occupational Code Number is given in brackets after the occupational title.

Table 7.2 (*continued*)

Occupational class		Unemployment rate %
6. Semi-skilled manual		
Postmen, mail-sorters	(203)	2·5
Bus and tram conductors	(205)	2·7
Chemical production process workers	(021)	1·9
Coalmine – workers above ground	(012)	6·0
Packers, labellers, etc.	(211)	4·2
Launderers, dry-cleaners	(264)	3·9
Drivers of road goods vehicles	(197)	2·8
7. Unskilled manual		
Labourers (engineering and allied trades)	(182)	7·3
Labourers (building and contracting)	(187)	9·5
Caretakers, office keepers	(260)	2·9
Boiler firemen	(170)	4·0

Source: Census of Population 1961: England and Wales (Occupation Tables). Census of Population 1961: Scotland (Occupation, Industry and Workplace, Part I)

While this is purely a moment-of-time impression, it undoubtedly gives a fair picture of unemployment experience in recent years. In general, the unemployment rate in Occupational Classes 1 to 4 is lower than the all-occupations average (by Census definitions) of 2·8 per cent.[1] Among the manual workers, however, the rate of unemployment tends to rise as the level of skill declines, with the highest rates in the general labouring categories. Nevertheless, as the table shows, there is even within an occupational class some scope for differences in unemployment experience.

An alternative approach, giving some corroboration to the evidence above, involves comparison of the numbers unemployed in an occupation with the number of unfilled vacancies notified by employers to employment exchanges. There are, however, some difficulties with this method, too.

[1] There is a complication here. For a variety of reasons, the numbers classified as 'out of employment' in the Census differ considerably from the number of persons registered as wholly unemployed in the Ministry of Labour Statistics. The Census figure includes many who are out of work for reasons of sickness or injury and who would not be included in the Ministry unemployment data. Thus, to be comparable with Ministry statistics, the results in the table should be deflated, but this is not possible on an occupational basis. The general pattern would probably not be significantly altered, however.

For example, in December 1966 the official statistics show 188,000 labourers to have been registered as unemployed, while there were barely 10,000 vacancies for labourers. On this evidence it would seem that about 19 workers were available for every labouring job available. But there is no obligation on employers to register vacancies, and where there is in any case a ready supply, employers will be less inclined to take the trouble of notification. Indeed, they may often get direct enquiries about job openings from this type of labour and so be aware of sources they can tap when necessary. Although there is some counter-balance to this in that not all those who are in search of work are necessarily registered as unemployed at employment exchanges, there is general agreement that the possible inaccuracy in the unemployment figures is less than in the vacancy data. Conversely, when employers have vacancies in occupations they know to be in short supply, they are more likely to try all means of recruitment available to them, including notification to the Department of Employment and Productivity. Thus the vacancy data in respect of 'shortage' occupations will normally be more accurate than those in substantial surplus.

Examination of vacancy and unemployment statistics bears out the earlier argument that the lower-skilled occupations are more often than not in a state of over-supply and unemployment is higher in consequence. Thus, over the years, there is a consistent pattern of vacancies much in excess of the unemployed available in occupations such as engineering fitters, turners, and machine-tool setters, draughtsmen and nurses, while the reverse is more true of occupations like shop assistants, clerical workers (especially men), ordinary motor drivers and general factory hands.

This imbalance raises many questions about the causes of relative surplus and shortage, about the extent to which workers can change their occupations, and the part played by wages in the allocation of labour to different types of work. But before we come to these issues in later chapters it is worth while giving some thought in concluding this chapter to the implications of unemployment in full employment conditions.

IV. Unemployment in a High Employment Economy

Unemployment in this country in the 1930s was at exceptionally high levels, and was widely dispersed through many industries, all parts of the country and nearly all levels of skill. The dominant problem was that of curing mass unemployment. In the post-war era, full employment (by most definitions) has been achieved and the unemployment problem has been small by comparison with earlier periods. Whether or not this residual unemployment constitutes a real problem depends on factors such as its duration, its geographical distribution and its incidence on the labour force. The full employment economy, in which at least as many jobs are available as there are workers to fill them, almost inevitably generates high levels of labour turnover on a voluntary basis. The worker who is dissatisfied with his job, whether because of poor working conditions, a lower level of pay than is obtainable elsewhere, unhappy personal relationships at work, or simply a desire for a change, will usually have a choice of several jobs. In this situation, which in any case is one where the worker will often have some savings at his disposal, labour is known to be more ready to leave one job before having fixed up an alternative, since the chances of his being long out of work are relatively small. For this reason the full employment society is generally associated with a certain amount of frictional unemployment.

If this were the only kind of unemployment existing, we could argue quite reasonably that unemployment was no longer a problem. What unemployment remained would be of short duration, would in a sense be voluntary and would in any case make a contribution to the flexibility necessary for the reallocation of manpower in a dynamic economy. Even then it might be thought that the level of frictional unemployment was excessive, and steps might be taken to improve the procedures by which unemployed workers and unfilled jobs were matched up, or to eliminate some proportion of voluntary turnover, unnecessary for the purpose of flexibility, by improving the market mechanism or industrial relations, by adjusting relative pay and so on.

However, enough has been said already in this chapter to suggest that the residual unemployment is not simply frictional in character. It is, too, generally recognised that while unemployment among certain types of labour, notably the unskilled, is high, there have been persistent shortages of white-collar labour and skilled manual workers. Evidently, quite apart from the point, to which we come in a moment, that the duration of unemployment is uneven, all is not well with the system and unemployment remains a problem, though one quite different in nature and in scale from that of pre-war days.

Who then are the unemployed? What are their personal characteristics? Is there, as is sometimes argued, a 'hard core' of labour that is virtually unemployable even in the best of times? We now know something about the regional, industrial and occupational composition of unemployment, but this is clearly not the whole story. Is there something in the personal characteristics of some workers, such as age, their inability to benefit from training, or their attitude to work that prevents them from obtaining anything but the most irregular employment?

In answering these questions we are helped by two sample enquiries into the characteristics of the unemployed, undertaken by the Ministry of Labour in 1961 and 1964.[1] Both enquiries were mounted at times when the level of national unemployment was fairly low, at 1·4 and 1·5 per cent respectively. In fact both studies produced remarkably similar results and for the present purpose figures are taken from the 1964 study, though reference is made to the earlier report too.

Rather less than one-quarter of the unemployed were classified as 'placeable without undue difficulty': in other words, the Ministry officials concerned regarded these as workers who were adequately qualified and experienced for the jobs they were seeking and were suitable in other respects for jobs which were available in their home areas. Almost certainly, many of these were voluntary job-changers whose period of unemployment would be short. Another category identified was that of workers who, though adequately experienced and employable, were likely to find difficulty in getting work in their home areas. These accounted for rather less than 20 per cent of the unemployed. It might be concluded, then, that only about 40 per cent of the unemployed could properly be regarded as a real reserve of labour, able to step immediately into employment as suitable jobs become available.

The remainder, well over half the total out of work, were classified as being difficult to place in employment, almost entirely because of personal deficiencies or characteristics, and it is worth while considering this.

Table 7.3 shows that roughly 40 per cent of the men and single women unemployed were regarded[2] as difficult to place on grounds of their age and physical or mental condition. Among married women these reasons

[1] The 1961 study is reported in the Ministry of Labour *Gazette* for February, April and September 1962; the 1964 study in the same publication, April and July 1966. The enquiries concerned only the 'wholly unemployed' as opposed to those statistically classified as 'temporarily out of work'. The latter comprise workers laid off by employers with the prospect of fairly immediate recall. This group tends to be quite a small proportion of the total unemployed (as in these cases) except at the onset of a cyclical downswing.

[2] It has to be remembered that much of the data is based on subjective opinions by Ministry officials, but there is no reason to doubt the accuracy of the general picture.

were less important, but roughly one in six of that group put some restriction on their availability for work. The only other really important reason for employment problems was 'attitude to work' (presumably lack of

Table 7.3

Analysis of the Characteristics of the Unemployed, 1964
(Great Britain)

Percentages

Classification	Men	Married women	Single women	Total
Should get work without difficulty	22·4	23·9	27·7	23·2
Difficult to employ due to:				
Lack of local opportunities	15·7	27·0	16·2	17·3
Qualifications, experience insufficient	1·4	2·5	2·3	1·6
Difficult to employ on personal grounds				
Age	23·2	7·9	14·6	20·2
Physical or mental condition	20·3	9·6	23·1	19·2
Prison record	1·6	0·1	0·1	1·2
Attitude to work	10·3	6·6	6·2	9·4
Colour	0·9	1·5	1·3	1·0
Lack of English	0·4	0·1	0·2	0·3
Restriction on availability	0·5	16·3	4·0	3·0
Lack of financial incentive	1·5	0·1	0·1	1·2
Non-members of trade union	0·1	—	—	0·1
Other reasons	1·7	4·3	4·1	2·3
Total (per cent)	100·0	100·0	100·0	100·0
(numbers)	236,520	41,450	34,960	312,930

Note: Totals do not always add to 100 per cent owing to rounding.
Source: Department of Employment and Productivity.

interest), involving just under one in ten of the unemployed. It is in fact interesting to find that some of the reasons frequently cited as giving rise to residual unemployment in an affluent, Welfare State society are really quite unimportant: less than 4 per cent of the unemployed owed their poor employment prospects to refusal to join a trade union, to lack of financial incentive, to possession of a prison record or to their being coloured. The two overwhelmingly important characteristics are age and health, and this has serious implications since it suggests that an important element in residual unemployment is due to factors which cannot easily be remedied, and that in consequence a significant number of the unemployed cannot properly be regarded as an immediately usable labour reserve at all. There is, however, no reason for regarding this 60 per cent or so of the unemployed who are difficult employment prospects as 'unemployable'. A better approach is to regard them as a special group who need some form of help to allow them some hope of re-absorption in regular employment, and it is one of the main differences between the present and immediate post-war situation that it is possible to think of such a particularised policy, rather than the general measures which were previously paramount.

There can be no doubt that there is an important problem here. Over 40 per cent of the unemployed in October 1964 had been out of work for 26 weeks or more, and just under 20 per cent had not worked for two years or more. In an economy which has been almost continually short of labour, this represents a considerable loss of manpower. The difficulty lies in the fact that the broad trend of technological change in the present era is towards an expansion in the use of skilled, qualified and technical labour, and a reduction in requirements for the unskilled who constitute a high proportion of the chronically unemployed. More is said about these problems, and policies to deal with them, in Chapters 16, 17 and 18.

In summary, at high employment levels, the remaining unemployment is largely comprised of frictional (often voluntary) unemployment, and that arising from deficiencies in the labour supply for some kinds of work. As is perhaps to be expected, many of the unemployed in such circumstances comprise older, less skilled workers of low efficiency and many whose health is poor. Many of these people cannot be reasonably regarded as an immediately available labour reserve, and to some extent it has to be accepted that the residual unemployment in today's high employment economy is as much a social problem as one of economics.

There is one final point to be made. Unemployment in the foregoing discussion has meant the lack of a job. Yet it is quite possible for a worker who wants full-time work to have a job, yet still in some sense be less than fully employed. Short-time working is one example of this, but there are other cases of a less obvious kind. The organisation of work may sometimes be such that more men are employed than are technically necessary to achieve the required schedule or target for work. This is often referred to as 'under-employment', for the workers in such a situation will usually have some spare time within working hours which is not used productively.[1] A prime example of this in Britain is the craftsman's mate, who may be called upon only occasionally during the working day to carry out the limited tasks for which he is employed. Over the last few years there has been a debate about the extent of under-employment in Britain, where a range of work practices originally designed to protect jobs in periods of depression has persisted into the more recent full employment environment. It is of course difficult to get any quantitative measure of the effect of these practices, but it is probably not unfair to say that Britain has a degree of under-employment which, if it could be tapped (as it is now in part being tapped by some productivity bargains), could add substantially to production without an increase in the labour force. In a period when skilled labour is in short supply, this is a problem which clearly requires serious attention.

Again, there is the possibility that low unemployment and labour shortage may conceal a misuse of labour, as a result for example of employers retaining labour by paying high wages even though it is not at the time being fully utilised owing to a drop in orders, while other firms are unable to meet commitments because of shortages of this kind of labour. This practice of 'labour hoarding' (again leading to under-employment) is not necessarily a foolish policy on the part of firms, for it may be advantageous to them to maintain work-teams with specialist abilities. When business picks up again, the firms might find it impossible to replace such men, and by taking the long view the 'hoarding' firms cover themselves against this possibility. Nevertheless, this practice does represent an under-employment of valuable labour resources, deriving from causes quite different from the institutionally-based protective practices mentioned above.

Thus unemployment – or its absence – need not be the most accurate reflection of the efficiency with which an economy uses its manpower resources. Certainly the unemployment rate does not tell the full story: the quality and degree of employment are in their own ways as important as its quantity.

[1] This is sometimes referred to as 'over-employment' – the viewpoint here being that of the employer rather than the worker, with the implication that too many workers are being employed for a given job.

SUGGESTED READING

Lord Beveridge, *Full Employment in a Free Society*, 1944.
L. C. Hunter, 'Unemployment in a Full Employment Society', *Scottish Journal of Political Economy*, November 1963.
Stanley Lebergott (ed.), *Men Without Work*, Englewood Cliffs, N.J., 1964.
National Bureau of Economic Research Conference, *The Measurement and Behavior of Unemployment*, Princeton, 1957.

Part III

The Operation of the Labour Market

8 The Labour Market: A Preliminary View

I.

In Part II we have been mainly concerned with the description of the institutional background to the British labour market and with the recent history of changes in labour force size, structure and employment. The stage has now been reached, however, when we cannot properly go on to further investigation of some of the most interesting but more complex issues which arise in such a labour market, without first developing a better understanding of the underlying determinants of labour market operation and the behaviour of individuals and institutions engaging in labour market activities. In this part of the book, then, we must begin to build up an economic theory of the labour market which will allow us to take up some of the more complex practical issues raised in Part V. At times this may seem to be taking the discussion well away from the real world problems that interest us, but it should be remembered that a theory which is to be of general application, and not just an account of particular events and relationships, must be based on some degree of simplification. In the theoretical discussion which follows, and particularly in Chapters 9 and 10, the degree of abstraction, resulting from the use of fairly stringent and unrealistic assumptions, is high. But as the discussion proceeds, the severity of these assumptions can be relaxed and a much more realistic – if still simplified – theory can be evolved. After all, we need theory not so much for giving a realistic account of *how* decisions are taken and changes in circumstances are introduced, as for enabling us to predict with some accuracy the *outcome* of such decisions and changes.

In view of the progressive nature of the argument on which we are about to embark, it may be useful at the beginning to provide an outline sketch of the overall functioning of the labour market, primarily to give a sense of perspective to the later stage-by-stage build-up of the discussion. This is one of the main objectives of the present chapter; the others are to give a general introduction to the concept of labour as a factor of production and to make preliminary observations on the nature of the demand for, and supply of, labour. It is with these latter aims that we begin.

G

II. Labour as a Factor of Production

In discussing the way in which any market works we have to employ a mixture of economic, social and institutional arguments. We live in an organised society, the circumstances and pressures of which condition our purchasing and selling practices. Government, as the major institution in our society, formulates many of the rules under which the economic system operates, and many other institutions, such as trade associations and specialised buying and selling agencies, also bring an important influence to bear on the operation of markets. Again, though we often think of firms as the major economic agents in many markets, they are themselves institutions and their actions are greatly affected by their rules and methods of organisation. Thus social and institutional factors are of such immense importance in determining the terms on which commerce proceeds that purely economic hypotheses are seldom fully adequate in themselves. As a result, although the economist usually deals with markets, consumer and producer behaviour, etc., by assuming economic rationality, a realistic analysis has to make allowance for the intrusion of non-economic influences. Social and institutional factors cannot simply be assumed away.

In these respects, the labour market is like other markets, though the range of non-economic factors which play a part in labour market operations is probably much greater than in most commodity markets. Furthermore, since in this instance it is men's work that is being priced, the need to pay attention to social and institutional influences is all the greater. The 'commodity' being traded is the services of men and women who are active rather than passive agents in the market and who are not without views on how their services should be bought and utilised; and partly because of this, the roles played by Government, trade unions, and employers' associations are of critical importance. The further we progress towards reality in explaining how the labour market works, the more we have to consider these social and institutional factors.

First, however, it is worth while giving some consideration to the implications of the differences between labour and physical capital. After all, it is possible to regard labour as a productive factor which is similar to physical capital in that it can be made more productive by means of investment in education and training. Just as new units of physical capital can be brought into use and old ones replaced, so do people enter the labour force and withdraw again at subsequent stages. Precisely what, then, is the real cause of difference between labour and physical capital, and what does this mean for the analysis of the conditions under which it is supplied and demanded?

Perhaps the most critical characteristics of labour is that, as Marshall expressed it, 'The worker sells his work, but he himself remains his own property'.[1] In other words, the worker is himself the embodiment of property or capital, but (except in a slave society, where human beings would be bought and sold no differently from other goods) the services of the capital are only made temporarily available to an employer, with no transfer of the capital itself. This has a number of immediate and important implications. It might seem initially that since only services are bought and sold, there might be less incentive for one person to 'invest' in another, say by paying for his training, than is the case with physical capital, since in the case of labour the ownership of the capital remains with the trainee and not with the employer or whoever else might make the investment. It is fairly common, for example, for a worker to change employers shortly after completion of training so that, from the point of view of the original employer at least, a loss is involved since he has incurred the costs of training but does not receive the benefit of output from the worker he has trained. One might therefore expect to find that societies are under-invested in human, relative to physical, capital, for the latter does remain in the possession of the investor as long as he wishes to keep it. On the other hand, most investment in education is financed from the public purse rather than by firms, and the society as a whole is less likely to lose the return to its investment than an individual firm. From another angle, the motives operating to determine the relative investments in human and physical capital may be distorted towards human capital. Rather than invest in physical capital, which might carry a higher rate of return, parents may spend more on the education of their children than their ability warrants, or the individual may over-invest in his own training: economic motives alone do not govern such personal decisions. Thus there are two possible sets of opposing forces in the case of human capital which are less likely with physical capital, perhaps giving rise to over- or under-investment between one person and another, or between human and non-human capital.[2]

[1] Alfred Marshall, *Principles of Economics*, 8th ed., 1952, p. 466.
[2] There is clearly also scope for misallocation of investment resources among different categories of education and training. It is one of the main questions of debate in discussions of economic growth and development, as to the 'right' amount of university education relative to technical or trade training, etc.

The second characteristic of labour is that 'when a person sells his services, he has to present them where they are delivered'.[1] A person selling a building or a piece of productive plant will not normally care how it is to be used, or in what environment. After the sale, he is separated from it. But a person selling his own labour services will engage to supply it in a given environment and so will be influenced in his decision by the physical surroundings and the relationships with those for whom or with whom he is working. As we shall see, in Chapter 11, this has important consequences for the rates of payment in different places of work and different jobs, since these rates generally have to compensate in some way for the good and bad features of specific employments.

These are the two main characteristics which distinguish labour from other forms of capital. In fact, Marshall went on to discuss three other properties which could be regarded as peculiar to labour:

(i) labour is perishable and so cannot be stored up from one day to another;

(ii) sellers, therefore, are often at a disadvantage in bargaining; and

(iii) a great deal of time is usually required to provide additional supplies of specialised ability.

But, as Marshall recognised, the difference in these latter cases is one of degree only, since there are examples of physical capital which possess very similar characteristics. The services of a factory building or a bridge can no more be stored up than labour. In some cases the perishability factor may put labour at a disadvantage, but equally it may prove an advantage when the employer's need for labour is urgent and immediate and the impossibility of resorting to the use of stored-up labour leaves the employer at a disadvantage in bargaining. Finally, any kind of specialised product, not just labour, may take a considerable time to increase in supply. However, although the first two points are the crucial ones, the others are relevant to an understanding of the conditions of labour supply and wage determination.

III. Labour Demand and Supply in General

One of the central problems of labour market theory is the pricing of labour services. In common with the pricing of other goods and services, the pricing of labour services is determined jointly by demand and supply,

[1] Marshall, op. cit., p. 471.

but largely because of the special character of labour as a productive factor the theories of labour supply and of the demand for labour raise some special considerations. These will be examined in more detail in the appropriate chapters below, but some of the groundwork may conveniently be undertaken now.

First, the supply of labour services incorporates a number of separate elements. One of these elements is the supply of workers themselves, the actual number of persons who are available for paid employment during a certain period. But this tells us only a part of what we want to know about labour supply. For the hours of labour made available on the market may differ considerably from worker to worker. Again, the output produced in these labour hours may vary from time to time, either because the skill composition of the labour force has changed (and the output of a more highly skilled labour force will usually be higher or better in quality than that of less skilled workers) or because of differences in the input of effort per hour of work. Thus the 'real labour content' of, say, one hundred hours of labour, as valued by the employer, will probably differ considerably over time and also between countries. A further problem is that not only are workers themselves not homogeneous, but even units of labour input by the same worker may differ from day to day or year to year, and may be subject to variation as work and wage payment conditions change.

This complexity of labour supply carries with it the implication that the worker has to make a number of conceptually separate decisions (though in practice they may be closely related) about his supply of labour. These decisions in turn, and the factors which determine them, have an influence on different problems within the theory of labour supply and the theory of the labour market more generally. In the short run, when the size and age structure of the total population is given, the problem is to determine what proportion of the population will engage in labour market activity, how many hours of labour they will supply, and what the skill and effort content of these hours will be. From the point of view of the firm, which is after all the principal source of demand for labour, the problem is to know under what conditions the requisite amount and 'skill-mix' of labour will be supplied, and how changes in economic conditions will affect supply. In the longer run, the problem is again different: is the growth and decline of population itself dependent on economic factors and, if so, what particular factors will affect it and what will be the outcome for the future supply of workers? Given this range of questions, it is not altogether surprising to find that there is no simple unified theory of labour supply, but rather a number of separate strands of theory, each of which bears on a particular problem.

Secondly, there is the nature of the demand for labour services. Some kinds of labour differ very little from consumption goods. If we think of the work of some professional men such as lawyers or chiropodists or piano-tuners, who use very little in the way of capital equipment, we can readily argue that their services are bought directly and for their own sake by the consumer in much the same way as ordinary goods. In such cases we want the labour for the 'utility' of the services themselves; at different prices we will usually be prepared to buy differing amounts. Then by bringing together the demand schedule and the supply schedule, which indicates how much will be supplied at different prices, we obtain a solution for the amount bought and sold, and the transaction price.

However, this kind of case, where more or less 'pure' labour services are being bought and sold, is the exception rather than the rule in the labour market transactions of a modern industrial society. Most of us work for an employer, and we have to regard the firm as the *locus* of most decisions about the demand for labour. This gives rise to a number of important consequences which, though they somewhat complicate the analysis, do not really involve a major change in the approach to the pricing problem. In the first place, firms will buy labour services not for the direct utility of such services to them but because of the contribution they are expected to make to the output, the sales revenue, and ultimately the profits of the firm. The firm's demand for labour, then, is not simply a function of the physical productivity of labour – the contribution it makes to physical output – but must also be influenced by the marketability and price of the total output available for sale. In effect, the value put on labour services by the employer is derived from the value of the output of these services in the product market, and for this reason the firm's demand for labour is often said to be *derived* demand.

Though the matter will have to be gone into much more fully in Chapter 10, we can suggest, even now, that a firm which is aiming to maximise its profits will hire additional units of labour so long as the costs of so doing are no greater than the addition to total revenue resulting from the sale of the higher level of output achieved. But while this provides us with a means of determining the firm's equilibrium employment, it does not in itself tell us how wages are determined; and wages are obviously the critical element in the cost to the firm of hiring extra labour. In fact, the productivity approach to the firm's demand for labour can be developed to give a solution to the wage determination problem, but at this point another question may be raised. Although the firm is the *locus* of employment decisions, we know that in most industrial economies the determination of wages for a great part of the labour force is the result of collective bargaining, in which negotiations on behalf of individual firms and workers are frequently conducted by employers' associations and trade unions. One of the possible implications of this is that the determination of wages might be regarded not so much as the outcome of economic forces but rather as the result of a bargaining process. As such, wage determination could be regarded at least as a part of political as well as of economic theory. This is one of the problems which will have to be tackled as we proceed, although in the earlier stages of the argument the role of the bargaining process will be excluded from consideration.

A further problem relates to the demand for labour in the economy as a whole. So long as we are dealing with the individual firm, we can with some justification ignore the external effects of changes in its demand for labour, but this is no longer possible when we move to a more aggregative level of analysis. If, for example, wages are cut in a small firm, the workers whose wages are reduced are likely to spend less and perhaps change their pattern of expenditure. But the effects of this on the total level and structure of effective demand (and hence on the total demand for labour) can safely be ignored. With a *general* wage cut, on the other hand, the effects on aggregate demand and ultimately on total employment levels cannot be ignored. In formal terms we can no longer conduct the analysis through partial equilibrium analysis, where only a small sector of the economy is examined and effects external to the firm can be left out of account. We must turn then to a general equilibrium model, with all the complications that entails.

Even in this preliminary look at labour supply and demand, it is obvious that there are many complex problems to be met with in labour market theory, and the need for a progressive build-up of a theoretical framework from simplified situations is more clearly seen. In the next section, however, it is possible to set some of these problems in a rather provisional and interim perspective of labour market theory as a whole.

IV. Allocation Problems and Labour Markets

The primary function of any market is to secure an efficient allocation of the goods which are exchanged within it. In a dynamic economy the demand for goods, and hence for the resources which help to produce them, is subject to a process of continuing change, and the efficiency of the market system can be assessed in terms of its ability to effect changes in allocation in the right direction and in the right proportion in a short period of time. In a market system the means of this allocation is the price mechanism, by which changes in demand are reflected in price changes and a consequent alteration in the allocation pattern. Depending on the circumstances of the market in question, and especially on the time period necessary for supply to adapt to the new conditions, the test of allocative efficiency will be the ability of the system quickly to remove imbalance in the market as reflected in shortages or surpluses of the goods in question.

Like other markets, the market for labour serves this kind of allocative function, and in fact we can identify two types of allocation. The first is the allocation of labour, relative to other factors of production, in such a way that full employment of each factor is achieved and pressures of excess demand are avoided. We might imagine, for example, a situation in which labour was over-priced in relation to capital and that as a result producers adopted more capital-intensive methods of production to save on the expensive labour factor. The result would be some unemployment or under-utilisation of labour, and the function of the labour market would be to eliminate this and to restore equilibrium. This first problem, then, is one of *inter-factor* allocation, and theory should be able to provide a means of analysing the process by which equilibrium will be regained. The second aspect arises because of the different kinds of labour that are to be found in the labour market. If we introduce change into a market system which is initially in equilibrium (where demand and supply of each type of labour are in balance at existing wages), a new allocation of labour will be required to restore equilibrium. By some means, labour will have to be transferred from sectors with an excess supply of labour to other sectors where there is an excess demand. This is the problem of *intra-factor* allocation.

Obviously, the efficiency of allocation in both these cases is of great importance to the smooth functioning of the economy and to the improvement of income and welfare on the part of the working population. Quite apart from the intrinsic value of having a satisfactory theory of the labour market, the question whether the market system can be left to bring about the necessary adjustments, or whether outside intervention is required, is one which has important policy implications. On this there are two opposing views, based on different conceptions of the operation of the labour market.

The first, which we will refer to as the competitive theory or hypothesis, presents the view that market forces, by acting on the price of labour, will automatically bring about the necessary adjustments in demand and supply. It then predicts that a competitive labour market will be capable both of regulating the price of labour *as a whole*, relative to other productive factors, so that the factor markets will be cleared and no excess demand or excess supply will persist; and of regulating the prices of *different* kinds of labour so that the market for each type of labour will be cleared and no shortage or surplus will remain. Thus the theory allows for differences in wages for different types and amounts of work, but asserts that in equilibrium the differentials in wages – the wage structure – will be such that they reflect the conditions under which labour is demanded and supplied. These differentials will thus reflect the difficulties and costs of training for different kinds of work and the difficulties and costs of moving between different types of work or different parts of the country. In equilibrium, the relationship between wages in different employments will take account of these costs so that there will be no incentive for individuals to transfer from one employment to another. When demand or supply in any sector of the market changes, the wage relationships will change, and labour will respond to the new wage structure until demand and supply are again equalised throughout the system. This process will not always be instantaneous for, as we have seen above in discussing the characteristics of labour as a productive factor, some kinds of labour take a long time to produce, owing to the length of the training process. In the longer run, however, the system will be able to readjust to a new position of equilibrium. The mechanism by which this adjustment occurs is that of a freely competitive market. Changes in demand and supply are quickly reflected in changing prices. It is assumed that firms set out to maximise profits, that labour is economically motivated (in the sense that it will move from lower-paid to higher-paid jobs as opportunities occur) and that there is no imperfection of market knowledge. Changes in wages then act as signals to employers and workers, encouraging them to change the direction of their demand or supply, until equilibrium is restored. The mechanism therefore operates through the assumed responsiveness of supply and demand to changes in the price of labour relative to other factors or to changes in the relative prices of different kinds of labour. And wages in turn are regarded as being responsive to changes in labour demand and supply. Obviously, both supply and demand will be more complex the more we introduce occupational and other distinctions between workers and jobs, but the general principles are much the same as outlined here.

G 2

Two qualifications to this central theoretical framework are usually made. First, the mere fact of *differences* in the wages paid for similar amounts and kinds of work need not give rise to movement from the lower-paid to the higher-paid employment.[1] It is recognised that some differences in wages will have to exist in equilibrium, to compensate for, or to neutralise, disadvantages or advantages attaching to certain kinds of work. For example, if an occupation possesses generally unattractive working conditions, few people may be prepared to offer their services in this occupation unless they are in some way compensated by a higher wage. Conversely, so many people may be willing to work in a pleasant occupation that a relatively low wage will be enough to secure an adequate supply. We will see later what kind of conditions are likely to affect choice in this way, but for the moment the main point is that even in equilibrium similar types of work may offer different wages as a result of the differing non-wage conditions of employment.

The second qualification refers to the degree of competitive freedom. It has long been recognised that the class structure of society is reflected in the labour market and that entry to some jobs is limited to people who belong to a certain social class. The result is an imperfection in the competitive system and in labour mobility, leading to enduring wage differences which are in no way to be explained either by differences in the type of work or in the non-wage conditions of work. The theory would also recognise that certain kinds of natural talent cannot be systematically produced by training, and in such cases the scarcity of such a resource may lead to relatively high levels of payment.

Apart from these qualifications, the competitive theory predicts that the market will set relative wages in such a way that similar types of work carry equal rates of pay; that different types of work will afford wages which differ just enough to bring forth the necessary amounts of labour of each type; and that when changes in demand or supply occur they will give rise to changes in wages and thereby induce sufficient labour mobility to restore equilibrium. This theory has been attacked on a number of counts, mainly deriving from empirical observations of behaviour in the labour market. For example, it has been argued that, in the short run at least, wages are determined not by market forces but by institutional factors through collective bargaining. A number of studies have shown that labour often appears to be unresponsive to changes in wage differentials, that workers have highly imperfect job information and in any case often

---

[1] These difficulties are of course distinct from those which are due to differences in the amounts and kinds of work.

take jobs for reasons quite unrelated to wages. Other criticisms related to the demand side, and particularly to the validity of the 'productivity' approach sketched in above.

In other words, both the assumptions of the competitive theory and its analysis of the processes of wage-determination and adjustment were challenged from an empirical standpoint which stressed the importance of institutional and social influences in the labour market. This line of criticism provides the basis for the second main approach to labour market analysis, which might be described as the socio-institutional hypothesis, although in fact no proper alternative theory has been developed from this starting point.[1] All that can be said is that alternative social and institutional explanations of particular parts of the labour market process do exist. But if there has been no counter-theory, the value of such criticism has been great, since it has led to a much better recognition of the complexities involved in labour market analysis, and amendments and additions have been made to the basic competitive theory to take at least some of these complexities into account.

Having now introduced the nature of the allocative problem in the labour market, and having sketched in two possible approaches to the analysis of labour market operations, a little more can now be said about labour markets in general. We have so far talked mainly in terms of *the* labour market, but it will already be clear that this must be an abstraction. While we will often refer to a country's labour market, we usually recognise that we are dealing with a complex of labour markets which will take on a different shape and structure depending on the standpoint adopted. For example, our interest may be in the problems of an occupation, in which case we will be concerned with the nature of an occupational labour market, such as that for school-teachers, or nurses, or engineers. Or we may be dealing with regional or area problems, in which case our interest will be in the geographical dimension of labour markets. What then constitutes a labour market, and in what ways do different kinds of market resemble or differ from one another?

One of the functions of a labour market, just like any other market, is to bring into contact buyers and sellers, and to do so it must be capable of providing information to interested parties – in this case to employers in search of labour and workers contemplating a change of job or otherwise seeking employment. The information here is about the availability of workers and their characteristics, and about vacant jobs and their conditions

---

[1] For a good example of this sort of critical approach, see Barbara Wootton, *The Social Foundations of Wage Policy*, 1954.

of employment. Where there is no information the market cannot operate, and so the extent of the market is defined by its coverage of the interested parties, and the efficiency of its operation within these limits will vary with its ability to achieve a good coverage of both the demand and the supply side.

From casual observation, we know that employers recruit most of their labour from localities near to their factory or office, and usually within daily travelling distance. In order to recruit this labour, employers will use many sources, but since they are primarily interested in the working population nearby they will concentrate on those channels of information which cover the immediately surrounding area. Thus they will advertise in local newspapers, they may consult with other local employers and they will make use of the facilities afforded by their local employment exchange. The form of these will depend on the particular institutional arrangements of the economy, but most developed countries now have a widespread network of public employment agencies operated by State or local government. In addition firms may use more informal channels, such as the local knowledge of some of their existing employees. Job-seekers, for their part, will again be mainly interested in locally available employment, and will tend to use the same channels, consulting their local employment service, examining the 'jobs vacant' columns of the local press, perhaps contacting previous employers and seeking information from their relations and friends. This suggests that there is, in most communities, a well-developed set of communications which provide the basis for a local labour market in which the bulk of workers in the area, and all employers for the major part of their labour force, will be actively concerned. And indeed most labour economists place a great deal of emphasis on the role of the local labour market.

It would be wrong, however, to try to link the local labour market too closely with the boundaries of an individual community. In a large city, for example, there may be a number of component local market areas which merge into each other and provide a mutual balance of employment. Or outlying communities may depend upon a concentration of employment opportunities in a central location, and so form part of a single labour market area. Again, we cannot define the boundaries of the market too rigidly in geographical terms, for changes in economic conditions may alter the area over which employers seek labour and workers seek employment. Nevertheless, as a working rule, it is usually possible to identify local labour markets by reference to daily travel to work patterns to and from centres of employment.

From another point of view, however, we must recognise that there are many workers who will not confine their search for work to the relatively limited area of the local market. The more specialised a worker is, the more is his concern to find employment which makes use of that specialism, and the alternative opportunities within any local market may be very restricted. His interest is then in the available employment openings *within his occupation* rather than within the local area, and again there are usually facilities to provide this kind of specialised information which will bring buyers and sellers of this specialist labour into contact. This may be done through the daily or Sunday newspapers, technical or professional journals, trade union or professional organisations or, less formally, through personal contacts within the occupation. These same sources will be used by employers who do not wish to confine their recruitment for key positions to locally available labour but who wish to draw on the wider sources to get a better range of selection. In such cases, the relevant labour market may be national or even international in coverage, though limited to one special stratum, the occupation in question. This will be most highly developed, of course, at the higher levels of specialisation, such as high-level management, administrators, and professional grades of worker such as doctors and engineers. But within regions and even in the larger towns and conurbations the geographical structure of the labour markets will be stratified occupationally, and in some cases these will have their own methods of disseminating information.

We have now been able to identify conceptually two different types of labour market, the local market and the occupational market. It might seem that we need to go on to define a third variety, the industrial labour market, dealing with the industry dimension of the hiring and sale of labour services related to particular industries. But while there is a little justification for this, its importance is slight in relation to the two already mentioned. On the positive side, it is true that some industries employ workers who are highly specific to the industry in question. But in the modern industrial economy these are relatively few, and the more common case is that of the industry which uses various types of labour which are also employed in a wide range of other industries. In short, it is the occupational rather than the industrial attachment which is important to most of the more specialised and highly skilled workers, and therefore the occupational aspects of job information are normally the most important. We should not, however, rule out the industrial dimension of the labour market, for it is important in some instances.

There is much more to be said in the course of this book on all the problems and concepts that have been introduced here. But we must now bring the introductory points to a close and turn to the development of the theory of labour market activity. As indicated at the start of this chapter, we must begin at a relatively simple level and build up towards a more realistic analytical framework. We begin this in Chapter 9 with a further discussion of the supply of labour. Chapter 10 takes up the theory of the demand for labour and, in conjunction with the supply analysis of the previous chapter, allows us to draw some preliminary conclusions about the determination of employment and wages. In Chapter 11 it is possible to remove some of the restrictive assumptions on which the earlier theory is based, and the analysis of wage structure and labour mobility can be further developed. Finally, in Chapter 12, the effects of collective bargaining on the processes of wage and employment determination can be introduced, at which point we will be much better equipped with a fairly realistic framework of analysis against which we can examine some of the more complex and practical problems in the final parts of the book.

SUGGESTED READING

Since Chapters 8 to 12 are all closely related, a consolidated list of reading has been provided at the end of Chapter 12.

9 The Supply of Labour

I. The Total Supply of Labour

The last chapter has already commented upon the various component elements of labour supply – the number of workers seeking paid employment, the number of hours each worker supplies per period of time, the effort and skill content of these hours. In fact there is relatively little that we can say at this stage about the effort and skill components, and attention is mainly confined here to the first two aspects, relating to the labour force participation decisions of the population and the factors which determine the hours of work they are willing to provide. These are the problems which are taken up in the first half of the chapter. Attention is then turned to the supply of labour to the individual firm, and this section of the analysis constitutes part of the foundation for the theory of wage and employment determination presented in Chapter 10. Finally, we look at the longer-run relationship between population and labour force growth.

(1) THE SUPPLY OF WORKERS

The total supply of workers from a given population obviously depends on the individual decisions of all those who are eligible to seek employment. Something has already been seen of the kind of factors that operate to determine the size of the labour force: age, marital status, family and domestic commitments, income and employment opportunity and so on. We must now go beyond the simple descriptive account to provide an analysis of the underlying mechanism. In other words, we must try to formulate a theory of the supply of workers in general, which will be capable of explaining such features as the growing importance of married women in the labour force, and the variations in activity rates between regions with different economic conditions. This involves a discussion of the general supply curve of workers, as opposed to the supply curve in respect of an occupation or a particular firm. That we can to a large extent deal satisfactorily with each of these almost (though not quite) independently of one another, is an indication that the factors determining supply in each case are rather different.

The worker in employment has already made a number of separate decisions. He has made a decision to work for pay or gain rather than remain out of the labour force altogether. He has made a decision between self-employment and being employed by others. He has made a decision to take a particular job rather than remain unemployed. He has made a choice of occupation – though in some cases this may be rather negative since the range of opportunities may be very limited. And he has elected to work for one employer out of a number who might have employed him. Ultimately there must be some interdependence between such decisions. For example, the acceptance of a particular employer's terms will normally be related to the worker's choice of occupation and his opportunities for employment therein. But for the moment we can proceed as though the decisions were really quite independent, an assumption which is perhaps most realistic in the distinction between the decision to enter the labour force and the others.

For many workers there is no real choice whether or not they will enter the labour force. Most of us must assume that we will become or will remain members of the labour force, and the only question is about the dates of entry and exit. The great majority of men, once they have entered the labour force, are more or less permanently attached to it until they approach the conventional retirement age, at which time some element of choice may again reappear. This is true of many single women, but not for certain other groups in the population.

Full-time students take vacation jobs. Wives and mothers may not be prepared to work on a regular basis but may yet be willing to take irregular or casual jobs when they are available, or jobs which, though regular, are regarded by them as in some way transitory; the same is true of many people above normal retirement age. This distinction, based on the degree of attachment of workers to the labour force, has been recognised and formalised in the classification of the labour force into *primary* and *secondary* groups. The primary labour force comprises principally the main bread-winners of the family, those whose labour force attachment is not likely to change (within normal working-age limits after full entry to the labour force has been made) either because of changes in family circumstances or in external economic conditions. On the other hand:

'the secondary labour force draws upon the following groups for its membership: those women whose labour force attachment changes in response to changes in one or more of several factors such as marital status, home responsibilities, family income, and types of job openings available; a relatively small number of men who are neither young nor old but who do not wish to work continuously and can get away with it; those young men and women who move into and out of the labour force while completing their education; and those handicapped and older persons who are employable but seek or hold only temporary employment'.[1]

Both for empirical and analytical purposes, this is an important distinction in relation to labour force participation decisions and hence for the analysis of changes in labour force activity by a given population. It provides a basis for differentiating between a 'permanent' and a 'transitory' element in the labour force and opens up the possibility that the two groups may be differently motivated in relation to their labour force participation. It also suggests that it may be useful to consider the family, rather than the individual in isolation, as the decision-making unit with respect to participation decisions, since it is evident that there is likely to be some interdependence between the supply of primary and secondary labour.

In the first place, most families probably have at least one, and often more, members capable of supplying labour in the market place. Again, for most families, the supply of labour services is the main source of family income on which joint plans for consumption and saving have to be based. This does not of course mean that each decision to purchase a good or service has to be jointly agreed, but simply that there should be an acceptable balance between income and expenditure plans for the family unit rather than for each individual in isolation. The economic theory of consumption behaviour now generally recognises the family or household as the decision-taking unit, and since consumption must be closely related to income expectations it is plausible to argue that income plans and hence labour supply decisions will be similarly based. Again, this does not mean that the decision to work in a particular occupation or for a particular employer will be jointly agreed, but rather that the decision whether or not individual family members will participate in labour market activity will be made in the context of the family and in the light of all its income and consumption plans and requirements.

[1] R. C. Wilcock, 'The Secondary Labor Force and the Measurement of Unemployment', p. 172, in *The Measurement and Behavior of Unemployment* (A Conference of the Universities – National Bureau Committee for Economic Research), Princeton, 1957.

Secondly, the decision to participate in labour market activity is really one to supply for sale in the labour market specified portions of time to be used in the production of goods and services. Such a decision cannot be taken independently of competing demands on the time of the potential worker. Time, after all, is not a free good, since time spent in one activity might have been allotted to other uses and thus it has an opportunity cost. Generally, the use of time which has the prospect of producing the greatest benefit will be chosen. Most approaches to the theory of labour supply have postulated a two-way division of time, into labour and leisure, which together provide an exhaustive use of time available to the individual; but perhaps a more useful distinction is that between time which is 'currently paid for' (the normal case of market employment) and time which is not so paid. The latter includes leisure as we normally regard it, but also time spent in education and the ordinary household services, such as cooking, cleaning, etc., performed by family members in the home.[1] When time is spent on such activities for which there is no monetary return, at least for the present, the opportunity cost is the money value of the wages which would have accrued had the time been made available in the market. In some cases this cost may be very low. Young children perform certain household duties, but since they could not be in paid employment anyway, the cost to the family (if not to the child) is nil. If there is no current demand in the market for the services which might have been provided, the cost of leisure or other time is again negligible. On the other hand, for the full-time housewife who could obtain paid employment as a secretary, school-teacher or factory worker, the opportunity cost of remaining a housewife could be considerable.

That many wives who could readily obtain paid employment do remain in the home on a full-time basis, and that young people forgo current earning opportunities to obtain better educational qualifications, is an indication of the higher values they set on the unpaid activities. The housewife probably regards it as more worth while that the household should be well run and children properly cared for than that a few pounds should be added to the weekly family income. The young person in full-time education probably expects to reap the benefits of giving up current earnings opportunities by obtaining higher earnings and better prospects

---

[1] Such services may make an important contribution to the market performance of labour force members and to the consumption of leisure. Some basic household services are relevant to the efficiency of labour, and the quality of such services may influence the preferences of family members for paid work, leisure, 'do-it-yourself' tasks and so on.

when he actually does enter the labour force. In these cases the current value of their services in the labour market will be known fairly accurately, but is obviously insufficient to outweigh the value implicitly imputed to the benefits of withholding supply and performing other non-market functions.

In short, the decision to supply labour is taken within the context of the family and with regard to the desired balance between income from employment and other objectives, such as consumption (including leisure activities), education or training, and the care of children and other domestic activities and responsibilities. This balance may, however, be subject to change for a variety of reasons, ranging from alterations in family circumstances or changes in family consumption or savings objectives to changes in income opportunity. How the family will react to any such change will depend on its own individual circumstances: for example, if a member of the family becomes unemployed, the response will depend on the importance of his or her contribution to family income, the flexibility of the family's expenditure pattern, the availability of additional earnings opportunities to other members at work or able to work, and so on. More generally, it is not possible to say *a priori* how the total supply of workers will change with alterations in economic conditions, such as a recession, though we can of course formulate hypotheses and test them against actual experience, as in the following illustrations.

Suppose the general level of economic activity falls off, and that many of the main family earners become unemployed. In these cases family income will fall fairly drastically, and even where the main earners do not become unemployed their earnings may be cut back through short-time working where previously they might have included substantial overtime payments. To meet this new situation, either family consumption plans may have to be revised downwards for the time being or income will have to be supplemented in some way. Attempts to supplement income may involve the wife entering the labour force in search of work (or if she is already employed, being prepared to work longer hours – though this really raises a new question about a change in the supply of hours of work rather than a change in participation).[1] Another possibility – which undoubtedly became reality both in this country and in North America in the depression conditions of the 1930s – is that young people will give up courses of education and training to enter the labour force on a full-time basis in order to boost family income. This line of argument gives rise to the 'additional worker' hypothesis, that a fall in the demand for labour will induce an inflow of

[1] Cf. below, subsection (2).

secondary workers into the labour force, responding to a fall in family income.

Conversely, however, it may be argued that the secondary workers already in employment will be among the earliest to be hit by recession. Then, since the drop in family income in these cases will usually be less severe than when the primary earner becomes unemployed, and since secondary earnings will often be for the luxuries and 'pin-money' in any case, the unemployed secondary workers will often simply withdraw from the labour force until business conditions pick up again. This hypothesis would suggest that a fall in the demand for labour will be met by a fall in participation rates due to the withdrawal of secondary labour.

In fact, both hypotheses may be supported by the evidence at one and the same time: some secondary workers may withdraw from the labour force and others enter as labour demand falls, and the outcome in any particular instance will depend on the relative weights of the two flows. The available evidence suggests that both these flows do exist, and that their relative weights vary from time to time and from country to country.[1] This in turn would seem to give support to the earlier analysis of participation as a decision taken in the family context and relating to income and consumption. It suggests also that one of the main variable factors in labour supply is the participation of secondary workers, and that their labour supply may be complementary to that of the primary earner.

It is worth mentioning at this point that the analysis of this section is also relevant to the trend, noted earlier in Chapter 6, towards increasing activity rates among married women. On the demand side, labour shortages have opened up employment opportunity for many married women and in many areas have raised their wage levels, so that the opportunity cost of their remaining outside the labour force has risen.[2] At the same time, there have been improvements in household 'technology' making available 'blocks' of time suitable for employment in the labour market. The addi-

---

[1] For a discussion of these hypotheses and some empirical results see, for example: C. D. Long, *The Labour Force under Changing Income and Employment*, 1958; T. F. Dernburg and K. T. Strand, 'Hidden Unemployment, 1953–62', *American Economic Review*, March 1966; also, by the same authors, 'Cyclical Variation in Civilian Labor Force Participation', *Review of Economics and Statistics*, November 1964; and for Great Britain, L. C. Hunter, 'Cyclical Variations in the Labour Supply', *Oxford Economic Papers*, July 1963.

[2] The recent Social Survey Report on women's employment found that the biggest single attraction for married women going out to work was financial, but less material motives were also important, e.g. a desire for company and a wish to escape from boredom. Cf. *A Survey of Women's Employment*, op. cit.

tional earnings accruing from this employment have certainly contributed to rising living standards and may have facilitated the trend towards increased numbers in full-time education, since the family able to supplement its income in this way will be able more easily to forgo the current earning potential of its younger adult members.

This discussion takes us some part of the way towards an understanding of the total supply of labour. But if we wish to know how changes in wages, or in employment conditions, are likely to affect the total supply of labour hours, we cannot do this solely on the basis of a theory of participation. We must, therefore, turn at this stage to the problem of the individual's supply of work once the participation decision has been taken.

(2) THE SUPPLY OF LABOUR HOURS

The problem of the supply of labour hours is again one which bears on the allocation of time among competing uses, so we can again make use of the distinction between time currently paid for and time that is not so paid for. In some circumstances, the individual may be free to work for pay exactly as long as he likes; this will be true of the self-employed person, for example, who can vary his hours of work more or less to the minute. In that case we might expect to find that the allocation of time to different uses would bear some relationship to the rate of remuneration he expected to receive.

It could be argued, firstly, that as the expected hourly rate of remuneration rose, it would become increasingly expensive for the individual to take time off work. The cost, in terms of earnings opportunities forgone, of leisure and other unpaid activities would rise. On this view, we would expect to find that this person had a 'normal' supply curve of labour, with the number of hours of labour supplied per period of time rising as hourly rates of remuneration increased. His supply curve of labour hours would be positively sloped (rising from left to right), and he would be substituting hours of work for hours of leisure as the rate of pay increased. This is what economists call a *positive substitution effect*.

But we could argue from a different point of view that the higher the hourly rate of remuneration, the greater will be the total earnings (income) from a given number of hours of work. Then since an individual with a higher income than before is likely to spend more on consumption, and since many consumption activities are intensive in their use of time – especially those relating to leisure – the individual may be tempted to forgo some part of the potential gain in income by working less than before and reallocating some time to leisure and other unpaid activities. This view would imply that a rise in the rate of payment would cause the person to trade off some income, in the form of hours of work, against leisure and other activities. In other words, the supply curve of labour hours would be negatively sloped (rising from right to left). This substitution of unpaid time for paid time as income rises is described by economists as a *negative income effect*.

These two views give us contradictory hypotheses about the supply of labour hours under changing pay conditions and suggest quite different supply curves of labour hours. We cannot tell, *a priori*, which is the more correct description of behaviour. We must therefore try to observe what happens in practice, and most observations suggest that at low rates of payment the substitution effect will be dominant, so that the supply curve is upward-sloping from left to right. At low income levels associated with low pay rates, any rise in the rates will have an incentive effect so that the worker is prepared to work longer, or, perhaps, at levels of income at or near subsistence an 'improvement' effect, enabling the worker to afford a better diet and thus making him physically capable of longer working hours. However, at still higher levels of income, the negative income effect becomes increasingly important, and ultimately, it is believed, will overcome the substitution effect, making the labour-hours supply curve 'bend backwards'. This is depicted in Fig. 9.1, where the SAS' shows how the

Fig. 9.1

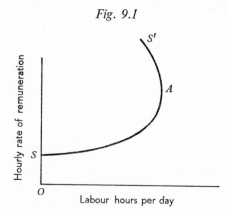

individual's supply of hours per day will vary as hourly rates alter. Below the rate of pay OS, no labour at all will be provided, either because the wage is below subsistence level or because rates less than OS would not be adequate to repay him for the trouble of working.[1] At rates immediately above OS the supply of hours will be fairly elastic, but gradually the effects of rising income and increasing possibility of being able to devote more time to other pursuits makes the curve more inelastic, until at point A the income and substitution effects cancel each other out. At still higher rates of pay, the income effect prevails and the supply of hours begins to decline, though total income may still be increasing.

So far, we have been discussing only the case of the person who can vary his supply of labour hours at will within a given period. But in most societies such persons are a small minority. Most people have fixed hours of work; their time is required by their employers in regular spells which allow the employer to organise flows of work in a reasonable fashion. The employer may, however, sometimes wish to obtain more work from his existing labour force and introduce overtime. For most manual workers overtime is paid at rates in excess of those for 'normal' hours. This premium rate could be interpreted as a sign of recognition by employers that additional hours of work will be supplied to them only at an enhanced rate (though it would probably be going too far to suggest that the historical development of premium overtime rates was due to an economic analysis of this kind).[2] Others, including many salaried workers, do not have such regular hours, though their employers will often expect some norm of attendance. Earnings in such cases are seldom related to hours of work, and it is commonly a part of the conditions of employment that when extra hours of work are required they will not be separately paid for, or not paid at premium rates.

However, the two facts – that workers cannot always vary their hours of work, and that there is sometimes no recognised or fixed hourly rate of pay – do not substantially alter the previous conclusions, though they do complicate the analysis. For example, the persistent problem of absenteeism in some industries (coalmining is a usual example in this country, but there

---

[1] A common situation in some countries with comprehensive social welfare schemes is that the unemployed worker will be guaranteed a certain minimum weekly income, the size of which will depend upon family circumstances. If he takes work, he will lose some or all of this benefit, and in the case of low-skilled, low-paid workers the change from unemployment to employment may mean that he is providing 40 hours for a *net* gain in weekly income of £2 or £3, which makes the real hourly rate of pay very low indeed. This wage-floor thus helps to set a minimum wage rate below which labour may feel it is not worth taking employment.

[2] Premium rates can also be viewed as a means of discouraging employers from asking workers to turn out for work at unreasonable times.

are many others) may be partially explained in terms of the predominance of the income effect: at existing hourly wage rates and earnings, the worker has enough income to secure his main consumption objectives and so, by occasionally absenting himself from a day's work, he adjusts his allocation of time between work and other activities. Again, the existence of a 'standard' working week need not mean that workers have to keep to it. Some may take a second job, while others may not have enough time to work the standard week and work only on a part-time basis. Those who want to earn more than is possible on the standard week and normal hourly rates will usually seek work in firms who are known to offer regular overtime, while those who are satisfied by the normal weekly pay will mainly take on jobs which do not normally require overtime.

Thus, in general, individuals may be able to change their jobs in such a way that they can adjust their allocation of time to labour and other uses according to changes in the wage-rate situation and in their personal preferences. Furthermore, the 'standard' length of the working week is itself subject to change, and in most developed countries has shown a long-run tendency to decline as incomes have risen. Although the individual at a point of time has to take the standard work-week as a datum, it is arguable that it is in the employers' interests to adjust, where possible, the length of the standard to satisfy the changing wishes or preferences of a majority of workers. As mentioned in earlier chapters, the length of the standard working week is one of the central issues in collective bargaining, and through such negotiations it becomes possible for workers' preferences to be made known. One qualification to this line of argument is necessary, however. Although the standard working week has declined historically, the number of hours actually worked on average has declined less rapidly. Since overtime normally carries premium rates, a reduction in standard hours without a comparable reduction in actual hours effectively means a rise in weekly earnings; and there is no doubt that in recent years, some British trade unions have sought a reduction in standard hours not because their members genuinely wanted a reduction in hours of work but because this was a means of achieving higher earnings.

The finding that the supply of labour hours varies with rates of pay brings with it further difficulties. First, how does this analysis relate to what was said earlier about the participation decision and the possibility of mutual adjustments in labour supply by members of the family unit? And secondly, there is a real problem about the money variable to which the supply of labour responds, since we have now suggested that the supply of labour hours is responsive to changes in hourly wage rates, while the earlier discussion centred on income. In fact, the two questions are not unrelated.

In the analysis of the participation decision it was argued that the family would plan its participation according to consumption and income targets consistent with available earning opportunities. Changes in circumstances, such as a fall in the demand for labour, could cause these targets to be modified or participation to be changed in order to raise income to a level closer to that originally planned. But a change in family participation rates would imply some change in the total supply of labour hours being made available in the market. If the fall in labour demand caused the main earner to be unemployed, and the wife or younger members of the family gave up unpaid activities to enter the labour market, the total supply of labour hours from the family would increase: the unemployment of the main earner would not mean any reduction in his supply of labour hours, only that this supply was not taken up by an employer. Similarly, if recession causes married women, as secondary earners, to withdraw from the labour force for the time being, and no other change in family labour supply takes place, the total supply of hours of labour from the family will be cut. In these ways participation rates – and hence the supply of labour hours – are responsive to alterations in variables which affect family income and consumption.

But we now have the added possibility that changes in these variables will lead to more direct changes in the supply of labour hours without a change in participation or as a complement to a change in participation. In the example we have been discussing, where the demand for labour falls, the unemployment of a family member may induce other members already in the labour force to increase their supply of labour hours: the wife working on a part-time basis may be prepared to work full-time, for instance, or the main earner may be willing to work more overtime than before if the wife becomes unemployed. Of course, in recession there may be no opportunity for these increased supplies of labour to be taken up, but similar kinds of response may well arise where workers become unemployed for reasons other than general recession.

This suggests that both participation rates and the individual's supply of labour hours may change in response to changes in circumstances. But now we see that a given change in circumstances may have quite different effects on the labour supply of different individuals within the family unit, and also between families. The unemployment of a secondary worker may mean that the worker withdraws from the labour force while the supply of labour hours from other family members may increase. And the net effect of this in one family may be quite different from that in others. Again, consider the effect of a rise in hourly wage rates. Such a rise may make it worth while for a full-time housewife to take a part-time job, thus inducing an increase in participation and hence in the total supply of labour hours. But the same change in hourly pay might induce a negative income effect on the labour supply of workers already in the labour force, causing them to reduce their supply of labour hours within the limits possible, for example by absenting themselves more frequently from work or refusing overtime opportunities. In other cases again the rise in wages may enable some families to meet their commitments and objectives more easily and so allow existing secondary earners to withdraw from the labour force.

Many other variations are possible, but the main points of the discussion should now be apparent. In the first place, changes in wage rates will affect the income or income potential of the family and so have an influence on labour supply. Secondly, changes in wage rates and other market circumstances may have quite opposite effects on the labour supply of primary and secondary workers, and the net result of a given change may vary from family to family. Because of this, it becomes impracticable to determine on *a priori* reasoning what the net effect of a given change in wages or the demand for labour will be on the total supply of labour hours. The change in this total supply is not simply a question of the predominance of the income or substitution effect for the individual but depends on the response of different kinds of labour to changes in wage and other conditions, with all that this implies for the cost of time used in unpaid activities, for consumption plans and so on. It may, therefore, be more appropriate to analyse separately the effects of a given change in market conditions on the primary and secondary elements of labour supply. Since these elements may respond differently, the ultimate effect of the change on total labour supply will depend on their relative weights in the labour force and on the elasticities of their separate supply curves within the relevant range.

This discussion does not leave us with a clear-cut theory which enables us to predict the outcome of changes in market circumstances for labour supply. It does, however, give us some conception of the complexity of the labour supply process and of the mechanisms which may be at work. It will be clear also from this approach that other non-economic factors may affect the consumption and income objectives of the family in such a way that they too may have some influence on labour supply. Also, we have been discussing the problem of labour supply without reference to the effects of taxation on the supply of labour. Obviously there is scope for much debate on the incentive or disincentive effects on labour supply arising from taxation on earned income, but this is again an area where empirical research rather than abstract analysis is required. As we will see in Chapter 14 below, the evidence needed to form a judgment on the income-tax effect is lacking. This does not, however, invalidate any of the foregoing analysis, which can readily be adjusted to take the effects of taxation into account.

(3) SKILL AND EFFORT

Two problems remain, though we can do little more than mention them at this stage. In the introductory remarks about labour supply in Chapter 8, we observed that labour supply was not simply a quantitative matter of hours of labour supplied, but that the skill and effort input of those hours was also of great importance for production. Taking the question of effort first, we have to admit that effort must be a largely subjective factor in labour supply. Two workers may be paid exactly the same for producing identical rates of output, but the effort input of each may be quite different, for what comes easily to one person may be highly taxing for another. In practice, it is not usually possible to measure the input of effort by different workers, and their payment does not so much reflect their effort as their ability to sustain at least some minimum standard of output or, where incentive payment schemes are in operation, their achievement in terms of physical output or time taken for a given task. Pay does not therefore provide a measure of effort in the sense of the personal cost in terms of physical and mental strain or exertion. Certainly there are interesting questions concerning the relation between wages and the effort which they will induce, but they perhaps belong more properly to the field of psychology than economics and we cannot usefully pursue them further.

Secondly, there is the question of the skill-content of labour hours. While there may be many factors other than wages which will affect the decision of a worker to acquire a degree of skill or not, wages are likely to be one of the relevant factors, and more will be said about this when we come to discuss the importance and causation of relative wages in Chapter 11. One point is worth while making here, however, since it is relevant to the main arguments of this section. The acquisition of skill or job-knowledge involves the individual in education or training, and during this period he may receive no payment or at least less than he could command in other jobs. He will accept this loss of current earnings opportunities largely because of the expectation of compensatingly higher earnings in later life.

A rise in current wage levels then might seem to increase the cost of continuing in training, in just the same way as it raises the cost to the full-time housewife of remaining outside the labour market. But in the case of the trainee, the cost of training would rise only if the rise in wage levels was confined to untrained labour or if it was proportionately greater for the latter than for more highly educated and trained workers. So long as the wage rise for trained labour is at least proportional to that for untrained labour, there will be no disadvantage in continuing to train. This is just one illustration of the relevance of the distinction made in the last chapter between the different uses of time 'not currently paid for'. In general, the more one probes the more complex problems of labour supply, the more useful does this type of distinction become as an aid to analysis.

II. The Supply of Labour to the Firm

We now turn to the labour supply position of the individual firm. For the moment we will assume away differences in the skill and efficiency of labour so that the problem reduces to that of the supply of workers and the supply of hours from them, where both workers and hours are homogeneous and the employer has no reason for discrimination.

(1) PERFECT COMPETITION

As a first step we will additionally make the assumption of perfect competition in the labour market, with many employers and workers, complete market information and no barriers to mobility arising from institutional or social factors. If we additionally assume that the attractiveness of the firms in ways other than payment is not an issue, workers would have no reason to prefer being employed in one firm rather than another, and even geographical mobility would be costless. We would then have a perfectly elastic supply curve of workers at a wage which was common to all employees and employers. Any firm which paid a wage below this competitive level would find all its workers leaving for other employments, and there would be no reason for firms to pay above the going rate; those that did in any case would not be maximising profits. In these circumstances, where the firm can increase its consumption of labour hours at a constant hourly cost by employing more workers, it has no need to resort to overtime to increase its supply. Overtime normally carries premium rates of pay so that additional supplies would have to be obtained at a higher hourly cost. Thus the supply curve of labour to the firm would be like SS' in Fig. 9.2, where the ruling wage is OS and firms could hire all the labour they required at that wage.

Fig. 9.2

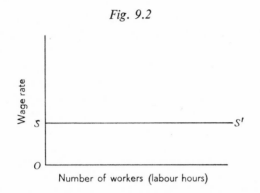

(2) IMPERFECT COMPETITION

(*a*) *The cost of mobility*. We can now relax the assumptions of perfect competition, while still retaining the assumption of homogeneous labour. First, let us introduce a geographical dimension into the labour market system. This means that wage differences may arise between local labour markets that are consistent with equilibrium in the market as a whole and that are to be explained by the costs of moving from one market to another. In that situation, where distance (rather than institutional or social obstacles) impedes mobility, the size of the labour force within any market area will be fairly inflexible in the short run. Now, so long as there is a margin of unemployed labour resources in the area, any firm will still be able to increase its employment without raising its wage level. But once full employment in the local market is reached, and no further reserves are available from within the area, the firm will either have to compete labour away from other firms in the area or induce workers in other areas to migrate into its own area. And to do this it will have to improve its employment conditions, probably by raising its wage relative to other firms or other areas. In other words, once we allow for the frictions implicit in geographical movement, the labour supply to the firm is influenced by the state of the local labour market in which it mainly operates. Under less than full employment conditions in the area, the worker supply curve is perfectly elastic, as in Fig. 9.2. But at full employment the curve will be inelastic, the steepness of the slope depending on the responsiveness of workers in other firms or areas to relative wage differences.

(b) *Worker preference.* Secondly, even though we assume labour to be homogeneous from the viewpoint of the employer, we need not assume that it all has identical preferences. As was pointed out in the last chapter, the attractiveness of a job is not solely a matter of its monetary remuneration, but includes its non-monetary attributes as well. The worker faced with a choice of jobs will then presumably choose a job which seems to him to afford the greatest 'net advantage' when the whole bundle of job-conditions, pecuniary and non-pecuniary, is evaluated. Employment with one firm may then give workers different degrees of job-satisfaction. For some, the wage together with the other aspects of work will be only just enough to make them want to stay there, and any change in the net advantage of this employment vis-à-vis alternative employments available will cause them to leave. In this case, the whole of a worker's earnings can be regarded as *transfer earnings*, by which we mean that he is paid exactly what is necessary to keep him from transferring out of the job. Other workers, in differing degrees, may obtain a greater degree of job-satisfaction from the conditions of employment, so that an adverse change in the net advantages of that employment relative to others available will reduce the amount of job-satisfaction but will not result in transfer out. In this case earnings include an element of *economic rent*, being the difference between what workers actually receive and the amount that would be just enough to prevent them from transferring to other jobs.[1]

The degree of attachment of individual workers to a firm will therefore vary, even if it is only a result of a worker preferring to work in a firm conveniently situated near his home, rather than a difference in actual working conditions or wages. For this reason, even in otherwise perfectly competitive conditions, a firm wishing to increase its labour force in full employment, and thus raising its wage level slightly, will not necessarily find itself able to attract all the labour it wants. It will only attract labour at the margin of satisfaction in other firms in the area. And for this reason, too, even in less than full employment conditions in the area, the labour

---

[1] The transfer earnings needed to keep a worker in employment with a given *firm* probably differ from those required to keep him within a given *occupation* or *area*, since the costs of mobility in each case might be very different.

supply curve of the firm may be rather less than perfectly elastic at the market wage, since there will be a limit to the amount of labour it can attract at that wage.

(c) *Overtime*. As yet, we have not touched upon the ability of the firm in imperfect competition to increase its supply of labour by having a given labour force work a greater number of hours. Assuming the normal condition of premium rates for overtime work, we would then expect that a firm in a local market with less than full employment, able to attract additional workers at a constant (or almost constant) hourly rate, would not wish to resort to overtime, which would usually be a more expensive expedient. On the other hand, once full employment has been reached in the market, overtime working, even at premium rates, *may* be a cheaper way of obtaining a greater labour supply than bidding up wages against other employers and other areas. Whether it is or not will depend on the frictions affecting inter-firm and inter-area mobility. But in any case the increased supply will only be available at an increased hourly wage rate, so that the supply curve will be relatively inelastic.

In general, once we introduce a geographical dimension into the labour market system, we obtain a highly (but not perfectly) elastic supply curve of labour hours at levels of employment below full employment; while at

Fig. 9.3

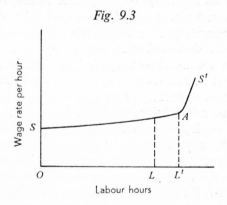

full employment in the local market area, the supply curve will be much more inelastic. This is illustrated in Fig. 9.3, where the firm is assumed to be in an area market just less than fully employed, and thus facing a labour supply curve that is still highly elastic around its current level of employment *OL*. Thus an increase in the firm's employment to *OL'* can be achieved with a very small rise in relative wages, but a rise sufficient to bring the total area market to full employment level will bring the firm on to a much more inelastic section of the curve SAS'.

(d) *Some further consequences of imperfect competition.* The degree of inelasticity in the firm's supply curve of labour may be increased by the smaller number of firms that we expect to find in the imperfect labour market. A rise in wages by one firm may now be matched by comparable wage rises in other firms who want to retain their present share of employment in the market, and successive rises in wages may have little effect in increasing the labour supply to the firm. Such a situation will often induce employers to try to differentiate themselves from competing firms by improving the non-wage conditions of employment, but again this can be matched by other firms.

Also, with the removal of the perfect competition assumptions, we can no longer assume complete market information on the part of buyers and sellers. There is in fact a good deal of empirical evidence to suggest that workers in general do not have a good knowledge of alternative job openings and wage conditions in other firms, and even the unemployed and others actively seeking work rely more often on casual and informal channels than on a systematic check on vacancies. In the extreme case, where there was no knowledge on the part of labour, the firm's supply curve of workers would be perfectly inelastic even at less than full employment levels. In general, the more incomplete the information available to workers, the more inelastic will be the supply curve of workers to the firm.

Finally, it is worth mentioning that in imperfect competition the firm may be able to reduce its wage relative to other firms without there being any noticeable effect on its labour supply. This will certainly be true where the market is well below full employment. Suppose that, as in Fig. 9.4, a firm is already employing OL workers at a wage OW and that there is a fairly high level of unemployment in the area. At point A, the firm can increase its employment without raising wages significantly: the curve is fairly elastic. But it may be able to reduce wages below OW without losing any labour, at least for relatively small wage cuts. This is partly due to the imperfections of the market, such as lack of information, the cost of inter-firm transfer and the element of economic rent in many wage payments. But mainly it is a reflection of unemployment and the lack of alternative work, causing workers to stay with the firm. Hence below A the curve may be highly inelastic over a range and the whole curve SAS' is kinked. The closer the area is to full employment, the smoother the curve will be, since transfer will be more possible in the presence of more job opportunities.

In summary, in the highly unreal conditions of perfect competition, the firm will have a perfectly elastic supply curve of labour. Once we remove these conditions, the firm's labour supply curve takes on a degree of

Fig. 9.4

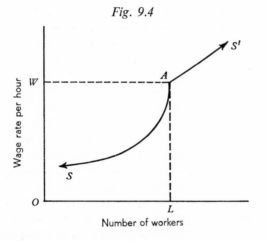

inelasticity, but this is likely to be most marked at full employment levels in the local labour market. A number of other factors, such as the coverage of market information and the number of employers in the market, may accentuate or modify this inelasticity. At least two major problems then remain. We have still to remove the assumption of homogeneous labour; and we have not yet discussed the effects of social and institutional barriers to mobility. These are problems which we must postpone until Chapter 11. But before leaving the labour supply side, something must be said about the supply of labour in the long run, to supplement the present discussion of the short run. As we now see, this is an area in which economic analysis is not well developed.

III. Population and Labour Supply in the Long Run

In classical economies one of the critical foundations of the theory of growth and distribution was the Malthusian population thesis, with its prediction that unless 'moral restraint' was exercised to restrict population

H

growth, poverty would persist and the great hopes of the Age of Enlightenment would be dashed. In economic terms, this meant that the long-run labour supply curve was infinitely elastic at a subsistence wage. Any rise in real wages per head would quickly be whittled away by earlier marriages, high birth rates and subsequently increased pressure on the limited productive powers of a fixed supply of agricultural land. This analysis is not altogether irrelevant to some of the less developed economies today, such as India and the Philippines, where the average level of real *per capita* wages has remained virtually constant despite vast inflows of economic aid and major attempts to achieve a higher level of economic development. In the Western world, however, although population has increased enormously in the last century and a half, as we indicated for Britain in Chapter 6, the rate of growth has been nothing like enough to keep the average real income down to its former level. Population theory of the Malthusian brand lost its relevance to the societies in which most economists lived, and no substitute was evolved. Yet the relationship between population growth and economic development, and its implications for the size and quality of the labour force, the need for employment creation, housing and consumption, is clearly an important one for the economist and there has been a revival of interest in recent years, more especially with the recognition that economic planning and policy rely to a great extent on population forecasts, which are likely to be improved by taking into account the impact of changes in a number of socio-economic variables.

As we saw in Chapter 6, changes in population size depend primarily on the birth rate, the death rate, and net migration, each of which is capable of being influenced by a number of economic factors, though none is completely determined by these factors. One such factor is the level of real income per head. Over the course of the trade cycle there has been some suggestion of a positive relationship between income and birth rates, and recent studies have confirmed this relationship for the longer secular cycles of economic activity.[1] Yet we also know that as economic development has proceeded in Western countries, birth rates have tended to decline, at least

[1] Cf. Irma Adelman, 'An Econometric Analysis of Population Growth', *American Economic Review*, June 1963, on which most of the following discussion of birth and death rates is based; also R. A. Easterlin, 'The Baby Boom in Perspective', *American Economic Review*, December 1961. It is as well to point out here that differences in the age and sex distribution of populations can themselves generate different overall birth rate and death rate patterns. Strictly, it is only the non-demographically generated changes which are examined in the text.

until the Second World War, which was the genesis of the so-called 'baby boom'. There must therefore have been counter-influences to rising real income, and these seem principally to have been the spread of intensification of education, the growth of industrialisation and the increasing urbanisation of the population. In addition, it is possible that both higher real incomes and improved medical care and knowledge have so significantly reduced the infant mortality rate that ideal family sizes are more easily achieved, so that the birth rate has fallen, without a similar fall in the number of children surviving to grow up in their family.

Death rates also are subject to economic influence as well as to the effects of improving public health services. Substantially better diets, superior housing, vastly improved working conditions, and many other factors associated with rising real income levels have undoubtedly played some part in lengthening life expectation, both at the very young and the older age levels. Higher educational standards, industrialisation and urbanisation are again important factors in explaining the falling death rate, presumably because people living in a developed industrial community are better able to understand rules of health and benefit from the presence of professional medical attention, of better sanitation and so on.

The implications of this for the labour force are clear. The greater chances of survival after birth will mean that more of those born will enter the labour force. Improved life expectancy implies that more of those entering the labour force will reach retirement age. In addition, of course, improved means and knowledge of birth control, by allowing families to be planned better and to be limited in size, mean that women have more opportunity to enter the labour force and to re-enter after completing their families. But while all this gives us some indication of the important economic influences on fertility and mortality, it falls short of an economic theory of population. This would require a theory of the demand for and supply of children, and while this may seem a curious use of economic concepts, interesting suggestions along such lines have been sketched out by Friedman and Spengler.[1]

Finally, mention has to be made of migration. The economic development of the United States has depended substantially on net inflows of migrants, initially largely from Europe and later from more nearby areas such as Puerto Rico; and other countries such as Canada and Australia are still experiencing this kind of process. On the other hand, countries with

[1] Cf. M. Friedman, 'Lectures in Price Theory', and J. J. Spengler, 'The Economist and the Population Question', *American Economic Review*, March 1966, pp. 14–15.

surplus population are often major net exporters of labour; this is true again of Puerto Rico, of India and Pakistan and of the West Indies. Economic motivation once more seems to be relevant, given the 'push' from countries with low average real incomes, high unemployment and poor economic environments, and the 'pull' of countries where labour is in short supply and living standards are high. If we regard the migration decision as a kind of investment, with the costs of movement being incurred in the expectation of high returns, the willingness of workers to undertake long journeys to lands which, though possessing different customs and attitudes, afford opportunities for higher standards of living, becomes more explicable. But this aspect of the problem is perhaps better postponed for further discussion until Chapter 11, where the question of labour mobility in general is taken up.

10 The Demand for Labour and the Determination of Wages

I. The Firm's Demand for Labour in the Short Run

Chapter 8, it will be recalled, provided an introductory account of the factors influencing the short-run demand for labour, in which two main problems were identified: the demand for labour at the level of the firm, which is generally the unit from which demand arises; and the demand for labour in the economy as a whole. It is with the problem of demand at the level of the firm that we begin. Mention has already been made of the demand for labour as a derived demand arising out of the productivity of labour and its expected contribution to the revenue and profits of the firm. The basis of this part of the labour market theory is the principle of marginal productivity which, despite a rather troubled history, still remains for most economists a useful tool in the explanation of factor pricing in general and the pricing of labour in particular. For the present we will refer to the marginal productivity principle as applying only to labour, though as we proceed its application in respect of other factors will become apparent.

Marginal productivity theory is only a theory of the demand for labour and does not in itself afford an explanation of wage or employment determination. Only when it is brought into juxtaposition with the theory of labour supply does a theory of wage and employment determination emerge. But as we have already considered the theory of labour supply, we can conveniently put it to use in this chapter by developing a theory of the demand for labour and simultaneously deriving the conclusions for wages and employment which follow when supply and demand are jointly considered. Since our supply theory only allows us to deal with homogeneous labour, we will retain this assumption here. Additionally we continue to assume that no social or institutional factors interfere with the free operation of the market, and that employers act rationally and seek to maximise short-run profits.[1]

In general, firms operate in market conditions which are far from those of perfect competition. But the analysis of the behaviour of firms in perfect competition allows us more easily to reach conclusions which can be

[1] Cf. Chapter 8 above, p. 198.

modified where necessary as various kinds of imperfection are introduced. We have already undertaken this kind of exercise in the case of labour supply, and we now follow a similar procedure for demand. But whereas we could in the case of supply confine attention to the labour market alone, we now have to take account of both product market and labour market conditions. This is because the demand for labour depends jointly on labour productivity and the marketability of labour's product. The need for this distinction becomes increasingly important as we proceed.

(1) PERFECT COMPETITION IN PRODUCT AND LABOUR MARKETS

One of the main conditions of perfect competition is that there are many buyers and sellers, none of whom is large enough to affect market price by changing his level of purchase or sales over any feasible range. In the product market under perfect competition, the firm is then a price-taker rather than a price-setter: it can sell as much of its product as it wants at the current market price. In the labour market likewise the firm is a price-taker, this time in the sense that it can hire as much labour as it wishes without affecting the price of labour. The problem for such a firm is not one of deciding what price to set or what wage to pay, but rather what levels of output and employment should be set if profits are to be maximised in the short run, given the ruling price of the product and the existing wage – and it is as well to stress that for the present we are only concerned with the short-run problem. Profits are the excess of total revenue from selling a given output over the total costs of producing that output, so that the firm's problem reduces to one of fixing output and employment at a level such that the margin between total revenue and total costs is maximised. What that level will be depends upon two factors: the variation of output as employment changes, and the variation of revenue as output changes. We begin with the output–employment aspect.

In the short run, by definition, the firm possesses a stock of capital equipment, implying a specific production technique, which it cannot alter. The efficient operation of this equipment will require a certain complement of labour. Fig. 10.1 (a) suggests how output will vary as the amount of labour employed on this fixed amount of capital is changed. At a very low level of employment, such as OL, the equipment will be operating inefficiently, with no real continuity of production and none of the economies of operation available at higher outputs. Further additions to employment will, however, reduce these inefficiencies of low capacity working and the rate of output growth will begin to rise for a time, as in the employment range *OL* to *OL'*. This increasing rate of growth of output cannot continue indefinitely after the diseconomies of low-level operation are overcome. As the plant begins to approach its designed level of operation, output will grow at an increasingly slower rate, until a point is reached at which further additions of labour (in the range *OL'* to *OL''*) will actually

Figure 10.1

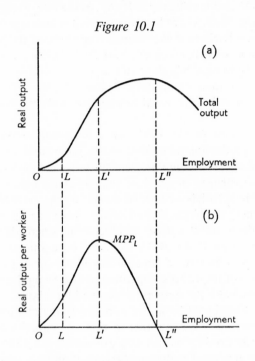

cause total output to fall. This analysis is in fact the basis of the *principle of diminishing returns*,[1] which states that if all factors of production bar one are held fixed and there is no change in other conditions, successive additions of the variable factor will after some point raise output by progressively smaller amounts and eventually cause output to decrease. The returns to the variable factor diminish and ultimately become negative.

We now turn to the productivity of the variable factor itself, in this case labour, and our interest is in the *changing* productivity of labour as more workers are employed with a fixed stock of factors. Our concern is therefore with the *marginal* productivity of labour, which is the change in total

[1] This is often referred to as the 'law of variable proportions'. Cf. R. G. Lipsey, *An Introduction to Positive Economics* (2nd ed.), p. 274.

output resulting from the employment of an extra unit of labour. (For simplicity we will assume that this extra unit is an additional worker.)[1] The path traced out by the marginal physical product of labour (MPP_L) is likely to take a form such as the curve MPP_L in Fig. 10.1 (*b*), which is drawn in conformity with Fig. 10.1 (*a*). Again starting at a low level of employment OL and moving towards OL', as the rate of increase of output rises, so will the MPP_L curve be rising, since it is here that the addition of extra workers is likely to make indirect contributions to the productivity of existing employees. Between OL' and OL'', MPP_L is falling, reflecting the fact that additional labour is still making a positive contribution to total output but in a diminishing degree. Beyond OL'' the marginal physical product of labour would be negative, and total output begins to fall.

The precise shape of the MPP_L curve is dependent on the technical conditions of production as implied in the given stock of capital equipment and its designed labour complement. In some highly advanced technological firms engaged in activities such as plastics manufacture or oil refining, additions to labour beyond a certain point will lead to a sharp reduction in marginal physical productivity, since there is little that extra workers can do to affect output. In other firms where the technology is much less sophisticated, the MPP_L curve will have a much less rapid rate of decline. This is important, because the MPP_L curve, subject to qualification in cases of imperfect competition, *is* the demand curve of labour, and its slope indicates the elasticity of demand for labour.

To see why this should be so, let us return to the relationship between output and revenue. We know that in perfect competition the firm is a price-taker in its product market and can sell all the output it wishes at the ruling market price. The revenue per unit of product sold is a constant, P. Total revenue, being the number of units sold times their unit price, will then have precisely the same slope as the total output curve in Fig. 10.1 (*a*). And just as we can measure the marginal physical product of labour, so we can conceive of a measure of the addition to total revenue resulting from the employment of an extra unit of labour; this is the *marginal revenue product* of labour (MRP_L). But since in perfect competi-

[1] In the strictest sense this is not quite correct, as the marginal unit should be infinitely small. It is also worth stressing here that the marginal product of labour is not necessarily the same as the *actual* output of *the* marginal unit of labour; for example, the addition of an extra worker may not only make a direct contribution to output but may indirectly help other workers to produce more. The marginal product is the change in *total* output arising from an addition to employment.

tion all units of output are sold at the same price, P, the MRP_L curve will be an exact replica of the MPP_L curve (since $MRP_L = MPP_L \times P$, where P is constant).

Thus the value to the firm of extra units of labour – and hence, implicitly, the price it will be willing to pay for these units – is traced out by the MRP_L curve, which is the firm's labour demand curve in monetary terms. Not all of the MRP_L curve is relevant for the present purpose, however. So long as the MRP_L curve is rising, it will obviously pay the employer to go on adding to his employment. It is only when the MRP_L curve begins to decline that the employer need seriously begin to consider whether it is worth while hiring more labour, since each addition to employment is going to add a decreasing amount to physical product and total revenue. Obviously, too, when MRP_L is negative, the employer will be in no doubt about the undesirability of hiring more labour. Thus the relevant section of the firm's demand curve for labour in perfect competition is the declining (but still positive) section of its MRP_L curve, as indicated by the unbroken line DD' in Fig. 10.2.

At this point we can introduce a new factor, the price of labour. Let us suppose that the employment of an extra unit of labour will allow production to be increased by 10 units, each of which can be sold for five

Figure 10·2

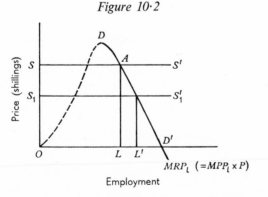

shillings: the marginal revenue product of labour is 50 shillings. Whether the firm will employ this unit of labour will depend on its cost to the firm. If it costs less than 50 shillings to hire, the firm will be able to add more to total revenue than the new labour adds to total costs, and the firm will increase its profits. If the labour costs more than 50 shillings, the addition to costs will outweigh the addition to revenue, and profits will be reduced.

H 2

If the labour costs exactly 50 shillings, the addition to revenue and to costs will exactly balance. Thus it will be worth while for the firm to hire labour up to (and including) that unit which equalises the addition to costs and the addition to revenue. To hire even one less unit would be to forgo a possible addition to total profit; to hire one more unit would reduce profit. More generally, if we define the addition to total costs by employing one more unit of labour as the *marginal cost* of labour (MC_L), we can conclude that the equilibrium level of employment for the firm will be the point at which MC_L and MRP_L are equal. In a perfectly competitive labour market, of course, the marginal cost of labour will simply be the ruling market wage rate and marginal and average cost will be equal.

This is illustrated in Fig. 10.2, where SS' is the firm's labour supply curve, perfectly elastic at a wage rate OS. At employment level OL the cost of the last unit of labour is OS and the marginal revenue product of that unit is AL (equal to OS). Thus the equilibrium level of employment for the firm is OL. If the wage rate now falls to OS, the firm will be able to increase its employment to OL', at which point the marginal cost of labour (MC_L) and the marginal revenue product of labour (MRP_L) are again equal, and the firm will again be in equilibrium. To remain at a level of employment less than OL' would mean that MRP_L was greater than MC_L – in other words, that by employing an extra unit of labour the firm could increase its revenue by more than the rise in costs; and it would not be maximising profits.[1]

From this analysis we have been able to derive an equilibrium level of employment for the firm which is faced with perfectly competitive conditions in both its product and its labour market. But since the assumptions of perfect competition are so unrealistic, we must see what changes in the analysis are necessary for conditions of imperfect competition.[2] First, then, we consider the consequences of imperfect competition in the product market while the labour market remains perfectly competitive.

(2) PERFECT COMPETITION IN THE LABOUR MARKET ONLY

Imperfect or monopolistic competition in the product market means that each of the numerous firms produces a product which is slightly

---

[1] The labour supply curves SS' and $S_1S'_1$ also cut the MRP_L curve in the rising section OD, but since within this range further additions to employment will lead to a rise in profits, the points of intersection cannot be points of equilibrium.

[2] 'Imperfect competition' is used synonymously with what is often referred to as 'monopolistic competition'.

different from any of the others. As a result, the output of different producers will no longer be regarded by purchasers as perfect substitutes, and changes in the relative prices of the differentiated products may produce changes in demand for them. In short, the product demand curve for any firm in imperfect competition is less than perfectly elastic. Increases in the volume of goods sold can only be achieved by a price reduction – which of course must apply to all the goods sold by the producer and not just those which represent the increase in output.

As in perfect competition, firms will aim to maximise profits, and by the same kind of analysis we can quickly see that they will be concerned with the effect of changes in employment on output, revenue and costs. They will in fact wish to set output and employment at a level such that the excess of revenue over costs will be a maximum. This is obviously a problem which can be stated, like that of perfect competition, in terms of marginal revenue product and marginal cost. On the side of marginal cost, there will be no change in the situation. Additional units of labour can be hired from the perfectly competitive labour market at a constant price. The other side of the problem, however, is rather different.

The marginal revenue product of labour has been defined as a function of the marginal physical product of labour and the price at which the extra units of physical product can be sold:

$$MRP_L = MPP_L \times \text{price of goods.}$$

In perfect competition price was constant and the MRP_L function took its shape directly from the MPP_L curve. Under imperfect competition there will be no change in the MPP_L curve, since it derives directly from the technological character of production. But now, as we have seen, additional units of output can be sold only at a decreasing price. Suppose the firm is currently producing and selling 100 units of a good per day at £1 each, so that its total revenue is £100 per day. The employment of an extra unit of labour would raise output to 110 units per day. But for the firm to be able to sell these extra units, price for the whole 110 units has to be reduced, say to 19s. 6d. Total revenue is then £107 5s. and the marginal revenue product of labour is £7 5s. Yet another unit of labour employed might raise physical output to 120 units of product, which could perhaps be sold only at 18s. 9d. each, so that MRP_L would be £5 5s.[1] Thus even if MPP_L were constant, MRP_L may be declining owing to the need for the firm to reduce its price if a larger quantity of goods is to be sold; and if MPP_L is declining, MRP_L will be more steeply sloped. But MRP_L is the firm's

[1] i.e. £(120 × 18s. 9d.) = £112 10s.; and £112 10s. – £107 5s. = £5 5s.

demand curve for labour; it relates the quantities of labour the firm would be prepared to hire to a number of hypothetical prices for labour services. The firm will only demand labour so long as the costs of hiring extra labour are no greater than the contribution of extra labour to total revenue. And furthermore, the profit-maximising firm will hire labour up to the point at which the marginal cost of labour and its marginal revenue product are equal. So long as the firm can hire labour at less than its MRP, it will increase its profits by hiring this labour; but if the cost of extra labour exceeds MRP_L, the firm will be reducing its profits.[1]

The differences between perfect and imperfect competition is important, as we see with the help of Fig. 10.3. Let us assume that a firm moves from a perfectly competitive situation (A) to an imperfectly competitive situation (B), while its MPP_L curve remains unchanged. In perfect competition, with a labour supply curve SS' and a labour demand curve shown by MRP_A, which takes its downward slope because of declining MPP_L, the level of employment in equilibrium will be OL at wage OS. In imperfect competition, the firm's demand curve for labour, MRP_B, will be more steeply sloped than MRP_A, reflecting the new condition that additions to output cannot be sold at a constant price but require a fall in price over the whole output sold. In this case with an identical labour supply curve SS', the equilibrium level of employment at wage rate OS will be OP, less than OL. One of the effects of imperfect competition, therefore, is to lower the equilibrium level of employment (and output) for the firm compared with a perfectly competitive situation in which technical and cost conditions are identical.

In this analysis the elasticity of the demand for the firm's product is

[1] A simple illustration may be useful here.

No. of workers	Total output	Marginal physical product	Price per unit (s.)	Value of MPP (s.)	Total revenue (s.)	Marginal revenue product (s.)
4	40	—	12	—	480	—
5	60	20	11	220	660	180
6	75	15	10	150	750	90
7	88	13	9	117	792	42

In this case, it will only pay the firm to employ the sixth worker if the addition to costs incurred is not more than 90s., even though the value of the MPP is 150s. The fall in price needed to sell the extra units produced has to be imposed on total output, so that marginal revenue goes up by much less than the value of MPP.

reflected in the firm's demand curve for labour. The more elastic the demand for the firm's product, the greater will be the fall in quantity demanded for a given rise in price, and the greater also will be the decline

Fig. 10.3

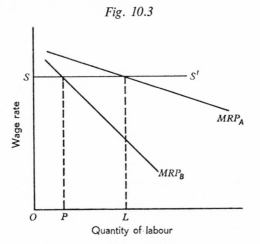

in the quantity of labour demanded, other things equal. The elasticity of the demand for labour is therefore determined in part by the elasticity of the demand for the firm's product.[1]

The most extreme situation, compared with that of perfect competition, is a pure monopoly in the product market. Only a brief mention of this case is necessary here since a pure monopoly is scarcely ever to be found. In fact, the characteristics of this case are similar to those of imperfect competition. Like the firm in imperfect competition, the monopolist will only be able to sell more output by reducing price over the whole range of output to be sold. The demand curve for his product will thus be downward-sloping. But also, as before, the output at which profits are maximised will be that at which marginal costs and marginal revenue are equalised, and labour will be hired up to the point at which the marginal cost of labour and its marginal revenue product are equal.

[1] In the real world, there will be other costs besides labour costs, and the ratio of labour to total costs will vary from firm to firm and industry to industry. The proportion of labour costs to total costs can be an important factor in determining the size of the effect of a wage rise on product demand and employment. The larger the proportion of labour costs, the greater will be the effect of a given percentage rise in wages on employment and output, *ceteris paribus*.

Finally, and perhaps more interestingly, there is the special case of *oligopoly* in the product market. This is the name given by economists to a market situation in which there are only a few producers selling differentiated products which are reasonable substitutes for each other. No collusion exists among the firms, for this would be tantamount to a monopoly, with a common price being charged and market shares adjusted to the firms' mutual satisfaction. In the oligopolistic market, each producer has to take account of the effects of changes in his own policy on the policies of other companies – or at any rate what he *thinks* these effects may be, for there can be no certainty in such matters. The characteristic situation is one where each producer feels that a rise in his price would not be followed by rival firms, so that he would lose enough of his existing customers to cause a fall in total revenue and in profits: for rises in price above its current level, he believes demand to be highly elastic. At the same time, he may believe that a cut in price would be met by a matching price cut on the part of his rivals, or at least that demand is sufficiently inelastic for a price cut not to yield an increase in profits.

The product demand curve for such a firm would then look like DBD' in Fig. 10.4 (*a*), where present price is AB; this is a 'kinked' demand curve, in contrast to the smooth curves we have so far met with.

Fig. 10.4

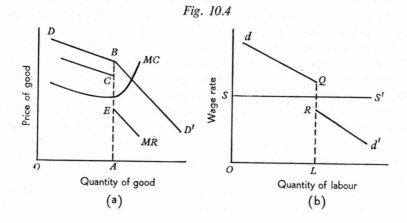

(a)

(b)

The firm is producing OA units of output and selling at price AB, and expects any rise or fall in price to lead to a fall in profits. The associated marginal revenue curve (tracing out the addition to revenue from successive increases in output) will then be *discontinuous* between C and E; but provided the marginal cost curve (MC) cuts the marginal revenue curve (MR) between E and C, the firm will be maximising profits. Thus small changes in costs within the range CE will not cause the firm to change its output or its selling price. This obviously has implications for the demand for factors, including labour. In Fig. 10.4 (b), the amount of labour employed to produce OA units of product is OL, and as in the previous example the labour supply curve (SS) is completely elastic at wage OS. Changes in costs within the range EC of the MR curve will not cause the firm to change its price/output position because cost changes cannot be reflected in price without departing from the profit-maximising situation. In consequence the firm has a discontinuous labour demand curve such as $dQRd'$, which is completely inelastic between Q and R, corresponding to the range EC in the MR curve in Fig. 10.4 (a). In other words, changes in labour costs within the range QR will not produce changes in the amount of labour demanded.

(3) PERFECT COMPETITION IN THE PRODUCT MARKET BUT NOT IN THE LABOUR MARKET

Where the producer sells his product in a perfectly competitive market but is a sufficiently large employer of labour for his labour market excursions to have an influence on wages, he can vary his output within all practicable bounds without affecting the price of the good. However, if he wants to increase his output by employing additional labour, he will no longer be faced with a perfectly elastic labour supply curve. Instead, additional quantities of labour will require a higher rate of pay, and unless the employer discriminates against his existing employees (and can get away with it), all units of this (homogeneous) labour will have to be paid the same wage. Thus by hiring an extra worker, wage costs will increase not just by the wage that has to be paid to engage him but by that amount *plus* the extra payment that has to be made to all the other workers already in employment. So far as the firm's demand for labour is concerned, it is *this total addition to the wage bill*, caused by the hiring of an extra unit of labour, that is important. And it is this marginal wage cost which will be compared with the marginal revenue product in coming to a decision on whether the additional labour should be hired. By the now familiar rule, the profit-maximising employer will only hire the extra worker where his marginal revenue product is equal to or greater than the marginal wage cost.

One consequence of this is that the equilibrium level of employment and the equilibrium wage will tend to lie below the level which would have prevailed in the perfectly competitive labour market situation. Fig.

10.5 (*a*) and (*b*) respectively represent the perfect competition and imperfect competition cases.

In Fig. 10.5 (*a*), *DD'* is the demand curve for labour and *SS'* is the labour supply curve, perfectly elastic at wage *OS* with average and marginal wage costs equal. Equilibrium employment is *OL*. In Fig. 10.5 (*b*), *DD'*

Fig. 10.5

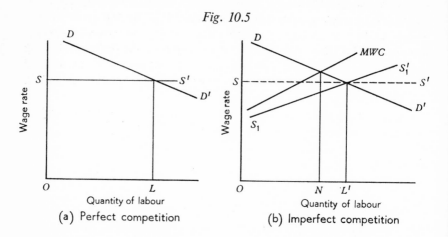

(a) Perfect competition

(b) Imperfect competition

is an identical labour demand curve, but instead of the perfectly elastic labour supply curve *SS* of the perfect competition case,[1] the labour supply curve is now the upward sloping curve S_1S_1'. That is, S_1S_1' is the curve which traces out the quantities of labour that will be supplied at various prices for labour services. We cannot conclude, however, that equilibrium employment will be at the point where the demand and supply curves intersect (i.e. at *OL'*, so drawn as to be equal to *OL* in Fig. 10.5 (*b*)). The reason for this is that in Fig. 10.5 (*a*) the marginal wage cost was simply the wage of the marginal worker. In Fig. 10.5 (*b*), on the other hand, the marginal wage cost will be represented by a curve such as *MWC*, reflecting the change in *total* wage costs as additional labour is employed; and since all workers must be paid the same wage, the rise in costs from hiring an extra worker at a higher wage than before will be greater than the wage of the marginal worker.[2] If the producer is to maximise his

[1] Shown as a dotted line in (*b*).

[2] For example, if a firm already employing ten workers at a wage of £15 per man per week decides to increase its employment to eleven, it may find that it has to pay £15 5*s.* to recruit this worker. The marginal wage cost is not however this £15 5*s.*, but £15 5*s. plus* the additional 5*s.* per week that has to be paid to each of the ten workers already employed. (i.e. £15 5*s.* + (10 × 5*s.*) = £17 15*s.*

profits, he will have to stop hiring labour at the employment level where the marginal wage cost equals the marginal revenue product of the extra labour. In Fig. 10.5 (*b*) this will occur at a level of employment *ON* (less than *OL'* or *OL* in Fig. 10.5 (*a*)) and at a wage *NQ* (less than *OS*). In this case, in contrast to those which have gone before, wages are no longer a datum for the firm, but are determined by the conditions of demand in the firm and by the costs of hiring extra labour.

(4) IMPERFECT COMPETITION IN BOTH PRODUCT AND LABOUR MARKETS

Finally, the analysis in the case where perfect competition is absent both in the product and labour markets involves a synthesis of the previous two cases. In the product market the producer is faced with a relatively inelastic demand curve which is reflected in a more steeply sloped *MRP* or factor demand curve compared with the perfectly competitive producer with an identical physical product schedule. In equilibrium, employment will be less than in perfect competition. In the labour market, the supply curve is positively sloped, and as in (3) above this will cause the wage and employment equilibrium for the firm to lie below that of the comparable competitive situation. When imperfect competition exists in both product and labour markets, the joint presence of the inelastic labour supply curve and the more inelastic demand curve, *ceteris paribus*, will mean that the wage and employment equilibrium of the firm tends to be pushed still further below that likely to exist in perfectly competitive conditions. A further consequence, however, is that a given change in demand or supply will produce relatively smaller employment effects than in more competitive conditions, where the higher elasticity of demand and supply curves converts even small changes in demand and supply into large employment effects. In other words, for given (percentage) changes in demand and supply, employment will be relatively more stable in less competitive markets. In the special case of oligopoly, changes in wages will have no effect on employment, provided the marginal cost curve continues to pass through the 'gap' in the marginal revenue curve.

More will be said about these conclusions as we go on to discuss some of the criticisms of marginal productivity analysis. For the moment, however, we have completed our discussion of the firm's demand for labour in the short run. So long as there is perfect competition in the labour market, the wage level for the firm will be a datum, and the marginal productivity analysis of labour demand allows us to derive only a theory of employment. There is then still a problem of the determination of wages in perfect competition, and in discussing this question further in the next section, we find ourselves able to enlarge the scope of the argument to give some understanding of the general equilibrium of the economic system and the long-run effects of competitive conditions on wages and employment.

II. Further Problems of Wage Determination

(1) WAGES AND GENERAL EQUILIBRIUM

For the moment we have to reinstate the assumption of perfect competition in both product and labour markets. We continue to assume short-run profit maximisation by producers, and no barriers to labour mobility. The problem of this section is to discover how the equilibrium level of wages is determined in such a way that the market will be cleared, leaving no unsatisfied demand or excess supply.

Consider an economic system in which there are a number of different industries, each employing homogeneous labour and capital in different proportions to produce different products. At a moment of time there will then be a complex structure of product prices and factor prices; given these, firms will adjust their output and employment until the whole system is in equilibrium. A change in any one of these prices will cause firms to adjust their demand for factors so that they return to a position of profit maximisation. In respect of employment, firms will adjust their demand for labour so that the value of the product of the last unit of labour employed equals its wage – that is, until

$$MPP_L \times P = W$$

(where P is the product price and W is the wage), or

$$\frac{MPP_L \times P}{W} = 1$$

By the same reasoning as in the case of the demand for labour, we can express the demand for any factor in terms of its marginal productivity, and we can determine the limit of its employment in the same way. Thus for capital, for instance, the firm will be in equilibrium when the following condition holds:

$$MPP_C \times P = K$$

(where MPP_C is the marginal physical product of capital, P is product price and K the price of a unit of capital),

or
$$\frac{MPP_C \times P}{K} = 1$$

Since the ratios of the marginal (revenue) product of both factors to their respective prices is the same (unity), they must be equal; and this is a more general condition of equilibrium for the firm. It means that every firm, to attain equilibrium, must so adjust its use of the factors it employs that the ratio of the value of the factor's marginal product to factor price is the same for all factors.

In the short run, this may not be possible. Capital equipment is fixed in the short run, for example. But in the long run all factors are assumed to be variable in supply so that the firm can choose a new combination of factors to take account of ruling factor prices. If the price of labour rises relative to that of capital, the firm will find it profitable to use more capital and less labour, and to choose its new technique accordingly. The demand for capital will rise, and its marginal physical productivity will fall as more of it is employed; at the same time the smaller demand for labour will lower its price, and lower employment will raise its marginal physical productivity. The system will then approach a new position of equilibrium in which the ratio

$$\frac{MPP}{\text{factor price}} \times P$$

is again equalised for each factor. Likewise, a change in the price of a product will cause a change in the pattern of product demand. Producers will want more of some factors, less of others, and factor prices will change, causing still further adjustments in factor pricing and utilisation until equilibrium is restored.

We must now consider another aspect of the problem. By assumption, labour is perfectly mobile and will move from lower-paid to higher-paid employment. In equilibrium, therefore, not only will all firms in a single industry have to pay the same wage to labour they employ, but all industries will have to pay the same wage. The same will apply to the remuneration of a unit of capital or any other factor of production. Thus the marginal revenue product of each factor ($MPP \times P$) must be equal in all its uses. Neither the price of factors nor the price of goods can then be set independently of one another. We are in fact in a world of general equilibrium where all prices – for factors and goods alike – are settled simultaneously and where any change in the system will have the effect of producing instantaneous readjustments to equilibrium. Wages will be equal to the marginal revenue product of labour, the remuneration of capital will equal the marginal revenue product of capital, and output and employment will be set in such a way that the price of a factor is equalised in all its uses and that the proportion of marginal revenue product to factor price will be equalised for all factors.

(2) SOME PROPERTIES OF THE SYSTEM

All this is undoubtedly a highly abstract approach, and not one which appears to have much to do with the real world. But before coming to the issue of its relevance to the real world, a few comments can usefully be made on some of its properties. For example, if we remove the condition of simultaneous adjustment throughout the system, we can still derive a conclusion about the equilibrium level to which it will tend. Changes will produce a chain reaction, the net result of which will be to push the prices of factors *towards* the value of their marginal product. The value of this marginal product will depend on the product price and hence on the demand for the product. If a product is subject to an increase in demand its price will rise, as will the value of the marginal product of labour (and of other factors used to produce the product). Resources will flow to this use from elsewhere in the system, raising MRP in the latter and lowering it in the former.[1] There is a built-in tendency towards a restoration of equilibrium. A further property of the model is that labour, in moving to jobs where wages are higher, is also moving to jobs where the value of its marginal product is higher, and improving not just its own position but that of society as well, since it allows consumer demand to be more adequately satisfied. Private and social interests coincide.

Another important point derives from this conclusion that factors tend to be paid the value of their marginal product, namely that it enabled economists to defend the system – and by implication the capitalist economy which depended on freedom of competition – against charges that it led to the exploitation of labour. Originally, in the terms of the Marxian labour theory of value, labour was the sole factor which gave rise to the value of a product, and if it did not receive the whole of that value it was being exploited. Subsequent developments redefined exploita-

[1] This is because MPP of the factor will rise as less of it is employed in a given use, and fall as more of it is employed, other things being equal.

tion in a less emotive sense to mean that a factor was being paid less than the value of its marginal product. But then if all factors were paid according to this same principle, and if (as was true on certain assumptions) this method of rewarding each factor completely exhausted their total product and left over no 'surplus', the charge of exploitation would be nullified.[1] In this respect, then, the model discussed above became 'morally defensible' – a fact which seemed not unimportant towards the end of the last century.

Furthermore, the system is one which seems to lead to all resources being fully employed in equilibrium. If workers are willing to work at the current rate but are unable to find employment, the system will not be in equilibrium. The unemployed will offer their services at a slightly reduced rate which will encourage employers to hire them. This will reduce the value of the marginal product of labour until all workers are employed at a wage equal to the value of labour's marginal product; and this of course applies to *all* workers, not just those newly hired, since all workers are homogeneous and employers will not discriminate among them. Wages will thus settle at this new level where all who want to work at that wage can find employment.[2]

There is, however, a major difficulty with this view. Certainly it was for a long time thought that excessive wage levels were responsible for unemployment, and that if wages were cut additional employment would be offered. For the individual firm this is so on the assumption that everything else remains constant and in particular that the demand for its product is not affected by a cut in the wages of its employees. It is true in terms of partial equilibrium analysis, in which the external effects of changes within the firm can be ignored. But if there is a general fall in wages, the effects of this on the economy as a whole cannot be ignored. A fall in wages leads to a fall in purchasing power and consumption expenditure on the part of wage earners. The effective demand for the products of industry will fall, and the demand for labour will further decline, leading to more unemployment. This cumulative process means that a general wage cut, far from restoring full employment, may well aggravate the problem. In line with the Keynesian analysis outlined in Chapter 7 above, we now know that the macro-economic demand for labour depends on the

---

[1] For further discussion see below, Chapter 14.
[2] There may be some who would work at a higher wage but not at the equilibrium wage, but they are not to be regarded as unemployed in that they are not part of the effective supply at the existing wage, but merely part of the potential supply at higher wages.

mutual interdependence of variables such as income, effective demand, saving and investment, and so on. We cannot therefore regard the aggregate demand curve for labour as the summation of individual labour demand curves which are based on the *ceteris paribus* assumption. This kind of understanding did not become an accepted part of economic analysis until the 1930s or later, however, and for a long period of time the existence of unemployment was simply regarded as a reflection of the fact that wages were too high in relation to the prices of other factors.

(3) CONCLUSIONS

There were, then, a number of reasons why this model seemed to be worth defending, based as it was on principles which bore a strong resemblance to the fundamental tenets of a free-enterprise, highly competitive economic system. But its principles could not really be sustained, partly because of the increasing recognition of imperfections in markets and competition, partly because of the failure of the system to secure even an approximation to the full employment of resources which led to a new trend of thought on the problem. The question must then be asked whether there is now any use in elaborating a theory such as this which is so inaccurate in its comprehension of the facts of the real world. Although economists are by no means agreed on this question, there are at least two possible reasons why it is worth while spending time on expounding it to the extent that we have done here. First, even if there are factors present in the economy which inhibit the competitive forces described in the model, or even if the system never has an opportunity to reach equilibrium because of the almost continual process of change which goes on within it, it may nevertheless be useful to know the direction in which the system, if left to itself, would ultimately tend. Quite minor departures from the assumptions of perfect competition, such as errors of judgment on the part of agents in the market place, or imperfections in information, will cause the system to deviate from equilibrium or keep it from reaching equilibrium. But we can still say something about the position to which it will tend in the long run, and many economists would maintain that the theory still has some practical use as a predictive tool in this sense, especially after the imperfections are taken into account.

A second reason for persevering with the competitive theory is that it gives a starting-point to the analysis which can then be modified to embrace different kinds of departure from perfect competition. In short, it provides a base of reference for further, and more realistic, analysis. We have now reached a stage in the development of the argument where we can go on in the following chapters to examine some other consequences of departing from the assumption we have used until now, and bring into the picture more of the real-world factors which contravene the assumptions of perfect competition or in some way cast doubt on the plausibility of the marginal productivity approach. In fact, the economists who worked in terms of the competitive model in its heyday did recognise that there were many sources of imperfection in the real world and, so far as they were able, adjusted the theory to take account of these.

11 Wage Differentials and Labour Mobility

I.

We have already touched upon the question of wage differentials, but we must now return to it in some detail. In perfect competition, with homogeneous labour, wage differentials can of course exist, but only in the short run where they are a symptom of disequilibrium. The existence of wage differences in perfect competition is a signal that readjustments are required in the system, and the process of readjustment will be effected through labour moving from lower-paid to higher-paid positions until the disequilibrium is removed. Whenever we depart from the conditions of a perfect market, there is a possibility that persistent wage differences will emerge. In this connection we have already observed the effects of worker preference, of the geographical immobility of labour and the lack of market knowledge. By creating a degree of inelasticity in the firm's labour supply curve, these imperfections make it possible for wage differences to persist which are not temporary but are quite consistent with labour market equilibrium – though a different equilibrium from that which would have resulted in perfectly competitive conditions. These factors are not, however, the only or even the main reason for the kind of differences in wages which were observed in Chapter 5 to exist in Britain.

In this chapter we must examine in more detail how some of these other sorts of wage differentials arise, and what effect they have on the working of the labour market and on the process of labour mobility. It should be emphasised, however, that the questions of wage structure and labour mobility are among the most critical in labour economics, and their importance is reflected in the fact that they are introduced into the discussion at various points in this book. We have already, in Chapter 5, seen something of the actual pattern of wage differences in Britain. In the present chapter our main concern is with the *process* by which differentials are created and changed, and with the theoretical relationship between labour mobility and the structure of wages. In the following chapter the question arises again as we introduce into the analysis the role of trade unions and employers' associations in the bargaining process by which wage rates are determined. Finally, in the chapters of Part V, where we examine a number of labour market issues, the problems of wage structure and mobility are never very far away from the centre of the discussion. In particular, however, Chapter 17 discusses education and training, which in themselves are major causes of differences in earned income levels, and Chapter 19, dealing specifically with migration and mobility, again explores different aspects of the wage structure and its functioning in a dynamic economy.

The real problem of wage differentials only begins to emerge when we remove the restrictive assumption of homogeneous labour. In this chapter, therefore, we abandon the labour homogeneity condition, and so open up the problems of wage relationships between different occupations, industries and areas. For the moment, however, we will continue to exclude the effects of trade unions and collective bargaining on the process of wage determination and on the relative wage structure.

II. The Meaning of 'Wage' in this Context

Before we proceed to the main problem of this chapter, however, there is one point which needs some attention. This is the meaning of 'wage' in the subsequent discussion. The concept of 'wages' can be used in a great many ways, according to the purpose in hand. Wages can be conceived of in monetary or in real terms. They can be regarded as the share of the labour factor in the national income or the share of the individual worker in the total income distributed to the labour factor. Wages can mean variously the 'basic' rate of payment according to a wage agreement; or the total earnings (inclusive of overtime and bonus) of a worker in a given period of time (per hour, per week, per month); or the annual income from work in a year or over some longer period. Yet again, the term may be used to denote any of the latter net of deductions for income tax, social security payments, etc. And wages may be regarded as inclusive or exclusive of the various fringe benefits which a worker may receive in addition to his money income from employment.

For some purposes, it is obvious enough which of these measures is the most appropriate. For others, the choice of a 'best' measure presents many difficulties. In the present case, where we are concerned with wage structure, the existence of non-homogeneous labour is, as we shall see, capable of producing a wage structure, so that different types and qualities of labour will receive differing rates of payment. This in itself presents no problem. But when we come to examine the part played by the wage structure in allocating labour to different uses, it becomes important to know whether labour is more responsive to some kinds of differential than to others. The relationship between the payment of two workers may differ considerably according to the measure we adopt; to give just one example, one worker may earn 30 per cent more than another before tax is deducted, but after tax the differential may be cut to 20 per cent. Which of these is more likely to be the one that is of interest to the worker? And does the worker respond to absolute monetary differences in income or is it the percentage differential that matters?

In fact we know very little about the responsiveness of labour to different kinds of differential. It is quite possible, indeed, that different types of worker, with different educational and social backgrounds, and working under different types of employment contract, will view the matter differently. The professional worker, such as a doctor or lawyer, may be more concerned with the longer-run flow of income – his annual receipts from work or the gross income he receives over a longer period in his working life. Conceivably the manual worker, being paid on an hourly or weekly basis, may be more influenced by differences in the immediate, short-term rate of earning. In some cases, of course, these two views might amount to the same thing, provided the weekly rate of earning is steady and can be maintained over a long period, but this will by no means always be the case. In short, this is an area where we are able to produce a large number of alternative hypotheses based on *a priori* reasoning but where there is no guidance for selecting among them except by empirical testing.

In recent years there have been a number of empirical studies of the relation between wages (variously defined) and mobility,[1] but they have not so far provided any proper basis for preferring one measure of wages rather than another. In part this is because these studies had other aims in mind, and simply used what data on wages was readily available; in part also it is because the problem of interpreting the results of such studies is a major one which has not been solved. This is not a purely academic question, and in fact is perhaps less serious in abstract analysis than it is in studies of real problems. Suppose an industry needs to expand its employment of labour and believes that the way to do this is to increase the differential between it and another industry employing the kind of labour it wants. If labour mobility is responsive only to a wage differential *after* deduction of tax and other payments, rather than to gross wage

[1] In particular, see P. de Wolff *et al.*, *Wages and Labour Mobility*, 1965.

differentials, gross earnings may have to rise very considerably to encourage labour to move, and this will be costly to the industry which is trying to attract labour. The efficiency of the labour market in reallocating labour between employments as demand and supply conditions alter is thus liable to be greater if labour responds to differences in gross earnings rather than net earnings, since in the latter case the degree of flexibility required in gross wages way be out of reach of many employers.

With little to guide us here, we will proceed on the basis that in the short run labour will be responsive to money wages before tax and other deductions. We will also concentrate mainly on (gross) average weekly earnings as a basis for job comparison, though as we go on we will have something to say about the way in which longer-term considerations may affect this. The justification for this is two-fold: first, workers do not seem to be completely knowledgeable about the effects of income taxation on earnings;[1] and secondly, there is some reason to believe that as collective bargaining is mainly concerned with establishing a basis for a weekly level of earnings, and as most of the working population is paid on a weekly basis, this is the measure of 'wages' which they are most likely to have in mind in contemplating job changes. This view has to be modified somewhat as we proceed, but at least it provides a convenient starting point.

III. Social and Economic Influences in Job Choice

When the assumption of homogeneous labour is abandoned, both demand and supply lose their 'amorphous' character and acquire a more structured form. On the demand side, workers no longer have the property of being completely interchangeable, and employers will exercise preferences for particular kinds of labour through the price system. They will be prepared to pay workers differing amounts according to their respective contributions to the firm's output and revenue. On the supply side, too, workers will have preferences concerning the kind of work they want to do, its location and its employment conditions. Workers will have differing abilities and training and will adapt more easily and efficiently to some types of work than to others. They will therefore seek employment where they think their maximum advantage lies. In such conditions of differentiated demand and supply it is inevitable that the unique wage of a perfectly competitive equilibrium will be replaced by an interrelated system of

[1] See below, Chapter 14.

wages at different levels, and this is of course a much more accurate reflection of the kind of situation we observe in real-world labour markets. A good deal remains to be said, however, about the origin of differentials and the interrelationships between wages in different jobs.

The supply of labour to different jobs depends on two main factors: the conditions of entry, and the 'net advantages' of the various jobs. For virtually all workers, whatever their qualities and characteristics, there will be some limitation on job choice deriving from those two factors, but the way in which these limitations operate will often vary according to the work experience of the individual. For example, many jobs require from those who are to fill them a certain amount of experience which cannot be supplied by young persons who are entering the labour force for the first time as full members. Even more established members of the labour force, however, may find that these jobs are not open to them because they require quite specific patterns of prior work experience, or acquired work attributes or skills. In other words, previous work experience is one of the major determinants of the job horizons – the range of jobs for which he is likely to be a serious competitor – which are open to any worker.

This, of course, is of major importance to the young person entering the labour force. Some of these will have made decisions about their intended job-career patterns even before entering the labour force: for example, those who commit themselves to a six-year programme of higher education to qualify as a medical practitioner. But the majority who have not made this kind of prior decision, in taking their first job, are frequently choosing an occupation or occupational level which will determine the future pattern and income prospects of their working lives. In many cases the sixteen-year-old boy who enters manual employment in a straight-forward semi-skilled or unskilled job is effectively eliminating his prospects of achieving craftsman status in later years, for he will tend to find himself embarked on a job-career progression which will not allow him easily to transfer to skilled manual work. Movement to other types of work, such as clerical employment, may be still more difficult. These difficulties of movement originate to some extent in the conventions which govern the processes of worker selection and promotion and which tend to give preference to workers already within a given occupational system, to the exclusion of those who have previously committed themselves to some other system. These conventional barriers are, however, supplemented and supported by institutional rules and regulations, operated in many cases by trade unions, as we see in the following chapter. Thus although natural or innate factors will influence the range of job choice of individuals, great importance also attaches to the work characteristics acquired by education, training and previous work experience, and as we shall also see, the social stratification of the economy may further affect the individual's ability to acquire the attributes required to gain entry to particular jobs and occupations.

(1) NATURAL AND SOCIAL BARRIERS TO ENTRY

Despite the great number of jobs, varying in occupation and industry, in existence in a modern technological society, the real range of choice at any time for the individual is by no means unrestricted. Several kinds of limitations on choice can be identified. In the first place there are the so-called 'natural' barriers. Workers are individuals possessing a certain array of talents, qualities and characteristics. Likewise, jobs require from those who enter them particular aptitudes and there will be a great many who do not possess the necessary attributes for a given job. This applies not only to work in occupations requiring high academic standards or rare innate abilities, but also to jobs which, though usually regarded as unskilled, demand qualities such as physical strength, a certain dexterity, or an ability to accept and adapt to a monotonous, routine task. Thus many people, aware of their own aptitudes, will rule out of account some types of work, while they may find that they are themselves ruled out from others because they do not possess (and are incapable of acquiring) the necessary characteristics. Where there is a demand for skills or qualities which are only rarely found in individuals, these people will then be able to command a high price for their services in the occupation in question: examples of this include film stars, artists, musical virtuosi and so on. Conversely, jobs which a great number of people are capable of performing adequately are likely to reap a lower rate of pay.

These natural obstacles to free occupational choice are reinforced by others which stem either from the conventions or customs of society or some sectors of society, or from institutional rules, regulations and practices which have been introduced for such diverse reasons as the protection of the public from inept and potentially harmful practice and the safeguarding of employment or the protection of wages in limited sectors of the labour market.

One of the main social barriers affects the employment of women. Although they now occupy positions in industry, commerce and the professions which not so long ago would have been inaccessible, many jobs remain closed to them which are quite adequately performed by women in other countries.[1] In some parts of the country there still seems to be social disapproval of middle-class women who take employment, and this disapproval has a deterrent effect. Even where attitudes are less stringent, much may depend on the kind of work involved. While secretarial work and school-teaching are 'acceptable', factory work may not be. A second barrier may be created by the educational system. The grammar-school pupil will often be at a disadvantage in seeking some types of work compared with the product of the public school, and even among the latter the status of the school itself may be important. Universities give rise to similar social advantages in employment: the Oxford–Cambridge background still eases entry to certain kinds of work. On the whole, however, these advantages and disadvantages are probably less important now than they were thirty years ago, and are less effective in restricting entry to an occupation than they are in respect of specific jobs in that occupation. This last conclusion is also broadly true of other characteristics such as creed and colour, in this country at least.

On the other hand, social factors influence the acquisition of, or attitude to, education and training. Considerable pressure, often without proper knowledge of the market, can be brought by family and friends on the young person choosing a career, so that a limited range of occupations, usually within the home community, and so familiar and acceptable to the group, are considered. Some of this is due to prejudice, but perhaps it owes its existence mainly to ignorance of jobs, conditions and prospects in fields which lie outside the experience of the advisers. This is often just as true of the son of the middle-class family who has manual skills and wants to become a craftsman, as of the son of the unskilled worker who wants and would benefit from further education as a means to occupational promotion. To go outside the known limits is to cut off important social contacts.

Another most important set of limitations, which we have already touched upon in mentioning the effects of educational background and the prejudices or lack of knowledge on the part of informal advisers, arises

[1] e.g. Israel and the U.S.S.R. It should be noted that although we are here concentrating on the effect of social attitudes preventing women from offering their services for some types of work, there are many cases also where social attitudes inhibit firms from recruiting women for certain posts. Sometimes it is difficult to separate the two influences: is the fact that we have few, if any, women working as professional engineers due to lack of employment opportunity or to the fact that this is not a job for which women offer themselves because of social conventions?

from the existence of separate and distinctive socio-economic groups. For a variety of reasons, ranging from inadequate information about occupations associated with other sectors of society, through the preference of employers for people with 'suitable' social and educational backgrounds, to the inability of some groups to acquire the necessary education or qualifications, and also a degree of socially-conditioned reluctance to pursue education, there is a stratification in society which results in 'non-competition' between the groups. Sometimes this means simply that the individual embarked on a career may find it difficult to switch to another job lying in a different class; in others, it means that even new entrants to the labour force may find it hard to enter jobs higher up the social scale because of their family background, especially if the move is not between neighbouring classes but involves a 'jump'. Even in the present state of British society, with free education, a system of university grants and an increased possibility of social mobility between classes, the influence of this stratification remains. If we are tempted to believe that this is dying out, it is perhaps salutary to recall the view of J. S. Mill, writing 120 years ago:

> 'The changes, however, now so rapidly taking place in usages and ideas, are undermining all these distinctions; the habits or disabilities which chained people to their hereditary condition are fast wearing away, and every class is exposed to increased and increasing competition from at least the class immediately below it. The general relaxation of conventional barriers, and the increased facilities of education which already are, and will be in a much greater degree, brought within the reach of all, tend to produce many excellent effects. . . .'[1]

The lines of demarcation between existing socio-economic groups may be reinforced in another way. For many jobs there are specific entry conditions which require the individual to obtain certain qualifications through some course of further education or training. These usually mean that costs have to be incurred. In most cases there is a loss of current earnings since trainee rates of pay are frequently less than the earnings which could be obtained in other jobs. There may also be direct costs for tuition and the purchase of books and equipment. Some professional associations require payment of a membership fee before recognised practice can be commenced. Even with the system of public grants towards the cost of higher education and other forms of training, some of the direct costs of training may still have to be met out of family income and in virtually all cases there is an indirect cost in loss of potential earnings.

[1] *Principles of Political Economy* (Ashley edition), p. 393.

Unless family expenditure on other items can be cut or family income supplemented in some way, young people from lower-income families may be obliged to seek employment where no extensive training period is required, which will usually result in lower lifetime earning prospects and lower status. Thus even with the present schemes of educational grants there is still some tendency for social barriers to be perpetuated by economic considerations.

In summary, this part of the discussion leads to the conclusion that the scarcer a natural aptitude or ability in relation to a given demand, the higher is the price that has to be paid for that aptitude likely to be. The same conclusion applies to the reward for abilities which are acquired by training and education, where the supply of certain occupational groups is limited by the need for training. Conversely, abilities, whether natural or acquired by training, which are plentiful in relation to demand will generally be able to command only a relatively low rate of pay. Personal attributes, generally supplemented by training, are therefore one of the factors which give structure to labour supply and hence give rise to wage differentials. Similarly, social divisions add another dimension to labour supply, resulting in a more limited competition for some jobs and greater competition for others than would be the case in a perfectly competitive market, and hence causing wages themselves to be differentiated rather than tending to a common level. One of the major causes of wage structure is therefore the barriers to entry and to mobility; the special case of trade unions and their influence in this respect is held over for discussion in the next chapter.

(2) NET ADVANTAGES

Even allowing for the entry barriers discussed above, there is still an important range of job choice for most members of the labour force. The question now is what factors are likely to be important in leading the individual to choose one job out of those that are available. Wages are only one aspect of job conditions, and even here, as we shall see, workers may have preferences about the pattern and timing of income receipts. There are also many important non-wage aspects of employment conditions. Thus it will normally be the case that job choice will depend on the *net advantages* of alternative employments; that is, on the individual's evaluation of the whole array of wage and non-wage conditions as he expects to find them. (This 'expectational' aspect is by no means unimportant: information about jobs is not always accurate and the realities may become apparent only when the worker experiences them.) In a competitive labour market without entry barriers, we might expect to find that the net advantages of different jobs tended towards equality, and this was indeed the view which characterised the classical approach to wage theory. But obviously, if net advantages are to be equalised and if non-wage conditions of employment vary considerably from job to job, the wage conditions themselves will have to differ. Here then is another source of wage differentials which we must examine in greater detail.

(a) *Non-wage factors*. One of the principal non-wage factors to be included in net advantages is the status or social regard of the kind of work. Traditionally, some occupations such as the medical profession and the Church have been regarded as conferring high social status on those who work in them. More generally, professional and white-collar work usually imply higher status than manual work, and within these broad groups much finer rankings are frequently implicit. In many instances the status of an occupation is not directly related to pay, perhaps because status is a partial substitute for income. However, high status may not permanently outweigh unfavourable wages and in the longer run supply may adjust accordingly, either by decreasing or by failing to attract workers of the same quality as before. Where quality deteriorates, society may recognise the fact and, by according the occupation a lower status, may further aggravate the problems of maintaining an adequate supply.

Conditions of work are another important factor. Where working conditions are dangerous, dirty or unhealthy, compensation in the form of higher money wages may be made to ensure an adequate supply. But even apart from the physical working conditions, other factors may be important, such as the extent and kind of personal relationships involved, the degree of independence at work, the creativity or routine involved, and so on. The economic assessment of such factors is not easy since satisfaction in a job will depend on very different personal weightings of the various elements, and no objective ordering of them can be considered.

The non-wage conditions of employment also include the wide range of 'fringe benefits', which extend from non-contributory pension schemes to the number of days' paid holiday per year. Many of these conditions will be at least as dependent upon the employment policy of the employing firm as upon the occupation, but there are nevertheless some occupations which have fairly generally applied standards for one or more types of fringe benefit: for example, the vacation periods for university teachers, or the free travel associated with railway and airline employment, or the

I

short working hours of bankers and school-teachers. Some of these are part of the popular mythology of occupations and, as such, may influence choice by the inexperienced individual, though the reality may be rather different.

Finally, among the non-wage factors should be included the promotion or 'mobility potential' implicit in a job. More will be said about this subsequently, but it is worth while observing here that jobs differ markedly in the extent to which they afford opportunities for promotion within their general occupational group, and occupations themselves differ in the extent to which they provide springboards for switches to other occupations at later stages in life. These are likely to be important factors in job and occupational choice.

(b) *Wage factors.* For most of us, monetary earnings probably have the largest role to play in job choice, but as noted at the start of this chapter, earnings may be expressed in a number of different ways. It was suggested there that the use of average weekly earnings as a basis for job comparison might be helpful, and this provides us with a starting point. Although there are exceptions, a choice of job frequently implies some degree of attachment, and it thus seems reasonable to think in terms of the income expected from a job at least over a period of months. But there are complications.

In the first place, some occupations are subject to a substantial degree of fluctuation in activity. This may be due to regular seasonal variations which affect some trades in building, agriculture and the tourist industries. In some periods of the year this may mean a good deal of overtime to take advantage of favourable weather; at others, reduced hours of working and perhaps even temporary unemployment. Another source of fluctuation is the cyclical variation in the level of economic activity over the economy as a whole, but this affects some industries (and some jobs within these) more severely than others. This kind of fluctuation is again likely to have its effect on earnings, especially in industries like motor-car manufacture, some parts of the building industry, and steel. In such circumstances the probability of unemployment, short-time working and, on the other hand, bonuses and overtime has to be assessed not just over a few months but perhaps over a few years. There is, of course, an important difference between the seasonal and cyclical cases since the former will tend to be fairly regular, while the latter may be much less predictable – especially in the extent to which the effects of unemployment and short-time working penetrate the labour force. Secondly, while some kinds of job offer a reasonable assurance of steady employment with no great variation in the *range* of expected earnings, others afford very occasional opportunities for very large earnings, coupled with a strong probability of very low earnings through irregularity of work and lack of pregress up the income scale. In the first category we should probably include civil servants, clerks, and office workers generally, and a number of skilled manual occupations such as precision fitters and electricians. In the second category could be included professional boxers, actors, authors, and generally the occupations associated with entertainment. Again, therefore, there is an important source of difference in the expected income of different types of work which cannot be gauged by observation of short-run rates of payment.

A third factor is the timing of earnings in the working lifetime. Two jobs may afford precisely the same total earnings over a period of years, but one may give higher earnings opportunities in earlier years with a subsequent falling off, while others may build up to an earnings peak fairly late on in life. People may put different values on present and future income, so that even although total earnings are the same, we could not predict how individuals would react if faced with such a choice.[1] This timing point gives rise to another issue. Many jobs require an initial investment in the acquisition of training or qualifications and the investment is made in the expectation, *inter alia*, of subsequently higher earnings. If a proper comparison is to be made, account should be taken not simply of the gross earnings stream over the period in the job, but rather of earnings net of the costs of training and forgone earnings, plus any additional special costs which arise in the practice of that job.[2]

This discussion leads us to an important conclusion. If an adequate supply of labour is to be obtained for a job which is subject to employment fluctuations, for example, it may be necessary to offer a slightly higher weekly rate than in comparable jobs where the regularity of employment is greater. Likewise, in jobs which require the individual to incur costs of training, a relatively higher rate of earning, sufficient to give the individual a satisfactory return on his investment of time and money, may be needed to bring forth a sufficient supply of labour. In other words, these kinds of

[1] In fact, a purely objective choice would settle on the first of these options wherever the rate of interest was positive, since the higher earnings of the early years could be invested, giving a higher present capital value to the stream of expected future earnings than in the alternative case.

[2] Ideally, a comparison of earnings in different jobs would have to be based on the present capital values of expected net incomes in each case. In such a comparison, too, it might seem reasonable to calculate on a post-tax basis, especially since a steeply progressive income-tax structure such as we have in Britain may considerably alter the differentials.

wage differences can be regarded as 'equalising differences' in the sense that the relatively higher wages in cases such as we have mentioned above perform a kind of balancing function, bringing the longer-run wage conditions of different jobs into greater conformity.

Taking a more general view, we might see wage differences as equalising in this sense if the differences can be interpreted as a means of compensating those in jobs which have some unfavourable characteristics, either in their wage or in their non-wage conditions. This is in contrast to the kind of differentials arising from natural or artificial barriers to entry, which are in no sense equalising. In the latter cases, imperfections in competition will tend to prevent the equalisation of the net advantages of jobs in separate sectors of the labour market.

But we must now stop to consider how far, if at all, this kind of ideal basis for comparison is relevant to actual decisions about job choice. Without much hesitation, we should have to admit that few people really go to such lengths to make sure that their choice is soundly based. And as we have already pointed out, non-financial considerations may also be very influential in choice. If this is so, we may be driven to the conclusion that people do not in general make their decisions on purely economic criteria, and we might even go on to conclude that the economic approach is not one which is appropriate for the study of such decisions. On the other hand, the importance in labour market analysis of job choice is such that economists must have some apparatus for understanding the basis for such decisions.

Fortunately, there is such an apparatus. There are undoubtedly some people who would accept particular jobs almost irrespective of pay earnings, at least above a bare subsistence level. Such occupations usually fall into the category of 'vocations', in the sense that those who follow them have a deep-rooted desire to do a certain kind of work; ministers of religion, and some medical workers and teachers, are the kinds of people we would expect to find in this category. For such people, any payment over and above subsistence is in the nature of an *economic rent*. But for a great many people, earnings from work constitute one of the most important factors which either keep them in a particular job or make them leave it. At the margin, there will be workers whose earnings will be wholly *transfer earnings*: in other words they are receiving only just enough wages (given the other job conditions) to make them want to stay in that employment.[1]

This in turn gives us a basis for understanding the process of labour

[1] See Chapter 9 above for discussion of these concepts.

mobility, to which we turn in the final section of this chapter. Of those who select any particular kind of job, there will be some who have only just been persuaded to enter. Any adverse change in the net advantages of that work, *relative to others which might be entered*, will tend to make those marginal workers consider transfer, and one of the principal variables in the array of net advantages will usually be the monetary conditions. Conversely, any relative improvement in net advantages will both enable existing job-holders to enjoy a kind of 'surplus' and may increase the supply of workers to that employment by attracting workers at the margin of other employments. In this way we have transfers of workers between jobs in response to changes in their relative employment conditions; this is the mobility process. But before taking up this problem, we have to consider the cause of wage differentials arising on the demand side.

IV. Employers' Hiring Preferences

So long as we could assume that all workers were identical, they could be regarded as perfect substitutes for one another. From the employer's viewpoint it made no difference which workers were hired. When this assumption is abandoned, employers will begin to exercise preferences. Not only will workers possess different kinds of skill, but even where the same training is common to a group of workers, their efficiency may vary considerably: some workers are old, others young; some are male, others female; some are black, others are white. The existence of these characteristics produces two effects. First, employers with a specific capital equipment will require specific types of labour in certain proportions. Secondly, for good economic reasons or for less rational but still understandable reasons, employers may prefer some types of worker to others, even though they possess equivalent skills by all objective tests. Young workers may be preferred to older workers, white workers to black, men to women, and so on.

The first of these effects means that the firm does not have a single demand curve for labour, but a complex of demand curves corresponding to the various types of labour. Thus there is a counterpart on the demand side to the sets of labour supply curves such as we suggested in the last section. In itself this makes little real difference, for we can continue to predict the wage and employment equilibrium for *each* type of labour in much the same way as we did before for a homogeneous labour force, but instead of a single wage rate for the firm there will now be a structure of rates.

The second effect, in which the employer exercises a preference for workers on grounds other than skill, involves different considerations. Some firms pride themselves on being 'good employers', which usually means that they are prepared to pay their workers a little more than other local employers for similar types of labour. The motivation for this sort of policy generally includes some belief on the part of employers that the offer of higher wages enables them to attract more workers, from whom they can select those they think to be worth most to the firm. They are then deliberately departing from the going rate for such labour in the market in order to exercise a better choice. In many cases this will be done for good economic reasons. A firm setting up a plant involving new techniques may want to employ a young and adaptable labour force and may pay something extra to attract more applications than would have been attracted at a lower wage; given the applications for employment, they can then choose according to the criteria they have set themselves. In other cases a higher wage may be thought to help in maintaining a stable labour force by eliminating some voluntary turnover and thus cutting down training and induction costs.[1]

In a sense this exercise of choice is a form of discrimination, though its basis is economic. More often, however, discrimination is based on non-economic grounds such as race and religion. Where this occurs, those who are discriminated against will not be able to obtain the wage and other employment conditions achieved by the remainder, even though they may be just as efficient in the job. This kind of discrimination arises when workers can be distinguished by some characteristic that cannot be changed. Sex and colour are obvious examples,[2] the result of which is that there are two separate and insulated sectors of the labour supply to an identical job function. The employer may hire from either sector according to his preferences, or even from both simultaneously; for instance, paying a higher rate to men or to white workers and a lower rate to women or coloured workers though they may work alongside each other and do identical work. Since the workers who are discriminated against cannot change over to the more favoured sector, two different rates for the same job may exist side by side.

[1] Of course, other employers may try to achieve similar objectives by paying the going market rate and offering better *non-wage* employment conditions, such as higher fringe benefits.

[2] This is not, however, the only reason for differentials based on these factors.

One consequence of this kind of situation is worthy of note. If, as we have assumed here, the two groups of workers are equal in skill (and by implication in productivity), it is clear that when they receive different wages at least one of the groups cannot be receiving the value of its marginal product. And since employers aiming to maximise profits will not hire labour when its wage is greater than its marginal product, we can conclude that the favoured group will be paid according to the value of its marginal product and the other will receive less. This situation, where labour receives less than the value of its marginal product, is usually termed 'exploitation'. We must, however, interpret exploitation carefully in this context since it usually implies an unfavourable value judgment against the employer who takes advantage of a defect in the labour market system to pay labour a wage less than it 'deserves'. This sense of the term implies a moral rather than an economic judgment and one which is not easily translated into economic terms.

Exploitation in the sense in which it is used by economists is a technical condition involving a factor being paid less than the value of its marginal product, and capital as well as labour can be exploited in this sense. Indeed, we have already encountered such a situation in the previous chapter where the employer is faced with a rising labour supply curve:[1] here, even without discrimination between sectors of the labour supply, the firm's equilibrium employment position implies a wage that is below the marginal revenue product of labour, and technically there is a condition of exploitation. But this comes about simply as a result of the employer following exactly the same rules of profit maximisation as the producer faced with a perfectly elastic supply curve. This need not mean that the employer is setting out deliberately to exploit his labour. On the contrary, it is very probable that many employers in this situation regard themselves (and are regarded by others) as 'good employers', paying wages above the going rate. On the other hand, it is just as possible that poorly-paid labour in other industries is being paid its full marginal revenue product, the difference being that in the more competitive situation more labour would be hired and the marginal productivity of labour would therefore be diminished, leading to a lower wage for labour.

From this it follows that the wages paid by a firm will depend to some extent on the degree of competition in the labour market. With non-homogeneous labour, the value of the marginal product of different kinds

[1] Cf. Fig. 10.5 (b). For a most valuable discussion of exploitation, see A. M. Cartter, *Theory of Wages and Employment* (Irwin), Homewood, Ill., 1959, pp. 65–70.

of labour will vary, and now we have seen that, depending upon the competitiveness of the labour markets in which the firm operates, it may pay a wage lower or higher than the marginal revenue product of labour.[1] Thus we have another possible source of wage differentials at the level of the firm. Obviously, however, firms hiring the same kind of labour in the same local labour market will not be able to disregard the wages paid by their competitors, so that although they need not all pay the same wage, potential mobility between firms will tend to prevent them from diverging too widely. How wide this differential will be in any particular market will depend upon the extent of non-wage competition among employers, and also on the degree of mobility among firms. This leads us to a fuller discussion of the mobility problem as a whole.

V. The Role of Labour Mobility

Once again the earlier analysis of perfect competition is a useful starting point, where wage differentials would be purely temporary phenomena, arising out of the time required for the labour market to adjust to changes in the pattern of demand or supply. Given such wage differences, labour would automatically move from lower- to higher-paid work and employers would alter their labour requirements until wages were again equalised at a value corresponding to that of labour's marginal product. By this means two functions are served: labour is able to move to employments where it achieves its maximum advantage, and at the same time the wishes of society as a whole are fulfilled, since labour resources are readily transferred from employments where demand has declined to those where it has increased. Public and private interests therefore coincide.

In the kind of imperfectly competitive world which we have been discussing in this chapter, obvious barriers to mobility do exist, enabling more permanent wage differences to arise, and the allocation of labour (and other) resources will differ from those of the perfect competition model. It is still quite possible, however, for the wage structure to act as an allocative mechanism, expressing through wage differentials the relationship between demand and supply in the various sectors and dimensions of the labour market, and thus providing a series of signals to give direction to the process of labour mobility. Against this background of differentials,

[1] Where a firm pays its labour a wage above its marginal revenue product, it is capital (or some other factor) rather than labour that is being exploited.

changes in the demand and supply of goods and services will be expressed in changes in the demand and supply situation in the labour markets of the economy, and the existing wage differentials will widen or contract in line with these changes. In this instance changes in the differentials between wages, as well as the differentials themselves, will act as pointers to the required direction of labour mobility. The allocation of labour resources among different uses – intra-factor allocation – will thus be effected through the wage structure and changes in the wage structure.

This analysis rests on a number of assumptions. It assumes firstly that the supply of labour is responsive to changes in money-wage differentials, so that if wages rise in one employment, more workers will want to work in it; while if wages fall in that employment, fewer workers will want to work there. How big the actual inflow or outflow will be depends upon the elasticity of labour supply to that employment; and the supply function itself will be determined in part by the freedom of entry to this and other available employments. A second assumption is that changes in the demand and supply of labour will be reflected in money-wage changes, and that money wages are flexible in both directions. As we proceed, more will be said about the validity of those assumptions.

Several important points relating to this analysis can now be made. First, labour mobility is as multi-dimensional as the labour market concept itself. Labour can transfer between local labour markets, between occupations, industries and firms, and a particular move may well involve more than one of these changes: for example, a worker may simultaneously change employer, industry and geographical location.[1] The existence of this kind of complex mobility is important in providing a relationship over wide ranges of the wage structure as a whole. For any individual worker there may be a large number of alternative sources of employment in other firms, other occupations, other industries, and other areas. An adverse change in the net advantages of his present employment relative to any of these alternatives may be enough to make him transfer, though as we have already suggested it is only the worker at the margin who is likely to be motivated to mobility provided only small relative changes are involved. However, we would expect from the earlier analysis that changes in relative wages (or other aspects of employment conditions) would give rise to *some* movement towards the new, more favourable employment, thereby bringing demand and supply more into balance.[2]

[1] Mobility can also occur within the firm, through promotion, transfer between departments, etc., so that occupation may change without a change of employer.
[2] The rise in wages may also eliminate some of the excess demand, but the

Secondly, the worker's present position will influence the ease with which he can undertake different kinds of movement. It was pointed out in Chapter 8 that a highly specialised worker, with a large investment in a particular kind of training, will usually wish to continue using this training and will therefore be more likely to move geographically in order to do so than to change his occupation and remain within his present local labour market. For the less specialised worker, and especially one who works in a large urban labour market, the degree of occupational attachment will be less, and changes between employers, occupations and industries within the local market will be more common. Some kinds of skilled craftsmen and other fairly specialised workers may be able to remain within their occupation, while changing from industry to industry. In this way we can interpret mobility as a kind of investment process, involving costs and returns. For any individual worker some types of movement will be very costly: for example, the specialised worker considering leaving his specialism, or the less skilled worker considering jobs outside his home area. In these cases the return would have to be relatively high for movement to take place: in other words, the wage differential between the present and the alternative employment would have to be great. For most workers, the most difficult form of mobility is geographical movement; for not only are the direct costs of movement great in comparison to shifts within the local market area (where no change of residence is needed), but there may also be important psychological costs involved in moving to unfamiliar surroundings in which new friendships and relationships have to be formed, and dependence on family and other ties may no longer be possible. On the other hand, if the local labour markets are competitive, an individual may be able to improve his position only very slightly by movement within the local market, and movement to another area may be the only means by which he can achieve a more substantial improvement in his position.

Thirdly, it is important to recognise that the existing wage structure may perform an allocative role, and that changes in relative wages need not be essential to changes in the relative employment share of a particular employment. This point can be usefully illustrated in the case of occupations (which is the most important in most instances), though the argument can be adapted to other circumstances. Provided an occupation enjoys a

existence of imperfections will often prevent equilibrium from being achieved, especially in the short run. In the longer run it may be more possible to increase the supply, or for employers to substitute other methods of production which economise in the use of scarce labour.

favourable wage position (towards the top end of the wage structure), it may be able to draw in more workers from other occupations simply by expanding its employment opportunities. The implication here is that at its existing wage level it has an extremely elastic labour supply, so that as the demand curve moves to the right, employment can be increased without a rise in wages. This will not always be so, of course, for there may be barriers to entry, or the costs of acquiring the skills necessary for this occupation may be too great. But in some occupations, such as business management and other jobs in administration, there will be workers ready to move up from lower-paid positions within the same promotion ladder. There are in fact many occupations of this type where workers enter in the expectation of being able to move up to better jobs in the hierarchy as they acquire experience and training in the job. It is then possible within limits for employers to accelerate or decelerate this process of promotion or mobility within the occupation, so changing the relative employment share of each grade, without changing the wage, except perhaps at the recruitment grades of the hierarchy as a whole. Other occupations, however, will not find this possible since there may exist no ready supply of additional labour. In these cases (where the supply of additional labour is highly inelastic) expansion will depend on attracting workers from other occupations with some common characteristics, and here relative wage increases will be an essential condition of employment expansion.[1]

The discussion of this third point introduces the idea of job systems, namely that workers, by gaining experience and skill in one set of functions, thereby open up for themselves new employment opportunities. Within any such system, the supply of labour to any level above the point of entry will be relatively elastic at existing wages, and an expansion of job opportunities at one or more of these levels will enable employment to be increased with little or no change in relative wages. Clearly, though, if this expansion is expected to be permanent, it will be necessary to increase the supply of new entrants to the system and at that point some rise in relative wages may become necessary, either to attract workers already established in the labour force away from their present jobs, or to divert the flow of those joining the labour force for the first time (or re-entering it) towards the expanding sector. Also, where the required expansion is large in relation to existing numbers, and incapable of being met by accelerated promotion without reducing quality, the need for a wage rise will be greater.

[1] Even then they will not *necessarily* induce an increase in supply, since entry barriers or some other factor may prevent workers from moving in.

Two additional points of a more general nature remain to be made. The first is that the adaptability of an economic system to change will be largely dependent on the mobility of its labour. Rapid adaptation of the system to shifts in product demand, to changes in tastes and in technology, requires that labour should exhibit a high degree of mobility. It does not, however, follow from this that a society in which the observed rate of mobility (for example the number of job changes per year per thousand workers) is high is necessarily efficient in its use and allocation of labour. Whether it is or not will depend further on the extent to which job changes are in the directions and quantities required. Where market information is inadequate or faulty, much of the observed mobility will be socially and economically unnecessary – and undesirable from an efficiency point of view, since it will lead to labour and other resources being under-used or misused. Thus the efficiency of the wage structure as an allocative device will depend in part on the adequacy of the labour market information system. However, a society in which the rate of job-changing is high evidently has a *potential* for adjustment to economic change, provided the direction and volume of job-changing can be channelled efficiently and based on sound information. In most societies there still remain numerous impediments to mobility so that even an effective system of market information may still not produce adequate mobility or, perhaps more commonly, may not give rise to sufficiently rapid adjustment.

This effect of market imperfections is the second of our additional points. As we have seen in the course of this chapter, these barriers to mobility derive from a number of sources. The existence of natural and social obstacles to mobility has been observed, and the difficulty and cost of some kinds of transfer have been mentioned. Likewise, the adoption by employers of certain selection criteria may restrict mobility, for example by making it difficult for older workers to change jobs or for women to enter some employments. As we shall see in the next chapter, other barriers owe their existence to institutional rules and practices operated by employers and trade unions. But there are still other factors which have the same effect. International migration of labour (which is often made difficult in any case by the cost of movement, language and cultural differences) is often rendered virtually impossible because of quota restrictions on immigration, by visa controls and the need for work-permits. Within a country, geographical movement may be hampered by imperfections in the housing market. Difficulties in selling existing accommodation, the extra expense of housing in areas where incomes are higher, the methods adopted by local authorites in the allocation of public sector housing, are all factors which may add to the other costs and uncertainties of geographical mobility.[1]

Despite the obvious obstacles to mobility, a great deal of job-changing of all kinds does take place in most societies. But even a casual inspection of the job-changing process indicates that by no means all mobility is voluntary. Workers are dismissed or laid off by their employers and are obliged to seek alternative employment. In these circumstances we would not expect all movements to be in the direction of jobs where net advantages are greater, especially as the worker is not able to choose the timing of his movement. This need not mean that workers no longer seek the best employment available, though it will often be the case that their range of choice is more than usually restricted and a drop in wages may be inevitable.

In conclusion, it is evident from this discussion that the process of labour mobility is likely to be far from perfect in most societies, though the location and severity of the imperfections will be determined by the structure of the society, the nature of its institutional arrangements (including the educational system, and the form and coverage of its trade-union movement) and the organisation of the economy as a whole. We have seen that, provided wages are influenced by demand and supply, both the wage structure and changes in wage differentials will tend to generate mobility, but that the elimination of labour shortages and surpluses may not be achieved because of the imperfections of the mobility process; or that this elimination will be effected only in the very long run, when social and institutional factors can be changed, and technology perhaps adapted to enable firms to be more flexible in their use of particular factors. In short, the effect of immobilities is to make the supply curve of labour to particular sectors more inelastic, and only in the longer term will this inelasticity be reduced by the possibility of substitution or social and institutional change.

It follows, therefore, that the competitive theory of the operation of the labour market must be considerably modified if it is to have any relevance for the understanding of everyday labour market problems. We obviously cannot expect a theory based on assumptions which are far removed from the facts of the labour market to provide an accurate prediction of the effects of change. But as we have seen in this chapter, the competitive

---

[1] It need hardly be pointed out that geographical migration often takes place for non-economic reasons. A change of location is fairly common when a worker marries, and shifts often occur after retirement from the labour force. Other reasons include climate, health, environment and similar factors. The subject of migration and mobility is further discussed in Chapter 19.

model does afford a useful basis for analysis, even of problems which arise from lack of competition, and, in the longer run especially, when the effect of at least some of the barriers to competition and mobility may be reduced, the competitive theory may provide results which are not too far removed from those observed in practice.

12 Wages, Employment and Collective Bargaining

I. Trade Unions and Wage Theory in General

In this chapter we conclude our adaptation of labour market theory to take account of the factors which are either ignored or under-emphasised in the basic competitive model of labour market behaviour. The main feature of the following discussion is the influence of trade unions on wages and employment and the relationship of the theory of wage determination as discussed in previous chapters to the process of wage determination through collective bargaining. The concluding section of the chapter makes a few general points arising out of the discussion of this and the preceding four chapters to round off this part of the book. While the discussion is mainly about trade unions, since their existence is the essential prerequisite of collective bargaining, it would be misleading to regard the discussion as being limited only to the organisations normally referred to as trade unions. As Chapters 2 and 4 have indicated, there are a number of important organisations in our society which, by imposing restrictions on entry to certain kinds of employment and otherwise interfering with the competitive mechanism, exert very much the same kind of influence as those we normally regard as 'trade unions'. Into this category come employers' associations, and also many professional organisations, anxious either to safeguard the public from malpractice or to protect their members (or both). Nor must we forget that Government itself may also play a major role in the labour market, both by creating a background against which collective bargaining can proceed and by organising the determination of wage and employment conditions where trade unions are absent or insufficiently influential. In addition, Government may exert a more indirect influence on the pattern of wage settlement by intervention in dispute settlement or by pronouncements on the range of wage settlement which is publicly acceptable in a particular period, and in such cases the wages resulting from the normal procedures of wage negotiation may be different from those which would otherwise have emerged. (We are here referring to the discussion of incomes policy which is continued in Chapter 21.)

In this chapter, however, we will mainly confine our discussion to the areas in which trade unions operate and where free collective bargaining prevails. Trade unions, of course, have many objectives which are not economic, but our only concern here is with the economic objectives and their effects and implications. In particular there are two questions which need to be considered. First, what are the economic objectives of trade unions; and secondly, how do they derive their influence on the areas where they pursue these objectives? In answering these questions we inevitably raise two further questions. One of these relates to the criticism that is often made of conventional wage theory, that wages are purely determined by institutional forces (sometimes conditioned by social factors) and that the economic explanation of wage determination is an arid exercise with no bearing on reality. We must consider how far this is a fair criticism, and in so doing we encounter a second question, relating to the economic effects of institutional wage determination, and trade-union action. For even if wages were determined by factors different from those allowed for in the economic theory, it would still be the case that economic theory would have something to predict about the consequences of the wage levels set through collective bargaining.

Collective bargaining itself, as indicated in Chapter 4 above, varies considerably in content, but two main subject areas can be identified in most cases. One of these may be regarded as the organisation of *payment*, in which the size and make-up of the worker's wage packet is the most important factor but in which fringe benefits, such as pension provisions and sickness benefit schemes, together with normal hours of work and holidays with pay, are also prominent. The second area is on a rather different level, and might be defined as the organisation of *work*. Not all of the items under this heading will appear in the terms of collective agreements themselves, but their importance in the conduct of negotiations may still be very real. Within this area will be included such items as the right of a particular union to organise certain workers, the manning schedules for specified types of capital equipment, the regulation of output or bonus earnings, the procedures to be followed when there is a cut-back in production, and many other matters of this type. By no means all of these will be taken up by every union, nor will they necessarily be imposed through formal collective bargaining procedures. But these are areas where trade unions normally have a considerable interest, and the bargaining process which bears upon them varies from the highly informal (such as the regulation of output by the work group on the shop floor) through the rather more constitutional negotiations undertaken by shop stewards and local trade union officers, to the completely formal collective agreement of the industry or occupational group itself.

This view of collective bargaining is one which sees the process as one of job regulation whereby rules about payment and methods of work organisation are developed by negotiation between employers and workers. From this point of view it would seem reasonable to identify the first group of aims, concerning payment, as the ultimate objective for trade unions, while the second provides a set of devices which enable the unions to make progress in satisfying these primary objectives. We now go on to see what these aims and methods of approach mean in theoretical terms.

II. Union and Employer Objectives in Bargaining

(1) UNION OBJECTIVES

Although trade unions are by no means entirely economic institutions, it is instructive to consider how far they can be so regarded. One possible approach is to view the union as a monopolistic association, acting as a seller of labour services and organising workers and marketing their services through a single agency. From this basis – especially if we choose the right examples – a fairly convincing picture of the union as a monopolist can be built up.

A craft union organising a single craft includes among its strategies techniques similar to those of a monopolistic producer who wishes to safeguard and advance his monopoly position. The monopolist tries to obtain complete control of his product and the union tries to achieve one hundred per cent organisation of its craft. The monopolist tries to limit entry into his market, while the union objects to dilutee labour and controls the intake and training of apprentices. The producer tries to control the marketing arrangements for his product (for example by resale price maintenance), while the union tries to enforce output limits both on the employer (by demanding certain manning standards for the operation of machinery) and on the worker (by setting limits on the volume of bonus working). Whereas the monopolistic producer aims at making his product as different as possible from possible substitutes, the union fights demarcation issues to maintain a clearly differentiated trade. The product is not supplied to those sales outlets and producers which do not observe the terms of sale laid down, while the union resorts to strikes and other forms of industrial action to force employers to comply with prescribed conditions. A monopoly agreement among producers who want to establish a monopoly lays down penalties for breaking agreements: the union enforces discipline on recalcitrant members.

The strength of the analogy between a craft union and a monopolistic producer is too great for it to be incidental. Furthermore, actual labour market situations, such as the long history of the preservation of the position of the skilled printing trades, or the successful preservation of high rewards in some professions, can be usefully analysed in this way, through a method of approach which is familiar to economists. But how useful is this as a *general* method of approach?

Even the example based on the craft union raises some difficulties. First, monopolists sometimes justify their actions by asserting the need to preserve specially high standards and to protect the public from inferior service. In some cases, this may also be true of the craft union which attempts to build up a *necessarily* high quality within its membership; by imposing restrictions on entry through the setting of qualifications and admission standards, for example, it may be doing no more than safeguarding the public in a way that might have been done by some external educational or governmental body. Thus there may be a real and necessary difference in the quality, training or experience of labour rather than an artificially created and unjustifiable distinction. In other cases attempts by trade unions to control the allocation of labour to particular processes may be a wise recognition of appropriate manning standards on grounds of efficiency or safety.

Secondly, action to obtain a high price for the sale of labour services is likely to require judgment on much wider and quite different social principles from our judgment of monopoly in the sale of a commodity. The effectiveness of a craft monopoly must depend on the unity of the craft in its loyalty to its union organisation, in the extent to which the whole craft is organised, and in its employment in virtually identical circumstances wherever it may work. The monopoly outlook suggested above can only be effectively sustained if the individuals concerned are prepared to forgo employment where conditions vary from those prescribed by the union, and this should apply not only to conditions which are inferior to those prescribed but also to those where conditions are better.

A third complication is that the monopolistic producer has to recognise that by raising prices he must expect to sell less units of product: in setting out to maximise profits he will have to restrict his output well below the competitive level. The trade union acting as monopolist must also accept some trade-off between wages and employment: by raising wages for its members it may have to forgo some employment. Certainly, a tightly-knit craft union might tackle this difficulty by limiting apprentice intake and could deal with occasional unemployment through a private unemployment compensation scheme. But this kind of policy may have dangerous consequences for the monopoly position of the union itself, for it means that the union must remain small and highly loyal within itself, and it must then be under constant threat of the formation of competitive unions or independent action by members who suffer from the effects of unemployment.

This of course assumes that we can properly regard the union as a 'maximising' unit, with the wage rate being the thing that is to be maximised. But given that employers will tend to use less labour as its wage rate rises, other things being equal, we must recognise that there are many other variables that the union might seek to maximise. For example, it might seek to maximise employment of its existing members, which might mean accepting a lower rate of wages. It might seek to maximise the wage bill. It might decide to maximise membership, which could involve it in expanding its organisation beyond a limited and specialised group of workers. The difficulty is that each of these hypotheses produces a different model of trade-union behaviour, involving different predictions.

In practice, it would seem that for different unions all these motives may be important, but in varying degrees, and that union policy in any particular case will be something of a compromise among them, depending on the circumstances of the union and the kind of employment conditions with which it is faced. In the present British situation there is hardly a true craft union left, and the much more typical situation is that of the general or multi-craft union in which there are different types of worker, with differing grades of skill, often working in different industries. In this kind of situation it is an almost inevitable consequence that the monopoly analogy loses force, since the policies pursued by unions of these types are complex and changing, and the application of any simple model becomes quite inappropriate.

As a general rule, however, we can probably assume with some conviction that *one* of the principal aims of a trade union will be to maintain and if possible improve the wage position of its members, though the degree to which it will pursue this aim will be governed by the union's need to take account of the consequences of that policy for employment, membership and other objectives. This in turn raises two important questions. Are unions more concerned with real wages or money wages? And where, if at all, do relative wages enter the picture?

Since real wages are the determinant of labour's living standard, we might expect that unions would be more concerned with the real value of wages than with their monetary expression. But we know from observation that unions do not threaten to strike every time prices go up and wages remain unchanged. Unions thus accept reductions in real wages for limited periods of time, though they will usually expect to catch up on rises in costs of living at the next wage negotiation. In an inflationary situation it often seems that the main concern of unions is with the relative wage position of their members, vis-à-vis the wage position of other unions. Obviously, unions will try to ensure that real wages are not eroded and that all possible gains in real wages are obtained, but the need to preserve the union's position in the *relative* wage structure frequently comes to the fore in wage claims. In a period of less than full employment, however, or where a particular union has many members unemployed, the union may be more intent upon securing an increase in employment than an immediate rise in real wages or an improvement in relative wages; or at least its wage demands may be tempered by concern for the unemployed. Finally, when in a deflation the demand for labour is falling, unions are generally thought of as being resistant to cuts in *money wages*, even though real wages may not thereby be affected, since prices may be falling too. On this view, labour would seem to be acting irrationally, basing their actions on what has been called the 'money illusion'.[1]

Keynes almost certainly exaggerated when he wrote about this resistance to money-wage cuts as an empirically observable phenomenon. Money wages do fall in depression, though there is no doubt that they are much more inflexible downwards than they are in the opposite direction and that money-wage cuts follow the decline in labour demand only after a considerable time-lag. There is no doubt either that this tendency is reinforced by the presence of a strong trade-union movement. This of course was important in Keynes's theory: cuts in money wages would lead to a fall in purchasing power and hence to further falls in the demand for labour, whereas Keynes sought employment stability through an increase in expenditure. In this respect he saw value in the typical union resistance to a cut in money wages. For the present purpose, however, the important points relate to union objectives, and on that score we can conclude that unions do in general resist money-wage cuts, though their ability to succeed will depend on the severity of the recession and the strength of the union relative to the employer. In more favourable circumstances, the union will

[1] This of course would also be the case where unions do not react – at least immediately – to falls in real wages through rises in prices.

not lose sight of the goal of raising real wages, but may in the short run be more concerned with money wages and especially the pattern of money wages among different groups of workers.

On this last point, there is little doubt that for many unions the need to preserve wage differentials between their own members and those of other *specified* unions is an important aspect of policy. In other words, certain unions see themselves as in an inextricable relationship to others, and their wage objectives will be framed in relation to what these other unions have achieved or are expected to achieve. This introduces a new element into the bargaining arena, the existence of *conventional* or *customary* differentials, which the unions concerned will try to uphold even when their respective economic circumstances change. If this kind of objective could be enforced, then the theory of labour resource allocation by means of changes in the relative wage structure would be inapplicable. In practice, the relative wage structure, especially with respect to wage rates, does tend to be relatively rigid even over fairly long periods of time, and it is probable that the unions' view of conventional differences has some part to play in this. But as we shall see subsequently, this rigidity is by no means complete; and in any case we have already stressed that resource allocation can occur through a competitive mechanism even though there are no changes in the relative wage structure: the existing wage structure can also serve to re-allocate resources as employment opportunities change.

In summary, then, we can say that while it is sometimes possible to analyse the role of trade unions by means of a fairly simple model of union behaviour, it is much more often the case that union objectives are too complex and dynamic to be considered in this way. Not only are there many possible objectives for a union, but these may be conflicting, so that some kind of compromise policy has to be adopted with the emphasis changing from one facet of policy to another as demand conditions alter. Unions, too, though not solely motivated by money wages, are apparently influenced more obviously by money wages than by real wages, not least perhaps because of the importance to them of their status in the wage hierarchy and the need to preserve customary differentials between themselves and other unions whom they regard as competing or otherwise closely related to themselves.

(2) EMPLOYERS' ASSOCIATIONS

Much less can be said on the objectives of employers' associations than about the aims of unions. Only to a very limited extent is it possible to adopt the analogy of the employers' association as a monopsonist (a single buyer) in the labour market. Certainly it may be the aim of many employers' associations to act in this way, and thereby to resist the pressures of a powerful union. From this point of view we can understand why associations try to exert control over their members, by preventing them from stepping out of line in wage matters, for example. Provided the association is able to exert such discipline, the monopsony approach may be of assistance in the understanding of its bargaining procedure. But there are many deficiencies in such an approach. Employers' associations have no control over new demand for labour. They do not usually cover the whole range of employment offered in any particular sector, since many firms – some of them important employers – prefer to remain outside such associations; and this of course weakens the association's position in relation to the trade unions. Furthermore, the power of discipline is weak, for the ultimate sanction available is expulsion from the association, which need not involve the recalcitrant firm in any real penalty. It can simply go its own road, and may in many circumstances do so more favourably than if it remained within the association. The problem for the employers' association is that its constituent firms are themselves complete economic organisations with an ability to command resources and conduct their own wage negotiations, and while it may suit a number of firms to come together for bargaining purposes, it is quite possible for them to proceed independently. Thus the basic unit of negotiation is ultimately the individual employer, and it frequently makes more sense to analyse bargaining situations from this point of view; even within the association, there has to be some common agreement among members about what offers can be made to labour while still remaining acceptable to all. In this type of situation the relevance of the monopsonistic approach is not readily apparent.

Another difficulty in the understanding of the objectives of employers' associations is that they most commonly assume a negative role, and exhibit few signs of positive policy. The initiative is usually left to the unions, in the timing, size and composition of the wage claim, while the employers' association exercises its function by resisting or moderating these demands, or by making counter-offers. It is this situation, of course, which gives definition to the real bargaining area, and which brings into play the strategic and tactical steps which characterise all bargaining processes. Yet, as we now see, there will be quite definite economic constraints and objectives which will influence both the determination of the bargaining territory and the process of reconciling conflict.

(3) ECONOMIC CONSTRAINTS ON BARGAINING

The basis of these economic constraints is fairly obvious. On the trade-union side, there has to be a recognition that some wage demands will be unrealistic and impracticable, either because they would leave nothing over for profits, and thus lead to inadequate investment or the closure of the firm, or because labour may be replaced by capital (or capital and less expensive types of labour) in a new technique of production. In either case the demand for the services of the union's members would decline and there must be a limit to the acceptability of such a policy on the part of the union's membership. On the other hand there will be some wage levels which will be too low for the unions to accept, either because they do not enable the union to maintain a parity with other unions or perhaps because they do not sufficiently compensate for rises in the cost of living. Thus there will be a limited range of wage positions for the union, all of which will be acceptable but some of which will be more highly preferred than others. This relatively simple view is complicated by the fact that unions do not bargain on wages alone, but on hours of work, fringe benefits and other issues which together comprise a bundle of employment conditions. But this complexity does have the merit of allowing a greater area of compromise, since it may be more easy for the union to accept less than it asked for on one score while getting rather more on another.

From the employer's standpoint, this complexity has the same kind of effect, but it has to be remembered that each item in the bundle of employment conditions will have its cost to the employer, even if it is not a wage matter. Once more, there will be economic limits to the range of acceptable settlements for the employer. Some settlements will be too costly in the sense that their reflection in selling prices will reduce demand and revenue and cut back profits. Others may be inaccessible because the wage conditions they imply will not be sufficient to bring forth an adequate labour supply or may lead to strike action. The employer clearly cannot ignore the wages which are being paid elsewhere in his industry to similar labour, nor can he ignore the wage standards being applied to the same sorts of labour in his own local labour market. In an imperfect market, of course, he need not pay precisely the same as others, but depending on the extent of competition, the degree of market knowledge and his expectations about turnover at different wage levels, the wage he pays must lie within a range which will enable him to get the labour he wants. The exact limits of this range will of course vary from producer to producer according to his product demand conditions, and even a single producer will experience changes as external economic conditions alter. In periods of buoyant product demand, larger rises in labour costs are likely to be granted than when demand is stagnant or declining.

There is another constraint on the employer which we have not so far introduced. Our previous analysis of the firm's demand for labour assumed a smooth and continuous marginal physical product curve for labour, implying that output and employment were infinitely variable.[1] But most modern firms are possessed of a technology which requires that if the plant is to be run efficiently it must operate in a narrow output range and with a fixed complement of labour. Short-term departures from this norm may be accepted by the firm in certain conditions, but over a longer period such a policy would not be feasible and some closure of capacity might become necessary. In such cases the plant cannot be regarded as an infinitely flexible means of production, but is more correctly conceived as a unit which is capable of producing output volumes at certain discrete size intervals. In other words, the employer in such circumstances is faced with a rigidity arising out of the technical process itself, and unless wage changes are so considerable that they force him to change to a new level of output, he must accept the need for hiring the appropriate quota of labour at the current wage. In view of this inflexibility, employers have much more interest in settling wages towards the bottom end of the bargaining range than if they were able to make small adjustments to output and employment as market and other conditions altered.

A second important consequence of this inflexibility – though it involves a slight digression – is that short-run changes in wages or (more generally) labour costs will not necessarily result in changes in numbers employed. The discussion above suggests that changes in employment are much more likely to be brought about by changes in product demand, affecting the level of output at which the firm can profitably produce, than by changes in wages. This is broadly consistent with everyday observation of the business world, where firms do not immediately change their employment levels following wage rises, but do shut down sections of plant or resort to short-time working when product demand is low.[2]

[1] The exception to this was the oligopoly case, where product market conditions were responsible for a kink in the demand curve.

[2] Strictly, this move away from a situation in which infinitely small adjustments to output and employment are possible, to one in which changes are discrete, means that the marginal analysis is no longer applicable. But if we are prepared to take a less pure view and to accept that firms are likely to miss their targets from time to time, we can reasonably maintain that the marginal productivity approach provides a satisfactory approximation. Even with infinitely

The conclusion that emerges from this discussion is that although both employers and unions will have preferences about the *locus* of wage settlements, these preferences will be defined at the extremes by practicability. Within certain limits, which vary from case to case and from time to time, there will be an area in which wage settlements could be acceptable to both parties. These limits are themselves largely the outcome of economic factors, as we have now seen. Precisely where the final settlement is located within these limits will depend on the bargaining power and skill of the respective parties, and the understanding and analysis of this process of determination would require a theory of bargaining which we cannot take up in this context. This does not, however, alter the fact that the general *locus* of such settlements is determined by economic factors. As one writer has put it:

> 'The unionization of an industry does not lead to the replacement of economic by political forces in the setting of wages; rather, the economic forces are filtered through political groupings, which can delay or redirect them but not reverse their flow.'[1]

III. Union Methods of Control

The analogy of the craft union as a monopolist, though in some ways imperfect, revealed the importance to the union of devising means by which it could control the supply of labour. This feature of control over the supply of labour and, by inference, the union's ability to exert pressure on the employer or employers' association, is by no means confined to the craft union, though it is in that sort of tightly-knit group that the degree of control may be greatest. In this section we will amplify the earlier discussion of these matters in Chapter 2 and examine the economic implications of some of the more important methods of control which are adopted by unions. There are three main methods of approach open to the unions: controls on entry, controls over effort, and sanctions.

---

variable production and employment, inaccuracies in scheduling, delays in adjustment, and the like would mean that firms could not in practice continually achieve equality between factor prices and their marginal revenue products. Besides, such continuous minor adjustments themselves, and the degree of recording data, etc., which they would involve, might themselves add more to costs than to revenue. For further discussion, see below, pp. 288–90.

[1] Albert Rees, *The Economics of Trade Unions*, 1962, p. 64.

(1) CONTROLS ON ENTRY

Controls on entry take many forms, according to the nature of the union organisation, but they all have one common aim: to limit the available supply of a particular kind of labour so that the supply is inelastic and any increase in demand will be expressed in higher wages per worker rather than increased employment. One of the most common controls here is the apprenticeship system, which limits the possession of particular types of work to men who have served a customary training period. This is not of course without value to the employer, for it means that he can hire such workers and be fairly certain of their competence over a given range of skills. But from the union's point of view it means that the competition for particular kinds of work is limited to its own members, and this may be further restricted by the union insisting on the maintenance of a fixed ratio of trainees to time-served workers. This latter restriction means that employers no longer have the sole discretion about training and transfers a degree of control to the union which can then, usually in the bargaining process, adjust apprentice ratios up or down as conditions dictate. Furthermore, this kind of control is backed up by union insistence on demarcation – the right of a union's membership to all work involving the handling of particular 'craft' tools or equipment or the carrying out of certain defined functions. The extent to which the union following such policies can succeed will clearly depend on its ability to achieve comprehensive coverage of workers, and this is often sought by means of a *closed-shop* policy, in which the union obliges employers to have only union members for particular types of work.[1] In this way the union increases its monopoly power by making it impossible for employers to find another feasible source of labour of the type in question.

In a few rather special cases, admission to the union is restricted to nominees from within the union itself, frequently relatives or friends of existing members. Examples of this practice are found in the docks and in some jobs associated with the wholesale food markets. Here again the aim is one of complete monopoly, with the union's power to nominate new members being extended in such a way that the possibility of 'outside' interests intruding, and perhaps breaking the union's grip on the organisation of labour supply, is virtually excluded.

In terms of our earlier analysis, all measures of this kind are effectively

---

[1] The closed-shop policy (or its variant, the union shop, requiring the employer only to have workers who are prepared to join the union) is not limited to the craft-based union.

aimed at introducing an artificial inelasticity into the supply curve of workers and, by adjusting the numbers available, to ensure full employment and high wages for the group concerned. This sort of control is not limited to craft unions – which in any case we have suggested to be relatively scarce, at least in a pure form. But there are many unions with a craft origin which still exercise similar kinds of control over labour supply, and of course other organisations – including a number of professional associations – use very similar methods, for example by restricting membership to those possessing specified qualifications and by insisting that employers hire only those who belong to the association. In this respect they differ not at all from the most traditional form of closed union.

Elsewhere, other methods of control on entry are adopted, perhaps the most important being the use of the *seniority principle*. Whereas the system we have just discussed depends on the possession of specific entry qualifications which, once possessed, allow the worker to take any job of this kind in any firm or industry, the seniority device is based on control of labour supply within the firm or industry. Jobs in the plant are ordered into hierarchies, with those at the top carrying the highest wages. Entry to the top jobs can only be effected by those in the rank immediately below, and this principle is continued down the scale. New entrants to the firm always have to begin at the bottom of the ladder, from which point they progress simply on the basis of seniority. For workers in this situation the firm itself becomes a complete labour market, through which they can move by changing occupational status within the well-defined boundaries of the particular job hierarchy. Whereas the worker in the craft-based union has an investment in a particular skill, the worker in an industry where the seniority principle is effective has an investment in his experience and service with the firm.

Promotion through seniority is often backed up by other measures to increase the employment and income security of established workers. It is in this kind of situation that we most frequently encounter the 'last in – first out' scheme, whereby any cut in the firm's employment falls on those most recently hired. Where necessary, those with most seniority may have to move down a grade temporarily, but their continued employment is relatively assured and the fall in income will usually be much less than if they were to become unemployed and had to seek alternative work. In many cases this arrangement is written into collective agreements and it is not uncommon for there to be an understanding that, when demand recovers, the firm will give priority to those it has earlier paid off, and that it will first rehire those workers most recently made redundant. There is thus an ordered supply of labour under this system, with ready-made substitutes for any job continually on hand and recruitment from outside the job system being limited entirely to jobs at the bottom of the scale.

The interest of the union in this case is very similar to the previous examples of control on entry. Both systems, by limiting the employers' ability to recruit from outside the system except at points of entry at the bottom of the scale, effectively control the supply of labour to established jobs. The seniority-based scheme is frequently coupled with a closed-shop or union-shop policy, just as in the case of the craft-based system. The main difference is that in the craft system it is frequently impossible for adult workers to effect entry, whereas this is not so in the seniority-based system, which is less selective at the points of entry. The other important difference – of rather a different kind – is that the two systems tend to generate quite different types of mobility. The craft-based system encourages attachment to the craft but may necessitate inter-firm and inter-industry movement, whereas the seniority-based scheme generates intra-firm mobility involving occupational shifts.

(2) CONTROLS ON EFFORT

The controls discussed in the last section are related to the supply of workers. Other methods of control exercised directly or indirectly by trade unions are related to the effort content of labour supply, but once again the main reasons for such policies are the safeguarding of employment and the maintenance of wages. Controls on effort are to be observed principally as restrictions on output or on bonus earning and arise more commonly where some form of piecework or incentive payment system is in operation. In some cases this may result from an official union view about the appropriate rate of output or earning, but in most instances it is the product of informal regulation through the setting of norms within work-groups on the factory floor.

The basis for such devices is relatively clear. In the system based on seniority, wage differences are a reflection of seniority, and those in a promotion line can be fairly certain that they will, in time, succeed to the better-paid jobs. In the craft-based system, all workers other than those in training are regarded by the union as of equal standing and for this reason one of their major aims in bargaining has been to secure a common rate for each type of job within their particular province. This conception of the 'common rule' can be interpreted as an integral part of the system since it produces a cohesion of interests and prevents the break-up of the common interest which might occur if it became obvious that the union was accepting wage differentials which were not a reflection of differences in productivity or in the type of work undertaken. But both in the craft-based system and in general unions, the existence of incentive payment schemes presents difficulties, by making it possible for individual workers, with particularly high abilities for a given job, to earn far more than their average colleagues. This differential in ability, and the fact that it may be reflected in earnings, represents a threat to the unity of the system, and the controls on output and earnings are in part a recognition of the need for such differences to be kept in check. A common consequence is that upper limits to the individual's production and earnings will be established informally by the work-groups, and anyone who persistently exceeds the norm will be disciplined by the work-group, often by 'sending him to Coventry' or by bringing pressure to bear on management to fire him.[1]

But this kind of pressure has other implications. The more it appears that higher output and earnings are readily achievable, the greater is likely to be the bargaining power of the employer to lower the payment per unit of output. Again, if workers are free to set their own production targets and are encouraged to raise them by the incentives built into the payment system, they may thereby be regarded either as working their fellows out of a job (especially if the order-book situation is known to be unfavourable) or as keeping others out of employment. The regulation of output and earnings thus has this second purpose of sharing work evenly, and of protecting income and employment. The rationale of this mode of control is of course more in keeping with an era of depression than one of prosperity, but even in today's fairly prosperous society some industries, such as ship-building, coalmining and others in process of structural decline, have some cause to maintain these traditional protective or restrictive practices. This is not, however, to imply that it is only in these more depressed industries that such practices are to be found, though elsewhere they may exist in a looser, more relaxed form.

(3) UNION SANCTIONS

The third and final source of trade-union control is their ability to invoke sanctions which bring pressure on employers to agree to settlements which lie closer to the union's preference path. These sanctions are basically of

[1] This pressure is usually based on some pretext, rather than on the fact that the unity of the group is being disrupted, so that the obvious cause of disputes is frequently not the 'real' or underlying cause.

two kinds, the one involving a complete withdrawal of union labour, thereby cutting off the firm's labour supply, the other involving a moderation of effort. Thus there is a reflection here of the two methods of control discussed in subsections (1) and (2) above.

The most extreme form of penalty the union can impose on the employer is the strike, but it is probably fair to say that unions prefer to avoid strikes except as a last resort, and most often use the *threat* of strike action as a means of influencing the employer. For although strikes inflict penalties on employers, they involve the union in certain dangers. In the first place they can be costly to the union in terms of the effect they have on union emergency funds. The strike imposes a cost, in terms of earnings forgone, on union membership; and the longer the strike continues, the greater the hardship on members and the less may become the enthusiasm of the participants. A failure on the part of the union to achieve 100 per cent withdrawal of labour, or to prevent a partial return to work before settlement of the dispute is reached, is indicative of a lack of cohesion in the union and a loss in the union's authority in negotiation. Finally, in circumstances of low product demand, the strike may be quite acceptable to the employer as it means that he can close down production completely at little cost, and again the effect of strike action as a means of bringing pressure to bear on the employer is nullified.

Sanctions involving controls on effort include devices such as working to rule, overtime bans and other actions of this type. The purpose and limitations are again very similar to those of strike action, though the effect on the employer is less immediate and the union is much more capable of maintaining such action over a long period, if necessary. But ultimately the intention is to impose economic penalties on the employer in order to convince him of the need to move closer to the union's preference path.

Two main conclusions arise from this discussion of union controls in the labour market. The first is that a primary purpose of control is to exercise an influence on the bargaining process, whether it be through limitations on entry, restraints on effort or the more straightforward use of direct power. Only if the union can achieve an effective means of control in one or more of these areas can it hope to influence the employer and bring him to a settlement which is closer to the union's terms. However, there is a second consequence, which may affect wages and employment more directly. Some of the sources from which unions derive their bargaining power themselves have a direct effect on wages and employment. This is so, for example, in the use of controls on output and earnings, which may influence both the numbers employed and the setting of piece-rates, which, though they should ideally be fixed by objective criteria, tend to be based on observed rates of achievement.

The effect of trade unionism, then, is to add a further dimension to labour market structure, superimposed on those which we have already seen to emerge from social, personal and other institutional influences. Unionism largely achieves its objectives by means of structuring the labour market into compartments which, though by no means always watertight, at least limit the ease of transfer or impose a regulated pattern on the movement that does take place. In this way it interferes further and deliberately with the competitive mechanism of the market, enabling individual unions to engage in bargaining over limited territories with a degree of power and authority which varies with the cohesiveness of the organisation and its ability to achieve complete control over labour supply. In the end, however, the ability of the union to benefit its membership is limited by economic factors. Its power is much less in depressed economic conditions since the costs it can inflict on employers are small. In the long run, it becomes more possible for producers to change their production techniques to cut out or reduce their dependence on certain types of labour. Some would argue, too, that trade unionism itself, by dint of its increasing age, has become respectable, and that its leaders have emerged as national figures who are regarded as bearing responsibility for union actions, so that there is a further constraint on the pressures unions can exert, especially where they seem to pose a threat to the public or national interest. As we shall see subsequently, in Chapter 15, it is by no means clear how far unions have actually been successful in altering the distribution of income in favour of labour – though there are many difficulties in determining this in a satisfactory manner. However, for the present purpose enough has been said to illustrate the objectives of trade unions, the methods by which they pursue these objectives, and their implications for the earlier theoretical analysis.

IV. Further Reflections on the Employer's Role

(1) MARGINAL PRODUCTIVITY AND THE EMPLOYER

As we have already seen, the firm's demand for labour in theory is based on the marginal productivity of labour. In perfect competition labour would tend to be paid the value of its marginal product; in imperfect competition, labour may well be paid less than the value of its marginal product, but in both cases the wage depends on supply and demand. According to the institutionalist view, wages will be the outcome of collective bargaining in which the relative bargaining power of employers and unions and their skill in bargaining will be the final determinants. How, if at all, can these two views be reconciled?

Those who favour approaches other than the use of marginal analysis have put forward a number of criticisms of the marginal productivity doctrine. First, it is asked whether the benefit to be derived from employing another worker can really be measured, compared with the change in costs thereby incurred. How, for example, is the employer to assess the marginal productivity of an office worker? And even in what might seem to be a more straightforward case, where a worker operates a machine, how can the value of labour's output be disentangled from that of the capital with which they work and the contribution of raw materials and component parts? Such questions concern the *measurability* of marginal productivity, and there is no doubt that in some circumstances this can be an important question.

Sometimes the problem can be side-stepped to some extent. An employer faced with a decision whether to buy a particular piece of equipment often finds that it requires a standard number of workers to man it. He need not concern himself with adjustments between labour and capital, since the ratio is technically fixed. Then, by assessing the output of the machine and labour concerned, and by deducting the expenses of the machine (depreciation and obsolescence) and the material and fuel costs incurred, he can get an estimate of the 'net product' of the labour. This, though not a direct assessment of labour's marginal product, will serve the same purpose of allowing him to decide whether the labour at a given cost is worth employing.

In other cases, when an employer is trying to estimate the worth of his existing labour force at normal levels of output, we can assume that he has an existing factory with a particular complement of machinery using given inputs of raw materials and set for a certain rate of output. Without necessarily implying that the employer can measure the marginal revenue product of an additional worker on any piece of plant, we can be fairly sure that he will know whether it will be worth while for him to incur the extra costs of hiring the extra worker. To suppose otherwise is really to deny that managements have any real awareness of the costs of extra labour and its value to the firm. Yet it is after all one of the main functions of management to make such investigations and to consider the effect on costs and output of changing the volume or structure of employment. Further, increasing use is nowadays made of management advisory services and consultants to explore cost–output relationships by means of even more sophisticated techniques. We ought not even to despair of the task of evaluating the contribution of marginal office staff, for it seems certain that management have some conception of this, arising out of the need to arrive at a satisfactory combination of administrative, technical, clerical and supervisory staff in relation to the manual labour force. Here it is not so much the 'output' of these workers that matters as much as knowledge of the delays and inefficiencies (and their costs to the firm) which have arisen in the past because of sickness, holidays, rush orders and downturns in demand.

The final problem in this connection is when major changes in technique are being considered. When an employer is thinking of general re-equipment of his establishment, of beginning a new line of production or greatly expanding his scale of operations, the issues of determining the merits of a particular combination of labour and equipment, or of deciding on a particular size of labour force, are much more open and many alternative combinations of the factors or levels of working are possible. When a new factory is being discussed, all the issues involved in estimating marginal product may come up. In advance planning all possible techniques may be considered and all manner of possible combinations of the factors. This will make the job of determining marginal product and lighting on the best combination of the factors specially important and specially difficult. On the other hand, in making such important decisions the employer can afford to check very carefully on the possible alternatives. As a single employer he is aware of the costs of each factor and can work to a known cost of the complementary quantities of capital and materials that any particular manning standard of labour would imply. It is very likely too that other employers in the industry will have arrived at particular ways of doing things, and an employer contemplating a new enterprise will often be able to study other cases in the light of what he knows of their experience and of the differences between their circumstances and his. Some idea of the marginal attractiveness of different courses of action seems likely to arise from such a study.

Because such large alterations in the pattern of labour demand of one employer occur infrequently, we can infer that a full reassessment of the marginal productivity of labour is much more likely in the long run than in the short. As we have seen,[1] wage changes in the short run may be

[1] Cf. section II (3), p. 280 above.

K

without effect on employment in the short run, either because the employer finds it too costly to make continual marginal adjustments and to carry out the costing and pricing exercises necessary if he is to know when and how to adjust, or because his existing plant requires a fixed complement of labour at a particular level of output. But in the longer run new technical possibilities, coupled with changes in the relative prices of different kinds of labour or of labour and capital, give him the opportunity to move to a more profitable combination of factors. In other words, it is in the longer run that major changes, affecting the return to factors at the margin, will be most influential.

This does not mean that the employer *thinks* in terms of marginal costs and marginal revenue, or marginal revenue product, but simply that however his decisions are taken, the objective of profit maximisation will lead to a position which can suitably be expressed in such terms. This leads us on to a second major form of criticism of the marginal productivity doctrine, which runs as follows: that businessmen do not work in marginal terms, that they generally do not know about marginal costs and marginal revenue product, and that they have little conception of the cost and demand functions which confront them. Hence, it is argued, it is quite meaningless to put forward a theory based on concepts of which businessmen are ignorant. But this line of attack entirely misses the point. At no stage does the marginal productivity doctrine purport to *describe* how businessmen reach their decisions. Instead, it assumes that businessmen set out to maximise profits and from this makes a series of logical deductions, resulting in a number of predictions about equilibrium output, employment and the reaction of firms to changes in certain economic variables. It says nothing about the way in which such decisions are reached and certainly does not depend on the assumption that businessmen work in terms of marginal analysis.[1]

These two forms of criticism, then, relate respectively to the measurability of marginal productivity, and its usefulness as a means of describing how the firm's demand for labour is formulated. What has emerged from our discussion of them is that neither criticism need lead us to abandon the theory developed earlier. But there is obviously a limit to the precision we can attribute to the employer in his assessment of the value to his firm of additional units of labour. Provided, however, that we are

---

[1] Other hypotheses, such as the so-called 'full-cost' approach to product pricing, or the 'bargaining' approach to wage determination, may well provide more realistic *descriptions* of the way in which certain decisions are reached, but they do not thereby necessarily invalidate the marginalist model as a predictive tool.

prepared to use the principle in a common-sense manner, and do not demand too much in the individual case, we can continue to derive from it a good deal that is valuable. As stressed above, much that is implicit in the approach is closely related to the everyday functions of management, and it is not unreasonable then to expect a tolerably close correspondence between what firms are observed to do and what the theory based on marginal productivity would predict.

The fact that wages are largely determined by collective bargaining need not affect these conclusions to any great extent. It is true that where collective bargaining is conducted by an employers' association on behalf of firms, wages are fixed 'outside' the firm and have to be accepted by it as a datum. Thus we might seem to be in a situation which has more in common with perfect competition, in which, wages being given, the firm adjusts output and employment to achieve equilibrium. Up to a point, this criticism is valid: the theory based on marginal productivity predicts that in the usual conditions of imperfect competition the firm's wage levels will be determined by the firm's demand for labour and its own labour supply, and these wage levels are not then a datum. One consequence of this is that whereas the theory predicts that short-run fluctuations in the firm's demand for labour will cause wages to vary, the collectively determined wage will remain fixed for the period of the agreement, and the whole burden of adjustment will fall on the firm's output and employment.

Yet there are several other points which weaken these criticisms. First, as mentioned earlier, the effectiveness of an employers' association depends on its ability to hold its membership together and it must therefore reflect the views of its constituents, so that the range of wage settlement envisaged must reflect – if indirectly – the economic circumstances of the member firms. In the short run the wage settlement reached by the association may differ somewhat from that which the individual member firm would have reached on its own. But in the long run, by changing production techniques and substituting cheaper for more expensive factors of production, the firm is once again able to have some influence on the total demand for different factors and the prices of these factors are more directly subjected to demand pressures which can be expressed in terms of marginal productivity. In this way the competitive influence is again brought to bear on factor pricing.

Secondly, even when collective bargaining is conducted by the employers' association, this frequently applies only to basic wage rates, additional elements in the wage packet being negotiable within the individual workplaces. In such cases the firm retains the final word on the total wage it is able and willing to pay, and this we would expect to be determined with reference to the estimated value to the firm of the labour concerned, at the margin: in other words, with reference to what we have called labour's marginal revenue product. The determination of these bonuses and other 'extra' payments above the basic rate will still of course be subject to collective bargaining, but it is now the individual firm, conscious of its own economic circumstances, which directly engages in negotiation, not the association. And as conditions within the firm change, it is often possible for the firm to reopen negotiations on these 'extras', leading to a prospect of greater short-run flexibility in wages and labour costs than we could expect in the more indirect form of collective bargaining involving the association.

Thirdly, many firms do not belong to employers' associations at all and engage in collective bargaining directly and on their own behalf. In these cases, too, we would expect the firm to have regard to the very factors that we have previously argued will determine the firm's demand for labour. Lastly, even allowing as we have done here that some short-run flexibility in wage determination is available to the firm in the context of collective bargaining, it might still be argued that this is not likely to lead to as many adjustments to output and factor utilisation as theory would suggest. But this makes the mistake of presuming that firms which are not constantly adjusting output and employment are departing from short-run profit maximisation. This need not be so. It will not be true, for example, in the oligopolistic situation where the marginal cost curve, though shifting up or down, continues to cut the MRP curve within the 'gap' – and this may be a very common position for firms, not limited to the case where there are a few large firms in one industry, but common also where a number of local producers have to take account of each other's policies and reactions. Again, the profit-maximising firm may not make changes in response to altered circumstances simply because they would involve the costly collection of information, possible losses through over-frequent alterations to schedules, and the like. Firms which do not make frequent responses to changing conditions may still be maximising short-run profits simply because frequent alterations would raise costs more than they would increase revenue.[1]

[1] This point is also relevant to doubts which have been expressed on the validity of the short-run profit maximisation assumption. Various other alternatives have been advanced, but we need not go into these here. It is enough to say for the present purpose that for a variety of reasons none of these approaches has so far seriously threatened to displace the basic structure of the marginalist analysis.

(2) THE EMPLOYER'S INFLUENCE

More briefly, we can round off this discussion by reviewing the influences the employer can exert in the course of collective bargaining. Whereas we have seen how the trade union formulates its objectives and derives its power to pursue these aims, we have said very little about the methods of control available to the employer to secure his own objectives. Indeed, if one were to adopt the strongest of institutionalist lines, it might seem that the only influences available to the employer are indirect, in the sense that once wages are determined externally to the firm, the employer has to accept the situation and must make the best of it by adjusting output and employment (if he can) in the short run or by changing his technique of production or withdrawing his capital in the long run. There is a degree of truth in this argument, though it would be wrong to minimise the importance of this indirect influence and the potential threat of such action, since these possibilities cannot be disregarded by the union in the bargaining process. But there are, additionally, a number of points which need to be made by way of qualification.

In the first place, this argument is at its strongest only when the employers' association is entirely responsible for the determination of the workers' total wage packets, and this, as we have already pointed out above, is by no means always the case. Further, even if this situation does hold, it is always possible for the firm to bring pressure to bear on the formulation of wage policy by the association or, if it cannot exert influence in this way, the firm may withdraw from the association altogether and pursue its own policy. On the other hand, to the extent that the individual firm does itself engage in collective bargaining as a follow-up to national agreements (and this perhaps is the more typical case in this country), it can, as we have seen, affect the course of negotiations directly and with full account being taken of its own special circumstances. In this respect it is also able to create conditions (e.g. by a 'change of practice' involving a small modification in work methods or materials) which will cause negotiations at plant level to be reopened.[1]

Secondly, while the firm in general is much less able than the union to

---

For a valuable discussion of this whole topic, see R. G. Lipsey, *An Introduction to Positive Economics* (2nd ed.), 1966, chap. 29.

[1] However, there will be an increasing constraint on the firm the higher is the basic rate in relation to the average gross wage paid by rival firms. In such cases the nationally negotiated basic rate may itself lie above the gross wage the firm would wish to pay.

enforce sanctions, it is not entirely without power in this respect. Although used much more rarely than the strike weapon, the 'lock-out' course of action is available to the employer, thereby barring workers from entry to the firm's premises and denying them the right to work. Such a course is likely, however, to be restricted to highly unusual circumstances. Perhaps of rather more importance is the ability of the firm to refuse negotiating rights to trade unions and to adopt an 'open-shop' policy, which may mean either that the firm discriminates *against* union members or that, although the firm may employ union members, it will not admit the right of the union to negotiate for these workers. Both circumstances are to be found in some measure in this country, though it is probably fair to add that such a policy cannot be adopted as readily in some industries as in others. Where the open shop exists, wages and employment conditions will be determined unilaterally by the employer. Sometimes these will be better, sometimes worse than the terms of settlement agreed by the employers' association. A great deal obviously depends on the firm's motives for remaining outside the association.

Despite these qualifications, it still seems that the general portrayal of employers as wielding a rather indirect influence on the bargaining process is not altogether unfair. The typical employer is one who belongs to an employers' association, who accepts the rights of his workpeople to belong to a trade union and who acknowledges the right of the trade union to negotiate on behalf of its members in his employment. In view of the means which the trade union has to employ if it is to achieve an effective degree of organisation and to engage effectively in bargaining, it becomes inevitable that the labour market should become highly structured and strongly demarcated according to the unions' ability to secure sole negotiating rights in different sectors of the labour market. The individual employer, despite the fact that he has at his command an amount of capital and an effective business organisation, finds himself enmeshed in a structure from which he can only extricate himself by abandoning certain commitments which may be valuable to him – his membership of the association, his recognition of worker and union rights, and so on.

It is true, of course, that the employer has voluntarily entered into this complex system that seems to limit his freedom of action, for collective agreements are not enforced unilaterally by trade unions but result from joint negotiation between employers and labour. The employer must, by implication, be willing to accept this kind of restriction on his role, but the fact remains that once he has entered into the spirit of the system and so long as he continues to accept its premises, he is bound by the rules which apply therein. In this connection, the increasing importance attached to the notion of productivity bargaining is illuminating.[1] For what productivity bargaining involves is essentially an attempt by the employer, almost invariably on his own initiative, to break out of the rigidities imposed on him by the system – of which, we should be clear, he has been a willing and acquiescent supporter in the past. Productivity bargaining, viewed in this light, can be seen as a deliberate attempt to move the settlement of wages (and employment conditions in general) from an atmosphere in which working practices, attitudes to bargaining and the whole conception of the wage–work nexus are frozen and customary, to one in which convention plays a much more subsidiary role and new approaches can be considered. Productivity bargaining, from this point of view, is a device by which the existing structure of the labour market can be shaken up and the boundaries between its compartments redrawn in such a way that greater flexibility of action is available to the employer. Thus firms engaging in negotiation of this type have been at pains to emphasise the need for changes in working practice, for more flexibility among crafts, for more productive use of employees' time in the workplace.

It would be misleading to suggest that no employers in this country ever thought and acted along these lines before the advent of the important agreements of the early 1960s, but there is undoubtedly now, towards the end of the 1960s, a much more widespread recognition of the value to the firm of such agreements and a greater and still growing range of coverage.[2] To pursue this further here would be to stray too far from the purpose in hand, and this whole area is one to which we shall have to return in the final chapters of this book. The main point here is simply that by this *kind* of approach the employer is still capable of initiative, and by a concentration of attention on the detailed relationship between work done and payment received within the individual workplace, the ultimate basis of wage payments in the productivity factor is still seen to underlie the institutional machinery of the labour market.

[1] Cf. Chapter 3 above and Chapter 21 below.
[2] It is perhaps significant to observe that productivity bargaining has attracted much more attention in this country than elsewhere. The reason for this almost certainly lies in the fact that the British labour market is one of the most highly structured by union activities and the observance of customs and convention, and that other countries have been much less restricted than ourselves in this respect. There are, however, notable examples in other countries where similar restraints on employers' action have existed.

V. Some General Conclusions on Labour Market Theory

In the course of the last five chapters we have outlined and developed an analytical view of the labour market and the process of wage determination. The argument has taken us from a fairly abstract theoretical treatment of supply, demand and wage and employment equilibrium, through a more realistic treatment of the effects of social and institutional factors in the labour market, to an analysis of the economic implications of wage determination by means of collective bargaining. We have therefore finished up with a view of the labour market which seems to include and take account of the main features of the labour market system. From this it is clear that the simple perfect competition model of labour market operations cannot be regarded as in any way providing an accurate *description* of the way the labour market really behaves, but then accurate description is less important in assessing the worth of a theory, than is its ability to stand up to testing against observed behaviour and to provide tolerably satisfactory predictions about the outcome of changes within the system. On this count, too, the simple competitive model is of little help, but this does not mean that time spent in elaborating this basic model is wasted.

For into this basic model we have been able to introduce the principal factors which interfere with the competitive process and to take note of the changes which these factors bring about in the operation of the system. There still remains a question of course as to how far – even now – we are possessed of a theory which satisfies the criteria we set for its acceptability. While it can be no part of our present purpose to extract the various hypotheses which emerge from the theory and to provide systematic tests of these, some clue to the usefulness of the approach that has been developed here can be derived from the remaining chapters of this book, particularly those which deal with important practical labour market issues.

One final remark of a general nature may be added. The approach which has been developed in the last few chapters is an attempt to provide a reasonably integrated analysis of the operation of the labour market, but it has of necessity involved a development and refinement of a central theoretical core, rather than a straightforward statement of a general theory. If there was such a thing as a simple, unitary labour market, this kind of approach would have been regarded as less than ideal, and indeed much important work in this field remains to be done. We have to remember, however, that the labour market is *not* simple or unified, that there are in fact a diversity of labour markets cutting across one another and interacting one with another. Employers are seeking different kinds of labour in different economic circumstances, while labour is not homogeneous but is differentiated occupationally, industrially and in many other ways. It may in these circumstances be no bad thing that we do not have a single theory but take a number of theoretical approaches from which, if we select carefully, we can draw the one most appropriate to the problem in hand. For example, analysis of a highly competitive sector of the labour market may benefit from application of the perfect competition approach, while in other cases it may be more relevant to account for wage movements and changes in market conditions in terms of institutional influences or social barriers to mobility. From this point of view, what matters most is not the lack of a general theory but rather the ability of the analyst to select the parts of theory which are most relevant to the problem in hand.

SUGGESTED READING (for Chapters 8 to 12)

A. M. Cartter, *Theory of Wages and Employment*, Homewood, Ill., 1959.
J. T. Dunlop (ed.), *Theory of Wage Determination*, 1957.
J. R. Hicks, *Theory of Wages* (2nd ed.), 1965.
E. M. Hugh-Jones (ed.), *Wage Structure in Theory and Practice*, Amsterdam, 1966.
National Bureau of Economic Research, *Aspects of Labor Economics*, Princeton, 1962.
A. Rees, *The Economics of Trade Unions*, 1962.
L. G. Reynolds, *The Structure of Labor Markets*, New York, 1951.
B. Wootton, *The Social Foundations of Wage Policy*, 1955.

Part IV

Income Distribution

13 The Growth and Distribution of Incomes in Britain

I.

This chapter and the two that follow it look at the problems with which this book is concerned from a much wider viewpoint and at a greater degree of aggregation. In this chapter we shall look briefly at income as a whole and the main constituents of income in relation to each other, and will therefore for the most part be talking about sources of income much wider than income from employment. The treatment will be largely descriptive and designed to show how wages are related to other forms of income, and how income levels and patterns in the community have been changing. Of course, the actual incomes that we have to spend and how much we can buy with them are very much influenced by taxation, so that Chapter 14 follows naturally on from this chapter. Chapter 14 also discusses some important ways in which taxation may directly influence the operation of the labour market. Chapter 15 takes up one of the great classical issues in economics – the factors determining the share of wages as a whole in the economy's income. Since most of the discussion in these three chapters will be in terms of broad aggregates, there is need for caution in applying the conclusions to specific examples. All three chapters are, from different angles, largely concerned with the same issue, that of how income from employment fits into the total pattern of incomes in our economy and society.

II. The Growth of Income per Head

The most general way of looking at the growth of income in a country is to construct and study estimates of its national income over the years. Two important difficulties, however, affect any attempt to use such estimates to indicate changes in people's well-being: the value of money has altered greatly, and the number of people dependent upon the national income has grown. Since the value of money is not constant we have to distinguish between *money* national income and *real* national income, or national income at constant prices after correction for changes in the value of money. Then we have also to divide the total of income at constant prices by the total number in the population at each date to get estimates of income per head which can be compared from year to year without the complications of changing numbers of people.

Apart from these conceptual difficulties, and others of less importance, the actual calculations also produce major problems. Official attempts to construct estimates of national income only began during the Second World War, are still meeting with problems in obtaining adequate data, and are likely to continue to have problems. Estimates for earlier periods are the results of private research and are based on much less adequate sources. Thus, while figures of the growth of national income give us a useful general picture, we must beware of expecting too much accuracy.

To convert money national income into real national income we must make use of some means of correcting for changes in the value of money and, since we are interested mainly in the value of money for consumers, this means relying on an index of retail prices. The various indices of retail prices (colloquially known as 'cost-of-living' indices) which have been used in Britain from time to time have all met with criticism. Earlier indices were based on rather inadequate information on the pattern of goods bought by the public and the proportions in which they were bought, and on actual price changes, and adjustments to obtain real income in the earlier periods are therefore by no means precise. Though the current index, produced by the Department of Employment and Productivity, and published in its *Gazette*, is undoubtedly the most satisfactory that we have had, there are still some difficulties in its interpretation as an indicator of living standards. The selection of goods and services which we use to create our pattern of living can nowadays change quite rapidly. Growing incomes have brought greater variety into our lives, and a single index based on one particular collection of goods can hardly do justice to the variety of actual spending patterns even among the wage-earning community. Though the index represents the way in which prices will have moved for an average working-class household, the actual spending habits of households can differ considerably from this average pattern and so be differentially affected by price movements. A very large factor in changing living standards derives not from prices but from changes in quality and performances, and these cannot easily be handled by an index. The older indices, which were concerned with movements in the price of bread and the like, did not have much difficulty in defining the goods being priced.

The current indices have to cope with rapidly changing equipment such as television sets, and new techniques such as frozen foods, and are considering price movements for a working-class population that can afford to buy a wider range of consumer goods.

Table 13.1

National Income per Head at Constant 1912–13 Prices,
1870 to 1939

Period	Index
1870–9	100
1880–9	117
1890–9	146
1900–9	158
1910–19	163
1920–9	173
1930–9	204

Source: J. B. Jefferys and Dorothy Walters, 'National Income and Expenditure of the United Kingdom, 1870–1952', a paper which appeared in International Association for Research in Income and Wealth, Income and Wealth, series V (1955). The estimates of national income per head in each year have been averaged over each decade and then related to the figure for the decade 1870–9 to give the index shown. The price index used by Jefferys and Walters to express all figures in terms of the prices ruling in 1912–13 was developed by them from several sources.

The estimates reproduced in Table 13.1 are subject to the reservations just outlined, but they are reasonably adequate to indicate long-term trends. Over these 70 years the income available per head in the United Kingdom doubled, despite the fact that during the same period the population increased by 40 per cent. Each decade showed an increase over its predecessor, though the growth of income per head was more rapid in the periods before 1900 and after 1930 than it was in the intervening period. Table 13.2 gives a related range of figures for some years after 1938 and again shows increasing real income per head, especially after 1950. Real product available per head of the population at present is more than three times its level in 1870.

Even though the British economy has been growing more slowly than most other economies, these are pleasing results which amply confirm the general impression of our economy as one which has greatly increased in well-being in the last century. The large reduction in primary poverty, which is evidenced by all studies of poverty over the period, and the expansion in the range and quantities of goods in our economy, for example, fall naturally into place alongside these figures.

An alternative way of looking at changes in national income, which is especially relevant to a discussion primarily concerned with labour, is to

Table 13.2

Gross Domestic Product per Head at Constant 1958 Prices, 1938 to 1966[1]

Year	Index
1938	*100*
1946	112
1950	114
1954	126
1958	133
1962	143
1966	164

[1] Gross Domestic Product at factor cost at constant 1958 prices, divided by mid-year population estimate.

Source: *Key Statistics of the British Economy 1900–1962* and *Monthly Digest of Statistics.*

assess growth in income or output, not in relation to the movement of the total population, but to changes in the quantity of labour used to produce it. This 'labour input' will be affected by all the factors determining the labour supplied by a population, which are discussed in Chapters 6 and 9 – such as the proportion of the population which is of working age, the proportion of the population of working age actually in the labour force, unemployment in the labour force, and changes in hours of work. The result of all these factors in relation to the growth in output of our economy is that the product per man-hour (i.e. changes in the total income or product divided by changes in 'labour input') has been growing at an average of 1·5 and 2 per cent a year since 1870, and the return to our economy from an hour's work by one man is now something like four times what it was in 1870.[1]

[1] This paragraph is largely based on Angus Maddison, 'Economic Growth in Western Europe 1870–1957', *Quarterly Review* of the Banca Nazionale del Lavoro, March 1959.

III. The Growth of the Wage Level

While all these figures strongly suggest an improvement in wage incomes, they do not precisely indicate the extent of the increase. The income we have been considering is not merely wage income but includes all forms: some part of it, for example, will have been used to increase our stock of capital and did not go directly into anyone's pocket, and we have not as yet said anything about labour's share of the product which it has helped to produce. It is safe to assume, on the basis of this discussion of income movements, that wage incomes have increased their purchasing power, but we ought to look at them directly to see by how much they have increased over this long period.

A study of the movement of wages again brings up a number of practical difficulties which have been discussed in earlier chapters. We have to rely mainly on wage-rate indices: these are unfortunately invariably based on a multiplicity of different kinds of rate payments in different industries, and use a definition of wages which leaves out salaried workers. Earnings movements have possibly been different from rate movements. Movements of differentials affect the extent to which different groups conform to the average movement of wages. And finally, we have once more to use price indices to convert money-wage movements into real-wage movements.

We begin by discussing real-wage movements in periods before 1914, where the ground is rather uncertain. Phelps Brown and Hopkins have, however, given us some guiding material.[1] Their data suggest that in southern England the level of real wages of builders in the first few decades of the nineteenth century was much about the same as it had been five and a half centuries before, in the late thirteenth century. In the intervening period there had been a good number of fluctuations: especially the real-wage level appears to have risen quite remarkably in the fifteenth century and to have fallen to a particularly low level in the later part of the sixteenth century, but the level in the later part of the thirteenth and the early part of the nineteenth centuries was fairly typical of the period taken as a whole. From about 1820 onwards real wage rates began a rise which eventually took them well beyond any known previous level. The impression conveyed by this study, however, is that it was about the 1880s before the real-wage level of these building workers exceeded levels already reached four centuries before, in the 1470s.

[1] E. H. Phelps Brown and S. V. Hopkins, 'Seven Centuries of the Prices of Consumables Compared with Builders' Wage Rates', *Economica*, 1956.

There are many possibilities of inaccuracies and misjudgments implicit in the use of an indicator of this type instead of a lengthy historical treatment. For example, the movement of the wages of builders need not have been typical of all wage earners, and even less typical of the standard of living of the peasant community who formed the larger part of our population in earlier times. Other parts of the country may have experienced very different conditions from those existing in southern England. The dates at which alterations in living standards took place must be very approximate. The beginning of the great rise in the conditions of life which has brought us to our present standards may have been under way before the Napoleonic Wars and have been put back by the war years. On the other hand, the general impression conveyed by Phelps Brown and Hopkins is not likely to be very wide of the mark. Certainly, around the third quarter of the nineteenth century, where Table 13.3 takes up the story, the effects of revolutionary changes in our commercial and industrial life began to take us to previously unknown levels of prosperity.

The general meaning of Table 13.3 is quite clear: the real standard of living of the wage earner has risen fairly steadily in the whole period since 1860. The figures before 1914 are specially subject to doubts and ambiguities, but they are certainly sufficiently accurate to justify the conclusion that the wage earner's standard of living was rising in that period, and it rose again both between the wars and after the Second World War. No earnings figures are given either before 1914 or between 1914 and 1938, since data for continuous series are simply not available; but there was probably no marked tendency for the earnings of wage earners to draw away from their wage rates at these times. Among other things, substantial overtime working was less possible: the regular hours of work in the latter half of the nineteenth century were still at around the level of 54 or 56 hours or more a week. The average earnings of wage earners may, however, have increased more than the index of wage rates because of upgrading of wage earners within wage-earning groups resulting in a shift from less to more remunerative occupations. Evidence exists to suggest that this has been happening.[1] Since 1938 we have had a much more rapid growth in earnings than in rates, with a consequent tendency to wider variety in the experiences of individuals as against the average. In the first few years after 1945 wage rates had hardly improved in real purchasing power at all, while the availability of goods had deteriorated considerably, and the possibility of getting goods – as well as their price – influenced the standard of living. On the other hand, earnings rose more quickly than wage rates

[1] Cf. A. L. Bowley, *Wages and Income since 1860*, 1937, and G. Routh, op. cit.

Table 13.3
Real and Money Wages since 1860

Year	(a) Wage-rate index	(b) 'Cost-of-living' index	(c) Real wage-rate index (a)÷(b)
(Average 1890–9 = 100)			
1860	68	130	52
1870	78	127	61
1880	93	121	77
1890	100	103	97
1900	108	105	103
1910	107	110	97
1914	115	115[1]	100
(Average 1925–9 = 100)			
1914	51	59	87
1920	159	159	100
1930	98	93	105
1938	104	92	114

(1938=100)

Year	(a) Wage-rate index	(b) Earnings index	(c) 'Cost-of-living' index	(d) Real wage-rate index (a)÷(c)	(e) Real earnings index (b)÷(c)
1938	100	100	100	100	100
1946	163	190	154	106	123
1950	186	240	185	101	130
1954	239	322	232	103	139
1958	299	408	272	110	150

(1958 = 100)

1958	100	100	100	100	100
1962	113·7	122·5	109·5	103·8	111·9
1966	134·7	156·2	125·6	107·2	124·4

[1] First half-year.

Sources: The figures up to 1938 are from E. H. Phelps Brown and S. V. Hopkins, 'The Course of Wage Rates in Five Countries, 1860–1939', Oxford Economic Papers, 1950. The figures from 1938 to 1958 are from the London and Cambridge Bulletin (wage-rate and 'cost-of-living' indices) and the Ministry of Labour Gazette (earnings). From 1958 the figures are derived from the National Institute Economic Review.

during the war years, and though in the post-war years both rates and earnings grew rapidly, earnings continued to draw ahead of rates until the middle fifties. While the increase in real wage rates since 1938 has been rather small, the increase in real earnings has been substantial. The data are not sufficient to permit dogmatism on the exact extent to which wage earners now are better off than in earlier times. We may guess, however, that by 1939 real wages were about two-and-a-half times their level in 1860; since then real earnings appear to have risen by about 85 per cent, though real wage rates have risen 20 to 25 per cent.

IV. Wages and Rewards to Other Factors

One way of appreciating the position of wage earners in our economy is to contrast the share of the income of the economy which they get with that going to other contributors to our product who receive other types of income. Table 13.4 selects data at ten-yearly intervals for the period from 1870 to 1950 from the work of Phelps Brown and Hart on this topic.

Table 13.4

Factor Distribution of Home-produced National Income, 1870 to 1950

	Percentages of national income					
Year	Rent	Salaries	Wages	Home profits	Wages plus salaries	Wage earners as % of population
1870	14	16	39	31	55	84
1880	15	15	40	30	55	82
1890	13	17	42	28	59	80
1900	11	18	41	30	59	78
1910	12	19	38	31	57	75
1913	11	18	37	34	55	74
1924	7	25	42	26	67	73
1930	9	26	41	24	67	72
1938	9	25	39	26	64	71
1946	6	23	41	31	64	—
1950	5	23	42	30	65	—

Source: E. H. Phelps Brown and P. E. Hart, 'The Share of Wages in National Income', Economic Journal, 1952.

Wages (including salaries) fully maintained their share of the national income over the years from 1870 to 1950 and indeed increased it. Wages alone (excluding salaries) kept very roughly to the same proportion of national income. A number of factors must have contributed to these results, and this subject is further developed, with more figures, in Chapter 15. One obvious factor that can alter is the number of wage earners involved in earning the total wage bill. Wage earners were by and large maintaining the same or a larger share of the national income from 1870 onwards even though they were becoming a smaller proportion of the total occupied population (as the last column of Table 13.4 indicates).

The Blue Books on National Income and Expenditure, which have developed from governmental attempts to create a system of social accounts for the United Kingdom, and are published each year by the Stationery Office, make it possible to take a more detailed look at changes in the distribution of different types of income since 1938. The figures in Table 13.5 indicate a marked increase since 1938 in the share of the total product of the economy going as earned income to employees. Some part of this is due to a larger number of employees at work, both from an extension of the labour force and a reduction in unemployment; but the increase in the share going to employed labour is largely the result of a real increase in relative earning power per unit of employed labour as against other agencies in the production process. The gain in income from employment is matched by a decline in the share of the total domestic product[1] taken out as rent and that taken by the self-employed.

Table 13.5 also shows an increase in the share of the domestic product taken by profits.[2] Some part of the size of this share is, however, illusory since, as the footnote to the table points out, the estimates of Table 13.5 are given before allowing for capital consumption and stock appreciation. Moreover, the share of profits is very much subject to cyclical variations, a point to which we return in Chapter 15. Estimates of capital consumption

[1] The figures in Table 13.5 are given in terms of gross *domestic* product or income rather than *national* product; the difference between these two concepts is accounted for by an item of 'net income from abroad'. This is added on to domestic product to give national product and is the balance between earnings on our capital invested abroad and earnings on foreign capital invested here. This balance was in our favour at the dates quoted and has generally been so.

[2] In Table 13.5 the profits item includes the gross trading surpluses of public corporations, such as the nationalised industries, and the gross profits of other public enterprises, such as the Post Office and local authority undertakings, as well as the gross profits earned by companies. Profits earned by companies are, however, by far the largest ingredient.

are attempts to quantify the extent to which capital loses value as time passes and as it suffers the wear and tear of its use in helping to provide our income. Estimates of stock appreciation are rather technical in character: their main object is, however, to adjust the value of stocks, of raw materials for example, for changes in prices since their purchase. Stock appreciation

Table 13.5

Shares in the Gross Domestic Income of the United Kingdom, 1938 to 1966

	1938	1958	1962	1966
Type of income	Percentages			
Income from employment	61·6	68·0	68·2	68·7
Income from self-employment	13·2	9·0	8·5	7·6
Gross corporate trading profits (including public enterprises)[1]	15·6	17·7	17·6	17·8
Rent[1]	9·6	5·3	5·6	5·9
Total domestic income	100·0	100·0	100·0	100·0

[1] Before allowing for capital consumption and stock appreciation.
Source: *National Income and Expenditure.*

can increase or decrease estimates of profitability made before allowing for changes in the value of stocks held; but, for simplicity, this will not be further discussed. Capital consumption is in any case by far the larger item and is always negative, so that estimates 'net' of it are always smaller than 'gross' figures. Capital consumption is applicable to estimates of rent as well as profits, since houses and often buildings generally deteriorate, as well as industrial equipment, and to estimates of income from self-employment, since farmers and professional people provide equipment which deteriorates with time and in use. It also affects Government property. But the most important part of deductions from the Gross National Product for capital consumption is related to the profits item in Table 13.5.

The last line of Table 13.6 shows the importance of corrections for capital consumption. This item is shown as a percentage of gross corporate income, which includes the profits of companies and public corporations but not those of other public enterprises. The greater importance of capital consumption in later post-war years than in 1938 explains some of the

increase in the share of Gross Domestic Income going to profits, which
Table 13.5 shows for *gross* profits.

Table 13.6 reveals a number of interesting trends. First, the share of the
income of companies paid out to their shareholders has gone down very
considerably since before the war. Nowadays more is kept in reserve and

Table 13.6

Allocation of Corporate Income, 1938 to 1966

	1938	1948	1958	1966
Type of income	*Percentages*			
Dividend and interest payments[1]	60	25	30	36
U.K. taxes and additions to tax reserves	9	28	17	13
Profits due abroad, net of U.K. tax, and taxes paid abroad	3	8	10	9
Balance: undistributed income after taxation	28	39	42	41
Total gross corporate income[2]	*100*	*100*	*100*	*100*
Capital consumption	−18	−16	−21	−23

[1] Including a relatively small item for dividend and interest reserves.
[2] Including income from abroad.
Source: National Income and Expenditure.

not distributed than is paid out. Though much of this undistributed income
is needed to meet capital consumption, quite a large part of the expansion
programme of companies can be financed from their reserves, and, while
this will yield increased income in the future, it means lowers dividends
at present. Taxation on companies was extremely high after the war, so
that the Government got more directly out of company profits in 1948
than the shareholders. It is now much lighter, though the shareholders are
likely still to have substantial taxes to pay as individuals when they receive
their dividends. The item for profits and remittances abroad has increased,
but companies are also receiving large incomes from abroad – much more
than they pay out to abroad.

Table 13.7 shows the composition of *personal* income before taxation
rather than national or domestic income. Two items distinguish personal
income estimates from the others. First, only the distributed portion of
profits is considered. Secondly, Government 'grants to persons' are
included. Quite a considerable part of Government expenditure takes the
form of grants paid out to persons in the form of pensions and the like,

and these grants are income to the persons who receive them. Admittedly such grants are paid for by taxation, which reduces incomes, and the Government does not create the income which its beneficiaries receive. But the recipients of grants are themselves subject to taxation, and Table 13.7 shows the distribution of total personal income after the Government's grants have been added to it and before its reduction by taxation.

Table 13.7 is best looked at first from the period from 1938 to 1958, and then for the more recent past. It again demonstrates the marked

Table 13.7

Composition of Personal Income before Tax, 1938 to 1966

	1938	1958	1962	1966
Type of income	Percentages			
Wages	37·8	41·8	39·7	37·8
Salaries	17·9	23·3	24·9	26·0
Forces' pay	1·3	2·1	1·7	1·6
National insurance and superannuation contributions by employers	2·5	5·0	5·2	5·7
Total income from employment	59·5	72·2	71·5	71·2
Professional persons[1]	2·3	1·6	1·6	1·4
Farmers[1]	1·4	2·4	2·3	1·9
Other self-employed income	9·1	5·6	5·1	4·5
Total income from self-employment[1]	12·8	9·6	9·0	7·8
Rent, dividends and interest	22·3	10·2	11·3	11·5
Current grants from public authorities	5·4	8·0	8·2	9·4
Total personal income[1]	100·0	100·0	100·0	100·0

[1] Before allowing for capital consumption and stock appreciation.
Source: *National Income and Expenditure.*

increase in the share of income from employment which occurred between 1938 and 1958. Income from self-employment, on the other hand, declined in importance. This tendency did not appear till after about 1950. Before then self-employed income had kept pace with income from employment, especially because of a marked improvement since before the war in the incomes of farmers.[1] Since 1950 the earnings of farmers have lagged

[1] Cf. H. F. Lydall, 'The Long-Term Trend in the Size Distribution of Income', *Journal of the Royal Statistical Society*, 1959.

because of less generous Government help and less buoyant food prices, while professional incomes have also been slow to move. The decrease in income from rent and the lower proportion of gross profits distributed to shareholders are shown up in the decline in importance of the rents, dividends and interest items which may collectively be described as 'investment income'. This type of income lost ground during the war years and thereafter, as the reduction from 22 per cent of personal income in 1938 to 10 per cent in 1958 illustrates. The increase in importance of Government grants to individuals is a reflection of the increased welfare provisions of the post-war years. Lydall[1] draws three main conclusions from his survey of changes in the shares of personal incomes analysed in this way. These are: '(1) the share of employment income has grown steadily throughout the period; (2) the share of investment income fell precipitately during the war and up to 1948, but has since maintained itself at the level then reached; (3) income of the self-employed maintained its position – and even increased somewhat – up to 1948, but has since declined.' The position changes somewhat after 1958. The trend upwards in Government grants to individuals and in salaries continues. The declining importance of income from self-employment, and the increasing importance of national insurance and superannuation contributions as a (sometimes elusive) part of payments continue to emerge. On the other hand the share of income from employment has fallen in the last decade, in part because of the increase in dividend and interest payments, shown in Table 13.6.

V. The Distribution of Personal Incomes

The most obvious way of presenting the pattern in which incomes are distributed in our economy, especially from the point of view of the individual trying to assess his own position, is to split up the total income accruing to individuals into various ranges of income and show how many income-earners come within each range, with perhaps a supplementary analysis of the importance of different types of income, such as wages or investment income, in the make-up of incomes of different sizes. This is precisely the objective of this section, but its realisation in an easy, complete and unambiguous form is not possible with our present statistical knowledge.

[1] Op. cit.

The Inland Revenue is the principal source of information on the distribution of incomes in the United Kingdom. But this source involves a number of omissions and ambiguities. The Board of Inland Revenue do not in their normal work assess the numbers or importance of incomes below the exemption limit for the payment of income tax, with the result that we do not know much about the pattern of incomes below the appropriate tax exemption limit at different dates, and the absence of adequate figures below this limit means that the total number of incomes in our economy has to be estimated. Incomes are assessed for income tax under a number of different Schedules, and it is not normally necessary for the Inland Revenue to add up the total income of individuals from all sources. The Inland Revenue assess the taxpayer and his wife together so that wives' incomes form part of a single 'income unit': the figures would therefore be affected, for example, by changes in the proportion of married women at work in our population. Finally, suspicions about tax avoidance and excessive expense allowances are frequently voiced and income which avoids tax avoids being recorded in the statistics.

The complications of income units which may include wives' earnings and of an unknown amount of tax avoidance cannot be eradicated from the figures, which have to be read with these points in mind. Estimates are available of the total number of incomes and of incomes between £50 and the exemption limit for tax; but distributions of numbers of incomes, especially for 1938, have to be treated with caution. Ambiguity about small incomes means that income distributions are far more accurate at the upper end of the scale than the lower. The difficulty which arises through assessments being made for separate Schedules rather than for total incomes has been specifically dealt with by the Inland Revenue, who have carried out periodic income censuses which provide firm data for 1938 and a number of post-war years, and enable more accurate estimates than would otherwise be possible to be drawn up for other years.

The distributions of income which are given in Table 13.8 are based on the Blue Books on National Income and Expenditure where the estimates are principally derived from Inland Revenue sources. These distributions indicate at first sight the very large growth in the size of incomes[1] which

[1] Table 13.8 (and also Tables 13.9, 13.10 and 13.11) are unfortunately distributions in terms of 'allocated' incomes only. The Central Statistical Office has found it impossible to allocate out all the income they include within personal income. To some extent the unallocated income is not the type of payment which individuals would regard as their income; but a gap between total incomes and allocated incomes remains and could affect deductions based on these tables to some extent.

has occurred since before the war. In 1938 most incomes were below £250 a year and less than 2 per cent of all incomes were of more than £700 a year. In 1965 one-third of all incomes fell within the £500 to £1000 a year category. (Central Statistical Office figures suggest that the annual wage

Table 13.8

Distribution of Allocated Personal Incomes before Tax
(Numbers of Incomes), 1938 to 1965

Range of income before tax	Percentage of incomes in income ranges			
	1938	*1958*	*1962*	*1965*
£50–250	(88·8)[1]	20·1	17·9	10·9
£250–500	7·9	27·2	22·3	22·8
£500–700	1·4	23·2	16·2	13·5
£700–1000	0·8	21·1	21·8	20·5
£1000–1500	0·5	5·6	15·9	21·6
£1500–2000	0·2	1·3	3·2	6·6
Over £2000	0·4	1·5	2·7	4·2
Total	(100·0)[1]	100·0	100·0	100·0

[1] The Blue Book does not give an estimate of the total number of incomes in 1938. An estimate by Lydall is used here.
Source: *National Income and Expenditure.*

in manufacturing industry in 1965 averaged £769.) Almost one-third of all incomes in 1965 were of above £1000 a year.

To some extent this is no more than a reflection of rising prices bringing rising money incomes with them, and the changes in the real purchasing power of incomes are much smaller: £820 a year, for example, had much about the same purchasing power in 1965 as £250 in 1938. But whereas between 80 and 90 per cent of incomes were below £250 in 1938, just over 50 per cent were below £820 in 1964, and this indicates a rise in money incomes offset largely, though by no means entirely, by changes in money values. The distributional pattern also appears to have changed. Table 13.9 shows that the growth in numbers of incomes over £2000 between 1938 and 1965 is much more evident between £2000 and £3000 than for incomes above £3000. At the extreme, the number of incomes over £20,000 before tax has grown least of all.

Lydall[1] uses a statistical device known as a percentile to analyse changes in the distribution of incomes. The meaning of this term is best explained by an example. Suppose we wished to set out the facts about the heights attained by the male undergraduates of a university. One way to do this would be to use percentages and say that 1 per cent were above 6 feet 2

Table 13.9

Distribution of Allocated Personal Incomes above £2000 Before Tax (Numbers of Incomes), 1938 to 1965

Range of income before tax	Numbers of incomes (thousands)			
	1938	1958	1962	1965
£2000–3000	46	218	410	702
£3000–5000	33	120	204	286
£5000–10,000	18	52	92	132
£10,000–20,000	6	12	20	30
£20,000 and over	2	3	4	7
Total number of incomes over £2000	105	405	730	1157

Source: National Income and Expenditure.

inches, 50 per cent above 5 feet 8 inches and so on. Alternatively we could cite the heights which divide up the group of undergraduates into percentages. If we used this form of words, then the heights which marked the divisions between one percentage and the next would be the percentiles of the distribution of heights. If we start with the tallest undergraduates, then 6 feet 2 inches would be the first percentile and 5 feet 8 inches the fiftieth. If we apply this terminology to the distribution of incomes, then the percentiles of the distribution at any date are the incomes which divide up the total number of incomes into one hundred parts. Thus 1 per cent of all incomes are larger than the first percentile, 10 per cent of all incomes are larger than the tenth and so on. Table 13.10 uses this terminology.

Table 13.10 once more emphasises the very small proportion of incomes in the upper income ranges. Less than 1 per cent of incomes were above £3500 in 1963, and it is an entirely safe deduction from general knowledge

[1] Op. cit. Lydall's work is a very thorough discussion of this whole subject, with figures for the period between 1938 and 1957. R. J. Nicholson, 'The Distribution of Personal Income', *Lloyds Bank Review*, January 1967, uses a similar method, and his figures are quoted here for the years after 1957.

of the purchasing power of £3500 in 1963 to suggest that there were not in 1963, and are not now, very many people in our society who are really rich in terms of their inflow of current income. The fiftieth percentile has

Table 13.10

Percentiles of Allocated Income Before Tax, 1938 to 1963

Percentile	Annual income before tax			Index (1938 = 100)	
	1938	1957	1963	1957	1963
	£	£	£		
First	1140	2450	3364	215	286
Fifth	393	1180	1697	299	424
Twentieth	185	792	1067	428	591
Fiftieth	110	512	645	465	609

Source: Lydall, op. cit., to 1957, and Nicholson, op. cit., for 1963.

Table 13.11

Percentiles of Allocated Income Before Tax
at Constant Prices, 1954 and 1957

	Index (1938 = 100)	
	1954	1957
First percentile	194	215
Index of consumer prices ('high-income' households)	231	256
∴ First percentile at constant prices	84	84
Fiftieth percentile	347	465
Index of consumer prices ('retail index' households)	235	263
∴ Fiftieth percentile at constant prices	147	177

Source: Lydall, op. cit. Lydall used material in the Ministry of Labour Report of an Enquiry into Household Expenditures in 1953–54 (1957) to construct separate price indices for the high-income households and for the more typical households which form the basis of the Ministry's own retail prices index.

grown since 1938 by more than the twentieth, the twentieth by more than the fifth, and the fifth by more than the first. Incomes before tax are now, therefore, much more equal than in 1938. This point is further emphasised for the period from 1938 to 1957 by Table 13.11, which is taken directly from Lydall's work. It shows that the value of the first percentile at constant prices was less in 1957 than in 1938, whereas that of the fiftieth was higher.

Two deficiencies of these tables must, however, be noted. First, they say nothing of the distribution of income below the fiftieth percentile – i.e. of the bottom half of incomes. The reason for this is simply that of inadequate information, but, especially in the context of assessing the extent of poverty in our society, this is a damaging omission from an account of income distribution. Nicholson rectifies this omission to a limited extent for the period from 1949 to 1963. He reckons that the seventieth percentile in 1963 was £400 per annum, and that it had increased between 1949 and 1963 by 228 per cent compared with 81 per cent for the first and 150 per cent for the twentieth percentile. (A few points about the extent of poverty are included in the last section of this chapter.) Secondly, indices of changes in the percentiles over the period between 1938 and 1963 can readily conceal changes in trend within that period. In fact, the trend did change around 1957, and since that date the move towards more equality in incomes before tax appears to have ceased. Between 1957 and 1959 the higher incomes increased more rapidly than those further down the scale, and between 1959 and 1963 all the percentiles except the first increased by about the same amount.

VI. The Effect of Investment Income on Size of Income

Wealth is much more unevenly distributed than income in this country. In 1946–7, 16 per cent of the total amount of capital in private hands in England and Wales was held by 0·06 per cent of adults in fortunes of over £100,000 each; 63 per cent of all capital was held by 2·7 per cent of all adults in units of more than £5000; and 84 per cent of capital was held by 11·6 per cent of adults in units of over £1000. This highly unequal distribution of wealth nevertheless represents greater equality in the distribution of wealth than prevailed before the war. In 1936–8, 21 per cent of private capital was held by 0·05 per cent of the adult population in units of over £100,000 and 65 per cent was held by 1·8 per cent in units of over £5000 –

and the purchasing power of this wealth was much greater in 1938 than in 1946. Both the 1946–7 and the 1936–8 figures, however, show a wider distribution of private capital than in earlier years: in 1911–13, 0·03 per cent of adults possessed 23 per cent of private capital in estates of over £100,000 while 83 per cent of all private capital was held by 3 per cent of the adult population.[1]

More recent figures derived from the Reports of the Inland Revenue suggest that there were in 1963–4 only twelve thousand people in Britain with wealth of over £200,000. Around five million people had assets of more than £3000. Another way of putting this is to say that most of the population had very little wealth.

Because most of us have little or no capital we rely on earned income. Because capital is unevenly distributed in large rather than small units,

Table 13.12

Sources of Income of Some Income Groups, 1937–8 and 1954–5

	Source of income (*percentage of income of each group*)					
	1937–8			*1954–5*		
Group	*Employ-ment*	*Self-employ-ment*	*Invest-ment*	*Employ-ment*	*Self-employ-ment*	*Invest-ment*
Top 1 per cent	24	18	59	35	27	38
Top 5 per cent	36	18	46	51	22	27
Top 10 per cent	44	17	38	62	18	20
Top 20 per cent	—	—	—	73	13	14

Source: Lydall, op. cit.

and because income and wealth are interacting, since income is needed to accumulate wealth and wealth produces income, investment income tends to be a more important element in larger incomes than it is in smaller. According to the data in Table 13.12 which is derived from Lydall, investment income was almost 40 per cent of the income of the top 1 per cent in 1954–5 but only amounted to 14 per cent of the income of the top 20 per cent. In 1954–5 incomes under £1000 on average drew at least 90 per cent

[1] All these estimates of the distribution of wealth are from Kathleen M. Langley, 'The Distribution of Capital in Private Hands in 1936–38 and 1946–47', *Bulletin of the Oxford University Institute of Statistics*, December 1950 and February 1951.

of their total from employment.[1] While the pattern of sources of income in 1954–5 was the same as it was in 1937–8 the emphasis on investment income had been reduced; this is in line with the changes in distribution of dividends by companies discussed earlier and with the weakness of rent income in post-war years. The increased share of self-employment income in the top 5 per cent in 1954–5 was probably more a result of the relative fall-back in investment income than due to some special strength of self-employment income.

Again, we may make some attempt to bring Lydall's results up to date. In 1964–5 over 96 per cent of the total income of those receiving incomes between £275 and £1000 a year came from their earnings, as compared with only 35 per cent for incomes over £20,000. The proportion of investment income to all income was well below 10 per cent on income up to £2000 a year, less than a third on income below £6000 a year but more than half on incomes over £15,000 a year.

VII. Family Income

For purposes of determining the standard of living of individuals, and their pattern of consumption, it is necessary to consider their incomes not as individual income earners, as in the previous sections of this chapter, but as members of families with responsibilities and possibly dependants. In addition this may be an important determinant of motivation to work. Since the income ranges into which the greater part of the British population fall are narrow, family circumstances can for most people be quite as important in determining well-being as the position the main bread-winner occupies on the ladders of skills and incomes. Though wives generally earn less than husbands, their contribution to the family budget often marks the difference between being affluent or merely average in living standards, compared with others of roughly the same social category in terms of the husband's occupational standing. This is a powerful motivation towards bringing wives into the labour market. In other cases, a contribution to earned income by the wife may be essential in keeping the family above the poverty level. Table 13.13 attempts to summarise the broad position on incomes in relation to family circumstances in 1964–5. It is based on the latest of the periodic Income Censuses conducted by the

[1] Calculated from the Income Census in the 99th Report of H.M. Commissioners of Inland Revenue.

Table 13.13

Family Circumstances and Incomes in 1964–5

% of cases in each range by family circumstances

£	Single	All married couples		Married couples with two children		Married couples with four or more children		All single and married
		Wife earning	Not earning	Wife earning	Not earning	Wife earning	Not earning	
275–500	41·3	1·9	7·0	1·2	2·6	1·4	5·1	19·4
500–700	26·2	4·5	15·3	2·9	9·2	3·1	8·4	17·2
700–1000	20·6	19·5	34·8	17·5	36·4	14·0	30·8	25·7
1000–1500	8·2	49·9	30·7	50·8	37·9	53·4	45·0	26·2
1500–3000	2·8	21·3	9·4	23·7	11·6	23·0	8·8	9·5
Over 3000	0·9	2·8	2·6	3·9	2·5	5·1	1·9	2·0
All ranges	100·0	100·0	100·0	100·0	100·0	100·0	100·0	100·0
% of All Cases	39·6	22·8	37·6	3·3	7·9	0·6	2·4	100·0

Source: 109th Report of H.M. Commissioners of Inland Revenue.

L

Inland Revenue and gives the percentage distributions of cases of incomes related to various types of family circumstances (above the minimum level of income £275) available for that Census.

The category of single men and women includes widowers, widows and divorced. Some of these people have children or other dependants but most of them do not. Young workers well below the peak of their potential earning power and older people in retirement are naturally important constituents of this group. Most single people have incomes of less than £1000 a year. Indeed, more than half of the single women have incomes below £500 a year, though, in contrast, the percentage of single women with incomes above £1500 is higher than that of men, presumably due to the tendency for some widows to have investment or annuity incomes.

Married couples have a better income distribution than single people. On the other hand the standard of living available to married couples is extremely sensitive to whether or not the wife is working and to the number of children which they have. For the most part Table 13.13 provides self-evident illustrations of these points. A fuller analysis than is given in the table shows that increasing family size for the most part is associated with increased income for those with families of three or fewer children, though families where the wife is not working are in a distinctly less favourable incomes situation than those in which the wife is out at work for all or part of the day. It is possible that such families have a more adequate family life in other ways, but that is, of course, a separate matter, and not one for discussion here. The proportion of low incomes is high in the case of families with four or more children, though the proportion of incomes between £1000 and £1500 is also high for this group. It is interesting to speculate on whether those with children are 'compensated' by higher incomes. They have some tax concessions and may have family allowances, which are mentioned in the next chapter, but these are somewhat less than adequate indicators of the cost of a child. The real difficulty, however, is that of deciding whether children should be fully compensated for in income. Are they not to some extent at least a part of the deliberate decision-taking of married couples on how they wish to live and spend their income?

Whatever might be said of the 'burden' of children on the average married couple and their income, the problem of families in poverty is clearly a matter of special public as well as individual concern. The Income Census, for example, shows that there were over 60,000 families with children living on incomes between £275 and £500 in 1964–5, as well as some single persons with family responsibilities, and quite a number of couples and single persons with such incomes and with other dependants to provide for. It is impossible to embark on a full discussion of poverty here. Two studies are, however, mentioned in the footnote.[1] The second of these studies states that of the 3·9 million families with two or more children who were receiving family allowances, at the time of the enquiry in 1966 'about 280,000 had initial resources – i.e. their incomes excluding any assistance allowances they received – which were less than their requirements, as measured by reference to the national assistance scales current at the time of the enquiry. Their children numbered about 910,000. If the supplementary benefit rates now current are applied, the number of families would have been about 345,000 and the number of their children 1·1 million.'[2] One special problem in giving help to such poor families which is highly relevant to discussion of wages, especially minimum wages, is that in a desire to prevent social provision from becoming competitive with taking a job, unemployed applicants for assistance who are thought not to be trying hard enough to find a job, or who have left their last employment voluntarily, are subject to a 'wage stop', by which their payments are held below what they would have available for spending if they were at work and being paid. Of the 345,000 families mentioned above, the same enquiry found that 20,000 would have been receiving restricted allowances because of the wage stop while another 125,000 families would be eligible for national assistance, but not receiving it because the wage earner was in full-time employment, though earning less than the national assistance rates. These figures provide quite ample evidence of the continued existence of a problem of poor families in Britain.

SUGGESTED READING

B. Abel-Smith and P. Townsend, *The Poor and the Poorest*, 1965.
A. L. Bowley, *Wages and Incomes since 1860*, 1937.
H. F. Lydall, 'The Long-Term Trend in the Size Distribution of Income', *Journal of the Royal Statistical Society*, 1959.

[1] B. Abel-Smith and P. Townsend, *The Poor and the Poorest* (1965), and Ministry of Social Security, *Circumstances of Families* (H.M.S.O., 1967).
[2] Supplementary benefits replaced National Assistance in 1966. The supplementary allowances are paid by the Ministry of Social Security to those who are not in full-time work and represent the amount by which a claimant's income requirements exceed his resources. Many of these allowances are paid to supplement unemployment or sickness benefits, or to replace them where a person is no longer eligible for insurance benefits.

E. H. Phelps Brown and S. V. Hopkins, 'The Course of Wage Rates in Five Countries 1860–1939', *Oxford Economic Papers*, 1950.

A. Maddison, *Economic Growth in the West*, 1964.

Ministry of Social Security, *Circumstances of Families*, 1967.

R. J. Nicholson, 'The Distribution of Personal Income', *Lloyds Bank Review*, January 1967.

United Nations, *Incomes in Post-War Europe*, Economic Commission for Europe, Geneva, 1967.

14 The Effects of Taxation

I.

The primary object of taxation is to raise revenue for the Government. In modern times, however, we have increasingly emphasised two other important functions. We would now take the view that it is the duty of the State in raising taxes, as well as considering its own convenience as a tax-gatherer, to study the wider social and economic effects of the types of taxes it chooses to impose. We also expect the State to manipulate the total size of its taxation in relation to its expenditure to produce desirable effects on the level of activity of the economy. These three functions are closely related in practice. Most of the expenditure of the British Government goes beyond the inevitable minimum activities of the State – provision of internal and external security and the maintenance of the machinery of government – and is devoted to furthering by direct means similar social and economic objectives to those which may also be pursued by manipulation of the tax structure. A large volume of Government taxation and expenditure is generated by these social and economic preoccupations as well as other items of Government, such as the need for defence expenditure: on some methods of reckoning about 40 per cent of the product of our economy passes through the hands of central or local government agencies, though much of it is passed back to individuals, and the large scale of governmental activities increases their impact.

In this chapter we shall be concerned with the effect of taxation, and to some extent of expenditure, on the structure of wages and the distribution of income, looking first at the effects of direct taxes and then at indirect taxes. We shall also have to consider some of the effects on income of governmental payments in the form of 'transfer to persons', which are payments to individuals made from public funds in the form of pensions, family allowances and the like rather than as payments for work. The chapter continues with a discussion of a particularly intractable subject – the effect of taxation on the incentive to work – and concludes with a brief discussion of some other taxes which affect the way in which labour is used in our economy. The role of the Government's budgetary activities as a regulator of the level and direction of activity of the economy as a whole is deferred for discussion in Chapters 20 and 21.

It is important to stress from the outset that it is not possible to regard the activities of the State in collecting taxes as simply a device for redistributing income in the interests of some particular social or political view of justice or equity. The State is committed to a relatively high level of expenditure, in large part because it wishes to maintain social policies which have redistributional effects, but also for general purposes of government. And this level of expenditure is such that the effect of the structure of taxation on the distribution of incomes which is given greatest social prominence, that of redistributing incomes away from the upper income group, has to be reconciled with the necessity of raising revenue. Whether the Government chooses to do so or not, the needs of the revenue force it into large-scale taxation of the big battalions of income earners who have smaller incomes. Direct taxes, such as income tax or surtax, can be constructed, and are constructed in our society, to take a higher proportion away from the larger incomes. But the current burden of governmental expenditure cannot be met by direct taxes alone, and the current revenue of our Government is derived for the most part in roughly equal parts from taxes on income and indirect taxes or taxes on expenditure. The latter tend to be placed on goods which are widely sold. These are bought by people with smaller incomes as well as those with large incomes, and tend to form a higher proportion of the total expenditure of small incomes. While direct taxation is designed to be 'progressive' in that it takes a progressively greater proportion of income as income rises, indirect taxes are usually 'regressive'.

Though there are many imperfections in the process, and plenty of political controversy associated with it, taxation and Government expenditure do, however, act to adjust the distribution of income arising from the workings of the labour market broadly in line with a country's social and political views on income distribution. Society determines formally or informally many of the rules and conventions which govern the behaviour of the labour market, and social forces help to mould the pattern of supply and demand for different types of labour. But the labour market need not necessarily arrive at a structure of payments which is socially pleasing or satisfies all the current social conventions. Extreme examples of poor wage levels or conditions of work which are not consonant with current political or social standards can be controlled by the Government adding in more rules, such as those relating to minimum wages or permitted hours of work for women, but the end product of the labour market's operations is still a price rather than an expression of social attitudes or political or social conscience. Clarity of thinking requires that we keep discussion of how the market operates apart in our minds from views about how the pattern of payments ought to work out on social or political grounds. These wider questions are the direct province of the State and its political decision-taking. It is proper and necessary to analyse the operations of the labour market without bringing in the broadest social and political contentions and so to discuss wages before taxation. If these wider considerations do not come wholly into the operation of the market it is also proper to charge the Government of the day with the duty of correcting the pattern of income in the light of politically acceptable assumptions, using redistributive taxation and social expenditure as its main instruments. And the wage and taxation aspects of the process of arriving at the incomes which people have after they have earned their pay and been subjected to governmental adjustment of incomes and benefits must be kept apart.

This distinction between social and political considerations and the results of the operation of the labour market has to be stressed, because it is unfortunately frequently forgotten, for example in controversy about equal payment for men and women. We are working within the confines of a discussion of the labour market if we suggest that market imperfections are the main barrier to equal pay, so that if social restrictions on particular types of job were altered more women would be employed and the distinction between the sexes in work and payment might disappear. If, however, we argue that women have a right to equal payment without studying the market situation, though we may hope that widespread use of such an argument will have its effect on market attitudes, we are really developing an appeal not to the market at all but to the community at large. A discussion of the rights of women is a matter for politics and for advocating appropriate policies on taxation and social expenditure rather than for the market. If on the other hand we choose to suggest that equal pay would be a mistake because men have families to provide for and women do not, apart from the dubious factual basis of such a statement, we ought in any case again to be thinking of Government action rather than suggesting that the market ought always to pay more to married men with families. Incidentally, such a requirement would have the unfortunate result of putting family men out of work, whereas the same difficulty does not arise when the family man's needs are reflected in tax allowances or social expenditure.

These examples are taken from the controversy on equal pay because it has been specially prolific in furthering confusion of thinking between the workings of the labour market and the duties of the State. Examples also occur in other types of discussion. A *maximum* wage has, for example, been recommended in the interests of social justice. This is quite different from advocating redistribution of income by taxation. Apart from the fact that a maximum wage, if it worked, would be the equivalent of confiscation of incomes above a certain level, the suggestion loses sight of the valuable functions of the structure of payments in sorting out the labour force. In sum, the pattern of payments which emerges after the effects of taxation have been taken into account is not the same thing as the wage structure or the structure of incomes determined by the operations of the labour market and related markets, and the two should not be confused.

II. The Structure of Incomes after Taxation

The State affects the distribution of incomes, apart from any effects that may be derived from legislation prescribing conditions of work or from its activities as a very large employer and a very large purchaser, by taxation, direct and indirect, and social expenditure. Direct taxation includes taxes on capital (death duties are at present the only taxes on capital used in Britain), as well as taxes on income of which the most important are income tax, surtax, and corporation tax. But taxation of capital operates on the distribution of wealth rather than directly on the distribution of income and so need not concern us here. We can also set aside corporation taxes levied on the income of companies as not being directly paid out of personal incomes. Social insurance contributions are a form of direct taxation and will be discussed later in this chapter. Indirect taxes comprise all the taxes on expenditure, purchase tax, duties on beer, spirits, labour, petrol, motor vehicle licences and so on. Public expenditure influences the distribution of income through transfer payments such as pensions and also via such social expenditure as the provision of education, subsidised housing, and the like.

The best way to outline the redistributive effects of taxes on income is to look again at some of the tables of Chapter 13 which show the pattern of income before taxation, and construct similar tables showing the position 'after tax'. Table 13.7 sets out the way in which the total of personal income in our economy was distributed among various types of income in 1938 and more recently. Personal income is the gross amount which the public have to spend or save; but before they get this income they have still to pay direct taxes on it. Thus the total income at the disposal of persons (in the sense that they have this income to spend or save as they wish, though some of it in the spending will be taken by taxes on expenditure) is the total of personal incomes less taxes on income. This latter total is known as personal disposable income, and some figures for it are given in Table 14.1.

Table 14.1

Composition of Personal Disposable Income, 1938, 1958 and 1966

	1938	1958	1966
Types of income	Percentages		
Income from employment[1]	61	73	71
Income from self-employment[2] ⎱ Rents, dividends and interest ⎰	33	18	18
Current grants from public authorities	6	9	12
Total disposable income[2]	100	100	100

[1] Including Forces' pay.
[2] Before allowing for capital consumption and stock appreciation.
Source: *National Income and Expenditure*. The figures slightly exceed 100 per cent because of deductions which are omitted from the table. The figures for 1966 are estimated, since the Blue Book now gives less detail about them than previously.

When contrasted with the figures of personal income given in Table 13.7, the estimates of personal disposable income in Table 14.1 indicate that direct taxation redistributes income slightly in favour of income from employment and more definitely to favour grants from public authorities. Investment income and income from self-employment represent a smaller share of personal disposable income than of personal income.

Table 14.2 contrasts the distribution of income by levels of income before and after tax in 1938 and 1965, reproducing the 'before-tax' figures of Table 13.8 and adding 'post-tax' figures.

It is apparent from Table 14.2 that direct taxation reduces the number of incomes in higher income ranges and increases those in lower ranges. In fact the proportion of income taken back in income tax and surtax rises rather rapidly from a start at around £400 to £500 for those with no family, but then levels off somewhat and climbs very slowly between, say, £1200 and several thousands. It rises steeply again, however, with the

L 2

emergence of surtax, which comes into play for earned incomes at about £5000. The actual proportion of income taken in tax is now lower than it was on smaller incomes in 1938 but much higher for larger incomes. But the reduction in the value of money between these dates has been such that

Table 14.2

Distribution of Allocated Personal Incomes Before and After Tax
(Number of Incomes), 1938 and 1965

| | Percentage of incomes in income ranges | | | |
| | 1938 | | 1965 | |
Range of income	Before	After	Before	After
£50–250	[88·8]	[88·8]	10·9	10·9
£250–500	7·9	8·1	22·8	24·8
£500–750	1·4	1·6	13·5	19·7
£750–1000	0·8	0·6	20·5	18·7
£1000–2000	0·7	0·6	28·2	23·4
Over £2000	0·4	0·3	4·2	2·6
Total	100	100	100	100

Source: *National Income and Expenditure.*
The figures for incomes between £50 and £250 in 1938 are estimates by Lydall, op. cit.

the burden of direct taxation on equivalent levels of real income is generally higher. The trend towards equality in the before-tax income distribution halted about 1957, and since that year the earned incomes up to about £5000 have not been liable to surtax. These two factors have combined to produce a distribution of incomes after tax which has shown a tendency to widen since 1957 as against the narrowing trend in the earlier post-war years.

Direct taxation on income takes account of family circumstances by a system of allowances of income which is not chargeable to tax. The allowances should be familiar to every taxpayer. As they stand in 1968, omitting certain complications introduced in 1968 to recover increases in family allowances from those with higher incomes, everybody is given a personal allowance of £220 with an additional £120 for a wife and £115 for each child under eleven, £140 for children between eleven and sixteen, and £165 for children in full-time education. The value of these allowances depends on the income in question; but for those paying the standard rate of tax and no surtax, the value of the allowance for a wife is approximately £50, a little less for a younger child and more for an older child. Those who pay less than the standard rate receive less differential advantage compared with people with similar incomes and fewer responsibilities. It seems improbable that these sums in any way represent the cost of maintaining such dependants, so that the direct tax structure may be said to do little to even out differences in the standard of living created by family responsibilities. The allowances themselves have not kept pace with changing money values. The allowance for a wife in 1938 was worth £22 in that year and that for a child £15 at the prevailing standard rate, but these amounts should be multiplied roughly three-and-a-half times to convert them into the equivalent purchasing power today.

Everybody in employment pays for social security and, except for variations in the case of married women, and some additional payments for graduated pensions reflecting income levels, the amount payable is the same for all men, and also, at a lower rate, for all women. These payments are direct taxation, in the sense that they are levied by Government directly on income, and even though they are to provide benefits and are called insurance contributions, the amounts payable in contributions are not closely related to the circumstances of the contributor as happens with private insurance. They are also regressive, since they bear proportionately more heavily on smaller incomes. Any complete account of the effects of taxation must, therefore, include this item.

An account of the effects of taxation only in terms of direct taxation would be very incomplete. Indirect taxation is levied on goods which are bought with income left after direct taxation. About as much revenue is raised from taxes on expenditure as from taxes on income, and in the interests of raising sufficient revenue such taxes are usually levied on articles in wide general demand. As a consequence the proportion of income paid in taxes on expenditure tends to be high on smaller incomes. On the other hand it is possible to evade such taxes by varying the collection of goods bought. Two of the largest items are the taxes on drink and tobacco, which account for two-fifths of the revenue from taxes on expenditure – and it is actually possible to live without drinking or smoking. One special further difficulty in making general statements on the effect of indirect taxes on income is to determine whether the tax is wholly paid by the consumer or is to some extent absorbed by the seller. If the latter is true, then the incidence of the tax is bound up with the operations of the producers. In practice attempts to assess the effect of indirect taxes on the distribution of income assume that the taxes are passed on to the consumer.

In contrast to the regressive effects of indirect taxation, much of Government social expenditure is in practice directed towards those with lower incomes and with more family responsibilities. All members of a family enjoy health service benefits. Pensions and social security payments support smaller incomes to a greater proportionate extent than larger. Education is a major item of Government expenditure which benefits families. In effect, though with difficulties in estimation, we may divide Government expenditure into a part which can be 'allocated' as likely to benefit people in particular income ranges and with particular family circumstances, and the remainder which is unallocated and includes items such as defence and roads and so on, the latter being paid for by those sections of the taxpayers for whom tax paid in direct and indirect taxes, including social security payments, is more than allocated expenditure received.

The Central Statistical Office[1] has provided data on the various effects on different sizes of families in 1966 of direct taxes, national insurance contributions, taxes on expenditure, and Government expenditure which can be allocated in this way – something like 50 per cent of all Government expenditure. The method employed involves the data on expenditure of families which are collected annually by the Department of Employment and Productivity in its Family Expenditure Survey. There are many snags in interpretation, but the broad picture which results is probably reliable and certainly interesting. The results they provide are illustrated in Tables 14.3 and 14.4 for households consisting of two adults and of two adults and two children. Apart from difficulties in estimation and assumption it is also important to notice that these figures are based initially on a sample, and its further subdivision into categories of families and ranges of income means that each item is based on a small number of cases. They are not, therefore, fully accurate or representative but are broadly indicative. The absence of data for higher income ranges is again due to the size of the sample. The actual income ranges used in the tables are those employed by the Central Statistical Office.

Both tables, despite the limitations of the data, show a remarkable consistency. Direct taxation rises slowly as a percentage of income. On the other hand national insurance contributions are regressive and the proportion paid out in national insurance is much more important than direct taxes for the smaller incomes. (The low proportion of national insurance contributions for the very small-income families in Table 14.3 is almost certainly due to the heads of these households being retired.) For the lower incomes shown in the tables indirect taxation is more important

[1] *Economic Trends*, February 1968.

Table 14.3

Taxes and Benefits of Families consisting of Two Adults in 1966

Original income range	Average original income	Types of payment as % of original income					Outcome	
		Taxes				Benefits	Final average income	As % of original income
		Direct taxes	Nat. ins. contributions	Indirect taxes	Total of taxes			
£	£						£	
260— 315	287	3	3	49	56	135	514	179
315— 382	347	6	4	43	53	120	582	168
382— 460	424	5	6	33	44	88	610	144
460— 559	510	10	5	29	45	73	652	128
559— 676	621	9	9	23	40	38	607	98
676— 816	759	10	8	21	39	27	670	88
816— 988	901	9	9	21	39	20	728	81
988—1196	1091	10	9	19	37	10	798	73
1196—1448	1314	11	8	18	37	7	922	70
1448—1752	1600	12	7	17	36	6	1112	70
1752—2122	1912	13	6	15	35	3	1307	68
2122—2566	2319	16	6	14	35	3	1572	68
2566 and above	3945	26	2	10	38	3	2540	64

Source: Calculated from *Economic Trends*, February 1968.

Table 14.4

Taxes and Benefits of Families consisting of Two Adults and Two Children in 1966

Original income range	Average original income	Types of payment as % of original income					Outcome	
		Direct taxes	Nat. ins. contributions	Indirect taxes	Total of taxes	Benefits	Final average income	As % of original income
£	£						£	
676– 816	766	1	10	21	32	42	837	109
816– 988	903	1	10	21	33	26	843	93
988–1196	1096	5	9	19	33	22	977	89
1196–1448	1326	7	7	19	33	19	1142	86
1448–1752	1596	9	6	18	33	16	1331	83
1752–2122	1918	12	5	17	34	15	1538	80
2122–2566	2341	12	4	13	29	12	1934	83
2566 and above	3744	19	2	10	32	6	2788	74

Source: Calculated from *Economic Trends*, February 1968.

than direct, and the tax burden of indirect taxes derived from this analysis based on what households buy is clearly regressive. On the other hand the benefits paid out to families with smaller incomes are higher in amount as well as a higher proportion of their incomes. The relatively high level of benefits to low-income families of two adults is no doubt also a direct reflection of the circumstance that many such family units are retired couples on pension. The final outcome of all these subtractions and additions is that for families of two adults without children benefits exceeded taxes in 1966 up to roughly £550 a year, while for families with two children this 'break-even point' beyond which the average family begins to contribute to the expenses of the Government for purposes not directly related to families, and, therefore, not directly allocable, was roughly £800.

Data such as these lie behind a number of suggestions for reform of the tax system. They strongly suggest that there is little point in talking of our direct tax system as 'progressive' for the broad range of wage earnings, since at such levels of income the combined effect of national insurance contributions and income tax taken together is to produce a tax which is broadly proportional to the income of those in work, with some adjustment for family circumstances. A proportional tax might then be simpler to understand and to collect and could be supplemented by progressive taxation on higher incomes. The fact that for low incomes tax is more than repaid in benefit suggests the idea of compounding tax liability with benefits and either collecting tax or paying benefits according to family circumstances, through the tax system. This idea has recently gained currency under the label of the 'negative income tax'. It is, however, a clearer idea in terms of averages than in detailed application. The difficulty of operating such an idea is largely that of taking account of individual circumstances – and this is the detailed concern of tax allowances and benefit regulations. It would not be easy to devise a simple method of compounding taxes and benefits which took account of all circumstances reflected in present regulations. It could be very difficult indeed to devise a scheme which included indirect taxes, since they are paid on everybody's purchases and it would be virtually impossible to provide for tax exemption. On the other hand, the fact that the total system is on average not progressive over a wide range of incomes suggests that some simplification is highly desirable and not likely to lead to loss of a purpose which in practice the tax system does not presently display.

This line of argument, which leaves the progressive element of the tax structure to the upper income levels, also highlights the question of the effective application of the progressive principle where it actually exists.

A damaging criticism on this is offered by R. M. Titmuss in *Income Distribution and Social Change*. To some extent Titmuss is simply concerned to draw out criticisms of analyses of income distributions, which, while of importance, leave such an analysis as an essential, though imperfect, part of our attempts at knowledge. Titmuss, however, also emphasises important possibilities of tax avoidance, and any account of income distribution should at least mention some of these. Four are listed here.

1. Discussions of income distribution take little account of benefits in kind which are often not taxed and can in some contexts be of considerable value. In the Forces, for example, there are various tax-free bounties and quite substantial parts of the necessities of life, such as clothing, are provided as part of the job. While various attempts have been made to tighten up the tax provisions here, managers and other senior executives may expect to be provided with a number of facilities which would otherwise require expenditure by them.

2. Savings for retirement, by those who can so save, are favourably treated for tax purposes.

3. While income from wealth is taxed, including capital gains, the distribution of wealth is much more unequal than that of income. Wealth gives to its fortunate possessor a flexible ability to improve his standard of living, and only some forms of income from wealth are included in accounts of the distribution of income.

4. It is possible to make various legal arrangements to avoid tax by taking advantage of intended provisions or of loopholes in the law, though the Chancellor of the Exchequer in most budgets makes some attempt to close some of them, including some that have emerged since he last spoke. For example, it is possible to arrange to provide for certain categories of dependants by making a tax-free covenant in their favour. It is difficult to describe this, or more sophisticated devices, as evasion, because it is within the law, but its effect on the command over the disposition of his resources by the individual may be considerable. It is also worth noting that legal avoidance of tax is an activity which inevitably consumes a lot of time and which is profitable so long as the tax avoided is greater than the outlay in doing so.

III. Taxation and Incentive

It is obviously true that, whatever other motives and aspects of the matter there are, people work for money, and therefore, in the broadest sense wages can be regarded as an incentive to work. Taxation reduces the return of income or of goods obtainable from working and this, therefore, naturally gives rise to the question whether taxation acts as a disincentive to work – a question of direct relevance to wages and the supply of labour. This section briefly reviews the position. It should be stressed, however, that the answer to be offered is very much of a 'not proven' variety. There is, of course, also the question of whether taxation is a disincentive to other types of economic activity, but this topic must be set aside here.

The choice which taxation is presumed to influence is that between working and not working, or in other words between work and leisure; but there is a further and most important effect of such a choice – its effect on income. The standard economic analysis of the effects of taxation on the incentive to work is one which distinguishes between the income and substitution effects of a change in taxation. The former, put quite simply, means that taxation reduces the quantity of goods that may be bought from a given income and hence from a given amount of work. If, then, people are intent upon maintaining a particular level of real income the presence of taxation means that they have to work harder to do so. If taxation should go up, then the income effect suggests that people will work harder since, while their real reward from working has been reduced, their need for income to maintain their real living standards has been increased. On the other hand, if leisure is regarded as having a value to the worker, an increase in taxation can be regarded as increasing the price of goods that can be bought with a given amount of work. This causes a shift in the relative attractiveness of work and leisure and on this line of argument a worker will substitute leisure for work as tax increases.

Evidently, therefore, we have two arguments pulling in opposite directions. A tax increase makes leisure relatively more attractive and might, therefore, reduce work; but it also makes it necessary to work harder to maintain a given income level. It may also be evident that a resolution of these conflicting tendencies to prove the proposition that taxation, and especially increases in taxation, reduces the incentive to work cannot be provided on general logical grounds. It all depends on the individual's position and priorities. Empirical studies have not provided a clear answer. One reason for the lack of clear empirical results which might aggregate individual reactions into a recognisable overall pattern is that the likely outcome of a choice between working harder or less hard as tax changes may be expected to vary according to circumstances – and the circumstances in question are themselves highly variable. Different meanings may be attached to the term work, leisure has implications for income, different taxes may have different effects, and incentives to work may vary with income levels. All of these points merit discussion.

Since it is not, of course, suggested that taxation will in practice cause work to stop, its effects, if any, will be at the margin where decisions are taken to reduce or increase the work load. The individual can choose to vary his work load in two ways. He may vary his rate of working or the hours he puts in. If he is on payment by results, variations in his rate of working are quickly reflected in payment, but the link between rate of work and payment, while less clear-cut and immediate, exists for most workers. Managers and professional people may seek or avoid more responsibility. Workers may eagerly, or not so eagerly, demonstrate their enthusiasm for promotion by their diligence. While most people have standard hours of work, variations in actual hours are usually possible. A certain amount of absenteeism may be tolerated. Paid opportunities for overtime are normally quite plentiful for British wage earners. It is always possible for people to seek a supplementary income in the form of a second job or casual extra earnings. There are indeed three distinct versions of the choice between work and leisure. The two obvious choices are of working hard or less hard at work, or of seeking or refusing longer periods of work. A third possibility must, however, also be mentioned because of its practical importance. The existence of direct taxes on income provides an incentive for those who wish to take advantage of it, even though it is clearly illegal and punishable if detected, to choose to limit their input of taxable work and seek extra casual sources of earnings which they do not declare for tax purposes.

A decision to work less hard at work must generally be regarded as a decision to take chances of leisure within the place of work or simply to have a quiet life at work. There are no doubt people who choose to do this anyway, and may be encouraged to do so, or to justify doing so, by tax considerations. But leisure at work is not of course the same thing as leisure away from work. Moreover, there is a positive incentive to maintain a place and a reputation while at work to be derived from considerations of status. A reputation for avoiding work is perhaps more easily acquired, and promotion less easily acquired, by the worker who is seen to be doing so while at work, than by the person who chooses leisure in preference to work and payment by staying away from extra periods of work. This judgment, however, depends upon the view that status and reputation in our society are associated with working hard or doing a good job. If there exists a social attitude in the work group which is opposed to working hard, and if taxation strengthens this view, then status considerations within the work group arising from the rate of working – as opposed to status considerations arising from obtaining promotion – may result in taxation reducing work and increasing leisure at work.

The effect of taxation on work which is most commonly cited is that which might cause a man to substitute leisure for work by reducing his hours of work. The most simple way in which this can be done without the kind of penalty which persistent absenteeism might incur is to avoid over-time and not to take an extra or casual job. In the logic of the argument there can be no doubt that tax exerts a substitution effect by increasing the relative attractiveness of leisure as against work. It should, however, be noticed that for the wage earner extra hours of work are generally remuner-ated at a premium rate, which acts, therefore, as an incentive to take on overtime. Casual work may also be specially well remunerated. Addition-ally, a decision to substitute leisure for work may well have implications for income. Many or even most forms of active leisure and entertainment cost money. On the other hand, leisure may take the form of 'do-it-yourself' activities designed to reduce the cost of possessions which would otherwise have to be acquired out of post-tax income. If taxation reduces income, leisure activities may be one of the factors pushing a worker towards extra work to maintain his income, and this naturally weakens the presumed substitution effect of leisure for work.

In brief, it is difficult to argue that the case for believing that taxation will in general reduce work is conclusive, since proof either way is lacking. Do different taxes affect this generalisation? National insurance contri-butions vary with income but not to a major extent. They can be smaller for part-time work, but most workers do not have the kind of flexibility in their commitments that would allow them to take much account of this factor. Married women may be an exception to this, particularly if they are interested in very part-time work, since different rules apply for less than eight hours a week. National insurance contributions are not, therefore, a tax which can be avoided once it is accepted that a full-time job is unavoidable for the majority of workers, though it is possible that they affect the amount and duration of part-time work. The contributions may have the effect of persuading workers to increase their rate of work to obtain post-tax income. Indirect taxes are avoidable since it is possible to work and to enjoy some forms of consumption without increasing tax. Apart from this point, however, the effect of indirect taxes are in general theoretically similar to those of direct taxes. On the other hand the link between income receivable and the level of tax is not at all obvious. Sub-jectively the worker is more likely to add indirect taxes in with prices, while he directly notes and reacts to the impact of direct tax upon his pay packet.

It is usually income tax which people are thinking about when the effects of taxation are under discussion, and the foregoing has looked at the effects of income tax in general terms. But what of the details? We may first note that there is evidence that British taxpayers do not accurately know the rate of income tax which they actually pay on their incomes, and possibly react to what they think they pay rather than the actual rate – a point which suggests that our tax structure is in need of simplification and greater explanation.[1] We noted earlier that the rate of tax payable per head of additional income under British income tax does not vary over a wide range of income from the point, dependent on family circumstances, at which reduced rates and allowances are exhausted to over £4000 a year. It seems probable that if the possibility of extra work and extra payment occurs at the same point of income at which the tax rate jumps up, we might anticipate some reaction from the worker. This effect, in which the marginal decision to increase earnings coincides with marginal tax increases, may occur for a man with a wife and two children if he is earning below £1200 a year or if he is earning more than £4000. It is said that workers avoid overtime because of marginal jumps in their tax rate, but it is observable that overtime has continued to be worked at a high level and also that workers really do not know their exact tax position.

It is indisputable that on the small number of earned incomes above £4000, and still more on the even smaller number above £5000, marginal rates of tax rise sharply as earned income allowances diminish and surtax begins to bite. This gives rise to the argument that in Britain higher-paid salaried workers – largely managers, administrators and professional groups – are more heavily taxed than in most other countries and that this important section of the labour force is therefore adversely influenced by a strong disincentive effect. There may be long-term consequences (such as emigration and a fall in recruitment) and it is possible on economic grounds to argue against as well as for more equality via the tax system, but it is not easy to prove a strong short-term disincentive effect of taxation even at this level. It has to be remembered that the kind of people who earn surtax-level salaries are likely to be those who are in demanding, high-status occupations which provide little opportunity for choosing leisure. It may be possible to assert that some such people deliberately choose to avoid new responsibilities because of taxation, but this would be difficult to prove. It is more possible to argue that those of the high income earners

[1] Cf. C. V. Brown, 'Misconceptions about Income Tax and Incentives', *Scottish Journal of Political Economy*, February 1968, pp. 1–21.

who are self-employed and can govern their own lives will choose more leisure because of tax considerations – popular authors are sometimes quoted as an example – while those self-employed who run their own businesses will be likely to suffer a shortage of risk capital because of taxes on their income. Another line of argument is that which suggests that post-tax income problems cause high-paid, and by inference high-productivity and valuable, employees to direct too much of their energy into doing work that could be done for them to the general advantage by less well-qualified labour. Again this possibility is difficult to document, but for some such people certain facilities that save their energies – such as chauffeur-driven cars – are certainly readily available.

In summary, the disincentive effects of taxation on work are more often argued over than proved. This discussion has, therefore, necessarily been inconclusive. One last point which might be made is to suggest – inevitably without proof – that a society which imagines itself to be heavily taxed develops a general attitude to work which is less satisfactory than it might be. British workers tend to believe that they are specially heavily taxed and wide publicity is given to the very high level of tax paid by a small number of highly remunerated individuals. It is possible that taxation may produce a general attitude and be a general disincentive even though its specific impact on incentives to work is obscure – but this is no more than a speculative statement.

IV. The Selective Employment Tax and the Regional Employment Premium

All taxes and Government expenditure have detailed effects on the nature and level of economic activity which it would, of course, be inappropriate to discuss here. Two recent introductions by the British Government are, however, intended directly to affect the allocation and utilisation of labour in our economy and must, therefore, find some mention in this chapter and in this book. These are the Selective Employment Tax, which was introduced in 1966, and the Regional Employment Premium, which began in 1967.

The Selective Employment Tax is levied on employers on the basis of the number of persons employed, with adjustments for part-time employees. All employers pay it but some receive an equivalent refund, and others receive both a refund and a subsidy. Firms classified as being in service industries pay the tax without refund, while those in manufacturing industries receive a refund and a subsidy. The subsidy element was, however, withdrawn, except in the Development Areas, when devaluation was announced on 18 November 1967, though this may prove to be a temporary arrangement. One of the motives of the tax was said to be to redress the balance of the tax system, since services had previously been less heavily taxed than manufacturing industry. Another motive was, no doubt, the familiar one of finding a new source of revenue. But the principal aim of the tax was 'to place a charge on employment in services and certain other activities to give a positive encouragement to manufacturing; and to be neutral for the remaining sectors of the economy'.[1]

The logic behind the proposed objective of the tax is simple. It increases the cost to the employer in the service industries of employing workers and reduces the cost, both relatively and absolutely (while the subsidy is being paid) in the manufacturing sector. Thus stated, while questions are raised of the extent to which mobility of labour between these sectors exists and can be encouraged, the tax seems well designed to its purpose. More questions arise, however, on further examination.

(i) The tax might reduce wage levels in the service sector relative to those in manufacturing, and the former tend already to be lower.

(ii) The tax shifts costs in favour of intensification of capital in the service sector, which may be desirable, but appears to favour an increase in the use of labour relative to capital in manufacturing, which is less desirable.

(iii) More generally, there is an inference that labour is specially wastefully used at present in the service sector, which might be true, but there is also the opposite inference that labour is really required in manufacturing and that making it cheaper will not mean that it is wasted.

(iv) The general trend in employment has been, and is likely to continue to be, from manufacturing towards services. The argument cannot, therefore, be about the fact of a move towards service employment, but rather on the timing and volume of its occurrence.

(v) Since the tax is taken in the first instance from everyone, it may have effects on the liquidity position of all firms.

(vi) By giving a subsidy to manufacturing the tax has an element of encouragement to the export sector of the economy, which is obviously desirable, but was lost when the subsidy was withdrawn at devaluation.

(vii) There are major problems of definition involved. Some typically service or distributional activities such as canteens and warehouses, being

[1] *Selective Employment Tax*, Cmnd. 2986, 1967.

attached to manufacturing plants, are differently treated from others which are counted within service industries. The definition of full- and part-time workers has given rise to difficulty, and perhaps to a tendency to reduce willingness to employ part-time workers.

(viii) The tax requires a substantial amount of administration.

None of these points is conclusive on the merits of the tax. They will, however, tend to show that a simple proposition in logic is more complex in practice and possibly that affecting the distribution of the labour force in this way by taxation is not specially satisfactory unless it is closely associated with governmental expenditure policies, which aim to help the labour market work more efficiently, and to encourage productivity.

The Regional Employment Premium uses the administrative mechanism of S.E.T., perhaps because it was convenient to do so, but has different purposes. It provides over a period of seven years from September 1967 a supplementary subsidy per employee in manufacturing industry in the Development Areas, which include most of Scotland and Wales, the northern counties of England, and Merseyside, and account for 20 per cent of manufacturing employment. By making labour cost less in the Development Areas, its intention is to encourage expansion of industry and employment there and so both reduce the demand for labour in the rapidly expanding areas of the country, where unemployment is low and labour is in specially short supply, and reduce unemployment and increase the effective utilisation of labour in the less rapidly growing areas. One intended result would be to even out the demand for labour over the country as a whole and so improve the prospects of effective management of the economy, avoiding a frequent dilemma by which general deflationary measures motivated by a desire to reduce an inflationary excess demand for labour in the South-East, have neutralised the benefit of a regional policy which has been trying to expand the economies of the under-employed regions. R.E.P., like other parts of regional policy, recognises the existence of twin problems, first of underemployment in the Development Areas which continues to exist, despite net emigration, and may even be intensified by the stagnation and lack of demand associated with emigration; and second, of the growing problems and rising costs of congestion in the rapidly-expanding South-East of the country. In effect, it is intended to reduce the costs and increase the competitiveness of the Development Areas.

Some of the comments made above about the Selective Employment Tax are also relevant to this measure. It may, for example, be a source of relative increases in wages which, though desirable as a longer-term reflection of success in regional policy, are deleterious in the short run. By subsidising labour costs it might artificially encourage labour-intensive expansion which would be disadvantageous for long-run competition. This point is, however, broadly neutralised by the fact that existing measures of regional policy – notably the investment grants – have been biased towards capital-intensive developments. It raises the general problem of the wisdom in a development situation of helping by a subsidy the declining as well as the expanding sectors of the regional economy and of helping the inefficient as well as the efficient. It favours manufacturing industry rather than services, and in most cases, but not all, growth in the regions must come initially from manufacturing. It raises inevitably some definitional issues of the so-called 'grey areas' which are neither Development Areas nor as prosperous as the South-East, though the extent of this definitional issue can be exaggerated. On the other hand, R.E.P. must be viewed in conjunction with other parts of a considerable apparatus of regional policy in the United Kingdom. This policy is, or ought to be, selective in giving particular attention to locations with favourable characteristics for growth, and in attempting, by encouraging new and immigrant industrial enterprise, to make the declining industries less important and change the structure of industry in the regions. The policy as a whole includes special attention to improvement of the social capital in the regions and the provision of facilities for industry, and to training of labour. It is particularly important to notice that R.E.P. provides a means of reducing costs for new enterprises during the settling-in period when running costs tend to be specially high. In other words, R.E.P. has clear faults when looked at on its own, but these are much less obvious and its benefits are much greater, when it is taken together with regional policy as a whole.

SUGGESTED READING

C. V. Brown, 'Misconceptions about Income Tax and Incentives', *Scottish Journal of Polical Economy*, February 1968.
C. V. Brown and D. A. Dawson, *Personal Taxation Incentives and Tax Reform*, 1969.
A. R. Prest, *Public Finance in Theory and Practice* (3rd ed.), 1967.
R. M. Titmuss, *Income Distribution and Social Change*, 1962.
United Nations, *Incomes in Post-War Europe*, Economic Commission for Europe, Geneva, 1967.

15 The Share of Wages in National Income

I. The Problem of Distributive Shares

In Chapter 13 we have already touched on the issue of what is often called the functional distribution of incomes: that is, the division of the national product among the main factors of production, traditionally labour, land and capital. Factor incomes have a dual role to play in the economic system. From one point of view, the return to a factor is a reflection of its price and therefore performs a function in helping to bring about an efficient allocation of resources. But secondly, factor incomes are also the means by which the social product is distributed, and it is this income-distribution aspect which is to concern us in this chapter.[1] What are the major determinants of the distribution of the social product? How, if at all, does this distribution change over time?

These problems are important for two reasons, the first of which is historical. David Ricardo and his followers regarded the 'laws' which governed the distribution of the product into profits, wages and rent as the principal problem of economics, and within the assumptions of the classical economic system, they developed a theory which was capable of solving this problem. The share of rent was explained by the principle of diminishing returns, while the share of wages was determined by the Malthusian theory of population growth, which predicted a perfectly elastic labour supply at a subsistence wage. The share of the third factor, capital, was then the remainder of the social product. But this theory was open to the charge that the economic system which it depicted was based on the exploitation of labour, a view which was advanced by Marx, who devised an alternative – but still unsatisfactory – theory of distribution. It was perhaps in some measure because of these attacks on the capitalist system

---

[1] Since the social product under discussion here is that which arises from the contributions of the factors it is, of course, the result of economic activity before the intervention of the tax gatherer. The discussion here is therefore concerned with the pre-tax position and not with the efforts of society, as represented by the State, to adjust the distribution of income in the light of certain objectives – the subject which was discussed in Chapter 14.

that a later generation of economists returned, with newly developed techniques of analysis, to the problem of income distribution. But whereas the Ricardians had developed a theory in terms of macro-economic variables, the new approach stemmed from micro-economic analysis, focusing on the behaviour of individual decision-takers such as consumers and entrepreneurs. Furthermore, instead of using *different* principles to explain the share of each factor, the neo-classical economists used a single principle – marginal productivity – to show not only how factor rewards would be determined, but also as a means of proving that when each factor's share was determined in this way the whole of the social product would be used up and no surplus would be left over. In fact this ethical defence of the system was valid only under certain restrictive assumptions, but it did lead to some theoretical advance and it is this rather than the defence of the system *per se* which is of most interest to present-day economists. Further developments came with the emergence of imperfect competition analysis, again of course along micro-economic lines.

The second reason for our interest in distributive shares arises from empirical evidence on the behaviour of these shares over time, and it is this which brings into prominence the problem of labour's share in income. Over long periods of time and in many different countries, empirical evidence reveals a long-run relative 'stability' in the share of wages. Many economists have regarded this as a sufficiently curious and important economic phenomenon to warrant a full-scale investigation and theoretical analysis. Kaldor, for example, has stated that:

'no hypothesis as regards the forces determining distributive shares could be intellectually satisfying unless it succeeds in accounting for the relative stability of these shares in the advanced economies over the last 100 years or so, despite the phenomenal changes in the techniques of production, in the accumulation of capital and in real income per head.'[1]

For the moment begging the question how invariant the share of wages has to be before it can be called 'stable' or 'constant', we can accept that the evidence is sufficient for us to take the problem seriously.[2]

Two other aspects of the main problem give added weight to the case for further investigation. First, there is the question of trade-union influence. One might have expected, at least in those countries like the United States where the emergence of trade unionism as a major economic force has been comparatively recent, that labour's share in the national income

[1] N. Kaldor, 'Alternative Theories of Distribution', *Review of Economic Studies*, vol. xxiii, no. 2, pp. 83–4.
[2] Some conception of this stability has already been given in Table 13.4.

might have increased in consequence. If labour's share has in fact been constant, does this mean that trade unions have no power to influence the proportion of total income going to the labour factor? Again, although the evidence seems initially to favour the case for long-run stability, it equally reveals a marked instability in relative income shares over the course of the trade cycle, with wages rising and profits falling relative to the total during recession, and vice versa in times of prosperity. Once more there is a question about the nature of the underlying mechanism.

These are the main problems which arise in relation to labour's share in the total product. A comprehensive account of work on this subject would raise some extremely difficult theoretical issues, for we cannot go very far without entering the territory of the economic model-builders, and this would take us far beyond what is necessary for the present purpose. The treatment in this chapter is therefore limited to an attempt to portray the behaviour of the main elements in the distributive process and to provide some indication of the kind of factors which have to be taken into account if the process is to be properly analysed. It falls short, however, of an attempt to provide complete summaries of different approaches to the problems.[1] Thus Section II reviews the behaviour of relative income shares in the United Kingdom, both in the short and long run. Section III takes up the problem of short-run variations in labour's share, and Section IV discusses the alternative approaches to the apparent long-run stability of the wage share. Section V provides a conclusion to the discussion.

II. The Empirical Evidence

We are fortunate in having for the United Kingdom a historical series on the functional distribution of home-produced national income dating back to the 1870s.[2] Table 15.1 shows for each decade since 1876–85 the various

[1] Admirable summaries do already exist. Cf. N. Kaldor, loc. cit.; T. Scitovsky, 'A Survey of Some Theories of Distribution' in *The Behavior of Income Shares*, National Bureau of Economic Research, Princeton, 1964; and K. W. Rothschild, 'Some Recent Contributions to a Macro-Economic Theory of Income Distribution', *Scottish Journal of Political Economy*, October 1961.

[2] This series is the work of E. H. Phelps Brown and P. E. Hart, 'The Share of Wages in National Income', *Economic Journal*, June 1952. The series reproduced in that article terminated with provisional figures for 1948–50. For the present purpose we have brought this series up to date and have replaced the earlier figures for 1948–50 on the basis of later statistics. The methods used here are the

Table 15.1

Distributive Shares as a Percentage of Home-Produced National Income: Decennial Averages
1876–85 to 1956–65

Period	Wages as % of national income	Salaries as % of national income	Wages and salaries as % of national income	Rent as % of national income	Profits as % of national income	National income £m.
1876–85	40·5	15·2	55·7	14·8	29·5	1053
1886–95	41·1	18·3	59·4	13·8	26·8	1231
1896–1905	40·3	18·9	59·2	12·4	28·4	1572
1906–13[1]	37·6	18·9	56·5	11·8	31·8	1543
1926–35	39·9	27·0	66·9	9·3	23·8	3624
1936–45	39·0	22·7	61·7	7·5	30·8	5890
1946–55	41·7	20·8	62·5	4·6	32·9	11,858
1956–65	40·6	24·5	65·1	5·8	29·1	22,273

[1] 8-year period only.

Source: E. H. Phelps Brown and P. E. Hart, 'The Share of Wages in National Income', Economic Journal, June 1952 (from which the averages up to 1945 are calculated; the figures for the final two decades have been derived by similar methods from National Income and Expenditure, H.M.S.O., 1965 (for 1946–55) and 1967 (for 1956–65)).

percentage shares in which we are interested (the only exception being the period affected by the First World War).

(a) *Wages and Salaries*. Wages, taken by themselves, exhibit a considerable long-run stability at around 40 per cent of home-produced national income, the degree of variation being much less than with rent, salaries or profits. Salaries have shown some tendency to rise in importance, but as a proportion of income have varied considerably from decade to decade, with what appears to be a major jump during the period affected by the First World War and its aftermath. More is said about this below. Taken together, wages and salaries have comprised on average around 60 per cent of total income, but as might be expected from what has been said about salaries, there is a suggestion of some long-term rise over the 90-year period.

(b) *Rent*. The share of rent has shown a long-run downward trend, comprising only about 5 per cent of income in recent years compared with 14 to 15 per cent at the end of the last century. The decennial averages show no real variation in the trend until 1956–65, when a small upturn occurred.

(c) *Profits*. Profits are again a variable item, with the long-run average just below 30 per cent, or about one-half of the joint wage and salary share. However, profits' share fell as low as 24 per cent in the depressionary period of 1926–35 and rose as high as 33 per cent in the post-1945 boom.

What is perhaps most remarkable about this is the relative stability of the pure wage share, despite the fact that the importance of wage earners in the total occupied population has diminished a great deal, from over 80 per cent in the 1880s to about 60 per cent in the 1960s, while the proportion of salaried workers has risen substantially. That the wage share has remained stable over time must then reflect a rise in the average income received by the wage earner, and some fall is perhaps implied in the average (relative) income of the increasingly important salary earners. And of course there have been major compositional changes in both wage and salary sectors which might have produced this kind of result, with the growth of manufacturing industries carrying high wages, and an expansion of employment in lower-paid salaried occupations, such as was discussed in Chapter 6 above. From this point of view, then, there is some

---

same as those used in the Phelps Brown and Hart study, as described in the Appendix to their article.

suggestion that the reduction in the proportion of wage earners has been compensated for by an internal change in the structure of wage earning employment. From another point of view, however, it might seem that the wage/salary distinction, though at one time fairly clear and unambiguous, is now much less so. Many wage earners have very much the same kind of income level as the average salary earner. Changes in the law affecting contracts of employment have diminished the importance of the earlier distinction based on the period of notice to be given on termination of employment. And the social distinctions based on dress and speech have both diminished and grown less important. One possible use for the distinction remains, namely the fact that wage earners may represent a prime cost to the employer while the salary earner represents an overhead, less subject to variation over the course of the business cycle with changes in demand and output. This is a point to which we return. There is then the probability that changes in the composition of the wage earning and salaried sections of the labour force have to some extent offset each other.

There are several reasons why we should not be surprised to find that the share of rent has fallen in an industrial economy such as our own. Technical changes in the agricultural and extractive industries, where we would normally expect the share of rent to be large, emphasise the contributions of capital. An industrial economy develops manufacturing and service trades where we may expect the share of rent to be relatively low. The increased amount of processing which today's more highly finished and more carefully presented goods undergo reduces the relative importance both of the rent of the land used for the factory and of the raw materials contained in the final product. An industrial economy like ours increases its dependence on imported food and raw materials, and transfers some part of its demand for the products of the land to the factors that contribute to the output of the industrialised export industries. The ultimate effect of this on the well-being of wage earners depends on the terms on which the imported food and raw materials are obtained; but it has an immediate effect in transferring emphasis from home food production to the export industries, and so reduces the importance of rent. Finally, rent payments tend to be fixed on a conventional basis and are revised only at fairly long intervals, relative to other factor prices and prices in general. This tendency has been strengthened over the years by legislative changes introduced to control the rent of housing and land. Rents thus almost automatically lag behind in times of rising prices.

Turning now to the short run, we can obtain a general indication of the behaviour of relative shares from Fig. 15.1.[1] The shaded areas represent recession phases in the economy so that we can, by inspection, get some impression of the behaviour of the shares over the course of the trade cycle.

Fig. 15.1: Relative income shares, 1926-65

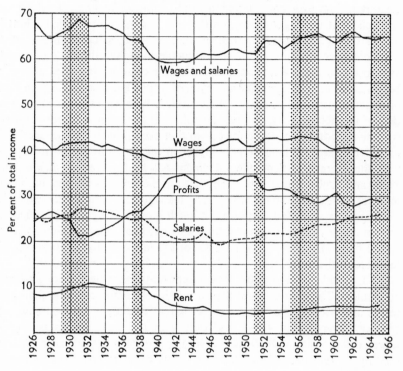

(1) Taken by themselves, wages as a proportion of total income vary a good deal from year to year, though always within fairly narrow limits (between about 38 and 43 per cent). There is some indication that this variation is anti-cyclical, the wage share rising in relation to total income during recession and falling back in more prosperous years. Thus the wage share has declined fairly consistently during periods when general business activity was on the upswing, and has usually been either maintained or

[1] The figures for the individual shares are given in Table 15.2, which appears as an Appendix to this chapter.

increased during the shaded recessionary periods – though behaviour during recession is more erratic.

(2) The share of salaries shows less year-to-year variation, but seemingly changes in the same direction for a period of years. The salary share rose from 1926 to a peak in 1931–2. This was followed by a prolonged decline to a low point of 19·7 in 1947, from which time it has again risen quite steadily to just over one-quarter of total income. This kind of behaviour is much what we might expect, on the view expressed above that salaried labour may be regarded as an overhead. As such, salaried employment will be slower to adjust to short-run fluctuations than direct labour, and as a result its share will tend to rise during recession. But when recovery begins, salaried employment and payment will be less responsive than that of direct labour, and its share will be eroded. Whether this is the explanation of the post-war rise in the salary share is conjectural, although there is some supporting evidence for this in that even though the average level of activity has been considerably higher in the post-war period than pre-war, the average level of unemployment has been increasing in the late 1950s and 1960s. But it is possible that another influence is making itself felt here – the change in technology and management organisation which is tending to expand staff employment much more rapidly than production worker employment. In that case any explanation of changing factor shares would have to include some analysis of the labour force implications of technological change.

(3) Like salaries, the share of rent appears to be subject to longer-term adjustment. The depression of the early 1930s, by 'squeezing' the shares of wages and profits, allowed the share of rent to rise, but the subsequent recovery reversed this trend, and only with the recurring bouts of enforced deflation in the 1950s and 1960s (and perhaps the change in the law relating to rent control in 1957–8) did this trend reverse itself to some extent.

(4) Profits are much more akin to wages in being variable from year to year, with some tendency to vary directly with the level of business activity, though the swings have been much greater than in the wage case. At the same time there do seem to be two main trends: the rise following the squeeze during the depression of the early 1930s, and after fluctuating on a kind of plateau for several years, the downward trend of the last fifteen years or so of the series.[1]

[1] This fluctuation round a downward trend has been analysed more fully elsewhere: see, for example, R. R. Neild, *Pricing and Employment in the Trade Cycle*, 1963, especially chap. 4.

More generally, it is usually accepted that the wages and profits shares are the truly variable elements in the short run, and that since their relationship is inverse their fluctuations tend to cancel each other out. As a rule, wages fall less than profits in recession,[1] but the share of both together tends to fall relative to the two 'stable' elements; the net effect of this has been to maintain the wage share of total income relatively steady.[2] The long-term repetition of this pattern would certainly seem to require some explanation, and indeed various interpretations have been advanced. We should, however, observe that the relative stability of the wage share in Britain appears to be somewhat accidental, arising out of the particular dimensions of the wage and profit shares. It may also be that the stability of the wage share is so much a curiosity that it diverts attention from other important issues. In view of what we have said about the diminishing importance of the wage/salary distinction, and given that the demarcation between direct and overhead labour is frequently rather blurred (and becoming more so), we should perhaps be more concerned with what might be called 'total employee compensation' as a share in national income. This would direct attention to the share of wages and salaries together (which is less stable than wages alone), and in addition we should have to include in this employers' contributions to National Insurance, etc., and other labour income such as fringe benefits and other items which represent a labour cost to the employer (but which are excluded from the above statistics). Aside from straight transfer payments, such a calculation would show a rise in the share of employee compensation greater than that for wages and salaries together in the above tables. This, taken with the downward trend in post-war profits, could then be taken as evidence of some measure of real redistribution of income in favour of the labour factor since 1939.

Before passing on to a consideration of some of the theoretical approaches to the problems of distributive shares, however, some mention can usefully be made of United States experience, where more detailed analysis has been carried out. The data show a rise in employee compensation from an average of 60·5 per cent in 1920–9 to 70·1 per cent in 1955–64. But two-thirds of this rise of 9·6 percentage points can be accounted for simply

---

[1] The change in component shares is of course dependent on the change in profits and wages relative to the price level; this is discussed more fully below, p. 355.

[2] Where W = wages, P = profits and Y = total income, we can say that in recession $W/(W+P)$ increases: but $(W+P)/Y$ falls in recession, the net effect being to stabilise W/Y.

M

by a change in the importance (as employers) of certain industries; for as it happens, industries characterised by a high employee compensation share in the industry's product have expanded relative to those with a low share. While this still leaves the nature of this change to be explained, the prima facie evidence suggesting a major rise in the share of employee compensation can be directly attributed to purely structural changes in the economy, leaving an increase of only about 3 percentage points to be explained in terms of other factors, such as the growth of trade unionism.[1] As for the other shares, rent has apparently undergone a long-run decline from around 9 per cent of national income in 1900–09 to just over 3 per cent since the 1930s, while profits have varied (fairly widely) about the 30 per cent mark despite major changes in composition.[2] To some extent, then, the American economy has been undergoing rather similar long-run changes in distribution, and even the relative proportions of the shares are not dissimilar.

III. Labour's Share in the Trade Cycle

The main points about the behaviour of wages and salaries over the trade cycle have now been established. As the national income declines (or dips below its long-run trend) during recession, the total wage bill also falls (at any rate relative to *its* trend). But profits tend to fall more than wages, while rent and salaries are less directly affected. The usual consequence seems to be a small rise in the *share* of wages in total income, while the share of profits declines. This at any rate appears to be the normal pattern, though exceptions exist, and we must now consider what kind of mechanisms are likely to be at work.

Consider first the depressionary phase of the cycle. At the onset of such a depression labour's bargaining power will be reduced and any labour shortages will diminish. We can therefore suggest that with the lapse of full employment wage rates will be unlikely to rise, while that part of earnings payments over basic rates which is due to labour shortages will be reduced. The most noticeable immediate change is thus likely to be a

[1] For further discussion of this, see A. M. Cartter and F. R. Marshall, *Labor Economics*, Homewood, Ill., 1967, chap. 15.

[2] Corporate profits have expanded relative to interest and entrepreneurial income. Cf. I. B. Kravis, 'Relative Income Shares in Fact and Theory', *American Economic Review*, December 1959.

general narrowing of the gap between earnings and rates. Overtime working will no longer be necessary either to produce extra output or to act as a recruitment inducement to scarce labour, and short-time working will affect some industries. Take-home pay will decline both absolutely and relative to wage rates first from the cessation of overtime and secondly because actual hours worked may fall below the standard hours in terms of which weekly wage rates are often quoted. The rates for bonus and other negotiated extras will not easily be changed, but the earnings which they represent in prosperity will be eroded by the fact that shortages of work will cut back output.

If the depression is severe (as in 1931–2), earnings will continue to sink towards, and even below, the negotiated rate for a standard working week. Pressures for reductions in these rates will be generated, but cuts in money-wage rates, as we saw earlier, are strongly resisted by trade unions, and while some individual reductions may be achieved, the wage level will tend to settle at or near the standard wage rate which effectively acts as a floor to money wages. Meanwhile, it is probable that prices will be falling, and may continue to fall more than wages. The effect of this is to raise costs relative to prices and revenue and hence to squeeze profit margins, which have no short-run 'floor' in the sense that wages have, and may even become negative in some cases. The only offset to this is the producers' ability to cut back on wage rates which is limited by trade-union policy, and on employment which again may be restricted by diseconomies which arise at sub-optimal levels of output and employment. However, in the employment cut-back it is production workers rather than staff who are likely to be most affected, and so salary income as a proportion of the total will rise, as will rental incomes on a contractual basis. In the end, however, it seems that neither wages nor employment are cut back sufficiently to prevent the share of wages in total income from increasing – though of course its absolute value may well fall, as it did in the early 1930s.

In the recovery phase wage rates will rise only slowly since the aftermath of the recession will often leave the unions in a fairly weak bargaining position. But the level of unemployment will fall and overtime, bonus earnings and other extras may pick up relatively quickly. This will help wages to maintain their share of a growing national income for a while, but as prices recover and demand rises, profits will improve their position, particularly at the expense of rents and salaries, which again are less responsive to the level of activity. It is interesting to notice in this connection that at the bottom of the recession the more drastic fall in prices than wages may well raise the real purchasing power of wages (and rents and salaries) – though it has to be remembered that many wage earners will be out of work.

A number of qualifications and additions now have to be made to this general account. In the first place, there must be some doubt whether this is an accurate statement of the course of events in the post-war period when recessions in this country have been very moderate, when a high level of employment has persisted, and when government policy has increasingly intervened to check continued inflation by short bouts of deflation, and subsequently by means of incomes policy and wage restraint. More is said on these matters in later chapters, but some observations are relevant here.

The 'typical' pattern of events in a recession such as we outlined above may well be modified when the recession is *expected* to be shallow and more of a breathing space in the inflationary process than a real change in the long-term trend. As a result the bargaining power of unions will be maintained. Also, employers will be much less willing to lay off labour or even to cut back severely on hours (since either course may cause them to lose labour which will be replaced only with difficulty when demand recovers, and even then at some expense through the need to engage in competitive bidding for labour). This tendency may also have been exaggerated by the secular growth in importance in the total labour force of staff workers who are less likely to be made redundant in such circumstances. And, indeed, there is some evidence that this was so during the 1950s, though the tendency may have diminished during the present decade as the attempts to check inflation have increased in frequency and severity,[1] and as other devices have been used to try to minimise the extent of 'labour hoarding'. The shallowness of post-war recessions may have had other effects on prices, for if demand contracts only slightly, prices will fall little if at all, and the recession may simply be a period of relatively greater price stability in a period of long-run increase. Even so, the slower growth of prices relative to wages will mean that profit margins are squeezed in fact if not in intention. In the end, therefore, the outcome may be rather similar to that in the more general discussion of depression conditions, so far as the shares of wages and profits are concerned, though the relationship may be less clear-cut.

In the prosperity phase of the cycle, during the kind of inflationary period we are now discussing, the relationship between cost changes and price is likely to be close, with any rise in costs quickly being passed on to the consumer in higher prices. At this time, however, trade unions will

[1] Cf. R. R. Neild, op. cit.

both be urgently pressing for wage increases and be able to impose their will on employers. In that case, with employers being unwilling to reduce man-hours during recessionary phases, the unions may be better able to maintain the share of wages in total income during the upswing of the cycle, and this may explain the very consistent level of the wage share during the cycles of the 1950s.

It does seem, therefore, that the distributional effects of a period of sustained inflation and full employment require an explanation which differs in detail from that of the earlier conception of events during the 'normal' business cycle, though the end result may not be greatly dissimilar.

IV. Labour's Share in the Long Run

The above discussion of the short-run behaviour of the share of wages and profits does not in itself amount to a theory, but rather an attempt to explain events by the application of relevant parts of the main body of economic theory to a specific set of problems. When we turn to the long-run behaviour of relative income shares we find a variety of theories. Some of these set out to explain the relative stability of the wage share, while others are simply theories of the interrelationship between selected variables, with no intention of accounting for a particular set of empirical results. In the end, of course, a satisfactory theory must be consistent with the facts and be capable of yielding reasonable predictions, but for a variety of reasons there are difficulties in formulating decisive tests for the alternative theories. As a result, most of the theories remain in existence and no clear-cut, generally acceptable single theory has come to dominate or to eliminate the remainder. Yet each in its own way adds something to our understanding of the economic system and the distributive process.

Perhaps the most basic and most generally acceptable theory is that which is built on the marginal productivity approach to the demand for productive factors. We have already seen that in long-run equilibrium a perfectly competitive economy will result in each factor being paid the value of its marginal product. The total income share of any factor in real terms, then, will be its rate of remuneration (its marginal product) multiplied by the number of units of the factor in employment. This can be regarded as a kind of 'market' theory of distribution, for the share of any factor depends on the demand for, and supply of, that factor. According to the competitive theory, substitution will occur as relative factor prices change, with producers using more of the (now) relatively cheaper factors and less of the relatively more expensive. In the short run the extent of substitution will be limited, since producers are already committed to a production technique involving the use of a fixed ratio of factors; but in the longer run they can switch to techniques using more favourable factor proportions in the new price situation. Thus, assuming a downward-sloping demand curve for each factor, changes in factor supply and in factor price will tend to offset each other. This, of course, would contribute to some stability in factor shares even with relatively large changes in factor supply, the degree of stability depending on the elasticity of the demand curve.[1]

Several problems remain, however. Can we be sure, for example, that if each factor receives its marginal product, the whole product will be exactly exhausted?[2] This was a question which much concerned the neo-classical economists, and is often referred to as the 'adding-up' problem. It turns out[3] that this will in fact be true under the restrictive assumption that the production function (the technical relationship between inputs and outputs) is such that a given proportionate change in all inputs will change output in the same proportion. This restriction seemed at the time to be unacceptable, leading economists to search for other possible approaches.

Other objections to the marginal productivity approach have been made, and must be taken seriously. There are several technical difficulties about the aggregation of individual marginal products into a composite whole. For example, it is questionable whether it is legitimate to use the marginal productivity principle, based as it is on micro-economic theory, to explain the behaviour of macro-economic variables such as the wage bill and total profits. Again, marginal productivity has its roots in perfect competition,

[1] The most notable use of this approach in relation to empirical data is the so-called Cobb–Douglas production function. Professor Paul Douglas fitted a production function to American data for a 22-year period and from it derived the conclusion that the stability of the income shares of labour and capital in the long-run could be accounted for if the elasticity of demand for labour and capital were respectively -4 and $-1\cdot33$: this was for a situation in which the ratio of labour's share to that of capital was 3:1.

[2] i.e. if P is the total product, and the factors of production are labour (l), land (m) and capital (k), with marginal productivities given respectively by $\partial P/\partial l$, $\partial P/\partial m$ and $\partial P/\partial k$, does the following relation hold?: $l. \partial P/\partial l + m. \partial P/\partial m + k. \partial P/\partial k = P$.

[3] By Euler's Theorem, which proves that this relationship holds when the implicit production function is homogeneous and of the first degree. The economic meaning of this is explained in the text.

whereas in the real world mobility, substitution and competition are far from complete. Though the basic theory can be modified to take some account of these difficulties and still leave us a qualified market theory of factor pricing and income distribution, the solution is less than satisfactory. A further objection relates to the role of technical progress – the development and application of scientific and technical knowledge to production problems, resulting in new techniques of production permitting new combinations of productive factors to be employed. There is no obvious reason why technical progress over long periods of time should have been 'neutral' – saving capital and labour in equal degree – in the sense that it has not markedly changed the relative income shares of labour and capital. It is generally agreed that an acceptable theory of the distributive process should in some way incorporate an explanation of the nature of the technical progress within its framework, but the marginal productivity analysis does not do so and this is a further reason why economists have turned to other methods of approach to the distribution problem.[1]

In view of the objections to the marginal productivity avenue of approach, it is necessary to give some further attention to those areas which give rise to criticism. The areas can be broadly identified as: technical progress, imperfections in competition and the more direct attempts to deal with economic aggregates through macro-economic theory.

(1) TECHNICAL PROGRESS[2]

Wage earners have frequently taken a rather gloomy view of the results of the introduction of capital even though it has meant a growth in output. Since the individual wage earner is inclined to have his mind fixed on the example of the existing equipment in his place of employment being replaced by new machinery, he argues that a given level of output will now be obtained with a smaller labour force and that the competitive position of labour will inevitably decline. A crude version of this approach lay behind the outbreak of riots in the early nineteenth century when workers broke up machinery which they thought would depress living standards and increase unemployment. Similar, though less violent, reactions are still

---

[1] One advantage of the marginal productivity analysis is, however, that it is virtually the only one capable of offering an explanation for the particular level of factor shares; for ultimately this can be traced back to the contribution of the factor to total production at the margin of its employment.

[2] The more practical problems of technical progress are discussed in Chapter 16.

to be found when labour is faced with large innovations such as auto-mation. The observable facts of our economy, however, certainly deny that the worker's living standards have fallen as output has grown and show that the share of labour in total product has actually remained much about the same. Besides, the theoretical answer to whether labour will maintain or increase its share of growing output or will inevitably lose ground to capital is neither as simple and clear-cut nor as adverse to labour as to warrant this type of reaction.

The crux of the simple argument that machinery is the enemy of labour, reduces wages and creates unemployment, is that capital is labour-saving. Capital is assumed to be introduced into a production process with the normal intention of its being substituted for labour. In the long-run con-text the introduction of capital will take the form of some innovation in production methods or product type. A businessman in putting an innova-tion into practice will hope to reduce unit costs of production, and the labour-saving assumption implies that the saving in cost is made at the expense of labour. This assumption of labour-saving innovation is quite usual. Both Hicks[1] and Rothschild[2] suggest that it is normally valid. But is it by any means invariably true? If an innovation results in a larger quantity of capital being employed for a given output it will mean a reduced labour force or a lower return to labour relative to capital, or possibly both. If innovations are for the most part capital-using, then the generalisation that capital is labour-saving is likely to be usually correct. But capital-saving innovations may readily be combined with unchanged labour utilisation, or with increased use of labour, or with labour-saving that is in excess of, or less than, the capital-saving.

Such capital-saving innovations may be much more frequent than is sometimes suggested. The introduction of wireless, which achieved the same volume of messages transmitted more easily than in less certain and slower forms of communication, is quoted as an example by both Hicks and Rothschild. A modern diesel bus is more efficient in several ways than its predecessors. It may economise in fuel. By being faster and more reliable it may allow a service to be maintained with a smaller amount of capital laid out on a fleet of buses. Greater speed and reliability is likely to mean a smaller labour force being needed to maintain a service. The net result is likely to be a saving in fuel, capital and labour, and the saving in capital may work out as greater than the saving in labour. A modern cargo liner may be much more expensive than a sailing vessel; but it is quicker and has

[1] J. R. Hicks, *The Theory of Wages* (2nd ed.), 1963.
[2] K. W. Rothschild, *The Theory of Wages*, Oxford, 1955.

a larger carrying capacity. The true comparison is not between one modern vessel and one older ship but between a given quantity of goods delivered at different dates. The modern ship may save capital by replacing a number of earlier vessels, and may also save labour by substituting one crew for a number. Whether more labour is saved than capital cannot be easily determined. In manufacturing processes the effect of innovation is frequently an integration of separate production stages. The new capital may save capital as well as labour and could easily save more of the former than of the latter. One power loom may replace a number of hand looms and in doing so both save capital and save labour.

We are apt to forget, too, that a large part of investment in manufacturing industry is in the form of buildings. A new factory building is not generally directed at reducing the labour force but is intended to improve the efficiency of all parts of the work. It may lead to economies in the size of stocks needed, to improvements in layout reducing the need for capital invested in transport, to improvements in the volume of work handled by each machine, and so on. A new building represents an increase in the capital invested in a business, but it may save capital in other ways and the relationship of capital to labour may not move as adversely to labour as might at first seem likely.

Another important item is the cost of raw materials. New capital is frequently introduced, not because it economises on older capital or on labour but because it can reduce unit consumption of raw materials. This is, for example, a primary objective for all equipment used in the generation of power or heat. The essential function of new capacity is to convert fuel into heat more efficiently. A great deal of capital in industry is devoted to making use of previously wasted segments of the raw material, the recovery of by-products, the elimination of 'waste heat', the recovery and re-use of processing materials, and so on.

Innovation, too, may have important structural side-effects which may not be unfavourable to labour. First, technical progress in production methods may alter the *industrial* structure, and while many of the industries which have expanded as a result of technical developments are heavily capitalised, they also involve a heavy outlay on labour in machine-tool and capital-equipment production, and in their servicing and maintenance. Secondly, technical progress may affect the structure of the labour force. We have to be cautious about thinking of the relation between labour and capital solely in terms of those directly engaged on production operations. Any kind of business requires people to carry out all the managerial, administrative and clerical duties connected with its operation. Greater

M 2

use of capital usually increases the complexity of a business's administration and so economies in labour actually enjoyed in production are usually to some extent offset by increases in supervisory personnel.[1]

The conclusion that emerges from this is that technical progress is by no means always labour-saving. But even if on balance there is some tendency for technical progress to economise relatively more on labour than on capital so that the immediate effects are unfavourable to particular groups of workers, the ultimate effects on labour as a whole, on labour as a productive factor, need not be so. In the first place, although there may be an initial drop on labour's employment, this may be accompanied by a rise in the productivity of labour, and wages themselves may rise, so that the share of labour in total income may remain relatively stable. Secondly, the reduction of unit costs may stimulate demand and create additional employment, even in the industry or firm which has been responsible for the innovation. It may be argued that industrialists are likely to be most disposed to introduce new equipment and techniques when they see a prospect of expanding sales by doing so. Thus, while in some cases technological change is forced on a producer to avoid declining sales, it often occurs along with a general expansion in the firm's activities and in its general need for labour. Thirdly, in so far as higher wages are obtained by some workers as a result of technical change while profits also reflect increased productivity, there is a prospect of a macro-economic effect on the general level of consumption, which will tend to rise. And it is well established that as incomes rise the amount of expenditure on the distributive trades, entertainment, professional services and other heavily labour-intensive services increases. Thus, although the direct and immediate effects of technical progress are often unfavourable to particular groups of workers, they need not be so to labour as a whole – and indeed the evidence observed earlier on labour's share in the social product would rather indicate that the balance lies in favour of the labour factor. (The macro-economic effects are more systematically discussed later in this section.)

(2) IMPERFECT COMPETITION AND PRICING POLICY

The problems of imperfection and immobility in the labour market have already been discussed at some length in earlier chapters, and we have seen how rewards to different workers or groups are influenced by institutional factors, lack of knowledge, and social considerations. Rather similar

[1] The implications of this are further discussed in Chapter 16.

imperfections exist in the capital market. Moreover, since large parts of the capital stock are not readily able to transfer among uses, no matter what opportunities for investment are available, it is inevitable that there should be uneven opportunities for capital investment at different periods. However, we would expect these sources of imperfection to have more effect on aggregate distribution in the short run rather than in the long period, when the temporary effects, though not disappearing entirely, will have an opportunity to work themselves out. We should not then expect to find any real explanation of the long-run behaviour of relative income shares in these shorter-run discontinuities and imperfections, and other factors have to be brought into the picture.

One important approach to this has developed out of hypotheses about pricing behaviour under conditions of imperfect competition, which can be illustrated by reference to Kalecki's theory.[1] The basis for this approach is that the share of wages in the national income will be determined by the importance of labour costs[2] in the value of a unit of output at the level of the firm. In imperfect competition, price will be set by adding a 'mark-up' to prime costs (wage-labour and raw materials), which were assumed to be constant in the range of sub-capacity production which Kalecki assumed to be the normal situation. The size of this mark-up was dependent on the firm's 'degree of monopoly'. The more command the firm had over its product market, the greater would the mark-up be, and so, therefore, would be the importance of profits in the unit value of output. This would determine the relative shares of wages and profits at the level of the firm and, by extension, for the economy as a whole. Though basically a short-run theory, the Kalecki approach has long-run implications. First, since different industries would be characterised by different 'degrees of mono-poly', changes in industrial structure *could* alter relative wage and profits shares. Secondly, Kalecki believed that the growth of industrial concentration, together with increases in fixed costs (including the growth of 'over-head' labour) and advertising costs, *would* increase the degree of monopoly as a result of which there would be an increase in profits relative to wages. The only counter-balance to this was the possibility of increased trade-union power, which would, however, only slow down the move in favour of profits.

If anything, the balance has in practice gone the other way, but the basic analysis is important, and has been taken up by others, with different

---

[1] M. Kalecki, *Theory of Economic Dynamics*, 1954.
[2] Kalecki confined this to the wages of direct labour; salaries were regarded as an overhead.

supplementary arguments. Among these, the foremost is perhaps that of Phelps Brown[1] who offers the hypothesis that the long-run stability of profit and wage shares is attributable to a 'stability in the propensities of management'. Changes in costs, demand and price will produce management reactions which do not readily alter over time, so that the end results, as far as the distribution of income is concerned, remain much the same. There may, however, be certain combinations of circumstances which can effectively intrude, and cause some (non-cyclical) shift in the dimensions of management reaction – which will then continue unchanged for a time. One example of such a shift is to be found in the collapse of the General Strike in 1926 and the subsequent rise of the profit share; though the general market environment will also play some part in determining how far industry can maintain profits in a phase of strong trade-union pressure.[2]

The difficulty about the pricing policy approach is that while it may help us to understand past events, it is less successful in predicting future outcomes. This is typified in the Kalecki approach where subjective judgments (e.g. on the growth of union power and industrial concentration) have to be introduced to develop predictions about the behaviour of the more proximate variables of the theory such as the degree of monopoly. However, some of the more direct attempts to produce a macro-economic theory of distribution have incorporated this kind of analysis to account for the stability of the profit–output ratio, viewed as one aggregate in a larger macro-economic system.

(3) THE MACRO-ECONOMIC APPROACH[3]

So far we have been concerned with theories which build up to an explanation of the behaviour of wage and profit aggregates from a microeconomic foundation. The alternative to which we now turn is that which derives from a much more Keynesian view of the economy at large, and attempts to explain the distributive mechanism in terms of the macroeconomic analysis typified by an emphasis on variables such as saving,

[1] E. H. Phelps Brown and P. E. Hart, op. cit.; and E. H. Phelps Brown and B. Weber, 'Accumulation, Productivity and Distribution in the British Economy, 1870–1938', *Economic Journal*, June 1953, pp. 263–88.

[2] Thus union power was probably strong in the period 1946–55, but with a weak competitive market, profits could be increased in line with wage costs and no significant shift in the wage–profit relationship occurred.

[3] The material in this section is, of necessity, more dependent on a knowledge of economic theory than the previous sections, and can be omitted by the non-specialist.

investment and aggregate demand. In this approach the classical three-factor model is reduced to one involving only 'labour' and 'non-labour', and concerning 'employment' and 'property' incomes. This kind of analysis inevitably becomes rather complex and involves a considerable degree of abstraction, and it is no part of the present purpose to provide a complete exposition of such theories. It is important, however, that we should have some understanding of the mechanisms and variables which are treated in this method of approach, and it is in that spirit that we now consider two rather different versions. The first and main example is that which has been developed by Kaldor.[1]

In full employment, it is argued, a rise in investment, and hence in aggregate demand, will raise prices and profit margins.[2] But at full employment total output cannot rise, so the rise in profit margins implies a redistribution of a given real income in favour of capitalists. At the same time the rise in investment will pull the system out of equilibrium by causing investment to exceed savings. However, provided we can assume that the marginal propensity to save attributable to capitalists is greater than that of workers, the redistribution of income to capitalists will give rise to an increase in saving, and this redistribution will continue until savings and investment are brought back into alignment, at which point the inflation is eliminated. The converse of this will occur to restore equilibrium when savings exceed investment, through a redistribution of income in favour of workers who have a higher marginal propensity to consume. From this Kaldor derives the proposition that, given the saving propensities of capitalists and workers (which are further taken to be fairly constant over the long run), the share of profits (and equally the share of wages) in income is determined simply by the ratio of investment to output (I/Y).[3] That is to say, as investment rises relative to income, the share of profits (P/Y) will rise and that of wages (W/Y) will fall, thereby redistributing incomes towards the group with the higher savings propensity and bringing the

[1] Initially stated by Kaldor in 'Alternative Theories of Distribution', *Review of Economic Studies*, vol. xxiii, no. 2, and further developed in 'A Model of Economic Growth', *Economic Journal*, December 1957, and elsewhere.

[2] This is essentially similar to the arguments of the previous section, that businessmen will adjust the mark-up according to the market environment.

[3] Kaldor's crucial equation is

$$P/Y = \frac{1}{Sp - Sw} I/Y - \frac{Sw}{Sp - Sw},$$

where P is profits, Y income, I investment and Sp and Sw the savings propensities of capitalists and workers respectively.

system back into equilibrium. Furthermore, Kaldor concludes, the stability of the system – the responsiveness of relative income shares to variations in I/Y – depends on the difference between the marginal propensities to save of the two groups: if there is little difference between them, small changes in I/Y will induce large changes in relative income shares, and vice versa.[1]

This gives some clue to what can be regarded as Kaldor's explanation of long-run stability in relative shares, namely that fluctuations in I/Y have been dampened in their effect on P/Y and W/Y because of a sizeable difference in the two savings propensities – which is probably not unreasonable as a matter of empirical fact. Further, the I/Y ratio is itself subject to stabilising forces, according to Kaldor, so that this stability of the profit share is enhanced.

Another aspect of this theory is the proposition that the rate of return on capital (P/K) will be stable in the long run (owing to the existence of a minimum rate, below which investment will be choked off) and the fact that a rise in the rate of return will raise investment until increased accumulation again depresses the rate. This has important consequences, for we now have reasoning which implies a stable share of profits in income (P/Y) and a stable rate of return on capital (P/K). These two ratios imply a third, K/Y (since $P/Y \equiv P/K . K/Y$), which is the familiar capital–output ratio and which also must be stable by dint of stability in the other two. Thus Kaldor deduces a stable capital – output ratio (though the reasoning on this point is changed in later articles) as a consequence of stability elsewhere.

The same three ratios have been the subject of other macro-economic analyses,[2] though the specific approach differs from case to case. Phelps Brown and Weber[3] account for stability in the P/Y ratio in the manner discussed in the previous section, but instead of explaining stability in P/K they divert attention to the capital–output ratio. The argument here relates back to our earlier discussion of technical progress. Productivity increases from technical progress can occur both in the capital goods and consumer goods sectors, but in the first case they will be capital-saving, and in the latter labour-saving. Phelps Brown and Weber put forward the

---

[1] This 'coefficient of sensitivity of income distribution' is

$$\frac{1}{Sp - Sw}.$$

[2] For an excellent summary, see K. Rothschild, loc. cit.
[3] Loc. cit.

view that there are market forces which will tend to keep the rate of productivity increase in both sectors roughly parallel, so that (again roughly) technical progress will be neutral. This neutrality, plus the stability of the relative shares, is taken to imply a stability in the capital–output ratio.[1]

To go beyond this point would be to embark on a discussion which would take us far from the limited purposes of this section. Several conclusions do, however, emerge. First, this method of attack on the problems of distribution enables us to bring directly into the picture factors which affect the supply of capital in the long run and the relationship between the capital stock and output, whereas other approaches tend to concentrate much more on the demand aspects. Secondly, this reversion to savings and the supply of capital pushes the analysis back to the more basic determinants of the economic system, such as the savings propensities of different sectors – but we still have to explain why they should have particular values and (as with Kaldor) why they should remain unchanged over time. In other words, still further questions are opened up. The character of technical progress can also be brought into the picture here, either as a resultant of the system or as a prime mover, but again the need for further explanation is evident. Finally, the place of trade unions and other institutional factors is not always explicit (again as in the Kaldor example), yet trade-union influence may be a force which protects labour against an unfavourable redistribution of income in periods of inflation.

V. Conclusion

Two final points remain. In the first place, it is clear that no completely satisfactory theory of income distribution is available, and in a sense this is perhaps not too surprising. An explanation of the distributive process requires investigation of the relations between labour, capital and output, where all three are changed relative to one another, and output is growing. The answer will depend on a multitude of factors, such as the changes occurring in labour supply and employment, the wage level, the quantity of capital, the effects of innovational capital compared with those of increased quantities of unchanged types of capital, the supply of capital and its rate of return, and many others. With this number of variables

[1] For further discussion of this, see T. Scitovsky, loc. cit., and the comments there by F. Modigliani.

involved it is inevitable that theories should be simplified and thereby leave themselves open to criticisms on grounds of omission. Yet the ultimate test of a theory's usefulness is its ability to identify the important relationships and to account for them in a manner which is at once convincing, in conformity with the empirical facts, and capable of yielding useful predictions. At present, such discrimination among the alternative theories is barely possible, partly because really critical tests have not been applied or developed, partly because of data limitations. Much remains to be done in this area.

Secondly, there remains the difficult problem of the effectiveness of trade unionism as a means of raising the share of labour in total income. Some commentators have tried to attribute monopoly powers to trade unions and have made them play the same role in relation to labour as they have suggested the degree of monopoly does for capital. We concluded earlier (in Chapter 12) that trade unions were at best rather ineffective monopolists. Nevertheless the market operations that determine the pattern of the productive processes are very imperfect and a strong labour movement may sometimes be able to push its claims to increased remuneration without coming immediately against the check of cost and price movements adverse to labour. This point can be of major importance in inflationary periods when labour's bargaining position is specially strong, and gains made at one time may be sustained by the imperfect operation of the market. But there is a market process and we cannot be certain whether labour's gains are due to the success of trade unions in applying pressure at weak points or to the changing needs of the economy.

We can be much surer of the contention that trade unions have had some success in establishing *minimum* wage levels. The market processes have always been ineffective in securing the well-being of the socially distressed groups in the community. The history of the conditions of labour in the nineteenth century in Britain is constantly beset with the troubles of casual labour, of unskilled groups generally, of isolated work-people in scattered industries lacking the strength of association, of out-workers, of unskilled women – in short, of all the groups in our community who were least able to protect themselves. Of course, the passage of time might of itself have rectified this position. We have as a society become more conscious of the problems of our least fortunate neighbours, and we have as an economy become richer, while labour has become scarcer. Moreover, changes in the labour market have put many of those who have little previous training into the position of acquiring semi-skilled status and substantial bonus earnings. Nevertheless, even our present society leaves pockets of distress, and the society in which trade unionism evolved certainly did so. Trade unions have been specially successful in obtaining minimum conditions of work mainly because the unity of their members is greater when the issue is one of minimum conditions, and also because it is easier to pursue an employer who is paying too little, than to exercise control over an employer who is paying rather more than some of his fellows. This power over minimum levels is specially important in depression conditions, which tend to bring extra earnings down to the minimum; on these occasions all trade-union members tend to have exactly the same outlook – that of preserving minimum standards.

More generally, the whole problem of trying to determine the effects of unions on wages is riddled with difficulty, especially in this country where trade-union influence is long-established and there is little possibility of examining conditions before and after the development of unions. This problem has been less acute in countries which have had more recent experience of union growth, such as the United States, where the evidence is that the average long-run differential between wages in unionised and non-unionised is no more than 10 per cent (in favour of the former), with this being increased in depression and eroded in prosperity and inflation. So far as labour's *share* is concerned, the issue is still more indeterminate. Given the historical stability of the pure wage share, which we would expect to be the part of employee compensation most subject to union influence, we might be tempted to conclude that the effect of unions has been nil. But in this we must be cautious, for in the absence of trade unions the wage share might have fallen, owing to a biased trend of technical progress, for example. In so far as trade unions have been effective in altering wages in individual sectors of the economy, they may have changed the whole course of history in these sectors by altering the rate of investment, the direction of investment, and even the direction of industrial research. We cannot therefore reach firm conclusions on this score.

If this is a negative note on which to end, there is a more positive side too. For the kind of analysis which we have here been reviewing is illuminating in tracing out the likely short- and long-run relationships between changes in the economy at large and in the labour markets. We have to remember that although labour markets are an important subject of study in their own right, in the last resort an understanding of labour markets is useful because it allows us to follow through the effects of changes in the rest of the economy to the level of the individual worker and employer and back again. It is from this point of view that the analysis of distribution theory is most relevant for a book of this kind.

SUGGESTED READING

E. H. Phelps Brown and P. E. Hart, 'The Share of Wages in National Income', *Economic Journal*, June 1952.

A. Rees, *The Economics of Trade Unions*, 1962.

K. W. Rothschild, 'Some Recent Contributions to a Macro-Economic Theory of Income Distribution', *Scottish Journal of Political Economy*, October 1961.

T. Scitovsky, 'A Survey of Some Theories of Distribution', in *The Behavior of Income Shares*, National Bureau of Economic Research, Princeton, 1964.

Appendix to Chapter 15

Table 15.2

Distributive Shares in Home-Produced National Income, 1926–65[1]

	(1) Wages as % of national income	(2) Salaries as % of national income	(3) Wages and salaries as % of national income	(4) Rent as % of national income	(5) Profits as % of national income
1926	42·0	25·7	67·7	8·2	24·1
1927	41·3	24·4	65·7	8·0	26·3
1928	39·8	24·4	64·3	8·2	27·5
1929	41·1	25·1	65·2	8·5	26·3
1930	41·0	25·6	66·6	9·3	24·1
1931	41·7	27·3	69·1	10·4	20·6
1932	41·5	27·2	68·7	10·7	20·7
1933	40·7	26·8	67·6	10·3	22·1
1934	41·0	26·5	67·5	10·0	22·5
1935	40·3	26·2	66·5	9·6	23·9
1936	39·8	25·6	65·3	9·2	25·5
1937	39·3	24·8	64·1	9·3	26·6
1938	39·2	25·1	64·4	9·4	26·2
1939	38·3	24·0	62·3	9·2	28·4
1940	38·2	22·1	60·3	7·8	31·9
1941	38·3	21·5	59·8	6·7	33·5
1942	39·1	20·3	59·3	6·1	34·5
1943	39·4	20·1	59·4	5·8	34·8
1944	39·7	20·7	60·5	5·8	33·7
1945	39·3	22·0	61·3	5·9	32·8
1946	40·9	20·4	61·2	5·0	33·8
1947	41·4	19·7	61·1	4·9	34·0
1948	42·1	20·1	62·2	4·3	33·5
1949	42·1	20·5	62·6	4·2	33·2
1950	40·9	20·4	61·3	4·5	34·2
1951	40·8	20·6	61·4	4·2	34·4
1952	42·5	21·7	64·2	4·4	31·3
1953	42·4	21·5	64·0	4·7	31·3
1954	42·2	21·4	63·5	4·8	31·7
1955	42·3	21·6	63·9	4·8	31·3

[1] Columns (1) and (2) do not always sum to the value given in column (3) owing) to rounding. Likewise the sum of columns (1), (2), (4) and (5) is not always equal to 100·0.

Table 15.2 (*continued*)

	(1)	(2)	(3)	(4)	(5)
	Wages as % of national income	Salaries as % of national income	Wages and salaries as % of national income	Rent as % of national income	Profits as % of national income
1956	42·9	22·1	65·0	5·0	30·0
1957	42·6	22·8	65·4	5·1	29·6
1958	42·2	23·5	65·7	5·7	28·6
1959	41·0	23·7	64·7	5·9	29·4
1960	40·1	23·8	63·9	5·8	30·3
1961	40·7	24·6	65·3	5·9	28·7
1962	40·6	25·5	66·1	6·0	27·9
1963	39·5	25·5	65·0	6·1	28·9
1964	39·2	25·5	64·7	6·0	29·3
1965	39·0	25·9	64·9	6·1	28·9

Sources: as for Table 15.1.

Part V

Current Issues

16 Technical Change and Automation

I. Introduction

In this final part of the book we come to an examination of a number of practical issues which are of major importance in understanding the problem of the labour market. By their very nature, the questions raised are not capable of ready answers. Many of them introduce important matters of policy which still give rise to argument and debate, even after long discussion: for example, the development of more security of income and employment, the means of developing a sufficiently mobile labour force to meet changes in the economy's pattern of labour demand, and the role of labour market policy in periods of inflation. The purpose of these remaining chapters is to indicate the main areas of debate and to illustrate some possible methods of approach to them. As we proceed, the practical relevance of parts of our discussion in earlier chapters will become increasingly evident, and we shall see how various pieces of the evidence and arguments so far set out begin to fit together in specific problem areas. In this respect the subject-matter of the present chapter is no exception, for the discussion of technical change gives rise to considerations ranging from its effects on employment, through the reactions of unions and workers to the prospect of new methods of production, to the need for adjustment on the part of those affected, both in their working and in their domestic circumstances.

Improvements in technology are of course one of the main sources of greater productivity and thereby contribute to the growth of the economy. Ultimately, therefore, the implementation of technical change is one of the main routes to an improvement in the general standard of living, both by providing better and more efficient methods of producing known goods and services and by giving rise to new goods which enable consumption demands to be satisfied in a new way or to a fuller extent. This at any rate is the usual longer-run consequence of technical progress, but the shorter-run effects are not always regarded as being so favourable. Some types of technical change give rise to changes in the level and structure of employment which require a redistribution of resources between industries and regions. At the level of the individual worker affected by such changes the advent of technical change may seem to imply a threat of insecurity, for which he may not be prepared. At the level of the economy, there may at times be serious difficulties in securing the necessary redistribution of resources without inflicting hardship on certain sectors of the community.

These short-term problems of adjustment are the price that has to be paid for the longer-term advantages of productivity growth through technological change. As we go on, we shall see in what way and to what extent these short-term problems arise and what measures can or have been taken to minimise the degree of friction. But there can be no doubt that in the longer run the economy has to take advantage of technical progress if it is to secure continuing improvements in the standard of living. This is true both in the straightforward material sense of the standard of living, and also for living standards and patterns of life in a more general sense. For just as in the past the advantage taken of technical developments has been a major contributor to the reduction in the length of the average working week, so in the future do further possibilities of increased leisure, and of increased real income to enable leisure time to be satisfactorily utilised, depend at least in part on the continued development of technology and its rapid application in industry.

II. The Nature of Technical Change

It is usual in economics to define a technique of production as a specific combination of productive factors (basically labour and capital) to produce a quantity of a particular good. Labour here is broadly defined to include all labour inputs – management and supervision as well as production workers – while capital is likewise broadly defined to include raw materials, spatial requirements as well as plant and equipment. Technical change is thus a change in the combination of labour and capital inputs to produce either an existing type of good or service or a new good or service. Three additional points require to be made here. First, we frequently think of technical change mainly in connection with the production of goods. But technical change is just as likely to occur in service industries, including office work, insurance, banking, transport and distribution, which after all account for roughly half our total employment. Secondly, technical change is not always 'technological' in origin; many changes are organisational, as we can readily appreciate when we consider the growth in the specialisation of management and administrative personnel in recent decades. Ultimately these may be a consequence of changes in the underlying technology of production, but they are nevertheless important in their own right. Thirdly, what appear simply as changes in the scale of productive plant may in themselves represent considerable technical change. In many branches of production, not only the size of markets but also the technical limitations on the size of plant may prevent managements investing in large-scale productive plant. As technical knowledge improves, so it becomes possible to build bigger plant where product demand and the economies of large-scale production warrant such a course, and this usually has the effect of changing the relationship between factor inputs and between factor costs per unit of output.

Technical change comes about for two main reasons. At a moment of time there will usually exist a number of different ways of producing a given product, involving different combinations of labour and capital and using capital equipment of differing designs and labour with different skills or job-functions. Some of these techniques will be old-established, others will be more modern and others still will be at the threshold of technical knowledge. For the entrepreneur who is considering a replacement of existing capital or an expansion of his activities, there is usually a choice of technique, and we would expect him to choose that technique which will be most economical in its use of productive factors for the chosen rate of output. His choice therefore depends to a large extent on the relative prices of the factor inputs required by different techniques, and hence changes in relative factor prices are the first source of technical change. As changes occur in factor prices, entrepreneurs will tend to choose techniques which use more of the relatively cheaper factors, and vice versa.

Secondly, however, technical change will come about because of improvements in technical knowledge. Though at a particular point of time there will be a given number of available techniques, over time the array of techniques from which businessmen can choose will tend to increase. The ultimate basis of this is research giving rise to new knowledge relevant to production problems. But even once the *technical* feasibility of a new process or product has been established, there is normally a development stage. What is satisfactorily accomplished on a small scale in controlled laboratory conditions is not always immediately transferable to large-scale operation under normal production conditions. Once such problems have been solved, the extent of the application of the new technique will depend on its *economic* feasibility and the extent to which it offers economic advantages over existing techniques of production. Even if these conditions are satisfied there may still be some delay in the actual adoption of the change, since there may be considerable time-lags in the 'diffusion' of the innovation, that is, in the spread of the new knowledge among firms, industries and even countries. However, it is this evolution and diffusion of technical knowledge that is the second source of technical change.[1]

Both these sources of technical change – alterations in relative factor prices and the acquisition of new technical knowledge – are fairly continuous over time. But there is a further factor which actually brings different techniques into operation, namely investment, which is the vehicle of technical change. Given a continuous change in the two factors we have mentioned, the process of investment will continually be altering the 'mix' of techniques in use, causing obsolete methods of production to be withdrawn because they are wasteful in their use of materials or rely too heavily on costly factors of production, and bringing into use new techniques which are more efficient and capable of yielding better rates of return.

Technical change may involve relatively minor technological improvements to existing capital equipment to raise productivity, or it may be on a quite different and larger scale, where complete units of plant are replaced and whole processes comprising many different operations are transferred to a new technological basis. Sometimes these developments apply quite specifically to a single industry or a limited production area, as for example with the intensive use of oxygen in steelmaking or the introduction of standardised containers in the transportation and distribution of goods. Other developments are more general, stemming from a technological breakthrough in one industry but leading to diverse applications and extensions in other industries; examples here include the technical advances which enabled steam power to be harnessed for industrial purposes, and the later growth in the industrial use of electric power which derived from the discovery of methods of producing electricity on a large scale and at low cost. At times there appear to have been quite marked 'waves' of change deriving from a major technical breakthrough which becomes extensively applied, and affecting the whole approach to production problems in a number of industries. The simple mechanisation of production, replacing a great deal of manual effort, was one of the earliest developments of this kind in modern times, though of course new and more complex forms of mechanisation are still being

[1] For a useful discussion of this process, see W. E. G. Salter, *Productivity and Technical Change*, 1960, chap. II.

devised even at the present time. The evolution of transfer equipment and the development of improved transport networks in the first two decades of the present century was the springboard for the subsequent spread of mass-production methods which revolutionised many industries. Further developments in the field of continuous production, coupled with the growth of the electronics industry and the increasing sophistication of automatic control devices, have led still more recently to what is generally regarded as the age of automation.

A great deal has been written in the last two decades on the definition, the technological potential, and the employment and social repercussions of automation. Here we will simply accept a definition of automation which regards it as a particular phase in the continuous process of technical change, marked out especially by its wide industrial and commercial applicability and by its use of complex control systems (including computers) to integrate and regulate production and other operations which were formerly separate stages with their own individual control mechanisms. Because of its heavily capital-intensive nature and the transfer of control and information analysis functions from labour to automatic devices, it has given rise to a new wave of speculation – and in some quarters pessimism – about the implications for employment. We return to this later.

On this view, automation is to be regarded as an extension and development of the historical process of technical change and, with other forms of change, it deserves attention for a number of reasons. First, technical change usually has some implications for labour, especially in the need for some form of adjustment to the new technological situation. Secondly, the *possibility* must be considered that the employment effects of technical change may be sufficiently serious to cause an imbalance in the labour markets of the economy – local, industrial and occupational, if not national – which cannot readily be rectified by normal market mechanisms. This, thirdly, requires that attention should be directed towards the pace and direction of change in individual sectors of the economy, so that if possible some predictions can be made about the dimensions of the adjustment problem, and the degree to which normal market processes can cope with it. This applies both to the possible changes in demand for labour already developed and to the development of new forms of labour demand, which may require the provision of additional training facilities and suitable improvements in the employment conditions offered to such groups of workers. And finally, it may have to be considered how current trends in technical change are likely to affect conditions of employment

and the availability of leisure, for example by altering the normal pattern
and level of working hours.

III. Employment Implications

As we observed in the last chapter, technical change need not always be
biased towards labour saving. Yet it will very often mean that workers
have to change jobs, by moving either to work on the newly introduced
capital equipment or to some other type of employment. In the latter case
especially, new jobs are not always to be found immediately, and it is this
unemployment, associated with technical change, that has given rise to
the greatest fears on the part of workers and trade unions. Even for those
who do find alternative employment immediately, there may still be fear
of reduced earnings and status, so that overall technical change is to be
seen as a threat to both job and income security – matters which are discussed more fully in Chapter 18 below. It is an easy step from this to a
belief that technical change is inevitably a cause of unemployment, and
that where major technical advances are involved, or where there is a
concentration of change in a particular period of time, the consequence
will be widespread and will lead to long-term unemployment, often
referred to as 'technological' unemployment.

Yet the available historical evidence does not generally seem to support
this proposition. What has happened, very broadly, is that the introduction
of change has been phased over a period of years; after all the volume of
gross investment in any year is not usually capable of bringing about more
than a partial replacement of existing capital and techniques. As a result,
the effects of change have been staggered and the need for instantaneous
absorption and adjustment has been reduced. At the same time, the effects
of technical change are to reduce unit production costs and to increase the
capacity of the firm or industry, so that demand for the product rises and
new (often additional) employment is created. In addition higher productivity tends to produce higher incomes and new demands are created,
though often in quite different areas of employment.

It may be argued that while this is all very well, technical change *can*
cause hardship and protracted unemployment for individuals (which is
undeniable); and further, that in a time like the present when a wave of
labour-saving change such as automation is appearing, the effects of dis-
employment may be so concentrated, particularly on certain groups in the

labour force, as to cause a rise in the general level and duration of unemployment (which is a more debatable proposition). On the one hand it is clear that American and West European economies are as yet at an early stage in the application of automation. Many sectors of industry where automated techniques are proven have still a long way to go before coverage in feasible areas is anything like complete. Computer and related technology is still in its infancy and much more sophisticated extensions and applications are predicted by experts in the field. Increasing resources are being fed into research and development, and there are indications that the rate of diffusion of new techniques is being speeded up by the growth of international and inter-industry communication of technical developments. On the other hand, there is no conclusive evidence that automation, as applied until now, has been any different in its effects from earlier waves of concentrated change. Individuals and certain occupations have certainly been adversely affected, but the threat of widespread and prolonged unemployment has not emerged. Productivity and *per capita* incomes have generally risen in the sectors most affected, leading to an improvement in the demand prospects of those sectors and, more generally, to a growth in labour demand elsewhere in the economy. It may be that there is no conclusive answer to this particular problem, and certainly there is no consensus of informed opinion on what the outcome will be. In any case it is not an argument that will be settled without resort to the facts, and without analysis of the processes of technical change and the nature of its impact on employment. It is to this aspect that we now turn.

Technical change can be expected to have two kinds of effect on employment. First, there may be some change in the *level* of employment, for the kind of reasons we have already mentioned; and secondly, there may be some effect on the *structure* of employment, especially in the industrial and occupational composition of the labour force. So far as the level of employment is concerned, British experience does not lend support to the view that rapid technical change leads to mass unemployment. Demand for goods and services has been quite adequate to maintain full employment, and instead we have been more concerned with how to obtain more growth than worried about what to do with surplus resources. Exceptionally high levels of employment have been sustained throughout the postwar years, and if the average level of unemployment has tended to rise somewhat in recent years, this seems largely to be explained by the greater frequency of policy-induced deflation and recession rather than by increased technological unemployment. But when we turn to the structural aspects the picture is less clear.

As illustrated in our earlier discussion in Chapter 6, there have been major changes in the structure of employment over the last 50 years. This, we suggested, was the result both of changes in the occupational structure itself, and of changes in the relative importance of industries which used different types of labour in quite varied proportions. Technical change is not the only explanation of these changes, for many of them have come about as a result of the growth in real *per capita* incomes, causing the demand for some goods and services to decline while the demand for other goods has increased, and entirely new demands have been created. But even in this respect technical change has been one of the moving factors in the growth of real incomes. Nor can there be any doubt that technical change has had a more direct effect on the structure of industrial employment. The development of modern manufacturing industry, with its large engineering and chemical sectors, is very much bound up with advances in technology. While technical change has by no means been absent in the slower-growing or declining industries such as coalmining and shipbuilding, it has not in itself been enough to contain the competition from emerging industries, like oil and electricity in the fuel sector, and improved road and air transport in the communications and distributive sectors. With their dependence on large-scale, capital-intensive methods of production, these expanding industries have come to require a higher – and growing – proportion of administrators, technical and qualified personnel. In this way the change in industrial structure has contributed to a change in the overall occupational structure of employment.

But technical change also affects occupations more directly. New techniques of production, and new methods of work organisation in both manufacturing and the service sector, frequently require quite different kinds of labour from those they replace, or use existing types of worker in quite different proportions. Thus welding has replaced riveting in the building of ships, and the demand for riveters has virtually disappeared. The decline of horse-drawn traffic and the growth of the motor vehicle has led to a great decline in the number of blacksmiths and a vast expansion in the number of motor mechanics. In office work the male clerk has been replaced by female typists, who may themselves be affected by current changes in office technology. In addition, the more recent scientific and technological developments have given rise to completely new occupations which had no real counterpart before, such as electronic engineers, computer programmers and analysts, operational research workers, and nuclear physicists.

All this is suggestive of a shift in the occupational structure towards what we may regard as the more highly trained and highly skilled occupations. More conclusive evidence of this for a recent period is given in Fig. 16.1, which shows the growth in the share of major occupational groups in total employment between 1951 and 1961. By far the greatest

Fig. 16.1

Percentage changes in main occupational groups as a proportion of the occupied population, 1951–61

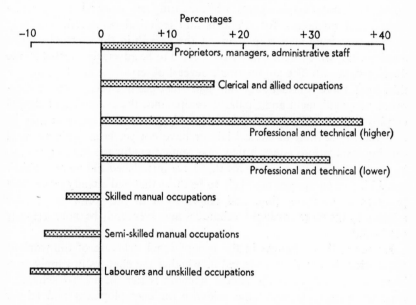

Source: *Occupational Changes 1951–61* (Manpower Studies No. 6), Department of Employment and Productivity, H.M.S.O., London, 1968

proportional increases have occurred in the professional and technical occupations, while substantial rises have also taken place in clerical employment and in the managerial and administrative types of employment.[1] By contrast, all the manual occupations have declined in relative importance, with the decrease becoming larger the lower the degree of

[1] The rise of 10 per cent shown in Fig. 16.1 is comprised of a virtually constant proportion of 'farmers, working proprietors, etc.' (who are heavily weighted in this group) and a 27 per cent rise in the proportion of 'directors, managers, administrative and executive staff'.

skill. The picture which emerges is thus one of relative expansion in the service occupations and especially those requiring higher training, and of contraction in the manual (or 'production worker') employments. Even so, the balance of total employment lies with the manual workers, who (on this classification) comprised almost two-thirds of the occupied population in 1961.

This is very much what we would have predicted on the basis of our previous discussion on the present course of technical change. For continued application of mechanisation and automation are most likely to affect the manual employments, while creating new demands for administrators and managers, for scientists and technical personnel. The only slightly surprising feature, perhaps, is the growth in the share of clerical employment, which we might have expected to be adversely affected by the development of 'office automation'. Several observations can be made on this. First, there is little doubt that had great use not been made of data-processing equipment and similar developments, the expansion of clerical employment would have been considerably greater. Secondly, it may be that the full savings in clerical labour have not yet been achieved from existing installations (since it may take some time for the full potential to be realised). Thirdly, those firms that have introduced the more sophisticated kind of equipment are likely to be those that had already made most progress to mechanisation, and employment in the sector not so far affected by the more advanced techniques may eventually be more seriously cut back.[1]

However, these changes in the occupational structure of the working population do not themselves tell us whether the changes in supply have been adequate to meet the altered demand requirements. To determine this, we have to consider the evidence on unemployment and labour shortage. Even if the economy at large has maintained very high employment levels, the possibility of persistent unemployment among certain groups still exists. And in conditions of general full employment, any bottlenecks in supply will be at once more evident and more serious. In fact, British experience does reveal just such a combination of persistent shortage and persistent unemployment. Shortages have been acute and continual among highly trained workers in the service occupations, and in the skilled manual occupations in some industries, particularly the engineering sector, where, in contrast to skilled manual occupations as a whole, the proportion of skilled workers has increased, if only slightly.

[1] For further discussion, see *Computers in Offices* (Manpower Studies No. 4), Ministry of Labour, H.M.S.O., 1965.

On the other hand, unemployment rates have been substantially higher among the less skilled and unskilled occupations than in any other group. Closer investigation of the characteristics of the unemployed shows that one-half to two-thirds of all unemployment is accounted for by unskilled workers and labourers, and that the incidence of long-term unemployment among these categories is high.[1] In addition, a high proportion of this unemployment is concentrated in the older (45 and over) age groups: in other words, the incidence is highest among those with a considerable work-experience behind them.

This combination of circumstances suggests that as the occupational structure of labour demand has changed, supply has not been able to adjust sufficiently quickly; and the lack of adjustment seems to be greatest among the established members of the work force who have a low degree of skill, rather than among the new entrants to the labour force. This pattern is perhaps what we might have expected from the continued application of mechanisation and automation. As technical change of this kind is introduced, it will tend to reduce the number of jobs available at the low end of the skill spectrum and to increase employment opportunity at the upper end. For new entrants to the labour force, with generally longer education and greater opportunities for training, this will not present too serious a problem. But for the older worker, who is probably less adaptable to a complete change of work, and for the unskilled worker, who may be incapable of acquiring a higher degree of skill, adjustment may be extremely difficult, and when lack of skill and high age are combined in particular individuals, the possibility of adaptation will be very slight indeed. Once such a worker is made redundant – whether for reasons of technical change or not – he will find it hard to obtain a new job.[2]

To summarise this part of the argument, we can conclude that although technical change is not the only factor causing changes in the demand for labour, it is one of the major determinants. While it does not seem in

[1] Cf. Chapter 7 above, and the references quoted there.

[2] As was noted in Chapter 7, the high unemployment levels in the United States between 1957 and 1963 gave rise to a major policy debate on the question whether the growth in unemployment was due to lack of effective demand or to a structural transformation, in which was usually included some reference to technological displacement. This discussion illustrated the need for analysis as a basis for policy. One interesting by-product of the discussion was the proposition that as improving technology raised productivity it also lifted the minimum wage level, so that the marginal productivity of the unskilled worker displaced by mechanisation fell below the minimum wage. Under these conditions re-employment for the unskilled would be virtually impossible.

N

general to be associated with widespread unemployment, even in periods of time when change seems to be particularly concentrated, it does affect the structure of employment and there are signs, both here and in the United States, that the adjustment of supply has been less than perfect. The problems of adjustment are probably greatest among the older, less skilled members of the labour force, though as we see in the next section, which takes up the problem of adjustment in more detail, they are by no means limited to one section of the population.

IV. Problems of Adjustment

The problems of adjustment to technical change exist at two different levels. First, it is important from the point of view of the economy at large that the labour required in industries and occupations expanding as a result of technical progress should be readily available. The development of serious bottlenecks in supply will tend both to delay the implementation of change and to hamper the growth of the economy. Likewise, the presence of unemployment of a technological nature represents a wastage of productive resources, as well as a serious social problem, for much of the unemployment is likely to be of a longer-term nature. For these reasons, Government itself may try to facilitate the adjustment mechanism in various ways, for example by providing greater training and educational facilities, by improving the flow of job-information in the labour market, and by cushioning the effects of redundancy on labour displaced by technical change.

Secondly, adjustment is important at the level of the individual worker. The loss of productive potential at the level of the economy is reflected in a loss of earning power and status for the individual, and if this is protracted it may raise serious social and psychological problems for the worker and his family, as well as the economic problems which result from inability to meet regular expenditure commitments.

In both cases, the essential need is for labour mobility, an issue to which we will return in more detail in Chapter 19 below. For the moment we are only concerned with the mobility problems associated with technical change. The need for mobility is evident enough. If the introduction of technical change within a firm causes the number of available jobs to be reduced, it becomes necessary for the workers whose jobs are made redundant to find new employment. Some workers may simply be transferred to roughly equivalent jobs on the newly introduced plant. Others may be transferred to different jobs within the firm, or perhaps to other branches of the company. In these cases mobility is internal to the firm, and usually raises fewer serious problems of adjustment. Even so, further training, or retraining, is often essential if the workers are to be so redeployed, and while some may acquire enhanced earning power and status, for others there will be a deterioration. Yet if they are not to face greater economic and personal difficulties, including a greater likelihood of unemployment, it may be necessary for them to accept internal redeployment rather than start looking for new work in another firm or industry.

It is often the case that not all the workers displaced by technical change can be re-employed by the firm initiating the change. In many cases, too, firms or departments may be closed as a result not of changes undertaken by themselves, but of changes adopted by competing firms and industries. This will come about, for example, where a new technique gives rise to considerable economies of scale, so that many fewer plants will be needed than before to produce a given amount of output; older, high-cost plant will then be withdrawn unless the growth of product demand is exceptionally rapid. In the case of closures, the possibility of internal redeployment is considerably reduced, and those who are displaced have to face the prospect of finding employment in another firm. Yet a change of this type will very often affect employment throughout the industry, or the employment of a particular occupational group, and those who are displaced may find it hard to find new work in the same industry or occupation. As a result, their search for new work must be directed towards other occupations or industries – and sometimes, as where a local labour market has a high concentration of employment in a single industry, to other areas. It is precisely this kind of movement, across geographical, occupational and industrial boundaries, that is liable to present the greatest difficulties.[1]

Geographical mobility is frequently the most difficult adjustment to make, for it can impose on the worker and his family not only the direct costs of movement but also indirect psychological costs, arising out of the transfer from an area which is known and familiar to one where new friendships and relationships, and new accommodation, have to be found. Occupational movement is difficult for a variety of reasons. The problem of the older and the unskilled workers has already been mentioned, but even for the more highly trained, more specialised worker, difficulties arise. Transfer to other skilled occupations, where comparable earnings and status might be attained, will often require very considerable retraining,

[1] Cf. Chapter 19 below, pp. 474–484.

and again this imposes a cost on the worker even if suitable training facilities are available. The alternative is a move to another type of job, perhaps of a semi-skilled nature where a short period of on-the-job training is adequate, but this will usually be accompanied by a fall in income and certainly a loss of status, and as such will commonly be resisted until all hopes of re-employment in the former occupation have faded. There are, of course, cases where an occupation is common to a number of industries – for example, painters, electricians, bricklayers, and so on. In these circumstances the worker may be able to remain within his occupation while transferring between firms in different industries. But inter-industry movement will itself involve difficulties at times, particularly where institutional practices dictate that virtually all new employees at manual level have to be recruited at the lowest grade, and where promotion is based on seniority in the firm.

This reference to institutional practices raises another aspect of the adjustment problem in general. The threat to wages and to employment security caused by potential technical change is one of the reasons why trade unions have erected protective mechanisms. Thus unions have variously devised methods of control on entry to particular types or levels of job, such as apprenticeship, promotion by seniority, strict demarcation of work and the like, which have the effect of restricting mobility and flexibility. For example, workers displaced from employment by technical change may find entry to other occupations blocked by the existence of rules which forbid the use of workers who have not served the appropriate apprenticeship period or who otherwise fail to meet certain requirements. Likewise, the seniority rule, with its accompaniment of recruitment at a low level, means that inter-firm movement is hampered, since previously high-paid workers will have to accept considerable earnings reductions.

From a rather different point of view, the existence of such protective devices and the presence of strong trade unionism may influence the application of technical change itself, and in this way the trade unions help to ease the burden of adjustment imposed on their members. Perhaps the most extreme case is where a union, fearing the employment effects of a new process, threatens industrial action if the process is introduced. More commonly, the unions will use normal bargaining procedures to achieve their objective. For management, the prospect of deriving a reasonable rate of return from investment in a new plant or process will be affected by the level and composition of manning on the equipment. If a trade union, in negotiating terms and conditions of employment on the new plant, is able to raise the level of manning above that proposed by management, the cost of operating the plant will be raised and the rate of return will be reduced. At times this may be enough to limit the application of the process in the industry as a whole. Unions will be most concerned to maintain the level of manning when employment prospects for the industry or occupation are deteriorating, and in this situation too the possibility of demarcation disputes is heightened, owing to different unions claiming the sole right of their members to operate the new capital equipment as a counter-balance to declining employment elsewhere.

On questions of wages, further disagreements may arise, for if the union cannot protect employment – or if it has no worries on that score – it may still try to improve the income position of its members. New plant almost invariably raises productivity and this becomes the basis of the union case for improved wages. Management may regard the change as one in which skill requirements have actually decreased – indeed, they may prefer, but be unable, to substitute less skilled, lower-cost labour for the more expensive labour previously employed – and will not be prepared to concede a wage rise. To do so would lower the rate of return on investment and again the industry's absorption of technical change might be restricted.

Many other illustrations of resistance to change could be given. The main point for the present, however, is that in falling back on restrictive practices, by emphasising the need for proper apprentice training, and by prolonging bargaining processes, the union is fulfilling its function of protecting its membership against employment and income insecurity. It may not, in the end, be able to prevent the widespread adoption of change, but it may be able to control its rate of application, or the conditions under which it is introduced, in such a way that the burden of adjustment on labour is not too severe or too sudden. How far this is justifiable from the overall economic viewpoint is often hard to determine. For on the one hand, delays in the absorption of technical advances may be to the disadvantage of the economy's competitive position in international markets, and may in the end retard the growth of living standards at home. Yet at the level of the union and the individual worker, anything which reduces the impact of technical change has to be seen as a benefit to the labour force – even if it is temporary.

Perhaps in recognition of this conflict, firms in this country and abroad have in recent years been paying increased attention to the planning of technical change, especially with a view to minimising the amount of worker redundancy, and to carrying unions along with the idea of change by sharing the benefits of productivity increases and by providing compensation for those who suffer a loss of employment or a drop in income. In most cases the main step has been an attempt to provide, at an early stage of the planning process, an accurate forecast of the number and composition of jobs likely to be available on the new process. Once this has been done, the scale of the redundancy problem becomes apparent, and methods can be devised to ensure that the amount of *worker* redundancy is as low as possible.[1] The methods used to achieve this are diverse, and vary considerably from firm to firm. But usually some attempt is made to avoid new recruitment in the occupations where job redundancy is greatest. The normal processes of voluntary turnover, retirement of older workers, and other forms of wastage will then reduce the labour force in these occupations, so that by the time the outmoded plant is withdrawn very few, if any, workers will be forced to seek employment outside the firm. Much depends on the length of the period taken to plan and install the new plant. Sometimes this will be very short, so that the time available for a rundown through non-replacement of wastage will not be adequate to avoid redundancy; in other cases the period may be as long as three or four years, and it may then be impossible to avoid some new recruitment. The success of internal redeployment such as is envisaged here depends on the willingness of workers to accept jobs available elsewhere in the works, and on the ability of the firm to arrange suitable retraining for workers who transfer to these jobs. This again raises the problems of potential loss of earning power and reduction in status.

Although there has been in the last few years a growth of legislation on periods of notice, redundancy payments and unemployment benefit, there is a good deal of evidence that even before this firms were taking on major responsibilities in these respects. Where internal transfers meant lower earnings, many firms were prepared to offer lump-sum compensation. Actual redundancy was frequently accompanied by payments to give the worker some reserves which could be used while a new job was being sought. Workers who were to be made redundant were given long periods of notice and were usually free to leave whenever a suitable job could be found. In addition, managements were making increased efforts to obtain the co-operation of trade unions by bringing representatives into discussion at various stages of the planning process. Usually this fell short of actual negotiation, but suggestions and advice were asked for, and frequently taken, and there can be little doubt that in some industries this

---

[1] i.e. although *job* redundancy occurs, workers may be redeployed within the firm so that they are not made redundant in the sense of having to seek work outside the firm.

had a favourable effect on the implementation and planning of change.[1]

This growth of management responsibility for the social aspects of technical change has been to some extent superseded by Government responsibility, in the form of new legislation, such as the Contracts of Employment Act, the Redundancy Payments Act, and the more recent provision of earnings-related unemployment benefit (which serves to ease the income and expenditure adjustments of the higher-paid worker who becomes redundant). In addition, there is the new Government support for industrial training, both through the Industrial Training Act and through the provision of more Government Training Centres; the latter particularly are capable of making a contribution to the retraining and re-employment of workers whose skills are technically obsolete. These specific measures have been introduced into a situation where the Ministry of Labour's employment service already operates, and again there is evidence that firms facing a prospect of redundancy have increasingly been making more intensive and more direct use of these facilities.

It is perhaps too early yet to assess the success of these interventionary measures. More will be said about training in Chapter 17. On the working of the Redundancy Payments Act, however, one interesting result does seem to be emerging, namely that the Redundancy Fund is being more heavily drawn upon than was expected when the Act was introduced. Various interpretations can be put on this, but it is at least possible that employers, in the knowledge that they will only have to bear a small part of the direct cost of any redundancy payments they make, have become increasingly prepared to declare labour redundant. In the new situation, and perhaps still more since the beginning of the earnings-related unemployment benefit, they may feel less of a social obligation either to carry surplus labour during the transition from a higher to a lower employment level, or to find jobs for older workers who have given them long service but whose productivity may now be lower than that of new recruits. On this interpretation, the new legislation may have to be regarded as transferring a social responsibility, once largely, but unevenly, accepted by managements, to the State.

Whether this is to be adjudged desirable or not is again a difficult issue to resolve. There is one view which regards State intervention as being a means of enforcing the acceptance of a minimum standard of treatment for all workers while, hopefully, some more enlightened employers will make provisions above the minimum. In the case of the Redundancy

[1] For more detailed discussion of these points, see *Technical Change and Manpower Planning* (ed. S. Barkin) O.E.C.D., Paris, 1967.

Payments Act there is as yet no sign that provisions above the minimum are at all common. On the other hand, if the Act and related legislation has had the effect of making employers more willing to cut back on their labour requirements, and tougher in their bargaining over the manning of new equipment, there will be gains in labour productivity and possibly some contribution to an easing of widely acknowledged labour shortages.[1]

In conclusion, it has to be stressed that the latter part of this argument is still somewhat conjectural, and more time and research will be necessary before a proper appreciation of the effects of the new legislation can be undertaken. On the issues of adjustment arising under technical change, there is less scope for disagreement. The problems which now arise are much the same as those that have emerged in the past, the only difference being that the general employment situation has in the present period been more favourable to redeployment. It is likely that the increasing attention now being paid to the planning of technical change and its labour force implications is due, in part at least, to experience of labour shortages and the need to conserve labour resources. It may be that the current lack of growth in the working-age population (observed in Chapter 6) will further emphasise this need.

V. Effects on Employment Conditions and Leisure Patterns

There is one further set of implications arising out of technical change which deserves attention here: the effects of technical change and automation on the work–leisure relationship. It is perhaps principally due to the debate on automation that this issue has been highlighted, though in fact the interaction between technical change and leisure availability is long-standing. The problem is one which is as much social as economic, but even the social aspects have important economic consequences.

In the course of the debate on the consequences of automation, it is commonly argued that a deliberate policy must be designed and put into effect to counteract the unemployment that will be generated by auto-

[1] This is, of course, relevant to the allegations, made against some sectors of British industry, of overmanning and labour hoarding. In this respect, the unwillingness or inability of management to achieve the lowest levels of manning technically possible may have had some effect in leading to continued over-manning – and the need for productivity bargaining as one way out of the dilemma.

mation. One of the main facets of such a policy, it has been suggested, should be a major reduction in working hours, with the result that the number of jobs available will be maintained. Exactly what is meant by a 'major reduction in working hours' is not always clear. If it means a reduction in the length of the standard working week by, say, 10 or 15 per cent, with a proportionate reduction in weekly pay, the idea would presumably be unacceptable to the unions – and it is the unions who in the United States have been most prominent in advocating a reduction in hours as a defence against automation. In any case, the fall in incomes would adversely affect the level of demand in the economy, and the effects of this on unemployment would be at least as serious as those feared from automation. On the other hand, if the reduction in hours means a reduction in the standard working week *without* any reduction in weekly pay, the result is likely to be quite unacceptable to employers and the economy as a whole. Labour costs per unit of output would rise sharply, so that unless other effects on cost reduction were very substantial, prices would tend to rise; and the subsequent fall in demand in home and export markets could again have a more catastrophic effect on unemployment levels than automation itself.

A more useful insight into the problem can be observed by taking a longer perspective. The length of the standard working week in this country has fallen slowly, but fairly steadily, over the last hundred years.[1] A century ago, the standard week averaged sixty hours, whereas today it is forty hours.[2] At the same time the pattern of hours has undergone considerable change, from a 'six-day, ten hours per day' system, through a 'five-and-a-half day, eight hours per day' system, to a general five-day week at the present time, although, as we have mentioned earlier, actual hours worked are still generally in excess of forty hours per week. As a result there are now two days' leisure in the week where previously for most workers there was only one. During this period, too, increased leisure has been made available through an extension of the number of days' paid holiday in the year, so that most workers now have at least two weeks holiday and many have three weeks or more. There is no doubt that technical progress has played a part in this process in two different ways. It has, firstly, raised productivity so that greater output could be achieved by fewer hours of work; and secondly, it has helped to raise incomes which themselves have made the prospect of additional leisure time more

[1] Cf. above, Chapter 3, Section V.
[2] For most white-collar workers the standard working week is around 35 to 37 hours.

N 2

acceptable, since leisure is commonly an activity which involves expenditure.[1]

Technical change has, however, had a different and less acceptable effect. The use of more highly capital-intensive methods of production has meant that productive plant has had to be kept in operation almost continuously, leading to extensive shift work. This inevitably has a disruptive effect on home life and leisure activities. Rota systems have been devised to try to even out the burden of this disruption on members of the company labour force, but this has meant that work and leisure patterns have been irregular – a rather unsatisfactory outcome in a society which was primarily geared to the habits of a population predominantly working during the daytime. If anything, the increasing use of automation will accentuate the use of shift work, and there are already signs that its effect is spreading from production workers to white-collar staff, who have to be represented during the night-shift as well as during the day. Nevertheless, we can reasonably expect some part of the productivity gains deriving from automation to be passed on in the form of increased leisure.[2] Exactly how this increased leisure will be taken, however, is more difficult to predict. In the past, the main source of extra leisure has been a reduced standard working week. Employers might resist the idea of a further cut in the number of hours worked per day, since this could in some industries lead to a fall in hourly productivity owing to discontinuities in production, or to serious problems in the scheduling of shift work.[3] A move towards a 'three-day week-end' is another possibility, but again there are problems since factories and offices cannot economically be closed for such an interval, and resort might have to be made to a system of staggered day work, with the attendance of workers being spread over a five-, six- or seven-day period, but each worker turning up on average only four days out of every seven. Despite the difficulties, some developments along these lines are likely to emerge in the near future, at least on an experimental basis.

If such developments did come about more generally, they would undoubtedly bring with them a need for further social adjustments, for example in the opening hours of shops, of centres of entertainment and

[1] Cf. Chapter 9, above.

[2] American evidence suggests that about two-thirds of productivity gains are taken in the form of higher income, and about one-third in increased leisure. 'The Employment Impact of Technological Change', Appendix, vol. II (*Report of the Commission on Technology, Automation and Economic Progress*), Washington, 1966, p. 362.

[3] This latter problem has already been encountered in continuous shift industries, following the reduction from 42 to 40 hours per standard week.

so on, which would in turn produce new patterns of working hours for those who are employed in these service occupations. Even now there is some evidence that shift work is spreading from manual to white-collar employment and that a greater flexibility of working hours is being required of many groups within the labour force. In this respect white-collar workers are becoming more like manual workers, but in another respect technical change is exerting an influence in the reverse direction. With the increased utilisation of automatic and semi-automatic production equipment, it may be that the traditional methods of wage payment – by basic rates with various additions, and by use of payment by results systems – will become obsolete. For the more automatic processes become, the less scope there will be for individual workers to affect the rate of output. Production workers will then become increasingly like salary earners at present: their presence and performance of duties will be necessary to production, but their contribution to output will be difficult to measure in any objective way. The logical result of this development would be a partial abandonment of the wage system as we know it, and a move towards a much more universal salary system of payment for production and staff workers alike. There are already, in some industries and firms, signs that this change is coming about; and other industries where the use of automation is important are beginning to discuss this approach to payment.[1]

In the longer run such changes in the pattern and character of working-hour arrangements may become much more important. In the shorter run, however, the main effects are likely to be related to holidays with pay. Although in the past the benefits of increased leisure have been taken mainly in the form of reductions in the standard working week, at present the average British worker, with two weeks paid holiday per year, is well behind his European counterpart, who commonly has three weeks and increasingly has four weeks holiday with pay. This too raises problems, for it is unlikely that three consecutive weeks holiday will be granted by employers, and one week may have to be taken during the winter months or in separate days spread throughout the year.

The conclusions that emerge from this discussion can be summarised as follows. First, it seems certain that as technical change proceeds, some part of the gain in productivity will be taken in the form of increased leisure. Secondly, in the short run this increased leisure is most likely to

[1] In Britain, the biggest step in this direction has been taken in the negotiation of a productivity and status agreement in the electricity supply industry, while the prospect of more general staff status is being actively discussed in some sectors of the chemiacl industry.

be reflected in longer periods of annual paid leave, though in the longer term adjustments may have to be made to the standard length of the working week. Thirdly, there are already indications of a trend towards increased use of shift work, which has important connotations for the timing and character of leisure activities. Fourthly, there is as yet no indication that the increased application of automation is likely to require a major reduction in working hours, which in any case would raise further difficulties for the level of employment, though automation does seem to be having an effect on status considerations and on attitudes to wage payment methods.

The inference to be drawn from this is that just as society has in the past adapted to situations of improved productivity performance, so it will continue to adjust in the present phase of change. This adjustment is likely to be slow and steady rather than sharp and discrete, not simply because this is the way change has occurred in the past but because the attitude of the working population towards leisure tends to be one which implies slow adaptation. While there are undoubtedly many workers who would quite unconditionally welcome an increase in leisure, there are many more whose demand for more leisure time is closely related to improvements in real income, and others still who are unwilling to accept a reduction in working hours because it leaves them with leisure time which they find difficult to use. As has already been emphasised, leisure activities are a consumption good which tends to involve expenditure out of income. While the reduction of the working day from 8 to $7\frac{1}{2}$ hours is not likely to have much effect on leisure patterns, longer week-ends and longer annual holidays are liable to have a more substantial influence, particularly in this age of the motor-car, and with the growing ease of foreign travel. But cars and other forms of travel are expensive in relation to average net incomes, and many other forms of leisure expenditure are likewise costly. Thus the reductions in the standard working week have not been matched by reduction in actual hours worked. Labour shortages have created this demand, but it is the need for extra income that has encouraged workers to work overtime. There has also been an increase in the number of people holding more than one job, both in this country and in the United States, where 'moonlighting' (as it is called) is an important phenomenon. This again is a reflection of an unwillingness to accept additional leisure opportunities without the extra income which extra leisure requires. Even the increased popularity of 'do-it-yourself' activities around the home can be seen in this light: by substituting one's own labour within the home for leisure, or for the hiring of services in the market, it is possible to save on some items of normal expenditure (e.g. home decorating, motor-car maintenance and repair, etc.) and simultaneously to use leisure time.

Both the widespread reluctance on the part of a large section of the working population to accept the full opportunity for greater leisure, and the development of different forms of leisure activity, are indicative of the way in which society regulates, and adapts to, new patterns of work and leisure. The improved general education of the labour force has undoubtedly been an important factor in the ability of the population to adjust to new leisure opportunities, and since the trend towards longer education is continuing, this influence will presumably remain operative in the future. There will inevitably be individual, personal difficulties of adjustment, perhaps most of all if it should become normal for workers to retire from their 'primary' jobs rather earlier than now, especially when the increased life-expectancy of the 60-year-old is taken into account. Some kind of further 'education' in the use of leisure time may become necessary in these cases, and this is one situation where deliberate policy measures may be required. On the whole, however, there is some reason to believe that the adjustments in work and leisure behaviour will be relatively slow and self-regulating.

VI. Conclusion

The discussion of this chapter has had to be wide-ranging, and it has touched upon problems which deserve, and have elsewhere received, more detailed analysis. The overall tenor of the argument, however, suggests that although technical change in general and automation in particular have brought about significant changes in the structure of employment and in the skill requirements of the individual, the process of social and economic adjustment has been relatively straightforward. More conjectural is the course of development in the future, but at least there are few current signs that serious maladjustment is imminent. This situation could change, given a continued expansion of research and development and a sustained period of investment boom which would allow technical advances to be introduced more rapidly than in the recent past. But what seems more important at the present time is that the individual and small-group problems which are thrown up by technical change should continue to attract attention by industry and Government alike. For there is no doubt that such problems of adjustment have appeared and will continue to emerge. The legislation which now covers this aspect of the labour market appears to have much to recommend it, but it is too early yet to assess its long-term adequacy.

SUGGESTED READING

International Labour Office, *Unemployment and Structural Change*, Geneva, 1962.
National Commission on Technology, Automation and Economic Progress, *Report* and *Appendices*, Washington, D.C., 1966.
W. E. G. Salter, *Productivity and Technical Change*, 1960.
J. Stieber (ed.), *Employment Problems of Automation and Advanced Technology*, New York, 1966.

17 Education, Training and Manpower Planning

I. Education and Training in General

The starting point for this chapter is the observation that it is only within the last decade that Governments and economists have taken a detailed interest in the role of education and training in their economic as opposed to their social setting. Why should this have been so? What is the economic role of education and training? And what is the importance of manpower planning, which has recently begun to loom large in discussions of overall economic policy? These are the major questions with which we shall be concerned in this chapter. It need hardly be added that in discussing this set of issues we are again dealing with matters which have relevance to the analysis of earlier and later chapters, especially Chapters 16 and 19, and which, because of their continual appearance, clearly require consideration in their own right.

There are several reasons for this growing emphasis on problems which, reduced to essentials, are those of the quality and utilisation of manpower resources. In the first place, it has become generally recognised that improvements in the quality of the labour force, by means of better education and training, can raise the productivity of labour and so make a contribution in their own right to the growth of the national product. Secondly, in a number of developed countries, among them Britain, the growth of the labour force has slowed down or stopped altogether, which makes a reasonable rate of economic growth increasingly dependent on an improvement in labour force quality and utilisation. Thirdly, the widespread experience of generally full employment in many countries in the last twenty years has highlighted important labour shortages, some of which have been coincident with relatively severe unemployment in limited sectors of the labour force. This again is the case in Britain. Since these shortages have frequently been more prevalent in skilled manual occupations requiring a lengthy period of industrial training, and in professional and technical occupations – the sectors of 'high-level manpower' – which require extended periods of general and vocational education, it is hardly surprising that concern has been growing for the ability of the educational and training systems of society to produce adequate supplies of such labour. Concern has also been shown over the ability of normal labour market processes to secure an optimal supply and distribution of trained manpower, and it is this that has led to a growing interest at company, industry, regional and national level in the benefits of some form of manpower planning. Manpower planning is basically the identification and measurement of potential future imbalances in labour supply and demand, and the development of plans or policies designed to avoid or minimise the incidence of such imbalance. It thereby casts attention forward to future developments in the demand for labour, and backward to the quantitative and qualitative adequacy of existing educational and training programmes.

The practical importance of this discussion is, then, obvious enough. However, before embarking on the main part of the argument, a few introductory comments on education and training may be helpful in avoiding difficulties at later stages. A distinction between education and training is difficult to draw, yet even if there is some blurring of the dividing lines, some kind of differentiation has to be made. As a first approach, education in general might be viewed as a process of learning, undertaken in schools, universities and colleges, which provides the individual in the educative process with two kinds of benefit. First, education will *at least* afford the individual a basis of knowledge and techniques which, though not in themselves specifically designed to enable the individual to undertake a particular job or type of work, will given him a better opportunity of absorbing job-related instruction. This must be regarded as a minimum effect, especially in view of the fact that many types of higher education go far beyond this stage, but we shall return to this presently. Secondly, education, as well as providing this basis which is likely to be indirectly useful to the person in his working life, is also to be regarded as a necessary condition for the individual to enjoy 'a full life', which we may interpret briefly as meaning that he can participate in, and contribute to, a wide range of social, cultural and political activities, if he wishes to do so. This second effect of education is less the concern of the economist than of other social scientists, but its importance cannot be dismissed by the economist, especially when the problems of developing nations are being discussed. For the present purpose, however, we can legitimately concentrate mainly on the first sort of benefit – the economic advantages of education.

Training, on the other hand, we might initially regard as a process of instruction or learning which is directly related to the activities involved in a particular kind of work. Such a view would mean that training is a complement to the educational process, by which a more general stock of knowledge is adapted to the performance of specified jobs. Thus we might take as a typical form of training the sort of trade apprenticeship whereby a youth works alongside a fully-trained craftsman, acquiring particular skills by assisting the craftsman and by informal instruction on the job. The same kind of 'on-the-job' training is common for many semi-skilled workers, with the training period lasting sometimes only for a few days but, more usually, for several weeks or months. On this understanding of 'training', we might conclude that it is, as a rule, a more job-related form of instruction which is therefore an important contributor to the economy and its growth but which is less important in producing the kind of social and cultural benefits to which education gives rise. In caricature, we might almost say that education is the process by which people acquire a foundation of theory and information, while training is the process by which people learn to apply this information to particular types of work. In this sense we would regard as education the university courses taken by a medical practitioner, and his post-graduate year in a hospital as training.

In practice, this can be no more than the roughest of working guides to the processes of education and training. For some groups of pupils in secondary education, considerable scope is often given to instruction in job-related activities such as book-keeping, secretarial work, and manual work in wood- and metal-work. In higher education, many students are acquiring job-related qualifications – in teaching, medicine and dentistry, engineering and so on. Conversely, young persons undergoing apprentice-ship training now increasingly attend formal courses of day-release instruction in technical colleges; and this instruction is not limited solely to the trade to which they are attached, but extends to much broader areas which might properly be regarded as part of general education. In another respect, training for certain jobs, such as nursing, allows the individual to acquire capacities and knowledge which have a far wider application than is implied by the strictly vocational nature of the training course.

In short, therefore, the division between education and training is far from being precise and unambiguous. For the economist interested in the economic implications of education and training, however, there is some merit in regarding education as comprising several stages. First, there is primary education, involving a basic standard of literacy and numeracy. Universal primary education is well established in all the developed countries, but is still beyond the resources and capacities of many developing countries. Primary education is a base which is essential for secondary and higher education, and which is also necessary for the performance of many types of work. The second stage is secondary education, which again can be regarded as a necessary condition for higher education, whether vocational or not, or for entry to the various professional training courses which are not usually regarded as being fully part of the higher educational system. Just as important, however, secondary education is an integral part of the preparation of young people for entry to other forms of employment, and indeed the individual's achievements in secondary education will to a large extent determine the kinds of offers of employment made by employers, *and* the opportunities for embarking on alternative courses of directly vocational training related to a specific job or to a general range of work. Thirdly, there is higher education, which generally depends on a full course of secondary education. Higher education may be either vocational, as we have seen, or general, in which case it is simply a basis for subsequent job-related training usually provided by the employing firm.

The various levels of education and the different forms of training for specific types of work are therefore fairly closely related and are complementary to one another. It is perhaps this aspect in particular which presents a problem in the developing countries, where lack of basic education may give rise to difficulties in the training of workers for many types of work. But even in the developed countries, the complementary aspect of education and training is important as an essential element in the development of an adequately trained and appropriately trained labour force, capable of meeting the demands for labour evoked in a changing industrial society. Here, as elsewhere, training for particular kinds of work cannot proceed independently of the educational basis achieved by the work force. Here, too, as we shall see, the institutional apparatus regulating entry to different jobs and controlling transfer between jobs makes considerable use of the educational and training systems of society.

The remainder of this chapter takes the following form. In Section II we go on to examine more carefully the economic role of education in general. Section III is concerned with some of the major features of the British educational and training system and the problems they generate at points of contact with the labour market. In Section IV we review some of the problems arising in the course of manpower planning, and the areas in which Government has intervened in the British labour market. Finally, in Section V, a few general conclusions are presented on the problems of education, training and manpower planning as a whole.

II. The Economic Role of Education

Education is only one of a number of forms of what is sometimes called 'human resource development'. Particularly in developing countries great importance, both socially and economically, is attached to improvements in the nutrition and health of the population at large, for these may influence for the better the ability of the individual to contribute more efficiently and for a longer period to the growth of the national product. However, in the developed countries it is likely that the economic gains that can be made by better nutrition and possibly even by better health are less than those attainable by improvements in education and training, and we can concentrate on the latter here with some justification.

The economic approach to education may seem, as it were, to put a money value on something which cannot be evaluated in money terms alone, but it is nevertheless essential that the economist should consider the economic costs and benefits of educational activity. For after all, the ability of a society to raise the educational standard and quality of life of its population depends on its accumulation of wealth and its ability to devote more resources to education; and the accumulation of wealth itself is dependent on improvements in the quality of the labour force.

It is the problem of economic growth which has served most to attract the attention of economists to the issue of education and training. The economic literature of the eighteenth and nineteenth centuries was by no means devoid of concern for the education of the labour force, and Adam Smith, J. S. Mill and Alfred Marshall in particular put a good deal of emphasis on the economic as well as the general value of education. In the present century, however, despite very considerable advances in the educational system of the more developed economies, little attention was given to the economic effects of this development until the late 1950s. The factors which combined to bring about this change have already been touched upon above but now require a little further comment.

(i) Although most economists in the past would have allowed that improvements in the quality of the labour force would have some contribution to make to the growth of the national product, it would have been virtually impossible for any of them to hazard an estimate of the size of that contribution. Almost certainly they would have accorded the educational process a very small share, compared with those of the accumulation of physical capital, the growth of the labour force and the effects of technical progress. As the attention of the economists in the postwar period turned increasingly to the problems of economic growth, a number of estimates of the contribution of various factors to growth became available. While there is now – and perhaps always will be – much dispute over the validity of this kind of measurement and the results, it is worth while noticing that one authority has assessed the contribution of education to the growth of G.N.P. in the United States at 11 per cent in 1909–29 and 23 per cent in 1929–57.[1] Even if this is no more than a crude guide to the magnitude of the contribution of education, it does suggest that education has a significant role to play in the process of economic growth, and one which may be growing in importance.

(ii) The second point relates to the problems of developing countries, and while this begins to open up a much wider field of enquiry which we cannot properly consider here, it is as well to be aware of the difference between the developing and the developed country situations. As it became clear that the more advanced countries were making an increased investment in manpower and that this was a concomitant (and probably a determinant) of economic growth, the developing countries became aware that if they were not to fall further behind, they not only had to develop their industrial base but also to procure a suitably trained and educated labour force. As is evident from the preliminary discussion in Section I above, this could not be achieved satisfactorily by purely job-oriented training but required both a widening and a deepening of the general education system on which industrial on-the-job training could be superimposed. Such an extension in turn required a greater supply of teachers at all levels, while the desire to secure better social and economic conditions also gave rise to demands for increased numbers of doctors, engineers and administrators.

This, however, generates two difficulties. First, the richer countries not only had a broad educational base from which to expand the output of certain types of high-level manpower, but they also had more adequate resources to invest in educational development. The poorer countries were starting almost from scratch, often with no more than a partial coverage of primary education and a fragmentary secondary and higher educational system. With a small national product, much of which in any case did not pass through normal market channels, it was difficult to divert resources towards educational provision. Consequently, many of the developing countries have become reliant upon international aid, both in

[1] E. F. Denison, 'Education, Economic Growth and Gaps in Information', *Journal of Political Economy*, Supplement (Investment in Human Beings), October 1962.

money and personnel, to bridge the gap until a more independent and self-generating system can be devised. Secondly, and of as much importance, it was much less possible for the developing countries to rely on 'normal' labour market mechanisms to effect an improvement in the quality of the labour force.[1] For with only a small proportion of the working-age population committed to regular market employment, the labour markets themselves are underdeveloped, and for the bulk of the population the economic incentives to the acquisition of greater skill and better-paid employment (which characterise the developed economies) are much less obvious. Once again, the existence of these problems, and the involvement of the developed countries – and their economists – led to a reconsideration of the economic role of education and training.

(iii) The third factor we have already encountered in the previous chapter: the effects of economic change on the structure of labour demand and especially the growing relative demands for workers in occupations which require a high level of job-training or of formal education. This is largely the result of the growing sophistication of technology, the growth in real income levels, and perhaps also the fact that if an economy is to continue growing as rapidly as its competitors, it must make some contribution to growth through its own scientific and industrial research. The high overall levels of post-war employment have served to highlight the existence of shortages in many of the high-level manpower sectors as well as in the skilled manual occupations where expansion has been taking place. Since Governments in the post-war period have taken an increasing political responsibility for economic growth, it is inevitable that obstacles to growth, such as bottlenecks in labour supply, should have attracted Government attention and given rise to centrally-directed programmes in the educational and training field. There is another factor which is less a reflection of economic demand than one of changing social standards. As real *per capita* incomes rise, Governments are able to set higher standards for many social and community services, many of which, such as education and health, require highly-trained, professionally qualified labour. But further, because of the now acknowledged relationship between the volume of high-quality manpower, economic growth, and national prestige, intercountry comparisons of social and technological performance and potential (notably on the part of the U.S.A. and U.S.S.R., but elsewhere also) are

---

[1] In some of these countries, at any rate, the prevailing ethos may militate against economic development and education because they are not orientated towards an 'acquisitive' or 'materialistic' view of society, and this may hinder the establishment and development of markets and market pressures.

commonly based on the *per capita* representation of doctors, scientists, engineers, teachers, etc., in the respective labour forces. Both from this source, and from the central regulation of social service standards in general, there may develop a somewhat 'artificial' demand for certain types of trained manpower. This is an 'administered' demand rather than one which evolves directly out of economic change, but it may nevertheless place additional pressure on the facilities provided by society, and require further diversion of resources if the demand is to be met.

These three sets of factors, then, have all contributed to the increasing interest in the economic role of education. One of the main points to emerge from this discussion is the conception of education and training as an investment process which, by making workers capable of combining with changing and improving techniques of production more efficiently, raises the productivity of the labour force and the productive capacity of the economy. Thus, in so far as the society requires children or young people to receive some minimum amount of compulsory education, we can regard society as making an investment in its future manpower resources.[1] By making education freely available in this way, up to and also beyond minimum school-leaving age, society is incurring two kinds of costs: first a direct cost in terms of the resources which it allocates to education, and secondly an indirect cost in terms of the production which could have been achieved had those in full-time education become full-time members of the regular labour force. For young children, of course, this latter opportunity cost is negligible, but it becomes less so when we consider those in the final years of secondary education and those in higher education courses.

As we noted in Chapter 9, this conception of education as an investment process applies equally to the individual, especially when he or she remains in full-time education beyond school-leaving age. This is a critical matter, for no matter how much opportunity for education is made available, the final decision rests with the individual. Even when the direct costs of education are fully borne by society rather than by the individual, there still remain the opportunity costs of foregone earnings during the period of 'optional' education. From the economic point of view, those who accept this cost, plus any extra costs for tuition fees, etc., must expect to receive a level of earnings after tax which, over the working-life cycle, is sufficient to compensate them and give some positive return.[2] And it is of course

---

[1] It will, of course, also be making an investment in its future citizens as voters, parents, consumers, etc., on which no economic value can be set.

[2] On a strict accounting basis, the present value of the expected after-tax

broadly true that jobs requiring higher education carry greater earnings than jobs where the training period is short. Similar arguments apply to many forms of training.

There is now a growing literature, mainly relating to the United States but for other countries too, giving estimates of the net rate of return on different incremental periods of types of education. It would perhaps be unwise to put too much reliance on the computed figures for particular rates of return, but it seems fairly certain that each increment to education up to postgraduate education yields a positive net return over any lesser training period. This is especially borne out where the individual completes the additional stage of education, and this despite the fact that each additional stage, per year of study, tends to be more expensive (i.e. undergraduate education is more expensive per unit than secondary education, postgraduate education more expensive than undergraduate education).

It is important to distinguish here between the private and social costs (and returns) of education. In a country like Britain, the young person who stays on at school past school-leaving age usually enjoys a high degree of subsidisation.[1] It is society at large, rather than the individual, who bears the cost, and the only real cost to the individual is that of the earnings he foregoes during training. Thus social costs of education in Britain will tend to be much higher than private costs. The same distinction between private and social appears in the consideration of returns. We have to make some assumption about the extent to which earnings differentials are a product of educational differences, rather than a result of differences in ability; and this is complicated by the fact that educational level and ability tend to be highly correlated. Certainly, some attempt to allow for this is usually

---

income stream over the worker's lifetime should be greater in the job for which training is required than for alternative jobs. Cf. above, Chapter 9, and also Gary S. Becker, *Human Capital*, Nat. Bur. Econ. Res., Columbia U.P., 1964, for a comprehensive discussion.

[1] This could be important in relation to the much-discussed differentials between, for example, medical practitioners in Britain and in the United States. Whereas the British undergraduate is highly subsidised, the American usually is not. Since the American may expect to cover his own *direct* expenses (as well as indirect costs which are common to both British and American trainees), he will require a considerably higher income flow. Thus the British doctor who emigrates to work in the United States has the best of both worlds: he does not bear the direct costs of training which his American counterpart incurs, but he shares in the extra high earnings of the American who requires them to offset his training costs. It would, however, probably be wrong to attribute the whole of the inter-country differential to this factor.

made in calculations of net private return, but when we turn to the social benefits the problem becomes still more complex. In the first place, the private return must be based on post-tax earnings figures, whereas the social return has to be on a before-tax basis. Secondly, we cannot translate the private return to education into a social return without some assumption about the relationship between earnings and productivity: for example, if earnings were assumed to be equal to the value of the marginal product for each different type of labour, we could convert the additional income attributable to each stage of education into contributions to the social product, and hence, with a knowledge of social costs, derive a social rate of return on investments in education. However, as we saw in earlier chapters, this relationship between earnings and productivity is one which is distorted by many kinds of social and institutional influences which obstruct and modify the competitive forces of the labour market.

The cautions which mark the various stages of this part of the discussion preclude the drawing of any unequivocal conclusions. We have, however, encountered some of the main problems requiring analysis and the difficulties which arise in the course of analysis. In this respect we now have a better understanding of the reasons why economists should be concerned with the relationship between the educational system as a source of suitably developed manpower, and the labour market as the institutional mechanism through which the demands for such manpower are expressed. Also, although the precise contribution to the process of economic growth is difficult to determine, there is probably now enough evidence for us to take seriously the proposition that education is *one* of the critical factors in growth.

III. Education and Training in Britain

Although it is no part of our purpose here to catalogue, even in summary form, the features of the educational and training system in Britain, some attention is due to the points at which the education and training arrangements of our society interact with the operation of the labour market. It is with this interaction that this section is principally concerned. Important points of contact can be identified in the three following areas: equality of opportunity in education; equality of opportunity for entry through the 'recognised' or customary training channels into particular occupations; and the capacity of the system to produce adequate supplies of high-level manpower.

(i) Without equality of opportunity in education there are bound to be imperfections in the operation of the labour market. If entry to a job requires a special educational background, and this education is limited to a select group or an *élite*, the supply of labour to that job will be restricted artificially, and this is likely to show itself in a wage level for that job which lies above the competitive rate. Thus for example the extension of basic education to all sectors of the population removed obstacles to entry into clerical employment, so that despite a major expansion of demand the relative wage position of the clerical worker has fallen vis-à-vis the average manual worker.

The present situation in Britain is that there does exist easy *access* to all stages of education, from primary school right into postgraduate courses. That is, provided satisfactory standards of performance have been achieved at any level of education it is possible for the individual to proceed without any direct cost to the next stage of education. This needs a little explanation. For young persons aged five to fifteen, full-time school education, including three years of secondary schooling, is compulsory. Current intentions are to raise the school-leaving age from fifteen to sixteen in the early 1970s. Although parents may still exercise a choice to pay for their children's education within the public-school system or in other forms of fee-paying schools, this period of education is available without charge to parents or children. Since it is unlawful for persons under fifteen to be employed on a full-time basis, the opportunity cost, as well as the direct cost, can be regarded as zero.[1]

But above the age of fifteen full-time employment is quite legal and the cost of continued attendance at school, to the individual or to the family, in terms of earnings opportunities foregone, rises each year. Thus although there need be no direct costs of education beyond the age of fifteen, it might be argued that equality of education opportunity does not exist, since family circumstances differ and the loss of potential earnings from children will be much more serious for some. To some extent this is rectified by families getting income relief for children undertaking full-time educational courses and by the availability of grants from public funds to students in most forms of higher education, though even then the loss of potential income is still unevenly shared.

The economic importance of this is that the ability of the young person to take advantage of educational opportunity is still somewhat conditioned

[1] Young people in full-time education may of course make some contribution to their own upkeep or to family income by taking paid employment, usually, in this country, during vacations.

by the financial circumstances of his family, and there is still a likelihood that the children of better-off parents will be at some advantage relative to the remainder. In terms of competition for certain kinds of jobs requiring a long formal education, therefore, the child of the higher-income family will be more favourably placed, and the competitive mechanism of the market will be impaired.[1] This tendency is further strengthened by the sociological influence of family background and circumstances on attitudes to education and employment.[2] There is little doubt, however, that the situation is now much more open than in the past, a fact that is reflected in the steady rise in the percentage of the fifteen-to-eighteen age group remaining at school and entering higher education. Even so, the majority of school-children leave school at the first opportunity: in 1965, only about 20 per cent of the fifteen-to-eighteen age group remained at school. For the majority who leave school at the ages of fifteen and sixteen, usually with little or nothing in the way of formal educational qualifications, there is an immediate step into the labour force where new training opportunities of a vocational kind are available.

(ii) Those who leave school at fifteen may already have had some pre-liminary vocational education: for boys this is mainly related to manual or lower-grade technical work, for girls towards office and commercial employment. An extension of this vocational aspect in the education of those leaving school at the first opportunity was advocated by the Newsom Report.[3] But most of those leaving school at fifteen will have their first opportunity for training related to a particular kind of work only when they actually enter employment. The significance of this is indicated in Table 17.1. The table shows that in 1965, of those entering employment for the first time at ages fifteen to seventeen, about two-thirds did so at fifteen. Of the fifteen-year-old boys, just over half took jobs with a recognised training period, the most important of which involved appren-ticeships. There are two important points here: first, that the proportion of girls entering regular training was very much smaller than that for boys; and secondly, that a great majority of boys entering apprenticeships did so at fifteen or sixteen. These facts reflect the relative lack of training facilities for girls, and the tendency for entry to apprenticeship training to

[1] It is also argued that so long as the public-school and fee-paying systems exist, they will attract some of the better teachers and so will give a better *quality* of education to those educated within them. This too may have an effect in distorting the flow of entrants to higher education by biasing opportunity in favour of children from better-off families.

[2] Cf. Chapter 11, Section II, above.

[3] *Half Our Future*, H.M.S.O., 1963.

Table 17.1

Analysis by Type of Employment entered and Age of Entry

| | Age at entry into employment (Thousands) | | | | | | | |
| | Boys | | | | Girls | | | |
Class of employment entered	15	16	17	Total	15	16	17	Total
Apprenticeship or learnership to skilled occupation (including pre-apprenticeship training in employment)	79·7	31·6	6·8	118·1	13·2	2·4	1·0	16·6
Employment leading to recognised professional qualifications	0·3	1·9	2·2	4·4	0·4	2·2	2·1	4·6
Clerical employment	7·6	13·8	7·7	29·1	53·2	39·3	15·7	108·2
Employment with planned training, apart from induction training, not covered in previous rows	27·1	7·1	2·7	37·0	28·1	3·9	1·7	33·7
Other employment	86·4	12·4	3·8	102·6	93·5	8·8	3·1	105·5
Total	201·2	66·9	23·2	291·2	188·4	56·6	23·6	268·5

Source: Ministry of Labour Gazette, May 1966.

be blocked beyond the age of sixteen. Of course, not all those entering jobs classified as 'other employment' went into jobs with no prospect of promotion or career development, but many of the jobs in this category would have precisely this dead-end character.

There is enough evidence here to suggest that equal opportunity for job-related training (as opposed to more formal education) is far from being achieved. Certainly there does not seem to be an equality of opportunity for boys and girls, even after allowance is made for the fact that girls may not be so interested in acquiring a job training which will serve them in later life. One obvious answer is that, for the employer, expenditure incurred on extensive training of girls may not be economic, since most will leave work in a very few years to be married and bring up families: in short, the pay-back period on training is too short for it to be worth while for the employer. There may, however, be doubts whether this kind of calculation is the correct one for the interests of society at large: on the broader plane, what may matter more is the benefits received by society over the whole working life of the individual, rather than the direct return to the employer who provides the training. The other restriction, relating to the age at which apprenticeship is normally begun, derives from trade-union rules. Most apprenticeships are for a five-year period, and tradition has it that a man should be fully qualified in his trade by the time he reaches the age of twenty-one; hence the starting age has become established at sixteen (often with a one-year pre-apprenticeship job). The questions which then arise are, first, whether the five-year period is really necessary or whether some curtailment of the training period might be possible; and secondly, whether the traditional view should hold in a society where the trend is towards an extension of full-time education. On both these questions there are growing doubts about the value of the customary approach, and the length of some apprenticeships has already been cut while a limited but increasing flexibility is being exhibited in regulations relating to starting age.

There is, however, a quite different aspect of this whole question of apprenticeships and extended training courses. Evidently, the number of places in firms made available for trainees will depend on their estimates of the future demand for different types of skilled (manual) labour and the extent to which employers think they will be able to fill vacancies either by recruitment of trained labour from other firms or by mobility within the firm. Given the nature of the apprenticeship system as it now exists, firms must try to estimate their requirements five years ahead. Such a long-term forecast must inevitably be subject to some margin of error, but even so a firm may be able to estimate roughly whether its demands are likely to increase or decrease. Further problems may then arise, for in some cases the firm may not be entirely free to restrict or expand its training places. Some trade unions, as in printing, enforce a fairly strict ratio of apprentices to journeymen in particular trades, either at industry or at firm level; and this ratio may be both a lower limit (since the union wishes to keep up its membership in future) and an upper limit (since the union will wish to preserve the income and job security of its existing members). The result of this may be either an over-supply or an under-supply of trainees, relative to future requirements, and adjustments in the apprentice ratios often lag behind changes in demand by several years. The problems here for manpower planning are evidently considerable, but should not, perhaps, be overstated since not all unions are able to enforce this policy, and even those who could are flexible in their approach. There is also the point that all firms are not prepared to make an equal contribution to the provision of training places and facilities, though the Industrial Training Act now makes it possible to ensure that virtually all firms in an industry make some financial contribution to training.

There are two further points to be made in relation to equality of training opportunity. In the first place, the flow of school-leavers into the labour force is by no means equal from year to year, but fluctuates (with appropriate lags) according to the birth rate. Britain experienced a major upsurge in the flow of school-leavers in the years 1960–4, for example, as a result of the high birth rate in the immediate post-war years. Not only does this kind of 'bulge' put a strain on educational facilities at all levels, but it requires some flexibility in the points of entry to working life. Yet the provision of training places may be affected (as it was in fact in 1962–3) by the trading position of firms, and recession may cause employers to reduce their intake of trainees. In consequence, the accessibility of training opportunity to school-leavers may vary considerably from year to year unless steps are taken to improve the absorptive power of the industrial training system.

The second and final point here is that for those who remain at school to obtain the General Certificate of Education or equivalent qualifications, there are many alternatives other than higher education at universities and other colleges or training institutions. Many professions have their own prescribed courses of vocational education – for example, accountancy, architecture and surveying. Again, these occupations are among the higher-income types of work, but during the training period, which may be as long as five years, grants may not be available as they are in other forms of higher education. It is generally the case that those in training are paid at a kind of 'apprentice' rate, but again this is likely to impose more hardship on lower-income families, and the equality of opportunity is thus by no means complete. The higher-income family is, on average, more likely to have its children enter high-paying occupations such as the professions simply because it can better afford the loss of contributions to family income, and can afford to subsidise children during extended periods of education and training.

(iii) The third topic for discussion here is the educational system's capacity for producing high-level manpower, including top-level management and administrators, professional groups such as scientists, engineers doctors, lawyers, etc., qualified teachers and 'technical' personnel such as foremen and supervisors, nurses and high-grade technicians. The discussion of Chapter 6 and Chapter 16, above, showed that these groups were among the most rapidly growing sectors of the working population. The training of such groups depends to a very great extent on the capacity of universities, business schools, colleges of education, polytechnics and other technical institutions engaged in the training of professional and other highly qualified manpower. On the assumption (which is not altogether justified by the evidence reviewed here) that we are continually moving closer to equality of opportunity in higher education, the main problem becomes that of the adequacy of the system to produce a sufficient number of high-level workers in the correct proportions to meet current and future demand.

From a general standpoint we have to recognise that because of the lengthy education and training periods for all these groups there is a considerable lag – often as much as ten years – between the time of entry to 'optional' education and the time at which professional or other qualifications are obtained. Concern over the adequacy of places in higher education led to the setting up of the Robbins Committee, whose terms of reference related to the long-term development of higher education and the principles on which this development ought to be based.[1] The main intention was to develop a programme for higher education which would carry through to the early 1980s, but there was also a short-term problem, reflected in doubts about the ability of the higher educational system to absorb the 'bulge' in the population likely to be seeking entry to higher education in the mid-1960s; this bulge resulted from the post-war rise in the birth rate already remarked upon. Here we need only to consider those

[1] *Higher Education*, Report of the Committee appointed by the Prime Minister under the Chairmanship of Lord Robbins, Cmnd. 2154, H.M.S.O., 1963.

of the Committee's recommendations which have immediate relevance for the problems of the labour market.

The Report recognised that an increasing number of young people each year were obtaining qualifications at least adequate to secure entry to higher education and that this trend would continue, while the proportion of those with the requisite qualifications applying for admission to courses would also grow. It showed that the provision of places was not keeping pace with this increase. The interpretation put upon this was that there was an increasing 'demand' for higher education on the part of young people, and it was thought that every effort should be made to satisfy it by the adequate provision of places. As a result it was proposed to raise the number of students in higher education from 216,000 in 1962–3 to 390,000 in 1973–4 and to about 560,000 by 1980–1. While recognising that over-production of particular kinds of expertise could be easily envisaged, the Committee was 'fairly confident that the Government would have to go much further than anything [the Committee's] present projections indicate before the country was over-supplied with trained talent in general'.[1] This method of approach, and the conclusions, require further consideration.

The concept of 'demand for higher education' adopted in the Report is not a 'demand' in the sense of quantity demanded at a price or a variety of prices. In the Committee's sense of the phrase, the demand for higher education is essentially a measure of educational performance on the part of the sixteen to nineteen age group, revealing its capacity – and perhaps its desire – for further (higher) education. This leaves unresolved the question of the economic demand for the output of the higher educational system as it joins the labour force; and this, it would seem, is just as critical as the supply side of the market. Admittedly the Committee considered the possibility of forecasting demand for the next decade, but rejected it as impracticable. And indeed, there are considerable difficulties on this score, as we shall see later in this chapter. The fact remains that from the point of view of future economic and manpower developments, it is every bit as important that the *composition* of supply, as well as the volume of supply, should mesh with demand, if we are to avoid unemployment, under-employment, and shortages of some types of highly trained man-power, and if we are to prevent a misallocation of educational and training expenditure to areas of less relative importance.

What makes this worse is that, in general, many of the occupations for which higher education is a necessary qualification are highly specialised,

[1] Ibid., p. 73.

giving rise to a limited possibility of inter-occupational mobility. Training for secondary-school teaching cannot readily be transferred to use in the medical or engineering professions, or vice versa. Even within engineering the different categories (such as civil, electrical, mechanical, aeronautical, etc.) are by no means capable of ready interchange. It would seem, then, that it *is* important that training places should be made available, so far as can be determined, in line with future requirements as predicted by industry and other users of such labour. Apart from a passing reference to the desirability for some *relative* expansion in the proportion of students taking courses in science and technology (and within this an expansion of technology), the Report gives little guidance to the structure of higher education by subject area that the economy of the future will require.[1] The Committee's solution to the problem we are posing here, the need for a structural balance between demand and supply, was mainly couched in terms of the removal of 'artificial barriers to mobility' and the adoption of 'educational methods to impart basic principles rather than narrow skills in specialised fields'.[2] Yet it is by no means certain that the barriers to mobility at this level of educational attainment are artificial, while it may be that the skills which industry and other users require are essentially of a kind that is highly developed within narrow limits.

Furthermore, as current experience shows, it may not be enough merely to provide places in particular subject areas, since without any positive guidance, or a policy designed to indicate the relatively greater need for some types of education than others, the inflow of students may take a shape which is inconsistent with that of future labour demand. Concern is being shown at the present time because of the unwillingness of students to take up available places in higher education in the scientific and technological subject areas. One is forced to consider whether, with a clearer idea of the structure of future demands, there might not be some case for differentiating grants to students according to subject area. It may be argued of course that it is the function of the labour market to effect this kind of adjustment (for example, by a change in income differentials) and in the longer run it may well do so, though undoubtedly with some imperfections. But this view overlooks the fact that the student who embarks on a specific course of higher education at seventeen or eighteen may be more influenced by current student income possibilities than by future income prospects, which may in any case have altered by the time he emerges from the course. Again we are back with the problem of the time-

[1] Ibid., p. 165.
[2] Ibid., p. 74.

lag involved in acquiring this kind of education, and the slow pace of adjustment in the market.

The existence of major problems in this area is evident enough, and it is clear that many of them can be traced back to the need for adequate manpower forecasts if a reasonable and continuing balance is to be achieved between supply and demand. The importance of this is that the provision of places in higher education, especially when it involves an expansion such as that envisaged in the Robbins Report, imposes a major call on resources both of capital for building programmes and of labour – itself largely the product of the higher education system – to undertake the teaching, research and administration which are implicit in higher education and in the schools which prepare children for such training. The supply of teachers themselves is, in fact, one of the critical issues, and one which has been brought to the fore by the expansion of education in general.

On the training side there have also been a number of developments. Within the secondary-school system itself, as we have observed, there has been an increase in the attention paid to vocational instruction for those likely to leave school at fifteen. This tendency is likely to be strengthened with the raising of the school-leaving age, for it seems essential that the extra year of schooling for those who leave at the first opportunity will have to include a greater amount of job-oriented instruction, if the extra year is to be effectively used as a means of bridging the gap between school and workplace. So far as job-related training is concerned, it is important to observe the considerable expansion which has taken place in the provision of training places outside the higher education system. Probably the largest development has been in the extension of day-release courses for apprentices, who are thereby enabled to take classes at technical colleges during working hours, leading to examinations in a number of trade subjects. The most important of these, with national recognition, are probably the Ordinary and Higher National Certificates, and the various City and Guilds courses. Also, quite apart from these provisions for training in manual occupations, there has been a growth in the number of training courses available in such areas as computer programming, commercial and sales work, the educational entry qualifications for which fall short of those required for entry to higher education. These provide alternatives to manual work for many young people.

Despite these changes, and the expansion of the system to cater for those who do not wish, or are in one way or another unable, to enter professional or higher education courses, a great deal of training that is done is still of the 'on-the-job' variety. The great advantage of this for the employer, of

O

course, is that he can often adapt labour with an existing stock of job-knowledge and experience to changing technological circumstances. This, however, is subject to two main sorts of qualification: first, that some sort of technological change, as seen in the last chapter, may involve such radical changes in labour requirements that normal retraining or adaptation processes are impossible; and secondly, that demarcation and other trade-union forms of control over labour supply may impede mobility within the firm. Nevertheless, the upgrading of labour within the firm, coupled with periods of training and familiarisation on the job, afford firms a valuable degree of flexibility in meeting changing labour force needs.

There remains, however, a discernible unevenness both in opportunities for training and in the quality of training provided by different industries and by individual firms within an industry. The Industrial Training Act of 1964 set in motion a programme designed to reduce this unevenness by setting up a number of Industrial Training Boards to be responsible for assessing the needs of the industry for trained labour of various types, and for implementing policies which would ensure that adequate training standards were being achieved while distributing the cost of training more equitably. It is still too early to determine the success of the Act, but there can be little doubt that such a step was overdue, and was certainly in the right direction.[1]

The conclusion to which the discussion of this section leads is that the pattern of education and training in this country is undergoing considerable change. In view of the conclusions reached in the last chapter, that the future trend in labour force requirements is towards an expansion of better-educated, more highly-qualified labour, the direction of change in the educational and training systems, and the growth of attention to these systems and their adequacy, is encouraging. Doubts must remain, however, about the compositional aspect of the relation between future labour supply and demand, and the capacity of the education and training facilities to produce a proper balance. It is at this point that we begin to enter into the new problem area of manpower forecasting and planning.

IV. Problems of Manpower Forecasting and Planning

Manpower planning has already been defined as a process by which impending deficiencies or surpluses of labour are identified and measures

[1] For further discussion, see below, Section IV, pp. 425–6.

implemented to avoid such imbalance. There are thus two essential parts in the process: the forecasting of future demand and supply and, where appropriate, the steps taken to bring these into line. Manpower planning can be undertaken at almost any level, and in this country many companies engage in this kind of planning, while Government – directly or indirectly through legislation or the setting up of committees or commissions – has been involved in many manpower planning exercises at national, regional, occupational and industrial level.

By now the reasons for some form of manpower planning will be apparent. Sustained full employment has meant that there is a very small national reserve of labour from which increased demands can be met in the short run. The slow growth of the labour force has meant that the inflow of new workers has been quickly absorbed. The changing structure of labour demands towards more highly-trained workers means that those who are unemployed are usually not capable of filling the jobs in which shortages are greatest. This changing structure also has the effect of making it difficult for the limited new supplies to be trained quickly, while transfers from other occupations may be difficult for the same reason. In this situation it becomes increasingly important that developing shortages should be identified early, and that efforts be made to raise the numbers in training or to find some alternative means of approach such as by using different production methods or restructuring jobs.

Different types of worker require different training periods. Unskilled and semi-skilled workers may require several weeks or months before they can perform the work required of them at a satisfactory pace and standard, but such a time-period presents few problems. Training is done mainly on the job, and so requires little in the way of additional equipment. It may not even require much formal instruction. The real problems arise with labour for which the conventional training period extends to three, five or even more years, for it is in this sort of time-span that future demands become much more difficult to predict. Yet if it is suddenly recognised that more of a particular type of labour will be required a year or so hence than is currently in the course of training, and if this labour cannot be produced from scratch in less than three years, there will be an intervening 'manpower gap'. For the individual firm the only solution may be an attempt to bid up wages or otherwise improve conditions, thereby attracting labour from other firms using this sort of labour, but this of course may simply lead to retaliation by these other firms. For the economy at large, the solution cannot be found in training new labour and the only real possibility may be to encourage labour with the necessary expertise to immigrate into the country from abroad.[1]

The initial problem is thus to identify and to measure the 'manpower gaps' of the future. This requires a projection of demand and supply for a period which is sufficiently long to allow any imbalance (and particularly any deficiency) to be avoided. In other words, the time it takes to produce any kind of labour is one of the principal determinants of the period over which the forecast should be conducted, if there is to be a possibility of implementing effective corrective measures. For many skilled workers in craft occupations this implies a forecast five years ahead;[2] for many grades of high-level manpower, as defined earlier, the period is not infrequently ten years and may even be longer in exceptional cases. But as the Robbins Committee on Higher Education observed, forecasting over ten-year periods is extremely difficult. Companies with fairly sophisticated forecasting procedures often set the upper limit of their forecasts at five years or less.[3] For industrial labour the problems are:

(i) uncertainty about the growth of the economy, and therefore about the sale of a firm's products either directly to consumers or to other industries;

(ii) uncertainty about the effects of technical change which, apart from its direct effects on the structure of employment, can bring about major alterations in product demand and give rise to substantial shifts in the composition of the firm's demand for labour even in a five-year period; and

(iii) uncertainty about changes in incomes and tastes, which in time may be influenced by the economy's growth and its experience of technical change and new product development.

For other types of labour the problems may be still more complex. Consider, for example, the demand for doctors, which will be affected by the size and age structure of the population, the ratio between doctors and

[1] Cf. Chapter 19, below.

[2] This need not always be so. Despite obstacles to mobility between crafts there is some degree of flexibility implicit in the system, and it is also true that a certain amount of interchangeability is possible within the first few years of some apprentice training courses. Where such flexibility is possible, the penalties of inaccurate five-year forecasts are less severe.

[3] As the Manpower Research Unit of the Department of Employment and Productivity has found, relatively few companies are capable of sophisticated forecasts. In the Unit's study of the metal industries, enquiries revealed that less than a quarter of 300 firms approached undertook forecasts for more than two years ahead; about one-half of these did some kind of manpower forecasting, but in most cases this was on a one-year basis. See *The Metal Industries* (Manpower Studies No. 2), H.M.S.O., 1965.

population which is regarded as socially desirable if satisfactory standards of health are to be maintained in line with the wealth of the economy, and by a variety of other factors such as the organisation of health services, the incidence of different types of sickness, etc. The difficulty of predicting the incidence of illness is obvious enough, but what might be seen to be a fairly straightforward task, the forecasting of population size and structure, is in fact a complex matter. For the birth rate can change suddenly and (literally) unpredictably, because of changes in social attitudes, changes in economic conditions, and a variety of other factors. It was precisely this circumstance which led the forecasts of the Willink Committee astray in 1957.[1] The Committee accepted the then current Government actuary forecast that the population would increase by 4·5 per cent between 1955–1971. By 1966, the rising birth rate had already produced an increase of over 7 per cent, and population in total was one million more than had earlier been predicted for 1971. Quite aside from any extra burden, the resulting change in age structure might have put on doctors, any estimate of the nation's demand for doctors based on a fixed 'doctor/population' factor would be quite misleading. In fact, the Willink Committee recommended in 1957 that the intake into medical schools might reasonably be *reduced* by one-tenth, and a subsequent Royal Commission, reporting in 1960, observing in the interim an actual fall in the number of medical students, concluded that 'the supply of candidates for training as doctors is reasonably close to requirements'.[2] The outcome of this is that there is already a 'shortage' of doctors, *in the special sense that target doctor/population ratios are not being met*, and that this will get worse throughout the 1970s unless measures are introduced to remedy the situation either by training more doctors, or by finding means to use the services of doctors more efficiently by supplementing their work with capital investment or more ancillary workers.

This, however, assumes there will be no change in circumstances, for example on the supply side itself. Just as a firm which trains a certain amount of labour to meet its future needs cannot be certain that it will retain all its trainees, so even the economy as a whole cannot be sure that all those it trains as doctors will remain as practising doctors in this

[1] *Report of the Committee to consider the future numbers of medical practitioners and for the appropriate intake of medical students*, H.M.S.O., 1957.

[2] Royal Commission on Doctors' and Dentists' Remuneration, 1957–60, *Report* (Cmnd. 939), H.M.S.O., p. 52. The Memorandum of Dissent by Professor Jewkes was less sanguine about the adequacy of supply; ibid., pp. 167–9.

country. In the British case, some of those in training are from developing countries and will return there on completion of training or after gaining some experience. Others will emigrate temporarily or permanently to work in developing countries under schemes of international assistance or for personal reasons. Others still may be attracted by higher earnings or different conditions of service in North America. There always has been some emigration of doctors, of course, but so far as can be ascertained, the rate of loss is variable over time and may be relatively high at present. Nor does the problem of emigration restrict itself to those just finishing their training period, for apart from the normal loss through death and retirement (which can be forecast accurately by actuarial methods), there may be changes in the existing stock of doctors as a result of emigration. Thus the effect of migratory flows on the adequacy of supply and of the numbers in training may be serious, and in fact there has been in recent years an extended debate on the doctor-shortage issue, relating particularly to the problems of estimating demand and the effects of migration.[1]

The case of doctors is illustrative of the forecasting problems which arise. In some ways, of course, it is a special case, because of its public service connotation and the fact that the organisation of health provision is almost entirely within the control of central Government. In this context, the concept of 'shortage' is rather special. The demand for doctors is in effect determined by the establishment of a target ratio for doctors per 10,000 population, which is used as a rough guide to the quality of service provided. The pay of doctors and the availability of training places in medicine is largely a matter of Government control. Thus a 'shortage' of doctors in this situation is *not* a shortage in the sense that the supply of doctors, at ruling *market* prices for doctors' services, is inadequate to meet effective demand. It is rather that there is some obstacle (which may be the conditions of service, the income level, the lack of training places, the career prospects, etc.) which prevents supply from reaching the levels regarded by Government as socially desirable. In a sense, then, the payment levels, the conditions of service, and the 'shortage' itself, are all 'administered', rather than the result of market forces.

However, this kind of yardstick, which gives rise to such an administered

[1] Cf. Deborah Paige and Kit Jones, *Health and Welfare Services in Britain in 1975*, Occasional Paper No. xxii, National Institute of Economic and Social Research, 1966; Alan Peacock and Robin Shannon, 'The New Doctors' Dilemma', *Lloyds Bank Review*, January 1968; and John Seale, 'Medical Emigration: A Study in the Inadequacy of Official Statistics', in *Lessons from Central Forecasting*, Eaton Paper No. 6, Institute of Economic Affairs, 1965. For further discussion of migration, see Chapter 19, below.

shortage, is by no means uncommon. In the first place, there are many areas of public service where some target is set up as being socially desirable, and from which, therefore, the adequacy of supply is determined. This is so in the case of the police service, where a target of one policeman per 500 people is implicit in discussion of manpower needs.[1] Similar targets exist in the cases of dentists, where a dentist/patient ratio is involved; of school-teachers, where a maximum size of class at various educational stages is a common factor in discussions; of nurses, university teachers, and many others. Secondly, even where there is no public service element, the setting of some target may result from a concern about national prestige. The Americans tend to view the adequacy of their supplies of engineers, scientists, medical practitioners, etc., by reference to the ratio of these groups to population achieved in Soviet Russia; in this country, we may have an eye to the position in North America or in Western Europe; and the same sort of reference process exists in the developing countries.

In all this, the outstanding feature is the emphasis on highly-trained manpower and especially on that which has a 'public service' or 'tech-nological maturity' implication. It is in these cases, of course, that the training period is generally lengthy and at least partly within the sphere of Government intervention. And it is in such cases that the role of man-power planning has proved to be most important, though in some econo-mies attempts have been made to forecast and plan on a national basis for the labour force as a whole.

Britain has had two attempts at this sort of planning. The first experience was part of the economic planning undertaken in the course of the Second World War. From 1941 until the end of the war, manpower budgeting was carried on at Cabinet level, on the basis of eighteen-month forecasts of demand produced by individual Departments and co-ordinated and reconciled as far as possible by a Ministerial manpower committee. Final decisions on manpower allocation were taken by the Prime Minister, at least as far as the broad distribution between branches of the Armed Forces and the various 'essential' industries were concerned. This was backed up by more detailed allocations, based on occupations as well as on industries, executed at lower levels largely through the Ministry of Labour. To some extent the additional problems created by war-time conditions, such as shortage of time for working out sophisticated techniques and difficulties in obtaining up-to-date information on labour utilisation, were counterbalanced by the existence of manpower controls such as

[1] Cf. Royal Commission on the Police, *Final Report*, 1962, Cmnd. 1728, H.M.S.O., p. 85.

conscription, the possibility of directing labour and the Essential Works Orders which could prevent workers from leaving an industry essential to the war effort (e.g. coalmining). The Government also had direct control of materials and production, which made manpower budgeting easier than in a situation where production decisions are the responsibility of individual managements and where the products have to be sold on the open market. Furthermore, many institutional rules were relaxed, so that demarcation problems were avoided and shorter periods of training were introduced for many jobs, such as welding. With the end of war-time controls, most of these advantages disappeared, although attempts at forecasting and budgeting were continued for certain key manpower sectors until about 1948–9.[1]

Secondly, there was the more recent attempt at manpower planning in the 1965 National Plan. Starting from an assumption of a 4 per cent annual growth rate in the economy as a whole between 1965 and 1970, the Government asked firms and industries to assess, among other things, what would be the effect on their labour requirements over the period. After a process of reconciling these estimates, it was forecast that on the particular growth rate assumption, manpower requirements in 1970 would be in excess of supply by about 400,000; and a number of policies were advocated to reduce this manpower gap to manageable proportions, mainly by raising the level of labour force participation and increasing the level of employment.[2]

While an exercise in manpower forecasting on this global scale is an inevitable element in a national economic plan of the kind envisaged in 1965, there is probably a much more extensive use of the more limited type of manpower planning which concerns itself with forecasts and programmes relating to sectoral or even company-level labour utilisation. Certainly, these forecasts will be dependent upon the overall rate of activity in the remainder of the economy, but this can to some extent be surmounted by two devices. First, a number of alternative assumptions may be adopted to suggest the outcome of opposite extremes (for example, the highest and lowest growth rates likely to be experienced) and of some more probable eventuality lying within the extremes. Secondly, a regular review of the future, undertaken perhaps every year or two years but depending on the length of the forecast period, gives a 'rolling' forecast which allows

[1] For further discussion, see H. M. D. Parker, *Manpower: a Study of War-time Policy and Administration*, 1957.

[2] *The National Plan*, H.M.S.O., 1965. In practice of course the economy has not achieved a growth rate of anything like 4 per cent, and the validity of the forecast *on its assumptions* was never tested.

existing measures to be reviewed in line with the current behaviour of the relevant variables. The basis of such forecasts may be simple or more complex statistical procedures, or may extend to a more sophisticated econometric model; much depends on the resources of the forecasting unit, the regularity or otherwise of its activity level and manpower requirements, and the availability both of regular, reliable data and of information on the determinants of demand and supply.[1]

The sectoral approach to manpower planning has been influenced considerably in Britain in recent years by a number of developments, stemming largely from Government or other official initiative. The Department of Employment and Productivity has for some years produced year-by-year forecasts of the total working population for ten or fifteen years ahead. But in 1963 a Manpower Research Unit was established within the Ministry of Labour, a major part of its function being to examine the trend of demand, and supply prospects, for individual industries. On the basis of enquiries among representative companies in an industry, a picture is assembled of expected changes in labour requirements for the industry as a whole, analysed by occupation. A prospect can then be obtained of the changing structure of occupational requirements.

This foreknowledge is the basis of programmes to rectify incipient shortages or surpluses. Individual firms, being better informed of the industry-wide situation, or of the supply prospects for particular kinds of labour throughout the economy, may set about adjusting the flow of trainees, though of course this in itself could lead to over- or under-supply if efforts are not co-ordinated. Some degree of co-ordination is perhaps more possible, following the Industrial Training Act of 1964. This Act resulted in the establishment of Industrial Training Boards, which numbered 21 in 1967, covering more than 11 million employees. The eventual target is for about 30 boards, to cover the whole of industry. While the boards do not have authority to control the volume of training by companies, they are able to exercise some control over training provision. Boards are empowered to raise a levy on all firms within their province and to make grants from this fund to firms which meet the training criteria and standards laid down by the board.[2] The boards also exercise a wide

---

[1] For further discussion of forecasting problems, see J. R. Crossley, 'Forecasting Manpower Demand and Supply', and 'Essential Statistics for Manpower Forecasting', in *Manpower Policy and Employment Trends* (ed. B. C. Roberts and J. H. Smith), 1966.

[2] A recent estimate is that boards distribute about £125 million annually by grants: Ministry of Labour *Gazette*, November 1967, p. 872.

o 2

advisory authority and they may be expected to exert increasing influence on the scope and direction of company training.

The specific functions of the 1964 Act were to ensure the quantitative adequacy of training, to improve its quality, and to spread the cost of industrial training more equitably, the latter particularly because firms which have a low standard of training or make a disproportionately small contribution to trained manpower supplies are now forced to contribute to the cost of good-quality training. The Act, however, still leaves the responsibility for industrial training within industry, though control is increasingly centralised, which may well be a precondition of reasonable co-ordination. In addition, Government has taken a more direct responsibility by the expansion of training places in Government Training Centres (G.T.C.s), which at present undertake training for about 40 trades. In 1962 there were only 13 G.T.C.s, but by 1968 the number had increased to 38 and the current programme to 1969–70 aims at a total of 48 Centres, with a throughput of 21,000 trained workers per year. As yet, however, the scale of these activities remains rather marginal, partly because there are some types of training which cannot justifiably be undertaken since the relevant trade unions will not accord full recognition – or any recognition at all – to these 'short-period' trainees, who normally spend six months at the Centre. Nevertheless, the scheme does make a contribution, particularly in the retraining of workers unemployed for reasons such as technological change, and who are least likely to benefit from company training programmes.

As these developments suggest, Government in this country, as elsewhere,[1] is becoming increasingly involved in the field of manpower planning – for clearly the forecasting and regulatory function of the Department of Employment and Productivity is closely associated with the programmes for training developed through the Industrial Training Act and the work of the G.T.C.s. However, this Government involvement extends to more closely integrated forecasts and programmes for particular types of labour, especially in the high-level manpower area. This involvement is expressed partly through the setting up of *ad hoc* committees (such as the Robbins Committee) and partly through the use of standing bodies which undertake

[1] Most European countries now have considerable experience of Government-directed or sponsored training, and in the United States a great deal of money is now being spent annually under the Manpower Development and Training Act and related legislation. For further discussion, see (e.g.) M. S. Gordon, 'The Comparative Experience with Retraining Programmes in the United States and Europe', in *Employment Problems of Automation and Advanced Technology*. (ed. J. Stieber), 1966.

periodic reviews of manpower provision in a particular sector. A notable case in point here is the Committee on Manpower Resources for Science and Technology which, among other functions, has conducted a series of triennial surveys of engineers, scientists, technologists and supporting staff, providing on an occupational basis information and recommendations about the trends in demand, the adequacy of training provision, the effects of migration and the priority requirements of different sectors.[1]

While Government can intervene in a variety of ways to encourage the identification of possible imbalances in demand and supply, its ability to initiate corrective measures may be restricted. It is true that if supply is evidently constrained by lack of training places, it can take more or less direct action by its control over funds to the educational sector or through its industrial training organisation. Likewise, it can make some contribution to regional or area employment balance through its distribution of industry policy, backed up by its ability to control some forms of industrial expansion and to make loans or grants to companies moving to high-unemployment areas.

There are other areas where Government influence is more remote, and where more reliance may have to be placed on the normal market-place mechanisms of adjustment.[2] Yet as we have already seen, the competitive mechanism may be greatly impaired, so that, for example, the wage structure and even changes in the wage structure may be ineffective in securing a reallocation of supply. This raises a number of questions about the adequacy of the labour mobility process, and the extent to which it can be relied upon to secure the necessary volume and composition of manpower redistribution. In our more theoretical discussions of Part II we have encountered a number of social, institutional and other factors which may be expected to influence the efficiency of the market processes. In Chapter 19 below, we shall examine more thoroughly the problems of labour

[1] Cf. *Report* on the 1965 Triennial Manpower Survey, Cmnd. 3103, H.M.S.O., 1966.

[2] In this general context, however, it is worth noting that even in areas where Government may seem to have little influence, there may be a means for Government to intervene. Thus the National Board for Prices and Incomes has investigated (or is now in the process of so doing) the fees payable to solicitors and to architects – which presumably could take into account the problem of labour supply in these occupations. Moreover, a recent reference to the Monopolies Commission involved enquiry into the justification for certain 'restrictive' practices invoked by various professions and their associations.

mobility in practice. But before doing so, a few general conclusions to this present chapter are necessary.

V. Towards an Active Manpower Policy

The discussion of this chapter has emphasised the increasing attention now being paid to education, training and deployment of the labour force. Although the relation between education and economic growth is not as clearly understood as we might wish, and although the quantitative significance for growth of improvements in education and training is still a matter for speculation, there is little doubt that these factors exercise an important influence on the process of development, together with the accumulation of physical capital and the progress of technology. This is true of all countries, developed and underdeveloped, but it may be of especial importance in the British economy. For with a labour force that is not expected to grow at all in size – and which may even decline – until the late 1970s, the need to draw fully on all sources of potential growth is re-emphasised. In the absence of growth in the quality of manpower available, attention must increasingly be turned to the quality of labour and the efficiency with which it is utilised. The need, in short, is for a comprehensive (or as it is now commonly termed, an 'active') manpower policy, which is concerned not simply with the quantitative adequacy of employment, but with its quality both in relation to the needs of the economy and of the individual. Having largely solved the problems of providing adequate amounts of employment, public policy in the more developed economies could – perhaps had to – move on to the promotion of 'full, productive and freely chosen employment', which is the essential objective of an active manpower policy.[1]

This is evidently dependent *inter alia* on the kind of educational and training provision made available by the society. It also clearly depends on the formulation, regulation and implementation of policies, designed to solve specific problems, being integrated and co-ordinated one with another. And it is here that there may be difficulties. For we have already seen that Government has been taking an increasing role in the manpower

---

[1] For a brief statement of what this policy comprises, see Solomon Barkin, 'Programming of the Technical Changes and Manpower Adjustments', in *Employment Problems of Automation and Advanced Technology* (ed. Stieber).

field at all levels in the last few years. Yet the traditional view in our society has tended to regard matters such as vocational training largely as a responsibility of industry. It is therefore a fairly important question whether a reasonable balance can be struck between the traditional values of our society and the needs of the future.

As yet, the answer to this is not clear, largely because the growth of Government intervention has not extended to full co-ordination of the variety of policy measures which now exist. Indeed, it is questionable whether the organisation of the Ministry of Labour, as it was constituted in this country until 1968, was suitable for such a co-ordinated approach. Despite considerable changes in its outlook in recent years it remained *organisationally* oriented towards a more old-fashioned 'employment' policy rather than the administration of a more positive manpower policy of the kind now being increasingly discussed. The formation of the new Department of Employment and Productivity in April 1968 was largely a matter of renaming the Ministry of Labour and giving it new powers on prices and incomes. Since its formation, however, the Department has shown some signs of a much broader view of its responsibilities than had been achieved by the Ministry. But it is still too early to attempt any judgment on the extent of the change in function and approach. Much will also depend on the reaction of trade unions and employers to the changing requirements. It is one of the aims of active manpower policy, as under-written by the O.E.C.D. and as accepted by most member-countries of that organisation, that managements and unions should actively participate in the initiation and implementation of such a policy. This participation would seem to be of great relevance in the areas which have been under discussion in this chapter, as well as in the processes of adjustment to technical and economic change described in the previous chapter.

Finally, there is the point that economic growth is itself a means to the end of better living standards and a better overall quality of life at work and in leisure. We have earlier suggested that we can expect the availability of leisure to increase in the future. If this is so, the growth of education (and perhaps a greater willingness on the part of the population to accept re-education throughout the life-cycle) may itself be a factor essential to the full utilisation of the benefits of improved living standards. In the long run, education may be as important to us as consumers as it is to us as producers.

430 Current Issues

SUGGESTED READING

Gary S. Becker, *Human Capital*, National Bureau of Economic Research, New York, 1964.

G. G. Somers, 'Retraining: An Evaluation of Gains and Costs', in *Employment Policy and the Labor Market*, (ed. Arthur M. Ross), Berkeley, 1965.

G. Strauss, 'Apprenticeship: An Evaluation of the Need', in *Employment Policy and the Labor Market*, op. cit.

John Vaizey, *The Economics of Education*, 1962.

Gertrude Williams, *Recruitment to Skilled Trades*, 1957.

18 Security of Employment and Incomes

This chapter is closely related to a number of others, especially Chapter 6, on Employment Trends and Structure, Chapter 7, on Full Employment and Unemployment, and Chapter 16, on Technological Change and Automation. It has, however, its own particular point of departure, since it builds on to these others a much more detailed view of the implications of security and insecurity for those affected by them and the possibilities of improving security. Of course large-scale unemployment creates a situation of extreme insecurity of incomes and of employment in which detailed prescriptions give way to a need for much more general remedies. Current public interest in the details of security is in part a reflection of the existence of full employment which makes concern for detail appropriate and possible. In this chapter we assume a degree of full employment akin to that which has been experienced in Britain during the 1960s.

Security of employment essentially means that a worker has a job and can with some confidence expect to keep it, while security of income means that a worker can count on having an income that is fairly stable and accrues regularly. The two concepts are clearly associated, since security of employment is likely to ensure some measure of stability in the income flow. But variations in income can occur, for example, if a worker has a job in which the system of payment gives irregular wage packets, or if he is not entitled to full payment when sick and absent from work. Arrangements to maintain the income of a worker when he is between jobs can take much of the sting out of the loss of employment. In a broader sense security of employment may be interpreted as a situation in which a worker knows that if he loses one job he will readily find another. Some aspects of the security of having and keeping the same job are likely to be lost to workers if they change their employer, but if income can be maintained between jobs, and if the expectation of finding another job is warranted, which requires an assumption of full employment, an overall sense of security can be maintained.

Some sections of the community are much more accustomed to security than others, and to some extent the attitudes that go with being secure are those of the middle-class salaried and professional groups, whose life is built upon such a foundation. Some workers undoubtedly see so little of security in their prospects that they think of the future with a very short perspective. For them it may be more realistic to discuss security in terms of their immediate fears of being unemployed which, though they are associated on a longer view with a loss of purpose and place in the community, are invariably concerned with having too little money for next week. For some people, therefore, the fear of insecurity may be more real than the advantages of potential security, but the advantages of security should be stated, nevertheless, both because they are advantages which many employees have, and because they are benefits to which others aspire.

The first and most obvious advantage of security is that so much of a family's standard of life, and way of life, depends upon it. Without a secure income, which usually means a secure job, it is not possible to maintain a stable pattern of expenditure, and the point that a stable pattern of income and expenditure is a valuable precondition of maintaining a regular standard of living hardly needs elaboration. This is more than a matter of knowing from one week to the next that the money will come in. A longer-term view of expenditure patterns depends on knowing that a job will yield a given level of income, and also that the job itself will continue, or can be assumed to be followed by another job with a comparable income. Many workers want to own a car or have already acquired one. This is very likely to involve them in continuing hire-purchase commitments and will require quite regular outlays on running costs. The usual way to obtain 'a home of one's own' is to pay for it with a mortgage over a period of years, and running a better house leads to further regular costs for rates, telephone rentals and so on. In other words, a long perspective of secure income is a necessary precondition of a rise in a family's pattern of living, whereas a high but ephemeral income level is not capable of maintaining a real improvement in living standards, though it can raise consumption levels temporarily.

Security of employment and of income are associated with high status. Status in the community is to some degree associated with being able to maintain a good standard, or pattern, of life. Status in employment is often associated with length of service, which in itself may confer standing in his place of employment on the worker. In some types of employment there are seniority rules which formally relate status and type of work to length of service. Promotion opportunities are often rather scarce for wage earners, and where promotion is by selection, as it should be, length of service can be an important factor in the selection process, since it means that the employer knows a worker's abilities, and values his familiarity with the work in hand. Most types of fringe benefits which increase security of income by providing against sickness or retirement or redundancy are related to length of service, so that here security is important as a means to further security.

Apart altogether from ways in which security helps towards a better, and more protected, standard of life, it is also important to remember a further, less tangible point. Security of employment induces a sense of belonging and having a place in life. A secure income, and help in meeting the problems of sickness and old age, without necessarily implying some sort of paternalism, again add to a sense of belonging and being wanted. While it is difficult to quantify such considerations, it would be hard to overestimate their importance.

The remainder of this chapter will look first at the causes of insecurity, then at the means of reducing it, and end with some discussion of the costs of providing greater security.

II. Causes of Insecurity

The causes of insecurity are both numerous and complex, and discussion of them impinges upon many of the other topics of this book. The main elements will be stated here for brevity and clarity in an itemised form, dealing first with insecurity of employment and then with insecurity of income, finishing with a summary of the problems which arise.

INSECURITY OF EMPLOYMENT

Insecurity of employment is a reflection of a failure on the part of the market to achieve a stable balance between demand and supply. Closer investigation suggests that the causes of this imbalance are usually associated with factors operating on the demand side of the market, but there may be occasions when rapid changes in supply, relative to the long-run normal position of demand, will create an abnormal degree of employment insecurity. This may happen, for example, when the effects of a rise in the birth rate begin to be felt in the increased flow of young people entering the labour market for the first time. In much the same way, an increase in the proportion of older workers may cause an excess of supply over demand for this age group, and job tenure may become more precarious. Demographic imbalances of this kind are clearly less amenable to solution by a process of adaptability (such as through retraining) than are imbalances arising out of the 'acquired' characteristics of the worker.

In a full employment context, such as is assumed here, the basic problem of insecurity is essentially that of a poor match between job provision and job-seekers in limited areas of the market, and for this reason insecurity tends to be more of a problem for specific groups of labour than for others. We see this most clearly when we look at the sources and effects of variations in demand.

There are many causes of variations in the demand for labour which can give rise to insecurity of employment by removing, temporarily or permanently, jobs which were previously available. The following are some of the principal causes:

(1) Cyclical variations in the level of activity of the economy change the demand for labour within industries and firms. In the inter-war period this point was of dominant importance and was associated with almost continuous under-employment in most sectors of the economy, even during the periods of cyclical recovery. In the post-war years such variations have continued to occur, but they have been much less severe and have been linked to governmental policies motivated by problems of the balance of payments and of inflation. The familiar stop–go movement of the British economy in the post-war period has produced a variation in the demand for labour which, though it has taken place within a general condition of full employment, has nevertheless produced problems of redundancy and fluctuations in employment levels which have had differential effects on industries and regions. The consumer goods industries, such as producers of electrical goods and motor-cars, have experienced short and sharp variations in demand and in labour requirements. Capital goods manufacturers have, as is to be expected, been slower to suffer from reductions in demand, but they have also been slower to recover as the economy has gathered way again. The less prosperous regions have tended to have more unemployment than others, and before full absorption of available labour reserves has been achieved, the growth of their employment has been checked by measures designed to deal with balance of payments problems and difficulties of over-employment and inflation created by expansion in the more prosperous areas of the country.

(2) Some types of employment are subject to seasonal fluctuations in labour demand. This may come about because of seasonal variations in

demand for the industry's product, as in the case of the tourist industry. Variations in demand for labour may also be due to seasonal factors in the supply of raw materials, such as occur in food-processing industries, or to other difficulties in maintaining a regular flow of production throughout the year as occurs, of course, in the agricultural industry itself, and also in activities affected by weather, such as building and window cleaning.

(3) In a number of industries short-run variations in labour requirements occur erratically in response to fluctuations either in the demand for the product or the prospect of producing it. Such a situation may result in workers being hired as casual labour when work is available, rather than being 'stood off' when the work ceases. The best known example of irregular work is that of dockers, whose work depends upon the flow of ships through the port and the nature of their cargoes. Many forms of casual selling – for example from stalls or on sporting occasions – are also manned by casual workers, because of irregular demand.

(4) Deterioration in the demand for an industry's product affects the security of its employees. Such changes may come about for a number of reasons, of which the most important are the following:

(*a*) An industry may lose all or parts of its market as a result of technical improvements in the products of other industries. Candle makers, for example, lost work when new forms of lighting were developed. Television affected employment in cinemas.

(*b*) Changes in taste may harm particular industries. The hatters, for example, have suffered from the abandonment of the conventional requirement that a man should wear a hat to his work.

(*c*) Changes in the level and distribution of income produce changes in the structure of demand and hence in the structure of industry and employment. It is unlikely that a general rise in incomes will of itself cause an absolute decline in the demand for a particular industry's products. But a general rise in the wage level is likely to be reflected in the wage level of industries which have not experienced the general rise in productivity, and the product of such industries is likely to become relatively more expensive than substitute products. Sluggish prospects in low-efficiency high-priced industries, especially if these are not recognised in a reduction in recruitment, will cause insecurity of employment to develop. Moreover, generally higher incomes will cause shifts in demand within product groups from less to more expensive categories of the same type of product, so that some categories of producers and their employees may suffer loss of demand for their services.

(*d*) Industries are in differing degrees subject to competition from imports and have differing opportunities, and consequential risks, in export trade. A number of British industries, among which textiles provides a notable example, have suffered from competing imports with consequent effects on security of employment. Others with a prosperous export business have nevertheless been subject to employment variations as export prospects have varied.

(5) Technical improvements have been a main source of variations in demands for labour. This point refers both to changes in demand for one industry's product owing to competition from new products in other industries, and to technical change within a particular industry altering methods of production without necessarily changing what is produced. This distinction need not be overstressed, however, since on a wide enough view of a 'product' or industry it tends to disappear. For example, if the provision of power, light and heat is regarded as a single activity, technical change might simply be regarded as a matter of substituting one form or method of production for another with consequential employment alterations. Technical changes which alter the method of producing a particular product, whether the 'product' is defined narrowly or widely, will create changes in the composition of the labour force required, and may actually reduce it. For example, agriculture in Britain has both greatly expanded output and reduced its labour force since before the war, while the nature of many agricultural jobs has changed.

(6) The demand for labour will vary according to whether workers are regarded as part of the variable costs and resources of an establishment, or are thought to be part of the permanent commitment of the enterprise and charged to overhead costs. In the former case employment will fluctuate directly with output, while in the latter the labour will be retained and maintained in much the same way as the capital equipment, to be ready to meet future demands on the firm's resources. In broad terms salaried workers are more likely to be thought of in the latter and wage earners in the former terms.

INSECURITY OF INCOMES

Insecurity of incomes tends inevitably to follow from insecure employment unless special preventive arrangements are made, and all of the foregoing items are also sources of insecurity of incomes. There are, however, further reasons for fluctuations in the income of those who are in employment.

(1) Some systems of payment, especially overtime and individual incentive schemes, result in an irregular flow of earnings even to people who are in relatively secure employment.

(2) Within a given occupational grade and a given system of payment which allows for variation with output and hours worked, income and relative living standards may vary with age both for manual workers and in those professions in which income depends on the individual's rate of work, since the older worker will feel less able to maintain a high rate of work or undertake extra hours. Moreover, his ability to keep up the pace may well vary from week to week. The occupational position of the older worker who is apprentice-trained is generally more secure than that of the process worker without formal training. In some cases seniority rules secure the place of the older man. In others, such as coalmining, a worker is liable to lose position and income with age. One problem of income prospects is common to us all as we become older – the change in income when we reach retirement.

(3) Ill health is an obvious source of loss of income; chronic ill health creates irregular rates of work and frequent absences. Spells away from work because of illness are generally, in the case of manual workers, financed by sickness benefit from National Insurance but still result in a fall in income. In consequence, those who suffer frequently from illness are likely to have very uncertain incomes accompanied by fears of ultimate loss of earning power, while any wage earner who is sick for more than a few days is liable to find his income cut back to the level of sickness benefit.

THE CHARACTERISTICS OF THE PROBLEM

The characteristics of insecurity emerging from the foregoing discussion of its causes may be put in three ways:

(1) Insecurity is a problem which potentially affects all or most of the labour force, and therefore may influence the actions and fears of many who are in practice at very little risk. The need for action is, therefore, partly one of providing assurance or reassurance so as to bring an exaggerated concern into perspective. This leads naturally towards answers in terms of some version of the insurance principle. An insurance company is able for moderate rates to insure householders against loss from fire, because most householders may reasonably hope to avoid such an eventuality. It is, however, important to the well-being of all householders that they should feel themselves protected against loss from this source. If they were not protected, their actions in spending current income

on fire prevention devices, and in acquiring capital in the form of houses and their contents, would be likely to be affected. Similarly, while the risk of insecurity of employment and of income is uneven, this does not mean that increased security is only relevant to those actually at severe risk.

(2) The risk of insecurity is in practice most unevenly distributed among the labour force. It is much more of a problem, both in employment and in income terms, for the wage earner than for the salaried employee. The risk of insecure incomes among wage earners varies with their risk of insecure employment as well as with the way in which they are paid and any arrangements made to maintain earnings as they become older or when they are sick. The catalogue of sources of insecurity of employment given above indicates special risks for those in industries which are specially subject to cyclical, seasonal or short-period irregular variations in employment, and again special risks of insecurity arise with exposure to technological change. Seasonal variations in the availability of work are more usual in some industries than in others. The vagaries of casual work are a particular hazard for some but not for others, and while redundancy from cyclical or technological causes may be feared by most types of workers, in practice it is uneven in its incidence. In present circumstances of full employment combined with interventionist Government policy designed to vary the level of activity of the economy, employees in some industries, including some of the most prosperous such as the motor industry, are particularly sensitive to sharp variations in the demand for their services. Technological change affects some workers much more frequently than it does others. Moreover, in its nature technological change may from time to time fall with great severity upon a group of workers with a special skill which becomes no longer relevant, so that they move rapidly from security in the possession of their skill to being misfits in a new technology.

(3) In this situation of an uneven distribution of risk it is natural that special problem categories should emerge from among those who are more at risk than the rest of the labour force. In such cases general remedies for insecurity are likely to be inadequate, so that they become individual problems which need special attention. It should, however, also be remembered that it does not follow that public concern or action will necessarily cause individual problems to disappear altogether.

(a) The best evidence of the uneven allocation of work is to be found in the rather distinctive characteristics of the unemployed in a fully employed economy. This matter was discussed in Chapter 7 above. All that need be said here is that the unemployed in such circumstances, and especially those who have been unemployed for some time, are a collection of people with special problems, rather than a mirror image of those in employment.

(b) The unemployed in a full employment society are largely unskilled, and for a number of reasons the unskilled are generally more at risk of redundancy than the skilled. Men and women without specific training predominate in seasonal and casual work. During short-period fluctuations in the demand for labour, firms are more likely to try to retain their skilled than their unskilled workers.

(c) In contrast, one of the more intractable problems of adjustment to technical change is that of the skilled group which is deprived of its functions and still clings to its skill in the face of declining demand for it and growing insecurity.

(d) Variations in income while in employment are particularly relevant to semi-skilled operatives in industries affected by sharp cyclical variations in demand.

(e) The operation of seniority rules and the like can keep an older man in his job when redundancy is in question, but older workers, once displaced, have more difficulty than younger workers in finding a new job, and are apt to find themselves with lower wages in new employment. This is true of older salaried workers as well as of wage earners. It is not surprising, therefore, both that older people should be specially fearful of insecurity even when they seem to be in a protected position, and that the re-employment of older workers is a matter of special concern.

(f) While most of us are absent from our normal activities from time to time because of illness, some unfortunately tend to be more at risk of absence through sickness than others, with obvious consequences both for insecurity of employment and insecurity of income.

In our contemporary industrial society, problems which affect large parts of the community tend naturally to become matters for governmental interest and initiative. Problems of insecurity give particular scope for such initiative, because insurance against a broadly-spread risk can be conveniently provided centrally by governmental arrangements, though partially financed by contributions from employers and workers. In any event the State has an interest in the whole subject because of its implications for labour efficiency, and because insecurity may produce social problems among those who are most at risk. On the other hand, matters of securing employment and incomes are obviously of direct concern to workers and their trade unions and also, because of the effects on their labour force, to employers. We may, therefore, expect means of increasing security to receive attention from workers and trade unions, from employers and from the State. The next section looks at the means of increasing security adopted by each of these.

III. Means of Increasing Security

(1) WORKERS AND UNIONS

Workers whose employment and income are insecure, in cases where this is a well-known and anticipated feature of the type of employment in question, will, unless their bargaining position is weak, have levels of payment which are adjusted to reflect insecurity. To some extent, therefore, anticipated risks of insecurity may be compensated by higher payments designed to maintain labour supply to jobs which lack the advantage of continuity of employment and income. This situation appears to arise, for example, in the case of workers recruited on contracts in the construction industry. However, whether the risk is well anticipated and compensated, or is a hazard which cannot be measured in advance, workers who think themselves likely to lose their work or income may be expected to try to do what they can to avoid or postpone the risk.

One of the means open to workers concerned about the preservation of their jobs is to seek help from others – the unions, the employers or the State. Alternatively, they may try to keep their work in existence by their own efforts. Employers tend to argue, with some truth, that the best way to keep work available is to attain a level of high productivity and low costs which will obtain them more business, but groups of workers, especially if they are hired on a short-term or casual basis with no secure prospect of sharing in the future activities of the firm, are more likely to seek means of making their present job last longer by slowing down their rate of work. This is the essential origin of restrictions on output by work groups, and points to one of the disadvantages of insecurity from the point of view of the employer. For groups with some special skill one obvious way of proceeding is to try to appropriate to themselves certain tasks which then become their own property and cannot be allocated by employers to other workers, thus protecting their work by demarcation and the restriction of access to the job by other groups of workers. More general devices are to try to force a particular pattern of labour utilisation upon the employer which requires him to have a labour force of a fixed size for the work he wants done (manning standards), or to form a collective view of a reasonable but modest day's work which all members of the group adhere to, thus preventing high productivity (a worker-inspired task or 'stint'). If the work group takes up a strong and united position on such matters, and is able to instil the same view in new recruits, they may be able to force their employer into accepting these worker-imposed standards. There is obviously, of course, a delicate balance to be struck between ensuring a moderate but not high rate of work and pushing an employer into retaliation by forcing the rate of work lower than he will tolerate without going to the trouble of fighting on the issue with his existing labour force, or trying to obtain an alternative supply of labour or an alternative method of production. One particular device, which is often used by workers on incentive payment schemes to regularise their flow of earnings from a system which essentially varies earnings with output, is to set a standard of work and earnings and to ensure regularity of payment by stopping output when that level is reached, or by holding back from recording output beyond their normal level if the system permits this and feeding the record of work done in excess in one week into the records for the following week.

The extent to which small groups of workers may succeed in this type of protective action will be limited by the strength of their individual situation. A trade union will clearly regard improvements in the security of the employment and income of its members as a matter of importance and may hope to be more successful than the unorganised efforts of groups of workers. There are two types of action that a trade union may take on its own. First, it may strengthen the working rules of its members – demarcation, manning standards, regulation of output – designed to maintain employment and income by protective and restrictive measures. If a trade union is able to secure the agreement of all its members to such policies, this will make it difficult for any one employer to circumvent them. Secondly, a union may introduce its own attempts to help members in difficulties by such things as small-scale insurance schemes, informal information on vacancies, and benevolent funds. There are again, however, obvious limits to the extent to which a union can push its policy forward on its own. If it has to operate its own policy on maintenance of work it must be protective and restrictive and will therefore arouse the opposition of employers with the prospect of costly industrial action, and its efforts at insurance and other benefits will be severely limited by the funds at its disposal. We may expect trade unions, therefore, to put a great deal of their effort into encouraging governmental action and into coming to collective agreements with employers which satisfy security as well as other conditions sought by the unions.

(2) EMPLOYERS

Employers can help to improve security by voluntarily adopting suitable policies of their own devising, by entering into appropriate collective agreements with trade unions, or being brought within the terms of governmental measures. One reason for increased interest in security by employers is evident in the foregoing. If security is left as a problem only for workers and their trade unions, they will tend to protect their interests by restrictive measures. Employers have found themselves acquiescing in demarcation, in manning standards, and in other devices, in a series of operating conventions designed by workers to protect their position. If employers find themselves obliged to come to terms with such arrangements and to sign agreements on them, it is proper that they should become interested in devising schemes to improve security which lack the element of restriction and are designed to reflect the needs of the labour force. At the same time a greater concern for the welfare of the labour force is a natural reflection of full employment and labour shortages, and of a general increase in interest in improved relationships between employers and workers and in improved conditions of work. In Britain, unlike the U.S.A., though some arrangements to improve security have been included in collective agreements, many of the improvements introduced by employers have not been incorporated in agreements even though they have often been made in consultation with, and sometimes under pressure from, the unions.

Employers can contribute directly to security of employment and of incomes (i) by attempting to manipulate their demand for labour and their methods of paying labour so as to reduce the extent of the worker's insecurity and (ii) by introducing 'fringe benefits' designed to help workers in periods of income insecurity.

(i) Casual workers are by far the most insecure group in the labour force in terms both of income and of employment. Casual work generally arises from variations in demand, but security of employment can be offered to that proportion of the workers whose services are likely to be required even when demand is slack. If this is not done then periods of slack demand are likely to result in the whole casual labour group interspersing occasional work with unemployment. The prospect of such work will tend to keep a sizeable labour force attached to the firm, whereas, from the point of view of fuller utilisation of the labour and security for the workers involved, it would be preferable that some should drift away to other employment. Casual work can be further reduced by accepting some degree of delay in meeting demand and generally by attempting to find ways of spreading the demand for labour more evenly over time. The effect of smaller earnings during periods of slack demand may be mitigated by some form of guaranteed minimum level of payment conditional only on the worker being available for work and not on the work being available for him to do.

Seasonal employment can provide interesting examples of attempts to combine a stable labour force with a varying demand for its services. One way of doing this is to introduce complementary demands on the labour force by producing in the one establishment goods with different seasonal demands. If the seasonality arises from natural supply, so that crops for food processing are available locally only for limited periods of time, a regular demand for labour may mean importing materials for processing. Another line of action is to introduce machinery designed to reduce the labour requirements of the most labour-using parts of the process. If this is done, then regularity of use of the plant is an added reason for efforts to provide alternative lines of production out of season. Both the introduction of more machinery and the attempt to reduce dependence on seasonal labour are, however, in themselves the result of a tight labour situation. It is notable that where a ready supply of casual labour exists, as in many underdeveloped countries, employers have little incentive to try to do away with seasonal labour.

A wider view of efforts by employers to regulate the demand for their goods and the utilisation of their labour in the interests of a stable labour force is implied by the increasing attention being paid by firms to the 'development' of their labour forces, involving the firm in taking a long-term view of its labour requirements. The ingredients of such a view are an estimation of future labour force requirements by type of worker and degree of seniority, an analysis of the existing labour force by age, skill and experience, and an estimation of the extent to which needs will be met by promotion and new recruitment. Such a policy will be complemented by the creation of suitable training facilities for new entrants, and retraining and development programmes designed to fit existing workers for new jobs or additional responsibility. These training and development programmes are likely to be associated with attention to the occupational structure itself and the creation of new promotion prospects. To achieve the labour force balance for which it is looking, a firm will also need to associate its active manpower policy with schemes of redundancy compensation and methods of payment designed to avoid unwanted labour turnover. It is not, of course, possible for a firm consistently to predict its future labour requirements with accuracy, and unexpected variations in demand may occur. It is, however, a straight implication of such an attitude that attempts should be made to avoid variations in demand in the interests of the long-run stability of the labour force. This may imply on occasion that work is accepted with a below-normal expectation of profit and that workers required for the longer-term needs of the firm are carried over short-lived recessions by some form of work-sharing which is likely to mean a controlled reduction of income for a period combined with continued security of employment. Alternatively, the employer, often with the encouragement of his workers, may operate seniority rules which protect long-service employees from unemployment at the expense of recent recruits, though rigid rules may unduly restrict the employer's ability to hold on to promising recruits. Obviously, there are dangers in keeping labour if temporary maintenance of demand for labour should give way to having more workers than are really going to be needed for some time to come; but it has the merit of recognising the importance to efficient long-term operation of designing and developing a suitable labour force, as well as helping to ensure security for the workers. In contrast to a 'hire and fire' attitude, this type of policy also requires the development of skilled labour management.

Income security can be improved by changes in payment methods and special payment arrangements made by firms. In so far as income insecurity occurs while a man is fit and in a job, its source will be either the reduction of income associated with overtime and incentive payment methods, or a temporary but more serious fall in earnings associated with short-time working. There is a big contrast here between the salaried worker and the wage earner. The salaried worker is assumed to do his work without it being directly measured, and without a direct incentive relationship between output and payment. He is also expected to put in extra time at his work without specific overtime payment, but is generally less subject to long overtime hours. If the volume of work drops temporarily, his salary continues. Changes in payment methods for wage earners designed to increase their security of income are essentially steps towards salaried conditions. The introduction of measured day work gives the wage earner a regular wage while retaining an element of output incentive. A number of concerns have gone further and have tried to consolidate overtime payments in an increased basic payment, while reducing overtime working by improved performance in normal hours, and to consolidate incentive payments in a 'status' agreement, which gives salaries to wage earners, as well as other 'staff conditions' which also tend to increase security.

The guaranteed wage is a more usual means to improve income security. The basic idea here is simply to say that if a worker has made himself available for work, but his earnings have failed to reach an agreed level, he will be guaranteed at least that amount. The reason for lower earnings might be failure by the individual to reach the level of production and earnings anticipated by a payment by results scheme, but the more usual case is probably that in which shortage of work has resulted in short-time working within a company. The guarantee may take various forms, such as the guaranteed annual wage which is to be found in American experience, and is designed to raise income in periods of slack demand. The U.S. guaranteed annual wage may be associated with supplementary unemployment benefits which are introduced either to 'cushion' unemployment for a man who is laid off without the prospect of resuming work with the same firm, or to keep up a worker's income in a period during which he draws unemployment pay from public sources and waits for recall to his old job when demand increases. The more usual British concept is that of the guaranteed week which prescribes a minimum, or fall-back, payment for a week's work; but British employers also make considerable use in appropriate circumstances of the 'temporarily stopped' category in our unemployment arrangements by which workers are paid normal unemployment benefit, but are waiting to resume their old job, and may be taking turns of being in and out of work.

(ii) Employers may contribute to income security on a voluntary basis by fringe benefit schemes[1] related to payments in periods of sickness, which are a typical part of a salaried worker's conditions but less common for wage earners, and to providing compensation in the event of redundancy, either as a lump sum or as payment for a stated number of weeks related to length of service. Obviously too the development of occupational pension schemes based on service with a firm contributes to longer-term aspects of income security beyond working age. Superannuation schemes, which have long been common for many salaried and professional employees, are still unusual for wage earners but they are now becoming a much more customary feature. It is, however, difficult for employers on their own to give adequate security against loss of income in cases of long-term sickness, redundancy and unemployment, to provide full

[1] Cf. G. L. Reid and D. J. Robertson (eds.), *Fringe Benefits, Labour Costs and Social Security*, 1965.

guarantee against loss of employment or to ensure that all workers have adequate provision for old age. The role of employers in these matters therefore tends to be supplementary to, and supplemented by, that of the State.

(3) THE STATE

The State has increasingly become involved in recent years in measures designed to improve the security of workers. Its actions have generally been based on some degree of co-operation between employers and trade unions in the development of appropriate policies, but the policies when introduced have tended to have elements of compulsion either in requiring contributions or in laying obligations upon employers. Taken together, the various policies developed by the State represent a very substantial incursion into matters relating to security. This section itemises the most important ingredients of the State's policies, beginning with quite specific measures and ending with some more general policies.[1]

Decasualisation. Casual work is one of the most obvious sources of insecurity. The above discussion of employers' policies for decasualisation is framed in terms of adjustments made by firms. The problem of casual work, however, may extend over a whole industry. In the most notable case, that of the docks, it is not easy to secure a solution at the level of the firm. The State, therefore, promoted policies designed to achieve some degree of security of employment and of guaranteed payments for dockers on an industry-wide basis using a national organisation, the National Dock Labour Board, to administer its schemes. In 1967 a further step was taken to give dock workers permanent employment.[2]

Highly variable rates of payment and conditions of service used to be characteristic of the catering industries and of agriculture, in both of which there are seasonal fluctuations in the demand for labour. The introduction of Agricultural Wages Boards for England and Wales in 1948 and for

[1] A White Paper, *National Superannuation and Social Insurance* Cmnd. 3883, 1969, was published as the proofs of this book became available and indicated a number of substantial proposals for change especially in relation to pensions. Changes in redundancy payments are also under discussion.

[2] The change introduced in September 1967 is essentially designed to attach registered dock workers to registered employers as permanent workers. It was preceded by considerable preliminary discussion, the most important documents being two Reports of a Committee under the Chairmanship of Lord Devlin which were published in 1965 and 1966 (H.M.S.O.).

Scotland in 1949 (following upon previous machinery dating back to 1924), and of a number of Wages Councils in the catering industry, reduced the variability of conditions of service in these industries by fixing statutory minimum wages related to standard hours of work and other conditions. It would be wrong to suggest that these agencies have eliminated seasonal unemployment, but they have regularised the conditions of employment of workers and helped to create more stable employment relationships. In the case of agriculture, other factors – especially mechanisation and full employment, which has reduced the number of casual workers available at times of peak labour demand – have reduced both the size of the labour force and the seasonality of demand.

Sickness Benefits. Since 1911 there has been a series of Acts arranging for the payment of benefit to workers during periods of sickness. The costs of the present scheme and those for Old Age Pensions and Unemployment Benefits are carried largely by contributions from employers and workers, but there are also Exchequer contributions. Payments are made into and out of the National Insurance Fund. While sickness benefits are some guarantee against a complete loss of income through sickness, benefits were until fairly recently on a flat-rate principle (though related to family circumstances), which meant that a worker with a good income from work had a considerable reduction in income if he was off work through illness. This deficiency was met to some extent by the introduction in 1966 of earnings-related benefits related to enhanced contributions. The supplement, however, may not exceed 85 per cent of earnings and, subject to detailed conditions, the additional payment does not exceed £7 per week. A worker who suffers from an industrial or permanent disablement caused by work may receive special injury benefits and, if the case justifies it, he can receive a disablement benefit for life.

Old Age Pensions. The State, of course, also operates a retirement pension scheme for men over 65 and women over 60, which is again related to contributions by employers and workers supplemented by the Exchequer. There is also a graduated pension scheme. The system of direct taxation is arranged to give concessions for income applied by those in work to the creation of personal provision for old age. Supplementary pensions may also be paid on a non-contributory basis to old people (and also to those not in full-time work) under arrangements designed to help people in need, which were formerly administered by the National Assistance Board and now come under the Supplementary Benefits Commission which was set up in 1966.

Unemployment Benefits. The National Insurance Acts apply with few exceptions to everyone over school-leaving age and under pension age. Thus every employee is covered by provisions for unemployment benefit as well as for sickness and for retirement pensions. Any employee who loses his job, unless this has been the result of misconduct or he has left of his own accord and without just cause, is therefore entitled to unemployment benefit at the same rates as for sickness benefit and with the same allowances for dependants. The same arrangements for income-related benefits apply as for sickness benefits. Thus, while a worker when he loses his job will certainly suffer a drop in his income, he is to some extent protected and will now receive a limited degree of supplementation if his income in work is much above the level of benefit. The extent of the drop in income will depend on his family circumstances, which affect the level of his benefit, and on the level of his previous income.

Redundancy Payments. The Redundancy Payments Act of 1965 provides for lump-sum payments to all workers under retirement age who, after two or more years of service with an employer, are made redundant because their job has disappeared. The amount of the lump sum is related to pay so that a redundant worker must receive half a week's pay for each year of service between 18 and 21, one week's pay for service between 21 and 40 years of age, and one and a half weeks' pay for service between 40 and 65. There are limitations on the amounts payable, however, since earnings over £40 are not reckoned in assessing a week's pay and the period of service that may be counted is limited to 20 years. These two points together mean that the maximum possible amount payable is £1200, but payments are usually much less than this. The payments are financed partly by employers in the form of contribution per employee per week to a Redundancy Fund, and partly by the State, which meets the cost of deficits in the Fund. Payments are made by employers who then receive a rebate from the Redundancy Fund, which covers two-thirds of the cost of payments to workers below 40, and two-thirds of the cost of payments at the rate of one week per year for workers over 40 plus all of the extra half-week's pay per year to workers over 40. This latter arrangement avoids the risk that employers might be penalised for employing older workers.

These arrangements improve the general situation of the redundant worker by giving him a greater prospect than he previously had of maintaining commitments on his income, and to that extent improving his security. On the other hand, the redundancy payment is a lump sum, which is probably more usually of the order of two or three hundred pounds than the theoretical maximum of £1200. Such a lump sum offers only a limited prospect of coping with the problem of extended unemployment, and there is a risk that lump-sum payments may be used unwisely in once-for-all expenditures instead of being rationed out by workers to provide for a period while they are looking for new work. The earnings-related benefit arrangements again present problems of income-reduction. In one respect the Redundancy Payments Act may possibly have resulted in an increased tendency by employers to reduce their labour force when changes in the method or volume of work justify such action. Since two-thirds of the cost of any particular redundancy is borne by the Fund, and since an employer has to pay into the Fund whether he declares redundancies or not, he may feel that he might as well have some of the money back, especially since he may take the view that the State scheme takes away his personal responsibility to redundant workers. This is a favourable effect from the point of view of adjustment of the labour force to change and is discussed in these terms in Chapter 16 above, but from the point of view of security of employment it increases the risk of redundancy.

Contract of Employment. The State has recently taken a greater interest than formerly in the terms of employees' contracts to give some safeguard against sudden dismissal. The Contracts of Employment Act of 1963, which came into force in July 1964, has two main provisions. First, it requires employers to give their workers written particulars of the main terms of their employment – including the period of notice which they will receive if their employment is going to be terminated. Secondly, it establishes minimum periods of notice which must be given to employees according to their period of continuous employment with one employer. If a worker has been with an employer for twenty-six weeks or more he must have at least one week's notice. The period of notice must not be less than two weeks for those with two years' service and not less than four weeks for those with five or more years of service. Prior to this legislation employers had much greater freedom to determine their own policy on periods of notice. Practice naturally varied very considerably, but a week's notice was very usual for all types of wage earners irrespective of length of service, and shorter notice was not uncommon. The effect of this change in the law was, therefore, to cushion the shock of redundancy, especially for those with long service for whom it would naturally mean a major change in established habits. Longer periods of notice undoubtedly expose employers to the risk of losing labour before they can do without it; but the obverse of this point is that the longer period gives a worker a valuable chance

P

to think out his future, and perhaps obtain a new opportunity, while his existing employment is running out.

Employment Exchanges. The Employment Exchanges have been in existence for over fifty years, having been first introduced as Labour Exchanges by an Act of 1909. At various times in their history they have been regarded as being more concerned with unemployment and the payment of benefits, and with finding work for unskilled men, than with providing a full range of placement services. However, in recent years the Ministry of Labour has been trying hard to extend the specialised work of the Exchange in the placement of skilled and even professional workers, and has greatly changed the old image. It is clear that if rapid change in the labour force is to avoid serious difficulties and insecurity for workers, the effective operation of such a service is essential. One important feature of the recent work of the Exchanges in the context of redundancy is the introduction of special arrangements, and if necessary special personnel, to deal with any extensive redundancy. The Department of Employment and Productivity is trying to develop a system by which it will be forewarned of such an occurrence and be able to make prior enquiries among employers who are likely to be seeking the categories of workers being displaced.

Training and Retraining. The previous chapter discussed the subject of training at some length. Here it is necessary to make only three points. First, the broader the basis of an individual's training, the wider the range of jobs open to him and the less is the risk that his skills will become redundant. The long-run effect of the process set in motion by the Industrial Training Act of 1964 seems likely to be to extend the coverage of training programmes and to broaden the knowledge of the skilled worker. Secondly, an expansion of training facilities combined with greater flexibility in the age of starting training will help the unskilled to improve their chances of secure employment. The growing number of Government Training Centres are engaged for the most part in providing training for the unskilled, and are particularly interested in giving an opportunity of training to those who missed their chance of it as youths. Thirdly, with the rate of technical change which is nowadays likely, older men are in danger of finding their function in the labour force disappear unless they can be retrained for new tasks. Retraining may involve a full alternative course of training so that those starting on it are, in relation to the new skills, wholly untrained, but it also raises much more intricate questions of adapting previous skills and experience to new needs. This could be a very complex educational process

requiring courses of differing lengths and changing design. A full programme of continuing adaptation of labour to new needs has yet to be
developed and perhaps requires more knowledge about the relationship
between jobs than we currently possess.

Manpower Forecasting and Planning. This subject has also been discussed in the previous chapter. Its relevance to security is obvious but
important. If the State can help to anticipate changes in the demand for
labour by industry and occupation, especially for trained men, it can hope
to avoid some of the imbalance between the supply of workers coming
forward and the demand for them, with clear consequences for the prospect of security of employment.

This list of policies which are now in existence in greater or lesser degree
is impressive indication of the interest of the British Government in so
developing the labour force as to ensure its relevance to the needs of the
economy and its secure prospects. The only remaining point of importance
that need be made is that the success of all these measures, and of future
action in filling in the gaps that still exist, depends on seeing and acting
on all this as an integrated and co-ordinated policy on labour force
development rather than as a series of isolated, *ad hoc* measures.

IV. Security in Relation to Labour Costs and Efficiency

Two general problems always arise in discussing security: first that of the
cost of measures introduced to improve security, secondly that of the relation between security and efficiency. The two are related, since most of the
measures that add to the employment or income security of labour also
add to labour costs, and therefore naturally raise the question of the
extent to which this extra cost is compensated by improved efficiency.

Though statistics on labour costs other than wages are not frequently
available, the Ministry of Labour conducted a survey of such costs for
1964 and its results are summarised in Table 18.1. The survey was for a
period before employers' labour costs were affected by the Selective
Employment Acts which added to labour costs in non-manufacturing
industry, the Regional Employment Premium which reduced labour costs
in manufacturing in some parts of the country, and the Industrial Training
and Redundancy Payments Acts, both of which incorporate levies on

employers related to the size of their labour force. The results, therefore, are more than likely to understate the extent of non-wage labour costs. There are also many problems of definition which affect any discussion of labour costs other than wages.[1]

The most striking feature of the figures in Table 18.1 is their diversity as between industries. In general those industries with a high proportion of administrative, clerical and technical employees as against manual workers have higher non-wage (or non-salary) costs, reflecting the fact that fringe benefits are more generously available to salaried workers than to wage earners. Insurance and banking is a good illustration of this point, especially in showing greater proportionate expenditure on private social welfare provisions – very largely for superannuation and pensions. The sectors with a high proportion of nationalised industry – mining, gas, electricity, and water and transport – have a rather higher proportion of non-wage labour costs than the private sector. Construction, the industry group which is likely to have the greatest volume of short-term employment, has a low proportion of non-wage labour cost. Miners' coal makes mining and quarrying the only group shown to have any substantial outlay on payments in kind. The most important item in column (2) is payment for holidays, and the most important subsidised service is the canteen.

Despite the diversity of the figures in Table 18.1 – and much greater diversity between firms is obviously concealed by these very broad averages – two conclusions can be drawn. First, non-wage labour costs are a far from insignificant item of costs, averaging 15 per cent in manufacturing industry in 1964 and likely to be more in service industries where salaried employment is of greater importance. Second, while not all such costs come under the heading of provision for increased security, a substantial proportion of them do, including almost all the cost of private welfare provisions, and all the cost of statutory national insurance contributions.

Since it is thus obvious that security directly increases labour costs, even if we grant the argument that it is beneficial to workers we must still go on to consider its implications for efficiency. There are, perhaps, three related issues here. First, does the worker's incentive to work become stronger or weaker if he feels his income and employment to be secure? Secondly, does a system of employment which embodies a fair measure of security of employment, and of income, lead to the development of more effective ways of utilising labour in a firm? Thirdly, is the operation of the labour market in allocating labour between employments seriously hampered by security of employment, or, to put this point differently, is

[1] These are extensively discussed in Reid and Robertson, op. cit.

Table 18.1

Categories of Total Labour Cost in 1964 (percentages)

Industry	(1) Wages and salaries other than in (2)	(2) Wages and salaries paid for holidays, sickness and attendance at training classes	(3) Statutory National Insurance contributions	(4) Private social welfare provisions	(5) Payments in kind	(6) Subsidised services	(7) Recruitment and training and other labour costs
All manufacturing industries	85·7	6·1	3·6	3·1	0·1	0·8	0·6
Mining and quarrying	77·9	7·9	2·9	4·4	4·8	1·1	1·1
Construction	89·0	4·6	3·7	1·2	—	1·1	0·5
Gas, electricity and water	79·8	9·4	3·0	6·4	—	0·9	0·5
Transport and communications	80·9	7·8	3·3	6·0	—	1·0	0·9
Insurance and banking	72·0	7·9	2·5	16·1	—	1·2	0·4
Non-industrial Civil Service and local authorities	78·9	10·6	3·2	5·8	0·1	0·8	0·5

Source: Ministry of Labour Gazette, December 1966 and March 1967.

security of employment compatible with adequate mobility of labour? One of the popular – and yet also one of the more distasteful – pieces of industrial mythology is that the fear of unemployment is the best means to get work done. It is an idea that is difficult to prove. In its strongest form it requires for its demonstration the sort of level of large-scale unemployment which is itself very wasteful of resources and associated with low total output. Moreover, fear of insecurity is an immediate cause of restrictive practices designed to maintain work. But this type and level of unemployment is in any event quite outside anybody's view of what is entailed in a commitment to full employment; it may be hoped that it is a matter of historical interest, and certainly not the commonly relevant context for the future. In contemporary full employment there will undoubtedly be workers at the margin of employability for whom unemployment is both an ever-present threat and a spur to somewhat marginal endeavour. Reactions to security or the lack of it may, however, be expected to occur among the non-marginal majority of the labour force. For them unemployment is rather unlikely, but is a worry which may induce them to try to make work spin out, to secure their position by restrictive practices, and to hold back some part of their mental and physical commitment to their work. The purpose of increasing security for the majority of workers is, then, to remove a potentially exaggerated fear of unemployment, to reduce their inclination to save work for the future and to increase their sense of participation in longer-term policies for development of the concern. It is worth noting that these are almost the traditional objectives of the salary types of payment.

Within a given establishment patterns of labour utilisation change with changes in demand and changes in methods of production. Efficiency in the utilisation of labour is, therefore, closely associated with flexibility and willingness to change on the part of workers. At the same time, there is value in having workers who know the firm and its ways of working, so that it is not a convenient answer to problems of flexible working simply to get rid of one set of workers and employ others with different characteristics, even apart from all the associated problems of availability, costs of recruitment and obligations to existing employees. Workers who see themselves as having a secure future in their employment, and a secure income in it, are more likely to be willing to adjust their methods of work and accept change than those whose prospect of employment depends on a continuation of current production which requires the type of work they are trained to provide. The former can identify their continued prosperity as lying with that of their employers and have an incentive towards flexibility of working if that is the means to maintain prosperity for the concern. The latter must seek to retain possession of their present skill and, as far as they can, try to ensure a demand for it, since their employment is related to a specific work situation. Flexibility also arises in relation to hours and duration of work, and method of payment. The employee with a short-term outlook in a firm will naturally wish to take as much out of the firm as he can and to be specifically paid for all that he does. The more secure employee can see the advantage of longer-term systems of relating payment to effort and be willing to consider variations in hours worked without developing a complex superstructure of overtime payments. It is notable that contemporary productivity bargaining has tended to stress flexible working arrangements, reduction of overtime working and consolidation of overtime payments, rather more than the actual rate of work, as contributions to increased productivity, and productivity bargains have tended to seek productivity gains in return for and in association with improvements in security.

Even though it is possible to argue, as in the preceding paragraph, that flexibility and efficiency of working within the firm will be helped by security of employment, there is still the question of whether the labour market itself can operate effectively if workers have secure employment. Of course it is true that complete security of employment would invalidate the labour market's function except in relation to new entrants into the market. (It is worth remarking in passing that such a system could, with sufficient change in institutions and attitudes, be made to work. A high proportion of Japanese workers in the large corporations have that degree of security, and labour market operations are, therefore, largely confined to special recruitment within the schools and to an underprivileged and underpaid sector of casual workers.[1]) It is also true that a firm which set security of employment for its workers as a prior objective to that of economical production and marketing might simply be over-manned. There is, therefore, some need for caution in pursuing security for employees. In practice, however, there are obvious categories of workers who are not held immobile by security of employment, and the central question is whether the labour market can carry out its allocative function largely on the basis of movements of workers in such categories.

Statistics of labour turnover showing the proportion of new recruits in manufacturing industry who leave within a short time of joining the firm are not available as national averages. There is, however, plenty of evidence

[1] Cf. special section on Japan in *British Journal of Industrial Relations*, July 1965.

from detailed studies of firms to show that a high proportion of recruits to a firm leave within a few weeks and that the numbers leaving within a year are also substantial. Many of those who stay with a firm only a short time will be 'shopping around' for a job which suits them, and since they are, therefore, demonstrating their mobility, efforts to secure their employment are rather irrelevant, while changing jobs naturally causes variations in income as well. However, particularly after a complete year of service with a firm, the rate of voluntary leaving declines fairly sharply. Most arrangements for security, whether at the instance of the State or of employers, are related to workers with minimum periods of service with an employer so that those who move frequently of their own accord do not infringe on security provisions to any considerable extent. (It also follows, on the other hand, that people who have recently moved into a job and want to stay there are less well protected than those who have longer service, and this sets some problems for policy.) It must also be remembered that arrangements which are made to improve the sense of security include provisions for redundancy compensation and periods of notice of termination of employment. In other words, they do not deny the need for labour force changes but try to temper the effects.

From the viewpoint of the operation of the labour market, then, even if a high proportion of the labour force are in secure employment there will be a number of workers who move voluntarily from one job to another – though not always with any great sense of purpose or direction. Additionally, many workers who have recently taken up employment lack security in their new jobs, including, from the viewpoint of mobility and adjustment of needs for labour, the all-important group of new recruits to the labour force. If it is needed, redundancy can achieve further adjustment. There remains, therefore, a considerable scope for mobility to bring about adjustment in the labour market – a topic which is taken up in the next chapter.

SUGGESTED READING

G. L. Reid and D. J. Robertson (eds.), *Fringe Benefits, Labour Costs and Social Security*, 1965.

19 Some Problems of Labour Migration and Mobility

I.

Labour mobility has already been discussed in Chapter 11, where it was observed that it is a complex process, depending not only on economic conditions and motivations, but being influenced as well by social and institutional factors which, at least in the short run, could impede and prevent economically desirable transfers of labour. The aim of the present chapter, however, is to focus attention on a limited number of practical problems relating to the patterns and processes of mobility in the present-day British context. These are matters with some important implications for public policy, much of it directly in the economic field, but they are also amenable to the kind of analysis which has already been outlined in our earlier discussions. Consideration will be given here to both aspects as they bear on the particular issues selected for discussion. It need hardly be added that there are many other problems which arise on practical issues, which cannot, however, be properly treated here.[1]

The present discussion is confined to three main topics. First, in Section II, we consider the problems of emigration and immigration in Britain, with particular reference to the so-called 'brain drain' and the part played by immigrants in the British labour market. Secondly, in Section III, we consider the inter-regional migration of labour, which evidently relates to the current discussion of regional economic policy. In Section IV we will examine some characteristic features of labour mobility in this country. In the light of the discussion of these three sections, we conclude with some observations on the role of Government policy in relation to labour mobility.

[1] For a fuller discussion of such problems see particularly H. S. Parnes, *Research on Labour Mobility*, Social Science Research Council, New York, 1954; L. C. Hunter and G. L. Reid, *Urban Worker Mobility*, O.E.C.D., Paris, 1968; and P. de Wolff *et al.*, *Wages and Labour Mobility*, O.E.C.D., Paris, 1965.

II. Emigration and Immigration

The imperfections which tend to exist in the internal labour markets of a country are normally exaggerated in the international labour market. In the internal market there are frequently two kinds of barrier to movement: 'natural' barriers, including the distance between present and possible alternative job opportunities, the lack of good communications, differences in social custom and even in language between areas; and 'institutional' barriers, such as specific educational requirements for entry to an occupation or trade-union restrictions on the employer's ability to hire freely. In the case of inter-country movements of labour the natural barriers may be greater, especially those of language and distance, while the immigrant also has to face the same institutional obstacles which confront the native worker. In addition, there may be an additional set of restrictions relating to the entry of workers to the country itself. By means of immigration quotas or the requirements that immigrants should hold a work permit or have a job previously arranged, countries are able to control the inflow of labour. Some countries will also make it difficult for their own population to leave, by imposing restrictions on the amount of assets which can be removed by emigrants, or by withholding exit permits.

Despite the existence of social, institutional and economic barriers to the international movement of labour, there has been, historically, a great deal of movement, particularly in the periods when 'new' countries like those of North America and Australia were in the earlier stages of development. The size of these flows has varied over time, responding to changes in the 'demand' or 'pull' of the developing countries for immigrant population (and labour), and to the changes in the economic or political situation in the country of origin, which may be regarded as the 'push' factor. Historical evidence suggests that migratory flows of labour in modern times have largely been determined by fluctuations in the relation between 'push' and 'pull', with immigration being highest when economic or political conditions in the despatching countries have been worst at the same time as the demands for new labour have been greatest in the developing countries. In short, although economic conditions in the countries of origin and destination are by no means the sole determinants of the volumes of international labour migration, these conditions seem to have been among the most important.

The existence of major migratory flows of labour is an indication of imbalance in the labour markets of the country of origin vis-à-vis other countries.[1] From this point of view, the country of origin may welcome the outflow as a means of reducing the pressure on its internal labour market, just as the destination country may welcome the inflow as a means of augmenting its labour supply. But the existence of barriers to exit and entry, such as were mentioned above, suggest that countries need to control movement. Sometimes these will be non-economic needs. For example, in the case of immigration, a country may wish to exclude the nationals of certain other countries for political reasons, or may impose quotas on the annual intake of particular races either as a deliberate racial discrimination policy or to permit people of different races to be properly absorbed without discrimination into the social and economic life of the country.

There are, however, economic reasons for controlling immigration. An uncontrolled inflow of labour, perhaps willing to work for wages that are low by the receiving country's standards, may have the effect of so increasing the competition for available jobs as to cause unemployment in the resident population. Even if the country is short of labour, immigrants might lack the skill to take jobs in sectors of shortage; they would simply add to the competition for jobs where the supply was already adequate. So far as emigration is concerned, free movement may involve not only a loss of population, which may have received considerable education and training at the expense of the sending country's resources, but also the loss of wealth and capital assets which the country cannot afford to lose. If the country cannot retain the human capital it can at least exercise control over the movement of 'detachable' assets and, by such control, may discourage the movement of labour itself. Even a country with a substantial labour surplus and heavy unemployment or under-employment may find such a course of action necessary. While continued net out-migration could be seen as a contribution to easing the surplus problem, it may well be that those who leave to seek employment in other countries are not the unemployed and low-skilled groups, but rather the better-off, regular members of the active work force who have skills which will be utilised elsewhere. It is clear, therefore, that it is not simply the quantitative aspects of migration that are important. The qualitative or structural character is often the most critical matter.

[1] Historically, of course, some of the most important migratory flows have been movements of population, rather than labour, though the labour market effects of these movements have also been significant. Such movements may be only indirectly be related to the respective labour market circumstances of the sending and receiving countries, being generated rather by political factors, and by the appearance of new opportunities in developing countries which are not confined wholly to economic prospects and advantages.

(1) EMIGRATION

It is against such a background that we must review the role of emigration and immigration in Britain. This country has had a long experience of outflow and inflow, and at some periods has experienced a net gain from migration, though more commonly there has been a net loss. There is at present a growing annual net outflow, which has caused public concern, not least because of the qualitative composition of the two flows. This is the problem we now consider.

The point has already been made on a number of occasions in earlier chapters that Britain in the post-war period has experienced a persistent shortage of labour, mainly but not solely in the more highly skilled and more highly qualified sectors of the labour force. In these circumstances almost any losses of labour through emigration might be regarded as serious to the growth of the economy, but a loss of high-level manpower and skilled manual workers would be particularly undesirable, since the effect of such emigration would be to aggravate existing bottlenecks in parts of the labour market and, by preventing or delaying productivity gains, to reduce the welfare of those who remained behind. It is precisely this sort of worker who seems to have been most heavily involved in emigration, but to this statement we have to add a number of qualifications. In the first place, many highly educated workers in science and the professions spend periods of a year or more abroad as a means of improving their skills and advancing their knowledge, but they may have no intention of remaining abroad. Further, on returning home they may bring with them superior skills which will aid the production of goods or knowledge in that country. From the sending country's point of view this period abroad is in the nature of an investment. Secondly, some of the high-level manpower which goes abroad, either for short one- or two-year spells or for much longer periods, goes to less developed countries not so much to advance its own personal expertise as to serve the developing country which is short of such skills, by teaching, technical advice, raising health standards and so on. Though this may impose economic costs on the sending country, most developed countries have traditionally rendered service of this kind and the economic costs and returns are not the only criteria in such cases.[1] Yet both those who spend time abroad to improve

[1] Even so, the economic costs must be counted. The gains from this 'export' may be political rather than economic, or they may be reflected in increased trade with the developing countries. Seldom will there be a complete loss to the sending country.

their expertise and those who go abroad to work in developing countries are generally included in migration statistics,[1] along with those who migrate 'permanently' and those who do so for personal reasons which may or may not include higher financial rewards. This kind of ambiguity has confused the discussion of the brain drain, but some sense of perspective has been put on the debate by a recent report on the subject, with special reference to engineers, technologists and scientists.[2]

Table 19.1

Estimated emigration of British and Commonwealth engineers, technologists and scientists going abroad for a minimum of one year (compared with new supply 1958 to 1963)

		Engineers and technologists		Scientists	
	Total emigration	Total	As % of new supply 3 years earlier	Total	As % of new supply 3 years earlier
1961	3200	1900	24	1300	22
1962	3500	2200	27	1300	20
1963	4000	2500	27	1500	20
1964	4700	3100	32	1700	22
1965	5100	3300	36	1800	22
1966	6200	4200	42	2000	23

Note: Figures rounded to nearest 100.
Source: Ministry of Technology (from The Brain Drain, op. cit.).

As Table 19.1 shows, the total number of engineers and technologists emigrating (in the sense of going abroad for at least one year) almost doubled between 1961 and 1966. There has also been a rise, from 24 to 42 per cent, in the proportion of those recently completing training – the

[1] Statistics of emigration and immigration for most countries, including Britain, are generally unsatisfactory for the purposes of this kind of discussion. International practice is, by convention, to include as emigrants those who go abroad with the intention of staying abroad for at least one year. But some of these will go abroad with every intention of returning within a period of two or three years.
[2] The Brain Drain, Report of the Working Group on Migration, Committee on Manpower Resources for Science and Technology, Cmnd. 3417, H.M.S.O., 1967.

source of replacement and net addition to the existing stock. For scientists the position has been rather different: the number has risen but the proportion emigrating has remained steady. This difference might be taken to imply a deterioration in the relative status or salaries of engineers and technologists in this country relative to North America, where most emigrants have gone; or it could be no more than a change in the desire of engineers for experience abroad or for travel. The first of these explanations seems most likely, for a number of reasons.

Table 19.2 shows that the deficit on the migration of all three categories of workers together has been growing since 1961 and that the proportion going to North America has increased from 40 to 50 per cent. Also, the United States has experienced an increase in demand for these workers

Table 19.2

Gross flows and approximate net balance of migration of engineers, technologists and scientists

	Outward flow	Inward flow	Net balance	% of outward flow going to North America
1961	3220	3215	−5	40
1962	3510	3170	−340	41
1963	3965	2535	−1430	42
1964	4745	3170*	−1575*	42
1965	5065	3290*	−1775*	46
1966	6215	3520*	−2695	50

* Estimated from incomplete data, and to be looked upon as orders of magnitude only.

Source: As for Table 19.1.

which has outrun the supply being produced there, owing to the vast aerospace programme, the requirements of the Vietnam war and the growth of demand in private industry and in Government service. It is in engineering and technology (as opposed to science) that the United States has believed itself to be most short of workers,[1] and it is in these sectors that emigration from Britain has risen. It is in these sectors also that

[1] The point is put this way, for there has been some academic discussion on the reality of the 'shortage'. See, for example, W. L. Hansen, 'The Economics of Scientific and Engineering Manpower', *Journal of Human Resources*, Spring 1967, and the sources quoted therein.

American companies and recruitment agencies have been active, in Britain and elsewhere, in trying to increase the flow to the United States; and the income differentials and working conditions, though not *sufficient* conditions for migration in themselves, have certainly been favourable to the success of such recruiting programmes. There has also been a strong 'push' factor on the British side, due to the uncertainty about the future of the British aero-space industry; and much of the emigration has been from this industry and the closely related electronics industry. And of course in the British–North American case, neither entry barriers nor those of language or custom have imposed much (if any) restriction on migration in the past. There seems little doubt, then, that in the case of engineers and technologists the brain drain is a reality. It is likely that in some other areas, such as medicine, the same process has been occurring, though the specific causes of 'push' may be rather different.[1] Three kinds of effects have to be considered: on the migrants themselves, on the destination country, and on the country of origin.

For the emigrant, the experience of working in another country may satisfy any one of a number of desires: more challenging work, better pay or higher prestige, better climate and so on. From the purely economic point of view, it is worth while mentioning that it is usual for the British graduate to have received during training a much higher subsidy from public funds than his American counterpart. For example, let us assume the existence of two countries which are identical except that one pays larger subsidies to education costs. If the rate of return on the individual's investment in education is to be equivalent in both countries, so that they will have equal long-run supplies of qualified labour, the earnings stream of the worker who has to pay more for his education will have to be higher than that of his counterpart in the other country. In other words, the higher training cost to the individual is repaid over the years in higher earnings. In the particular case of the engineer who receives his training in Britain, largely at public expense, and who emigrates to the United States, there is double benefit. He avoids the higher private cost of education which prevails in the United States; and he receives a level of payment there which reflects both higher *per capita* income in the United States and the fact that 'native' engineers must have a sufficient differential to induce them to enter a long course of education with a relatively high private cost. For the emigrant in this case the private rate of return (even aside from

[1] For further discussion, see J. Seale, 'Medical Emigration: a Study in the Inadequacy of Official Statistics', in *Lessons from Central Forecasting* (Eaton Paper No. 6), Institute of Economic Affairs, 1965.

tax differences, which also seem to lie towards the favour of the American side of the market)[1] is considerably increased.

So far as the destination country is concerned, the ability to attract, through migration, workers who possess skills that are especially scarce in relation to demand is a clear advantage. Most of those who emigrate are in the twenty-five- to thirty-five-year age group, and thus have most of their productive working life ahead of them. The training cost has already been largely incurred by another country, so that the product of the immigrant over the years is a net gain to the receiving country. Immediate labour shortages will be eased, and it may be more possible for resources which would otherwise have to be diverted to increase supply to be used elsewhere. By taxing the immigrant's income and expenditure, the receiving country will be able to derive a contribution to the social overheads imposed by the immigrant (the education of his children, his use of roads, hospitals, etc.).

Thirdly, there is the problem of the country of origin. It is easy here to adopt a nationalistic viewpoint which regards the loss of all labour as undesirable. From a strictly economic viewpoint, much depends on the condition of the economy at large. If, as in the present British situation, net emigration on a considerable scale is occurring in manpower areas where there are already more vacancies than workers to fill them, there is an immediate exaggeration of existing market imbalances which may delay development programmes or even cause them to be cancelled. The less easy it is to substitute other labour, and the longer it takes to train replacements, the longer will this situation of imbalance be continued. Furthermore, a continuing net loss from emigration means that to meet a given demand the country will have to devote an increased amount of resources to the education and training of the labour in question – and the opportunity cost of these resources may be high. A ready supply of new trainees may not be available: competing demands from other users of high-level man-power, a slowly growing working population and a rigid, unfavourable wage structure may make an increased supply in a 'shortage' occupation still more difficult to achieve. In greater or lesser measure, all of these strictures apply in the discussion of the brain drain in the British–American context.

There is also a rather different implication of this sort of migration for the country of origin. The emigrant not only reduces the potential produc-tion of the country, but he also removes a source of Government revenue from taxation, and this taxation might be regarded in part as a means of paying back the society's earlier investment costs. It has been argued that

[1] Cf. *The Brain Drain*, op. cit.

the financing of education can be regarded as a transfer of resources from one generation to another; the adult population of today forgoes consumption to finance the education of its children, who will subsequently do the same for their children. But the emigrant removes not only his contribution to Government revenue, but his children as well, who would have incurred social educational costs. From this point of view, the emigrant is *not* guilty of failing to repay a debt to society.[1] But it may also be argued that taxation on today's working population is in part a means of providing for the older population, who have previously contributed to the education of today's working population. In that case the emigrant *does* fail to repay his debt to the previous generations who have invested in his education in the expectation that this education would contribute to their welfare in old age.

There are, as yet, too many unquantified aspects of this whole process of emigration of high-level manpower for a proper assessment of the overall costs and benefits. Evidently, there are some offsetting advantages to the country which loses such labour, and under some sort of non-nationalist welfare index there may be net gains. Yet the individual country with a shortage of high-level manpower cannot but be concerned about the implication of a continuing drain on its resources. However, it may reasonably be asked why, if there is a shortage in the country from which emigration is taking place, it is not possible to redress the outflow by an improvement in the conditions of the group in question. There is indeed some point in considering just what is meant by references to a 'shortage' of engineers in Britain, for example, and whether a change in the salary levels, career structure or utilisation of engineers in industry might not bring about an improvement in the balance of demand and supply.

(2) IMMIGRATION

Rather briefer mention can be given to the question of immigration into Britain, especially as we have now covered many of the possible lines of argument that arise in the analysis of international migration. In the first place Britain itself has experienced some immigration of high-level manpower (apart from the return of earlier emigrants), mainly from Commonwealth countries in course of economic development. Just as British engineers, for instance, find attractive prospects in North America, so highly qualified workers from developing countries find British conditions more attractive than those in their own country. However, the

[1] For fuller discussion see H. B. Grubel and A. D. Scott, 'The International Flow of Human Capital', *American Economic Review*, May 1966, pp. 268–74.

situation is not quite the same as in the British–American case, for some of the immigrants will have received part of their education (often at first-degree level) within Britain because of inadequate facilities in their own countries. Having made some contribution to their education, Britain will derive some benefit to the extent that students after training remain in this country, either to gain practical experience or to take up more permanent posts; in the former case the country of origin may have to wait a little longer for a more highly qualified and experienced worker on his return, but in the latter case the benefit of education is transferred from the sending country to Britain – an outcome which may be most unwelcome to the developing country in great need of engineers, doctors, teachers, etc.

However, by far the greatest proportion of immigration into Britain in recent years has been in sectors other than that of high-level manpower. A great deal of the immigration that has occurred has comprised lower-skilled workers from the West Indies, India and Pakistan, who enter a fairly narrow range of employments.[1] As suggested earlier, many of those who emigrate from developing countries are drawn from the industrial labour force and have some degree of training or work experience which may make the adjustment to British conditions easier, even though their previous training may not be used here, owing either to lack of demand or to the training not being of a high enough standard. As a result, the industries and occupations into which these immigrants go tend to be the lower-paid, lower-skilled. They are, however, acceptable to the immigrants because although such jobs are at the bottom end of the scale in this country, they will still afford a standard of living well above that which would have been attained in the country of origin.

The absorption of such immigrants into employment has been made easier by the existence of full employment and labour shortage. Although we have stressed the shortage of supply in the more highly qualified occupations, there have also been deficiencies of supply elsewhere, and perhaps especially at the bottom end of the wage scale and in jobs where working conditions are awkward or unpleasant (owing to continuous shift working, poor work environments, etc.). Such jobs have become less attractive to British workers in the full employment situation, since it is easier to find better-paid work with better conditions elsewhere, and more selectivity has been exercised than in past periods of higher unemployment. As a result, there have been persistent labour shortages in industrial sectors like public

---

[1] This is in addition to the traditional flow of immigrants from the Republic of Ireland, who are rather a special case. With the growing prosperity of Ireland, this flow may be becoming less important.

transport, especially in the high-employment areas of the Midlands and London, and it is to these areas that most of the Commonwealth immigrants have come. Comparatively little training is needed for such jobs; and elsewhere, as in the Yorkshire woollen textile industry, the Indian and Pakistani immigrants may have brought with them a certain familiarity with the work. In consequence, it has been relatively easy to absorb most of the immigrants into employment in these sectors, and undoubtedly labour shortages would have been much worse in these cases, had immigration not occurred.

Despite such labour shortages, and the slow growth of the working population, Britain has not adopted the policy followed by some other European countries (notably Switzerland and West Germany, who have had serious labour shortages in the post-war period) of setting out deliberately to recruit labour from labour-surplus countries such as Greece, Turkey, and until recently the south of Italy.[1] Indeed, in recent years British policy on immigration appears to have been based more on its political and social implications than on economic considerations. Economic effects have not, however, been entirely overlooked. A voucher scheme for immigrant workers from Commonwealth countries is now weighted in favour of work 'which is, in the opinion of the Ministry of Labour, of substantial economic or social value to the United Kingdom'.[2] Also, before foreign (non-Commonwealth) workers can be employed in Britain, permission must be received from the Department of Employment and Productivity. The conditions that have to be satisfied here are that the employment is 'reasonable and necessary, that no suitable labour is available in this country, and that the wages and conditions offered are not less favourable than those commonly accorded to British employees for similar work in the district concerned'.[3] Thus the country's manpower needs are by no means left out of account, but at least, in comparison with other European countries, it remains true that the economic considerations occupy a secondary role.[4]

[1] For further discussion of post-war European migration patterns, see, for example, G. L. Reid and L. C. Hunter, 'Integration and Labour Mobility', in *International Labour* (Industrial Relations Research Association) (ed. Solomon Barkin *et al.*), 1968. It should be added here that Britain did import workers as a deliberate policy in the early post-war years, the most notable example being the employment of Italians in the coalmining industry.

[2] Ministry of Labour *Gazette*, April 1968.

[3] Ministry of Labour *Gazette*,, March 1968.

[4] Though we cannot develop the point here in any detail, it seems fairly clear that both net immigration and net emigration are capable of affecting the level of

III. Internal Migration and the Regional Problem

In addition to the inward and outward flows of labour to and from the country as a whole, there is each year a considerable volume of labour mobility between regions and within regions.[1] From the economist's point of view these internal migratory flows have to be considered as responses to changing conditions of labour demand, due, for example, to the diminishing importance of some existing centres of employment and

Table 19.3

Distance travelled on occasion of last move (within Great Britain)

Distance moved	Percentage of those moving
Remained in same town/borough	64·0
Another town/borough – up to 10 miles	15·0
11–30 miles	9·2
31–100 miles	6·4
Over 100 miles	5·4

Source: Labour Mobility in Great Britain, p. 12.

the growth of new employment in developing communities such as the New Towns. The spatial distribution of the labour force is in many respects as important as its industrial and occupational distribution, and since geographical movement over any significant distance is usually subject to greater constraints than other forms of movement, the efficiency of

aggregate demand in the economy. In an inflationary economy suffering from labour shortages, it may matter a great deal whether, for example, net immigration will increase or reduce aggregate demand in the receiving economy. This in turn may have further implications for the future conditions of the national labour market. For an interesting discussion of this approach to immigration, see E. J. Mishan and L. Needleman, 'Immigration, Excess Aggregate Demand and the Balance of Payments', *Economica*, May 1966.

[1] For the present purpose, 'regions' are the Standard Regions designated for statistical convenience by the Department of Employment and Productivity. Although these are basically administrative areas, which include a diversity of social and economic conditions, and are not always the most appropriate units for economic analysis, it is possible to derive from the statistics a good deal of information about the internal migration of the labour force.

this part of the adjustment mechanism is a matter for concern to the economist.

Movement between regions almost invariably involves a simultaneous change of job and change of residence. But this kind of movement is much less common than either changes of job without change of residence or changes of residence with no job-change. As was pointed out earlier, in Chapter 11, the average worker is able to change his job within the local labour market area in which he resides, simply by an alteration in the journey to work. Again, people who move residence will most frequently do so for reasons unconnected with their jobs: marriage, change in family size and composition, slum clearance, and preference for better environments, are among the most important causes of change in residence. When such moves do occur, they tend to take place within the broad area of present residence, as is shown in Table 19.3, based on a sample survey of mobility in Great Britain.[1]

The table indicates that only 20 per cent of those who changed their place of residence between 1953 and 1963 had moved more than ten miles on the occasion of their last move. But further evidence from the same source suggests that roughly half of the 20 per cent were engaged in inter-regional shifts. Almost certainly, a very high proportion of inter-regional migrants would be involved in a job-change of some kind, though they may not have moved for job-related reasons. The evidence is, therefore, that by far the greatest amount of residential mobility is over very short distances, but that there is an important amount of longer distance-movement, much of which involves a change of job. In addition, it is known that while there is a substantial part of the labour force which is not likely to move geographically, there is a small part which is responsible for a high proportion of the movement that does take place, so that the total number of moves across regional boundaries will be higher – often much higher – than the total number of workers who have so moved.

In the past the Ministry of Labour has provided estimates of the volume of inter-regional migration. Between 1954–5 and 1963–4, the average number of *employees* migrating across regional boundaries was about half a million per annum, but the number has risen over the decade from just over 400,000 to over 600,000, with a major rise about 1959.[2] These

---

[1] Amelia I. Harris, *Labour Mobility in Great Britain, 1953–63*, Government Social Survey, H.M.S.O., 1966.

[2] Ministry of Labour *Gazette*, June 1965, pp. 299–303. Unfortunately it is not possible to give later figures of inter-regional migration. A note in the Ministry of Labour *Gazette*, February 1968 (p. 120), explains that more recent published

figures relate to *gross* movements of employees; the *net* flows into and out of individual regions are small by comparison, indicating that in any year the normal situation is one of considerable inflow *and* outflow. This is borne out by the data in Table 19.4. However, what is most striking about

Table 19.4

Migration of Employees by Region: Totals for 1954–5 to 1963–4

	Males			Females		
Region	In	Out	Net gains (+) or loss (−) by migration	In	Out	Net gains (+) or loss (−) by migration
South-East England	1095	903	+192	544	422	+122
South-Western	308	307	+1	146	141	+5
Midland	414	419	−5	166	178	−12
North Midland	354	340	+14	144	149	−5
East and West Ridings	336	347	−11	141	168	−27
North-Western	461	484	−23	210	219	−9
Northern	217	278	−61	87	111	−24
Scotland	189	274	−85	92	125	−33
Wales	199	221	−22	78	95	−17

Source: Ministry of Labour *Gazette*, July 1965, p. 300.

the figures is the clear pattern of net movement which is revealed over the ten-year period. Three regions – South-East, North Midland and South-Western – have experienced a net gain; and of these only the first is really significant. The seven remaining regions have had a net loss, the highest being in Scotland, where the net outflow was almost 120,000. Casual observation suggests that the net movement of employees between regions is highly correlated with average unemployment rates in the regions. Empirical investigation indicates that regional differentials in unem-

---

estimates (1962–6) had been cancelled owing to the discovery of serious deficiencies in the information available to the Ministry. Even the later figures given here in Table 19.4 are apparently subject to some degree of unreliability and must therefore be interpreted with some caution. It seems that in general the Ministry's published data have *over-estimated* the volume of inter-regional migration of employees.

ployment rates are important in explaining inter-regional migration of employees, but that they do not account for all differences in regional migration experience; it also seems that inter-regional migration of labour is most closely connected with the differences between regional and national unemployment.[1] Evidence pointing to a similar relationship between unemployment and geographical movement has been provided by others,[2] but closer examination suggests that the underlying mechanism is a good deal more complex than the simple relationship might suggest.

Most notably, perhaps, we have to recognise that net movements are the result of gross movements in opposite directions, and as Table 19.4 revealed, the regions of net immigration experienced a great deal of gross out-migration, while even Scotland with its large net loss had a gross inflow of almost 300,000 over the decade. If we are satisfactorily to explain the net flows, we must begin by explaining the gross flows – and unfortunately, perhaps, the relationship between gross flows and unemployment is by no means as clear as in the case of net flows. We must then reconsider the possible implications of the unemployment–migration relationship.

Our earlier discussions have pointed to the function of labour mobility as an adjustment mechanism. Movements of labour between regions, in that light, are to be interpreted as responses on the part of workers to differences in wage or employment conditions (or more generally, net advantages) between regions. As in our discussion of emigration, we can analyse movement in terms of 'push' and 'pull'. High unemployment or low earnings in one region relative to other regions will make labour more prepared to undertake movement from the poorer areas. The areas where labour is in short supply, and hence where earnings will be highest and unemployment lowest, will exert a pull. The movement of labour from poorer to better-off regions will act as an equilibrating force. To a large extent, the pattern of post-war labour migration bears out this view, for the areas which have received a net inflow of labour, such as the South-East and Midlands of England, have been the areas of labour shortage and high earnings, while Wales, the North of England, and Scotland have been experiencing a persistent net loss of labour. But if the direction of net flow seems to be in line with the predictions of economic theory, how are we to explain the sizeable reverse flows to the areas of higher unemployment,

[1] For fuller discussion, see F. R. Oliver, 'Inter-regional Migration and Unemployment, 1951–61', *Journal of the Royal Statistical Society*, Series A, 1964.

[2] Notably the work done in the 1930s by H. Makower, J. Marshall and H. W. Robinson; see, for example, 'The Response of Labour to Economic Incentives' in *Oxford Studies in the Price Mechanism* (ed. T. Wilson), 1938.

lower earnings, and less buoyant labour demand? Or, to put the point differently, the gross outflow from the North and from Wales, and the gross inflow to the South-East and the Midlands, is what we might expect, but the gross outflow from the regions of high labour demand and the gross inflow to the regions of lower labour demand do not seem explicable in terms of inter-regional differences in wages and unemployment. How then are we to explain them?

There are in fact a number of possible solutions, all of which may have some part to play, though it must be admitted that we do not have enough evidence to assess their quantitative importance. First, and perhaps most importantly, the higher unemployment, lower average wage regions are by no means lacking in attractive employment opportunities. There may be certain areas within the region, or certain industrial or occupational sectors, where prospects are less favourable than in other parts of the country, but there are nevertheless other areas or sectors which will be competitive with their counterparts in other regions. Thus the individual who moves from, say, London to Scotland will probably more often than not be making a move to increase his personal advantage. Secondly, we have previously mentioned the importance of personal attachment to an area. Workers who may at one time have left an area because of lack of employment opportunity may then be attracted back to it when prospects improve; and a great deal of new employment has been brought to such areas through the Government's regional economic policy. Thirdly, it is a normal part of the career of many types of worker to spend some time in head offices or the main works of a company – and many of these are located in London and the Midlands. Undoubtedly some part of the reverse flow is due to the return of such people to their regions of origin. Similarly, companies located in the south of England may send their employees to work for a time in branch plants in other regions. In all these cases, the direction of movement is perfectly explicable in terms of gains in personal net advantage. There are undoubtedly other reasons, many of which will be non-economic, but this of course will apply also to moves towards the better-off regions.[1] Finally, it has to be remembered that some job changes will be involuntary, as a result of redundancy for example, in which case the worker will be forced to make a job-change at a time that is not of his own choosing. In such cases, those who have previously emi-

---

[1] For instance, just as some people will be attracted to jobs in London for non-economic reasons, such as the availability of entertainments, shops, etc., others will leave London because of congestion, the housing problem, and so on.

grated may decide to return to their home area where financial help and other means of adjustment will be more readily available.

In summary, it would be misleading to attribute all regional migration to economic causes. From the resource allocation point of view, what matters is that the direction of *net* movement should be correct (i.e. to areas of higher wages and better employment opportunity); and in general this seems to be the case, especially for male workers. For women, the relationship is less strong, perhaps understandably, since many women will move residence as a result of job-changes by husbands, and their job-changing behaviour will be less closely related to the market conditions for female labour.[1] It is also important from the resource allocation point of view that the volume of movement should be approximately adequate to achieve or maintain market equilibrium, and this poses a number of difficult problems. Despite the amount of migration which has taken place in the last twenty years (as well as the improvements in job-provision afforded by Government policy and the restrictions on employment expansion in areas like the South-East), the relative positions of the regions in terms of unemployment and earnings has not altered significantly, though there has been some indication of a narrowing differential.[2] The difficulty is that the problem of employment imbalance cannot be solved in a once-for-all fashion, since its origin lies in a continuing long-run process of structural change, requiring equally continuous adjustment. Thus, for example, both coalmining and shipbuilding, both of which have traditionally been important employers in Scotland and the North of England, are by no means at the end of a period of contraction which has already been going on for many years.

The continuation of imbalance, because of gradual decline, means that net emigration itself becomes a continual process, and for many communities, perhaps even for a region as a whole, this may have serious consequences for the prospects of attracting new employment to replace that which is disappearing. For migration is most common among the twenty-five to thirty-five-year age group, and a prolonged outflow of this group will eventually produce an age structure in the community which is biased towards the upper age groups. Additionally, there is a good deal of evidence

[1] It will not be *unrelated* to the availability of jobs for women, however. For if, as we argued in Chapter 9, labour supply decisions are commonly taken on a family rather than on an individual basis, it is likely that the earnings of the family unit, and not simply those of the main earner, will be taken into account in decisions about migration. In that case the employment and income opportunity of the wife may be important at the margin.

[2] Cf. Chapter 5, above.

to show that migration is highly correlated with educational attainment and high job qualifications, so that continuing net emigration may also leave the community with a poor skill balance, biased towards the less well educated or lower skilled groups. This may not be encouraging for potential new employers in the area, for whom an adequate supply of trained or trainable labour will usually be a necessity. Thus, in the longer run, continued net emigration may result in a deterioration in the demographic and skill structure of the population which itself becomes a deterrent to the creation of new employment, and the cycle perpetuates itself, until the outward movement begins to decline owing to the fact that those who remain are the older, immobile, hard core of residents.

Of course, it may be that what is required from the national resource allocation standpoint is precisely this kind of rundown of existing communities and the creation of new communities or larger towns elsewhere. It may be that such a redistribution of labour is required to secure effective use of these resources, and that by migration to new employments workers will raise their productivity. At this point it is obstacles to migration that assume greatest importance – the factors which impede the desired mobility of the labour force. Mention has already been made of the costs, direct and indirect, of geographical movement: the costs of removal, the psychological costs of breaking up old relationships and forming new ones, and so on. We have also observed that it is the twenty-five- to thirty-five-year age groups which tend to be most mobile. Beyond thirty-five, the mobility of the working population declines strikingly until retirement age. Again, much has been written about the effects of housing on labour mobility – though in fact the picture now appears to be much more complex than was once thought.

Much depends on the character of the housing market in the country in question. There are, for example, significant differences between the situation in the United States (where home-owners are less mobile than renters) and in this country (where the reverse is more true). A large part of the British labour force is housed in accommodation rented from local authorities, and much of this is provided at heavily subsidised rents. The demand created by low rents is one factor – though by no means the only one – which has created a continuing housing shortage, and has led to strict rationing procedures in which high priority is given to the length of time a family has been on a specific local authority waiting list. Except in rather unusual circumstances, as for example where the worker is eligible for 'key worker' housing through a scheme operated by the Department of Employment and Productivity, the migrant worker will have to join at the end of the queue, with no real prospect of getting a house for several years. It is fairly certain that in many cases this system is a deterrent to mobility between local authority areas. The alternatives to local authority housing are renting private accommodation (which in most parts of the country is extremely scarce and expensive) or home-ownership (which is beyond the means or aspirations of many workers).

For home-owners the problem is rather different. Owner-occupiers in depressed areas, who consider movement to jobs in other areas, are constrained in two ways. First, they may not be able to find a purchaser for their houses; or, secondly, if they do, the price they receive will often be quite inadequate to permit purchase of a house in the destination area, especially if it is one of high incomes. The private housing market, like the labour market, is highly structured, and conditions vary enormously between declining and expanding areas. Again, mobility may be subject to serious constraints. Yet it is not clear exactly how far housing problems in themselves are responsible for restricting migration, for home-ownership and attachment to low-rent housing are themselves highly correlated with other immobilising influences, such as age, larger family size, service with a company and so on. It is in fact one of the greatest problems of mobility analysis that many of the variables are highly correlated with each other, so that it is difficult to determine the relative significance of individual variables. Thus, although we can be fairly sure that housing has some effect on mobility, we are much less sure how important it is in quantitative terms.[1]

Since geographical mobility is far from perfect, the redistribution of the population required by structural and locational changes in economic activity may be delayed or even blocked entirely. Public policy has to choose between taking work to the workers in depressed or declining areas and helping workers to overcome obstacles to movement by measures designed to increase the flow of workers to places where jobs are available. In the post-war period, Government policy in this country has been predominantly of the first variety, mainly on the argument that unrestrained expansion in the areas of highest labour demand, such as London, would cause increasing congestion and external diseconomies, while leaving social capital under-utilised in the outlying areas.[2] In other words, private and

---

[1] For an admirable discussion, see J. B. Cullingworth, *Housing and Labour Mobility*, O.E.C.D., Paris, 1968; cf. also the discussion in Hunter and Reid, op. cit., chapter VI.

[2] For an opposing view, see H. W. Richardson and E. G. West, 'Must we always take work to the workers?', *Lloyds Bank Review*, January 1964.

social interests conflict and measures have been required to ensure that the latter are accounted for. There has been a very limited amount of aid to geographical movement by Department of Employment and Productivity grants to individual workers, but the total expenditure on this has been minute in comparison to the sums spent on industrial location policy and related measures. The total number of workers aided by such grants is just as minute in relation to the total amount of movement. Yet the Department of Employment and Productivity has undoubtedly played a part of some importance in the geographical movement of labour, including inter-regional movement. The work of the Employment Exchanges in providing information about available labour and job vacancies extends far beyond the immediate labour market area. This information service is a crucial part of the whole interrelationship among labour markets, and probably taps a section of the market which is less well catered for, in terms of inter-area or national flows of job information, than others.[1] In addition, the increasing amount of retraining being carried out in Government Training Centres, many of which are located in areas of higher unemployment, and under the Industrial Training Act,[2] is a further factor contributing to the solution of unemployment problems in declining areas. Both the interest and the influence of Government in the regional problem, and its symptoms, are much in evidence, though questions remain about the scale of its operation and the direction of additional expenditure on regional policy.

IV.　Some Further Aspects of Mobility

A few observations can usefully be added on some non-geographical aspects of mobility. First, it is important to recognise that labour mobility involving a change of employer is reflected in turnover at the level of the firm. It is sometimes maintained, rather loosely, that a high level of mobility is 'good' for the economy since it implies a high degree of flexibility on the part of the labour force, and hence provides an index of its ability to absorb change. But high levels of mobility may equally mean that the labour market is functioning inefficiently and that job-changes are

---

[1] The limited evidence available suggests that the Employment Exchanges are most helpful to the unemployed and the less skilled. Cf. Hunter and Reid, op. cit., p. 118.

[2] As discussed in Chapter 17 above.

being made which are not only economically unnecessary but also undesirable; this will happen, for example, if workers are taking jobs on the basis of faulty information. The effect of this will be that movement takes place which leads to output being lost as a result of imbalances of labour supply and demand. Costs will also be incurred by employers who lose labour for reasons that are not connected with improvements in the efficiency of labour resource allocation. For such losses of labour will have to be replaced, and this involves expenditure on recruitment, induction and training.

The study of labour turnover is concerned both with the separation of labour from a firm, and with the engagement of new labour to replace losses from the stock or to add to the stock. Separation may be voluntary, when the worker leaves of his own account; or involuntary, when the worker loses his job through redundancy or dismissal. The former is obviously much less subject to control by the employer than the latter, and this is a point of some significance in a full employment society with persisting labour shortages in certain sectors. Workers are rather more willing to change jobs when employment levels are high or rising (especially when we consider the evidence that many, perhaps most, workers do not have another job arranged when they leave their present job voluntarily.)[1] The greater the relative number of outstanding vacancies, the better are the chances of a job-changer finding new work of a suitable kind quickly. It has to be remembered, too, that a new job may not always turn out as expected, and if expectations are not fulfilled, another job-change may follow quickly. This is one of the main reasons why the turnover rate is much higher among short-service employees, for the first few weeks' employment in a firm will test the validity of job-expectations, and certainly within the first year of service with a company the worker will be able to decide whether the job is suitable from a longer-term point of view. Thus the longer the service of a worker in a particular firm, the greater is the probability that he will stay with the firm.

On the other hand, if unemployment is fairly high, or if the unemployment level is rising so that job opportunities are becoming harder to find, the worker is less likely to consider job-changes – though of course the chances of his losing his job involuntarily, by redundancy, will increase. Thus there tends to be a strong inverse relationship between unemployment

[1] This is based on American evidence, which bears out that the majority of voluntary job-changers have no job previously arranged. For institutional reasons, such as the long-established, widespread network of Employment Exchanges, this may be less true in Britain.

and voluntary turnover, and there is some evidence to suggest that in several countries the *gross* rate of turnover (voluntary and involuntary job changes) tends to vary directly with the level of employment.[1]

These rather general conclusions have to be qualified to some extent to take account of other factors affecting turnover. Some industries, like construction and agriculture, have fairly wide swings in labour demand due to seasonal factors, and turnover rates are correspondingly high relative to industries with a more stable demand. Different occupational groups have different turnover rates: in general, the greater the skill, the lower the rate of employer change. The size of firm may also have some effect on turnover, since larger firms usually offer more opportunity for job-mobility *within* the enterprise and may be able to pay higher wages or better fringe benefits to keep turnover rates down. This is particularly true for workers in higher occupational levels, who are also likely to have better standards of job protection. Two other factors, age and sex, are also important. The older a worker, the less likely is he to change his job voluntarily, though there is a positive correlation between age and length of service and it is hard to distinguish the respective contributions of each factor. It is often maintained that women have higher turnover rates than men, and there might seem to be an explanation for this in the higher propensity of women to move in and out of the labour force at different stages of the life-cycle; but again it could simply be that the kind of jobs normally held by women are themselves characterised by higher turnover rates.

The amount of mobility in the economy is therefore subject to a great many influences, originating in social and personal as well as in economic characteristics. There is, however, some reason for believing that voluntary mobility is likely to be more favourable to an efficient allocation of labour resources, since the involuntary job-changer, especially in times of higher unemployment, will generally have less freedom of job choice and may have to make the best of a poor situation by taking a job which is only a stop-gap. Given this, and the tendency for voluntary mobility to be highest when employment opportunities are most favourable, we might reasonably conclude that both the flexibility of the labour force between employments and the efficiency of the labour market processes of resource allocation will be greater when full employment prevails. The only qualification to this conclusion is that when employment is at an exceptionally high level, an amount of labour mobility or turnover may be generated which is in excess of the economy's real requirements for labour redistribution.

[1] Cf. Hunter and Reid, op. cit., pp. 103–6; and P. de Wolff *et al.*, op cit., pp. 65-8.

A second point which now arises is that even when the *general* economic conditions for an adequate level of labour mobility are established, there may be important sectors of the economy where economic or institutional factors prevent transfer into or out of a range of jobs. There are several factors which may be of critical importance here.

(1) INFORMATION

The existence of an adequate market information system, providing details about existing job vacancies and labour availability, is essential to an efficient mobility process. Where information is lacking, the market will be inoperative and desirable transfers will be impossible. Where information is inaccurate or misleading (for example because full details are not available), misinformed decisions may be taken about job-changes, and either economically desirable movement will not take place or movement will occur which is not in the interests of the individuals concerned or of the economy at large. As we have already seen, information services are provided in a number of ways. The more specialised the labour, or the more expensive it is, the greater will be the interests of both employers and workers in ensuring that there are efficient communication channels. However, for a large part of the labour force, especially the semi-skilled and unskilled manual groups, the lower degree of specific occupational attachment and the greater scope for substitution of one worker for another will usually mean that no specialised information service will be established privately, and it is for these groups that the role of the public employment service as a recognised source of job information is most important.

In Britain, there is a well-established nation-wide network of local Employment Exchanges organised by the Department of Employment and Productivity. There is no compulsion on employers or workers to use the Department's services, although the unemployed must register at an Employment Exchange to be eligible for unemployment benefit, and this of course allows the Department's officials to derive information about a substantial proportion of job-seekers. On the employers' side, practice varies from firm to firm, from industry to industry, and with the state of the labour market. Many employers automatically notify job vacancies in their works to the local Exchange, in addition to any other forms of market coverage they think appropriate. The Exchange office then becomes a central point of the market, possessing a profile of jobs and job-seekers and the means of bringing about a contact between the demand and supply sides of the market. Short of compulsory registration of job vacancies and job-seekers, of course, market coverage will be incomplete,[1] but even so the provision of such a means of contact may make an important contribution to a quicker rate of placement, and particularly to a better quality of placement, for groups that might otherwise have considerable difficulty in obtaining acceptable jobs. The placement function is by no means limited to the local labour market area, though the majority of placings will in fact be local. There is frequent interchange of information among Exchanges, so that the coverage of the market is extended. In addition, the 'matching' function is backed up by other advisory services which cater for the information needs of young workers and adults considering occupational changes.[2]

(2) TRADE UNION RESTRICTIONS

A second source of resistance to mobility derives from the 'insulation' devices adopted by trade unions and professional associations. It is easy to overstate the importance of these barriers, and while we cannot ignore their presence we must admit that we do not know much about their quantitative significance. Mention has already been made in the course of this book of most of the important restrictions: the use of age limits and apprenticeship ratios to control entry to skilled trades, the specification of qualifications for practice of a particular occupation, the seniority principle and so on. Undoubtedly these restrictions are *capable* of restricting mobility, and especially occupational transfer, since many of the protective practices are formed on narrow occupational lines. Whether they *actually* cause movement to be seriously restricted is another question. Many of the trade-union practices derive from fears about secular declines in employment opportunity, and if in fact an occupation is declining it is to the advantage of all that workers should be discouraged from entering the occupation. The real problem arises when employment opportunities are expanding, and where restrictions on entry prevent the transfer of workers from other occupations or an increase in the intake of new labour force entrants. Yet there are indications that in these circumstances the relevant

---

[1] There have been occasions where emergency conditions have led Government to control the registration of vacancies and the process of engagement.

[2] These functions are carried out by the Youth Employment Officers and by the Occupational Guidance Units of the Department of Employment and Productivity, and of course their work is related to the provisions now made for industrial training.

unions do appreciate the position and, while not perhaps going as far as employers would wish – which may be a complete relaxation of entry barriers – they do make some attempt to ease the supply situation. A further point here is that even if entry barriers were entirely relaxed, this might not in itself be a sufficient condition for the generation of net mobility into the occupation. Much would still depend on the nature of the job, its standing in the earnings structure, and other factors bearing on the elasticity of supply to that type of work. This is a point to which we return in (4) below.

(3) COMPANY EMPLOYMENT POLICIES

The employment policies of companies may have at least as much effect on mobility as the employment protection practices of labour organisations, though again it is difficult to quantify their importance. A number of different types of restriction may be briefly noted. First, employers may adopt recruitment policies which discriminate against particular groups: among these, discrimination on grounds of age, sex, race and religion are of greatest importance. Even though, as was noted in Chapter 11, there may sometimes be objectively acceptable economic grounds for such discrimination, the fact remains that it will result in a potential restriction on mobility, and as such may give rise to a less than optimal distribution of labour resources. Secondly, employers may enter into informal agreements designed to eliminate labour 'poaching' (i.e. making direct offers of employment to labour already employed in neighbouring or rival firms). While the effect of this may be to restrict mobility, it will not always be disadvantageous, for with a labour supply that is inelastic in the short run, competitive bidding for labour may simply inflate earnings and labour costs without making any substantial change in either the supply of labour or its distribution. Thirdly, quite apart from other reasons for providing fringe benefits, employers may try to use these benefits to secure labour to their own firms. Perhaps most important in this respect are company pension provisions, the benefits of which will increase with length of service. It is frequently maintained that such schemes, especially if they are of the *non-vested* variety (where the employee on leaving the firm has no entitlement to the contributions made by the employer), inhibit the process of employer change. However, the evidence on this question does not seem to bear out the immobilisation hypothesis. A recent Report[1] on

[1] *Preservation of Pension Rights*, National Joint Advisory Council, Ministry of Labour, H.M.S.O., 1966.

Q

the subject indicated that pension arrangements were not an inhibiting factor and that many employees did not want preservation of their pension rights; it was found, for example, that 30 per cent of those in occupational pension schemes had the opportunity to preserve their rights on changing jobs, but only 8 per cent actually did so. For the older worker with long service, the pension scheme will usually assume increasing importance, but even though mobility does seem to be inhibited in such cases it is hard to tell how far this is due to pension rights and how far due to age and seniority, themselves factors which make for immobility.

Lastly, there is the effect of 'labour hoarding' by employers. There is a general presumption that during periods of slacker activity firms will pay off labour which may then be employed by other firms with better current trading conditions. However, if employers during such slack periods continue to employ their existing workers, they will restrict the amount of employer change and may exacerbate shortages of labour in other firms. Obviously, for firms to maintain their work forces will add to operating costs; and in a tight labour market situation they may actually have to engage in competitive bidding to retain their present employees, even though their own business is rather slack. Why then should they do so? The basis of this kind of policy lies in the labour shortage situation itself. Firms know from experience that if they lay workers off – especially skilled workers in generally short supply – they may not be able to re-engage them or find suitable replacements when activity picks up again, since they will have been absorbed by other firms, in the same or different industries. Also particular teams of workers, through working together over a period, may have special value to the firm and will not be lightly broken up or discarded. In such cases, there is a certain amount of economic justification for the practice of hoarding, though the individual employer's gain may not be a gain overall, if other firms are held up in their production programme by a shortage of the labour in question.

(4) WAGE STRUCTURE

The final major factor to be mentioned here is that of the wage structure itself. The importance of relative wages as an incentive to job-change is, to say the least, problematical. The view we have taken in this book is that we certainly cannot ignore the wage structure as one of the factors giving rise to mobility, and that in certain circumstances *changes* in the wage structure may be necessary to induce the necessary net flows of labour between occupations, industries, etc. We have, however, stressed that the *existing* wage structure may be capable of inducing much of the necessary mobility so that an expansion of job-opportunities in employments where the 'wage-signal' is in any case in the right direction (towards a higher point in the structure) may be enough to generate movement into these jobs. We must also acknowledge, however, that in the short run especially the pattern of relative wages, or changes in the structure, will not be *sufficient* conditions for movement. Thus, as the empirical evidence shows, it is quite possible for there to be significant changes in the numbers employed in particular sectors of the labour market without substantial changes in the relative wages of these sectors, while changes in wages need not be accompanied by changes in employment.[1]

Nevertheless, the achievement of adequate mobility in the desired direction may well depend on the wage-signal being in the right direction: in other words, if the wage in the sector requiring more labour is in excess of that in sectors from which labour might be drawn, the wage structure will at least not inhibit the required movement. If, however, the wage-signal is in the wrong direction, the pay structure may serve only to lock labour into existing areas of employment, even if opportunities there are shrinking, for there will be no financial incentive to encourage workers to move out. In a world of perfect markets, of course, this kind of deficiency in the wage structure would quickly be redressed, but in the real world situation a locking-in of labour is quite feasible owing to the effect of institutional influences on wage determination preventing wages from reaching their competitive levels.

In practice, this has not so far proved to be much of a problem. The greatest expansions in labour demand have occurred in occupations already favourably placed in the overall wage structure, and changes in employment opportunity within these grades seem to have been enough to generate net flows in the right direction, though other factors may have slowed down the pace of adjustment. In most advanced economies, the demand for labour in this century has tended to expand most rapidly in the relatively well-paid manufacturing sector; and particularly in the skilled and semi-skilled jobs within that sector; the wage signal has been in the right direction in any case. From our discussion of technological change, we have seen that manufacturing industry is likely to suffer a reduction in the relative numbers employed in the unskilled grades; and it may be that this effect will spread further up the scale with the development of automation, so that at least the relative rate of growth of employment in the semi-skilled and skilled occupations there will slacken. To some extent, this slackening

[1] Cf. Chapter 11, above; see also P. de Wolff *et al.*, op. cit.

will be compensated by growing demand for higher-paid service labour, so that, provided the educational and training programmes adjust accordingly, one of the problems of adjustment will be removed. Here again the wage-signal will be in the right direction.

But, as at least one American observer has pointed out,[1] the growth of service industries in recent years involves a growth of two quite different occupational groups – the 'higher' service occupations, including administrators, professional groups, etc., and the 'lower' service occupations (repair workers, barbers, some types of public service employee, etc.) whose current position in the wage structure is relatively unfavourable. Already in the United States the decline of the blue-collar (manual) worker in manufacturing industry is well established and the rise of the service industries equally clear; and there is evidence that other countries in Europe and elsewhere are beginning to share the American experience. If this is so, and if full adjustment of the labour force requires that labour should move out from manufacturing industry, the mobility problem may become more difficult than it has been in the recent past. Either it will be necessary for manual workers to move into the higher service occupations, where although the wage-signal is right the other factors inhibiting mobility may be more significant; or it will be necessary for them to transfer to the lower service occupations, where the wage-signal is in the wrong direction. Especially where wages in such occupations are determined 'administratively' (e.g. in some form of public service), it may prove difficult to adjust the wage-signal appropriately.

It remains to be seen whether the United States or other countries find that this is a serious difficulty, for there are several determining factors, such as the efficiency of retraining schemes, the ability of at least the skilled manual worker to be increasingly upgraded to the lower grades of management,[2] the pace of changes in the employment structure and the longer-run adaptability of the wage structure. Nevertheless the issue could be an important one in practice, and serves to point up the potential importance of the wage structure in relation to the mobility process.

[1] R. L. Raimon, 'Labour Mobility and Wage Inflexibility', Industrial Relations Research Association, *Proceedings*, December 1963.

[2] This in itself might be a problem in some countries. In Britain, for example, full employment and extensive overtime in manufacturing has made supervising jobs less attractive to skilled craftsmen since the gain in income is often slight and may at times be entirely adverse to movement to lower management positions.

V. Conclusions

Enough has now been said to demonstrate the proposition that the labour mobility process, though essential to the smooth functioning of the labour market and indeed of the economy as a whole, is by no means free from obstacles. The question then arises, whether and to what extent a policy for mobility is a necessary element in a country's manpower policy. We have seen that mobility is subject to influence from the general level of activity in the economy, and from that point of view the Government's regulation of business activity can be regarded as a means of regulating mobility. However, the arguments of the last section suggest that it is not possible to rely entirely on such a general method of control, which will tend to act unselectively in any case. Mobility problems, when they arise, will usually be of a fairly specific kind, such as an impediment on movement from occupation A to occupation B or from area X to area Y. The specific nature of these problems implies that there may need to be equally specific measures to remove the obstacles. To some extent this can be done on a broad scale; if we really believe, for instance, that housing policies of local authorities are an inhibiting factor, action can be taken to liberalise the allocation of houses to mobile workers. Likewise, attempts may be made to loosen the controls of trade unions over retraining, or to alter the attitudes of employers to the hiring and training of older workers or coloured workers.

Thus mobility measures do seem to be an important element in total manpower policy, quite aside from the general influence which Governments may have over the mobility process as a result of policies designed to regulate the behaviour of other variables in the economy. A considerable amount is already known about the economics of mobility, but there is much that we do not yet know, and it may be that an adequate policy for mobility will have to await the outcome of further research into the determinants of different kinds of mobility and the relationships between different sorts of job. In the interim, the importance of factors such as market information and some institutional obstacles is beyond doubt, and increasing Government attention to such problems is evidence that this is becoming more widely recognised.

SUGGESTED READING

The Brain Drain (Report of the Working Group on Migration), Cmnd. 3417, H.M.S.O., 1967.

L. C. Hunter and G. L. Reid, *Urban Worker Mobility*, O.E.C.D., Paris, 1968.

H. S. Parnes, *Research on Labor Mobility*, Social Science Research Council, New York, 1954.

P. de Wolff *et al.*, *Wages and Labour Mobility*, O.E.C.D., Paris, 1965.

20 The Labour Market and Inflation

I.

While full employment is in many ways preferable to heavy unemployment such as the British economy suffered between the wars, it carries with it some dangers of its own. It is a very short step from full employment to the type of strain on resources, and changes in prices and costs, which are associated with inflation. This has been the continuing problem of the British economy, and of many other economies, since 1945, and it has, of course, been attended by balance of payments problems as well as by domestic effects.

The aim of this chapter is to set out in quite a simple way some of the broad situations and problems which characterise the behaviour of wages and of the labour market in conditions of inflation, largely in preparation for the following chapter, on incomes policy. The approach of both chapters is rather heavily directed towards policy-making. This is a deliberate choice made for two reasons. First, it is not easy to enter into a theoretical analysis of inflation and of the movement of the key variables in the British economy with any prospect of a rapid treatment, and in any case such a discussion would go beyond the scope of the present volume. Secondly, the important task here is to try to show the elements of the policy dilemma and of alternative policy solutions, both as the most relevant and topical issue and as that most calculated to yield returns to the student. Since, however, the approach in this chapter is both simple and related to the aspects of inflation in this book, it necessarily follows that the account given here is in no way a substitute for a full discussion of inflation. However, further analytical discussion is available in a number of sources, some of which are quoted in the bibliography.

This chapter describes inflation and gives some account of the behaviour of wages, and of the labour market generally, in inflationary conditions. Chapter 21 begins by considering a number of alternative ways in which the level of money wages may be prevented from rising faster than the growth of productivity, and then moves on to discuss recent incomes policy in Britain.

II. The Meaning of Inflation

The first task of this chapter is to provide a very preliminary outline of the meaning of inflation. A demand inflation occurs when the total demand for the community's output is in excess of the community's ability to produce. If such a situation is not controlled, the gross national expenditure of the economy can be balanced with its gross national product only by means of a general price rise. But price increases are no substitute for additional supplies of goods and, while the economy reacts to excess demand by increasing prices, any balance between demand and production achieved by this means will be superficial in the sense that planned expenditure on actual goods and services will not be met. If the ability to demand the same quantity of goods is still present in the economy, then the gap between the volume of goods demanded and that available will continue and further price increases become likely. If one type of demand, for example Government spending in excess of its tax revenue, rises and continues to run at a level in excess of what can be provided without contraction of other demands on the economy's resources, then a continuing struggle for an insufficient quantity of goods is likely to breed a continuing tendency for prices to increase. In practice the level of output in most developed economies has shown a considerable capacity for growth, but so too has the level of expenditure, and the lack of balance has then taken the form of a continuing tendency for the growth in demand to exceed the growth in output.

Excess demand in an economy may be offset to some extent at least by a balance of payments deficit created by a fall in exports, or a rise in imports, or both. While immediately helpful in relieving internal inflationary pressure by making more goods available in the home market, such reactions in international trading relationships are associated with balance of payments deficits and with international distrust of the inflating economy's currency. Indeed, international difficulties have forced remedial action on economies suffering from inflation. Whether or not an economy is prepared to put up with the domestic inconveniences of inflation, if it is as open to international effects as the British economy it cannot for long tolerate a rate of inflation much greater than exists in the rest of the world.

Internal consequences of falling money values will appear in difficulties for those on fixed incomes such as pensioners, in difficulties in negotiating contracts in money terms, and in general unrest and competition to restore incomes to their previous purchasing power on the part of those who are capable of doing so. An unplanned redistribution of the purchasing power of the community will result. In addition to price rises, demand inflation also produces a whole crop of difficulties for the economy through shortages of all types. The excess of demand over supply will not be equally severe for all goods, and producers will differ in their preparedness to react with prompt price increases. Queues, postponements and uncertainties in delivery dates, and 'bottlenecks' in production due to failures in obtaining adequate supplies of particular raw materials, or sub-components, or types of labour, are all familiar features of a demand inflation.

Rising prices are the most characteristic symptom of inflation. But prices have actually been rising, and the value of money falling, more frequently than not for many centuries. While this long-period tendency can be described as inflation, it is more usual and useful to associate inflation with rapid price increases in a short period. The rise in prices must be general and more than a scattering of particular increases for particular commodities; and it may well be great enough to cause the economy in which it occurs to become uneasy and to begin to anticipate that money values will be unstable. At the extreme inflation can possibly lead to the rejection of the currency of the inflating economy as a measure of value.

While, however, for the most part inflation results in rising prices, it does not always do so. An economy may be suffering from excess demand which is being held in check by Government action. A 'suppressed inflation' occurs when price increases are prevented by price controls, and by controls over demand in the form of quotas, rationing, licences and the like. This condition differs from other forms of demand inflation only by reason of the steps adopted by the Government with the idea of making the burden of excess demand more bearable. It will show a strong tendency to develop all the disadvantages of an open demand inflation if, as is likely, the system of controls is not completely successful. Though the rapid increase of prices and its consequences will be moderated, this is likely to be at the cost of having a black market. The economy will also suffer the disadvantages which follow from the controls themselves: controls are expensive and burdensome and can be cumbersome in operation.

A 'cost inflation' occurs when price rises originate in increases in the costs of production such as rising import prices or wage increases. While excess demand pulls prices up by creating an excess of demand over supply, cost increases push prices up by making goods more expensive to produce. Because a cost inflation does not require demand to be in excess

Q 2

of supply before it can start, it carries the implication that costs and prices are capable of rising significantly over a short period of time without being stimulated by demand. Without excess demand we are unlikely to have the special problems of shortages and bottlenecks associated with demand inflation; but a serious rise in prices created by a cost inflation will cause all the consequences of falling money values, including an unplanned redistribution of incomes, and in practice cost inflation usually leads on to demand inflation.

III. Wages and Inflation

While there is plenty of theoretical argument about the validity of distinguishing between demand and cost inflation, such a distinction is necessary for an understanding of how wages behave in inflation or near-inflation. There are difficulties in practice in diagnosing the type of inflationary situation existing at any moment of time, but for exposition we shall use the distinction between demand and cost inflation here without apology.

1 WAGES AND DEMAND INFLATION

In demand inflation most prices, both for products and factors, will rise, and demand at existing prices will generally be in excess of existing supply and of any potential short-period increases in productive capacity. Wage increases and shortages of labour in the labour market are only one of many signs of excess demand and cannot readily be distinguished from similar phenomena in other markets. If a demand inflation suddenly arose from a period of stability, it might be possible with adequate statistics to form a final judgment on whether wage increases were the immediate source of excess demand. In such circumstances we could contrast the ways in which the product of the economy was allocated before the inflation and what alterations had taken place with inflation, and we could make some estimate of the source and strength of initiating forces. Unfortunately the start of an inflationary process is rarely as clear-cut as this. Moreover, once an inflation begins, all those capable of doing so generally make an effort to increase their money incomes and expenditure and so compensate for rising prices. If this did not happen, an inflation would stop once prices had risen enough to offset the original excessive increase in demand. Since it does happen, inflations have a habit of continuing and it becomes progressively more difficult to distinguish cause and effect as prices and incomes continue to rise. Price rises may be a reflection of higher excess demand for goods, or of rising labour costs. Wage increases may be represented as following price increases, or may themselves be the cause of price movements. Moreover, an inflation may develop a tendency to go in waves as reactions and adjustments are lagged: many price increases, including wage rates, are altered at intervals, while Governments are inclined to have spasms of specially energetic attempts to check inflation. This makes the whole problem of diagnosis difficult, since particular increases in incomes or prices may be argued as being in advance of the general movement or as catching up on previous movements. In practice, therefore, we must expect to find difficulty in isolating the particular contribution of wages to demand inflation.

Despite the difficulty of distinguishing cause and effect in the movement of wages under conditions of demand inflation, we can say some useful things about the *way* in which wages appear to move. Total wage payments – earnings – do not necessarily follow exactly the same path as changes in the rates (minimum, standard, etc.) which are negotiated in formal, and frequently national, negotiating procedures. In general earnings movements are smoother than the irregular upwards steps induced by negotiated changes. Moreover, earnings movements, as well as earnings patterns, are more responsive to demand pressures. If there is general excess demand for labour, earnings appear to keep going up, even if wage-rate changes are infrequent and not very extensive. This tendency for earnings to move away from rates is known as 'wage drift' or 'earnings drift'. In part it reflects extra hours of work, and perhaps also extra effort pulled out from workers in conditions in which there is obviously more than enough work for them to do, but it also reflects a genuine tendency for changes in the price of labour in the market place to move separately from the price changes formally fixed for it. The earnings drift does not of course affect all sectors of the market evenly; for structural reasons some sections of the labour market are under more severe demand pressures than others. Some formal wage bargains are more detailed than others and allow less scope for independent movement. And some jobs are organised in a way which provides fewer opportunities for offering and obtaining extra earnings.

The suggestion that the earnings drift is to some extent independent of changes in negotiated wage rates does not mean, however, that wage-rate changes have no influence on earnings. Wage-rate changes are settled by negotiations where a number of facts are important in decision-taking. Under demand inflation not the least of such factors is the extent to which there appears to be generally unrequited demand for labour. Once a wage-rate change is decided for an industry or any group of workers it appears to be largely added on to existing payments and so, though it may possibly narrow the gap between rates and earnings a little, its major effect seems to be to raise the level of both rates and earnings.

Wage-rate changes occur at intervals which, in post-war British experience, have shown some tendency to be of about a year's duration, and we have also found them occurring for most wage earners at around the same time of year. To the extent that there is some regularity in this pattern we have what is called a 'wage-round'. Even if the pattern is not regular, the whole wage level of the economy, both in rates and earnings, and the spending power of wage earners, are subject under demand inflation to a periodic boost upwards (sometimes called a 'ratchet' effect). The interval between these occasions is obviously of importance in studying wage movements and so the characteristic features of the 'wage-round' have been much discussed. For example, attempts have been made to identify 'wage leaders' who set the round in motion and fix the general level of advance in wages for the period. These studies have not, however, led to very definite conclusions: the wage leaders, if they exist, appear to change from time to time, and the 'wage-round', while a useful expository device, is less than precise in practice.

(2) MIXTURES OF DEMAND AND COST INFLATION

There are two types of situation which appear to be a mixture between a demand inflation in the labour market and a cost inflation in the product market. The first of these, however, is really a particular variety of demand inflation since it occurs when there is excess demand for both products and factors. The second depends on the proposition that excess demand may continue to exist in the labour market when it has been eliminated from the produce market. In each type both wage rates and earnings are on the move, and it depends on the frequency and extent of alterations to negotiated rates whether the gap between earnings and rates widens or otherwise.

(a) Excess demand for both products and factors may be accompanied by reluctance on the part of producers to raise prices in response to demand while wage increases occur, through negotiated wage-rate changes and increases in earnings associated with labour shortages, and lead to price increases through rising unit costs of labour. This is best regarded as a type of demand inflation where all prices are rising but wages are taking the lead and outrunning other price increases. It can, however, also be loosely described as a type of cost inflation, since the initiation of rising prices comes from costs. This situation, in which excess demand *could* be pulling up prices, but in fact prices have not risen unless pushed by rising costs, appears to have occurred in our post-war experience of inflation. There have been occasions when, while prices have been rising, they have not risen rapidly enough to come within reasonable distance of balancing market forces. The main burden of inflation has then been carried by shortages and lengthening delivery dates. In such circumstances producers have not been allowing demand to determine their prices but have been content to price on a conventional percentage above costs ('cost-plus' pricing).

(*b*) A cost inflation from the point of view of the prices of products may occur when the product market is stable but the labour market is still exhibiting signs of excess demand. Wage costs will then rise through demand pressures on labour raising wage rates and earnings as in a demand inflation, while product prices will rise through cost increases as in a cost inflation.

There is no general excess demand when the total quantity of goods demanded is not in excess of total supply at ruling prices. This does not mean that all items are exactly balanced, since there are bound to be many examples of over-supply and under-supply, resulting from structural mal-adjustments of the pattern of production to the pattern of consumption. But we tend to assume that the product markets are reasonably quick in adjusting these excesses and deficiencies, which do not therefore overthrow the general balance. Overall balance could, however, for a short period be accompanied by fairly evident signs of excess demand due to structural deficiencies. If we assume a tendency for prices to be reluctant to fall, even for commodities where demand is poor, while the prices of those goods which are temporarily short are rising, the general price level may rise even though there is no overall excess of demand over supply. In the labour market such structural factors are more important and more long-lasting, since the labour market is particularly slow to adjust to structural changes. Men hang on to occupations and skills which are no longer wanted, or are reluctant to move to new areas. A new occupation develops slowly, and a new community takes a long time to form. Because wage rates are slow to fall, and to some extent increases in them are based on comparisons between groups – the 'comparability' principle – rather than on the demand/ supply relationships for one particular group's services, structural im- balance in the labour market will mean that the presence of a group in excess demand may tend to exert upward pressure on the whole wage-rate structure. Excess demand and increases in wages and in unit labour costs arising out of structural rather than general imbalance will therefore tend to be more frequent in the labour market than in the markets for products.

The labour market may also show signs of excess demand when the product market is balanced, apart altogether from such structural difficulties due to regional or occupational imbalance. The demand and supply of products will be balanced if enough labour can be found in the labour market to produce the necessary volume of goods. But the number of regular members of the labour force does not always expand rapidly in response to demand for its services, and extra labour can be obtained only by more work from existing workers or by bringing into the labour market those marginal groups who are able to choose between working and staying at home, or who, alternatively, find it difficult to obtain employment when the market conditions are tighter. Thus a balance of demand and supply in the product market may be accompanied in the labour market by substantial overtime and bonus-working and by the appearance in employment of large numbers of married women and previously retired workers, possibly on a part-time basis, and of physically or mentally handicapped workers. These expedients will produce the necessary volume of goods but at the same time they represent an unsatisfied demand for workers which has forced expedients and higher real costs upon managers, who would prefer to recruit more of their regular type of employees. There will then be excess demand for workers though no excess demand for work.

(3) WAGES AND COST INFLATION

In a 'pure' cost inflation neither products nor labour are in excess demand: costs are increased, and prices are raised to cover rising costs. In the absence of excess demand in both product and labour markets an earnings drift is highly unlikely and generally rising labour costs must originate in increases in the negotiated rates of payment. Cost inflation by wages therefore involves the assumption that negotiated wage rates can be increased by more than the growth in output of the economy without there being a shortage of labour. Collective bargaining and allied processes are consequently taken to be capable of initiating a push on costs. If such wage-rate increases could be accompanied by reduced extra earnings per hour, total unit wage costs might not increase. But negotiated increases whether for minimum or standard rates have by convention typically been passed to all workers covered by the particular agreement concerned whatever their present level of payment. Moreover extra payments, which when added to rates give the earnings level, usually have a specific as well as a general purpose and cannot easily be taken away. Earnings reductions do not therefore generally offset rising wage rates, which in consequence initiate a push on costs. Such a cost inflation could topple an economy over into demand inflation. Labour has a high propensity to consume, so that a differentially high increase in labour's income is likely to have a greater impact on final consumption demand than an increase in income to other sections of the community such as profit-earners. Moreover an increase in the share of income and of the economy's resources going to labour will cause those dependent on other forms of income to attempt to maintain or increase their share of the community's resources. In demand inflation, where excess demand exists in both the product and the labour markets or in the latter alone, earnings as well as rates will be rising. In the 'pure' cost inflation case wage-rate increases are most important and an earnings drift is initially less likely.

IV. Inflation and Labour Utilisation

The way in which the labour market operates is changed by inflation in a number of important respects, most of which are touched upon in other contexts in this book. (i) Inflation produces changes in the characteristics of the supply of labour. (ii) Inflation puts the processes of adjustment of demand and supply in the market under special strain, and is associated with the emergence of shortages in some market sectors. (iii) Inflation may change some of the ways in which labour is utilised by employers.

(i) In a situation in which the demand for labour tends to run ahead of its supply we may expect means of increasing supply to emerge. Three changes may be mentioned. There will be an increase in the participation or activity rate associated with the movement into the market of people, especially married women and older persons, who would not in other circumstances have seen ready inducements or opportunities to do so. There will be an increase in the number of people taking the opportunity of holding two jobs. Both because some of the new entrants into the labour force are not available for full-time employment and because 'second jobs' are often part-time, there will also be an increase in part-time work.

(ii) The chief function of the labour market is to bring about an allocation of available labour to the jobs where it is wanted. The effect of inflation is to make success in this task impracticable in two ways. First, shortages develop in some sectors of the market more rapidly than others, both because of longer-term supply situations, and because of uneven short-period expansions of demand. For example, some types of skilled workers become specially scarce and the intensity of demand for labour relative to its supply is greater in some regions than in others. Secondly, unemployment has a function as a stock of labour needed to operate the adjustment mechanism of the market, and definitions of full employment recognise this by expressing full employment in terms of a minimum necessary level of unemployment: that is, the reserve should be kept to the minimum scale required to be consistent with labour force flexibility. Inflation erodes this usable stock of resources and reduces the unemployed to an unrepresentative selection of largely unskilled men who are difficult to train and include a high proportion of people with disabilities of one kind or another.

Firms react to the possibility or actuality of shortages in a number of ways. First, they will naturally try to make shortages good, which is one very understandable reason why wages, like other prices, should rise in inflation. Secondly, they will attempt to change the ways in which they use labour to find a road round their shortages – a point discussed in (iii) below. Thirdly, they will anticipate the risk of shortages and try to retain scarce categories of workers to meet future needs. This, of course, simply makes the collective problem worse, since it means that firms indulge in 'overmanning' and holding on to workers at a time when others are going short. In the nature of things the result is that firms may have too many workers, and yet having too many of most sorts of workers does not insure them against having too few of some categories. This type of situation is liable to produce high-cost production by overmanning, by over-bidding for scarce workers, and by bottlenecks and difficulties in maintaining smooth production flows when short of some necessary types of workers.

(iii) Since demand inflation is a situation in which both the demand for goods is high and the supply of resources is short, employers will obviously attempt to increase production by changing their utilisation of labour, though they are likely to begin with the handicaps of shortages of particular skills, mixed possibly with some degree of overmanning in other sectors due to their anxiety to hold on to some reserves. One way of avoiding the effects of a particular shortage is by introducing 'dilutee' labour. If the skill is not all that difficult to learn this will be successful, but it may in other circumstances be a wasteful procedure. Another possibility is to increase hours of work of existing labour by overtime, or the periods of operating machinery by shift working. Both practices, however, increase unit labour costs per hour. Means of increasing the rate of working, such as incentive schemes, may be used extravagantly and in inappropriate contexts. A general inflationary tendency in price levels will make it possible to introduce various means to encourage output without giving rise to too much worry about the effects of costs, but the payments which follow, though partly a reflection of the desire to increase output, also involve an increase in the price of labour and constitute a principal element of wage drift. Improved performance, moreover, also requires more effective management, with accurate programming of work flows, materials and deliveries, and the dilemma of the manager in inflation is that of having a market but lacking full control of his production, since he will be subject to arbitrary shortages and hold-ups in production caused by excess demand on resources. Labour shortages in inflation force attempts to improve labour utilisation, but also create real difficulties in achieving efficiency.

V. The Objectives of Policy

Having discussed some of the ways in which the labour market and wages behave in inflation, we may now conclude this chapter by trying to set out the problems which policy on this matter should try to deal with, and then in the next chapter consider policy alternatives in the light of what has happened in Britain. The discussion of policy will centre on policies designed to ensure that rising prices do not originate in wage increases which cannot be met from output; but an effective policy on wages must recognise the issue of efficiency in the utilisation of labour as well as issues of wage movements. A list of the main points that arise from the discussion in this chapter of problems of wages and of labour utilisation in inflation is an appropriate conclusion to the chapter, but it is also an appropriate check list of the main problems for incomes policy. (Incomes policy is a term which properly includes policies related to the movement of dividends, rents and other incomes under inflationary pressures as well as to wages and salaries, but here we shall mainly discuss it in relation to payments to labour.)

1. Under conditions of full employment and with existing forms and conventions of collective bargaining in Britain, wage increases can create a cost inflation.

2. There are two major elements of wage movements in full employment: wage rate increases and earnings or wage drift, the latter developing momentum especially with demand inflation. Wage rate increases are based on negotiated wage bargains, generally on a national industry-wide basis. Wage drift arises in part from bargains at a more local level. In part extra earnings reflect productivity improvements and longer hours of work. Wage drift is also simply a reflection of uncontrolled responses to market pressures.

3. National wage negotiations have shown a tendency to be instituted by trade unions as a matter of regular routine. They have been lacking in a detailed relation between wage increases and improvements in the rate and type of work done, and increases have to a degree been based on comparisons with each other, leading to 'wage rounds'.

4. Inflation creates strong pressures for more output and involves expedients to increase labour supply and productivity. At the same time, however, inflation removes cost restraints, giving rise to high-cost production methods, routine and inefficient overtime working, and degenerate payment-by-results systems.

SUGGESTED READINGS

The American Assembly, *Wages, Prices, Profits and Productivity*, 1959.
Organisation for European Economic Co-operation, *The Problem of Rising Prices*, Paris, 1961.
A. D. Smith (ed.), *The Labour Market and Inflation*, 1968.
United Nations, *Incomes in Post-War Europe*, Economic Commission for Europe, Geneva, 1967.
T. Wilson, *Inflation*, 1960.

21 Incomes Policy

I

In the previous chapter we indicated some of the broad relationships between inflation and the movement of wages, and some of the characteristics of the wage problems that emerge. The essential issue foreshadowed there was the capacity of, and the tendency for, the money-wage level to exceed increases in productivity under full employment conditions, and thus to be a major source of pressure towards rising costs and prices.

The term incomes policy essentially has a wide meaning covering all collective, or more strictly governmental, efforts to influence the level and structure of all forms of income, including, therefore, taxation and some forms of governmental expenditure. In practice, however, it has come to refer very much to attempts to control the movement of incomes under full employment in the interests of stable prices and of keeping aggregate incomes and consumer expenditure in line with the aggregate flow of goods and services available to meet such expenditure. In all recent pronouncements by the British Government the full description given to the policy as a whole is that of 'prices and incomes policy', thereby distinguishing between efforts to stabilise prices directly, and affect the level of incomes in that way, from efforts to control income movements directly, and affect price movements by so doing. Incomes policy in the hands of British Government has generally been intended to affect the levels of dividends, costs and other forms of incomes. However, the greatest emphasis in governmental statements and public awareness, and the greatest activity, has been in that part of incomes policy which is sometimes more accurately described as wages policy, and the wider term is now generally used to describe the set of policies related to earned incomes. In this chapter we shall discuss the issues mainly in terms of policies for wages and the labour market, without entering much into policies for other types of income except where specially relevant. Even so, as our subsequent discussion will show, there are variations in policy alternatives for incomes policy in this narrower sense, and related variations in objectives. Policies may be designed to obtain their results by general or by more specific measures. They may be thought of as short-term or as long-term. They may be essentially a form of negative control, but may also, however, be given a more purposive look, especially in their longer-term manifestations, and be related both to changes in the structure and pattern of wage payments and to specific efforts to improve productivity.

The approach followed in this chapter is that of first setting out the broad policy alternatives in general terms in the next section and then discussing recent British policies in a further section. This particular method is followed for two reasons. First, it may help the reader to begin with the various alternatives without overmuch attention to the somewhat complicated details of actual current policies. Secondly, the precise form of incomes policy can change considerably at short notice and at frequent intervals. Any account of current policy such as that in Section III below is therefore bound to date very quickly, whereas the alternatives remain.

II. Policy Alternatives

(1) THE LEVEL OF DEMAND

One of the principal approaches to the problem of wages rising faster than productivity is to contend that stable prices can readily be maintained by policies designed to reduce the level of aggregate demand. The classic statement of that position is associated with a remarkably influential article by A. W. Phillips,[1] which analyses statistics over almost a hundred years to show the extent of changes in wage rates at different levels of unemployment. This article has resulted in a whole literature on Phillips curves which relate wage increases to different levels of unemployment. The most general proposition in Phillips's article, namely that wage increases are likely to slow down as unemployment rises, is not one with which there would be much dispute. The essential questions are of the degree to which this occurs, the level of unemployment at which relatively stable prices emerge and whether such a point, if it clearly exists, is acceptable as full employment. Phillips argued that at $2\frac{1}{2}$ per cent unemployment, wages were unlikely to grow faster than productivity so that prices would be stable. The relevance of Phillips's calculations has been questioned for

[1] A. W. Phillips, 'The Relation between Unemployment and the Rate of Change of Money Wage Rates in the United Kingdom 1862–1957', *Economica*, November 1958.

the contemporary period. His analysis refers to a long period generally characterised by much heavier unemployment than that of the post-war years, and his data are on wage rates only for periods when wage-rate data were none too reliable. These criticisms rather reduce the validity of Phillips's conclusion that $2\frac{1}{2}$ per cent unemployment would give price stability, and leave open to question the view that to relieve stability by reduction of demand alone might mean going to more than that degree of unemployment. At this point it has to be said that even $2\frac{1}{2}$ per cent unemployment as a U.K. average, which implies somewhat higher figures in some areas, has been above what appears to be politically acceptable, as well as being wasteful of resources in terms both of excess capacity and of under-utilised labour. Moreover, the short periods in which unemployment in Britain has been almost $2\frac{1}{2}$ per cent recently – for example, in 1963 and late 1967 – were also periods in which, despite efforts to achieve a contrary effect, wages were clearly very much on the move.

We are still left with the proposition that reductions in demand will damp down wage movements, even if the Phillips view is thought either not fully persuasive, or inaccurate in estimating the level of unemployment now needed for stability. On this residual part of the thesis two comments are appropriate. It does not deny that wage movements may be cost-induced within full employment, or that direct action to restrain wages may be both necessary and to some degree effective. On the other hand, it does suggest that some moderation of demand, even if it does not go to the alleged point of stability implied by $2\frac{1}{2}$ per cent (or more) unemployment, will be necessary or helpful to wage moderation even if not wholly sufficient or effective.

This view is quite compatible with the analysis of the previous chapter, which suggested that under conditions of demand inflation the price of labour, like other prices, can hardly do other than rise. It also gave reasons for supposing that there exists an intermediate situation, less than that in which it can be clearly shown that aggregate demand is too great for current capacity at current prices, where nevertheless there will be substantial tendencies to demand pressures upon labour, met by extra work and marginal extra workers but carrying with them implications for demand-induced wage increases for sections of the labour force and for earnings drift. In other words, if aggregate demand is high enough to generate sectional labour shortages and a general tightness of supply, we may expect first that wage rates will rise for demand reasons, even without pressures from wage negotiators or with little resistance to such pressures, and secondly that earnings other than wage rates will also rise, because of built-in connections between rising wage rates and parts of the earnings structure – such as the overtime premium and the base rates for calculation of incentive schemes – and because demands for labour will cause a demand – induced upward drift in earnings. Though we may suspect the view of some exponents of the 'demand-pull' thesis who seem to be advocating a solution *solely* by demand reduction, there is none the less a place for a demand-pull approach, even if we consider that demand reductions should not be pushed to the point at which prices are stabilised, or will not work on their own without more specific wage policies. Since deflation, and the management of the economy in general, require to be implemented by measures to restrain demand, we must now look and see how such general economic policies affect wages.

Fiscal and monetary policies. Both fiscal and monetary policies may be operated to secure at least a temporary reduction of demand, and can create overall balance of demand and supply at current prices in the product markets. We may, therefore, be reasonably satisfied with their ability to control earnings movements originating from excess demand for products, but not those which come from specific shortages of labour. Systems of payment related to output may also continue to produce increases associated with output changes, but not necessarily in a way which ensures that productivity improvements are commensurate with improvements in payment. An economy which has committed itself to full employment, even if it reduces aggregate demand to some extent, must still face the issue of inflation by wage movements at its most difficult, within the narrow bounds which can be described as full employment without excess demand for products. In such circumstances the general bargaining strength of labour will be less than it would be when there is excess demand but it may nevertheless be extremely strong. The control of wage rates arising from bargained settlements cannot automatically be assumed to follow simply from some reduction in the level of demand. Full stability will depend on what happens in the actual process of negotiation and bargaining.

Fiscal and monetary policies can produce 'side effects' on wage bargaining and the demand for labour, and some of these effects will run counter to the general intention of the policy-makers. Fiscal policy reduces the level of demand in the economy by increasing taxes, or by reducing Government expenditure, or by a mixture of both. Reductions in Government expenditure will have an immediate general effect on aggregate demand. While, however, some types of expenditure cuts – a reduction in defence expenditure, for example – will not be specially likely to influence the wage bargain in any more direct way, others – a reduction in subsidies or social services, for example – will raise the cost of living and so form part of an argument for wage-rate increases. If a budget surplus is attained by increases in taxes there is more likelihood of arguments for wage increases. Indirect tax increases, which are regressive by nature, will be specially likely to affect wage bargains since they will increase living costs through price increases in necessities, or widely-bought and widely-desired consumer durables. A mild increase in items of household expenditure may sometimes, indeed, be made the subject of quite disproportionate wage claims: increases in the prices of pots and pans resulting from the Autumn Budget of 1955 reverberated in wage claims for most of the following year. Indirect taxes may also influence the bargaining position of some categories of workers directly by cutting down the demand for labour in the industries which have been specially taxed. Increases in profits taxation or in progressive income tax will not be likely to bias wage bargaining specially towards wage increases and may help restraint on the principle that others are also suffering. But they are also not likely to be as effective or as certain as indirect tax changes in reducing consumption. Moreover profits taxes may in practice be passed on at least partly into prices, and income-tax increases may affect the incentive to work.

Fiscal policy attempts to bring the planned expenditure of the economy into line with its expected output, but it will not directly or entirely control any renewed growth in the public's spending. Though increased tax yields arising from a growth in expenditure and additional income will take away some part of increased purchasing power, some increase in demand will remain. If a wage-rate change takes place it can be passed on into demand and probably into increased total earnings. This may be anticipated by overestimating the size of budget surplus required on the basis of existing expenditure, but a larger surplus needs further tax increases or expenditure cuts, which for the reasons mentioned above may invite more wage claims. Fiscal policy cannot prevent cost inflation by wage-rate increases unless it has pushed the economy well below full employment and so greatly reduced labour's bargaining strength; and some aspects of fiscal policy may actually encourage wage claims, for example by raising the price level for consumption goods.

Monetary policy attempts to control demand by reducing the availability of credit and increasing its price, and by controlling liquidity and the money supply. Compared with fiscal policy it has fewer side effects which bear particularly on the wage bargain. Increases in interest rates may increase prices, but the extent of this for the wage earner will probably be slight. Special controls on hire purchase are much more likely to be of immediate concern, but while such controls may reduce purchasing power they do not increase prices, other than from relatively unimportant rises in interest charges, and can hardly be the source of strong claims for increased wages. Monetary policy may to some extent be used in a discriminatory way to curb specially marked inflationary demand for goods and for labour in industries supplying consumer durables and capital goods, and so reduce the strength of labour's bargaining powers in these sectors; but discrimination against these sectors is in practice rather an automatic consequence of using monetary policy at all, than evidence of its flexibility between sectors.

The most important distinction between fiscal and monetary policies in controlling wages, however, relates to their respective reactions to a wage-rate increase which takes place after restraining policies have been applied to the economy. A budget surplus has to be based on an estimate of the amount of excess demand in an economy. If wage-rate increases upset this estimate, increased yields on existing taxes will skim off some of the ensuing increased demand, but a large part of it can be passed on into increased earnings and generally increased spending power. Monetary restriction on the other hand can be represented as being capable of imposing a positive limit on demand, since it operates to reduce purchasing power and to keep it from expanding by reducing liquidity and the supply of money. If it is not possible to expand demand, either wage-rate increases will not take place, because their sterility will be realised, or they will be offset by compensating reductions, possibly initially in profit margins, and eventually in the total wage bill. It can therefore be argued that wage-rate increases will bounce up against monetary restrictions and fall back again, since it will be impossible for the excess purchasing power which they require to be produced. There is truth in this argument, but there are probably few who regard it as complete. There are many difficulties in the application of monetary stringency in as rigid a way as it would require. There are doubts about the extent to which increases in the velocity of circulation could offset reductions in its supply. The post-war economy has shown itself to be highly adaptable in developing new agencies for supplying credit.

Direct controls on purchasing and prices. Quota and licensing systems, rationing and price controls can be used in a demand inflation to suppress excess demand and prevent a general increase in the price level. Such measures can hardly be regarded as a complete alternative to fiscal and monetary policies since they aim to suppress the inflation rather than remove it; but they are sometimes advocated as an alternative or, more frequently, as a complement to other policies. If controls are successful they will eliminate earnings increases induced by demand, and generally stabilise wage movements arising from the effective presence of excess demand. But if demand has to be kept in check by controls for long periods it becomes rather like sitting on a volcano without knowing when and where it is likely to erupt. Since the excess demand continues to exist and is only kept out of sight, it becomes progressively more difficult to sustain such a policy. The premium for successfully getting round the controls is high, and a black market is likely. There will be continual small appearances of excess demand for products and labour and these will always threaten to become extensive. The prospects of movements in wages on relative grounds increase as break-outs from controls occur.

While rising earnings levels due to excess demand will be checked by such controls to the extent that the controls are good enough, we have also to look at their efficiency in reducing wage-rate movements. Claims for increases in wage rates are put forward by trade unions frequently in large-scale negotiations and are carried through in a welter of arguments and counter-arguments from the opposing unions and employers. If it is possible to remove the arguments which trade unions use to justify wage claims, or alternatively to strengthen the arguments with which employers try to reject them, wage-rate stability may be achieved. Unions are most favourably placed when their members are in short supply in the labour market; if excess demand is controlled or does not exist, then this strong argument is removed. In practice, however, unions have not used excess demand as a major debating issue in wage negotiations, though it has been a powerful force in the background to negotiations. The most important ground for wage claims in most of the post-war period, though less so recently, has been the rising cost of living. Wage-rate increases in line with changes in the cost of living are widely held to be be socially proper on the ground that they insulate workers from falling real wages, and the practice of granting or awarding increases in wage rates in proportion to increases in the cost of living has had wide application. The use of general price controls can help to do away with rising prices as a ground for wage claims. However, a variant of general price controls is usually given more emphasis as a means to wage-rate stability. There is a recognisable group of goods, including essential foodstuffs, which play a special part in wage-earners' expenditure and also in social arguments on living standards, and price controls on essential commodities may therefore be advocated as a method of keeping down the volume of wage-rate claims. Another variant carries this idea a good way further and suggests that a carefully selected list of commodities concentrated on essential goods should be subsidised. Such a subsidy policy may be particularly important in damping down wage claims based on the hardships of the lowest levels of wage earners. A further variant is to concentrate price controls and subsidies on the major items which appear in a cost-of-living index. This involves using an index which is unduly influenced by the movements of the prices of a few commodities, with the risk that the index will become discredited. This type of policy has occurred from time to time in various places; it appears to have been pursued in Britain in relation to the rather inadequate Index of Retail Prices which was in use in the early years after the Second World War, until the Index became distrusted and was replaced in 1947.

Rising profits are frequently cited by unions as justifying claims for rising wages, and controls on profits are asked as the price of moderation in wage claims. Price controls can be used to hold profits by squeezing profit margins, but direct controls on profits, especially profits distributed to shareholders, have also been suggested as part of a policy for wage-rate stability, and additional taxes on profits have been advocated for several reasons. Controls on profits could, for example, take the form of an insistence that previous levels of distribution of profits should not be exceeded, or could be implemented by the negotiation of a voluntary policy of dividend limitation.

Price and profit controls can be put forward as means of preventing employers from being able to grant wage-rate increases. The intention of the controls in relation to the unions is to dissuade them from pushing wage claims, but, in addition, if the price level obtainable by the employer is rigidly controlled, wage-rate increases are possible only as far as profit margins can be squeezed. Thus it can be argued that price controls will prevent employers from granting wage increases.

Enforcement of such a policy of controls becomes progressively more difficult as time passes and the controls proliferate, and it does not necessarily stop wage-rate claims but only removes some of the grounds for them. There are many other grounds available: for example leapfrogging claims based on relative wage comparisons can be substituted for claims based on price movements. Subsidies cannot be indiscriminately increased. Controls on prices and profits can hardly cover all employers' circumstances and therefore cannot with certainty restrain all employers from granting increases in wages, especially if as a result of an increase an employer is able to obtain more labour, greater output, and possibly greater profit, through increased sales. The most important doubts about controls, however, arise less in relation to their uncertain effects on wages than their much more general effects on the economy. A system of controls is clumsy and difficult to operate, and it tends to grow alarmingly as time passes and people begin to find ways round it. Changes in production methods and the range of products are always a possibility; these cannot readily be incorporated into the control system as rapidly as they occur, and so desirable developments may be stultified, while undesirable changes may be encouraged.

All the policy proposals discussed up to now have aimed to control wage-rate changes by controlling the backgrounds against which they take place – by removing excess demand, or by making it difficult for employers to give increases, or by trying to counter in advance the arguments on which wage-rate increases might be justified. *Undoubtedly control of excess demand is necessary to the success of any wage policy.*[1] It seems quite unrealistic to suppose that wage increases can be avoided if there is general excess demand; even if wage rates do not go up, earnings will do so and are likely in the end to force wage-rate changes on comparative grounds. But though price controls may sometimes be helpful, and control of excess demand is essential, if a wage policy is to succeed these measures are almost certainly not sufficient to stop wage movements on their own.

Since indirect influences on the labour market exerted by general economic policies related to the level of economic activities are not of themselves sufficient to achieve wage–price stability, it has been necessary to look further at more direct ways of influencing wage movements.

(2) ADVICE AND EXHORTATION

The weakest form of direct influence is to offer advice. Three versions of offering advice may be mentioned. First, the Government may simply keep reiterating the need for restraint in wage movements. There are various ways in which this can be done, of which the most obvious are by ministerial speeches and by featuring the point in published appraisals of current economic problems. This general level of encouragement for wage restraint is a familiar part of life in Britain and has been increasingly so for some years. It is, however, obviously difficult to assess the effectiveness of its contribution, except that it may help to develop the public's education in economic matters and indirectly at least have some effect on the social

---

[1] 'A firm and effective incomes policy is not a substitute for fiscal action as an instrument of demand management', Chancellor of Exchequer, Budget Speech, March 1968.

acceptability of certain measures of economic policy. Secondly, the Government may seek to offer advice on particular wage claims to try to bring them into line with its views. This may be done by direct contact, in the case of the nationalised industries and other public sector employees, though the Government's view has not always prevailed in such instances. The Government may also make a special effort on a particular occasion to influence an industry's decisions by urging its views on the employers or trade unionists concerned.[1] A more extensive version of the same process may take the form of a request to all parties to negotiations to give the Government a chance to express its view before a settlement is reached. Some versions of the 'early warning' procedure, by which the Government seeks to have prior notice of wage claims, may be purely advisory in character, while others may have elements of compulsory notification. Thirdly, the Government may seek to route its advice through an advisory body which can be regarded as offering an independent view. Such an advisory body may be invited simply to express an authoritative opinion on the general issues of prices and incomes. The best example of this was the Council on Prices, Productivity and Incomes, which existed from 1957 until 1961. An advisory body may also be charged with looking at and advising upon more detailed matters relating to wages, either in respect of particular claims in particular industries or particular types of payment. Both the National Incomes Commission, which operated from 1962 to 1965, and the National Board for Prices and Incomes, which took up its task in early 1965, are bodies of this type, though the N.B.P.I., which will be discussed in the next section, has become rather more than an advisory body.

(3) POLICIES OPERATED BY THE TRADE UNIONS AND EMPLOYERS' ASSOCIATIONS

One version of incomes policy which has frequently been advocated is that of an organisation representing the trade unions and employers, possibly diluted to a greater or lesser extent by representatives of the Government, which could be established by agreement and would then proceed to make decisions on the degree of change in wage and salary levels to be permitted in stated periods. The Declaration of Intent, signed on behalf of representative organisations of trade unions and of employers and by Ministers in December 1964, seemed to foreshadow something of

[1] One such instance is fully described in H. A. Clegg and R. Adams, *The Employers' Challenge*, 1957.

this kind. Presumably such a body would consider the economy's position and would be expected to recommend increases which would be possible without inflationary consequences. It is a bold assumption that agreement on the level of increases to be recommended is a possibility. The trade unions might, for example, be intent on imposing sacrifice on the employers, who would be unprepared to put up with the proposed increases. The unions, if they were able to resolve conflicting interests among themselves, might possibly suggest a level of increase which might be accepted by the employers, but would be inflationary and as such unwelcome to the Government. It is also by no means certain that the unions and employers would allow themselves to be persuaded into forming such a joint body at all.

Another version of a policy controlled by the parties to wage bargaining is based on the view that trade unions might restrain themselves. The most convenient body to represent the trade unions is the T.U.C., since it is the central organisation of the trade unions and its General Council includes the most important trade-union leaders. But the T.U.C. has no formal authority over its members. If it reaches an agreement with employers or the Government it cannot guarantee that the unions will support its decisions. If it sets itself up as a guide to the actions of its member unions they may simply reject its advice. It will certainly have difficulty in making individual trade unionists who have been outside the debate see the reasons for particular agreed measures. Even if most of the member unions go with the T.U.C. in its decisions there may still be some who act independently; they cannot be controlled by the T.U.C. and if they are successful then the general policy is immediately jeopardised. If all are in agreement the T.U.C. can speak for them, but since its authority depends on prestige and acceptance, it cannot continue to lead a policy which is beginning to be set aside by individual unions. Thus in the 'wage freeze' period from 1948 to 1950 the T.U.C. only continued to support voluntary wage restraint so long as there were few major dissenting unions, and it did not wait for a rejection of the policy by a majority before swinging away from it in 1950, as doubts among member unions grew.

Similar issues arise for trade-union leaders who agree to their powers of wage negotiation being centralised in the T.U.C., since they may then lose a major justification of their existence. Though they are empowered to forward their members' interests, they would have given a major part of the job over to the T.U.C. They may also find that they invite trouble from local leaders and members by doing so. This is especially likely since a central decision is likely to mean that sectional interests – a main reason for the existence of separate unions – are denied. A time would almost inevitably come when a union leader was asked to put the T.U.C.'s interests before those of his union. This could be a difficult decision; but in practice the direction in which individual union leaders are likely to move is set by the strong probability that a failure to put their own union first will result in their losing power to dissenters within their ranks.

The same kind of remarks can be applied to employers' associations. The Confederation of British Industries, like the T.U.C., can only lead as long as its members are prepared to follow. Individual employers are hardly likely to abide by the decisions of their employers' association if they are short of labour and can get it by a little judicious bargaining, which increases the wages of their own workpeople and encourages recruits and possibly productivity. Indeed, both trade unions and employers' associations are likely to have their centrally determined arrangements altered by local decision-taking. The circumstances for such local initiative become ideal when general wage changes are decided centrally, since a local modification can then be made against a known general alteration. Eventually such local adjustments could become so usual as to be self-cancelling and could destroy the whole foundation of centrally-controlled wage determination.

One suggestion which has occurred from time to time is a device to avoid the creation of a joint central body representing trade unions and employers while still obtaining the effect of a co-ordinated view. This approach is usually coupled with plans for improvements in the extent to which unions and employers stick to their agreements, though this usually boils down to recommending a greater sense of responsibility. The most important idea on this line of thinking is to recommend that one or two sectional agreements, such as, most typically, those relating to the engineering industry, should be regarded as the leading wage negotiations, as 'key bargains' or 'master agreements'. The decisions there should be taken with the full consciousness of their critical national importance and other wage decisions should merely follow them. This is in many ways a variation of the proposals we have already considered, with the same difficulties, except that sectional discussion of the key bargains could intrude on the national interest, and there are even greater problems of ensuring that any further centrally-determined policy actually operates.

(4) AN INDEPENDENT WAGE AUTHORITY

If a Government wishes to move from a policy of persuasion to one

which includes some element of control, and if the possibility of a 'voluntary' policy administered by the employers and trade unions is ruled out,
the next question is evidently one of the machinery that a Government
might itself introduce. There is typically some reluctance to take on the
job as simply part of the processes of Government, since there is a natural
desire to avoid the impression of enforcing a view without appeal to
independent judgment. This reluctance is closely related to the length of
time for which a controlling policy is envisaged. A short-period policy
may be very negative in its approach (a wage freeze) and, while a Government will wish nevertheless to create the impression that it has a consensus
for its actions, it may enforce these by direct administrative action. The
British Government, as we shall see in the next section, has been showing
itself increasingly willing to act directly. But as an incomes policy extends
in range and duration more questions of detail come up, and so to an
increasing extent the Government has to come out of an essentially
negative role and enter into specific situations and recommendations.
At this point the idea of some kind of independent wage authority has
considerable attractions. It can develop a more detailed view of the grounds
for particular wage changes and can hope to build up some degree of
consistency in the policy. And, from the point of view of the Government,
it is helpful to have an agency somewhat independent of itself to take the
brunt of detailed criticism of the operation of a policy of restraining the
growth of incomes.

The device of creating an independent authority has been followed elsewhere, especially in the Netherlands.[1] In Britain there are precedents for
Government-appointed bodies independently initiating or by administer-
ing policies. Royal Commissions are to an extent of this type, and N.I.C.
and N.B.P.I. were created as standing Royal Commissions. (The N.B.P.I.
is now a statutory body.) The University Grants Committee administers
something like an independent policy for allocating finance to individual
universities on behalf of the Government.

(5) ESTABLISHING CRITERIA FOR WAGE MOVEMENTS

Once a Government decides to try to implement a wages policy, whether
by agreement with representatives of the trade unions and employers or

[1] For a valuable survey of incomes policies in various countries see John
Corina, 'Can an Incomes Policy be Administered?', *British Journal of Industrial
Relations*, November 1967.

on its own authority, and whether simply as advice or with some degree of enforcement, questions both of method and of content arise. We have been talking mainly of *methods* of exerting direct influence on wages; but a Government must also state what it wants to happen, and indicate the context of its proposed prescription for wages. This is a very large but necessary question with several parts to it.

The need for a wage policy arises from the desirability of constraining the growth of wages to avoid a level of consumer demand which will mean inflation, or of preventing an increase in labour costs unmatched by productivity. The policy objective in terms of wages is usually stated as that holding the average rate of increase of wages to a certain percentage increase. One of the central features of a governmental statement on wages policy will therefore be the promulgation of a target figure for the percentage increase in wages which would, in the Government's opinion, be reasonable. This percentage is generally arrived at by estimation of the expected increase in overall output per head. There are problems about this measure, however: on the assumption of stable prices the effect of applying it will be broadly to maintain labour's share of the proceeds of economic growth, but this also implies maintaining labour's existing share of the allocation of the national product, which may not be a welcome implication to trade unionists. Questions also arise about adjustment for price changes. If prices are rising, whether because of prior movements in labour costs or for other reasons, a wage increase might do no more in real terms than maintain the wage earners' real purchasing power. This point can lead to debate about the genesis of price changes and the extent to which the rate of wage changes should be adjusted to take them into account. Some price changes, from a deterioration in the terms of trade or from devaluation, cannot be compensated in the percentage formulation without creating an increased share of national product for labour. Others may reflect past wage movements, but they could also be due to increases in profit margins. There is, therefore, no wholly unambiguous answer to the question of allowing for price movements, though the policy-makers seeking stable prices are likely to hold strongly to the view that price changes should not be taken into account in determining the appropriate degree of change in wages which should be permitted. The increase of output per head to which the percentage increase has to be related is prospective rather than actual and here there is room for much further debate. It is possible to base such an estimate on past trends in productivity, but these will be suspect since there may be latent capacity for growth which successful economic policies would release while current difficulties and economic restraint could make past trends too optimistic. An argument and a bargaining process are inevitable.

Despite the difficulties of finding a satisfactory answer, a view, or possibly a compromise, on what is the overall desirable level of increase in the wage level is the first step in giving substance to a wage policy. Such a view has appeared in each successive formulation of wage-policy advice in Britain with titles such as the 'guiding light' and the 'norm'. The American effort to produce the same idea has been termed 'the guidepost'.[1]

Once a 'norm' is set up there is next the problem of considering whether all wage claims should conform to it, or if there should be exceptions. If the policy advocates a standstill on wage movements, as in the latter half of 1966, then it is logical to suggest that there should be no exceptions. But a freeze is a very temporary policy, since economic circumstances change, including the prospect of readily being able to afford increased wages, and pressures for changes from the unions and their members increase; the more usual context is one in which a Government is advocating or trying to enforce longer-term restraint. Arguments or attempted justification of particular changes in wages follow and a general view is needed on which criteria for increases should have special attention. There are essentially two issues here, first that of trying to determine the grounds on which exceptional increases above the norm would be appropriate and also what in general are to be regarded as reasonable grounds for wage increases at all. If the norm is to mean the average, and if exceptions are to be considered, then some should receive less than the norm or nothing in the way of an increase, and normal increases will also require argument. (If, however, the norm is set at zero, as it has been at times in Britain, and, as in current circumstances, there is no likely prospect of wage cuts, all increases would require to be justified in terms of criteria for exceptions to the norm.) We shall discuss the detailed criteria for exceptions in Britain later, but at this stage we may note that there is a very clear measure of agreement between successive British and American formulations. The exceptions tend to be based on the case for favourable treatment of wage increases for the low-paid workers on social grounds in periods of general restraint and probably also because of rising prices, for those whose increases may be related to productivity improvements, for increases designed to help to recruit to sectors which are specially in need of labour,

[1] For a further account of these matters see D. J. Robertson, 'Guideposts and Norms: Contrasts in U.S. and U.K. Wage Policy', *Three Banks Review*, December 1966.

R

and for increases to those who are generally regarded as having lost their place in the wage hierarchy and have been left behind.[1]

Each of these concepts bristles with difficulties. Who is low-paid? What kind of productivity improvements? Should workers receive all the savings from productivity improvements? What about people for whom productivity is difficult to measure, or easy to see but dependent on technical change, even to the point that the increase in productivity of the process goes along with less work or less demanding work from the individual worker? If we say that an increase is necessary to obtain a change in the distribution of labour in favour of a particular section, how do we assess the effectiveness of such a policy? It is possible that there will be no quick return from a change in relative wages in a shift in the distribution of labour towards an area of labour shortage. But can we really deny the long-term depressive effects on labour supply of not maintaining the attractiveness of an occupation which we desire to favour with good-quality recruits in sufficient quantity? Are there not serious dangers in lending any credence to the view that those who have missed their turn should have a turn? Is this not just another way of approving of a continued series of wage rounds where the criterion is that everyone should retain his accustomed place in the wage structure without question? And yet it is clear that people can genuinely have fallen out of line in a real and significant way, and this can have adverse long-term effects. Ideas of 'fair comparison' can be simply automatic devices for wage increases, but there may be a stage at which they cannot appropriately be ignored.

This catalogue of questions that face those who try, in constructing an incomes policy, to determine the way in which particular wage movements should be considered for exceptional treatment, indicates the inevitability of a movement from generalised propositions towards detailed debate. It therefore strengthens the view that an effective incomes policy will require machinery capable of entering into detailed as well as general discussion. This view is confirmed when we consider the implications of two other questions that have still to be asked about establishing criteria for wage movements. First, how often should wage changes take place, and secondly, what in this context should be included within the meaning of wages and wage changes?

One way of operating a policy of restraining the growth of wages is to try to increase the length of time between wage changes, and hence the duration of any particular wage settlement. It might seem that the general

[1] For further discussion of the contemporary British context see Section III (4), below.

objective will be achieved if wage changes happen less frequently. This is after all the intended effect of a wage freeze, and wage policies try to break the rhythm of wage rounds and extend the period between settlements. But the matter is more complicated. Postponing settlements may give temporary and valuable advantage, but it will be largely eroded if subsequent wage movements are larger than they would have been, so that labour costs lurch upwards whenever the policy ceases to function. Moreover, there are difficulties in delaying some wage movements if others are proceeding. If the policy grasps those wage and salary changes which are formally negotiated and spaces them out while leaving wage drift to proceed unhindered, the drift will cause pressures for wage change in those sections which are held by the policy, and the overall prospects of delaying changes will be reduced. These points suggest that a wages policy, unless all it has to do is to achieve a temporary delay, will require to continue in existence, if not more permanently, at least into a transitional period to modify the movement of wages as the policy relaxes. They also suggest that a wages policy has to contemplate control of wage drift as well as more formal and larger-scale wage bargains. This last point leads on to the question of what wages and wage changes should be included within the context of a wages policy.

The object of the whole exercise can be put either in terms of restraining the growth of unit labour costs, or of restraining the growth of labour's income and purchasing power. These are not, however, identical concepts. The movement of both should be influenced by productivity, but labour costs have to reckon with changes in hours of work and holidays, which raise labour costs per unit if they are associated with unchanged weekly payment and not accompanied by proportionate increases in productivity per hour at work. Reductions in the duration of work ought, therefore, to be reckoned as wage increases if the weekly wage is maintained. Labour costs also include a number of items which add to the employers' costs but do not go directly into the income and purchasing power of wage earners. Fringe benefits such as improved pension schemes and payroll taxes are of this type. In so far as the object is to hold labour costs, increases in these are contrary to the policy; but the taxes will effect a reduction in purchasing power and the fringe benefits may in the short period increase institutional savings, or increase purchasing power, according to the details of how they are framed, and when, and how, they are distributed.

Negotiations for salaried workers at the national level are usually centred around incremental salary scales; but the increments are not usually regarded by their recipients as a general salary increase, which means an improvement in the whole scale. In the case of salaried workers there is, therefore, a formal mechanism by which money salaries will rise without new negotiations, though the extent to which salary costs increase on average will depend on the balance between those leaving the salaried group and new entrants, assuming the former to be generally further up the scale than the latter. In the case of wage earners there are other extensive ways in which earnings and incomes may rise without formal wage changes – the whole apparatus of extra rates, rising bonuses and overtime, i.e. of wage drift. If a wage policy is to be successful it must in some measure control these movements. The emphasis of forms of machinery for direct influence on wages levels necessarily has to be on the process of formal wage negotiation. The norm is, however, related to all wages, since it is concerned with increases in wage incomes and not simply negotiated rates, and the criteria for exceptional wage changes ought also to apply to wages in general and not merely to wage changes at the national level. If low wages are to be a criteria for special consideration, then the actual level of wage payment is relevant, and not simply that expressed in an agreement. If we are to be concerned with the relative levels of payment, then again we should be thinking of the whole payment situation. If productivity is to be a particularly influential factor in discussing wage changes, there is no way of doing so without considering the earnings position. Since it is here that productivity and payment are most closely related, there can then be little doubt that giving body and context to a wage policy requires going beyond wage rates and into earnings. But this is a long and untidy job in the context of our complicated wage structure and structure of wage payments (Chapters 3, 4, and 5). The dilemma of wage policy in Britain is that to do its work fully it requires a grasp of all wage movements, and the longer the policy lasts, the more true this becomes. Yet beyond the negotiated settlements in large-scale bargains there may be great diversity both in payments and in methods of determining wage changes. To operate here requires extensive machinery of investigation and leads us to the view that if wage policy is designed as more than a temporary experiment it will become involved in changing the structure of bargaining and hence affect the character of wage payments to a considerable extent.

(6) TEMPORARY OR PERMANENT WAGE POLICIES?

The discussion in (5) above takes us back to some of the points made in the concluding section of the last chapter. Wage policy has to concern itself with earnings as well as negotiated rates. Discussion of criteria for wage change and the needs of economic growth leads on to examination of the utilisation of labour, productivity and the effects of wage structures and methods of payment upon them. A policy to be effective even in the short run has to be discriminating between competing candidates for increases and so has to question existing structures both of rates and of earnings. Any attempt to control earnings requires study of the methods of wage settlement and a move into the less formal areas of bargaining which lie behind national negotiations. If a policy is of the 'wage freeze' variety and of short duration it may be possible to fend off these issues, but the longer a policy continues the more they will become obtrusive. It therefore happens that as a wage policy continues it becomes increasingly concerned with reform of wages bargaining and methods of payment as well as with short-term restraint.[1] It may indeed be argued, even for the short period, that a proper wages policy should be concerned with productivity as well as wages so as to offer some prospect of enhancement of the national product and wage advance as well as controlling the level of wage movements.

In short, the continued existence of wage policies alters their direction and content and leads on to the possibility of some degree of permanent existence of a policy for wages which concerns itself with the growth of incomes as well as restraint upon them, and which seeks an extension of the scope of collective bargaining to embrace matters related to productivity and performance, as well as a changing structure of bargaining to improve on the uncertain relationship between wage rates and earnings from which many of the initial problems of wages policy seem to stem. In effect it becomes expedient in the operation of a short-term incomes policy to develop criteria for wage increases and to consider their application to earnings as well as to wage rates. These exercises, originally introduced for short-term reasons, then begin to develop their own momentum of reform so that a case for a more permanent wage policy emerges to supplement shorter-term policies or because it is seen that short-term policies are inadequate or ineffective. Such a more permanent policy would, however, be based less on the need for restraint of wage movement, and more on the improvement of productivity and of methods of bargaining and on the development of a policy for income growth.

The subjects of concern in this type of more permanent wage reform are

[1] It is not, therefore, surprising that in respect of this point as well as others the Report of the Royal Commission on Trade Unions and Employers' Associations, 1968, has advocated reform of the structure of collective bargaining in Britain.

potentially numerous. Essentially, however, the issues raised are those, first of improvement in the utilisation of labour, achieved in part by changes in working practices, and in part by improvements in methods of payments; and secondly of reformulation of bargaining structure and negotiating procedures associated essentially with productivity bargaining, in a somewhat wider and looser sense than that now current. Any degree of permanent effort towards this type of objective requires some form of mechanism of change, the most obvious way of providing this being through a body issuing advisory reports, since an educational process of steering both public and national opinion is involved.

III. Wage Policy in Britain

This section moves from the foregoing long list of alternative formulations of wage policy to describe and comment upon wage policy in Britain. This is a difficult task. Though there was a marked quickening of interest and activity dating from the 'pay pause' introduced by a Conservative administration in 1961, and this intensity of activity increased after the Labour Government came to power in October 1964, wage policy has been a topic of discussion in Britain since the 'wage freeze' of the 1948–50 period, and this is not surprising as problems of rising prices and costs have been with us right since the end of the war. Moreover, while the approach of the preceding section of this chapter was to present various versions of the policy as alternatives, the present situation is essentially one in which most, if not all, of the policy alternatives coexist. It is as a result inevitable that a description will give the impression of successive layers of policy one on top of the other – that has, indeed, been the situation. We shall concentrate here on two tasks, first to give an impression of development of policy broadly since the Labour Government took office in October 1964, and secondly to provide a statement of the incomes policy current in Britain at the time of writing. An outline of the sequence of governmental action on incomes policy since 1964 is given in the Appendix to this chapter. It should be noted, however, that any summary account such as this, while useful as a broad outline, lacks the detail, and more especially the inferences, which are essential to a full understanding of the sequence of events. This defect of the bare chronology will be remedied to a very limited extent by the discussion in this section, but a full account would merit a book of its own and is not attempted here. Our description of the contemporary situation is as it stood in mid-1968. Here another caution must be offered: wage policy has been changing so frequently in the last few years that it is not possible to be wholly up to date in any form of publication other than a daily or weekly newspaper. Inevitably the detail given here will be changed even before this book appears, and will continue to change. On the other hand a snapshot of the situation at one point of time is a useful illustration, even though it loses immediate accuracy as time passes.

During the whole period of the 1960s Britain has been in balance of payments difficulties, sometimes severe and sometimes sufficiently ameliorated as to give grounds for spurious optimism. This history led eventually to devaluation in November 1967. Both before and after devaluation fiscal and monetary policy has been used with varying intensity to control the level of demand in the economy, with improvements in the availability of labour and restraint of wage growth as important parts of the overall objective. These measures have undoubtedly helped the labour supply position, with the result that by 1968 there has appeared to be some consensus for the view that the economy should preferably be run at a rather lower level of intensity, and hence with more unemployment, than had been customary in earlier post-war years, though the figure at which policy has seemed to aim has still been below 2 per cent. On the other hand, the economy has continued to exhibit many signs of cost inflation, with the consequence that there have been successive attempts to develop satisfactory incomes policies, and appeals for moderation in increases in wages have formed a constant refrain in the public announcements of politicians of all the major parties. The actual form taken by the policies is perhaps best explained by a list of their various parts.

(1) CO-OPERATION OF TRADE UNIONS AND EMPLOYERS

Unless a wage policy takes the form of a complete freeze on all wage movements, which is very difficult and certainly short-lived, appeals for restraint, and efforts by the Government to obtain restraint, essentially require at least the tacit support of the trade unions and employers. If employers wish to find ways of getting round wage restraint they can do so. If a policy has to be fought through against industrial action by a number of unions it will be so disruptive, and so potentially difficult, as to be self-destroying. Lack of trade-union co-operation made the work of the National Incomes Commission set up in the latter days of the Conservative administration very difficult. The Labour Government succeeded in achieving formal acceptance of incomes policy in the form of a Statement of Intent signed by representatives of employers, trade unions and the Government in December 1964 as a consensus on the need for wage and price restraint, and initially developed its incomes policy as purely voluntary and based on this participant support. Events in the following months gave little evidence of success for this voluntary policy. On the other hand, as the Government moved towards more direct intervention and control, while the C.B.I. played rather a passive role in detailed action as distinct from pronouncements, the T.U.C. began to take an active part in restraining wage movements. It introduced its own procedure for examining proposed pay claims by its member unions and advising unions on whether a claim could be regarded as reasonable in the light of its details and of the general economic situation. The T.U.C. insisted that this 'vetting' of claims would achieve effective voluntary restraint from unions. Thus, even though the present system has elements of compulsion, it runs beside a trade-union policy with more modest objectives, and it still depends to a large degree on the willingness of trade-union leaders to give broad consent to the idea of restraint both in their claims and their actions.

(2) EARLY WARNING

The trade union 'vetting' of wages movements occurs before claims have been presented or fully processed. The Government in attempting to supplement this system has introduced its own 'early warning' procedure by which wage claims are notified to it through the C.B.I. or T.U.C. or from individual firms. This system also is voluntary, though legislative provision exists for making it more compulsory. A similar 'early warning' system exists for price increases as well. The obvious purpose of an early warning is to give the Government a chance to influence the decision taken by the parties, or to bring reviewing machinery into action.

(3) NORM AND CEILING

During the 'standstill' period in the second half of 1966 no wage increases were permitted and the Government took powers to enforce its wishes largely by means of requiring employers not to pay increases and protecting them from actions in the courts if they refused to apply increases which were frozen for the duration of the standstill. At other times, however, the policy has centred round a norm, which, during the period of 'severe restraint' in the first half of 1967 and up to early 1968, was set at zero. An innovation was attempted in April 1968 when a 'ceiling' of $3\frac{1}{2}$ per cent per annum was introduced. This new device was presumably intended to avoid the lack of realism of a zero norm, but also to prevent the prospect that any positive norm would become the accepted level for a minimal increase. It was now argued that no increase should be granted unless it met the criteria for wage increases under the incomes policy and that increases justified in this way should not exceed 3½ per cent per annum. These criteria are the same as those which have appeared in successive pronouncements since the Labour Government came into power, but also bear a strong family resemblance to the ones produced by the previous Conservative administration. It is intended to apply the ceiling at the local as well as at the national level, but not apparently to restrict 'increases in earnings under payments by results systems resulting directly from increased output'.[1] Since payment by results is not without faults and is a source of earnings drift, there are problems here, as well as in achieving a ceiling for all the numerous forms of local increases in wages.

(4) CRITERIA

Criteria for wage increases figure in all recent statements of incomes policy. Sometimes, however, they have been held to be applicable as justification for increases above the norm (and, therefore, as criteria for exceptional treatment); sometimes they have been stated as the necessary basis for any increase with a zero norm. In the case of the 'ceiling' approach the criteria become for the policy-makers the justification for any increases at all, but increases justified by them are limited to the ceiling of 3½ per cent per annum. There is, however, still an 'exceptional' element in the criteria since increases in payment justified in terms of the productivity criterion are singled out as alone being thought entitled to exceed the ceiling.

The criteria as they have appeared in the most recent document[2] are worth stating in full.

'(i) Where the employees concerned, for example by accepting more exacting work or a major change in working practices, make a direct contribution towards increasing productivity in the particular firm or industry. Even in such cases some of the benefit should accrue to the community as a whole in the form of lower prices.

'(ii) Where it is essential in the national interest to secure a change in the distribution of manpower (or to prevent a change which would otherwise

---

[1] *Productivity, Prices and Incomes Policy in 1968 and 1969*, Cmnd. 3590, H.M.S.O., April 1968. This is at the time of writing the current statement of incomes policy.　　　　　　　　　　　[2] Cmnd. 3590.

R 2

take place) and a pay increase would be both necessary and effective for this purpose.

'(iii) Where there is general recognition that existing wage and salary levels are too low to maintain a reasonable standard of living.

'(iv) Where there is widespread recognition that the pay of a certain group of workers has fallen severely out of line with the level of remuneration for similar work and needs in the national interest to be improved.'

All of these criteria are somewhat ambiguously worded, and perhaps inevitably so. The clearest perhaps is that relating to productivity, which has been embellished by further guidelines for productivity agreements produced by the Prices and Incomes Board. It clearly is intended to encourage productivity bargaining in one form or another. The obvious difficulty and source of argument about the low wage criterion is that it does not specify the level of wage to which it refers! The trade unions appear to put this at a higher level than the Government, though the position of the latter may only be judged broadly and by inference from the way in which the Government has reacted to particular cases of wage increases to lower-paid workers. There is also the difficult problem of distinguishing between the level of the negotiated wage rate and the prospects of enhanced earnings. The second criterion on the distribution of manpower is guarded by the justification that specific problems of labour supply should be cured, and are in fact likely to be cured, by wage changes. As was suggested in our earlier Chapters 11 and 19, there is room for considerable doubt about whether a change in wage is likely to be usually effective as a short-run means of remedying a labour shortage. The last criterion seems to mean simply comparability, but it has tended to be interpreted, by Government at least, with emphasis on the 'seriously out of line' qualification and not, therefore, as a statement that everyone should follow their neighbours.

(5) PRICES AND DIVIDENDS AS WELL

It is the strong view of trade unionists that restraint on workers' incomes should be accompanied both by restraint on other incomes and by attempts to hold down the cost of living. There is a history of efforts to achieve voluntary dividend limitation. In the situation introduced in April 1968 dividend increases must be notified to the Treasury and are expected to be held to not more than $3\frac{1}{2}$ per cent. Early warning of price change has been a growing feature of the policy and the current position is that changes in prices can be referred to the Prices and Incomes Board for examination and increases may be delayed for a maximum of twelve months, or possibly prices reduced, if the Board so recommends.

(6) DELAYING POWERS

During the period of standstill and to a lesser extent in the period of severe restraint, the Government's powers to hold up wage changes were temporary but considerable. Subsequently they were reduced to a maximum of seven months' delay, if a case was sent to the Prices and Incomes Board, and the Board thought an increase was not warranted. The policy introduced in April 1968 extended the maximum delaying power on both price and pay increases to twelve months in the context of a reference to the Board. It is important to comment, however, first that the delaying power does not preclude, though such action would be strongly discouraged, the possibility of back-dating an increase to the original date once it becomes permitted; and secondly, that this delaying power like all its predecessors is intended to work mainly as a means of discouraging increases outwith the active use of the policy framework, in the hope that voluntary restraint will normally work with the powers being kept in reserve.

(7) NATIONAL BOARD FOR PRICES AND INCOMES

Apart from being charged with continuing responsibility for certain standing references – currently the Armed Forces and academics – the N.B.P.I. has at least three roles in the current context. First, it is an essential part of the delaying mechanism since reference to it is part of the procedure of delay and its report is the basis of a decision whether to continue to delay. Secondly, the Board is used, as the National Incomes Commission was before it, to investigate particular wage (and price) cases in some detail and thus to help to make new structures of payments in particular industries. Thirdly, the Board has increasingly become an agent of policy formulation. By its specific judgments it builds up a body of opinion on good and bad increases, methods of payments and wage structures. It also produces general reports – on productivity bargaining and payment by results, for example – which pull together evidence from a number of industries. In this latter role it has become a major source of change in wage negotiation with a tendency to encourage the relation of wage changes to productivity and also more detailed bargaining – based on smaller units and furnished with more evidence. In this way its function is only to some degree that of a short-term instrument of incomes policy and it can also be regarded as a more permanent instrument of guidance towards change.

That, in rather brief compass, is the outline of incomes policy in 1968. It would obviously be possible to tell this story in much greater detail, and then to offer a long commentary upon it. It will suffice here, however, simply to list a few of the more obvious points that emerge.

(1) The policy is rather a disordered mixture of diverse parts.

(2) While it has elements of compulsion it relies heavily on voluntary elements and on the threat of compulsion rather than its reality. In simple terms, it is a compromise.

(3) It has elements of long-term policy-making in the work of the N.B.P.I. and in its attempt to push certain criteria for wages changes in preference to others – most notably to claims based on changes in the cost of living.

(4) It makes some attempt to deal with earnings as well as rates, but is rather incomplete in its coverage of earnings. On the other hand, its longer-term aspects would, and should, change the nature of the relationship between rates and earnings.

(5) It is sufficiently full of compromise that it can hardly be expected to be successful in any complete sense. Judgments on the degree to which it has been successful have to consider the extent to which it can be said that it (a) postpones increases while productivity rises; (b) can be argued to reduce the rate of increase of wages even slightly; (c) changes attitudes of bargainers and causes them to reflect on wider issues outside their own bargaining context; (d) induces the beginning of changes in the structure of bargaining; and (e) increases attention to productivity improvements in the utilisation of labour. Unfortunately all of these are difficult to measure. Even though an incomes policy is only partially respected, and only partially able to hold wages down to its recommended norm or ceiling, it may, however, be worth having because delay is important and because longer-term changes are needed.

How may we sum up on incomes policy? There can be little doubt that the context of wage changes in Britain has been altered by successive doses of incomes policy, and that not all of these alterations are temporary. Wage bargaining now emphasises different arguments – especially those relating to productivity. Systems of payment such as payment by results and overtime are being critically examined. These are important long-term gains which are worth having even if the policy has little short-term success. One clear danger must, however, be stressed. If in the pursuit of its policy objectives the Government were to alienate the trade unions, their opposition could be destructive of long-term as well as short-term aims. While this danger is real, and much discussed, it is however observable that trade-union opposition in recent years has been far from complete or unanimous. In fact the trade unions have moved, along with most people, into a frame of mind in which the need for incomes policy and for broader changes in methods and content of bargaining is recognised,[1] so that the debate has been more on ways and means. It may be suggested that the trade unions have a clear interest in improvements in bargaining, in improvements in productivity, and in avoiding a clash with Government. However, the situation obviously requires careful handling and some degree of compromise. There is less likelihood of disagreement between employers and Government, at any rate on the wages aspect of incomes policy, while the policy itself has stimulated employers into a more active interest in labour market changes.

The quantitative question of how far incomes policy has in fact restrained the growth of incomes is both important and difficult to answer, because the existence of the policy necessarily means that comparison with what would have happened if there had been no policy is not possible except in terms of comparison with different time periods and hence different circumstances. It is clear that wages policy has had more impact on wage rates than on earnings. It is clear that it can temporarily reduce wage increases – most notably in the 'standstill' period. The real ambiguity arises in discussing whether subsequent wage changes make good the delayed increases in the period of restraint. They clearly do so to some extent, but it looks as though the forgone increases are not wholly recovered. It may in any case be argued that a delay is well worth having. For example, it is important to keep costs down as far as possible after devaluation, and subsequent increases in wages may then, it may be hoped, occur later in easier balance of payments circumstances, and with an increase in production available to permit increased consumption. Moreover, we appear to have arrived at a situation in which wages policy is in some form or another likely to be continuous for some years. In this context the prospects of making good the level of increases that might have occurred in a previous period if there had been no policy are now affected by the restraining influence of the current policy.

[1] The view that this is necessary has now (June 1968) been strongly endorsed by the Report of the Royal Commission on Trade Unions and Employers' Associations.

It is evident that a wages policy does not stop wage increases for very long and may not hold to its prescribed targets for moderate increases. This, however, does not mean that it has failed – partial success in the form of some delay and some degree of moderation is an important gain, which may help towards the kind of growing economy in which larger money increases are acceptable, and greater increases in the standard of living are possible.

SUGGESTED READING

John Corina, *The Development of Incomes Policy*, Institute of Personnel Management, 1966.
J. R. Crossley, 'Wage Structure and the Future of Incomes Policy', *Scottish Journal of Political Economy*, June 1968.
National Board for Prices and Incomes, *First General Report* (Report No. 19), 1966; and *Second General Report* (Report No. 40), 1967 (and also the Board's Reports on particular wage issues upon which it was asked to make a recommendation – especially *Productivity Agreements*, Report No. 36, 1967).
Organisation for Economic Co-operation and Development, *The Problem of Rising Prices*, Paris, 1961.
B. C. Roberts, *National Wages Policy in War and Peace*, 1958.
Royal Commission on Trade Unions and Employers' Associations, *Report*, 1968.
Scottish Journal of Political Economy, Symposium on Wages Policy, 1958.
United Nations, *Incomes in Post-War Europe*, Economic Commission for Europe, Geneva, 1967.

Appendix to Chapter 21

Prices and Incomes Policy under the Labour Government

THE TIMETABLE OF GOVERNMENT ACTION

October 1964. Government announces intention of introducing new incomes policy.

December 1964. After much discussion, *Joint Statement of Intent on Productivity, Prices and Incomes* signed by unions (T.U.C.), management (C.B.I.), and Government. They acknowledge desirability of 'keeping watch' on incomes, and agree to co-operate with Government in giving 'effective shape' to machinery for reviewing and examining incomes and prices.

February 1965. National Board for Prices and Incomes (P.I.B.) established, with a majority of independent members and an independent chairman. Cases to be referred to P.I.B. by the Government.

April 1965. White Paper *Prices and Incomes Policy* (Cmnd. 2639) gave criteria for price increases and wage increases related to growth of national productivity, and 'norm' for wage increases based on this. 'Increases in wages and salaries above the norm should be confined to cases in which exceptional treatment can be shown to be required in the national interest.' Few exceptional criteria.

(i) Major change in working practices directly leading to increased productivity;

(ii) where change in manpower distribution is essential, and a pay increase would be necessary and effective;

(iii) where 'general recognition' that existing pay levels are too low to allow a 'reasonable standard of living';

(iv) where 'widespread recognition' that pay has fallen 'seriously out of line' with pay for similar work and needs to be improved.

April 1965. T.U.C. affiliates support policy, but several large unions, including Transport and General Workers, vote against.

May 1965. P.I.B. begins hearings, and first report issued June 1965.

September 1965. Prices and incomes policy strengthened because of very high wage increases. Government proposes compulsory early-warning system of notification for certain price changes and wage claims. T.U.C. proposes its own wage-examination scheme.

November 1965. White Paper *Prices and Incomes Policy: An Early Warning System* (Cmnd. 2808). Details of price and wage changes required; provision for notification to P.I.B., whose report should be awaited by parties before proposed changes occur.

February 1966. Prices and Incomes Bill introduced, providing penalties for those not notifying proposed price and wage increases. Standstill period (during P.I.B. investigation) made mandatory. P.I.B. made statutory and given powers to compel evidence. The Bill was not introduced at this time because of the election in March 1966.

July 1966. Following 'comprehensive and tough policies' to deal with exchange crisis, new policy announced. White Paper *Prices and Incomes Standstill* (Cmnd. 3073) issued. All pay and price increases prohibited for 6 months, except with Government approval. All existing agreements to take effect after July 1966 deferred. During period of 'severe restraint' (January–June 1967) the norm would be zero. P.I.B. given role of examining difficult or doubtful cases.

July 1966. Prices and Incomes Bill reintroduced. Part II repeated earlier proposal, by providing for 1–4-month standstill in prices or wages, with fines for violators. Part IV, which was new, provided that no prices or wages could be changed without Ministerial consent. Part IV not immediately enacted, but regarded as 'reserve powers'.

October 1966. Part IV enacted after legal challenge to the pay standstill. Part IV lapsed in August 1967.

November 1966. White Paper *Prices and Incomes Standstill: Period of Severe Restraint* (Cmnd. 3150) gave criteria for January–June 1967. Further deferment of existing agreements to end June. New increases held to a minimum, and only where justified by increased efficiency or low pay.

December 1966. P.I.B. issues stringent criteria for productivity increases deserving higher pay.

March 1967. White Paper *Prices and Incomes Policy after 30th June 1967* (Cmnd. 3235). Early warning system retained; norm still zero, with increases to be justified according to criteria of April 1965. P.I.B. to remain statutory. Part II – with delaying powers – to remain in effect and to be used unless voluntary machinery could be guaranteed. Two interesting points: (i) twelve months regarded as minimum period between wage increases; (ii) parties should not make good increases forgone under standstill and severe restraint.

July 1967. Further legislation on delaying powers in Prices and Incomes (No. 2) Bill. Where compulsory notification was required, Government could delay price increase or wage settlement for up to six months if there was an adverse report by P.I.B. Where settlement was already in operation, it could be suspended for three months until P.I.B. report published. Six-month delay could then operate from date of original Government intervention. However, employers not forbidden to backdate delayed increases to date of original settlement.

The statutory notification and delaying powers were designed to operate for one year, until August 1968.

November 1967. Devaluation of sterling, accompanied by deflationary measures, with promise of further deflation in 1968.

November 1967. T.U.C. forecasts productivity growth of 6 per cent allowing wage increases of 3½–4 per cent. Forecast 'too optimistic', according to Government. This T.U.C. economic policy accepted by union executive conference February 1968.

March 1968. Chancellor announces intention of seeking further reserve powers over prices and incomes after August 1968. Budget is seen to be highly deflationary.

April 1968. White Paper *Productivity, Prices and Incomes Policy in 1968 and 1969* (Cmnd. 3590). Ceiling of 3½ per cent on income increases, with criteria of April 1965 being applied to decide exceptions; however, productivity and low pay much more significant than comparability or redistribution of manpower. Early-warning system continued and voluntary arrangements to be used.

However, reserve powers sought:

(i) delaying power increased to twelve months;

(ii) P.I.B. recommendations of price increases to be required;

(iii) divident notification required.

July 1968. A Prices and Incomes Act to give effect to these proposals becomes law.

22 Future Trends and Problems

This is not the kind of book which requires a fully integrated conclusion pulling together all the arguments of the preceding chapters. Indeed, its proper function as a textbook is to open up a number of separate subjects within the general area which it covers, and a conclusion attempting to bring all these issues together again would be either impossibly long or an oversimplification. On the other hand, it does seem appropriate to indicate in this brief concluding chapter a few of the labour market issues which we think are of particular importance to the British economy at present, and are likely to develop in importance over the next few years. Some of these topics arise out of general trends and problems in the economy at large, such as growth, inflation and the related economic difficulties. There is another group of problems, however, which, though they have never been far below the surface of labour market discussions, have been given added point and emphasis by the publication of the Report of the Royal Commission on Trade Unions and Employers' Associations. The Royal Commission was deliberating while this book was being written and the Report appeared just as the book was receiving its final revision. Since its Report will certainly play an important part in the next few years in deliberations on many of the topics in this book, the opportunity is taken here to comment upon some of the most relevant and important views of the Royal Commission.

The issues which we wish to raise have already been discussed explicitly or by inference in earlier chapters, and they may, therefore, simply be itemised here.

1. Many commentators have observed that the rate of growth of the British economy, both in total and in output per head, is slower than that of most other developed countries, and have suggested that it is important, and possibly essential, that this growth rate should be improved. The labour force necessarily plays a crucial part in any process of growth, and yet the British labour force is unlikely to grow in numbers to any great extent over the next few years. Indeed, even to assume that it will not

decline requires further assumptions about the participation of married women in employment and about success in bringing into active employment some reserves of labour which are thought to exist in the less fully employed regions of the economy. It follows that labour's contribution to whatever growth may be achieved in the next few years will mainly take the form of growth in output per head, without the benefit of the stimulus to expansion and to changes in the utilisation of labour which can come from a rising volume of labour supply. However, the nature of the productivity improvements for which we should be looking needs to be understood. Something is naturally to be achieved by harder work, but it would be retrogressive to think that this should mean longer hours and shorter holidays. Indeed, the trend is likely to be in the opposite direction, and in the longer period this is certainly right. Productivity improvement is more closely related to effective work by the labour force and this has to be viewed alongside the growth of capital and technical change. The need is to develop a labour force with the requisite degree and types of skill to meet the requirements of a changing economy, and with the adaptability to keep up with these changes.

2. It is not possible to mention the subject of the rate of growth of the British economy without very shortly thereafter moving on to discussions of balance of payments problems and of inflation. The operation of the labour market comes rapidly into the discussion, because of the marked tendency for wages and salaries in Britain in post-war years to run ahead of the growth of output – with consequential effects upon prices. This subject is tied up with the question of the adaptability of the labour force, because the wage movements have not merely to be of a size which the economy can afford but must occur in ways which are themselves helpful to the contribution of labour to the process of economic growth. Points 1 and 2 may be summed up by saying that the British economy is particularly in need both of manpower policy and of long-run policies on incomes from employment.

3. We would not wish to repeat here a discussion of the elements of manpower policy, which is to be found running through many of the preceding chapters. It is, however, clear that Britain needs to pay particular attention to the education and training of its labour force to develop both a higher proportion of trained workers and a wider variety of types of training. The form of training which has in the past been most favoured in industrial occupations in the British economy is that of the apprenticeship. This represents an honourable tradition producing a set of clearly marked skilled groups, but with some degree of inflexibility both in the duration

and type of training and in the distinctions between one craft group and another. Over the next few years, discussion is likely to centre increasingly on the need to change the apprenticeship tradition into a more flexible system of training and retraining, combined with more interchange between particular categories of trained manpower. This is almost certainly more than a simple matter of breaking down the status of existing skills, since it must involve a continuing process of developing new patterns and types of training in which restrictive arrangements relating to present skills may be seen as out of date in relation to new opportunities. In this situation trade unions (and also professional associations) with a contemporary outlook are, of course, essential.

4. One of the other strongly marked features of the British labour market is the existence of distinctions between the wage earner and the salaried worker. A process of assimilation of the apprentice-trained skilled man into a wider conspectus of skill levels and types of training needs properly to be associated with a general tendency to abandon the distinction between wage earners and salaried workers. This, of course, has immediate and major implications for the terms and conditions of employment of manual workers and for the special privileges which salaried workers have enjoyed in Britain. Issues of the status of the wage earner, and of the development of increased opportunities for wage earners to move up the ladders of occupation and of payment, including the opportunity, to move into managerial grades and status, are going to assume increasing prominence.

5. The whole topic of increased opportunities can be confidently expected to arouse interest over the next few years in a number of respects. There are already signs of increased interest in equal pay, but if this is to be more than an artificial creation, it must be accompanied by wider opportunities for women in employment. Improved opportunities provide a surer route to equal payment than legislation or lobbying simply on equal payment. The right of workers to participate in management is reflected in discussion of direct worker representation, as workers, in managerial decision-taking, and in claims for much-improved methods of communication and consultation, as well as in more open opportunities for promotion.

6. In Britain in recent years there has been an unusual inclination to emphasise a short-period relationship between output and payment by the use of incentive schemes, and to develop a tendency to increase payment through increased overtime. Thus wage earners receive a multiplicity of payments for what is essentially a single job, and working hard will only

really result in extra money if it is done in conformity with a particular system of payment which emphasises output on incentive schemes and hours beyond the normal. Attempts to develop a more satisfactory relationship between payment and work, and a more long-term view of the contribution of workers to the needs of their employers, are already of growing importance. There are many signs of this in the new interest in status agreements, and in growing emphasis on fringe benefits, as well as a marked growth in disquiet about both traditional incentive systems of payment and overtime.

7. Formal negotiating procedures in Britain have been dominated by the national bargain. In recent years there has been growing interest in plant bargaining and in intensifying the content of collective agreements to bring them to grips with the issues of relating payment to productivity, interpreting productivity not so much as simply higher output, but also as the adaptability and adjustment of the labour force to the work required from it. It is unlikely that national bargains can themselves carry the whole burden of a more intensive study of the relationship between work and payment. Moreover, they have typified a situation in which regular wage increases have run in excess of productivity gains. A change towards more professional and more continuous bargaining at more local levels is desirable and likely to develop at an increasing rate. A new emphasis on company or factory bargaining will, however, only be an improvement on the existing situation, both in terms of the structure of wage payments and of incomes policy, if it is procedurally well organised and has the resources to produce detailed agreements which are the product of joint study.

8. One of the obvious consequences of a move away from the older-style situation of confrontation will be a bigger demand upon the professional competence and strength of the trade unions. Reform of trade unions has been much discussed in recent years. Most of the discussion has been concerned with the damage which strikes and other forms of industrial action have done to the British economy. The discussion over the next few years about trade unions should shift towards matters more closely related to their efficiency in an increasingly complicated job, such as those of their organisation and their resources.

9. Since there is very little in the operation of the labour market that is not to some degree undergoing a process of change, one immediate requirement is to think more about manpower forecasting and planning. But this is more than simply a matter of prediction. Manpower policy is also a matter for governmental decision and action – in relation to training, redundancy, employment services and many other topics. It is equally

clear that the management of labour is a part of the management function in industry which will require specialist and concentrated attention, not as a side issue from general management but as an important and growing part of general management requiring some specialist training for some managers and understanding of the issues by all managers.

The issues raised in these preceding paragraphs, as well as many of those developed in other parts of this book, are likely to be discussed over the next few years, with the Report of the Royal Commission on Trade Unions and Employers' Associations[1] as a primary source of ideas and controversy. It is, therefore, appropriate to end with a brief reference to it.

The central theme of the Report can be summed up in a single quotation. 'Britain has two systems of industrial relations. One is the formal system embodied in the official institutions. The other is the informal system created by the actual behaviour of trade unions and employers' associations, of managers, shop stewards and workers.' Apart from various legal issues affecting the status of trade unions and the rights of individuals, the Commission's recommendations are concerned almost entirely with improving the system of industrial relations by eliminating these two overlapping and sometimes contradictory systems. This leads it into discussion of a number of topics covered in this book – payments systems, informal bargaining, wage drift, restrictive labour practices, and the relation between collective bargaining and incomes policy. The central resultant recommendation is that factory or company bargaining should be encouraged, national bargains in industries in which they are retained being reduced to a subsidiary role in regulating some standard conditions, or in providing 'guidelines' for company bargaining. The Report also advocates the extension of collective bargaining by improving the means by which trade unions may achieve recognition and hence the right to bargain on behalf of their members – a recommendation which would be specially relevant to white-collar workers – and by suggested changes in the law relating to Wages Councils, which would make it easier to replace Wages Councils with collective bargaining and make it possible to exempt from the provisions of Wages Council orders those sectors of a Wages Council industry which have their own collective agreements.

If company agreements are to be preferred to national agreements, how does the Report see this happening? Four points should be made. First,

[1] Cmnd. 3623, op. cit. A summary of the Report and comments upon it are contained in a special issue of the *British Journal of Industrial Relations*, November 1968.

the Report suggests that companies should review industrial relations in their undertakings to develop procedural arrangements for 'comprehensive and authoritative collective bargaining machinery' covering terms and conditions of employment, 'the rapid and equitable settlement of grievances', the position of shop stewards, redundancy, discipline and safety. Secondly, the Report recommends that agreements, initially for firms with over 5000 employees, should be registered with the Department of Employment and Productivity under the provisions of a proposed Industrial Relations Act. Thirdly, the Report recommends the establishment of an Industrial Relations Commission, to which the Department could refer problems arising out of the registration of agreements. The Commission would also act as a standing reference body on problems of industrial relations in a factory or industry. Fourthly, the Report recommends more mergers between unions, more rationalisation of union representation within factories, closer working arrangements between unions, a new look at the status of shop stewards in unions and their training, and improvements in the financial position of trade unions.

It will be apparent that much of this is in harmony with the line of reasoning followed in this book. Questions about the recommendations do, however, readily come to mind. It seems likely that five subjects will play an important part in discussion on those aspects of the Report which are relevant to this book. First, the duties of the Industrial Relations Commission are not well delineated. It has an advisory role but has no powers. Good company bargaining may follow from its advice but need not. Secondly, the Report does not appear to give enough emphasis to the weaknesses of the resources of trade unions for the exacting task of conducting many complex company bargains. Company bargaining will only work well if both sides can give it very full attention. There is a risk that bad company bargaining could be more inflationary and less conducive to efficiency than present arrangements, though it offers the chance of considerable improvements. Thirdly, the Report says very little about the complementary need for labour management. Fourthly, the continuing role of national agreements is unclear. Fifthly, the Report relies on productivity bargaining as a means of reducing restrictive practices and makes no clear recommendation on action to be taken if this approach proves inadequate. There is more than a slight tendency on the part of the Royal Commission to confuse the possibility of productivity bargains creating large changes in the utilisation of labour accompanied by special increases in payment with the continuing tasks of plant bargaining, which are more concerned with well-ordered relationships between managements and their employees in payment and other matters, and offer less prospect of spectacular changes either in labour utilisation or in payment. By so doing the Royal Commission overemphasises immediate gains from plant bargaining and thereby diverts attention unduly from what may in the longer run be more critical matters, especially the long-term relationship between earnings and productivity (as opposed to once-for-all productivity bargains), and the procedural arrangements governing the relations between managements and workpeople.

It seems likely that some of these issues will give rise to further legislation to regulate and steer the system of industrial relations and thereby the operation of the labour market. The last decade has witnessed a series of actions on the part of Government which have altered the character of the British labour market and its institutions, and there has been increasing recognition on the part of Government that its ability to manage the economy depends a great deal on its ability to manage the labour market, since so many parts of general economic policy have to take effect through the labour market. It therefore becomes essential that the way in which labour markets work should be better understood, and this conclusion may well be of increased importance in the next decade, when the Government's interest in the control and operation of the labour market is more likely to be heightened than diminished.[1]

[1] A White Paper, *In Place of Strife*, Cmnd. 3888, published in January, 1969 when this book was in proof, announced the Government's proposed policy for industrial relations. A Commission for Industrial Relations has been set up with the retiring General Secretary of the T.U.C. (Mr G. Woodcock as its first Chairman. The C.I.R. will be concerned with ways of improving and extending procedural arrangements, on references from the Secretary of State, and will also be asked to consider problems of the recognition of trade unions by employers in collective bargaining. An Industrial Relations Bill is proposed. The Secretary of State would have the power to introduce a compulsory 'conciliation pause' of 28 days in unofficial strikes. During this period, in which a strike would not be permitted, conciliation or other discussion would take place. A ballot before official strikes could also be required. The Bill is also to include other changes – to create an Industrial Board which will assess financial penalties for breach of the provisions of the Bill, to require registration of certain collective agreements, to protect workers from unfair dismissal – and many other matters.

Index